X

Tragedy in Dedham

BOOKS BY FRANCIS RUSSELL

THREE STUDIES IN 20TH-CENTURY OBSCURITY

THE AMERICAN HERITAGE BOOK OF THE
PIONEER SPIRIT (co-author)

THE FRENCH AND INDIAN WARS

THE GREAT INTERLUDE

LEXINGTON, CONCORD AND BUNKER HILL

THE WORLD OF DÜRER

THE MAKING OF THE NATION, 1783–1860

THE CONFIDENT YEARS: The Period between
the Civil War and World War I

THE SHADOW OF BLOOMING GROVE

FORTY YEARS ON

TRAGEDY IN DEDHAM
Fiftieth Anniversary Edition

TRAGEDY IN DEDHAM

The Story of the Sacco-Vanzetti Case

BY

Francis Russell

FIFTIETH ANNIVERSARY EDITION

◇◇◇◇◇◇◇◇◇◇◇◇◇◇◇◇◇◇◇◇◇◇◇◇◇◇◇

In his Ingersoll Lecture at Harvard, Lowes Dickinson inquired, "Is immortality desirable?" I almost think it is, if only to get at the truth of the Sacco-Vanzetti case.   —FERRIS GREENSLET

◇◇◇◇◇◇◇◇◇◇◇◇◇◇◇◇◇◇◇◇◇◇◇◇◇◇◇

McGraw-Hill Book Company
New York   St. Louis   San Francisco
Düsseldorf   Mexico   Toronto

Contents

	CHRONOLOGY	vii
	FOREWORD	xi
	MAPS	xxiv
ONE	THE TRAGEDY IN DEDHAM	1
TWO	HISTORY, WRITTEN AND OTHERWISE	10
THREE	APRIL 15, 1920	28
FOUR	BRIDGEWATER AND WEST BRIDGEWATER	49
FIVE	THE NIGHT OF MAY 5	60
SIX	THE MEN AND THE TIMES	71
SEVEN	THE PLYMOUTH TRIAL	93
EIGHT	THE YEAR BETWEEN	107
NINE	THE TRIAL—I	129
TEN	THE TRIAL—II	158
ELEVEN	THE TRIAL—III	176
TWELVE	POST-TRIAL—I	216
THIRTEEN	POST-TRIAL—II	237
FOURTEEN	THE CONFESSIONS	270

FIFTEEN   MORE HISTORY,
          WRITTEN AND OTHERWISE   302

SIXTEEN   1926   326

SEVENTEEN 1927   349

EIGHTEEN THE PUBLIC
          AND THE LOWELL COMMITTEE   380

NINETEEN AUGUST 1927   404

TWENTY   AFTERMATH   451

          SOURCES
          AND ACKNOWLEDGMENTS   469

          INDEX   473

Chronology

1919

June 2. Attorney General Palmer's house bombed, Washington, D.C.

November 7. First of the Palmer Red raids.

November 23. Buick belonging to F. J. Murphy stolen in Needham.

December 22. License plates stolen from Hassam's garage, Needham.

December 24. Bridgewater holdup.

1920

January 2. Red raids in thirty-three cities.

January 6-7. License plates stolen from car, Needham.

February 25. Elia and Salsedo detained in New York by Department of Justice.

April 15. Holdup and murders in South Braintree.

April 17. Discovery of abandoned Murphy Buick.

April 20. Stewart interviews Boda.

April 25. Vanzetti goes to New York.

May 5. Sacco and Vanzetti arrested.

May 6. Orciani arrested. Katzmann questions Sacco and Vanzetti. Sacco's preliminary hearing on South Braintree charge.

May 11. Orciani released.

May 18. Vanzetti's preliminary hearing on South Braintree charge.

June 11. Vanzetti indicted for Bridgewater holdup.

June 22-July 1.	Vanzetti tried for Bridgewater holdup.
August 16.	Vanzetti sentenced.
August 19.	Fred Moore takes up defense of Sacco and Vanzetti.
September 16.	Wall Street bomb explosion.

1921

January.	Negotiations between Angelina DeFalco and Defense Committee.
May 31-July 14.	Trial of Sacco and Vanzetti.
October.	Mass demonstrations in Europe against verdict.
October 29, November 5.	Motion for new trial argued.
November 8.	First supplementary (Ripley) motion filed.
December 24.	Thayer denies motion for new trial.

1922

May 4.	Second supplementary (Gould-Pelser) motion filed.
July 22.	Third supplementary (Goodridge) motion filed.
September 11.	Fourth supplementary (Andrews) motion filed.

1923

March 8.	William Thompson agrees to argue supplementary motions.
April 23.	Sacco committed to Bridgewater State Hospital for the Criminally Insane.
April 30.	Fifth supplementary (Hamilton-Proctor) motion filed.
September 29.	Sacco discharged from Bridgewater Hospital.
October 1-November 8.	Hearings on the supplementary motions.

1924

August.	Moore withdraws from case.
October 1.	Thayer denies all five supplementary motions.

1925

January 2-May 28. Vanzetti committed to Bridgewater Hospital.

June. International Labor Defense takes up case.

November 18. Madeiros confesses.

1926

February. Renewed demonstrations overseas.

May 12. Massachusetts Supreme Judicial Court rejects Thompson's appeal from Thayer's denial of the supplementary motions; convictions of Sacco and Vanzetti confirmed.

May 15-20. Madeiros' second trial.

May 22. Herbert Ehrmann finds trail of Morelli gang.

May 26. Motion based on Madeiros confession filed.

June 2. Samuel Johnson's house bombed.

September 13-17. Thompson argues Madeiros motion before Thayer.

October 23. Thayer denies Madeiros motion.

1927

January 27, 28. Thompson appeals Thayer's denial of October 23 to Massachusetts Supreme Judicial Court.

March. Frankfurter's *Atlantic Monthly* article.

April 5. Supreme Court affirms Thayer's denial of October 23.

April 9. Sacco and Vanzetti sentenced.

May 4. Governor Fuller receives Vanzetti's clemency petition.

June 1. Fuller appoints Advisory ("Lowell") Committee.

June 3. Calvin Goddard tests shells and bullets.

July 27. Lowell Committee reports findings to Governor Fuller.

August 3. Fuller refuses clemency.

August 5. Bombings in New York, Philadelphia, Baltimore.

August 7. Lowell Committee report made public.

August 15. Juror McHardy's house dynamited.

August 23. Madeiros, Sacco, and Vanzetti executed.

1932

September 27. Thayer's house bombed.

1959

April 2. Massachusetts Legislature Committee hearing on posthumous pardon for Sacco and Vanzetti.

1961

October 11. Re-examination of ballistics evidence by Jac Weller and Frank Jury.

Foreword

FIFTIETH
ANNIVERSARY EDITION

This year, the ninth since *Tragedy in Dedham* was first published, is the fiftieth anniversary of the Dedham trial and conviction of Sacco and Vanzetti for the murders of a paymaster and his guard in South Braintree, Massachusetts, on April 15, 1920. My 1962 book marked, if it did not originate, a period of revision in the case, a slow thaw of the frozen dogmatism that had so long regarded any questioning of the two men's innocence as secular heresy. In the years since the 1927 executions, those who considered themselves the intelligentsia continued to maintain the innocence of the defendants and the infamy of the trial. In 1948, G. Louis Joughin could write in *The Legacy of Sacco and Vanzetti* that "the literary verdict is unanimously sympathetic to the executed men. Prosecution, judges and the hostile Massachusetts public majority have not in twenty years found a single literary defender of their position."

According to the dogma, Sacco and Vanzetti were two philosophical anarchists done to death for their political beliefs by fearful and corrupt "hangmen in frock coats." Arrested in a period of wild anti-Red hysteria, they were executed for a murder that they not only did not commit, but of which they had no knowledge. The police who arrested them knew they were innocent. So did the prosecution. The Yankee jurors who convicted them were blindly biased against foreigners and radicals. Vanzetti, in his speech to the court after his sentencing, claimed that "not even a dog that kill chickens would have been found guilty with the evidence that the Commonwealth have produced against us." The district attorney deliberately framed them. The judge was a vindictive bigot, "a black-gowned cobra" in Vanzetti's words, and the trial itself little better than a kangaroo court. Massachusetts' Governor Fuller and Harvard's President Lowell, who reviewed the case, preferred to commit judicial murder rather than to cast reflections on their state's judiciary system.

Even to examine this dogma with an open mind was considered intellectually contemptible, an earlier equivalent of supporting the late Senator Joseph McCarthy or joining the John Birch Society. For after all, if Felix Frankfurter, Walter Lippmann, John Dewey, Norman Thomas, Edna St. Vincent Millay, Jane Addams, Robert La Follette, Sherwood Eddy, H. L. Mencken, John Dos Passos, Harold Laski, H. G. Wells and hundreds of others of equal note in the literary and educational world were so volubly convinced of Sacco's and Vanzetti's innocence, how could any cultivated man think otherwise? Several years ago I was talking about the case with a young woman instructor from an Eastern university and I suggested that in the light of the new ballistics tests conducted in 1961 the dogma should at least be re-examined. "No," she said pontifically. "They *had* to be innocent!"

For four decades they *had* to be innocent. Intellectuals accepted this as an article of faith. To doubt it would have been to doubt their own integrity. With the benighted exception of official Massachusetts, the dogma became so universally accepted that it rubbed off on nonintellectuals, crept unchallenged into popular history books, with the tacit assumption that there was nothing to challenge. Until 1960, in all the vast literature about the case, the only effort in book form to defend the prosecution and verdict was a little pamphlet written by a prissy and forgotten reporter of decisions of the Massachusetts Supreme Court.

After the global reverberations following the executions, interest in the case blazed up periodically, then died down. But the underground fire continued to smoulder. In 1959 a public hearing was held in Boston's State House on a resolution recommending a posthumous pardon for Sacco and Vanzetti. Although the legislators rejected the resolution, the hearing was dominated by Sacco-Vanzetti sympathizers, with only one speaker opposed. A year later Reginald Rose presented his two-part television melodrama, *The Sacco-Vanzetti Story*, in which two almost angelic Italians were shown as betrayed by the satanic reactionaries of Massachusetts. Rose's play was later transposed for the West German television by Peter von Zahn who also compiled a similarly oriented documentary. Subsequently a play with the same conclusions, sponsored by Group

W of the Westinghouse Broadcasting Company, was presented on Broadway and simultaneously televised. Marc Blitzstein at about that time was in Italy working on an opera on the theme of Sacco and Vanzetti for which he had been commissioned by the Metropolitan Opera Company.* In 1962 when I was in East Berlin I found a fictional autobiography of Vanzetti in a booklet sponsored by the East German military publishers, and three years later I saw Sacco-Vanzetti posters for sale in Leningrad. Within the last few years a play about the case has been produced in Italy, and an edition of Vanzetti's letters published there. In October 1967 the surviving Sacco and Vanzetti relatives in Italy brought an unsuccessful libel suit in Milan against the German science writer Jürgen Thorwald who in his book, *The Century of the Detective*, had suggested that in the light of later ballistics tests the two men might after all be guilty. That same month marked the dedication by Ben Shahn of his 60-by-12-foot Sacco-Vanzetti outdoor mosaic on the campus of Syracuse University. In 1969 the last surviving defense lawyer, Herbert Ehrmann, elaborated the whole defense position in *The Case That Will Not Die*. So each year has brought some new turn to the old case that enshrined the two alien anarchists as the century's American martyrs.

Intellectual opinion so solidified behind Sacco and Vanzetti that it was not until thirty-one years after their execution that the first crack in the monolith of dogma appeared: the publication in 1958 by East German Professor Johannes Zelt of his *Proletarian Internationalism in the Battle for Sacco and Vanzetti*. In writing his book Zelt was allowed access to the government files in Moscow. Using these to attack the bourgeois liberals, he demonstrated, beyond question, that the European protest movement at the time of Sacco's and Vanzetti's deaths was organized, led and directed by the Communist Party. All innocently, Zelt demolished the myth of the workers of Europe rising in spontaneous indignation against American capitalist injustice. The giant demonstrations, as he proved, took place because the order went out from the Communist European central headquarters in Berlin's Alexanderplatz. In extolling his party, Zelt undermined his cause.

Then in 1960 a conservative Boston lawyer, Robert Montgomery, long a student of the Sacco-Vanzetti case, published the first direct challenge to the dogma of innocence with his *Sacco-Vanzetti—The*

* Blitzstein received a Guggenheim Fellowship for the projected work. Since his death the manuscript has vanished.

Murder and the Myth. In his angry defense of the Massachusetts judiciary, Montgomery could see nothing in the two anarchists but a couple of sleazy criminals. Nevertheless, the facts that he marshaled for the prosecution, the holes that he punched in the various defense alibis, are impressive. After his book appeared, anyone glibly asserting the innocence of Sacco and Vanzetti had a formidable obstacle to reckon with. James Rorty, an earlier dogmatist, a Sacco-Vanzetti street demonstrator and poet of the cause, in reviewing the book for the *New Leader* wrote that it stood like a lion in the path of Sacco-Vanzetti defenders.

Two years later a liberal New York lawyer, James Grossman, made his own independent examination of the trial evidence and the later proceedings. His careful analysis, appearing in an article in *Commentary*, concluded that Sacco and Vanzetti were indeed guilty. *Protest: Sacco and Vanzetti and the Intellectuals,* published in 1965 by the New York history professor David Felix, is another landmark in the re-evaluation of the case. With no ax to grind and no emotional commitments to either side, Felix concerned himself chiefly with the symbol and the dogma in relation to the facts. Were Sacco and Vanzetti guilty? Was the trial, with its aftermath of appeals and hearings, fair? His first conclusion, after a re-examination of all the evidence, is that the two were guilty. As to the question of the fairness of the trial, he has read the transcript with unblinkered eyes. He has interviewed a surviving juror and just about everyone else left who was once connected with the case, even managing to talk over the whole trial process with the highly respected justice of the Massachusetts Supreme Court, Harold Williams, who as assistant district attorney shared in the prosecution of Sacco and Vanzetti. In his summary view the trial was reasonably fair, the judge—whatever his outside limitations—conducted himself on the bench with propriety, and in the light of the dubious post-trial evidence produced as exceptions "the Supreme Court and the Governor had no alternative but to uphold the verdict."

If this is true, how was it then that the intellectual world felt so overwhelmingly otherwise? Intellectuals, in Felix's opinion, identifying themselves with two portrayed idealists in rebellion against Philistines and Pharisees, were caught up in an act of faith. Believing "in innocence and betrayal through a burst of revelation; they began with pure emotion and applied their best intelligence to the proof of it."

When in the autumn of 1958, with Tom O'Connor and the old

anarchist Aldino Felicani, I spoke on the Sacco-Vanzetti case from the platform of Boston's Community Church, I had then just begun to gather material for my book. I was convinced, as I told the congregation, that the two Italians were innocent men, and hoped in the course of my researches to come across additional evidence that would prove this once and for all. In speaking to the members of the Community Church, I was not telling anyone a thing he had not believed for a long time. Yet that very unanimity of opinion according to status had perplexed me ever since I began to study the case. It seemed almost impossible for people to be objective about it, even forty years afterward. Anyone who joined the undogmatic Community Church accepted automatically the dogma that Sacco and Vanzetti were innocent persecuted radicals, just as members of the American Legion—at least in Massachusetts—assumed automatically that they were subversive criminals who had got just what was coming to them.

I considered myself as unemotionally objective, ready to accept whatever facts came to hand, to follow wherever they might lead. Yet in reality I was much more committed to the dogma of innocence than I myself realized. How I finally came, reluctantly, to change my mind I have indicated in the last half-dozen pages of *Tragedy in Dedham*. Three-quarters of my manuscript was completed before then. There were warning signs along the way but I chose to disregard them, to push aside such unwanted intrusive facts as Sacco's absence from work on the day of the crime or that both men were armed when arrested or the later ballistics evidence. As the months stretched into years, the pages on my desk piled up, and what I had originally planned as a sixty- to eighty-thousand-word narrative grew to over 200,000 words. Most of my characters I found unsympathetic, but increasingly I found myself drawn to three individuals: the Bohemian radical defense lawyer, Fred Moore, who had transformed an obscure murder trial into an international event (and whom Frankfurter had unkindly called a "blatherskate"); Carlo Tresca, the large-hearted and impetuous anarchist leader who had organized the defense and had brought Moore into the case; and Vanzetti himself, that gentle, winning and most eloquent man.

Moore's later guarded opinion that "Sacco was probably, Vanzetti possibly guilty" came as a great surprise to me halfway through my labors. I learned about it first indirectly, then had the story confirmed by Upton Sinclair. Other warning signs began to look more ominous. Yet, however uneasily, I still held to my belief in innocence betrayed. The turning point, the way down the mountain for me, was when I learned that Tresca had told Max Eastman flatly, "Sacco was guilty, but Vanzetti was not." Only then did I finally confront myself and realize that I could no longer sustain my old belief. For if Tresca, Eastman's long-time friend, had said this, then I could see no alternative but to accept it. He, above all others, must have known the truth.

I spent a day with Eastman on Martha's Vineyard talking of Tresca and the great case. "I don't know why I never thought to ask Carlo about it until a few weeks before he was murdered," Eastman told me, "but we were interrupted then, and I never did get the chance to see him again. That was what he said."

"Of course," I told him, "there'll be two objections to your story. First of all, some of the Sacco-Vanzetti vindicators will say that you are lying because of your guilty conscience, because you once were a Communist and took part in the October Revolution and knew Lenin and Trotsky and the others. And then in your later years you turned conservative."

He laughed. "Do you think I seem a liar?" he asked me.

"Not from the ones I've known," I said. "But then there'll be others who will say that you're crazy."

"Perhaps I am," he added. "But Tresca still said it."

There was a third possibility that I had overlooked. Judge Musmanno, when he heard the story, maintained that Tresca spoke such thick English that Eastman had misunderstood him. Vanzetti's friend Felicani, a less bombastic and more honest man than Musmanno, told me simply, "I knew Max Eastman. If he said that Carlo said it, then Carlo said it. But why," he added in an anguished voice, "did Tresca never tell me? Believe me, I never knew this. I never knew!" And he put his hands to his face and cried.

I had often visited Felicani in his little print shop on Boston's Milk Street, talking with him for hours about the great case which had been by far the most important, the most engrossing fact in his life. Always he treated me with kindness, opening his files, supplying me with photographs, showing me the originals of certain Vanzetti letters that had been altered and doctored by Gardner Jackson and Marion Frankfurter in a published edition. "Tell the truth," he told me when I first visited him and told him I planned to write a Sacco-Vanzetti book, but I know that what he hoped for from me was the ultimate vindicating work. Once I had changed my belief in innocence betrayed, I felt that I must tell him to his face rather than let him find out secondhand after my book had appeared. But on the summer morning I went to see him I walked round the block twice before I could finally bring myself to cross the threshold of the little print shop. It is an unhappy memory I still have; the after-image of him sitting there, the hulking bald-headed man hunched over his desk, his face covered by hands still not large enough to conceal his tears. On the filing cabinet behind him is a small plaster bust of Tresca.

To establish the innocence of Sacco and Vanzetti had been his preoccupation ever since he had first helped organize their defense. He had to continue to believe, and I had to be a villain. After my book appeared he attacked me in issue after issue of his minuscule anarchist publication *Controcorrente* as a *"vulgare sbirro,"* a police spy, an unctuous pseudo-historian, a "Maramaldo of the pen," whose book was "permeated with the prejudices" that I had inherited from my father, "a reactionary lawyer." And so on, each month. I suppose I could have sued the old man for libel. But I understood. In attacking me, he was defending himself against his own inner doubts. I liked him then; I still like him in memory.

Tom O'Connor, founder and chairman of the Committee for the Vindication of Sacco and Vanzetti, was another for whom the case had become the engrossing and enveloping object of his life, for which he had sacrificed his own career as a journalist and whatever money he had earned or inherited. He helped me much, and he too died at about the same time as Felicani. "I have had a wife and a mistress in my life," the old bachelor once told me. "My mother was my wife and my mistress was the Sacco-Vanzetti case." As I finished each chapter, he read my piecemeal manuscript with a voluble enthusiasm that tapered into silence when I let him understand that I had changed my mind. Only after his death, when his papers had been transferred to the Brandeis Library, did I learn that from that point on he had been photostating my pages and sending them off to potentially hostile critics; that, with Judge Musmanno and others, he had been organizing what he called "Operation Assault" to keep *Tragedy in Dedham* from being reviewed at all. I could not blame him. For in his impassioned and life-long defense of the two Italians he had really found both wife and mistress, and he could not live without this love. Unamuno wrote that at the core of every belief is disbelief. Rather than face the Medusa's head of their own doubts, Felicani and O'Connor had to consider me a traitor, a *sbirro*.

The decade of the sixties saw the disappearance of most of those remaining who had been directly concerned with the case: Felicani; Tom O'Connor; Judge Musmanno; Justice Frankfurter; Justice Williams; Governor Fuller and his pugnacious secretary, Herman MacDonald; Gardner Jackson, whom I met at the home of Arthur Schlesinger, Sr., and who showed some embarrassment when I asked about his doctoring of the Sacco-Vanzetti letters; Max Eastman; Upton Sinclair; John Dos Passos. And there are the vanished lesser figures: Dedham's Sheriff Capen; the South Braintree expressman, Shelley Neal; Angelina DeFalco, the Dedham go-between; Albert Carpenter, last of Moore's investigators; Vanzetti's first lawyer, James Graham. Finally in June of 1970, the sole surviving lawyer, Herbert Ehrmann, junior defense counsel in the last stages of the case, died.

O'Connor and Felicani had sacrificed themselves and their careers for the great case that had become so integral a part of their lives. Ehrmann and Musmanno, on the other hand, had made their careers out of the case. Musmanno arrived in Boston in the summer of 1927 a few weeks before the execution with a petition to Governor Fuller from the Sons of Italy, and entered the case via the bedroom window of one of the more belligerent females connected with the defense. His principal function, in Ehrmann's sardonic summing up, was to carry somebody else's briefcase for two weeks. But in that time he managed to dramatize himself on several occasions, ending with a lachrymose personal appeal to Governor Fuller a few hours before Sacco and Vanzetti died. Returning to Pennsylvania as the champion of his ethnic group, with one foot in the radical door and the other resting on the threshold of the Church, he gathered in the united support of the Italian community to win election as a municipal judge, and some years later, through the flamboyancy of his oratory, he was elevated by the voters to the state supreme court. The case had been an open sesame to him.

It was perhaps less so for Herbert Ehrmann, a more astute and capable lawyer. Yet he too was able to build a career on his far more extended connection with the case, for he, as a young lawyer, a stranger to Boston, found liberal doors in the city open to him that would, in more ordinary circumstances, have remained closed. Through the years he continued to regard Sacco and Vanzetti as his clients, and indeed his book, published the year before his death, is no more than an extended lawyer's brief, an exercise in special pleading rather than a search for truth. When in 1961 I sponsored

new ballistics tests, to determine whether or not a bullet taken from
the body of a South Braintree guard and a shell picked up at the
scene of the crime had been fired from the Colt automatic found on
Sacco after his arrest, I withheld the findings until the publication
of my book. The tests, conducted in the ballistics laboratory of the
Massachusetts State Police by the honorary curator of the West
Point Museum, Jac Weller, and Colonel Frank Jury of the New
Jersey State Police, were unambiguous. With officials and newspapermen present, Jury and Weller sat on opposite sides of the
room, each behind a comparison microscope. While one compared
the South Braintree shell with test shells fired in 1921 and in 1961,
the other made the comparison with the murder bullet and similar
test bullets. Then, after revealing their findings to me but not to
each other, the two exchanged places and each repeated the test.
Jury and Weller both concluded that the fatal shell and bullet had
been fired from Sacco's Colt "and could have been fired in no other
weapon."

When Ehrmann asked me if he might see the Jury-Weller report,
I lent him a copy, specifying only that he keep the contents secret
until after my book appeared. Without my knowledge, he had the
report photostated and turned it over to a ballistics expert of questionable reputation and qualifications, who later challenged Jury
and Weller not only as to their competence but as to their integrity.
Jury and Weller, in dealing with the belatedly evolved theory that
the prosecution might have made a fraudulent substitution of the
fatal shell and bullet, stated that the bullet's lopsided shape—caused
when it struck the hipbone of the murdered guard—could not have
been duplicated artificially. Ehrmann's expert maintained that it
could have been, and Ehrmann publicly denounced the 1961 test as
a fraud.

On learning this, I wrote asking him where he considered the
fraud lay. Did he believe that Jury and Weller had pretended to
match shells and bullets that did not match? Or did he believe that
during the trial the fatal shell and bullet had been secretly replaced
by a shell and bullet fired from Sacco's Colt? Any substitution theory
seemed to me to fall apart for the simple reason that to accept it
one had to accept that both shell and bullet had been substituted.
And in the primitive state of ballistics analysis in 1921, it was not
then realized that the breechblock markings on the base of a shell
are as telltale as the striations on a bullet. No one in the district
attorney's office would have then known enough to make a shell

substitution. I pointed out to Ehrmann that if he believed Sacco's Colt had not fired the murder bullet on that April afternoon in South Braintree, then only two alternatives remained. Either: (A) the 1961 Jury-Weller tests were a fraud; or (B) the Jury-Weller tests were accurate, but the bullet tested was not the one taken from the dead guard's body, and the shell not the shell found at the scene of the crime. "If A is true," I wrote, "then B must be false. If B is true, then A must be false. A and B cannot both be true. Which do you accept?"

Astute lawyer that he was, he saw no need to throw away a debater's point. To my question, repeated several times, he always refused a direct answer. "Yours," he wrote finally "is an exercise in logic."

In the nine years since my book appeared, much additional evidence has come to light, all of it confirming my evolved belief that Sacco at least was guilty. On that murder afternoon in South Braintree there were five occupants in the getaway car. Two of them, I am now convinced, were Mike Boda and Ricardo Orciani, two dubious Italians who had been with Sacco and Vanzetti earlier on the night of their arrest. Orciani was picked up by the police but then released after he was able to show his factory timecard, punched (by himself or somebody else) for the day of the crime. Boda disappeared, to show up months later in Italy. The third man in the car was, I believe, Ferruccio Coacci, another Italian with whom Boda boarded in West Bridgewater and who was deported as an anarchist a few days after the South Braintree crime. The probable driver, whom I had mentioned only in a footnote, was William Dodson, not an Italian at all but a professional car thief, described in his police record as "sallow complexion, long nose, hazel eyes." Those who noticed the car on the morning of the crime, as well as most of those who saw it later, testified that the driver was a pale man, not an Italian, with blue eyes, light hair and a long nose.

Judge Musmanno maintained with some vociferousness that no mere bullet tests could undermine Sacco's "ironclad" alibi of having been in Boston on the fatal day. Half-a-dozen witnesses testified that they had seen him there then. But years later a former Boston anarchist, Anthony Ramuglia, reduced the ironclad alibi to paper thinness when he admitted that he had been approached by his comrades to testify falsely to having seen Sacco in the city. By chance I learned from a former Hanover factory owner, long after my book had appeared, that one of his Italian workers, who had known Sacco previously, had seen and identified him during the holdup but had been too fearful to come forward at the trial or to mention it until long afterward. And, for what it is worth, I learned from James Burnham that James Cannon, of the International Labor Defense, had admitted in the course of a convivial evening that Sacco was guilty. I also discovered that Tresca, some years before his brief and broken-off admission to Eastman, had amplified his remarks to a group that included Norman Thomas. Tresca had then said that he had known from the beginning of Sacco's participation in the South Braintree holdup-murders, and he had tried to persuade Sacco to admit his guilt in open court in the defiant anarchist tradition and so allow the innocent Vanzetti to go free. But Sacco refused, holding stubbornly that he could win his case and Vanzetti's too.

Upton Sinclair, in planning his huge novel *Boston*, had come to the city just after the executions, and in 1953 related how he had visited Sacco's family and sensed that there was some dark secret there. The secret has persisted. Sacco's son, Dante, lives with his family in Norwood only four miles from the courthouse where his father was convicted. Ines, Sacco's daughter born after his arrest, is married and lives in a Boston suburb, while his wife, who some years after his death married his anarchist friend Ernanno Bianchini, lives in almost pathological seclusion in West Bridgewater. In over four decades of demonstrations, forums, debates, memorial meetings, anniversary banquets, agitation for posthumous pardons and other activities to keep the memory of the two anarchists green, the Saccos have taken no part. Never once have they even appeared on a public platform to encourage the defenders of their dead husband and father. In Maxwell Anderson's play *Winterset*, based on the Sacco-Vanzetti case, the son of an unjustly executed man gives his life to tracking down the real criminals. But Sacco's son has always refused to take any part in his father's vindication. To all queries he has replied with polite brevity that he refuses to discuss the case. After long hesitation I finally wrote to him in 1970 asking if he would at least say that he believed his father innocent, since the silence of the Sacco family had come to carry with it the implication of guilt. To this letter I never received an answer. Rosina Sacco and Ines have remained equally apart, equally silent. When in 1959 the newly formed Committee for the Vindication of Sacco and

Vanzetti was arranging for a legislative hearing on a posthumous pardon for the two men, the Sacco family, to the rage of Felicani, protested against having the issue raised at all.

But if the Saccos after half a century are still bound to their dark secret, the friends of Vanzetti have nothing to hide. When I visited Alfonsina Brini and her married daughter, LeFavre, in Plymouth, in the little house where Vanzetti used to board, they treated me as if I were, myself, a returned friend. Guileless and open, they showed me letters he had written to them, told me little intimate tales of his kindness, answered every question I put, still as convinced of his innocence as they were at the time of the trial and of his death.

For all that I shared the Brinis' basic belief, I grew more and more convinced that the Harrington & Richardson revolver found on Vanzetti was the one taken by the bandits from the dying guard, Berardelli. Vanzetti's revolver had had a new hammer installed recently. Late in March of 1920 Berardelli had brought his revolver to Iver Johnson's in Boston to replace the hammer. Unfortunately Iver Johnson's did not then make a practice of recording the serial numbers of repaired guns, so that this positive identification failed. At the trial Moore had brought in several witnesses to testify to their previous ownership of the revolver, the last witness being a moulder who said he had sold it to Orciani. Orciani, though present every day as Moore's chauffeur, refused to take the stand and explain how he had passed the revolver on to Vanzetti. I was left with the conviction that Vanzetti, whatever his innocence, had known the truth, he was in the technical legal sense an accessory after the fact. Moore, so I was told by one of his investigators, had come to believe that it was Boda who had engineered the South Braintree holdup. The Boda theory has a Copernican simplicity about it that confronts with simple logic the Ptolemaic involutions of the Sacco-Vanzetti defenders.

Ever since I began seriously to study the Sacco-Vanzetti case I have been haunted by the knowledge that there are those still living who know—beyond all bullet tests and identifications by witnesses —what happened on that long-ago spring afternoon in South Braintree, who the five men in the car were and what each of them did. Boda, if he is still alive in Italy—as he was in 1963—knows; so do Orciani and Coacci, wherever they may be. Dante Sacco must know the bitter truth that has sealed his lips. So must his sister Ines. Rosina Sacco in her self-imposed isolation knows. And there are others, elderly people now, still tenaciously prepared to carry the weight of their secret to the grave. Barring a sudden revelation by one of them, I do not see how any more clarity can be added to the case. Some of the mist has at least been dispersed in the last decade. We know that Sacco's Colt was guilty, and that he shared that guilt. We do not know if he pressed the trigger, although Tresca's two statements indicate that he did. We sense that Coacci, Boda and Orciani were involved. But beyond everything else we know that the passionately held belief that Sacco and Vanzetti were innocent philosophical anarchists done to death by a reactionary and fearful capitalist society is, after all, a myth.

Francis Russell
"The Lindens"

January, 1971

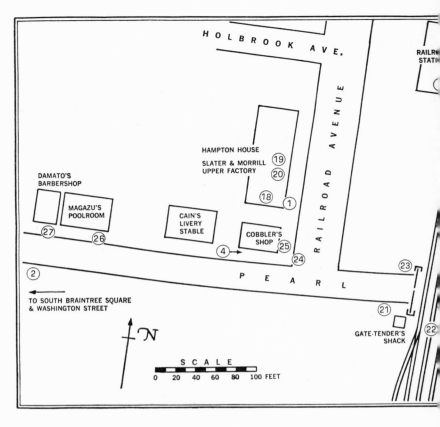

Scene of South Braintree Holdup

BEFORE THE SHOOTING:

1 Neal
2 Tracey
3 Heron
4 Novelli
5 Behrsin

DURING THE SHOOTING:

6 Where Buick waited
7 Where Berardelli fell
8 Where Parmenter fell
9 Bostock
10 Wade
11 Nichols
12 McGlone
13 Langlois

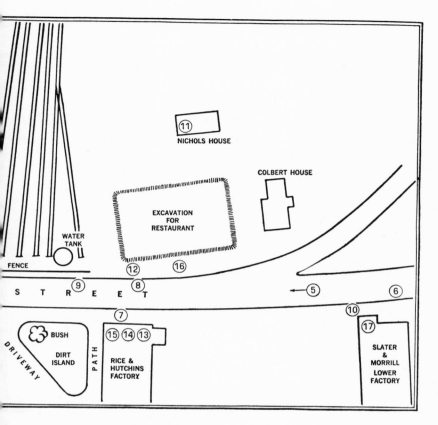

14 Pelser
15 Liscomb
16 Laborers at excavation

AFTER THE SHOOTING:

17 Kennedy, Hayes
18 Splaine, Devlin
19 Carrigan
20 Pierce, Ferguson
21 Levangie
22 Workers on railroad
23 Gould
24 Burke
25 DeBeradinis
26 Goodridge
27 Damato

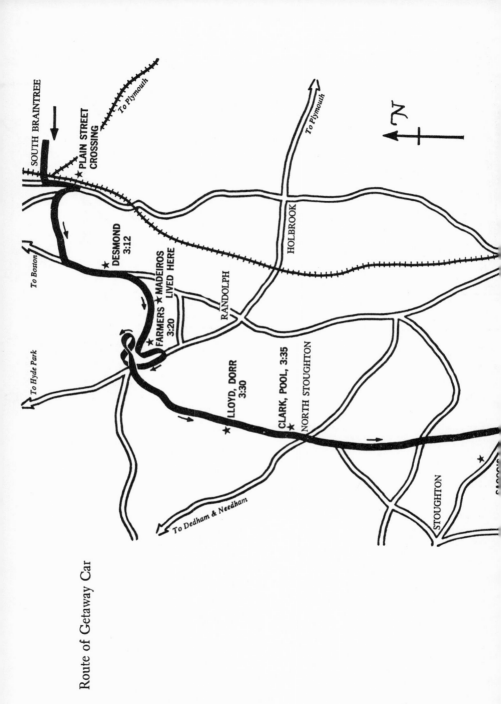

Route of Getaway Car

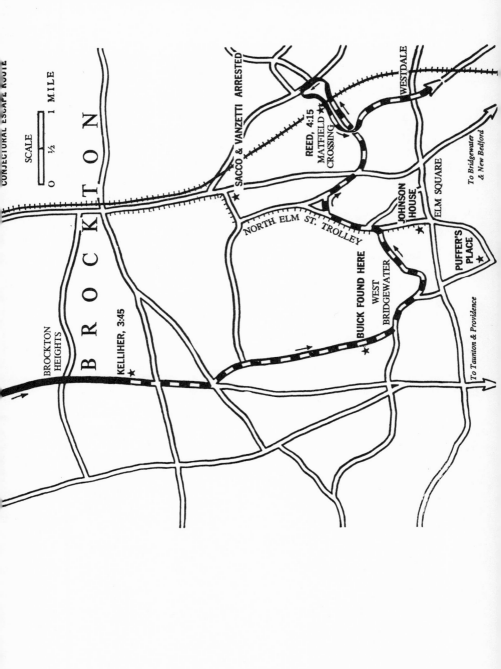

CONJECTURAL ESCAPE ROUTE

SCALE

0   ½   1 MILE

B R O C K T O N

BROCKTON
HEIGHTS

KELLIHER, 3:45 ★

SACCO & VANZETTI ARRESTED ★

REED, 4:15
MATFIELD
CROSSING ★

WESTDALE

NORTH ELM ST. TROLLEY

JOHNSON
HOUSE

ELM SQUARE

PUFFER'S
PLACE ★

BUICK FOUND HERE
WEST
BRIDGEWATER ★

To Bridgewater
& New Bedford

To Taunton & Providence

◇◇◇◇◇◇◇◇◇◇◇◇◇◇◇◇◇◇◇◇◇◇◇◇◇◇◇◇◇◇◇

CHAPTER ONE

The Tragedy in Dedham

The case of Sacco and Vanzetti, which began as the prosecution for a commonplace if brutal murder, developed gradually into one of the world's great trials. In the end it was much more than a trial. It became one of those events that divide a society. Although the issues that it raised have been overlaid by war and political events, they never wholly die. Even today middle-aged men and women, hearing by some chance the names Sacco and Vanzetti, still find themselves stirred by the passion and violence of their younger days. Sacco and Vanzetti have become a symbol, and, like all symbols, the meaning varies with those who adopt it.

I myself do not have any memory of the trial, being then in the sixth grade of the Boston public schools, but I do remember from my eighteenth year the agitation and excitement of those summer weeks in 1927 preceding the two men's execution. The day they were to die I spent the better part of the afternoon walking over Beacon Hill and across the Common in the muted August sunshine. Police were everywhere, hard-faced and angry, some of them carrying rifles—a thing I had never seen before. Pickets with placards marched up and down before the Bulfinch façade of the State House. Periodically the police carted groups of them away in a patrol wagon to the Joy Street Station. Almost at once their places were filled by others. Buses kept arriving from New York hung with signs proclaiming SACCO AND VANZETTI MUST NOT DIE! and trailing red paper streamers. As the buses pulled into Park Square those inside began to sing "The Red Flag." They looked like foreigners, most of them. I did not like their looks. I sensed in myself the hostility of the bourgeois world toward those two men. In spite of any pickets and red-streamered buses from New

York, I knew that they were going to die that night. As I walked under the lindens on the Tremont Street side of the Frog Pond I felt a sense of oneness with the community that was asserting itself. I was glad Sacco and Vanzetti were going to die.

It never occurred to me that they might be innocent. In the shabby-genteel private school I went to in Roxbury none of the masters would have dreamt of such a thing. We took our opinions from them and from our parents. The father of one of my classmates was Reporter of Decisions of the Massachusetts Supreme Court. He published in 1927 a much-approved pamphlet on the trial in which he demonstrated the quasi-divine status of Massachusetts justice, a status that made even the appointment of the Lowell Committee to investigate the case a reflection on the Commonwealth's judicial system. According to the reporter, that system, sanctified by the past, could not err. Such a conservative position was common enough in Massachusetts then. Nor did it change. Thirty years later the reporter still listed his pamphlet in *Who's Who* as his single literary accomplishment.

By and large one's view of the case depended on one's status in the community. If one was middle-class and Republican and read the *Herald* mornings and the *Transcript* nights, one thought Sacco and Vanzetti guilty. Any latent doubts subsided after President Lowell of Harvard issued his report. But if one was a university liberal, one tended to think the trial unfair, and if one read the *Nation* or *New Republic* one was sure they were innocent.

My father was a lawyer and a Republican. He believed the two men guilty not from any particular study of the trial itself but because of his acquaintance with Captain Van Amburgh, a ballistics expert who testified at the trial. Van Amburgh, through laboratory examinations, was certain that one of the recovered murder bullets had been fired from Sacco's gun. This convinced my father, although—as it came out later—it never convinced Captain Proctor of the State Police.

My Aunt Amy, who was a social worker and lived in the Elizabeth Peabody House, was equally convinced of the two men's innocence. This again was not from studying the evidence—it was simply the way one had to feel if one was a social worker. Nobody could have continued to stay at the Elizabeth Peabody House who felt otherwise—not that such a person would ever have been there in the first place. One of the proud moments of Aunt Amy's life was when she was arrested for picketing the State House and taken away in a patrol wagon. I think she was almost disappointed that the policeman who arrested her was so courteous about it.

I do not know when my views about Sacco and Vanzetti changed. It must have been sometime in the thirties, when I happened to read a book of their letters. Those letters were just not congruous with the sordid and mercenary Braintree murders. As to the question, Who were the murderers if Sacco and Vanzetti were not? I thought I found that answered later by one of their counsel, Herbert Ehrmann, whose book *The Untried Case* seemed to prove that the men who did the killing were from the Morelli Gang of Providence. If one accepted that explanation, reinforced by other evidence as time went on, everything apparently fitted together. One of the Morellis looked enough like Sacco to have been his brother.

Dedham, where the trial took place, is a colonial backwater. For the most part it is a mill town stretched along the loops of the Charles River, but the older section near the High—not Main—Street is a well-preserved relic, with spacious frame houses of the mid-eighteenth century and later and more grandiloquent mansions of the century's end. The courthouse, built in 1827, is a stone building with massive Greek-revival columns. Its Roman dome, soberly proportioned to the columns, is the most conspicuous object in Dedham. From the flat country beyond the river it looms above the elms, flanked by white meeting-house spires, a symbol of authority. Almost always when I see the great dome so secure above the peaceful community I find myself thinking back to the Sacco-Vanzetti trial. Whatever one's feelings about the trial, its presence still seems tangible in the courthouse and the High Street.

I felt the presence in 1953, thirty-two years after the trial, when I was called on to serve for a month as a juror in the same paneled room where Sacco and Vanzetti were tried and found guilty and, after all the exceptions and delays, were sentenced to death six years later. Scarcely a day of that month passed but there was some reference to the case.

Sometimes during the lunch hour one of us would ask the old sheriff about the trial. In his blue serge cutaway he had served the Dedham court for forty years. For him the law revealed there was majestically certain. I do not think he ever entertained the idea that it might err or that the Sacco-Vanzetti decision might have been unjust. To think this would have been to challenge the things that had become part of him—his engraved brass buttons, his white mace with the blue state seal on it. His office did not, however, keep him from having his personal feelings. He had come to like Sacco and Vanzetti. "They were good boys," he told us. "I knew Nick best, but they were both good boys. Never any trouble."

At the end of the afternoon session he occasionally took a few of us through the jail, two streets away, and—after showing us the reception hall and the dining room and the laundry—he would point out the cells Sacco and Vanzetti had occupied. "I was in the court," he told us one afternoon, "that day when Judge Thayer sentenced them. Vanzetti made his speech first, that long speech—maybe you heard about it. And all the time he was talking Judge Thayer just sat there with his chin in his hand looking down at his desk. Never moved. But when Vanzetti finished, then he let him have it."

On our way into the courtroom we would pass the prisoners' cage, used in all Dedham murder trials. In this cage Sacco and Vanzetti had sat. The cage is often mentioned in the literature of the case, as if the men had been exhibited in court like monkeys in a zoo. But in spite of its name the cage is no cage at all. It is a topless enclosure of metal lattice about three feet high in front, rising to five feet in the back. Except for its symbolism there is nothing very formidable about it.

I was on a civil jury. Most of our cases concerned personal injuries. One of our last, involving a woman who had cut her leg in the door of a car, made the courtroom buzz as the lawyer for the plaintiff appeared. The clerk came over to the rail and muttered something to our foreman.

The lawyer was a portly man in his seventies, with a manner so assured that it was almost contemptuous. He was nearly bald, his face florid, with the flesh sagging under the cheeks. Behind his rimless spectacles his pale blue eyes watered. He was dressed with the conservatism of a Boston banker, wearing a hard-woven worsted suit cut in characteristic pear-shaped style. Two points of a linen handkerchief projected sharply from his breast pocket. His shoes were of Scotch grain. His voice was upper-class Bostonian—with that elastic prolongation of the vowel sounds that has come to be known as the Harvard accent. As soon as he opened his argument he lapsed into Victorian rhetoric.

The clerk's remark was passed along the jury box. The man next to me nudged my elbow. "That's Katzmann," he said, "the fellow that got Sacco and Vanzetti."

He seemed a culmination of the ghosts of the month. There he was again, in Judge Webster Thayer's old courtroom, at the scene of his triumph of a generation before. As he faced us, spinning poly-syllabic phrases out of nothing, I tried to form an impression of him divorced altogether from the Sacco-Vanzetti case. If I had seen him only at that moment, I should have thought him empty and pompous, but I should also have admitted his basic honesty.

He died the following autumn. Some months later I talked with a judge who had known Katzmann. When I told about seeing him at Dedham he asked me my opinion of the man. I said he was verbose, third-rate, not wholly grammatical. He laughed. "That describes most of us lawyers," he said. "As for Katzmann, he was average—an average district attorney, a little tricky like most of them, but no worse than most out to get a conviction. He thought Sacco and Vanzetti were guilty. I'm sure he never changed his mind."

Four decades have passed since the trial. Judge Thayer, Katzmann, President Lowell, Governor Fuller, and most of the jurors and wit-nesses are dead. What remains out of this shadowed past? Beyond all else, doubt. Refusing to face this doubt, the two sides became irreconcilable. One side felt, as did the court reporter in his pamphlet, that anything less than the execution of Sacco and Vanzetti would undermine the Massachusetts judiciary. The other side demanded that the whole proceedings of Judge Thayer's court be repudiated. There should have been some middle way out, some face-saving for-mula that would at least have pacified if not contented the reporter and his kind and yet given the men their lives. Whatever the defense's private opinion of Judge Thayer, it would have been better to have said less about him and to have concentrated on the evidence dis-covered after the trial. That this evidence changed nothing was pre-eminently the responsibility of President Lowell. Working as he did in private with his committee, unhampered by the strict rules of legal evidence, he had the opportunity to examine all the facts. A word from him, an indirect indication, and Governor Fuller would have stayed the death sentences and ordered a new trial.

Governor Fuller, of course, took his cue from the Lowell Report. If he, the parvenu, had not been so in awe of Lowell and the Back Bay ascendancy he represented, perhaps he would have acted other-wise. His jail meetings with Sacco and Vanzetti are said to have been friendly.

Once or twice a year in the decade after World War II, going into the State Street Trust Building, I used to see Fuller. The doorman would see him first and swing the door open with a ringing "Good morning, Governor." I could slip through in the eddy. The old financial clipper would billow ahead of me under full sail. Self-esteem carried him along like a favoring wind. His was the pride of manner that had reached its goal. An Alger story of the new century. From a Malden bicycle shop to the head of the Packard agency for New England when Packard was the Rolls-Royce of America. A mansion on the water side of Beacon Street hung with Gainsboroughs and Romneys and Raeburns. That was the first stage. Then the governorship. And when Packard slipped in the Depression, the ex-governor sensed the moment of ebb and shifted to Cadillac.

There was a cragginess to his features in age. More and more he came to resemble the Back Bay Brahmins he so much admired. I suppose Sacco and Vanzetti, those men whose hands he had shaken so long ago in the death cells, had become blurred impressions, overlaid by eighteenth-century paintings and the tailfins of Cadillacs. "Our reputation is your protection," said the governor's used-car ads. Yet I never saw him sweeping into the State Street Trust but I thought of his role in the case.

Public opinion in Massachusetts was against Sacco and Vanzetti. To the community they were two murderers who had been given a fair trial and every opportunity for appeal afterward. The whole thing had gone on for much too long. Radicals and anarchists and Communists were trying to use the case as a lever to pry apart the foundations of law and order. But Massachusetts was not going to be dictated to by such people. There might be demonstrations in front of American embassies throughout the world, there might be more bombs planted in the houses of those concerned—as had already happened to a witness and one of the jurors. Nothing like that was going to change the course of justice! Conservative opinion more and more adopted the point of view that Sacco and Vanzetti had become a challenge to society that could be answered only by their deaths.

Literary talent was the forte of the other side. That side consisted of the literary left, radicals, liberals, Communists, woolly well-meaning progressives like my Aunt Amy, plus a large scattering of people who could not be labeled politically but whose sense of justice had been outraged. Some of these latter were starched conservatives. The crystallized view of the opposition was that Sacco and Vanzetti were the victims of a malignant conspiracy. Neither judge nor district attorney had really believed them guilty of murder. The trial was a put-up job to get rid of two troublesome agitators.

For the Communists—to whom this case in its later stages gave their first opportunity for an international mass appeal—Sacco and Vanzetti were martyrs of the proletariat, murdered by reactionaries trying to preserve an unjust social order. Seen from this point of view, two alien Reds could expect no justice from a Massachusetts court or a Dedham jury.

During my month in Dedham I used to wonder about that earlier jury. Drawn in much the same way that we were, the jurors could not have been so very different from ourselves. And what were we? Some middle class, some working class, a few of us stupid, a few opinionated, but most of us reasonable enough to weigh an issue. At least we tried to overcome our prejudices. The jury I sat on would have been prejudiced against Reds, but it would not have convicted a Communist on a capital charge because of his political beliefs. It did not seem to me the Sacco-Vanzetti jury could have been otherwise. Granted even that the foreman was prejudiced, some of the others would have stood out against injustice. I felt sure that when the jurors decided that Sacco and Vanzetti were guilty, it was because they were convinced that they were guilty of murder.

Thinking of the great trial, I found myself wondering how I should have voted, had I been on that jury. As soon as I had the time I read the transcript of the record. Much it could not offer—the atmosphere of the court, with its tensions, the appearance of the witnesses and the defendants, the subtleties that could be gathered from a tone of voice but could not be preserved in black and white. Yet the substance, the prime matter of the trial, endured, each word spoken during that six weeks pressed and dried between the now-yellowing pages. As the inchoate mass gradually took shape for me, I tried to disavow any preconceptions, to imagine myself in the jury box at Dedham occupied solely with the question of whether two men murdered two other men, and knowing no more about it in advance than the evidence offered. How should I have judged?

I knew one thing—that I should have disregarded the testimony of the experts. My month had taught me that. Experts canceled each other out as the paid bias of either side, and a jury then decided on other grounds. The real grounds in this case were the half-dozen or so witnesses who identified Sacco—and to a lesser extent Vanzetti—as being at or near the scene of the murder on that April day. In opposition to them were an equal number of witnesses who testified that these two were not the men. It was a question finally of which group to believe. The weakest part of the Commonwealth's case was that it never established an adequate motive for the crime.

On the other hand Sacco and Vanzetti were armed the night the police picked them up, Sacco with an automatic of the type that fired the murder bullet, Vanzetti with a revolver that might have been taken from the murdered guard. This was the most damaging evidence against them. Sacco maintained that he had tucked his gun inside his belt that afternoon and forgotten about it. Vanzetti said that he carried his for protection. Both statements may have been true. Often the lame excuse is the truthful one. Yet here were two philosophical anarchists who maintained that the use of force was never justified, not even for the advancement of their beliefs, who boasted that they had never shed blood, but when they were picked up, they had on them weapons of force. If they had not been armed the chances are they would never have been tried.

The trial may well have been more unfair than seems apparent in the record. There the most glaring fault is the district attorney's harrying interrogation of the two men as to their beliefs, their lack of patriotism, and their reasons for running away to avoid the draft. The impropriety stares out of the printed page. Here certainly was error, yet I cannot believe that this was primary in the jury's verdict. On the other hand, the judge's charge, which Felix Frankfurter so condemned, seems reasonable enough in cold print. I was finally left with the feeling that if I had been on the original jury, I should have voted with the others. Yet I was not really certain.

Looked back at over the lapse of years, the case of Sacco and Vanzetti becomes a tragedy in the classical sense. It was no melodrama, as many have seen it, with good neatly divided from evil. Katzmann was as sharp as most district attorneys out for a conviction, a limited man but not a bad one. Judge Thayer could not hide the bias of his obsessions. He was indiscreet and he was weak, but he made an effort to conduct the trial fairly. Both he and Katzmann believed to their dying day that Sacco and Vanzetti were guilty.

It was not a conspiracy of evil men against noble men, as Maxwell Anderson saw it in his play Gods of the Lightning. There was something more, something deeper and more embracing in the case. It was in fact fate that was the mover behind the events at the Dedham courthouse in the spring of 1921. And it was fate in the ironic Greek sense, dwarfing all the participants, ending in inexorable disaster.

Sacco and Vanzetti were figures of Greek tragedy: the doomed king's son becomes in modern dress two Italian workmen. Fate lurks behind them at each step. Sacco scarcely misses a day at his factory except the day of the murders. If he had missed any other day, the

factory records would have been his alibi. Without him it is agreed
that Vanzetti could not have been convicted. Fate engineered the
almost accidental arrest of the two men as they were riding on the
Brockton streetcar. But for fate, Sacco would have been off to his
native country in three days.

And as in Greek tragedy the hero condemns himself unknowingly
in his own words, is doomed by his own inner weakness, so in the
end are Sacco and Vanzetti doomed by theirs. The men of peace go
armed. Fate plus human weakness—that is the basis of high tragedy,
a tragedy such as theirs that they played out to the end with bravery
and dignity. It was a tragedy for everyone concerned with the case,
and in the end it is best accepted so, as it was by the Greeks.

◇◇◇◇◇◇◇◇◇◇◇◇◇◇◇◇◇◇◇◇◇◇◇◇◇◇◇◇◇◇◇◇◇◇

CHAPTER TWO

History, Written
and Otherwise

Walking up State Street a third of a century after the executions, on another August afternoon, I wondered again about the enigma of the case. The whole drama had been played out within twenty miles of here: in South Braintree, in Bridgewater, in sedate Dedham, in the gilt-domed State House beyond the Common, and finally just across Prison Point Bridge in the granite fortress of the now-demolished state prison. Would it ever become as clear-cut as the Dreyfus affair, where everyone was at last satisfied of the grossness of the injustice done? That still seemed unlikely. In 1950 the seven surviving jury members were interviewed as to their later opinions. The decades had only confirmed their belief in the rightness of their verdict. In 1959 a judiciary committee of the Massachusetts legislature had refused to consider granting Sacco and Vanzetti a posthumous pardon.

Where the past is reduced to shelves of documents in a library it becomes manageable enough for the scholar or historian to make his evaluation. But where it is still an actual present in the contradictory minds of living men, what yardstick can one use except that of preconceptions? Was the chief of police who arrested Sacco and Vanzetti a forger of evidence? Did their first lawyers betray them? Was the district attorney a barrator with his hand out under the table? Was the judge mad? Was President Lowell of Harvard a Yankee bigot? Many upright men had maintained these things. Were Sacco and Vanzetti quietistic anarchists, or did they believe in the politics of the deed?

Boston seemed downcast, heatstruck. The Old State House at the head of State Street had, I noticed, been steam-cleaned, and the clock over the balcony had been replaced by a more authentic sundial. As I reached the subway entrance under the ancient foundations, an eddy of heat snapped in my face like a dirty towel. At that moment a herd of tourists following the Freedom Trail had paused at Point 9 to get Freedom Stamps from the slot machine for their souvenir albums. A shiny-faced man in a Hawaiian sport shirt was maneuvering against the sun to get a photograph of the lion-and-unicorn supports on the Old State House façade, no doubt thinking they went back to 1776 instead of merely to a twentieth-century Armenian tinsmith's shop. Watching the tourists, I felt I ought to have some sort of souvenir book myself to paste with self-congratulatory stamps for interviewing people on an afternoon like this.

My first call was on a corporation lawyer who had spent years writing a book to prove that Sacco and Vanzetti were guilty. His firm, occupying the sixth floor of a large old-fashioned building on Federal Street, was ostentatiously shabby with a well-preserved Edwardian décor. A horseshoe-shaped receptionist's desk dominated an outer office.

The man in his seventies who showed me into his private office without shaking hands was less the calcined Boston type than I had expected. There was a metallic quality about his eroding features. His wiry gray hair fluffed over the collar of a rumpled white shirt. He had taken off his coat, exposing waist-high trousers held up by police galluses. His eyebrows were tufted and he wore round gold-rimmed spectacles.

"I did not," he announced, "like the tone of your Sacco-Vanzetti article in *American Heritage* at all. Nevertheless I am willing to see you. What is it you want to know?"

I told him I was trying to write an impartial study of all the events in the Sacco-Vanzetti case, that I knew he thought they were guilty, and that I wanted to include his point of view.

His knees creaked a little as he sat down opposite me. A smile broke through his clouded face. "If you want to write a book like your article you could probably finish it in four or five months; but if you really want to be honest, it will take you two years just to do the preliminary reading. The fundamental thing is to make the proper comparisons between the trial record and that of the governor's committee. Of course if you tell the truth you'll never find a publisher. Because if you really go into the case you can only conclude that those two Italians were guilty. And you'll never get a hearing on that. Why?

Because their innocence has become a liberal trademark. There has never been any real doubt about this case among those who know about it. It was just used by people—by the anarchists and that radical lawyer of theirs and then the Communists.

"The case was open and shut. Everyone at the Dedham trial was convinced they were guilty, except a few old women social workers and Frank Sibley of the *Globe*. Sacco and Vanzetti said the night they were arrested they were out to pick up anarchist literature from their friends because they were afraid of the Department of Justice raids. That was May fifth, though. All those anarchists knew beforehand that the raids were going to take place on May first. No, they weren't out to pick up their anarchist papers that night. They were going to Bridgewater with guns on them to get a car because they knew that next day was payday at the factories. They needed money for the defense of their comrade Elia in New York, and they were going to get it in the only way they knew."

I said that I could not imagine why, if a man had shot someone, he would be foolish enough to have the murder weapon in his belt three weeks later. Any sensible murderer would have thrown the gun away.

"Ordinarily, yes," he went on, "but they had those guns on them very simply because they needed them, because they were planning a robbery next day. That radical business was an excuse they concocted afterward—and don't forget it was the defense that introduced anarchism into the case. During the trial they had some Italian professor from the North End testify that he had seen Sacco in town the day of the South Braintree murders and that Sacco had left him to go to the Italian Consulate. But it took him over a year to tell that tale. If, as soon as he'd heard Sacco was arrested, this man had gone to Katzmann and told him he'd been with Sacco that day, then they could have gone directly to the Italian consul. And if the consul had confirmed the story, that would have been the end of the case. But they didn't because they couldn't fake that fast, because the whole alibi was something they concocted months afterward.

"Moore, their counsel, knew they were guilty. He was just in it for the money. Why, all in all they collected a third of a million dollars for their defense fund. They say that Italian anarchist printer fellow who organized it made himself a small fortune. Moore finally had to quit the case or they'd have arrested him for perjury. He chased one witness, that poor fellow Goodridge, to Maine after the trial and pretended he was going to have him arrested if he didn't change his testimony. The Andrews woman from Quincy who identified Sacco—he had her beaten up. Orciani—the third one they arrested —he probably was the one who did it. Orciani had a time-clock alibi for the day of the robbery so they couldn't touch him, but you know it's easy enough to get some other man to punch your time card. He was in the court for the early part of the trial. He was the one the defense said sold the gun to Vanzetti, but Moore could never get him to testify. That was the way it was all through with the defense—lies, cheating, evasion."

I mentioned that some of the prosecution witnesses had changed their stories several times between the preliminary hearing and the Dedham trial.

"Sacco and Vanzetti weren't convicted on the testimony of the witnesses," he said. "It was the evidence of the bullets that convicted them. Some of the bullets they found on Sacco were so obsolete that the State Police experts couldn't find any duplicates when they wanted to make firing tests. Yet the same kind of obsolete bullet was found in the guard's body. As far as witnesses go, you may not be able to describe a man properly but if you see him again you'll recognize him. Could you describe our receptionist now?"

I had to admit that I could not.

"Yet you just talked with her. But if you went out there you would know if another girl had taken her place. You see!"

He paused and I could hear the squeak of his swivel chair. "Maxwell Anderson wrote a play about the case just after the executions. He had dinner with me afterward and I told him he was barking up the wrong tree. I explained why, and I think I convinced him. Then he wrote *Winterset*, and in that he saw the case quite differently. To my mind the greatest wrong, the greatest injustice in the whole trial, was done to Webster Thayer. He was an upstanding man, and they took years off his life. The trial grew to be an obsession with him later, but it's small wonder the way he was threatened. He once told me that every day at noon he telephoned home to see if his house was all right, and every day he felt sick inside thinking it might be blown up. You remember they finally did dynamite it.

"One of the jurors, Dever, became a lawyer afterward and he wrote an account of his experiences during the trial. Simon and Schuster would have published it. They found it all very interesting, if he'd only put in a happy ending: tell how he changed his original opinion and decided they were innocent. But Dever wouldn't do it, so he never did find a publisher. That's the situation I've been up against.

That's what you'll face if you're honest. It'll take you five years, and you'll come up against a stone wall."

He stood up abruptly and stalked to a table on which were two piles of manuscript, each over a foot high. "Here's my answer," he said, patting them. "This is my book on the case, the definitive answer. But do you think any publisher will touch it? Of course not. Can't you imagine what the *Times* and the *Herald Trib* and the *Saturday Review* would say to anything like this?"

The chapters of the book were bound separately. He let me leaf through the one on the ballistics testimony while he moved over to a row of filing cabinets labeled S-V. "Look," he said, rolling open the drawers one after another. "That's the raw material. It would take you years to get all that together, years. Much of it's not even in the record. There's the report from the Attorney General's office, for example—never been released. I can't even tell you how I got it.

"You aren't a lawyer, your mind isn't trained to evaluate," he said, leading me out to the elevator. "If you'll take my advice, kindly meant, just give up the whole business."

When I stepped from the air-conditioned building onto sun-baked Federal Street the city growled. The sky beyond Post Office Square looked rancid. I remembered the World War II British Army expression for accumulated paperwork: *bumf*. Those tight-packed filing cabinets with their formidable accumulation of details were bumf. The transcript of the record itself ran to over six thousand pages, and on top of this was enough additional bumf to bury me.

My next call was to be on Aldino Felicani, the man the lawyer had dismissed as "that Italian anarchist printer fellow." An extraordinary old man, Felicani. The organizer of the Sacco-Vanzetti Defense Committee, he seemed so much a part of the past that I could never quite get used to the idea of his still being around. He was an anachronism. Whenever I saw him in public he wore the red shirt, the black Latin Quarter tie, and the wide-brimmed hat that had been the anarchist uniform in Bakunin's time. So I had seen him last at the legislature's Judiciary Committee hearing for a posthumous pardon for Sacco and Vanzetti. As I watched him listening to the proceedings I thought of the charge Vanzetti had given him: "Avenge our blood! Clear our names!" I had heard Felicani repeat it many times in his heavy accent.

Sacco and Vanzetti had about as much chance of getting a pardon from that legislative committee as Benedict Arnold. The gum-chewing faces behind the oak desks in the State House's Gardner Auditorium were implacable. When my father had been in the legislature during World War I, the characteristic member had been a lawyer, Republican, middle- to upper-class, interested more in maintaining the *status quo* than in himself. In 1959 the social revolution of forty years was apparent enough in these lower-middle-class legislators whose interest was mainly in keeping their feet in the trough.

Yet from these men representing a new emergent class I should somehow have expected more charity for the two dead Italians. Instead there was entrenched hatred, concentrating in the chairman as he interrogated Judge Musmanno.

Justice Michael Musmanno of the Supreme Court of Pennsylvania, one of Sacco and Vanzetti's final counsel, was the main speaker in favor of the committee's bill. Silver-maned and silver-tongued, he unwound reels of words until he was stopped by the chairman's hard voice. The latter had the features of the ur-Celt: savage blue eyes, gray shaggy hair looped over the back of his collar like an old-time United States senator.

"Look, Judge, why did Vanzetti have the loaded revolver on him, and a pocketful of slugs that fit it and why did he go for it when the police grabbed him?"

Musmanno tried to explain that carrying revolvers was then a common custom in America, especially among Italians, and that it was a right guaranteed by the Constitution. The chairman's voice, burred as a cat's tongue, broke in.

"You mean to tell me that the district attorney, the judge, the jury, the governor, the president of Harvard, the Supreme Court of Massachusetts, the Supreme Court of the United States—they're all wrong and you're right?"

Musmanno maintained that this was just what he was trying to tell him. Applause from the audience, in which I saw old Felicani join, brought the familiar threat to have the hall cleared. That audience was a curious conglomeration of the elderly, a scattering of students, and a cluster of beatniks at the side in beards and blue denims tied up with rope.

The elderly were survivors of an old storm, their eccentricities accentuated by age, the crackpot label attached to their clothes, their hats, their gestures. Emotionally they were drawn to lost causes, and here they gathered again like old soldiers at a reunion. The Sacco-Vanzetti case with its drawn-out tragic climax had been for them a generation ago a self-fulfillment in indignation that they were now reliving. At one point a woman near the exit caused a stir, almost a suspension of the hearing, by holding up Sacco's and Vanzetti's death masks.

Felicani's Excelsior Press was on the ground floor of a decrepit building near the foot of Milk Street under the shadow of the new John F. "Honey" Fitzgerald Expressway where the business district fringes into the Italian North End. Every time I saw the large red and green linoleum squares on the floor of that familiar little office I thought back to the hopscotch games of my childhood. The walls were of pebbled tin sheeting painted with mauve Chemtone. Next to Felicani's desk was a pay telephone and just above it an oak-framed clock, invariably six minutes fast. On top of a filing cabinet next to a spindly philodendron plant was a plaster bust of the dead anarchist leader, Carlo Tresca.

I was glad to find the old man there on this hot August afternoon. A man who towered in any crowd and looked more like a viking than a Latin, he was wearing a brightly patterned sport shirt. His gray eyes peered with astigmatic blankness until he recognized me and smiled. I told him of the mass of bumf I had just encountered.

"Yes," he said, offering me a chair, "but what were they, those papers? I have almost as many papers myself. If your lawyer's wrong at the start, it doesn't matter how many files he has. There are not many of us left from those days, the ones who really knew."

I asked Felicani what he had done immediately after the two men's arrest. He thought for a moment.

"It's strange," he said. "When you begin to think, then all the memories come back, just as clearly as if it all happened yesterday. I knew Vanzetti best. He was one of my closest friends. As soon as he was arrested he got word to me and I got the others together. We went to see them at the Brockton police station. We raised money— two or three dollars here, another dollar there. It's all down in writing, every penny. Then, at the first trial for the Bridgewater holdup, Thayer gave Vanzetti twelve to fourteen years. When Tresca heard that he came on from New York. 'What is going on here?' he asked us. 'Fourteen years? Is that what you do?' So then he got Moore, the lawyer from the Lawrence strike, to come in and take charge of the case."

"I know this may be painful to you," I told him, "but I have a letter from Upton Sinclair, who talked with Moore after the executions. Moore told him then—his exact words were: 'Sacco was probably, Vanzetti possibly guilty.' "

Felicani's sport shirt rippled as he shrugged his vast shoulders. "I've heard things of that kind, so many rumors. You know, Sinclair wrote most of *Boston* right here in this office. I don't see why he didn't mention it to me. Moore was angry after he left the case. His anger just got too big."

I knew that Sacco had come to distrust Moore, but I did not know the details of Moore's leaving. Felicani was roundabout in answering me.

"I never say Moore kept money for himself. He was an honest man. But for all the money you gave him, he wanted more always—for witnesses, for travels, for new investigations. He had no idea of money. If you gave him a thousand dollars every other day Moore was all right, but we didn't have that much, the committee. Finally I tightened the purse strings. Then Moore started his own committee to raise money. That was why he got into a fight with Sacco, how the bitterness started. That was why we let Moore go and got Thompson."

His voice was heavy with regret. "Ah, if we had had Thompson from the beginning, then we would have got them off. When we first went to him he was cold. He listened to us and he said he'd take the case for twenty-five thousand dollars. When he started he didn't know the difference between an anarchist and a Communist. You could tell that by an appeal he drew up that Vanzetti corrected. After he talked for some time with Vanzetti, he understood. It made all the difference. He took part then as if we were friends. A wonderful man, Thompson. An aristocrat, the way the word should mean. He would have made mincemeat of a man like Katzmann, if only we'd had him instead of Moore."

One thing I had been wanting to ask was about the various bombings connected with the case. Would he agree that anarchists had been responsible for them? Sacco and Vanzetti themselves were said to have been philosophical anarchists, as opposed to violence as Tolstoy was. But where did the dividing line come?

Felicani stared at me with his guileless eyes. "You know," he said, "there are times when a man is so desperate that he will do such a thing as set off a bomb. When that happens and to what man, I don't know. Vanzetti never could have done anything like that—but, yes, in certain circumstances Sacco might have. That is the type of man he was. But a holdup murder, to kill innocent men like that? It was quite impossible.

"Think of the times," he said, lifting his hands palms upward. "I carried a pistol in my pocket then. I never fired it, I didn't even know how to load it, but it gave me strength to feel it in my pocket." He stopped as if he were thinking again of those far-off days. I watched him, the peaceable elderly printer who had outlived his party and his time. Where the word *anarchism* had once aroused fear, it now brought a kind of nostalgia. Violent some of the anarchists may have been, but there had been an integrity about them, a trust in human nature that I could never have. Now here he was, gnarled and sturdy as an old oak, speaking to me of the lost comrades of his young manhood.

Afterward, as I walked out into the reverberant street, I felt I had put the bumf into perspective. I knew it was intuition rather than reason, that the historical method had fallen by the wayside, yet I did not see how anyone could spend an afternoon talking with Aldino Felicani and still feel that Sacco and Vanzetti were guilty. But that was the difficulty in trying to form any picture of an event by talking with the survivors. The three principals in the case whom I had seen in the flesh and who were now dead—District Attorney Katzmann, Governor Fuller, President Lowell of Harvard—I had judged harshly. But others I met, whom I had expected to find fools or knaves, I had found neither.

Among these was Michael Stewart, the Bridgewater police chief whose suspicions started the events that led to the arrest of Sacco and Vanzetti. Some time after the trial Stewart had left Bridgewater to become police chief of Scituate, a seaside town southeast of Braintree. He had a speech about the case that he liked to deliver at men's-club meetings. Now retired, he lived with his son in a white bungalow near Scituate Harbor. I knew the inside of it well: the gumwood trim, the nicknacks on the tapestry-brick mantel, the Child Jesus of Prague under cellophane, the sofa and the overstuffed chairs. Whenever I rang the bell I could see Stewart through the glass as he came limping to the door, lame from some old police injury. There was an unmistakable Celtic look about him from the cut of his mouth to the blueness of his eyes and the wave to his white hair.

Never since the night in 1920 that he had driven down to the Brockton police station to interview Sacco and Vanzetti had he ever had any doubt about their guilt. To him, it was all very simple. Godless men, atheists like Sacco and Vanzetti, were capable of any crime. Yet his relations with them after their arrest were for a period amiable, and he had liked Vanzetti.

"Sacco I never paid much attention to," he told me. "He was just a sap, but Vanzetti was a real interesting man. I used to drive him to the Plymouth trial from the jail, and each morning I saw him I'd say 'Hello, Bertie,' and he'd say 'Hello, Mike.' Sometimes he used to sing songs for us in Italian on the way over, and he had quite a voice. After he heard me testify in court though, the next time he saw me he raised his hands—he was handcuffed—and shook them at me. And he never spoke to me again. The thing I remember most about him is his eyes. He had terrible eyes, like fire when he looked at you."

Though Orciani, who was with Sacco and Vanzetti just before their arrest, had produced a watertight alibi after he was picked up, Stewart was nevertheless convinced of his guilt. "For my money Orciani was the cleverest of the lot," he told me. "That's how he managed to rig himself up such a good alibi. He was one of those wise guys. During the trial he used to go to court every day. There was a little room in back the defense had for exhibits and things like that, and he had charge of it. Most of the time he'd stand in the doorway watching what went on in court. Well, Katzmann spotted him there and the day they were cross-examining Vanzetti and asking him about where he got his gun, Katzmann looked straight at Orciani and said, 'I'll tell you, Mr. Vanzetti, where you got that gun.' You could hear his voice right down the corridor. 'You got it from your friend Orciani after he took it off of Berardelli's dead body.' Katzmann pointed his finger right at him and Orciani ducked. That was the last time he ever showed up."

One late-summer afternoon I drove to Billerica to meet Dr. Warren Stearns, dean emeritus of Tufts Medical School, who as state prison psychiatrist had seen Sacco and Vanzetti regularly in the years following their conviction. I found him in the study of his classically square colonial mansion facing the common. He was listening to a middle-aged man in heavy tortoise-shell spectacles who held an open book in his left hand and pointed to a passage with his right.

"It says here," the man explained, "ten thousand people were there to see him hanged. That was 1820. I wonder what would draw all those people to an execution?"

Stearns, with his wreath of kinky white hair surrounding a bald dome, looked amiable, but his voice was tart. "Cruelty. If it were announced that I was going to be publicly tortured and hanged next

Monday morning on Boston Common there'd be at least a hundred and fifty thousand people there to see it."

He beckoned to me apologetically and then, when the other had left, pointed to a chair. "I'm the Billerica antiquary," he said. "The local historians all call on me with their problems. Seventy-five years old I am. That gives me a life expectancy of five years—and it would take fifty for me to do all the things I have to do. You came here to ask me about Sacco and Vanzetti. What do you want to know?"

Without waiting for my answer he went on. "I don't think the truth will ever be known. As to whether they did it or not, I don't know and I've made a point of not trying to know. I tell you this, though. They weren't criminal types. For a while I think I saw them as much as anyone. Sacco had a very winning way about him. Of course he was a more settled type, with a wife and family. Vanzetti reminded me of a trade-union leader. That rigid mentality. He once said to me that where he came from in Italy there was a castle above the town and one family living in it had been oppressing the ordinary people in the valley for eight hundred years. I told him that it wasn't so in America, that a family scarcely lasted three generations here. He'd read a little, but he'd not digested it too well—an unstable, wandering type, paranoid at times. When I saw him once over in the Charlestown Prison he said to me, 'I don't deny the right of the state to execute a man, but they have no right to castrate me and make me a laughingstock.' "

The doctor had known personally almost everyone connected with the case on both sides. Katzmann was to him lazy and incompetent, though he thought better of his assistant, Harold Williams. Judge Thayer he gave credit for honest intentions, but found him irascible, a snob, and obsessed with the idea that the Communists were just about to take over the United States. Governor Fuller was merely a successful automobile salesman. Thompson he respected, but felt that he had gone into the case merely for the fee.

"I thought," I said, making another stab at it, "that seeing Sacco and Vanzetti so closely, you might have formed some opinion as to their guilt or innocence."

"I feel," he said, "as William James did about psychic phenomena. I just do not know."

When I left, he walked out with me through his back garden blooming with zinnias. "If you are interested," he said finally, "I'll try to find my files on Sacco and Vanzetti for you. There may be something there. I've had so many cases since that I can't remember the details. But drop in when you're by this way again."

Three weeks later he was dead.

By chance I discovered that Beltrando Brini was living in Wollaston, a twenty-minute drive from my home in Wellesley. When a boy of thirteen, Brini had testified at Vanzetti's first trial that the two of them had been delivering eels in Plymouth the day before Christmas, 1919—the day Vanzetti was to be found guilty of attempting a holdup in Bridgewater. As he grew up, Brini had broken away from the Italian community. He had graduated from Boston University and was now an elementary school principal. Community affairs seemed to take up most of his spare time. Two weeks passed before he could find a free evening to see me. I found his house easily enough, a decent inconspicuous house in a decent inconspicuous street. He was a small man in his fifties. Like many of the second generation he still looked Italian, but to a diminished degree. He showed me into his living room. His wife was standing near the fireplace, a thin fair-haired woman, not Latin at all. After he had introduced me to her we sat down, taking each other's measure while she went into the kitchen to make coffee.

"You know," he said finally, "I could have been a musician. I really could at one time have gotten into the Boston Symphony Orchestra. But I thought it was safer to be a teacher. That's why I never seem to be home nights—always something they want a school principal to be doing, somewhere they want him to be." He looked at me sharply. "You want to know about Vanzetti. He lived with us a long time. He paid more attention to me than my parents did. He was kind to all children. I remember one Halloween we all had jack-o'-lanterns. The others had theirs lighted but mine didn't have a candle in it. Vanzetti came along and asked me why I didn't get a candle. I said I hadn't any money. He asked me how much candles cost and I said two cents, so he fished in his pocket and gave them to me. When I got to the hardware store I found he'd given me a cent and a dime. So I got my candle and I brought him back the nine cents. I'd never had that much money in my pocket before, but I remember how proud of myself I was that I brought that nine cents back to him.

"I remember the last time I saw him before his arrest. It's a thing I somehow still feel ashamed about. A bunch of us were playing ball in Suosso's Lane and somebody hit one over the fence into a garden. While I was climbing over to get it I trampled on some vegetables and the man who owned the garden came out and started to bawl me out. I answered him back, like any fresh kid. Then Vanzetti came along, took me over by the fence, and talked to me. He wasn't angry, he didn't raise his voice, but what he said made me feel ashamed. I didn't feel like playing ball any more. I've often wished it hadn't been that way, the last time I saw him free.

"You know, of course," he went on, "that I testified I was delivering eels with him the morning he was supposed to have been holding up the pay truck in Bridgewater. That's been the terrible thing for me. I *was* there with him all that morning long, and I couldn't make them believe me. Sometimes I've asked myself, Could I have been wrong, could I have dreamed it all? Was Vanzetti really at Bridgewater? But then I know, I *know* that I was delivering eels with him that morning. It couldn't have been any other day, because that's the one day Italians always eat eels, no matter what they cost. And I remember how I started out that morning to go to Vanzetti's house. It was muddy and I forgot my rubbers. At the corner I met my father and he sent me back for them, so I was late. Vanzetti was waiting for me with the pushcart. We delivered eels until, it must have been, two o'clock. It's funny the things you remember. I remember a two-family house where I made a mistake and went to the wrong door. When we got all through Vanzetti paid me off at the corner of Cherry Lane and Court Street. And I know that it happened that way, that it was the day before Christmas, the same day and the same time they said he was holding up the truck in Bridgewater. When I told my story in court Katzmann complimented me on learning my part so well.

"I was only thirteen then and I was scared. I'd never been in a court before. Katzmann would go at me like a tiger, fire three questions at me at once. Thayer would never help me out. His face was so stern. He never said anything, but you could feel his hostility."

Brini's wife came in with a tray, and Brini took a pile of magazines from the coffee table to make room.

"Tell me," I said, as she joined us. "If you had a friend in trouble you knew was innocent, could you lie to establish an alibi for him?"

He leaned back in his chair for some seconds, frowning slightly, while his wife poured the coffee. "I thought you might ask me something like that," he said finally. "No, I couldn't. I suppose you wanted me to say yes, but I couldn't. I don't know why I couldn't, either."

"Could you?" his wife asked me.

"Yes," I said truthfully, "I could quite easily. Under oath too."

"So could I," she said, looking at her husband as if she thought he was being foolish.

"Well," he said, "I know this, that I didn't want to go to court. Young as I was, I knew what a disadvantage it would be for me to get mixed up in it. I wanted to be a musician, and whatever I might want, once I testified, I knew I'd find the way blocked. And it's shadowed me ever since. They've pointed me out—Brini, the boy who testified for a murderer. In 1927 I told my story to Governor Fuller, and he said he believed me, but he never did anything about it. The day before they were executed I tried to see the governor again, but I couldn't get past his secretary. I shouted at him, 'If I lied, why don't you arrest me for perjury?' All he said was, if I was so brave why wasn't I out picketing on the Common. I told him I'd been there the day before, and I asked to be locked up, but he just turned his back."

He set down his coffee cup. "I don't suppose what I've been telling you helps you much. These are just my feelings. Those others, where we delivered the eels that morning, they didn't want to testify either. They were all good Catholics and Vanzetti was an anarchist. But they'd bought the eels, they'd seen Vanzetti, and my father talked to them. They had respect for him, not fear but respect, so they went."

As we talked the lights of the suburban street began to wink out, and I could see it was time for me to go. "You'll probably think of things you forgot to ask me," he said at the door. "Just telephone me or come down, if there's anything more you want to know. Any time."

Driving home, I thought over what Brini had told me. What had a respectable school principal to gain by lying? If he had had anything to hide, forty years after the event, he could simply have refused to see me. Yet if Brini was telling the truth, Vanzetti was innocent of the Bridgewater holdup. And if he was innocent of the first crime, it seemed to me he was most probably innocent of the second. But Brini knew. If he had told me the truth, Vanzetti was an innocent man.

"I think you can sense whether a person is telling the truth or not," I told a sergeant at the State Police headquarters a few days later. "You can judge a man by the sort of person he is, by the general impression he gives as much as by what he says. You can size him

up, don't you think?" The sergeant did not reply directly, but his
laugh had a jeering ring.

For weeks I had been trying to get an interview with Michael
Dray, Katzmann's old law partner, but always, without quite turning
me down, he had eluded me. Katzmann had been dead six years, but
Dray still kept the firm's name. After the trial Katzmann had never
made any public comment on his great case. Nor since his death had
his partner been less reticent.

Finally, unexpectedly, Dray offered to see me. I drove through
Dedham again, past the rain-wet courthouse with its glistening
columns, down the empty High Street and across the empty square,
and then through the mean industrial section of East Dedham, following the loops of the Neponset River to Hyde Park. It was a strange
feeling to be on that journey, as if I might at last be heading toward
the center of the maze.

Katzmann & Dray—there was the name on the downstairs directory
of the modernized office building on River Street. Upstairs it was not
quite so modern. I followed the dark, creaking corridor until I faced
the name painted on an open door, then walked into a narrow brown
room with nothing in it but a table, a lamp, and a gilt-framed photograph of Katzmann. I recognized him at once from the afternoon at
Dedham: the square domineering head with the close-cropped hair.

Dray came suddenly out of a back room, a short, pudgy man in his
sixties, with thin mouse-gray hair and blue eyes. "Just go in there,"
he said pointing to another room, "and I'll be right with you."

On the oak door were the faded letters F. G. KATZMANN, Room 12.
Stepping inside, I found myself alone. An oak desk faced me. On its
plate-glass top I noticed the issue of *American Heritage* containing
my Sacco-Vanzetti article with the Ben Shahn illustrations—to my
embarrassment, for my description of Katzmann in it was not flattering.

Dray strode in briskly, sat down at the desk, and stared at me
several seconds before speaking. "I could have seen you at any time
within the last two months," he said finally, "but I couldn't make up
my mind whether to or not. This is what decided me." He tapped
the magazine. "You write here that though you thought they were
innocent, just by reading the evidence alone you'd have found them
guilty. When I read that I decided you at least were honest. But for
that I'd not have seen you.

"You know that Fred, as long as he lived, refused to discuss this case publicly with anyone. Of course he mentioned it to me. I don't suppose a day went by that he didn't think of it in one way or another. I saw him come in sometimes with tears in his eyes and say, 'Why do they say these things about me? Why do they keep on attacking me?' Don't think he wasn't hurt.

"Now he's gone, thinking it over, I'm willing to tell you a few things I know to set the record straight, because so much has been said against him. Fred was almost like a father to me. I was twenty-four when I came here just after the trial, and I studied what law I know right here in this office. Fred never had a son of his own, just his two daughters, and I think he came to look on me sort of as a son. All I know is this: My son's at law school now, and if I can teach him as much decency and as much law as Fred Katzmann did me, I'll think I'm a lucky man. You think I admire Fred. I do."

He opened the *American Heritage*. "Here you speak of Katzmann as being, in spite of his name, a Mayflower descendant. He wasn't. His father was a German, his mother Scotch and came from Roxbury. They were poor. His mother used to work. Fred had nothing. I think when he went to Harvard an aunt helped him out a little, but he used to tend furnaces to work his way through. Sometimes he earned a bit singing. He had a fine voice. Even when he was starting up his practice he still used to sing sometimes at churches and funerals.

"We got pretty close over the years. I don't think in the end there was anything he kept back from me. I knew about his family, his social life, his practice. I knew how he felt about the Sacco-Vanzetti case. In that he never changed. He didn't just think they were guilty, he *knew* they were guilty. He wouldn't have avoided the case, for he never did put off dirty jobs onto other people, but sometimes he'd say to me, 'Mike, if I had my life to live over, I'd never want to go through that again.' He always felt it shortened his wife's life, the whole business. For years they had to have guards round his house. He said whenever he woke up nights he'd hear them tramping round.

"A lot of things I set myself out to tell you," Dray went on, "but they slip through my mind right now. Just this, though. I've built up a good practice in Hyde Park. I've done all right here. But I always have the feeling somehow that it was Fred's practice, that anything I've amounted to has been through him. I want to defend his memory, and that's why I'm talking to you.

"I'll tell you another thing. When Jerry McAnarney was on the Sacco-Vanzetti defense, he thought his clients were innocent. I never heard any of the Defense Committee boys criticize Jerry. He went to the governor's committee afterward and he still thought they were innocent. But he and Fred stayed the same good friends all through the years. They were partners together on that Willett-Sears case. Maybe you remember, that case lasted fourteen months—the longest jury case in the history of Massachusetts. I suppose if anyone asked Fred to name his ten best friends, Jerry McAnarney would have been among them. And if Jerry named his best five, Fred would have been on the list. I remember, too, just a short while before Jerry died he said one day right in this office: 'No matter what they said about you, Fred, you were all right.' "

So we talked—or rather, I listened—as the lawyer talked through the afternoon. Katzmann had avoided the Dedham courtroom the day Thayer passed sentence, but Dray had gone there deliberately, and had heard Vanzetti's speech to the court and watched him point his finger at the judge. For Dray, Vanzetti had seemed a sinister figure at that moment with his glaring eyes, his heavy bobbing mustache, and his passionate foreign voice.

Inevitably, we got to the subject of the guns.

"There's a church just across the street," Dray said. "The priest, Father Fraher, had a brother who was in here after the trial. He told Fred, 'You want to know where Berardelli got his gun? He got it from me, that's where he got it.' There was a crack or nick or some sort of mark on the handle, and this Fraher said, 'If the one you found on Vanzetti has that mark on it, it's the same gun.' He hadn't even seen the gun then, mind you, but when we showed it to him, there was the mark, just like he said.

"Ah," he said at last, sadness in his voice, "I wish I could explain to you in words what Fred really was. You couldn't really understand him, seeing him just that once. Perhaps you were fed up with being on a jury. Fred wasn't tricky. He was honest all the way through. I remember some man came in here once and wanted Fred to defend him in a robbery case, offered him five thousand dollars. That was a lot more money then than it is today. When he came to pay Fred, he brought the money in a box, all in bills, done up in little piles. As soon as Fred saw it, he wouldn't touch the case. That money looked too much like payroll money. But an assistant district attorney over in Suffolk County didn't mind taking it. No, you couldn't get Fred to do anything that had even a suspicion of being wrong. He was that kind of man."

I left Dray in the anteroom. We shook hands beside Katzmann's picture. "I'm glad you came," he said finally.

Out I went into the slashing rain, to my car parked by the dark bulk of the Catholic church where Father Fraher or his successor was probably still hearing confessions. If only Dray could have whipped open one of his filing cabinets and taken out the ultimate document that would have satisfied everyone from Aldino Felicani in his sheet-metal office to the corporation lawyer on Federal Street. I would have settled for a villain, but I had found only decent-enough people in irreconcilable positions, and still at the core of the labyrinth two men who had died a third of a century earlier in the electric chair.

◇◇◇◇◇◇◇◇◇◇◇◇◇◇◇◇◇◇◇◇◇◇◇◇◇◇◇◇◇◇◇◇◇◇◇

CHAPTER THREE

April 15th, 1920

Thursday mornings Shelley Neal, the South Braintree agent for the American Express Company, met the 9:18 local from Boston to pick up the payrolls of the Slater & Morrill and Walker & Kneeland shoe factories. Until January 1920, the payrolls had been sent down on Wednesdays, but recently there had been so many holdups around Boston that the head office had altered its delivery schedules.

It was an uneasy time, that year after the soldiers returned. In November the savings bank in the neighboring town of Randolph, a few miles west of Braintree, had been held up and robbed. A month later, on the day before Christmas, four men in a touring car had tried to rob the paymaster of the L. Q. White shoe factory in Bridgewater, sixteen miles to the south. An unknown gang had recently stolen several freight-car loads of shoes belonging to Slater & Morrill. Almost every week Neal received a notice from the Boston office warning him to take every precaution, particularly to watch out for suspicious strangers. He now carried his 38-caliber Colt in his pocket with the pocket flap tucked inside so that he could reach for it quickly.

South Braintree was the other side of the New York, New Haven & Hartford tracks, at the wrong end of town. Had there been a national-bank branch there, the payroll money would not have had to be sent down by train, but the triangle of factories and narrow streets and workers' houses was not commercially important enough. Braintree itself, lying ten miles south of Boston, was an undistinguished community of about fifteen thousand inhabitants that one passed through almost absent-mindedly on the old turnpike road to Cape Cod.

On Thursday morning, April 15, Neal, in his customary dark suit, derby, and overcoat, waited on the station platform with Art Stevens, one of his expressmen. The 9:18 was late. Neal drew out his gold Waltham on its heavy chain with the Masonic seal. Nine twenty-one. He could hear the wail of the steam-whistle—two long notes, a short, and a long—as the train approached the Braintree crossing. It would take another five minutes to reach South Braintree.

His express wagon was backed up to the curb, the driver hunched forward on the seat, his coat collar over his ears. Between the shafts the horse jingled his brasses, stamped, steamed, and tossed his head. Although the sun was four hours up, the air still held an aftermath of winter. Neal's blunt hands with their hairy knuckles showed red, the diamond set in the thick gold band on his left ring finger reflected the light coldly.

A cumulus puff from the invisible train billowed up, blurring the horizon outline of the water towers on Penns Hill, Quincy. Within a minute the engine rounded the curve, growing larger as it moved soundlessly against the wind. Then the whistle echoed again and suddenly the train loomed up on the Union Street crossing by the Victorian brick aggregate of Thayer Academy. The station windows began to vibrate with the sound.

Almost before Neal was aware of it the train had slipped into the station, the brass bell on the boiler clanging, the driving wheels slurring to a halt. He waved to the engineer as the cab passed. Below the station at the Pearl Street crossing Mike Levangie, the lank-mustached, one-legged gate-tender, hobbled out of his shack and cranked down the double gate, then clumped over the tracks and lowered the single one.

Several passengers got off, a man and a woman got on, the station-master came out to check a bundle of Boston newspapers. Neal and Stevens walked to the baggage car where the freight clerk was waiting for them. Neal did not know his name—he was a new fellow—but he was a Mason. "Cold morning," he remarked as he shoved an iron box across the floor. It contained some thirty thousand dollars in bills and coin. After Neal had signed the receipt book the clerk handed him the box's key in a sealed envelope.

Neal and Stevens carried the box across the platform to the wagon and pushed it under the seat. Then Neal climbed up beside the driver. The driver flicked the reins and the horse started forward. Stevens, who had climbed over the tailboard, remained standing. Just as the wagon began to move, the locomotive backed up suddenly with a clank of couplings. Its piston rods reversed, a jet of steam shot from the cylinders, and the train started off in the direction of Weymouth, Hingham, and the South Shore.

The shadow of the wagon moved diagonally across Railroad Avenue toward the Hampton House, a mansard-roofed structure, four stories high, that had been built in the seventies for a trunk factory. It now housed the Slater & Morrill offices as well as the cutting rooms of the upper factory—Slater & Morrill's lower factory was some distance away on Pearl Street. On the ground floor of the Hampton House, to the left of the center entrance, was the express company's office. The gilt sign over its door, unchanged from an earlier day, read *New York & Boston Despatch Express Co.*

Its clapboarding flaked and blistered, the gray building lay full in the slanting sunlight that burnished its windows. A narrow grass border divided the avenue from an indented strip of pavement in front of the porticoed Slater & Morrill entrance. Six or seven cars were parked along the outside of the border. Neal recognized them. It was still possible to know all the cars in town at sight. "A lot of autos here this morning," he remarked to the driver. There was one auto parked by the granite curb near the central entrance that Neal had never seen before: a touring car, dark and shiny as if it had just been polished. The top was up, the rear side curtains were fastened in place, and the motor was running. Neal's driver had to turn out sharply to avoid scraping its fender. A man slumped down in the driver's seat did not turn or look at them. He wore a felt hat, and his shoulders were hunched so that all Neal could see was the back of his neck, and his right hand on the steering wheel. Then, standing in the doorway under the portico, Neal noticed a second man, thin and fair-haired, with a pale sunken face. He had on a brown coat like an old army overcoat and he wore a gray hat pulled over his forehead. Neal did not like his looks.

The driver backed the wagon into the space in front of the express office, and Neal and Stevens carried the box inside. After the outside chill the office was warmly pleasant, smelling of floor oil and cigars. Neal took the key from the envelope and opened the box. Inside were the payrolls for the two companies, each in a brown canvas bag stamped National Shawmut Bank. He took out the Slater & Morrill bag and put the box containing the Walker and Kneeland money in the safe. Then he closed the safe door, pressed down the nickel-plated handle, and spun the dial.

With the bag tucked under his arm Neal motioned to Stevens and they started out the door toward the building's center entrance.

Neal now noticed another strange car. This one was parked across the avenue, facing south. He could not tell what kind it was. It was streaked with mud. He heard its driver call out "All right!" to the man in the first car. The pale man was still standing under the portico leaning against the door post. His hands were thrust into his overcoat pockets, and he held his head low, but as Neal and Stevens passed he stared up at them, moving his eyes without lifting his head. Neal felt for the reassurance of the Colt in his pocket. The man did not move. He had blue bulging eyes, the whites muddied, and his skin was yellowish, sickly, as if he were tubercular.

There was something queer about him, about his being there, Neal felt as he trudged up to the second floor. "Some funny-looking people round here today," he told the girl at the desk. Margaret Mahoney, the paymistress, was at her desk by the water cooler. Neal had known Margaret Mahoney for years. The payroll bag was heavy for her so he walked across the office and put it in the safe himself. She gave him the receipt for it, and he and Stevens started downstairs.

From the top of the landing Neal could see the pale man still standing in the doorway but when he was about halfway down the man took his hands out of his pockets, walked over to the touring car, opened the rear door, and got in. Neal kept his hand on his Colt. By the time he reached the doorway the car had started up and swung round the corner of Holbrook Avenue. The mud-streaked car had already disappeared.

South Braintree Square was empty at half-past ten when Harry Dolbeare, a piano tuner, finished a cup of coffee at Torrey's Drugstore on the corner and started up Washington Street to Cuff's Music Store. Cuff had called him the day before to see about the felts on a secondhand upright, and Dolbeare told him he would have a look at it. As he reached Gregor's Restaurant he noticed a black touring car turning left from Holbrook Avenue to Washington Street. He could see two men in front and, although the rear side curtains were up, three more men in the back seat. One of the men in back was leaning forward talking to the driver. Dolbeare had never seen any of them before, or the car either. They looked to him like foreigners, maybe some of that Dago bunch from the Fore River shipyards. Tough tickets, the lot of them, he thought to himself after the car had passed him.

At 11:15 Lola Hassam, a hard-faced woman in her forties, got off the train from Quincy with Julia Campbell, the old woman who rented one of her two rooms in the Alhambra Block there. Lola now called herself Lola Andrews, her name before her divorce, although some people said she had never been married. At various times she had been a waitress, a cleaning woman, and a practical nurse. Men often used to come to her room in the Alhambra. Since things were slack in Quincy, she and Julia had decided to come to South Braintree and look for work in one of the shoe factories.

They crossed the tracks by the gate-tender's shack at the end of Railroad Avenue, walked down Pearl Street past the double pipe fence in front of Rice & Hutchins, and continued another twenty-five yards to the lower Slater & Morrill factory. Julia Campbell was developing cataracts, and she took the younger woman's arm going downhill.

About thirty feet from the factory they passed a black touring car parked at the side of the road. A dark stocky man with high cheekbones was bending over the raised hood adjusting the motor. Lola Andrews saw another man sitting in the back of the car, a pale, sick-looking sort of fellow in a khaki overcoat.

The men paid no attention to them and the women walked up the steps of Slater & Morrill. Once inside they could not locate the employment office. As they stood there undecided, a middle-aged man in a business suit came down the corridor and asked them what they wanted.

"We want work, mister," Lola Andrews said. The man said that three months ago he could have given them both jobs. Now they were not taking on any new help. She was not to be put off so easily, insisting she had heard in Quincy that the factory needed people. He told her she had heard wrong. "Isn't this Rice and Hutchins?" she asked him finally.

No, he told her, Rice & Hutchins was up the road.

When the women again passed the touring car, the pale man in the overcoat was standing behind it and the dark man had crawled underneath and was working on the motor from below, his head and shoulders just visible through the spokes of the front wheel. Lola had almost to step over his feet to get by. He had a screwdriver in his hand, and just as she was opposite him he glanced up at her.

"Pardon me," she said, "could you tell me how to get to the factory office?"

He crawled out from under the car, stood up, and asked her what factory she wanted. When she told him Rice & Hutchins, he pointed out the brick building and told her to take the driveway to the left; that was the office up there.

Lola and old Julia went down the gravel walk along the side of the brick building, up the stairs, and through the double folding doors. They could see the Employment Office sign there plainly enough.

Whenever William Tracey drove to the square on an errand, as he did two or three times a day, he liked to drive by his building, the wooden three-decker he had built in 1907 at the corner of Hancock and Pearl. Torrey's Drugstore occupied the ground floor. That Thursday morning as he parked on Pearl to pick up his wife's groceries at Dyer & Sullivan's, just across from the drugstore, he noticed two strangers standing with their backs to Torrey's window where the big glass vase of red water hung from its chains. The men were swarthy, about medium height, one just a little taller than the other. If it had been twelve o'clock the streets would have been full of factory hands and he probably would not have noticed them, but it was still half an hour before the noon whistle and the square was empty. He could not help but notice them.

After Tracey reached home with the groceries he found he had forgotten bread, so he drove back again, past his building and left to Schrout's Bakery on Pearl Street. The strange men were still leaning against the window as he went in. When he came out they were gone.

Not quite an hour later William Heron, a railroad detective, noticed the same two men in the station. They were sitting on a bench by the gents' toilet smoking cigarettes and talking in some foreign language. Dagos, he thought they were. He had come down on the 12:27 from Boston, and he was scarcely off the train before he spotted a fresh kid who had climbed on top of the Union News stand and was trying to tip it over. Eleven or twelve years old he was, one of that gang that hung around the station afternoons. Heron grabbed him by the collar and ran him into the operator's room. The Dagos didn't even look up as he went by.

McNamara was the kid's name. The operator said his old man was all right, worked for the railroad, so Heron told the kid what he'd do to him if he ever caught him hanging round the station again, and let him go. He was not in the operator's room more than five minutes, but when he stepped out again the Dagos had left. Somehow they stuck in his mind, and he wondered where they had gone to.

By trade Ralph DeForest was a shoemaker, though he had been unemployed for two months now. When he had nothing else to do, and that was most of the time, he wandered around South Braintree Square or sometimes dropped in at Magazu's poolroom on Pearl Street. At 2:20 he was talking with Officer Shea on the corner next to Torrey's when he spotted two men in front of the jewelry store. In the last two months he had seen everyone in town, but he had never seen those two before. Shea left to go up to the town hall and DeForest walked down by the fruit store past the jeweler's. The two men looked him over as if they wanted to make something of it. Dark men they were, tough babies. He wasn't going to let them think he was scared of them, though. Deliberately he turned round and walked past them again. They stared at him, and he stared at them, and finally he said: "I don't think I owe you fellows anything."

Without answering him they started off down Pearl Street, one about five feet ahead of the other. DeForest decided he would follow them. At the crossing they turned left toward the station. Just in front of the station a pinch-faced man in a brown coat was tinkering with the engine of a black touring car. The other two paused on the platform and DeForest brushed right by them and through the station into the toilet. When he came out the car and men had disappeared.

At ten minutes to three Jenny Novelli, a nurse, was on her way down Pearl Street to call on her friend Mrs. Knipps, who lived on Colbert Avenue, a dead-end dirt road just beyond Rice & Hutchins on the left. As she passed Schrout's Bakery she noticed a large curtained touring car abreast of her and going in the same direction scarcely faster than she was walking. The car kept level with her until she reached the cobbler's shop on the corner. At first she thought the man next to the driver was a friend of hers, William Mooney, but at second glance she realized she was mistaken. The pale driver she scarcely noticed.

For sixteen years Lewis Wade had been working in the sole-leather room at Slater & Morrill. Then, late in 1919, the boss had put him in charge of the shed and gasoline pump in front of the lower factory. Any time the company cars needed gas he went out to take care of them. Every afternoon at the same time Hans Behrsin, Mr. Slater's chauffeur, would come round to fill up Slater's Marmon sedan, and Wade was always ready for him with the shed door open and the pump unlocked.

On this April 15 just before three o'clock, Behrsin dropped by as usual and said he was on his way to the garage and that he would be back in ten minutes. A couple of minutes after three, as Wade was hitching the hose onto the pump, he happened to see a touring car below the factory in front of the little wooden house that belonged to the carpenter at Rice & Hutchins. A man was bending over the hood of the car fixing something.

Behrsin pulled up alongside the shed with the gray Marmon and Wade put in about eight gallons of gas. While he was cranking he kept watching the black car until before he knew it the tank had overflowed. Behrsin and he wiped up the overflow, then Behrsin drove off up Pearl Street toward the station.

As he passed Rice & Hutchins he saw two men sitting on the pipe fence near the end of the building, their feet on the lower bar. He knew they were strangers, but that was all he noticed about them.

From the time Shelley Neal brought in the payroll money, Margaret Mahoney had been dividing it to make up the envelopes for the lower factory. There were almost five hundred separate envelopes to be filled, and dividing the $15,776.51 took her right up to three o'clock, with only about ten minutes off for lunch. After she had sealed the envelopes she packed them in two wooden cases that went inside steel cashboxes with Yale locks. Hardly had she got the locks fastened before Mr. Parmenter and his guard Berardelli, the one everyone called the detective, stood there waiting for them.

Frederick Parmenter was in his middle forties, a full-faced man with a short mustache. The solidness of his body, his slightly sagging features and thinning brown hair made him seem older. Margaret Mahoney and the other girls in the office looked forward to his weekly visits. He liked to joke and pretend to make dates with them, though it was only in fun, for he had been married for years and did not play around. He was always very careful of his dress. That day he wore a white shirt with black and pink stripes and a new brown felt hat. Before he left he kidded a bit with the bookkeepers, Frances Devlin and Mary Splaine. He said he would take his pay now while there was still some money, and Margaret Gabney, the assistant bookkeeper, told him he had better, for there might not be any tomorrow. Then he took one of the cashboxes by the handle, and the detective took the other. The detective was just another Italian who never said anything.

Margaret Mahoney remembered afterward how Parmenter stood for a moment in the doorway and then how the stairs creaked as he and the detective walked down. It was a few minutes past three.

Outside the main entrance of the Hampton House, Parmenter, with Berardelli behind him, met Albert Frantello from the lower factory. Frantello said he was on his way to the office to get some cardboard tags. The paymaster and his guard walked on out of the shadow of the Hampton House.

Frances Devlin and Mary Splaine watched them for some minutes from their window on the second floor. Parmenter, without an overcoat, kept to the outside of the gravel walk and the detective, his overcoat buttoned up, walked a little way behind him. Just before they reached the crossing Parmenter shifted the cashbox from his left to his right hand. Fifteen feet beyond him the gate-tender was out washing a window of his shack.

From the cutting room on the third floor, Mark Carrigan, also looking out a window, kept his eye on the paymaster and the detective with their boxes as they passed the cobbler's shop on the corner and went on toward the railroad-crossing sign. Just beyond the crossing, they stopped to talk with a man coming uphill from the other direction. Then they went on down, behind the high board fence by the water tower.

The first-floor windows of the lower Slater & Morrill factory were open, and Minnie Kennedy and Louise Hayes at their workbench noticed a touring car parked by the side of the street only about ten feet from them. A slight fair-haired man in a blue suit was fussing with the motor, lifting one side of the hood and then the other. Finally he stood by the front mudguard and lit a cigarette. A sickly young man he seemed, but not bad-looking. While he was standing there with a screwdriver in his hand, Thomas Treacy drove up with a wagonload of coal for Slater & Morrill, noticed the man's light hair, and remembered that he had seen the same car with another man in front of the railroad station early that morning.

After a while the two girls watched the fair-haired man get into the car, drive down Pearl Street toward the swamp, turn round, and start back again.

Roy Gould had invented an oil-and-pumice paste for sharpening safety razor blades. All you needed to do was smear a little on the edge of a blade, run the blade a couple of times around the inside rim of a glass tumbler, and it was as good as new. He used to go to the different South Shore factories on paydays and sell his paste at the gates as the men came out. On April 15 he arrived at South Braintree on the 2:59 train. There was a young fellow standing on the platform and Gould asked him if he knew where and how they paid off at the shoe factories. The other pointed to two men walking down the street to the railroad crossing. "There goes the paymaster now," he told him. "Just follow him."

Gould started off toward the gateman's shack. He could see the paymaster stop briefly at the crossing to talk with someone, then disappear behind the board fence the other side of the tracks.

Jimmy Bostock, the bandy-legged machine repairman, hurrying up Pearl Street from the lower factory to get the 3:15 trolley to Brockton, was near the water tower when he saw Parmenter and Berardelli coming down the street. He crossed over to meet them.

"Bostock," Parmenter said as he came up, "there's a pulley off one of the motors up at Number One."

"I can't look at it, not today," Bostock told him. "I got to get this quarter-past-three trolley to Brockton to do a job there."

"Well," said Parmenter amiably, "they just told me to tell you if I saw you. That's all." While they were talking, Behrsin drove by in the Marmon sedan, honking and waving as he passed. Bostock said he would have to leg it to catch his trolley. "Don't let me keep you," Parmenter told him. He and his guard continued down the gravel walk.

Parmenter shifted the cashbox from his right to his left hand. The afternoon sun was warm on his back. To his right was the garage with the tin roof, and beyond it the tower of Rice & Hutchins. The lilac bush on the little dirt triangle in front of the factory was just coming into bud. A flock of pigeons circled over the tower, then headed back to their loft in Cain's livery stable. Across the street, beyond a pile of bricks, some Italians were digging the cellar for a new restaurant. A loaded truck had just started up out of the excavation. Jim McGlone's dump cart was pulled up to the curb beside a couple of little carts into which the Italians were shoveling dirt.

Parmenter passed the telephone pole with the red fire-alarm box on it. Two strangers were standing by the fence in front of Rice & Hutchins, dark squat men, their hands in their pockets. One wore a cap, the other a felt hat. He kept on past them, one step, two steps, three . . .

As his guard, still following, reached the telephone pole, the strangers whipped their hands from their pockets, and the man in the cap lunged forward, pinning Berardelli by the shoulder with his left hand while his right brought up a pistol. Berardelli tried to grapple with him, but before he could get a grip the man fired into him three times. Parmenter turned like a cat to find the same man now facing him, pistol in hand, and Berardelli just behind, his knees buckling. Then the gun muzzle flashed and a bullet struck him in the chest. He flinched, took a few steps sideways, and the man fired again. This time the bullet struck him in the back, and as he staggered across the street his legs began to go limp. Berardelli lay in the gutter, his arms twitching, the second cashbox just beyond the reach of his right hand. The man in the felt hat snatched up the box, then darted out toward the box Parmenter had dropped.

The man in the cap, who had followed Parmenter halfway across the street, now signaled with his pistol and fired again. As he did so the dark touring car that had been parked below Slater & Morrill seventy-five yards away started jerkily uphill with a grinding of gears.

The staccato sound of the shots echoed from the factory walls. From the loft of the livery stable the pigeons swirled up into the sunshine, then wheeled over the Hampton House. At the end of the wooden fence, almost at the crossing, Jimmy Bostock turned to see Berardelli doubling up and the gunman firing. Parmenter was walking jerkily across the street, and Bostock did not realize the paymaster had been hit until he began to sag. Seeing him fall, Bostock took a few steps toward him, but as he did so the man in the cap froze him by the fence with two shots.

The touring car churned along the street, sputtering and skipping, the driver furiously working the spark lever on the steering wheel. Berardelli had managed to get to his hands and knees. Before the car stopped a man, crouched on the running board, sprang off near the brick pile. He had an automatic in his hand. Stepping to the swaying Berardelli, he fired point-blank. Berardelli collapsed in the gravel. The first two bandits had piled into the back seat with the cashboxes. After firing several shots at the upper factory windows, the third bandit climbed in the back seat after them. As the car whined toward the crossing he crawled over into the front seat, leaning out, pistol in hand.

Wade was just snapping the lock on the gas pump when he heard the noise and looked up the street, thinking the Italians had started a fight. He saw Parmenter drop behind the cart and then watched a wavy-haired man shoot at Berardelli.

Along the front of each floor of Rice & Hutchins were nine rows of frosted-glass windows. Even if the sash of the middle cutting-room window on the first floor had not been jammed several inches above the sill, the cutters at their benches might still have heard the shots above the noise of the machinery. The jammed window made this certain. At the sound William Brenner leaned forward from his cutting board to peer through the slit, as did Louis Pelser on his right. As they looked down they saw Berardelli writhing in the gutter almost directly below them and a man with a pistol standing over him. Afterward they found it difficult to remember just what or how much they had seen in that one glimpse. As Pelser later testified, "We seen a glance of the whole thing." From behind them Peter McCullum sprang on top of the bench, kicking the cutting boards aside and throwing the window up to the sash. What he saw was a dark man pushing a box in a car with his right hand. The sunshine was flickering on a whitish pistol in his left hand.

"Duck!" McCullum yelled, "There's shooting going on!" Another shot echoed, and there was a tinkle of broken glass. McCullum, Brenner, Pelser, and the rest of the cutters threw themselves on the floor under the benches. A few seconds later a cutter at the other end of the room shouted that the automobile was crossing the tracks. They crawled out from under the benches, and Pelser pushed down to the end of the room where someone had opened the last window. He managed to see only the rear of the car jolting over the tracks but he could still make out the license plate. Going back to his cutting board he wrote down the number: 49783.

From the treeing room on the floor above, the foreman, Edgar Langlois, glanced incredulously down at the slumped Berardelli and the two strangers. "Someone's been shot!" he shouted and ran for the wall telephone in the corridor. Barbara Liscomb peered from the window to see the paymaster and his guard on the ground, and just below her a dark, short, hatless man with a pistol in his hand. As she looked, he lifted his head and stared directly at her, a face that she could never afterward get out of her mind. He pointed his pistol, but before the bullet crashed through the pane over her head she had fainted. Langlois, dashing back, looked out again to see the dark car rolling toward the crossing. The glass had been removed from the back window and a rifle or shotgun barrel was sticking through the opening.

In the Slater & Morrill lower factory Minnie Kennedy and Louise Hayes had gone upstairs to the ladies' room. When they heard the shots they dashed to the window just in time to catch a glimpse of the vanishing car.

From the kitchen of the frame house in back of the excavation Annie Nichols, so startled that she could hardly breathe, had watched the shooting, seen Berardelli and Parmenter fall, and the laborers scatter and dodge toward her fence. Then the touring car appeared and a man tossed the cashboxes into it. In his house next door Maurice Colbert, a carman for the railroad, had just gone into the kitchen to take off his coat when he heard the shots and saw the Italians running. He started for the front door only to find that his wife, sensing trouble, had locked it and removed the key. All he could see from the window was the auto and the two men with boxes running toward it.

As the car approached the railroad crossing, it came so close to Bostock that he could have reached out and touched it. Levangie, washing the windows of his shack, had heard the shots without heeding them until he saw a man come out from behind the brick pile and commence shooting. At that very moment the warning bell began to ring for the Brockton train, and he left his cloth and bucket to crank down the gates. Just as he brought the bars horizontal the touring car came to a halt in front of him, a man leaning out with a pistol that he jerked up sharply, shouting "Up! Up!" The train was still beyond the Hood Rubber Works, the engine just rounding the bend. Again the man jerked the pistol, then pointed it. Levangie raised the barrier. The touring car jolted across the ties, passing within a few feet of Roy Gould on his way to the factories with his razor-blade paste. A bareheaded gunman fired at Gould almost point-blank, the bullet piercing a lapel of his overcoat. Gould fixed the man's look in his mind: the blown wavy hair, the blue suit, and oddly enough the watchchain that he was wearing across his waistcoat.

Mary Splaine and Frances Devlin from their Hampton House office, Mark Carrigan from the cutting room above, watched the top-heavy car with its flapping curtains as it crossed from the tracks to the cobbler's shop on the corner. The gunman in the front seat was firing at random. Workers scurried out the side entrance of Rice & Hutchins. Someone was chasing up the street from the factory calling "Stop them! Stop them!" A railroad gang working beside a sandpile stood gaping, their shovels still in their hands, Angelo Ricci, the foreman, trying to keep them back.

On the corner of Railroad Avenue in front of the cobbler's shop the car almost brushed Frank Burke, an itinerant glassblower down for the day from Brockton. The gunman in the front seat aimed directly at him and pulled the trigger, but the hammer merely clicked. "Get out of the way, you son of a bitch!" he bellowed at Burke, the curtains blurring his face.

Louis DeBeradinis in his cobbler's shop was giving an order to a salesman, Merle Averill, when he heard the tattoo of shots. "What the hell's that?" Averill asked him, dropping his order book and running to the door. DeBeradinis followed. Together they saw the touring car sputter past the shop. The gunman leaned out and fired almost in DeBeradinis' face. Again the weapon misfired.

At the poolroom at 66 Pearl Street, beyond the stable, Carlos Goodridge, a Victrola salesman, had been having a quick game with Peter Magazu, the proprietor, who also owned the shoe store next door, when he heard the first shots. He walked to the window, saw nothing, came back, and was chalking his cue when he heard more shots and people shouting. This time, stepping out to the edge of the sidewalk, he saw the dark touring car only twenty feet away and a swarthy man leaning out of it pointing a revolver at him. He ducked back inside and slammed the poolroom door, then peered out through the glass as the car spun by. The gunman had lowered his hand now, but he still held the revolver. Goodridge, his stomach tightened in a knot, watched the car swerve past the bakery, a gun barrel protruding from the gap of the rear window.

It gathered speed, running more smoothly, rolling past the stores and the frame two- and three-family houses and the barber shop with its spiraling striped pole. At 54 Pearl Street Nicola Damato, the barber, watched it pass, as did a shoe worker, Olaf Olsen, who had just come out of Torrey's Drugstore. Both of them saw the gunman leaning out. Olsen noticed how he kept his left hand over his mouth as he held the pistol in his right. As the car swung left onto Washington at the top of Pearl Street, the tires spewing up the gravel, one of the men in the rear seat threw out several handfuls of tacks.

Elmer Chase, loading a truck in front of the Co-operative Society a hundred yards down Washington Street, heard the squeal of brakes and the grinding of gears. He looked up at the oncoming car, expecting a smashup. It slowed slightly as it passed him, and he had a glimpse of a sickly-looking driver and a stocky dark man with blowing hair bent over next to him.

Scarcely a minute had elapsed from the first shot until the getaway car vanished, but with its disappearance the actuality faded and the myth took over. All in all there were more than fifty witnesses of the holdup in its various stages, yet each impression now began to work in the yeast of individual preconceptions. The car was black, it was green, it was shiny, it was mud-streaked. There were two cars.

The men who did the shooting were dark, were pale, had blue suits, had brown suits, had gray suits, wore felt hats, wore caps, were bareheaded. Only one had a gun, both had guns. The third man had been behind the brick pile with a shotgun all the time. Anywhere between eight and thirty shots had been fired. On some points there was a rough agreement: The car was a touring car, there were five men in it, the driver was a fair, sallow man, and the two men who had begun the shooting were short and clean-shaven.

The three gunmen had scarcely climbed into their car before Jim McGlone crawled from the excavation to where Parmenter lay sprawled on a stone. "I got him by the shoulder," McGlone related two days later at the inquest, "and asked him where he was hurt and he didn't answer, and I lowered his head to the ground. I went to the double team and got a horse blanket to put under Parmenter's head and my brother came along and we lifted Parmenter up and they spread the horse blanket out and we put Parmenter in, and my brother and two other fellows took hold of a corner of the blanket and we carried him into the house."

As soon as the car had passed the water tower Jimmy Bostock ran back to Berardelli. The detective lay on his side, his lips open, and with every breath blood foamed from his mouth. Bostock propped the guard's head up slightly and wiped his face with a handkerchief.

Berardelli gave a shudder, the bright bubbling at his mouth stopped, and Bostock knew that the man was dead. In the gravel Bostock noted four spent shell cases. He picked them up and put them in his pocket.

All the factory entrances were now clogged with gesticulating figures. Those who remained inside lined the open windows. From the shops and tenements and the Hampton House beyond, people were streaming across the tracks to where the two men were lying. Around Berardelli they gathered ten deep. Fred Loring, who had run out with the others from the lower factory, saw a dark cloth cap lying a foot or so from the guard's body. He picked it up and tucked it into his pocket. McGlone kept pushing the crowd back from the groaning Parmenter. Then he and his brother and Bostock carried the paymaster into the Colbert house, just behind the excavation. Crowds swarmed into Pearl Street: men in shirtsleeves, women in work aprons, small boys underfoot pushing their way through the others. The roadway was soon blocked from the factories to the railroad crossing. The voices of the men and women mingled, a collective murmur of incredulity that a thing such as they might have read about in newspaper headlines could actually have happened in South Braintree.

Shelley Neal arrived with his special police badge pinned on his coat and his Colt in his pocket just as they were carrying Parmenter into the Colbert house. The paymaster looked almost gone. As soon as Neal saw him in the blanket his one thought was to get back to the office and call the man's wife. It took him five minutes, bucking the crowd, to reach the Hampton House and once there he found all the telephone lines busy. After trying several times to get central, he hurried down the steps to his harnessed wagon and headed for the telephone exchange.

Police Chief Jeremiah Gallivan, driving up in his Ford, passed the careening wagon, Neal with his feet braced against the dashboard and slashing at his galloping horse. By the time Gallivan covered the mile and a half from his home to Rice & Hutchins, Parmenter had been taken inside and Berardelli was dead. The chief shouldered his way through the crowd until he stood looking down at the familiar body with the unfamiliar glazed eyes. The mill workers pressed about him, their voices clamorous as they pointed out where the shots had been fired and the route of the car. Fire Chief Fred Tenney, already on the spot, told him it was a touring car with a green body. Its motor was acting up, Tenny said. He thought there might still be a chance to catch the gunman. Gallivan was willing to try. Together they started off in the red department runabout, forcing their way up Pearl Street, Tenney sounding the brass bell mounted on the radiator. After a left turn onto Washington Street they had to stop to brush away the scattered tacks, but after that they were in the clear. At the Plain Street railroad crossing Gallivan shouted at Joe Buckley, the gate-tender, that there had been a killing. Had he seen a car pass? Buckley had not. Gallivan and Tenney continued straight south toward Holbrook, two miles away.

At Holbrook Square they found a soldier who had seen just such a green touring car ten minutes before on the way to Abington. They swung east on the Abington road, Gallivan gun in hand, Tenney clanging his bell as he held the accelerator to the floor. The flat wooden town came on them with a rush, but beyond, in the network of roads between Whitman and Cox's Corner, they lost the trail. Back and forth through the barren landscape they circled, along dirt ways that looped back on themselves or ended in the litter of some

squatter's chicken yard. The dust rose behind them and the afternoon shadows lengthened as the red runabout pushed on—until after
almost two hours of driving they gave up.

Gallivan's revolver was back in its holster and the fire chief's bell
silent when they again reached the Plain Street crossing. Buckley
waved for them to stop. "I forgot to tell you about a car that came
down here and went up that way," he told them, pointing north. "It
went out of my mind. The brakes screeched so much I thought it
was going into the river."

"Well," said Gallivan, "it's too late now."

Instead of continuing over the tracks at Plain Street the car—with
the screech that Buckley noted—had made a hairpin turn and headed
back toward South Braintree on the almost parallel Franklin Street.
But at the hill corner by the white-spired South Congregational
Church it had swung west on Pond Street, following the curve of
Sunset Lake on the right, and past the cemetery and the Torrey
Elementary School on the left. After following Pond Street west
for a mile, slapping and jolting, side curtains billowing and the
motor roaring, the car turned south on Granite Street toward
Randolph.

Mrs. Alta Baker saw it near the Randolph line, moving at fifty
miles an hour. At twelve minutes after three it passed Walter
Desmond, a tobacco salesman, on his way from Randolph to South
Braintree. Then at the junction with the Randolph highway it swung
right along the broken surface of Oak Street, cut through the scrubby
outskirts of the Randolph Woods for a mile and a half, and took the
left fork near an old cemetery into Orchard Street. On this obscure
lane it passed Albert Farmer and his wife Adeline with their horse
and wagon that they had just taken from the barn where the two
roads joined. The Farmers noticed the swirl of dust as the car moved
toward them and they watched it make the abrupt turn south into
Orchard Street.

The driver must have soon realized he was off course, for ten
minutes later George Chisholm, a road laborer working on Main
Street, a stone's throw from Oak, saw the car beating up north with
flaring curtains, hurtling by him so fast he thought the tires were
coming off. It turned right into Oak Street and continued a quarter of
a mile east, bearing down Orchard until it again arrived at the
junction. The driver stopped, hesitated, then swung the car into the
yard of the Hewins house on the corner just across from the Farmers.

Mabel Hewins was standing on her porch when the swarthy man in the front seat leaned out and asked her the way to Providence. She told him to follow Oak Street to Chestnut across North Main and keep going. He grunted, reversed the car jerkily, and started back the way he had come. She could see both men in the front seat clearly, but not the others.

Not quite two miles farther, a mile beyond Tower Hill where Chestnut Street merges with the Stoughton Post Road, John Lloyd and Wilson Dorr, working in a sandpit, saw the car jouncing south along the road that was "all hills and hollows and ruts." Dorr noticed that the glass was missing from the back window. On the sharp gradient of Tucker Hill leading into Stoughton it overtook Francis Clark and Elmer Pool in their bakery wagon, veered out, and continued on the left-hand side of the road and over the crest. Clark, too, noticed the oblong gap in the back of the cloth top and told Pool to copy the license plate. All Pool could spot was 49.

The car disappeared south in the isolation of the old turnpike and was not glimpsed again until it reached the outskirts of Brockton at a quarter to four. A high school girl, Julia Kelliher, saw it coming down very fast over the hill from Brockton Heights, churning the dust behind it, the curtains fluttering in the wind. As it went over a bump she saw something tossed up in the back seat behind the curtains. There were two men in front. After the car passed she tried to take down the license number. She could made out an 83 at the end and a 9 and a 7, and these she wrote in the sand beside the road.

At 4:15 Austin Reed, the railroad-crossing tender at Matfield, a small settlement on the outskirts of West Bridgewater, eight and a half miles southeast of Brockton Heights and twenty-two miles from South Braintree, stepped out of his shanty at the approach of the train from Westdale. As he stood in the middle of the road with the yellow STOP sign in his hand, he saw a touring car racing down the hill from West Bridgewater. He walked toward it holding up his sign. The driver did not seem to want to stop, but finally he pulled up about forty feet away. A man sitting next to the driver leaned out and shouted, "What the hell are you holding us up for?" Then the train passed between them. After it had rumbled by, the car started up over the crossing and the man in the front seat pointed his finger at Reed as if it were a pistol and bellowed again: "What the hell did you hold us up for?" He was only four feet away.

The rattling car took the right fork on Matfield Street, then, as if it had made a circle, returned three minutes later on the left fork of

Belmont Street and recrossed the track. Reed saw it edge over the hill and watched the cloud of dust that slowly settled behind it. That was the last seen that day of the touring car.

Parmenter lay propped up on the sofa in the front room of the Colbert house. Scarcely conscious, he managed to whisper that one gunman was dark, short, and stocky and the other short and thin.

When the Weymouth medical examiner, Dr. John Chisholm Frazer, arrived at four o'clock there were several other doctors already in the room with Parmenter. Frazer stopped by Berardelli's body—it had been carried into the Colbert kitchen—only long enough to note that he was dead and that blood was oozing from his back and arms. Shortly after the medical examiner's arrival, the ambulance from the Quincy City Hospital came for Parmenter. As the paymaster was carried down the steps the onlookers surged in toward the stretcher. They surged in again twenty minutes later when Berardelli's body was taken away in a wicker basket.

After the hearse had disappeared the crowd began to thin. Most of the workers headed home, leaving behind a diminishing core of the young and idle. The long shadow of the afternoon moved along the factory fronts and the sun turned the Slater & Morrill windows orange. A group—mostly boys in corduroy knickers—still stood around the stains in the gravel where Berardelli had fallen.

Later, as the sun edged toward the Blue Hills and the light began to fade, the crowd increased again. Workers and their wives strolled down Pearl Street after supper for a second look, voluble witnesses repeated the details, and as the news spread to the neighboring towns the curious and the morbid began to arrive from the compass points —Randolph, Quincy, Holbrook, Weymouth.

Dr. Nathaniel Hunting operated on Parmenter shortly after his arrival in the hospital. A bullet that had apparently glanced off his ribs, causing an elongated but superficial wound, was shaken out of his jacket. The second bullet, the one that had struck him after he turned, had cut horizontally through his abdomen, perforating the *vena cava*, the body's largest vein. Hunting was able to remove it easily from a mass of blue flesh just below the surface of the abdomen. He marked the bullet with a cross on the base. After the operation Parmenter recovered consciousness for a few minutes and managed to tell Assistant District Attorney George Adams, who had been waiting at his bedside, that he did not recognize the men who shot him.

APRIL 15, 1920   47

Then he drifted off again. He died at five in the morning, some fourteen hours after he was shot.

Dr. George Burgess Magrath, the medical examiner of Suffolk
County, made the autopsy on Berardelli, assisted by the Norfolk
County examiner, Dr. Frederick Jones. He found four visible wounds:
the first in the left back upper arm, the second near the left armpit,
the third lower down on the left side, and the fourth at the right
shoulder. According to Dr. Magrath, Berardelli might have recovered
from the first three wounds, but not from the fourth. The bullet there
had pierced the right lung, severed the great artery issuing from the
heart, and continued down through the intestines until it lodged in
the hipbone.

All four bullets had remained in the body. As Dr. Magrath recovered them he took a surgical needle and scored each in turn on
the base with a Roman numeral. The mortal bullet he marked with
three vertical scratches.

The shell cases that Jimmy Bostock had picked out of the gravel
he handed to Thomas Fraher, the Slater & Morrill superintendent.
These consisted of two Peters shells, one Remington, and one Winchester—the last identifiable by a W stamped on its base. Fraher in
turn gave them to Captain William Proctor, the head of the State
Police, who had driven down from Boston as soon as he heard of
the shootings. Several hours later Fred Loring gave the cap he had
picked up to Fraher, who kept it overnight and then passed it on to
Chief Gallivan.

Over that week end South Braintree bubbled with gossip. State
Police and Pinkerton detectives, occasionally at crosspurposes, combed
the town, interviewing and filling out their reports. Chief Gallivan
spent Sunday with a state policeman searching the Braintree woods
for abandoned cashboxes. He found nothing. That was his last discouraged gesture in the case.

A rumor floated round that Berardelli had recognized the man who
shot him, that he had known in advance something was up, and that
was why he had been killed. There was a lot of such talk in the
Hampton House. Mary Splaine and Jimmy Bostock told a young
Pinkerton operative, Henry Hellyer, they thought a man named Darling who worked in the order department might have been the front
man for the bandits. Darling had a bad reputation. Two of his friends
had been arrested some years back for stealing shoes from the factory,
and only a few weeks ago the police had found some stolen shoes at

his house. Mary Splaine supposed that Darling had probably hatched the scheme and tipped off his accomplices as to the time the payroll went out. But when Hellyer asked Fraher about this, the superintendent told him that Darling was completely trustworthy and that Mary Splaine was too irresponsible for anyone to take her seriously.

On Saturday, when the inquest was held before Judge Albert Avery in the Quincy District Court, several witnesses said they had seen two cars during the holdup, a large touring car and a small sedan. Levangie, the gate-tender, described the driver of the touring car as having a "dark complexion, dark brown mustache, soft hat, and brown coat." Everyone else described him as a pale, fair-haired man with a smooth yellowish face.

Detectives brought down a selection of rogues'-gallery pictures from Boston. Bostock, Wade, and several others who riffled through the assortment picked out a New York bank robber, Anthony Palmisano, as one of the South Braintree bandits. On April 23 a group that included Bostock, Wade, Albert Frantello, and Mary Splaine was taken to Captain Proctor's office in the State House and shown a number of photographs, including Palmisano's. Mary Splaine positively identified his picture as that of the man she had seen leaning out of the car with the revolver. Frantello and Bostock said it was an excellent likeness.

Unfortunately for their promising identification, it was soon learned that Palmisano—also known as Tony the Wop and Baby Tony—had been arrested in Buffalo in January and was still in jail there.

CHAPTER FOUR

Bridgewater and
West Bridgewater

The attempted robbery of the L. Q. White Shoe Company payroll in Bridgewater, on Wednesday, December 24, 1919, resulted neither in loss of money nor life. At twenty minutes to eight on that freezing overcast morning Alfred Cox, the company paymaster, was taking the week's payroll of $33,113.31 in his delivery truck from the Bridgewater Trust Company to the factory at the foot of the hill by the railroad station. The truck, a Ford with a tarpaulin top and solid rubber tires, was driven by Earl Graves, with Constable Benjamin Bowles beside him. Cox sat just behind Graves, on a large galvanized-iron box containing the money.

Graves drove from the bank along Summer Street to the square, then turned down Broad Street—divided in the middle by a single streetcar track—moving at a cautious ten miles an hour because of the ice on the road. A streetcar moving in the same direction had just stopped at the corner of Hale Street, seventy-five yards away. At the same moment a curtained touring car swung over the tracks and pulled up on the corner, its wheels on the sidewalk. Three men jumped out and dog-trotted toward the oncoming truck. The man in the lead, bareheaded, with a dark mustache and wearing a long black coat, carried a shotgun. The two behind him held pistols.

Graves had first noticed the touring car—a Hudson, he thought it was—while he was passing Harlow's blacksmith shop. He watched the men get out and start running, but it was not until the mustached man knelt and took aim that he realized he was in for a holdup. Yanking on the gas lever, he veered the truck across the tracks. Bowles

49

reached for his revolver. When the truck was some twenty-five yards away the mustached man fired both barrels. A few pellets rattled against the truck's metal body without doing any damage. One of the men with pistols, standing eight feet behind the man with the shotgun, exchanged random shots with Bowles until the streetcar came between them. Then the mustached man dashed across the street and fired again at the slithering truck.

Cox, from his seat on the cashbox, saw the kneeling figure and the smoke from the discharged shotgun, "everything like the snap of a camera." As the truck skidded, Graves lost control of the wheel. Bowles grabbed it out of his hands. Wavering from one side of the street to the other, the truck finally crashed against a telephone pole, smashing headlights and radiator. In the meantime the three gunmen had scurried back to their car with its waiting driver and spun out of sight down Hale Street in the direction of the normal school.

When Frank ("Slip") Harding, an auto-parts salesman on his way to Bassett's Garage just across from the corner of Hale Street, first saw the men carrying guns, he thought it was some kind of movie stunt. He was only four feet away as they began firing and he watched them, too astonished to move. Then within seconds they had run back to their car and driven off. Harding later described the car as a black Hudson Six with the license number 01173C.

Dr. John Murphy, a young general practitioner with his house and office at 76 Broad Street, was getting dressed when he heard the shots. He looked out his window just in time to glimpse the touring car moving away. By the time he reached the street, about the only thing he could see was the litter of glass where the truck was rammed against the pole. Then he noticed a spent shotgun shell in the gutter. He picked it up and put it in his pocket.

For Bridgewater's police chief, Michael Stewart, the robbery attempt lay outside the range of small-town peccadilloes with which he was used to dealing. His force consisted of two officers, one patrolman, and one night patrolman. In addition there were the specials, one at the normal school, one for the night performances at the Princess Theater, one at the L. Q. White factory, and six for the Fourth of July only. Stewart, in his forties, had held his job since 1915. Before this he had spent four years as chief of the two-man force in Rockland, another of the flat semirural manufacturing towns lying inland between Boston and Cape Cod. In Rockland most of his trouble had come from the foreign workers. The same was true in Bridgewater, where a third of the population was now made up of

Poles, Russians, Greeks, and Armenians. As a second-generation Irish-American Stewart tended to be suspicious of these newcomers. He had an idea that the holdup men might be Russians, with a confederate working in the factory. Inspector Albert Brouillard of the State Police, who was sent down to Bridgewater to work with Stewart, was more inclined to think the holdup the work of one of the gangs that had moved into the area after the recent Boston police strike. Graves thought the men were Italians.

The license number that Harding had written down was traced through the Registry of Motor Vehicles to George Hassam's garage in Needham, a Boston suburb, twenty-three miles northwest of Bridgewater. It turned out to be a dealer's plate. Hassam owned five sets of them.

On Monday, December 22, a foreigner had come into Hassam's office and asked if he could borrow a set of plates. In broken English he told Hassam he had just bought a car in Wellesley and wanted to take it away. When Hassam said he could not lend his dealer's plates, the man left. He was a surly man of about forty, as Hassam remembered him, dark, with a close-cropped mustache.

Hassam forgot about him until the police telephoned regarding the plates on the Bridgewater car. Then, as he went to the back of his garage to look at a secondhand Hupp that had been carrying a set of his dealer's plates, he found them missing. When or how they had been taken he did not know.

On December 26 the Pinkerton operative Henry Hellyer noted in his report that on Sunday evening, December 21, a Buick touring car belonging to Daniel H. Murphy of Natick had been stolen from 115 Fair Oaks Street, Needham, not far from Hassam's Garage. Hellyer was right about the Buick though not about some of his other details. The car, belonging to a Francis J. Murphy had actually been stolen in Needham a month earlier, on November 23, from in front of a house in Fair Oaks Park.

That same November night a Dedham police officer, Warren Totty, standing under the arc light in the granite shadow of Memorial Hall, had seen the car speeding across Dedham Square. He had stepped out with his hand raised, but the car swung past him down the hill and under the railroad bridge toward Hyde Park. The license number that Totty managed to copy down turned out to be Murphy's.

"It is thought," Hellyer reported, "that this car may have been used by the men last Wednesday." The connection between the Murphy Buick and the Needham license plates appealed to Stewart, even though both Graves and Harding had said that the car was a Hudson. Hellyer now interviewed Richard Casey, a student at Rhode Island State College, who had seen the car on Main Street before the shooting, and John King, who noticed it afterward near the normal school. Whether or not Chief Stewart had prompted them, both said it was a Buick.

Stewart and Brouillard had managed to trace the car as far as Stoughton. Beyond that point, although they called at all the garages in the vicinity, their leads came to nothing. Chief Shine of Dedham had a notion that an Italian gang in East Dedham might be involved. Stewart visited Dedham, Needham, even some suspects in Newton, and arranged meanwhile for circulars describing the car to be distributed to the local garages and gas stations. He now began to think the car was hidden somewhere between Stoughton and Dedham.

Meanwhile the Pinkerton agents had been spreading out through the Italian districts of Quincy and Boston. On December 30 Assistant Superintendent Henry Murray reported:

Today informant telephoned in; later met him at supper and in the course of conversation stated that he had learned that the Italian mentioned yesterday had said that the men who were implicated in the Bridgewater holdup had occupied temporarily a shack in close proximity to Bridgewater and that the car that had been used was left there along with some overalls or disguise of a similar nature, used by one of the men implicated in the holdup; that these men were Italians, had deserted the car, returned to Quincy by trolley; that they are believed to be residing in the vicinity of Fore River Shipyard and are known as Anarchists.

The "Italian mentioned yesterday" was a floater who spent most of his time hanging around the Boston American Building near Summer Street or in Monahan's Bar in the North End. It took the Pinkerton agents several days to track him home to 31 Waverly Street, in the massed tenement district of Brighton. The house was a brick three-flatter, and there was a SCARLET FEVER card on the front door. Hellyer, Stewart, and Brouillard went there the afternoon of January 3, 1920. By ringing the three doorbells until they got an answer they learned that the man they wanted had left for Allston earlier in the day. They waited almost five hours on the upper landing until he came back. He turned out to be a flashily dressed Sicilian, Carmine Barasso, who had anglicized his name to C. A. Barr. Quite willing to talk, he invited the three men in to his flat. According to Hellyer's report:

Barr related a rambling statement about a machine that he had invented with which he could detect who had committed a crime no matter where it was committed. He stated that one Mrs. Vetilia of 2 Lexington Street East Boston, had looked into the machine and saw the holdup happening and saw the man plainly but did not know who they were.

As Stewart drove back to Bridgewater along the empty snow-edged roads of the Blue Hills he added another piece to the puzzle he was fitting together in his mind. If the Pinkerton information was right, the holdup men were anarchists. It was not a difficult conclusion to come to in the winter of 1919–1920. A group of 249 anarchist and Communist aliens that included Emma Goldman and Alexander Berkman had just been deported to Russia. That very day, January 3, the headlines of the papers were flaring with the news of Attorney General Palmer's raids that had taken place all over the country the previous evening. RAIDS TO HEAD OFF REVOLUTION was the heading of the weekly Bridgewater *Independent*. DEPARTMENT OF JUSTICE MAKES PUBLIC COMMUNISTS' PLAN TO OVERTHROW GOVERNMENT. ARRESTS IN FIFTY TOWNS.

But such incidents and antagonisms, the social change and struggle of the postwar period, were sensed only vaguely in Bridgewater. By the time the wave of history reached the inland cape towns it was scarcely a ripple. The same issue of the *Independent* made Charlotte Randall's twenty-first birthday party in West Bridgewater the subject of its editorial.

When the Eighteenth Amendment went into effect on January 16 the December holdup no longer seemed worth discussing. The Pinkerton men had gone. The thousand-dollar reward posted by Loring Q. White for the gunmen's capture was unclaimed. At his headquarters in the back room of the wooden-pilastered town hall, Chief Stewart still thought about the crime, but he could find no more pieces to add to his puzzle.

It was the snowiest winter in fifty years. The weeks followed into the lengthening afternoons of February. On the sixth a mockingbird was seen by the members of the Bridgewater Bird Club. Five days later a blizzard swirled in from the northeast and the town was snowed under again. In the Superior Court in Brockton Judge Webster

Thayer fined a young Brava (the local name for the colored Cape Verde Island Portuguese) two hundred dollars for manslaughter under extenuating circumstances, and asked that the fine be turned over to the victim's family for funeral expenses. The thaw began on March 19, and the basement of the Bridgewater Central Square Congregational Church was flooded.

Then on April 15 a South Braintree paymaster and his guard were killed during a holdup. Having already gone to press, the April 17 edition of the *Independent* made no mention of the murders. Yet the event had already impinged on Bridgewater. Shortly after the passage of the 1918 Deportation Act, Chief Stewart had assisted the Immigration Service in arresting six Italians charged with spreading literature advocating the overthrow of the government. The six were marked down for deportation and released on bail. Stewart supposed they had all long since been sent back to Italy.

But that spring at least one of the six, Ferruccio Coacci, was still living in a section of West Bridgewater called Cochesett. Coacci, sometimes known as Ercole Parrecca, had come to Quincy in 1915 and taken up with a woman named Ersilia Buongarzone. Ersilia had borne him two children, both delivered at the state almshouse in Tewksbury. For a period Coacci was employed at the L. Q. White Company. At the time of his arrest, Joseph Ventola, an anarchist friend from Hyde Park, had posted the thousand-dollar bond, and Coacci was released on condition that he marry Ersilia and support her children. While awaiting his deportation order he worked for Slater & Morrill in South Braintree. Early in April 1920, after receiving his notice to report on the fifteenth at the East Boston Immigration Station, he quit his job.

Since the first of the year Coacci had been living in Puffer's Place, at the corner of Lincoln and South Elm Street, in the empty flatland about a mile from West Bridgewater's Elm Square. Puffer's Place was a small, decayed two-story structure with a rust-colored mansard roof and irregularly spaced gables. Once it had been the office of the long-since-defunct Alger Iron Foundry. Then Clarence Puffer, a local handyman, had turned it into a dwelling. Mario Buda, a young Italian who called himself Mike Boda, had rented it early in the winter, and a month or so later Coacci had moved in from Quincy. Ersilia, who was pregnant again, kept house and did the cooking.

The Italians in Puffer's Place were scarcely noticed by their scattered Yankee neighbors. At times cars would be parked on the corner on Sunday afternoons and talk and singing would echo from inside, but for the most part the newcomers were orderly enough. No one knew what Boda did for a living. With the Eighteenth Amendment in force, some people on South Elm Street suspected the Italians might be engaged in selling liquor. In this they were right. At one time Boda and his brother had run a dry-cleaning shop in Wellesley, adjoining Needham, but after prohibition he became a bootlegger. His avocation was anarchism. All his spare time and his enthusiasm he devoted to distributing radical pamphlets and journals to the Italian colonies of eastern Massachusetts.

Boda was a dapper man, five feet six inches tall, with a short mustache, aquiline nose, and deep-set hazel eyes. If anyone happened to ask him what he did, he replied that he was a salesman for a New York fruit-importing firm. Since coming to West Bridgewater from Hyde Park he had bought a green Overland which he kept in a shed beside the house. The car was a 1912 model, more often than not laid up for repairs. Boda had not registered it for 1920.

During the two years he had been out on bail Coacci had maintained that he wanted to go back to Italy and that he was just waiting for a free ride. When his bondsman, Ventola, learned from the Immigration Service that Coacci had not turned himself in on April 15, he was as surprised as he was dismayed. He drove at once to West Bridgewater, arriving at Puffer's Place at half past four. There was no one home but the door was open. He went into the kitchen to wait. About five o'clock he at last saw Boda coming down the road from Elm Square, wearing a green velour hat and carrying a leather bag.

Boda said he had just come back on the trolley from Brockton. Ventola told him that Coacci had not reported at the immigration station and that he was worried about his bond. Boda assured him that Coacci would report next morning. For the time being Ersilia and the children would stay in the United States. Ventola, relieved, offered to help them.

The following afternoon Coacci telephoned the Immigration Service and told Inspector Root that he could not come in. His wife was sick, he said, and he needed a few extra days to take care of her. Root in turn called Chief Stewart in Bridgewater and suggested they both drop in on Coacci that evening. But Stewart had to attend a dress rehearsal of *Aunt Jerusha's Quilting Party*, a play in which he had a part. Besides, West Bridgewater was a separate town outside his jurisdiction. However, he agreed to send his night patrolman, Frank LeBaron.

Root and LeBaron arrived at Puffer's Place after dark. Coacci admitted them and announced that he was ready to leave. There seemed to be nothing wrong with his wife. Root, who had a lodge meeting that night, offered to have the deportation postponed another week, but Coacci refused, saying that he wanted to get back on the first steamer to his sick father. When Root suggested that Coacci leave his wife some money, Coacci—who had two hundred dollars with him—said she did not need any. As the inspector led him down the steps with his baggage, Ersilia and the children stood in the doorway crying.

After his rehearsal, Chief Stewart hurried back to headquarters. LeBaron was already there, behind the desk. "That Dago," he said. "There wasn't nothing wrong with his wife. Just a stall." As Stewart walked home from the town hall, under the elms of the deserted common, he kept mulling over LeBaron's remark. He suddenly recalled what Barr-Barasso had said in December about some anarchists living in a shack near Bridgewater. On April 15 these anarchists had been—where? It was in this evening moment, in Chief Stewart's responding mind, that the Sacco-Vanzetti case had its origin.

On the afternoon of April 17, Charles Fuller, the business manager of the Brockton *Enterprise*, locked his office, walked over to the Fair Grounds where he kept his horse, and started out with his friend Max Wind on their usual Saturday ride. They left the Fair Grounds at half past two, riding out the back gate toward West Bridgewater. Once over the railroad track on Manley Street, not far from the Poor Farm, they headed down a bridle path through the thick secondary growth of maple and scrub oak and alder known as the Manley Woods. Fuller rode ahead. About six hundred feet in from the road, he came face to face with a Buick touring car. So close were the bushes that he and Wind had to dismount and lead their horses past it. The car had apparently been there overnight, for the windshield and hood and fenders were streaked with dew. Fuller glanced in as he went by and saw a few coins on the front seat and a coat in the back. A moment later when he looked back to see if Wind could get by, he noticed that the glass was missing from the rear window.

Before remounting the two men stopped to look at the smeared dark-blue car. It had no license plates, but otherwise it seemed to resemble the holdup car they had read about the day before. Just ahead of the car they made out the thin tracks of a smaller car, perhaps a Ford, leading to Manley Street. They rode back the way they had come, stopped at the first house, and called the Brockton police. Within fifteen minutes City Marshal Ryan arrived with Officer William Hill.

Together the four men examined the car inside and out. Besides the coins and the old brown overcoat, they found a phial that was thought afterward to have contained dope, and on the floor the glass from the rear window. Since Fuller was more familiar with a Buick than the others he drove it out through the snagging bushes. Reaching Manley Street, he turned the car over to Hill, who drove it to the police garage in Brockton. The next morning the police, examining the car a second time, found a bullet hole in the rear door.

Stewart and Brouillard were notified, and they inspected the car Sunday evening. The Buick's spare tire was missing, and the maker's number near the gas tank had been chiseled off. The engine number, however, was still intact: 560,490. It was the number of the Murphy car stolen in Needham on November 23. The Registry of Motor Vehicles had reported that the license plate, 49783, had been stolen from a Ford belonging to Warren H. Ellis of 602 Webster Street, Needham. Just after ten o'clock on the night of January 6 Ellis had put his car in his garage. Next morning the plates were gone.

Stewart learned about the Ellis plates on Monday. In December he had connected the missing Needham Buick with the Bridgewater holdup. Now it turned out to be the car used in South Braintree. And both the Bridgewater and the South Braintree license plates had been stolen in Needham within an interval of about two weeks. The two crimes now seemed to him to be the work of the same gang— another piece added to his puzzle. It was curious too—a kind of corroboration of his theory of the other night—that the car should have been found less than two miles from Puffer's Place. Coacci again!

Unfortunately, Coacci was at this point somewhere on the Atlantic. Nevertheless Stewart felt there might still be some evidence to be found in the South Elm Street house. He telephoned Brouillard and they arranged to go over to Puffer's Place on Tuesday.

That same Monday Joseph Ventola turned up at Puffer's with a truck to move Ersilia, her children, and her belongings to a house in South Braintree. Not long after he had gone Simon Johnson and his brother Samuel arrived from their Elm Square Garage with a tow truck to haul away Boda's broken-down Overland. Boda helped them push the car out of the shed at the side of the house. After they had hitched it up, Boda, who had known the Johnsons ever since he had moved to Cochesett, rode the mile to Elm Square with them in the truck. The Italian wore his velour hat and was carrying his leather bag. The Johnsons let him off at the car stop and he boarded the Brockton trolley.

Tuesday afternoon Stewart picked up Brouillard and they drove to Puffer's Place. In the fading light, the ramshackle gabled house with the gnarled apple tree in front of it and the leafless grapevine in the rear looked as if it might have been cut out of cardboard. Broken windows in the shed had been tacked over with burlap.

After Stewart knocked several times, Boda came to the door in his shirtsleeves. Stewart said he and Brouillard were from the Immigration Service and that they wanted a photograph of Coacci. Boda said Coacci had already sent in two photographs. Stewart explained that one of them had been lost. Boda let the men in. When Stewart asked about Coacci's friends, Boda said that they sometimes came to the house but he did not know who they were. They were, he told the chief, "bad peoples." More than that he could or would not say. When Stewart asked if Coacci had owned a gun, Boda said he had kept one in the kitchen drawer. Stewart opened the drawer. Though he found no gun, the drawer contained the manufacturer's diagram of a Savage automatic.

Still ostensibly looking for photographs, Stewart and Brouillard searched the house while Boda tagged after them. When they asked if he himself had a gun, Boda produced a Spanish-type automatic from his bureau. He said he had no license, but that he never carried the gun outside. Brouillard removed the clip and examined the three cartridges. Each was of a different make; all were American.

When the three men went out on the porch, Stewart asked about the padlocked shed. Boda said he kept his car there, but just now it was at the Johnson's garage. Stewart asked if he could look inside the shed. Boda unsnapped the padlock and slid the door back.

On the right of the dirt-floored shed stood two planks on which the Overland had rested. To the left of the planks the floor had recently been raked. Stewart and Brouillard inspected the shed carefully. Afterward Stewart claimed that a small unraked patch near one of the planks showed the clear imprint of a U. S. Royal tire, much too large for an Overland but the right size for a Buick.*

Boda locked the shed again and Stewart thanked him for his cooperation, saying he might have a chat with him later.

* Several years later another investigator measured the shed and said that it would have been impossible to maneuver a car from the right-hand threshold to the area on the left.

The more Stewart thought about Boda afterward the more dubious the Italian began to appear. Later, he felt he should have arrested him on the spot, but at the time there had seemed nothing tangible except the pistol. Early the next morning he drove over to Puffer's Place alone. Boda was eating breakfast at the kitchen table when he glimpsed the chief's car coming down South Elm Street. By the time Stewart knocked on the door, he had slipped out of sight. Stewart knocked several times, peered through the window at the breakfast table, and then drove off.

For Boda that second visit was conclusive. The police would be coming back. Whatever they might want, he preferred not to be there. An Italian friend came down from Brockton and helped him get his belongings together. He left on the Boston train that afternoon, and for the next few weeks stayed under cover with an Italian family in East Boston.

Just as Boda had suspected, Stewart returned the following evening. But this time, when he flashed his light through the kitchen window, there was nothing to see. Except for a few tin cans in the corner the place was empty.

Stewart drove to the Elm Square Garage. Boda's Overland was still there. Stewart told Simon Johnson ominously that there was some pretty serious business afoot and that if Boda or anyone else should come for the Overland, Johnson was to string him along until he could call the police.

CHAPTER FIVE

◇◇◇◇◇◇◇◇◇◇◇◇◇◇◇◇◇◇◇◇◇◇◇◇◇◇◇◇◇◇◇

The Night of May 5

A week after Stewart's visit, Simon Johnson received a long-distance telephone call at his garage from Boda asking if the Overland was ready. Johnson told him it was. Boda said he would pick it up next day. Next day he did not appear. Another week passed, and Johnson began to worry about his bill. He asked Stewart if he could sell the car for what was owing on it. Stewart told him to wait.

On the evening of May 5 Johnson had felt out of sorts and gone to bed early. At a little after nine o'clock his wife, Ruth, was sitting in the front bedroom of their one-story wooden house on North Elm Street, a quarter of a mile from the garage, when she heard a knock at the front door. Going to the vestibule, she asked who it was. A voice replied that it was Mike Boda and that he had come for his car. From the bedroom Johnson recognized the foreign voice. As his wife came back, he whispered to her to go next door and telephone. She nodded, then said loudly enough to be heard outside: "Mr. Boda is here for his car. While you're getting up I'll go over for the milk."

As she opened the front door and stepped outside she found herself caught in a beam of light. At first she could make out nothing beyond the whiteness, then she saw Boda vaguely outlined against a telephone pole ten feet away. As her eyes grew more used to the glare, she noticed two strangers walking toward her from across the railroad bridge thirty feet south of the house. She could hear them talking— in Italian, she thought. The glare caught them. They looked foreign. One was wearing a derby and an overcoat. The other, who wore a felt hat, Ruth Johnson remembered afterward because of his drooping mustache. Boda called out something to them and then walked toward her.

60

"Mr. Johnson isn't feeling good," she told him, "but he's getting out of bed to get your car for you."

Boda nodded as she walked past him toward the Bartlett house next door. The light, she now saw, came from a motorcycle. A man in a checked mackinaw with a hat pulled over his eyes was sitting in the saddle with one hand resting on the empty sidecar. After she had passed into the darkness she had the uneasy feeling that the men were following her. But there were no steps behind her as she turned up the Bartletts' driveway. To her relief, the lights in the house were still on downstairs.

One of the Bartlett children let her in. Over the hall telephone, in a voice barely under control, she told the operator to get through to the police. For the moment that was all she could think of to say. West Bridgewater then had no police force, only two part-time policemen. The operator connected her with the house of one of them, Warren Laughton, who was also fire chief and water commissioner. Laughton had just stepped out, his wife said, but she took the message that the Johnsons had agreed on with Stewart: "Boda has come for his car."

Johnson dressed slowly. When he finally stepped out of his house the first thing he noticed was Boda walking toward him from the bridge. Farther off he saw the motorcycle with the indeterminate outlines of the driver and the two other men. The usually dapper Boda was wearing a crumpled brown suit and an old slouch hat. He said he wanted to take the Overland away at once. Johnson asked him if he had brought license plates. Boda said he had not. Johnson told him he could not drive without plates. "I will take the chance," Boda said. Johnson said that when his wife got back, they would go down to the garage.

Boda, watching Mrs. Johnson return, said he guessed it was too late for the car now, that he would send someone with plates for it next day. He said good night and turned away. The man in the mackinaw kicked the motorcycle's starter pedal and the other two men stepped back. Ruth Johnson, as she passed, sensed that they were watching her and she thought she caught the word *telephone* mixed in their foreign speech.

Boda stepped into the sidecar, squatted down, and the motorcycle spluttered off north toward Brockton. The taillight was out, but Johnson had already noted the license plate: 871. As the motor echoed away, the two strangers, the man in the derby and the man with the drooping mustache, started back over the railroad bridge.

The Johnsons watched them hesitate, turn, and disappear in the direction the motorcycle had taken.

Along empty North Elm Street they trudged for a mile, following the Bridgewater-Brockton trolley line. Meeting a solitary woman, they asked her where the car stop was. She pointed just beyond them to a white-striped pole on the corner of Sunset Avenue. They thanked her. A few minutes later the electric car from Bridgewater hummed along the track. It was 9:40 when the two men stepped aboard it.

Until he had a closer look at him, Austin Cole, the twenty-three-year-old conductor, thought that the man in the derby and the walrus mustache was a Portuguese named Tony. Cole asked if they were going to Brockton and the other man, who was clean-shaven, said yes. At that hour the car was almost empty. The newcomers walked stiffly down the aisle and sat in the first cross-seat at the rear. Somehow they reminded Cole of a pair who had got on at the same place about the same time a few weeks back.

The car swayed and rattled through the darkness. Where North Elm Street crossed the Brockton line it became Copeland Street, and the houses—most of them with their lights out now—began to give way to small shops and an occasional church. Cole, counting transfers, eyed the strangers in the back seat. They were aliens. Anyone could see that. The high-cheek boned man with the drooping mustache was easy to spot, but beyond his obviousness there was a quality about them both—a stiffness of feature, a fixed look to the eyes, just the awkward way they wore their clothes—that set them apart. Americans were put together more loosely.

When Warren Laughton arrived home and received Ruth Johnson's message, he had no idea what was back of it but called Chief Stewart at once. However, by the time Stewart arrived at the Johnson house the two strangers were already on the Brockton car.

How Stewart knew they were on that car is not wholly clear. One account has it that Johnson followed them and saw the car stop at Sunset Avenue. It may be that the unnamed woman at the corner of Sunset Avenue reported them. In any case, Stewart went to the Bartlett house and called the Brockton police headquarters.

A few minutes before 10 P.M. Michael Connolly, the officer on duty at Station 2, Campello, received a call from the Brockton central station telling him that two foreigners on the trolley from Bridgewater had just tried to steal an auto. The trolley was due in Brockton any minute. Connolly put down a sandwich, nodded to the sergeant at the desk, and hurried off to Main Street with Officer Earl Vaughn.

Vaughn walked north, Connolly headed south. It was four minutes past ten. Connolly saw the trolley's headlight as it turned into Main Street from Keith Avenue. A hulking, florid, pugnacious man who liked a good pinch, he hoped that the suspects had not got off. He signaled to the motorman and swung aboard while the trolley was still moving.

As Connolly steadied himself and glanced down the aisle he saw the foreigners in the rear seat. A year later at the Dedham trial he gave his version of the arrest:

I went down through the car and when I got opposite the seat I stopped and I asked them where they came from. They said, "Bridgewater." I said, "What was you doing in Bridgewater?" They said, "We went down to see a friend of mine." I said, "Who is your friend?" He said, "A man by the—they call him Poppy." "Well," I said, "I want you, you are under arrest." Vanzetti was sitting on the inside of the seat . . . and he went, put his hand on his hip pocket and I says, "Keep your hands on your lap, or you will be sorry."

They wanted to know what they were arrested for and I says, "Suspicious characters." We went on—oh, it was maybe about three minutes' ride where . . . Officer Vaughn got on . . . and I told Officer Vaughn to fish Vanzetti, and I just gave Sacco a slight going over, just felt him over, did not go into his pockets, and we led them out the front way of the car.

Vaughn found a loaded revolver in the hip pocket of the man with the mustache and gave it to Connolly, who kept it in his hand all the way to the Brockton central station. Officers Spear and Snow of the central station had driven down to meet the trolley.

I put Sacco and Vanzetti in the back of our light machine [Connolly continued], and Officer Snow got in the back seat with them. I took the front seat with the driver, facing Sacco and Vanzetti. . . . I told them when we started that the first false move I would put a bullet in them. On the way to the station Sacco reached his hand to under his overcoat and I told him to keep his hands outside of his clothes and on his lap. . . . I says to him, "Have you got a gun there?" He says, "No." He says, "I ain't got no gun." "Well," I says, "keep your hands outside your clothes." We went along a little further and he done the same thing. I gets up on my knees on the front seat and I reaches over and I puts my hand on his coat but I did not see any gun. "Now," I says, "Mister, if you put your hand in there again you

*are going to get into trouble." He says, "I don't want no trouble." We
reached the station, brought them up to the office and searched them.*

The revolver taken from the mustached man was a 38-caliber
Harrington & Richardson, its five chambers loaded with two Remington and three U. S. cartridges. Taken from him at the Campello
station were four shotgun shells, a pocket knife, a handkerchief,
twenty dollars, and several pamphlets. The smooth-faced man was
searched by Officer Spear, who found a 32-caliber Colt automatic
tucked in his waistband. The Colt had eight cartridges in the clip
and one in the chamber. In the man's pocket were twenty-three loose
cartridges. Though all 32-caliber, the cartridges were of assorted makes
—sixteen Peters, seven U. S., six Winchesters, and three Remingtons.
In addition the man had in his pocket a penciled announcement in
Italian that read:

*Proletarians, you have fought all the wars. You have worked for all the
owners. You have wandered over all the countries. Have you harvested
the fruits of your labors, the price of your victories? Does the past
comfort you? Does the present smile on you? Does the future promise
you anything? Have you found a piece of land where you can live like
a human being and die like a human being? On these questions, on
this argument, and on this theme, the struggle for existence, Bartolomeo Vanzetti will speak. Hour____Day____Hall____Admission free.
Freedom of discussion to all. Take the ladies with you.*

Within a quarter of an hour Chief Stewart arrived at the station,
heady with excitement at the springing of his trap. With him were his
night patrolmen Frank LeBaron and Warren Laughton, and Simon
Johnson. Johnson at once identified the prisoners as the men he had
seen standing by the motorcycle. Stewart then questioned them indi-
vidually. He talked to the mustached man first, taking care to repeat
the cautionary formula that the latter did not have to answer questions but that anything he said might be held against him. The
prisoner did not hesitate. He said his name was Bartolomeo Vanzetti,
that he was an Italian, thirty-two years old and a fish peddler, and
that he lived at 35 Cherry Street, Plymouth. For the last two days,
he said, he had been visiting his friend, Nick Sacco, in South Stoughton. The two of them had gone to Bridgewater that evening to see
Vanzetti's friend Poppy, but it was so late by the time they arrived
that they decided Poppy had probably gone to bed and they might
as well go home. They were on their way back to South Stoughton
when the police picked them up. As for Poppy, that was only the

man's nickname. Vanzetti did not know his real name or even his address in Bridgewater, but he was a big man who usually wore a blue shirt. They had worked together in the Plymouth Cordage plant.

Vanzetti denied knowing anyone named Boda or Coacci. He said he had never before been in West Bridgewater. He had walked some distance before he had taken the trolley, but he had seen no motorcycle all evening. Stewart suddenly asked Vanzetti if he was an anarchist, if he approved of the government. All Vanzetti would admit was that he was a little different and that he liked things different. As to why he was carrying a revolver, he said that he was in business and needed it for protection. He had no permit.

Stewart's questioning of the second man followed the same line. The suspect said his name was Nicola Sacco, that he was married, lived in South Stoughton, and had been in America eleven years. For the last two years he had worked at the Three-K factory in Stoughton. He had once looked for a job in Bridgewater, but he had never been in West Bridgewater until tonight. He did not know any Boda or Coacci. He had not seen a motorcycle. He was not an anarchist or Communist. As for the automatic in his waistband, he carried it because there were a lot of bad men about. He had bought it a long time ago at some shop near Hanover Street in Boston. The cartridges were from a box he had bought and they just happened to be in his pocket. He had planned to shoot them off in the woods with his friends.

Stewart's questioning of both men lasted about ten minutes. They were then locked up.

Neither Sacco nor Vanzetti had been behind bars before. Now, in adjoining cells under the shadowless glare of the overhead light, with a wooden shelf to sleep on and a seatless toilet in the corner, they sensed the isolating fear of arbitrary impersonal force. To the policemen going on and off duty they were curiosities and as such subject to a certain amount of crude horseplay. When the two men requested blankets the reply was that they would find it warm enough when they were lined up in the hall for a little live target practice, and one patrolman showed Vanzetti a cartridge which he then slipped into the barrel of his revolver, cocking it and pointing between the bars. When Vanzetti did not move, the other spat on the floor contemptuously and turned away.

According to the Registry of Motor Vehicles records the motorcycle in which Boda had ridden off belonged to Ricardo Orciani. A

molder in a Norwood foundry, Orciani boarded at 1532 Hyde Park
Avenue with Angelo Ventola, whose brother, Joseph Ventola, lived
across the street. Orciani was picked up in his room the night of
May 6 and taken to Brockton. Still wearing the checked mackinaw
of the night before, he was identified by Simon and Ruth Johnson
as the driver of the motorcycle. A short, cocky Italian with an assured
round face and clipped mustache, he was unperturbed by his arrest.
He refused to answer questions. Where he went, he told the police,
was his own business. The revolver found in his bureau was one he
just happened to have.

On Thursday, May 6, the district attorney for Norfolk and Plymouth
counties, Frederick Gunn Katzmann, appeared at the Brockton station to take over the questioning, bringing with him a stenographer
and an interpreter.

Katzmann was then in his late forties, a plump, ambitious man
whose presence seemed underlined by the smartness of his dress, his
snap-brim hat, and his raglan Burberry coat. He had grown up on
one of the poorer streets of Hyde Park, a gray semi-industrial adjunct
of Boston, attending the Boston Latin School and then crossing the
Charles River to enter Harvard with the class of 1896. As an un-
athletic poor boy from Hyde Park, his years at Harvard were obscure.
He belonged to no clubs, took part in no sports or undergraduate
activities. Nor, on the other hand, was he a scholar. At the end of
his senior year his one distinction was an honorable mention in
engineering. Returning to Hyde Park with his diploma, he worked for
several years as a meter-reader for the local electric-light company.
What he really wanted was to be a lawyer. If he had had the money
he would have gone on to the Harvard Law School. Instead he
attended night sessions at Boston University, receiving his bachelor
of laws degree in 1902.

For the next year he served as an apprentice with one of the established firms of Boston's Pemberton Square. But the staid legal world
of Beacon Hill and State Street was a fenced-off Brahmin preserve.
A Hyde Park boy with a B.U. law degree and a dubious name would
not penetrate that circle.

Katzmann was sensitive about his name. His mother's maiden
name—his own middle one—was Gunn, and he tried to emphasize
its Anglican propriety in his signature. After his year at Pemberton
Square he returned to the familiar puddle of Hyde Park and set up
his office on the second floor of a wooden building on River Street.
There, in a small ocher room with a creaking floor smelling of oil,

he hung his two diplomas and filled several sectional bookcases with secondhand volumes of *Corpus Juris*. He prospered. From 1907 to 1908 he represented Hyde Park in the Massachusetts legislature. The following year he was appointed assistant district attorney. From 1909 until Hyde Park was absorbed by Boston in 1912 he served on the school committee. In November, 1916, he ran for district attorney and was elected to a three-year term. In 1919 he was re-elected.

Katzmann's personality, like his figure, expanded with success. He could plan to go back to his Harvard twenty-fifth reunion with pride, the chill of his undergraduate years forgotten. As an active, conforming Republican, the prospect of a judgeship in the superior court or even, with luck, the state attorney-generalship lay ahead of him. The drawback of his name scarcely bothered him now. He lived with his wife and two young daughters in a Victorian frame house on the Mattapan side of River Street, within walking distance of his office. He was a member of the Hyde Park Lodge of Masons, the Cebra Tennis Club, and the Wollaston Golf Club. He became Hyde Park counsel for the Family Welfare Society of Boston. As district attorney he was popular if undistinguished, a routine prosecutor addicted to the McKinley-baroque style of oratory. The district had re-elected him in spite of the war-fanned prejudice against German names. As with many criminal lawyers, the law was for him, like politics, a game where at times one might have to cut a few corners, but in the end the best man usually won, and the loser congratulated the winner. It was a game played with other men's years and sometimes with their lives—but still a game. Such was the man, soon to become a symbol of chicanery and deceit for indifferently informed protestors all over the world, as he arrived at the Brockton police station for the routine questioning of two holdup suspects.

Especially in questioning foreigners the district attorney favored the disarming approach, bluff, fatherly, confidential—you deal straight with me and I'll deal straight with you. It is particularly effective after a suspect has spent a night in a cell. Katzmann first questioned Sacco. For some time he put merely routine questions to him about his acquaintances, about the gun and the cartridges. Sacco said he had bought his gun two years before in the North End. He had not given his right name then because he was afraid. As to Orciani, yes, he knew him but Vanzetti did not. Boda he had never heard of. Boda did not sound like an Italian name. Suddenly Katzmann asked if he knew anyone named Berardelli. Sacco asked him who Berardelli was. In the course of the interrogation Sacco said that his mother had died recently and that he was planning to return to Italy. When Katzmann asked if he had heard about the South Braintree murders, he said he had read in the *Post* "there was bandits robbing money." He had worked in various shoe factories, he admitted, but never in Braintree. He had taken a day off early in April to go to Boston for his passport, but thought he had been working in Stoughton on April 15, the day of the holdup. That was all—the opening gambit—but both men were now aware of the South Braintree crime in relation to each other.

When Vanzetti appeared, Katzmann asked him if he spoke English. He said that he spoke a little. When reminded that he was free not to answer questions, he said he was willing to answer any. He had known Sacco for a year and a half. He told of taking the trolley from Stoughton to Bridgewater with him to see a friend, and of changing cars at Brockton. During the wait he had gone into a fruit store to buy some cigars and to a lunchroom for a cup of coffee. At no time, the evening of May 5, had he seen a man on a motorcycle. The name Boda meant nothing to him. His revolver he had bought four or five years before for eighteen or nineteen dollars at a shop on Hanover Street. At the same time he had bought a box of cartridges. Some of these he had fired off on the Plymouth beach. The remaining six were in the revolver. Katzmann led him indirectly to the date of the South Braintree crime. Vanzetti remembered Patriot's Day, the nineteenth of April, because it had fallen on a Monday. He had no particular recollection of what he had done the preceding Thursday.

Katzmann had already discovered, before questioning the men, that Sacco had been absent from his work on April 15. When he left the police station he was convinced that Sacco had been involved in the South Braintree murders. Of Vanzetti he was not so sure.

After their questioning, the two Italians, unshaven and bedraggled, were photographed. They were then taken to the Brockton police court and charged with carrying concealed weapons. A local lawyer, William Callahan, was engaged for them. They pleaded guilty. The judge, after consulting with the district attorney's office, held them without bail under an unrepealed wartime act that empowered him to hold men suspected of major crimes.

Later in the day several dozen witnesses were brought from South Braintree and Bridgewater to see if they could identify the prisoners as participants in either of the holdups. In the small Brockton police station there was no attempt to have the two Italians mixed with other suspects in a lineup. They were merely led into the emergency room by themselves where they stood docilely until ordered to kneel, put on and take off their hats, raise their arms, and assume the crouching position of a man firing a pistol. The various witnesses walked around them slowly observing them from every angle.

Mary Splaine, Frances Devlin, Minnie Kennedy, Louise Hayes, Mark Carrigan, Albert Frantello, Frank Burke, Hans Behrsin, Louis DeBeradinis, Jimmy Bostock, Mike Levangie, and Lewis Wade were among those who came from South Braintree. Minnie, Louise, Carrigan, Burke, and Bostock could not identify either man. Frantello was certain that they were not the ones he had seen on April 15. Wade thought Sacco resembled the man he saw shooting Berardelli.

Frances Devlin and Mary Splaine studied the two men separately several times. Sacco was again ordered to raise his arm as if holding a pistol. The two women finally decided that he might possibly have been the man they saw leaning out of the car and shooting, but they were certain they had never seen Vanzetti before. Of all the South Braintree witnesses only Levangie, the gate-tender, picked Vanzetti as the driver of the getaway car. Jenny Novelli, coming to the station with a later group of witnesses, said that Sacco resembled the man she had seen in the bandit car, but she could not be positive about him.

The shotgun bandit in the Bridgewater holdup had been described by Constable Bowles as having a close-cropped mustache, and Slip Harding had so described him to a detective the afternoon of the crime, adding "I did not get much of a look at his face, but I think he was a Pole." Nevertheless, he no sooner caught sight of the droop-mustached Vanzetti in the Brockton station than he pointed to him with great positiveness as the man with the shotgun. Cox, on the other hand, was inclined to think Vanzetti was not the man. Bowles thought that he might have been.

While these identifications were being made, Chief Stewart and Assistant District Attorney William Kane took the handcuffed but still unperturbed Orciani on an identification marathon from Brockton to Needham to Braintree to Bridgewater. Faced with Sacco and Vanzetti, Orciani smilingly declared that he had never seen them before in his life. In Needham George Hassam said Orciani was not the man who had tried to borrow his dealer's plates in December. When Orciani was displayed in the Braintree town hall, three witnesses identified him as one of the April 15 gunmen. In Bridgewater Harding was positive that Orciani had been one of the gunmen in the December 24 holdup.

Back in Brockton, Orciani was taken to court and charged with exceeding the speed limit on his motorcycle and not having a tail-light, the only things the police could pin on him for the moment. Like Sacco and Vanzetti, he was held without bail. Although state and local police combed their districts for Boda they could find no trace of him.

The headlines of the Boston *Evening Globe* of May 6 announced that Governor Calvin Coolidge had vetoed the 2.75 Beer Bill. Tucked away on page six were several short paragraphs about "Bert Vanzetti, 32, of Plymouth, and Mike Sacco, 34, of South Stoughton . . . arraigned this morning in the Brockton Police Court charged with carrying concealed weapons." The last paragraph mentioned that an unnamed witness was almost sure that one of the men under arrest had driven the getaway car the day of the South Braintree murders.

These few lines were the first notice in print of what would in the next seven years become the Sacco-Vanzetti case.

◇◇◇◇◇◇◇◇◇◇◇◇◇◇◇◇◇◇◇◇◇◇◇◇◇◇◇◇◇◇◇◇

CHAPTER SIX

The Men and the Times

An introspective man, the sensitivity of his features concealed by prominent cheekbones and the drooping thatch of his ferocious mustache, Vanzetti was well known in North Plymouth's Italian settlement. Unmarried, he boarded with the Fortini family in a house halfway up Cherry Lane. Daily he sold fish to the Italian and Portuguese families, pushing his cart with its clanking brass scales and load of haddock, cod, halibut, and swordfish along Cherry Lane and Cherry Court and Standish Avenue. The fish for his regular customers he carefully wrapped in newspapers, marking the packages with the name and price.

Most of the Italians of North Plymouth worked at the Plymouth Cordage Company. Vanzetti had been employed there for eighteen months during 1914 and 1915 but had quit when they wanted him to shift from an outside to an inside job, preferring to work outdoors on the Plymouth breakwater. He had been on the strikers' fund committee in the Cordage strike that broke out over a wage dispute in January 1916. At that time the men were receiving eight dollars a week, the women six. The strikers demanded twelve and eight dollars, but finally accepted the company's offer of a general raise of a dollar. After that, Vanzetti never worked or attempted to work for the Cordage again. In the spring of 1919, in an effort to be independent of bosses and foremen, he bought his pushcart and scales and knives from a friend who was going back to Italy.

Each morning at the Fortinis' he would come downstairs in his slippers, take his boots from the zinc platform under the coal stove, and put them on before having breakfast. Then he would push his cart either to the town pier or the railroad station, returning to the

Fortinis' with his load of fish, which he could clean in the cellar. When fish were scarce he would go clamming on the flats between the town pier and the Cordage plant. He liked being on the windy beach.

Everybody knew the fish peddler, Bart the Beard, along the narrow lanes of his route, even the Yankee policemen. Children loved him. At mealtimes he was welcome in the Italian kitchens along his route, where he would sit at the table with his elbows on the checkered cotton tablecloth drinking coffee (for some years he had drunk nothing stronger) while the others downed glasses of homemade red-eye. He liked to talk and he liked to read. Over the years he had read Darwin, Marx, Spencer, Hugo, Tolstoy, and Zola, in random persistent efforts to overcome his lack of formal education. And he had read the anarchist fathers, Kropotkin, Proudhon, Malatesta, long since convinced that only anarchism could strike off the chains that fettered human freedom. His best-thumbed books, however, were *The Divine Comedy* and Renan's *Life of Jesus*. Anarchist that he was, in his personal relations he was not a doctrinaire. At one time he had enrolled in an evening course given by a liberal Protestant minister in Plymouth.

Sacco would never have set foot inside a church. Like his friend a member of the loose-knit Galleani group of New England anarchists, he was rigidly class-conscious. Yet in his private life he was much more the petty-bourgeois than Vanzetti. Domesticity, which meant little to Vanzetti, touched Sacco more deeply than anything else. He lived with his wife Rosina and his seven-year-old son Dante in a five-room bungalow rented from Michael Kelley, the owner of the Three-K Shoe Company, where he worked. His wife, who was expecting another child, was a delicately featured auburn-haired woman of the northern Italian type. As is often the case with Latin women, she left politics to the men and held to her inherited Catholic faith.

Sacco, as a skilled piece worker, often earned sixty or seventy dollars a week. A short, muscular man, he read little except the daily paper and repetitious anarchist tracts, preferring to spend his free time in his garden. Often he would be there at sunrise of a summer morning before going off to the factory, and after hours he would be working among his vegetables until dark. Sometimes he gave Michael Kelley beans and corn and tomatoes to distribute to poor families in the vicinity. Kelley thought well of Sacco. During the cold months he gave him the small extra job of tending the factory furnace. When Sacco stoked the fire in the evening he always checked the premises.

Mornings he always made sure that the place was warm by the time the workers arrived. Whenever he went to the factory after hours he carried his 32-caliber Colt with him. Kelley warned him several times to get a permit from the chief of police if he wanted to carry a pistol.

Sacco had come to the United States in 1908, the same year as Vanzetti. In the dozen years since their arrival they had both kept close to the immigrant community. They spoke scarcely more than a pidgin English.

"Nameless, in the crowd of nameless ones," Vanzetti described himself in his twenty-page autobiography, "The Story of a Proletarian Life," that he wrote in the Charlestown prison.

He was born in June 1888 into a prosperous family of Villafalletto, Piedmont, a village on the Magra River. Life in northwest Italy had the harshness of most peasant life, but the landscape itself could have served to illustrate the *Georgics*. Villafalletto was a rich agricultural community raising corn, wheat, beets, silkworms, and three crops of hay yearly. In the surrounding Alpine hills were apples, pears, cherries, grapes, plums, figs, and peaches. Vanzetti's earliest memories were of his father planting peaches, of blue flowers in the garden of his house, and of his mother giving him honey every morning from a beehive.

Vanzetti lived with his parents, a brother, and two sisters until his fourteenth year. At school, loving study "with a real passion," he won examination prizes that included a second prize in religious catechism. Under other circumstances the eager introspective boy might have developed into a teacher or scholar. William Thompson, who became Vanzetti's counsel in 1924, thought he was one of the most gifted men he had known and—applying a Boston yardstick—felt that with an education he might have been a Harvard professor.

Vanzetti's father was a practical peasant-minded man. For some time he could not make up his mind whether to apprentice his son or to let him continue his studies. But when he read in the *Gazzetta del Popolo* that forty-two Turin lawyers had applied for a position paying thirty-five lire a month, he decided then and there that education was a waste of money.

And so [Vanzetti wrote] *in the year 1901 he conducted me to Signor Conino, who ran a pastry shop in the city of Cuneo, and left me there to taste for the first time, the flavor of hard, relentless labor. I worked for about twenty months there—from seven o'clock each morning until ten at night, every day, except for a three-hour vacation twice a*

*month. From Cuneo I went to Cavour and found myself installed in
the bakery of Signor Goitre, a place that I kept for three years. Conditions were no better than in Cuneo, except that the fortnightly free
period was of five hours' duration.*

Later he became a caramel-maker in Turin. Scarcely out of his
childhood, drifting from city to city, reading whatever came to hand,
he found nothing to replace the memory of Villafalletto. His companions, the casual workers of the urban proletariat, were blasphe-
mously Marxist, and he, still loyal to his heritage, would occasionally
defend his religion with his fists. Yet, as the hard years of his
adolescence passed, he too was drawn to the socialist image of a
better world. His Catholicism eroded to a vague deism.

Early in 1907, working again in Turin, he fell ill of pleurisy, and his
father came from Villafalletto to take him home. In spite of his
suffering, when he saw from the train the deep green of his native
countryside Vanzetti felt renewed.

*And so I returned after six years spent in the fetid atmosphere of
bakeries and restaurant kitchens, with rarely a breath of God's air or
a glimpse of His glorious world. Six years that might have been beautiful to a boy avid of learning and thirsty for a refreshing draught of the
simple country life of his native village. Years of the great miracle
which transforms the child into the man. Ah, that I might have had
the leisure to watch the wonderful unfoldment!*

After two months in bed, nursed by his mother, he began to recover. He was now twenty years old. Later he was to describe the
period of his convalescence as one of the happiest of his life, a time
of gardening, of talking, and wandering through the woods bordering
the Magra. The happiness was brief, for his mother developed cancer
and after three agonizing months died. Vanzetti cared for her as she
had cared for him. He remained at her bedside day and night. For
the last two months of her life he did not even undress. She died
in his arms.

In after years he recalled that death in all its immediacy:

*It was I who laid her in her coffin, I who accompanied her to the final
resting place, I who threw the first handful of earth over her bier.
And it was right that I should do so, for I was burying part of myself
. . . the void left has never been filled.*

It was in the days following her death that he decided to go to America, to that land across the ocean where the past might be erased. On June 9, 1908, he left Villafalleto, accompanied far down the road by his tearful relatives and neighbors. After traveling across France he embarked at Le Havre in the packed steerage of a giant liner.

New York, the impersonal sky-swept metropolis, seemed to him from the huddled deck both inviting and threatening. In his autobiography one can sense the bewilderment of the immigrant coming down the gangplank.

How well I remember standing at the Battery, in lower New York, upon my arrival, alone, with a few poor belongings in the way of clothes, and very little money. Until yesterday I was among folks who understood me. This morning I seemed to have awakened in a land where my language meant little more to the native than the pitiful noises of a dumb animal. Where was I to go? What was I to do? Here was the promised land. The elevated rattled by and did not answer. The automobiles and the trolleys sped by, heedless of me.

That depression year of 1908 was a sorry time for a friendless stranger to arrive in the United States. Like all immigrants facing the unknown, Vanzetti sought out his fellow countrymen; one of them found him a job in a fashionable restaurant where he worked as a dishwasher and slept in a vermin-infested garret. Three months later he moved on to a similar job at Mouquin's. As in so many such places the glittering dining room bore little relation to the squalid kitchen. The scullery where Vanzetti worked was windowless.

When the electric light for some reason was out, it was totally dark so that we couldn't move without running into things. The vapor of the boiling water where the plates, pans and silver were washed formed great drops of water on the ceiling, took up all the dust and grime there, then fell slowly one by one upon my head, as I worked below. During working hours the heat was terrific. The table leavings amassed in barrels near the pantry gave out nauseating exhalations. The sinks had no direct sewerage connection. Instead, the water was permitted to overrun to the floor. In the center of the room there was a drain. Every night the pipe was clogged and the greasy water rose higher and higher and we trudged in the slime.

We worked twelve hours one day and fourteen the next, with five hours off every other Sunday. Damp food hardly fit for dogs and five

or six dollars a week was the pay. After eight months I left the place
for fear of contracting consumption.

Three months he tramped the streets of New York looking for
work. Behind the bright towering façade of the world city he saw the
human refuse that slept out of doors and rummaged in garbage barrels.
There were two worlds—he could see them for himself—the world of
those who sat at the tables of Mouquin's, and the world of those like
himself who worked in sculleries. And for him they were irreconcilable. At an employment agency he met a young Italian who had
not eaten for two days. Vanzetti bought him a meal. They decided to
strike out into the country where they thought there would be a
better chance of finding work and where at least the air would be
clean.

With Vanzetti's last savings they bought tickets and took a steam-
boat up the Connecticut River to Hartford. They then set off, aimless
and hopeful, knocking on doors and asking for work but rarely finding
any. A farmer they encountered took pity on them, fed them, and
let them stay two weeks on his farm although he had no real need of
their labor. Vanzetti never forgot the man's kindness.

Their wanderings took them from village to village. Penniless, often
soaked by rain, they were glad to find a few slices of bread at the end
of the day or an abandoned stable to sleep in. Finally they managed
to get work in a brick factory near Springfield, Massachusetts. The
other man soon quit, but Vanzetti stayed on, the hard labor at the
furnaces compensated for after work by the gay spirits of a little colony
of his countrymen, natives of Piedmont, Tuscany, and Venice. In the
evenings, someone would strike up a tune on a violin or an accordion.
Some would dance. Vanzetti liked to watch them, keeping time to the
music with his foot.

Later he went to Meriden, Connecticut, where he worked almost
beyond his strength in the stone pits. His friends kept urging him to
go back to his trade as a pastry cook, insisting that the unskilled
worker was the lowest animal in the social system. After two years
Vanzetti returned to New York and took a job as assistant pastry
chef in the Savarin Restaurant on Broadway. Eight months later he
was unexpectedly discharged. He found a new job in a Seventh
Avenue hotel, only to be discharged again after five months. Finally
he learned the reason. The employment agencies were splitting their
fees with the chefs, who found hiring and firing more profitable than
keeping regular help.

Again he was out of work, walking the streets, unable to find a job even as a dishwasher, buffeted by the weather, sometimes sleeping in doorways, his clothes lined with newspapers to keep out the cold. After five months he learned of an employment agency that was looking for pick-and-shovel workers.

It was necessary [he recalled] to present one's self with unbuttoned shirts, because they wanted to see what one was like, they wanted to see the hair on the chest of the worker, and good for me that I am Latin with haired chest. They used to say: "You are too small—you are too old."

He was sent to a barrack settlement near Springfield, Massachusetts, and put to work on the railroad. After he had swung a pick several months and saved enough to pay off his debts in New York—a little over a hundred dollars—he moved on to Worcester, first working on the Boston & Albany Railroad, then in various factories.

In 1914 he arrived in Plymouth where he was employed as a gardener, then with a loading gang in the Plymouth Cordage Company. Through all his working years he spent his scant free hours in reading. "Ah, how many nights I sat over some volume by a flickering gas jet," he wrote, "far into the morning hours! Barely had I laid my head on my pillow when the whistle sounded and back I went to the factory or stone pits." His reading was now mostly political: Gorki and Merlino, Reclus, Marx, Leon de Labriola, the *Testament* of Carlo Pisacani, Mazzini's *Duties of Man*.

He boarded at first with Vincenzo Brini and his wife Alfonsina in Suosso's Lane, one of the unpaved unnumbered streets, like Cherry Street and Cordage Lane, of North Plymouth's Little Italy. The houses were either the barracklike structures of the Cordage Company or else square boxes with haphazard additions, always with a grape arbor in the rear. They clustered round the Cordage plant like houses round a medieval cathedral.

The Brini house was a wooden double tenement opposite the Amerigo Vespucci Club, the social center of the Italian colony. Vanzetti had been drawn to Brini by his anarchist beliefs. Brini was a forceful, outstanding man, respected in the community for an integrity strong enough to overcome the suspicion of his free-thinking. For, in the pattern of immigrant groups, the Italians of Plymouth were more devout than those of the old country, their religion reinforcing their nationality in a foreign land. The Brini house was a way station for every passing anarchist. Luigi Galleani had stopped there, and big, genial, bearded Carlo Tresca, and the poet Arturo Giovannitti, and Malatesta himself, the aristocrat turned radical, with his beautiful voice. Night after night they used to sit in the Brini kitchen, talking, talking, talking of the brave new world to come.

Vanzetti felt himself more a relative than a boarder in the four years he lived at the Brinis'. He was fond of the little girls, LeFavre and Zora, but their brother Beltrando came to seem almost a son to him. Vanzetti always had time for the children when the parents had none. He used to take Beltrando on walks, showing him the kinds of flowers, or in the early evening pointing out the constellations. On Saturdays Beltrando would sometimes help him with the pushcart. Vanzetti liked to listen when Beltrando practiced his violin. Though he could not read music, Vanzetti had a sharp ear for the wrong note. "Paganini" he called the boy.

Although the Cordage strike had left him blacklisted in the local factories, Vanzetti stayed on at the Brinis' taking odd jobs: carting bricks, digging cellars, building breakwaters, cutting ice, or after a northeaster shoveling snow for the town or the railroad. He continued in this casual way until the spring of 1917.

Nicola Sacco had been baptized Ferdinando, a name he sometimes used in later life, but when his eldest brother, Nicola, died, he inherited the name by which he came to be generally known. The third of seventeen children, he was born in 1891 into a prosperous peasant family living on the outskirts of Torremaggiore, an Adriatic village in the foothills of the Appenines. His father, who owned olive groves and vineyards and who had married the daughter of an oil and wine merchant, was not made conservative by his prosperity. He belonged to a local republican club. Nicola's older brother Sabino went one step further and became a socialist.

Recalled from his Dedham prison cell, those early years at Torremaggiore became a sun-drenched idyll that Sacco would sometimes describe in letters that were at the same time exercises in English:

About sixty step from our vineyard we have a large piece of lant full of any quatity of vegetables that my brothers and I we used to coltivate them. So every morning before the sun shining used comes up and at night after the sun gos out I used to put one quarts of water on every plant of flowers and vegetables and the small fruit of little

*trees. While I was finished my work the sun shining was just coming
up and I used always jumping upon well wall and look at the beauty
sun shining and I do not know a long I used remane there look at
that enchanted scene of beautiful.*

At fourteen he left school to work in the fields. He became the
reliable son. Sometimes his father would send him off in a cart paying
off workmen or buying supplies. When the grapes were ripe he used
to sleep in a hayrick to guard the vineyards. Summers he tended the
steam engine that threshed all the wheat of the region. He liked
machines.

When Sabino was called up for his three years in the army, Nicola
took over as the head of the family. A trustworthy boy, old for his
age, he still did not want to settle down in Torremaggiore. Sabino had
long been fascinated by the dream of going to America and his
younger brother absorbed the idea from him. Their father had a
friend who had some years before emigrated to Milford, Massachusetts, and when they wrote to him he replied enthusiastically,
urging them to come over as soon as possible.

Sabino finished his army years in the spring of 1908. In April he
and Nicola sailed from Naples on one of the White Star ships. They
landed in East Boston just before Nicola's seventeenth birthday, and
went at once to Milford.

The realities of immigrant life were too much for Sabino. Within a
year he returned to Italy. Nicola stayed on. For his first few months
he worked in Milford as a water boy with a road gang. Sometimes the
engineer would let him tend the steam roller. He liked to stand beside
the clanking shining engine, stoking it with coal or squirting oil into
it from the long-nozzled can. After three months, however, he was
given a pick and shovel. Then for a year he worked in the foundry
of the Draper Corporation in Hopedale, trimming slag off pig iron.

As an unskilled foreign laborer he was at the bottom of the heap
and he knew it. He decided to learn a trade. In Milford, Michael
Kelley, then superintendent of the Milford Shoe Company, ran a
school where immigrants could learn edge-trimming, lasting, stitching,
and the other processes of shoe manufacture. The course lasted three
months and cost fifty dollars. More burdensome than the fee was the
necessity of spending a quarter of a year without earning anything.
But Sacco took the chance and the course. He became a skilled edger.

The benefits were immediate. Where before he had been earning

$1.15 a day, he could now earn $40 or $50 or more a week. After a short period in another factory, Sacco went to work in the Milford Shoe Company, remaining there from 1910 until the spring of 1917.

Three evenings a week he attended English classes, then compulsory for foreigners working in factories. Most of the pupils showed up in their work clothes, sweaty and indifferent, but Sacco always arrived washed and shaved, in a decent suit of clothes. His teacher remembered his courtesy, his eager mind. She liked him, as did everyone else in the clanbound community, even though they all knew that he was a radical.* Sacco joined the Italian dramatic society and took part in most of the neighborhood social events. It was at a benefit dance he got up for a crippled accordion player that he met Rosina Zambelli. She was sixteen that year, 1912, and had arrived from a convent school in Italy only a few months before to live with her parents. Father Zambelli heard a lot about Sacco as soon as he began to court Rosina. A *sovversivo*, a free-thinker! When the *sovversivo* eloped with his daughter, Zambelli was furious. "That one will end on the gallows!" he shouted. Later he became somewhat reconciled with his son-in-law.

Sacco was happier in his married life than he had ever been before. But for this it is probable that in a few years he would have followed his brother back to Italy. He never identified himself with America. He kept to the society of Italians and gave up his efforts to learn English. Like many radical-minded Italian immigrants of the time, he found himself drawn to anarchism. Until coming to America he had been a republican. In Milford he read *Il Proletario*, a paper edited by the poet-anarchist Giovannitti, Galleani's *Cronaca Sovversiva*, and other more fugitive sheets. Sometimes he and Rosina acted in fund-raising propaganda melodramas with titles like *Senza Padrone* and *Tempeste Sociali*.

In 1913 he joined a local anarchist club, the Circolo di Studi Sociali. He helped organize meetings in neighboring towns, distributed crudely printed apocalyptic pamphlets, raised small sums of money, and occasionally welcomed visiting leaders like Tresca or Galleani. In 1916 his club held a meeting in Milford to raise money to support a strike Tresca was running in Minnesota. The meeting did not have a police permit and the speakers were arrested, among them Sacco. He was convicted and paid a fine for disturbing the

* According to his teacher, no one in Milford ever believed Sacco was guilty of murder. After his arrest the Italian community ran benefits to raise money for his defense. It also contributed to his funeral expenses.

peace. It was the only time he was ever arrested until the May night when he was picked up on the Brockton streetcar.

For most Americans the belated entry of the United States into World War I was an exhilarating experience. The bloody reality of the Civil War had long since been embroidered by legend. After half a century of peace—the Spanish-American affair was, after all, little more than a maneuver—combat could again seem the grandest of human hazards. For Sacco and Vanzetti the complex tragedy of the war was simplified to the formula of predatory capitalism. Their attitude was summed up in the Anarchist-Communist Anti-Conscription Appeal, which demanded that the workers refuse to serve in the Army at any cost.

A month after Congress declared war, President Wilson signed the Selective Military Conscription Bill, requiring every male between the ages of twenty-one and thirty-one, whether or not a citizen of the United States, to register on June 5, 1917. The official notice explained that registration did not mean liability to military service except for citizens or those who had taken out first papers. Sacco and Vanzetti were not liable, but so remote were they from ordinary American life that neither of them understood this. The passage of the act filled them with panic. A week before the registration date they left for Mexico. It was only a week before this that Sacco and Vanzetti had first met.

Some thirty New England anarchists formed a cooperative community in Monterrey. Those who could found jobs. Sacco worked in a bakery, sometimes taking his pay in bread and carrying a sack of it back to the others. But life in the adobe huts was difficult. From the United States letters came telling of high wages there and how easy it was to avoid the draft. Gradually the Monterrey anarchists slipped back across the border. Sacco, who had suffered much from the separation from his family, returned to Massachusetts late in August. Under his mother's maiden name of Mosmacotelli he rejoined his wife in Cambridge and worked briefly for the New England Candy Company, going on to a succession of poorly paid jobs in East Boston and Haverhill, and a better one in Brockton. This he gave up rather than buy a Liberty Bond. For a short period in October 1917 he was employed by Rice & Hutchins in South Braintree, but quit when he found that he was making only thirteen dollars a week.

A few days before the Armistice, when it was obvious that war was ending, Sacco reappeared under his own name at the Three-K Shoe

Factory in South Stoughton. It was a small plant of about 125 workers, owned by the same Michael Kelley who had run the apprentice school in Milford. Sacco walked into his office and said, "I am Nick." At first Kelley could not place him. Then he remembered the deft young Italian he had taught six years before. He called his elder son and told him, "George, if you need an edge-trimmer, here's a good man." And Sacco was a good man: steady, arriving early and staying late, "a great fellow to clean up everything."

Unlike Sacco, Vanzetti had no personal goal. Returning to the United States at about the same time as Sacco, he wandered for a year: first to St. Louis; then Youngstown, Ohio; Farrell, Pennsylvania; and finally, in the summer of 1918, back to Plymouth. For a few months he stayed again with the Brinis, then Vincenzo found him a room with the Fortinis in Cherry Lane. But though Vanzetti no longer lived at the Brinis', the old intimacy remained.

For a year Vanzetti worked at various jobs. Then he bought his pushcart. He had no competitors in North Plymouth, and there were days when he would sell up to two hundred pounds of fish. The difficulty was the supply. Often the trawlers did not go out until April, and sometimes they came back with empty holds. During the slack summer of 1919 Vanzetti worked for the town, but in the autumn he again pushed his cart. Sometimes he had to go to the Boston docks for his fish. When he was in the city he would drop in to see his friend, the printer Aldino Felicani, in the press room of the Italian daily *La Notizia*, or else would take the one-cent ferry to East Boston to visit some of his anarchist comrades there. After the first of Attorney General Palmer's Red raids in November, Vanzetti told Felicani they should plan to set up an underground press.

In 1917 the slogans that after the war came to seem as shabby as a last-season's theater poster had rung taut and true. *Beat the Hun! Stand by the President! Keep the World Safe for Democracy!*

It had been a time of sauerkraut turned liberty cabbage, of Wagner turned John Philip Sousa, of the conductor of the Boston Symphony Orchestra, Dr. Karl Muck, driven from the podium and dachshunds driven from the streets. Several states had even passed laws against speaking German. High schools dropped the language from their curricula. Upper-school boys of my school, Roxbury Latin, who were still allowed the choice between Greek and German, used to joke that it was better to choose Greek because you could study it on the streetcar.

Except for the scapegoat Germans, all American racial and religious groups were welded into the unity of the war years. Only a meager minority, a few hundred thousand at most, continued to stand aside. What opposition to the war still remained came from the foreign-born of the big cities with their inherited dread of conscription, from the dwindling Socialist Party, the still belligerently confident Industrial Workers of the World—the Wobblies—and from the anarchists.

War unity, seeming at the time to be forged in steel, has a way shortly afterward of showing its puttylike consistency—as 1919 soon demonstrated. In a soothing-syrup speech that year Senator Warren G. Harding coined *normalcy,* a word that has endured because it somehow expressed the common yearning to return to the idealized prewar period.

Instead of normalcy, 1919 was a year of fragmentation that began with President Wilson triumphant on his European journey and ended with him in America broken and defeated. It was the year of the High Cost of Living (as inflation was then known), the year of the great steel strike, the Seattle general strike, the outlaw railway strikes, coal strikes, textile strikes, maritime strikes, telephone operators' strikes, the Boston police strike, actors' strikes, even strikes of rent-payers. At one point almost three million workers were out.

Above all it was a year of antitheses. The first year of peace, it saw the United States reject the peace treaty. In Versailles the League of Nations was born, while in Berlin the Spartacist revolt was bloodily suppressed. The AEF paraded under Madison Square's plaster triumphal arch in New York, and just before Christmas the Spanish-American War transport *Buford*—nicknamed the Soviet Ark—left Ellis Island for Russia with a load of assorted radical deportees that included Emma Goldman. Within a few months of each other the American Legion and the American Communist Party were founded. "Hell will now be for rent," Billy Sunday announced triumphantly as Nebraska became the thirty-sixth state to ratify the prohibition amendment; at the same time a crime wave surged from coast to coast.

It was a year of violence. When President Wilson landed in Boston on February 23 after his return from the Paris Peace Conference, Secret Service men lined the roofs and all windows were ordered closed as he drove through the streets. The day before, two members of the Groupa Pro Prensa, a Spanish anarchist circle in Philadelphia, were arrested by Secret Service agents and accused of plotting the President's assassination. On April 28 Mayor Ole Hansen of Seattle, who had been denouncing the Red Menace, received a bomb package in the mail. The following afternoon a maid at the Atlanta home of Senator Thomas Hardwick, former chairman of the Committee on Immigration, opened a package that blew off her hands. Subsequently, thirty-four bomb packages were put in the mails addressed to Attorney General Palmer, the Postmaster General, the Secretary of Labor, the Commissioner of Immigration, Justice Oliver Wendell Holmes, Judge K. M. Landis (who had recently presided at an anarchist trial), Senator Lee Overman (chairman of a committee investigating Bolshevism), J. P. Morgan, John D. Rockefeller, and others.

May Day, the first since the Armistice and the second since the Bolshevik *coup d'état* in Russia, was anticipated by the police in all major American cities. Attorney General Palmer had announced that there was a plot afoot to kill high officials and force American recognition of Soviet Russia. But the bomb packages were followed by nothing so drastic. In New York a Tom Mooney protest meeting that overflowed Carnegie Hall was charged by ex-servicemen in uniform. The New York offices of the socialist *Call* were sacked by a mob of soldiers and sailors. There were demonstrations and counter-demonstrations in Chicago, and in Cleveland a man was killed when paraders carrying a red flag were attacked. The worst street fighting took place in Boston when the Communist-dominated Lettish Workmen's Society attempted to hold a parade after a mass meeting in the Dudley Street Opera House.

In mid-May Luigi Galleani, the leading anarchist figure in the United States, was taken to the East Boston Immigration Station for deportation. A man of leonine bearing and much charm, Galleani had edited the brilliantly inflammatory *Cronaca Sovversiva* in Paterson, New Jersey, in Barre, Vermont, and finally in Lynn, Massachusetts. "Our master," Vanzetti called him.

Following his deportation, on the evening of June 2, bombs exploded in eight cities. The chief target was Attorney General Palmer, whose house at 2132 R Street, Washington, had its front blown in just as he was going to bed. Windows of neighboring houses were shattered, including those of Assistant Secretary of the Navy Franklin Roosevelt directly across the street. Apparently the bomb had gone off prematurely, killing its carrier, for parts of a body were found up and down the street, one fragment lying on the Roosevelt doorstep. The police also found a cheap suitcase large enough to hold about twenty-five pounds of dynamite, two pistols, a derby, a sandal, and shreds of a pin-stripe suit and a polka-dot bow tie. About fifty printed pink flyers entitled PLAIN WORDS were scattered over the neighborhood. Several of these were picked up by Secretary Roosevelt. They read:

The powers that be make no secret of their will to stop, here in America, the world-wide spread of revolution. The powers that be must reckon that they will have to accept the fight they have provoked.

A time has come when the social question's solution can be delayed no longer; the class war is on and cannot cease but with a complete victory for the international proletariat. . . .

Do not say we are acting cowardly because we keep in hiding, do not say it is abominable; it is war, class war, and you were the first to wage it under cover of the powerful institutions you call order, in the darkness of your laws, behind the guns of your boneheaded slaves. . . .

There will have to be bloodshed . . . we will destroy to rid the world of your tyrannical institutions. . . .

Long live social revolution! Down with tyranny!

The Anarchist Fighters.

The same evening a watchman was killed in New York when a bomb exploded on the steps of the town house of Judge Charles Nott. Our Lady of Victory Church in Philadelphia was bombed, and in Pittsburgh there were blasts at the homes of United States District Judge W. H. Thompson, who had once presided over a prosecution of Carlo Tresca, and Chief Inspector W. W. Sibray of the Bureau of Immigration.

In Boston Judge Hayden, who had dealt severely with the arrested May Day paraders, had his house almost demolished by a bomb made of iron pipe stuffed with shrapnel and dynamite. In suburban Newtonville, a similar bomb blew off the side of the house belonging to Representative Leland Powers, who had sponsored an anti-anarchy bill in the state legislature. Copies of PLAIN WORDS were found in the vicinity of both explosions.

Except for the watchman and the obliterated carrier, no one was injured in any of the bombings, but the effect over the country was one of dismay at the recurring challenge and indignation against the alien radicals held reponsible. The New York *Times* might consider the bombings of "Bolshevik or I.W.W. origin," but the public generally believed them the work of anarchists. Ever since Chicago's Haymarket Massacre of 1886, when six policemen were killed by a bomb thrown at an anarchist meeting, Americans had been haunted by the image of the terrorist alien. President McKinley's assassination by the half-mad half-anarchist Leo Czolgosz hardened the image. Such acts were in the tradition of the propaganda of the deed, as proclaimed by anarchist patriarchs like Malatesta and furthered gleefully by disciples like Johann Most in his *Science of Revolutionary Warfare— A Manual of Instruction in the Use and Preparation of Nitroglycerine, Dynamite, Gun Cotton, Fulminating Mercury, Bombs, Fuses, Poison, Etc., Etc.*

But for their rare spectacular gestures of political violence, the anarchists would doubtless have been left to wither in the obscurity of their cult. The nobly absurd anarchic conception of a governmentless future when, in Vanzetti's words, man would no longer be wolf to the man, was held in America by only a miniscule group—mostly immigrants from the more backward countries to whom it seemed quite feasible that workers could run factories cooperatively. Because by his philosophy of freedom each anarchist made his own basic decisions, there was no way of separating the theorist from the activist. Sacco and Vanzetti were said to be quietistic anarchists—as opposed to the activist bombers of June 2—yet the dividing line was as difficult to establish in 1919 as it was two generations before with the abolitionists, whose ranks could include John Greenleaf Whittier and John Brown.

"Property is theft," Proudhon had said, and some anarchists accepted this literally, asserting, in Galleani's words, "the right to expropriate the bourgeoisie—which lives by theft—whenever the need presses or the struggle against the evil social order demands it." During the 1880s in Paris, one such anarchist expropriator, Clement Duval, was convicted of robbery and sent to Devil's Island. His successor, François Ravachol, became one of the saints of anarchism through his bombings of the houses of judges. In the course of various robberies Ravachol committed several brutal murders.*

Galleani spoke well of both Duval and Ravachol, and when Duval escaped from Devil's Island and reached the United States, published his prison memoirs and a biographical sketch in *Cronaca Sovversiva.*

---

* The most sensational of the anarchist criminal groups in this century was the Bonnot Gang of Paris. In December 1911, the members attacked two bank messengers on the street, shot one, grabbed their bags, and made off in a waiting car in what was apparently the world's first motorized holdup.

In 1917 this material appeared in book form, edited by Andrea Salsedo, a forty-year-old Sicilian who had helped Galleani with his newspaper.

The bombing of his house may well have caused Attorney General Palmer to believe that "resident aliens in large numbers and of a desperate type" were conspiring to overthrow the government by means of a "physical force revolution." Certainly from then on Red plots became his phobia. Appointing William J. Flynn, former head of the Secret Service, Director of the Bureau of Investigation, Palmer ordered him to conduct "a dragnet for Reds all over the country."

The first raids took place on November 7, the second anniversary of the Russian Revolution. Suddenly, an army of government agents, local police, and special deputies, augmented by a haphazard swarm of private detectives, many of dubious background, swooped down on the various headquarters of the Communist Party, the Communist Labor Party, the Union of Russian Workers, and the Russian anarchists. During that wild and vengeful night the raiders smashed their way into buildings in all the large cities, wrecked property, broke open safes, and indifferent to warrants and the niceties of habeas corpus hustled thousands of citizens as well as noncitizens to the lockup.

But the November raids were only a prelude to the sweeping raids of January 2, 1920. These were timed to take place simultaneously in thirty-three cities. Six thousand warrants were issued, and thousands of aliens were picked up with or without warrants. Subsequently, about three thousand were held for deportation—although in the end only 446 of these were deported.

In Massachusetts there were fourteen such raids, and in Boston five hundred aliens were marched through the streets in chains and taken to the Deer Island House of Correction, where they were isolated in brutally chaotic conditions.

The callous illegalities of the raiding procedures caused much indignation among native Americans. In Boston, Federal Judge George Anderson spoke out sharply against the mob actions of government agents. Twelve nationally known lawyers, among them Zechariah Chafee, Roscoe Pound, and Felix Frankfurter, all of the Harvard Law School, collaborated on a report condemning the illegal practices of the Justice Department.

If the raids caused indignation among the native-born, among the alien radicals they caused terror. No one seemed safe from the midnight knock on the door, the hard-faced men with clubs, the blinding lights and the hammering questions of the night-long interrogation. Rumor exaggerated the Palmer proceedings to outright murder as they were discussed by Sacco and his friends in Stoughton and by Vanzetti and his comrades on Sunday afternoons in the Italian Independent Naturalization Club of East Boston.

After months of following each clue, even to tracing the polka-dot tie to the store that sold it, Department of Justice agents concluded that the man blown to pieces in the bombing of Attorney General Palmer's house was an Italian anarchist, Carlo Valdinoce, a member of the dynamite-minded group in Paterson, New Jersey. Valdinoce had been associated there with Galleani in the printing of the *Cronaca Sovversiva*. In addition, Flynn, the new Bureau of Investigation director, had collected enough evidence to convince him that an explosion of the same date in Paterson was the work of another local anarchist, Ruggero Baccini, who had since been deported. There were no clues in the other eleven bombings, though Flynn was certain that they were all the work of anarchists and that the dynamite had come from Paterson. Efforts to determine the origin of the PLAIN WORDS flyer failed.

Then, in February 1920, Flynn received a tip from an ostensible direct-action anarchist named Ravarini. Recently, in Boston, Ravarini had sold subscriptions to Malatesta's *Umanita Nuova* to Sacco, Vanzetti, Boda, and Orciani, among others. He told a federal agent that a Roberto Elia, a printer at Canzani's Printing Shop in Brooklyn, New York, was engaged in publishing anarchist literature, including flyers. On the night of February 25, Bureau agents picked up Elia in his lodgings. At the print shop the agents turned up pink paper similar to that of the flyer and unearthed from the Canzani fonts the peculiar s that had not matched the typeface used for the first nine letters of the title PLAIN WORDS. Canzani's typesetter turned out to be Galleani's old associate, Andrea Salsedo.

Salsedo and Elia, questioned separately, at first maintained they knew nothing about PLAIN WORDS. They were taken to the Manhattan offices of the Department of Justice at 21 Park Row and there they remained until the morning of May 2 when Salsedo's smashed body was found on the pavement, fourteen floors beneath the window of his room. It was believed by the anarchists at the time, and afterward by many liberals, that Salsedo had been tortured by Bureau agents and then thrown from the window. Actually, Salsedo was a suicide. Neither he nor Elia was under formal arrest at Park Row, although the agents made it clear that the alternative to staying was jail or deportation. According to a Department of Justice report, Salsedo confessed that he had printed PLAIN WORDS. Elia admitted that he had been in the shop and that he had delivered a bundle of the flyers to Carlo Recchi, a member of the Galleani group. After consulting with their lawyer, Narciso Donato, the men agreed that they would remain in the Department's offices, "that their whereabouts should remain unknown to all except their families, their attorney, and certain of their friends, and, further, that neither should be subjected to interrogation or examination without the presence of their attorney." Donato later said that his clients had been well treated and had been questioned only when he was present.

Subsequently, Elia was deported. Before leaving the country he set down his own version of the events at Park Row in an affidavit for one of the Sacco-Vanzetti defense lawyers. On March 8, he related, while being taken to an interrogation room, he had passed another room where he had seen Salsedo surrounded by four agents in their shirtsleeves. Then, while he himself was being interrogated, he had heard Salsedo scream. The next morning he had been taken to Director Flynn's office.

I was alone in the outer room [Elia deposed] until Salsedo came in with Mr. Donato. Salsedo's face and forehead were bruised from the beating he had received. He had red spots and scratches on his cheeks and temples and his eyes were vacant. He was depressed. I never saw him normal during all the times after that we were together.

In Mr. Flynn's waiting room Salsedo told me about his interrogation the night before. They showed him a bloody sandal and said "You see this blood? This is the blood of the man who was blown up. Tell me whose blood that is." He would say that he did not know, and they would swear at him and strike him in the face or body with the heel of the sandal. They did this over and over again.

Mr. Donato told me that we were charged with murder in the first degree. Salsedo said "I do not want to die. We have done nothing, but we are in a trap. What are we to do? I will admit that I printed PLAIN WORDS, because I cannot stand any more, and maybe I will help myself.". . .

On the next day we were questioned by Mr. Flynn. Salsedo said that he had printed the leaflet in May 1919; that I had nothing to do with it; that it had been ordered by one Recchi. I stated that I had seen Salsedo printing it, but had nothing to do with it. . . .

After that we were not formally questioned any more and we were very well treated. A room was fitted up for us with two beds. We had good meals; we were taken out for walks; once we were taken to the movies. When any one asked me if I was content or if I was willing to stay at the Department of Justice I always said "Yes," because I did not want to go to prison and I thought that all depended upon the good will of the agents. . . .

Mr. Donato came to see us frequently. So did Salsedo's wife, who sought to tranquillize him. But Salsedo was always despondent and in fear. He would say, "We who are innocent, are in jail. Maybe those who are guilty are out there in freedom." I would tell him that we would be free, but he did not believe it. He would lie groaning and lamenting all the night. He complained continually of pains in his stomach and head. He was always nervous. He refused absolutely to eat. He showed clear signs of an unbalancing mind. . . .

On the evening of Sunday, May 2nd, Salsedo walked a little with me in the corridor as was our custom. He went to bed about nine o'clock. Then I sat with the Department of Justice agents who were smoking and telling stories. About eleven o'clock I came into our room with Palmera the interpreter. Salsedo begged me to turn off the light; he said "I have a terrible headache. That cigarette you gave me hurt me."

I went to bed. For a long time I heard Salsedo groaning and lamenting. Then I fell asleep. I know nothing more until I was awakened by the watchman who came to call us every morning between five and six o'clock so that we should be up before the cleaning women came to the offices. I said "Is it not early?" He answered, "Your comrade is dead. He has jumped from the window."

To the anarchist groups of New York, New Jersey, and New England the detention of Elia and Salsedo was ominous. Tresca, who had succeeded the deported Galleani as leader, consulted with Donato, but was unable to see the men. He suspected the lawyer of back-hand dealings with the Department of Justice.

On Sunday afternoon, April 25, fifteen or twenty of the East Boston anarchists, meeting in their hall overlooking the docks, discussed what they could do for Elia and Salsedo. Sacco, Vanzetti, and Orciani were present. Ever since they had learned of their comrades' mysterious detention these men had been raising money and sending it on without, however, knowing just where it was going. Somebody from Boston, they now decided, must go to New York and find out what was happening. Vanzetti, being self-employed and having no family responsibilities, was chosen. He left that evening on the train.

In New York he found that Tresca could give him little new information. Luigi Quintiliano, the chairman of a committee to defend Palmer raid victims, warned Vanzetti that there would soon be more raids and urged him to tell his Massachusetts friends to get rid of any anarchist literature they might possess.

Vanzetti passed on this warning when he returned to Boston, but about Salsedo and Elia he had no more to tell than was known before.

In spite of the Attorney General's prediction that a gigantic bomb plot and general strike would erupt on May Day, the day was for the most part a quiet one all over the country. Palmer's zeal produced only a few victims, among them members of the Association of Harvard Clubs who, marching in Washington behind their crimson banners, found themselves mistaken for a Red parade. Public opinion began to turn against the Attorney General, even as his shadow still loomed large over the alien radicals.

At their Sunday meeting on May 2, the East Boston Anarchists were not aware of any change in the public temper. To them the times seemed desperate, with the possibility of a police ambush at the next corner. Most of their talk was about getting rid of their anarchist literature. Orciani, who had recently seen Boda, reported that the latter still owned a car; he thought they might use it for rounding up the literature. Sacco suggested that he and Vanzetti and Orciani should meet with Boda some time early in the week. Vanzetti reminded everyone that there would be a meeting in Brockton on May 9 to raise money for Salsedo and Elia.

After the meeting Sacco told Vanzetti that on the ninth he and his family would be on their way to Italy. He suggested that Vanzetti come back to Stoughton with him for a last visit. Vanzetti promised to come down the following afternoon.

Monday morning Vanzetti visited the Boston piers but found that fish was still scarce and too expensive for his pushcart customers. He had lunch with some Italian friends near Haymarket Square and heard the news of Salsedo's death. Late in the afternoon he took the train for Stoughton.

Only Rosina and the child were at the bungalow when he arrived. Sacco had quit his job on Saturday, but had gone back to the factory to help break in a new man. He returned just after five o'clock.

Tuesday morning Sacco had to go in to Boston to the Italian

Consulate for his passport. Vanzetti spent the day reading. After Sacco had picked up the passport he rode out to Hyde Park on the el to meet Orciani, who had come down from Readville on his motorcycle. They talked again about the books and pamphlets that had to be collected, and Orciani said they could arrange with Boda to get the car the next evening. He gave Sacco a ride back to Stoughton. As they chugged into the yard of the bungalow they saw young George Kelley, the factory superintendent, who lived next door. Sacco intoduced him to Orciani. They stood there a few minutes talking about motorcycles and the weather. Orciani said he would be over again next afternoon.

On Wednesday Sacco stayed home all day. He and Vanzetti chopped wood in the morning, had lunch, took a walk, and then sat down in the kitchen while Rosina went on with the packing. Vanzetti said afterward that he happened to notice several shotgun shells on top of the kitchen cabinet. Rather than see them thrown out he put them in his pocket, thinking he might sell them to some comrade in Plymouth and perhaps make a quarter for the cause.

Orciani arrived on his motorcycle about half past four, the elusive Boda in the sidecar. Boda told them he had telephoned the garage man about his car; they could pick it up that evening. After the four ate supper, Orciani and Boda left on the motorcycle, having agreed to meet Sacco and Vanzetti at Elm Square in West Bridgewater.

Sacco and Vanzetti caught the 7:20 streetcar for Brockton. There they found they had to wait for the Bridgewater car. It was growing dark. Vanzetti went into a store on Main Street and bought several cigars. Then the two men had a cup of coffee in a lunchroom. While they drank it Vanzetti took out a paper and pencil and began to write the notice for the Sunday meeting in Brockton.

He continued to work on it after they boarded the Bridgewater car. Just before they reached West Bridgewater he gave the notice to Sacco and told him it was ready for the printer. At the Elm Square they waited a while under the street light by the Johnson brothers' garage, which was shut. Then, after starting toward Bridgewater, they turned back, recrossed the square, and walked in the direction of Brockton. As they reached the railroad bridge they saw the solitary beam of a motorcycle headlight snaking toward them.

CHAPTER SEVEN

The Plymouth Trial

The first of the East Boston comrades to visit the Brockton police station was Professor Felice Guadagni, a graduate of the Institute of Naples and editor of the *Gazzetta del Massachusetts*. He was proud of being an educated man and in spite of his anarchism liked to call himself and have others call him Professor. He found that his two friends did not seem to understand the reason for their arrest. Vanzetti told him with a shrug that even if they were going to be deported now, they would at least go to Italy at Uncle Sam's expense. The point of Katzmann's opaque questioning was suddenly clear when Guadagni explained that they were being held, not because they were anarchists, not for running away to Mexico during the war, but because they were accused of murder.

When the news of Vanzetti's predicament reached Plymouth, Vincenzo Brini gathered his friends together to decide what to do. Like most aliens they felt confused when faced with governmental authority. Whenever such difficulties came up in North Plymouth—troubles with police or courts or town officials—the Italian community turned to Doviglio Govoni. Govoni, the Plymouth court interpreter, was also the local fixer. He knew English, he knew the judges and the district attorney and the sheriff, he knew the routine of the town hall and the heads of the various departments, most of whom he called by their first names. Whether it was a tax abatement, a couple of boys caught robbing a fruit store, a matter of filing first papers, or getting a runaway son out of the Navy, Govoni was the man to go to.

After Govoni had listened to Brini and the others, he told them straight off that they must get rid of their lawyer, Callahan. What they needed was a good smart lawyer, like Judge John Vahey of the district court. Not only did Vahey know his way around Plymouth, but his brother was a big Boston attorney who might come in handy in case things didn't turn out right.

Vanzetti's friends agreed. They and Govoni went down to the Brockton station the following evening with a declaration of discharge. They explained to Vanzetti that they would do everything they could for him, but that they needed a lawyer they had confidence in. Vanzetti, though he had come to like Callahan, signed the declaration.

Meanwhile Sacco's comrades had engaged a Boston lawyer, James Graham. An Irish Catholic, Graham had built up a large practice in the Italian North End, where he was noted for his ability to get on with politicians and to get his clients off. The latters' guilt or innocence did not concern him. He assumed that most of the Italians who came to him in trouble were troublemakers.

Harding's positive identification of Vanzetti as the Bridgewater shotgun bandit had been enough to convince Chief Stewart, and on May 11 he filed a complaint in the Brockton police court charging that Vanzetti "being armed with a dangerous weapon did assault Alfred E. Cox with intent to rob him." That same afternoon, to Stewart's disgust, Orciani had to be released, since his time card showed that he had been at work in Norwood on the date of both crimes.

The preliminary hearing on the Bridgewater charge against Vanzetti was held in the Brockton police court before Judge Herbert Thorndike on May 18, 1920.* Graves, the truck driver, who had thought the bandit car a Hudson, had died in the interim, but Cox the paymaster, Bowles the guard, and Slip Harding appeared as witnesses for the Commonwealth. The three still described the man with the shotgun as having a cropped mustache but picked out the droop-mustached Vanzetti as the man. Bowles and Cox, who had been vague when they first saw Vanzetti in the police station, had by this time become much more positive. "I think he looks enough like the man to be the man," Cox told the court, although under cross-examination he admitted that he was still not completely sure. Bowles was sure. "That is the man who had the shotgun that morning," he said.

---

* The preliminary hearing on his participation in the South Braintree murders followed on May 26 before Judge Avery in the Quincy District Court. Sacco, against whom the evidence seemed more substantial, had appeared in the Quincy Court on May 8.

Harding remained as certain about Vanzetti as he had been at the station, but the car he had originally described as a Hudson Six had now firmly become a Buick. In addition to the three repeaters the Commonwealth had a new witness, a Mrs. Georgina Brooks, who a few minutes before the Bridgewater attempt had been walking down Broad Street with her five-year-old son. She had crossed just in front of the bandit car and had noticed the four men inside. The driver had followed her with his eyes as she passed. Now she picked Vanzetti as the man she had seen behind the wheel of the car. "I am positive," she said.

Vahey having not bothered to produce any defense witnesses, Judge Thorndike held Vanzetti for action by the grand jury, and on June 11 two indictments were found against him: for assault with intent to rob, and assault with intent to murder. At the conclusion of the May preliminary hearing Assistant District Attorney Kane told the court that he had witnesses who would positively identify Vanzetti in connection with the South Braintree murders. On learning this, Judge Thorndike refused to admit Vanzetti to bail and remanded him to the Plymouth county jail. His trial was scheduled for June 22.

In the intervening weeks Vanzetti continued to insist that he had spent December 24, the day of the Bridgewater attempt, delivering eels to his customers in North Plymouth. Among Catholics the day before Christmas is a fast day, and among Italians it ends in a feast that always includes eels. Even the poorest or the most free-thinking of Italian families manages to have eels on that traditional day. Brini rounded up several dozen witnesses to testify that they had bought eels from Vanzetti or seen him with his pushcart the day before Christmas.

Sacco's lawyer, Graham, became associated with Vahey in Vanzetti's defense. Six years afterward, while in Charlestown State Prison, Vanzetti wrote a pamphlet, "Background of the Plymouth Trial," denouncing both his Plymouth lawyers. One of his chief complaints was that Vahey had refused to allow him to testify in his own behalf. Vanzetti wrote that when they discussed the matter,

He asked me how I would explain from the stand the meaning of Socialism, or Communism, or Bolshevism, if I was requested by the district attorney to do so. At such a query, I would begin an explanation on those subjects, and Mr. Vahey would cut it off at its very beginning.

"Hush, if you will tell such things to the ignorant, conservative jurors, they will send you to State prison right away."

Graham set down his version thirty years later. According to it he and Vahey went to the Plymouth jail one evening and spent hours discussing whether or not Vanzetti should take the stand. Graham said he told Vanzetti that when a defendant failed to testify in Massachusetts he was usually found guilty.

Vanzetti [Graham wrote] *was carefully advised as to the evidence that had gone in as to what inference the Jury might draw if he failed to take the stand despite what the Judge would tell them in his charge, and as to what information might be elicited from him if he did take the stand.* "But you," *Vahey told him,* "are the one who has got to make the decision as to whether you will testify or not."

Sacco had been moved to the Dedham jail and Vahey, at Vanzetti's request, went there to discuss the matter with him. When he returned, Vanzetti, according to Graham, said in substance: "I don't think I can improve upon the alibi which has been established. I had better not take the stand."

Vanzetti was sure afterward that he had been betrayed, and attacked Vahey in the bitter language of his pamphlet. Part of his bitterness was undoubtedly caused by the fact that in 1924 Vahey became Katzmann's law partner.

May passed into June. Except among the Italians of North Plymouth and the small anarchist circle in East Boston, Vanzetti's forthcoming trial caused little interest. There was a flurry in June when the Boston *Sunday Advertiser* reported—it later turned out to be a newspaperman's hoax—that a letter, signed the "Red X Society," had been found near Plymouth Rock demanding Vanzetti's release "or take the consequences." But for most people the trial was just a routine affair coming at the end of the spring criminal session. The newspapers and public were much more interested in the trial of Jennie Zimmerman in Springfield, accused of murdering her cousin and lover, Dr. Henry Zimmerman.

Although Chief Stewart had received a setback with Orciani's release, he still stuck to his theory that the deported Coacci and the missing Boda had been mixed up in both crimes. Boda, he was convinced, was the man who had appeared at Hassam's garage in Needham looking for license plates. But Boda had successfully vanished.

Actually, during all the time the police were looking for him, he was living quietly with friends in East Boston. In August he moved on to Portsmouth, New Hampshire, where he stayed for two months, then went to Providence where—under his old name of Buda—he received a passport from the Italian vice-consul and returned to Italy. Several attempts were made later to induce him to come back to Massachusetts and testify for Sacco and Vanzetti, but each time he refused, maintaining that his life would be in danger.

When Stewart went to North Plymouth and searched Vanzetti's room at 35 Cherry Street, he discovered nothing except odds and ends of clothing. He took away a black coat, a shirt, a sweater, and a brown cloth cap. An earlier search of Sacco's bungalow in Stoughton had produced a gray cap and a rifle, along with a few books and a few anarchist pamphlets that Rosina had neglected to burn. In Joseph Ventola's garage in Hyde Park the police turned up a box that had belonged to Coacci. It contained forty dollars' worth of shoe material stolen from Slater & Morrill. Of the missing South Braintree payroll there was no trace anywhere.

Vanzetti's trial began in the second-floor courtroom of the brick-pilastered Plymouth courthouse on Tuesday, June 22, with the selection of the jury. This ran off quickly. There were no challenges by either side, even though one of the jurymen, Arthur Nickerson, a foreman at the Cordage, might well have been challenged by the defense. Vahey and Graham were opposed by District Attorney Katzmann and Assistant District Attorney Kane. Judge Webster Thayer presided.

At the opening of the trial Judge Thayer was within two weeks of being sixty-three, although the leathery texture of his face made him seem a decade older. He was about five feet two inches tall, with the edgy vanity of many short men, and a voice that easily turned petulant. On the bench he looked the part of a judge. He had a high forehead, a sudden little hawk nose bridged by pince-nez, thin gray hair and mustache, dark-circled eyes, and a narrow Yankee line of mouth. Governor Samuel McCall, a fellow graduate of Dartmouth, had appointed him to the bench in 1917.

Thayer was born in Blackstone, Massachusetts, twenty-five miles south of Worcester, the son of the local slaughterer and provisions dealer. After going through the local public schools and Worcester Academy, he entered Dartmouth with the class of 1880. Known there as Bobby, he was more noted as an athlete than a scholar. While a sophomore he organized the first college baseball nine and was its captain for three years. Once he was suspended for a half-year as the result of a rowdy prank, but he returned to graduate with his class. His undergraduate pictures show a fair-haired young man with a sprouting mustache, a quizzical expression, and eyes so deep-set that they seem almost hooded.

On graduation he briefly considered going in for big-league baseball, but instead returned to Worcester, where for two years he read law on his own. He was admitted to the bar in 1882. For the next thirty-five years he remained in that small city, rising higher in its restricted social world than might have been expected of a butcher's son. He married early and well. He became an Odd Fellow, chairman of the Worcester Athletic Association, and a member of the Dartmouth Alumni Council. Indicative of his popularity, he was elected a Democratic alderman in Republican Worcester, the youngest alderman the city ever had. Later he conformed more strictly to his social group and became a Republican. His greatest regret, for which his appointment as Superior Court Justice was only partial solace, was that he had not been young enough to join the Army in 1917.

Webster Thayer—the Anglo-Saxon coupling had a bell-like resonance in which were blended the Mayflower tradition and that of the young federal republic. Yet there was a hollowness to the ring, as the butcher's son well knew. Thayer, even as a justice of the Superior Court, was haunted by an inner sense of doubt that made him seek the approbation of other men, constantly, uncritically. In his three years on the bench he appeared a run-of-the-mill justice, causing no particular attention adversely or otherwise. The court attendants noted his irascibility, and his vanity came out in a fondness for buttonholing lawyers in the corridor to tell them about the charge he had just written. As an old-line Yankee, he had no great sympathy with foreigners, but no one had ever questioned his fairness.

Other than Vanzetti's Italian neighbors and a couple of cub reporters from the Boston papers, there were scarcely any spectators at the trial. The routine was the same each morning. Vanzetti was brought in handcuffed and taken to the prisoner's box in the center of the room, where his handcuffs were unfastened. Then Vahey and Graham conferred with him, and the set melanchoy face with the drooping mustache would take on a momentary animation. Katzmann and Kane always nodded affably to the defense lawyers as they came in. Then there was a wait of several minutes until Judge Thayer appeared, consciously delaying the daily drama of his entry, sweeping over the threshold in his black robe, inwardly satisfied that the room was standing for his presence and would remain standing until he took his seat. The crier intoned: "Hear ye, hear ye. All persons having anything to do before the Honorable Justices of the Superior Court now sitting at Plymouth within and for the County of Plymouth, draw near, give your attendance and you shall be heard. God save the Commonwealth of Massachusetts!"

With his intoning, the ritual of the court took over. The actuality of the outside world, the muted summer noises of the town entering with the sea air through the open oval-topped windows, became less real than this legal world where all action had been reduced to verbalizations. Symbolic in more than one sense was the statue of Justice in a niche of the courthouse, holding up her gilded scales and covered by a protective layer of chicken-wire.

During none of the trial sessions was there discussion of Vanzetti's political beliefs. The prosecution's case was merely an elaboration of the preliminary hearing. The district attorney relied chiefly on the primary identification witnesses—Bowles, Cox, Harding, and Mrs. Brooks—reinforcing them with corroborative evidence that would in itself have been insufficient even to indict. Bowles still maintained that Vanzetti was the man with the shotgun, but the mustache he had earlier described as close-cropped now became merely trimmed. Cox denied that he had said, on seeing Vanzetti in Brockton, "I think there is doubt." Even now, though he had become much more certain, he was not wholly sure of his identification, and the best that Katzmann could get out of him was "I am not positive but I feel certain he is the man."

All three men had been shown the car found in the Manley Woods. Harding, disregarding his first statement about a Hudson, again described the Bridgewater car as a seven-passenger Buick. The "croppy" mustache of the bandit that he "did not get much of a look at" was now "a heavy dark mustache that had been trimmed." On December 24 he had described the shotgun bandit to a Pinkerton investigator as "slim, five feet ten inches, wore a long black overcoat and a derby hat." Now he described him: "Long coat, no hat, high forehead, hair was short, dark complected man, I should say, high cheekbones, rather hard, broad face and the head, perhaps, more a round head, bullet shaped."

Mrs. Brooks repeated her story of crossing in front of the parked car and looking through the windshield at the driver. She had picked Vanzetti out of a lineup of four men in the Brockton police station as that driver. Facing him in the courtroom, she was still certain he had been the driver. After she had entered the railway station, she testified she heard shots and, looking out the window, saw the flashes from two gun barrels as the L. Q. White truck lurched down Broad Street. In cross-examining her Vahey questioned whether it was possible (as indeed it was not) to have an unimpeded view of the street from the station, and whether in fact she had seen the shooting at all. Mrs. Brooks became confused and hesitant, but Vahey did not press the point. Neither did he bring out the fact that Vanzetti did not know how to drive.

The only other witness to identify Vanzetti in court was Maynard Shaw, a schoolboy who had been delivering papers at the time of the attempt. From one hundred fifty feet away on Broad Street he had seen a dark-mustached man with a shotgun get out of a touring car on the corner and fire at the payroll truck. "He is the one I saw," the boy said, pointing at Vanzetti. He added that even at a distance he knew the man was a foreigner "by the way he ran." Vahey made much of this remark, asking Shaw whether Italians and Russians ran differently from Swedes or Norwegians and how anybody could tell the difference. Shaw had not paid much attention to the bandits' car, thinking it a Hudson or a Buick. Later, though he did not explain why, he concluded it was a Buick.

The other witnesses were routine. John King of Grove Street had been in his upstairs bedroom when he heard the car roar by. Looking out, he noted it was a seven-passenger Buick. Dr. Murphy once more told of picking up the spent shotgun shell. Simon and Ruth Johnson appeared and told their stories, and George Hassam, the Needham garage owner, told his. Officer Connolly told of arresting Vanzetti. Chief Stewart submitted a transcript of his interview with the defendant. Most of it was excluded because of its references to political beliefs.

Captain William Proctor of the State Police, testifying as a ballistics expert, claimed that the 12-gauge Winchester shell Dr. Murphy had found in the gutter and the Winchester shells found in Vanzetti's pocket were identical, except that one was empty and the others loaded. Vahey objected that the shell in the gutter might have been dropped there by any passing hunter and that there was no connection between it and the shells found on Vanzetti four months later. Judge Thayer overruled Vahey and admitted the shells as evidence for the jury to pass on.

Sacco's name was mentioned only once during the trial, when

Austin Cole, the streetcar conductor, testified that he had seen Sacco and Vanzetti on the Brockton car not only the night of their arrest but also on the fourteenth or fifteenth of April, when the two men had got on at the same Sunset Avenue stop at the same time and had got off at Brockton. On that first night, according to Cole, Sacco had paid the fares with a quarter and a nickel. "I changed the quarter," Cole continued, "and I said to him 'To Brockton?' He says 'Yes.' I said, 'It will be thirty cents.' 'I know it,' he says and he handed me a nickel and the other hand was thrust into the pocket, and he asked for two transfers. When I was talking with him he smiled and I noticed the gold tooth on Sacco."

Vahey wanted to know how the conductor could remember a particular day of no special significance among many days he could not remember at all. Cole maintained that he had worked Wednesday and Thursday, the fourteenth and fifteenth, and not again until the following Tuesday. He remembered those dates particularly because he associated them with Patriot's Day, the nineteenth.

Katzmann's efforts to link Boda with the holdup attempt were fumbling. One witness, Napoleon Ensher, who lived a quarter of a mile from Puffer's Place, said that early in the spring he had seen Boda drive past in a Buick and that Boda had waved to him. At the Dedham trial a year later Ensher's evidence was ruled out as unsubstantiated. Another witness, Richard Casey, had watched the bandit car stop near his house at the corner of Broad and Main Streets. He described the driver as a man with a short mustache and prominent nose, wearing either a velour or a black soft hat. All that Casey could remember of the man next to the driver was that he wore a brown cap. When Stewart showed him half a dozen caps, Casey picked out the one that the chief had taken from Vanzetti's room.

District Attorney Katzmann took three and a half days to present his case. On Monday, June 28, just before the noon recess, he announced that the Commonwealth rested.

The defense lawyers did not search Bridgewater for refuting witnesses. Their strategy was to rely on Vanzetti's alibi as established by his North Plymouth neighbors. Judge Thayer charged the jury that if they could conclude Vanzetti was in Plymouth on the morning of December 24, the case was ended. In addition the defense had collected several witnesses to testify that during all the years Vanzetti had lived in Plymouth he had never worn anything but his present shaggy mustache.

Awed and uneasy, the Italian witnesses marshaled by Vahey sat together in the back of the courtroom talking in whispers and waiting for their names to be called. Except for those who were American-born, they spoke through the interpreter, Govoni. First to take the stand was Vittorio Papa, the elusive Poppy Vanzetti had claimed he was trying to visit the night of his arrest. Papa merely said that he had been friendly with Vanzetti in Plymouth and that when he moved to East Bridgewater he had asked his friend to come and visit him. He had not given Vanzetti his address there.

Papa was followed by Mary Fortini, Vanzetti's landlady, who told how on that day before Christmas she had gone upstairs and called her lodger at a quarter past six. A few minutes later he had come down in his stocking feet, wearing overalls and a green sweater. She had warmed some milk for his breakfast. After drinking it, he had put on his boots and gone out.

A day or two before, a barrel of eels had come down from Boston for him by express, and she happened to be at home when it arrived. Vanzetti had spent the evening of the twenty-third in the kitchen cleaning and weighing them, wrapping them in newspapers, and ticketing them for delivery next day. After he left the house the morning of the twenty-fourth, he came back again about eight o'clock with a boy who was helping him, and the two of them had loaded the pushcart and a wheelbarrow with the packages of eels.

Carlo Balboni, a night fireman at the Cordage, said he had left the plant at six in the morning and gone directly to the Fortinis' to pick up the eels he had ordered the day before. Vanzetti was still in bed when he got there and Mrs. Fortini had gone upstairs to wake him. John DiCarlo, a shoemaker on Court Street, said that on December 24 he had opened his shop as usual at 7:15 and was just starting to sweep the place out when Vanzetti came in with a package of eels. DiCarlo could even remember that they weighed a pound and a half. Rosa Balboni of South Cherry Street said that Vanzetti had delivered the eels she had ordered in the afternoon, but she had also seen him early that morning as she was going to the baker's. Enrico Bastoni, the Cherry Street baker, told the court that Vanzetti had come to his shop the day before Christmas just before eight o'clock to see if he could rent a horse and truck for the day. But that day Bastoni needed them himself. It was a little before eight when Vanzetti arrived, for just afterward Bastoni heard the second Cordage whistle blow. Terese Malaguti, also of Cherry Street, said that she had bought eels from Vanzetti the same morning and that he had come about seven o'clock, when the first whistle blew. Adeladi Bongiovanni remembered that she had bought three pounds of eels at forty cents a pound. The boy brought them to the door and she had offered him two dollars, but as he had no change she had gone out in the street and paid Vanzetti herself. Just as the boy arrived she had been cooking polenta, and while she was out chatting with Vanzetti the polenta caught fire. Her next-door neighbors, Margherita Fiochi and Emma Borsari, told how they had also bought eels from Vanzetti that morning, as did a high school student, Esther Christophori, living in Suosso's Lane, and young Vincent Longhi of 42 Cherry Street, both of whom testified in English.

In dealing with this solid block of testimony Katzmann tried to discredit it generally. He asked the witnesses how they could recall the details of one particular day among all the other days of the year. Might not Vanzetti as easily have delivered his eels on the twenty-third as the twenty-fourth? His landlady, for example, although she said she had called him at quarter past six the day before Christmas, could not recall what time he got up the day after Christmas, or New Year's Day or Washington's Birthday or any other specific day.

The most important witness for Vanzetti was thirteen-year-old Beltrando Brini. The defense claimed he had been Vanzetti's helper on his morning round delivering the eels. Nicknamed Dolly, he was an intelligent, nervous boy, small for his age, looking rather helpless in his Norfolk knickerbocker suit and high boots. On the night of December 23, he told the court, two men had brought a half a pig to his house in Suosso's Lane. His father had ordered the pig for Christmas. That same night Vanzetti had stopped in to ask if the boy would help him deliver eels next day. Dolly promised he would. On that damp and muddy morning before Christmas he met Vanzetti first in front of Maxwell's Drugstore. Near the drugstore Dolly's father had run into him, taken one look at his boots, and told him to go home and get his rubbers. At first the boy could not find them. By the time he had located them under the stairs and hurried back to Vanzetti's house in Cherry Street it was eight o'clock, for as he trotted along he could hear the Cordage whistle blowing.

Vanzetti was putting his packages of eels in his pushcart and an extra wheelbarrow when Dolly arrived. He told the boy he had wanted to hire a horse and cart but could not find one. The two of them started out with wheelbarrow and pushcart, making their deliveries to the regular customers up and down Cherry Street, Cherry Place, Cherry Court, and finally down to Court Street. Dolly had worked from eight in the morning until two in the afternoon, when Vanzetti paid him off.

On Christmas Eve, Vanzetti dropped in at the Brinis'. When he left he noticed the children's stockings hanging by the mantel and put two half-dollars in each one. On Christmas Day Vanzetti stopped in again, and Dolly thanked him for the half-dollars and showed him his Christmas presents.

Katzmann began his cross-examination with deceptive gentleness, calling the boy "son" and asking if he would like to testify sitting down. As he continued, his voice hardened and he began to box the boy in with questions. How many times had he told his story? How many times had he gone over it with his parents? With Mr. Vahey? Had he learned it just like a piece at school? Who corrected him when he left something out? The district attorney stalked him through all the details of the morning: the houses where the boy had left packages, the weight of the basket he carried, the time he started and the time he finished his deliveries. Had he finished at one-fifteen, or was it one-twenty? The boy squirmed and looked pleadingly at Judge Thayer, but there was no relief coming from that stiff-robed parchment-faced figure. Young Brini had to admit that he had repeated his story a number of times to his parents and others, and that when he repeated it and omitted anything his father would correct him.

Beltrando's parents, Vincenzo and Alfonsina, both testified. Vincenzo told of meeting his boy in the lane on the morning of December 24 and sending him back for his rubbers. He also mentioned the side of pig that had arrived the night before, when Vanzetti dropped in for a visit. Vanzetti's mustache was untrimmed then, just the same that night as it was now. Alfonsina corroborated her husband. In a lengthy cross-examination Katzmann tried to force her into admitting that she had coached her son in his story, but the most she would say was that she had listened to him tell it a number of times.

John Vernazano, the Court Street barber who had shaved Vanzetti and cut his hair for the last five or six years, now took the stand to say that he had never trimmed Vanzetti's mustache, that it had always been just as it was today. He received unexpected confirmation from two non-Italian members of the Plymouth police force. Officer John Gault said that he knew Vanzetti and had seen him three or four times a week for several years. Gault had never noticed any change or alteration in the Italian's mustache, but under Katzmann's cross-examination he admitted that he had not paid any particular attention to it. Officer Joseph Schilling had seen Vanzetti off and on several times a week in the months before his arrest, and his mustache had always looked the same. It might not have been the same, Schilling admitted, but he had never noticed any difference.

Cross-examining Vernazano, Katzmann asked him if he knew William Douglass, the proprietor of the Samoset House, and if the man had a mustache. The barber said he knew Douglass by sight and that he had a small light mustache. Katzmann then produced the clean-shaven Douglass on the stand to say that he had never had a mustache.

On this inconclusive note the defense ended its case on Monday morning, July 1. Judge Thayer, in a short, conventional charge to the jury, instructed them that no inference should be drawn against the defense witnesses because they were Italians. However, in spite of the judge's words, the Italians' embarrassment as they spoke through their interpreter undoubtedly made the Anglo-Saxon jury feel that—in Vanzetti's later words—"all the wops stick together." If the headmaster of the Plymouth High School or the wife of the local Congregational minister had testified to buying fish from Vanzetti on the morning of December 24, that would have been as good as a directed verdict. But these swarthy aliens were suspect.

The jury retired at 10:15. Henry Burgess, the foreman, was curious about what was inside the shotgun shells and just before lunch he opened two of them. They were loaded, not with birdshot, but buckshot. Simon Sullivan and several of the other jurors took a few of the pellets as souvenirs.

After the lunch recess the jury resumed deliberation. At 4:18 it brought in its verdict, finding Vanzetti guilty of assault with intent to rob and guilty on three counts of assault with intent to murder. As the foreman pronounced the word "guilty," a protesting wail broke out from the thickset peasant women in the back of the courtroom. Vanzetti remained calm. "*Coraggio!*" he called out to them as he was led away.

The echo of Vanzetti's voice subsided into the dusty calm of legal decorum. Vanzetti's friends moved toward the exits, looking back now and then at the men filing out of the jury box. Judge Thayer, after Vahey and Graham had stepped forward to consult with him, extended the time for filing exceptions to August 18 and set bail at twenty-five thousand dollars.

Several days later Juror Sullivan happened to run into Judge Thayer in a Brockton store and mention that he and a couple of others had taken away some of the buckshot. Judge Thayer ordered him to see that all of it was at once returned to the district attorney. The chastened Sullivan brought the pellets back, and Katzmann warned him not to say anything more about the matter.

On August 16 Vahey filed a bill of exceptions in which he requested that the shotgun-shell evidence and the testimony of Simon and Ruth Johnson be excluded. The exceptions were not allowed, and Vahey did not carry the matter further. On that same morning, in the almost-deserted courtroom, Vanzetti appeared for sentencing. He stood in the dock, an alien, slightly bent figure, flanked by his guards, with high forehead and high cheekbones and flowing mustache. The heat of the day had not yet set in, and the oval windows were open. If the prisoner had glanced to his left he could have looked down Brewster Street to the blue line of Plymouth Harbor. Instead, he stared ahead at Judge Thayer sitting on the dais beneath the Plymouth seal, and the judge stared back from the mask of his withered face.

Then Judge Thayer began to pronounce sentence in his precise dessicated voice, the phrases falling like a curtain: "The Court having considered the offense whereof the said Bartolomeo Vanzetti is convict does order and adjudge that the said Bartolomeo Vanzetti suffer imprisonment for a term of not less than twelve years nor more than fifteen years, one day thereof solitary imprisonment and the residue of said term confinement to hard labor, in and within the limits of our State Prison situate in Boston in our County of Suffolk."

◇◇◇◇◇◇◇◇◇◇◇◇◇◇◇◇◇◇◇◇◇◇◇◇◇◇◇◇◇◇

CHAPTER EIGHT

The Year Between

A few days after the arrest of Sacco and Vanzetti their typesetter friend Aldino Felicani organized a defense committee among the East Boston anarchists. The seventeen members were skilled workers —one was a building contractor—but they were men detached from American life, distrustful of outsiders. The freeing of their comrades from the ominous charge hanging over them was, they felt, their affair. Their first pamphlet, published in Italian, appealed to "Men of Good Will."

Two of our active good friends and comrades . . . have become involved in one of those tragic, dark legal plots in which innocence has all the semblance of guilt, and honesty has the hypocritical mask put on by the subtlest of rogues. . . . In a country where subversive ideas are persecuted with Inquisitorial fury, anarchists are beyond the pale. . . . We are convinced that an attempt is being made, through the persons of Sacco and Vanzetti, to strike at all subversive elements and their libertarian ideas. A sentence . . . would serve, in the hands of our enemies, to show that lovers of liberty are common criminals and that their ideas are not entitled to any of the civil freedoms. . . . We face a severe, a terrible test.

Energetically the committee raised a defense fund from the nickels and dimes and quarters of their countrymen in the crowded streets of the North End and East Boston. It was the committee that hired Graham as counsel, counting on his American skill to mediate between the two Italians and the complexities of Massachusetts justice. For the committee, the result of the Plymouth trial was a disaster.

In New York, Carlo Tresca and his fellow anarchists were appalled by the verdict. Tresca sent Elizabeth Gurley Flynn, with whom he had been living since he met her in a 1912 May Day parade, to talk matters over with Felicani. "Gurley," the founder and secretary of the Workers' Defense Union, was bound for Boston in any case, to see what could be done for the aliens imprisoned on Deer Island as a result of the Palmer raids. With Mrs. Marion Emerson, secretary of a workers' defense organization in Boston, she made her way through the twisting streets of the North End to the offices of La Notizia, and there, under the shadow of the Old North Church spire, they talked with the tall, indignant Felicani, who at that time could speak only through an interpreter. So it was that Gurley and Mrs. Emerson on a July afternoon in 1920 were the first non-Italian sympathizers to hear the story of Sacco and Vanzetti. Later Felicani took them to see the other now thoroughly worried members of the committee, who asked them to try to arrange English-speaking protest meetings and to help find a lawyer who would understand the defendants' radical viewpoint.

Returning to New York, Gurley hired the Forward Hall on East Broadway for a Sacco-Vanzetti protest meeting. She, the president of the Free Speech League, and the veteran anarchist Harry Kelly, were the speakers. So few people showed up that the caretaker of the hall insisted on immediate payment. "You'll never get it in a collection," he explained. Shortly afterward Mrs. Emerson organized a similarly uneventful meeting in the rickety Grand Opera House in Boston's South End.

It was through Tresca and Elizabeth Gurley Flynn, both of whom had known him and worked with him over the years, that Fred Moore now entered the case. It was a fateful entry. At this point, while Sacco and Vanzetti were still inconspicuous foreigners whose names meant nothing, a capable conservative lawyer like their later counsel William Thompson might have secured their acquittal. Moore, the radical labor lawyer, was to make them internationally famous, to link their names indissolubly, but he may well have signed their death warrants in the process.

Tresca had met Moore eight years earlier during the Lawrence Textile Strike of 1912 and the murder trial that was its by-product.

Lawrence, Massachusetts, an industrial city of unrelieved drabness on the banks of the Merrimack, was in 1912 a polyglot company town owned by the Lawrences and the Lowells, and worked by Italians, Germans, French-Canadians, Poles, Lithuanians, Belgians, and Syrians, with a scattering of Russians, Jews, and Greeks. When the Massachusetts legislature in its 1911 autumn session reduced the work week from fifty-six to fifty-four hours, the Lawrence textile mills countered by reducing wages correspondingly. Weekly pay then averaged $8.76 a week for adults, $5 or less for the many child workers.

The calculated meanness of the reduction, amounting only to about twenty-five cents, so infuriated the workers that on January 12, 1912, they spontaneously downed tools, in some cases smashing the looms. There followed a bitter struggle that brought twenty-three thousand workers onto the streets. After a number of riots between strikers and police, Governor Eugene Foss called out the militia.

The strike was taken over and managed by the I.W.W. with anarchist assistance. From New York came Joe Ettor of the I.W.W. executive board, and Arturo Giovannitti. Ettor was an organizer, Giovannitti a persuasive speaker who kept up the strikers' courage through the bitter winter. In finally winning the strike the I.W.W. reached the peak of its influence in the East.

One afternoon while police and militia were charging a picket line, a girl worker, Annie Lopizza, was shot dead. No one knew who fired the shot, but the police at once arrested "the troublemakers" Ettor and Giovannitti as accessories to murder. They were held without bail until the end of the strike.

With the leaders in jail the I.W.W.'s Big Bill Haywood, the one-eyed giant who was already almost a legend, came to Lawrence and took command. With him he brought Elizabeth Gurley Flynn. By the time of the Sacco-Vanzetti trial she had become enormously fat, but in 1912 she was a slim young firebrand with flashing blue eyes and a lacerating tongue. Theodore Dreiser had called her the East Side Joan of Arc. An Ettor-Giovannitti Defense Committee was at once formed, and Haywood had Fred Moore brought on from California. The strategy of the committee was to have the indefatigable and ingenious Moore help in selecting the witnesses and collecting evidence but to have the case tried by a well-known local conservative. James Sisk, a staid Lynn lawyer, was chosen to represent Ettor and Giovannitti in court.

The results of this strategy were highly successful. In spite of the pressure of moneyed opinion against them, Ettor and Giovannitti, appearing before the Irish-Catholic Judge Joseph Quinn and a native-American jury, were acquitted.

It was this pattern that Tresca had in mind when he sent Moore to Boston in the fall of 1920. Moore was again to be the assiduous and inspired fact-gatherer. He would again prepare the brief and then some irreproachable Massachusetts lawyer would try the case. Such, too, was the intention of the Sacco-Vanzetti Defense Committee when it accepted Moore. It was not Moore's intention at all.

Moore, then in his late thirties, was the barrister bohemian in looks, dress, and manner. His long hair seemed to flow back from his forehead, he often wore sandals, and the broad-brimmed Western hat he brought with him from California became almost his trademark in Boston. He had started out as a railroad attorney in Seattle, then moved on to Los Angeles where for a time he seemed a brilliant young corporation lawyer on the way up. But money and an established bourgeois existence meant nothing to him. When a casual I.W.W. acquaintance arrested in a free-speech fight in San Diego telephoned him for help, Moore picked up his broad-brimmed hat and a revolver, told his associates he would be back shortly, and walked out of the promise of his law career. After that he went wherever his underdog interests took him. He became a labor defense expert, particularly devoted to serving the I.W.W., drifting from one labor fight to another, taking on the hopeless, desperate cases that could not afford better-known lawyers.

When he ran into Tresca in New York in the summer of 1920, he had just come from Tulsa, Oklahoma, where he had defended "Big Boy" Krieger, an I.W.W. organizer charged with dynamiting the house of a Standard Oil official. The charge was a frame-up, a fact cheerfully accepted by the townspeople, the prosecution, the defense, the judge, and the jury. Fortunately for Moore, one of the jurymen with a personal grudge against Standard Oil held out for acquittal. In a second trial the fraud was too apparent and Krieger was freed.

As Moore headed for Boston he was certain it would be a similar story with Sacco and Vanzetti, and the more he reflected on the ramifications of the South Braintree crime the more convinced he became that this backwater New England affair could be his big case, the culmination of his career.

Eugene Lyons, the young left-wing labor journalist who had been with Moore in Oklahoma and who later followed him to Massachusetts to work for the Defense Committee, was awed by the lawyer's dexterity. Moore, he wrote long afterward,

was at heart an artist. Instinctively he recognized the materials of a world issue in what appeared to others a routine matter. A socialist newspaper-man spent a few days in Boston and returned to New York to report that "there's no story in it . . . just a couple of wops in a jam." Not one of the members of the defense committee formed immediately after the men's arrest suspected that the affair was anything larger than it seemed. When the case grew into a historical tussle, these men were utterly bewildered. But Moore saw its magnitude from the first. His legal tactics have been the subject of dispute and recrimination. I think that there is some color of truth, indeed, to the charge that he sometimes subordinated the literal needs of legalistic procedure to the larger needs of the case as a symbol of the class struggle. If he had not done so, Sacco and Vanzetti would have died six years earlier, without the solace of martyrdom.

With the deliberation of a composer evolving the details of a symphony which he senses in its rounded entirety, Moore proceeded to clarify and deepen the elements implicit in the case.

Arriving in Boston, Moore installed himself at 5 Rollins Place, a small four-story brick house in a cul-de-sac of Beacon Hill in that no-man's land where proper Boston tapers off into the improper. The house, masked by a wooden porch with Greek-revival columns, and the brick-paved roadway, too narrow for any vehicle, seemed to suggest that whoever might live there would be gone tomorrow, a feeling that harmonized with Moore's personality. Shortly after moving in, Moore married Lola Darroch, the handsome young woman who had been with him during the Krieger trial. Their marriage lasted officially a little over a year, though unofficially it was concluded much sooner when Lola was supplanted by a Lithuanian stenographer. In the environment this seemed rational enough. Wherever Moore went in his travels he pursued his weakness, which he considered a need, for pretty young women.

Five Rollins Place was a catchall: a home for Moore and his assorted associates, an informal office, a dormitory for out-of-town enthusiasts, Italian and otherwise, a lodging house for prospective witnesses and intellectuals and freshly minted college girls heavy with purpose. There were nights of talk and more talk, of makeshift Prohibition drinking, of song and vacillating affections. Eugene Lyons, an almost daily visitor, later wrote that:

Commonplace stenographers accidentally drawn into this tense atmosphere developed into flaming radicals. Roughneck detectives sprouted a social conscience. Cautious A.F. of L. officials hobnobbed with foreign firebrands. A milk-white, golden-haired little poetess swept like a tornado through the defense group, working havoc among the harassed men and spreading despair among their wives and sweethearts; she dominated the lives of a writer, a strike leader, a lawyer and a Boston newspaperman in quick succession, with forays into the domestic preserves of half a dozen others, while composing soulful verses in defense of the accused Italians. A gawky, half-savage boy lured from the Maine woods to plead with his mother, a crucial identification witness, to retract her perjured testimony, had to be forced, literally, to take a bath; soon he blossomed into a spic-and-span U.S. Marine. One of the closest comrades and most ardent defenders of Sacco fell hopelessly in love with Sacco's wife (he married her after Sacco's execution). Within the larger drama of the case, there developed complicated cycles of lesser dramas of private emotion.

Before going to Boston, Lyons had gone to Italy in pursuit of revolutions. Moore wrote him there, persuading him to create propaganda for the case and to interview potential witnesses. In that convulsive period of red-flagged cities and rising Fascism the arrest of two Italians in a New England mill town was a small enough pebble on an eroding beach, but Lyons—through Sacco's brother Sabino, now the mayor of Torremaggiore—managed to get Leon Mucci to bring the Sacco-Vanzetti affair to the floor of the Italian Chamber of Deputies for its initial foreign mention.*

Coacci, Lyons found in a sleepy village in the Marchesan hills, posing grandly as an international revolutionary:

His shelves were lined with brochures on the home manufacture of bombs and he professed himself a terrorist of the Galleani school. So deep, however, had the fear of American law and the police entered his heart that it needed a week of pleading and threatening and pressure by Merlino, the grand old man of the anarcho-syndicalist movement, to bring this terrorist to the point of signing an innocuous affidavit in support of Sacco's alibi.

Sacco and Vanzetti were to typify a cause, Moore explained to a friend, adding, "In saving them we strengthen our muscles, develop our forces preparatory to the day when we save ourselves." The more extreme anarchists of the Defense Committee were critical of such

---

* Like Sacco a native of Torremaggiore, Mucci had spent some time in America and had been one of the defending counsel in the Ettor-Giovannitti trial at Lawrence.

an attitude, feeling that Moore was more interested in building up the biggest labor case in history than in the fate of the men involved. This, too, was Rosina Sacco's feeling from the first time she met Moore. Not interested in issues, she merely wanted her Nick back to resume their old family life, to see the new baby Ines, born four months after his arrest. Instinctively she distrusted the sparkle of the bohemian lawyer.

Moore's initial objective was to expand the case beyond the parochial limits of Norfolk County. With this in mind he worked up a number of sensational appeals, following the pattern customary both in American criminal cases and in charity drives. He wrote, he telegraphed, he traveled, he sent out assistants, volunteers, anyone whom he could persuade to lend a hand. His salary ($150 a week) never seemed to cover his expenses. He was lawyer, detective, fund-raiser, and propagandist combined. At their annual conventions the Amalgamated Clothing Workers and the American Federation of Teamsters found themselves demanding the release of Sacco and Vanzetti, although few of the delegates had ever heard their names before some official friendly to Moore introduced the resolution. If Moore sent word that there was a frame-up in the offing, his word was enough for the central labor unions in Boston, Chicago, Detroit, Worcester, Seattle, and Salem, just as it was for the United Mine Workers, the Minnesota State Federation of Labor, and dozens of other organizations Moore had known or assisted. Although their resolutions may have been quickly presented and quickly put aside, their effect was to be cumulative.

By the end of 1920 there were stirrings across the country, and echoes from overseas. To anyone with as sensitive an ear as Moore's they were a promise of what was to come.

Moore's temporary office in the Olympian Building at 3 Tremont Row, echoing with talk and typewriters and shuffling feet, was like a bus terminal in its comings and goings. In one corner the blond Lithuanian stenographer hammered away at the keys. Opposite her John Nicholas Beffel, a free-lance socialist journalist from New York, sat chain-smoking and preparing press releases in English. Art Shields, sent on by Elizabeth Gurley Flynn, assisted him. Frank Lopez, a young Spanish anarchist, a cabinetmaker by trade, preserved somehow by Moore from a deportation order, got out propaganda for the Spanish-speaking world. Felicani and the committee, from an upstairs room on Battery Street, took care of the Italian publicity.

Only gradually did Moore bridge the gap between the Italian anarchists and the indigenous Boston liberals. When he approached John Codman of the New England Civil Liberties Committee, Codman asked for satisfactory proof that Sacco and Vanzetti would not be given an impartial trial. He had served recently on a jury in Dedham and said he had been impressed by District Attorney Katzmann's ability and fairness. Moore eventually managed to convince Codman to the extent that in February 1921 the Civil Liberties Committee contributed five hundred dollars to the Defense Committee. Later in the year it published its own pamphlet: "Sacco and Vanzetti: Shall There be a Mooney Frame-up in New England?"

Through the Civil Liberties Committee link a number of elderly Boston women of assured position and belligerent good works began their participation in the case. In the social-worker tradition of Elizabeth Peabody, with the inherited wealth to be cultured as Boston understood the word, they functioned as nonconformists within the Back Bay circle of conformity. The most conspicuous and determined of these was Elizabeth Glendower Evans, a pacifist and campaigner for women's suffrage. Level-headed and charming, she avoided the crackpot label so easily attached to middle-aged female reformers. Hundreds of prisoners in Massachusetts jails were indebted to her often-anonymous kindness. Dozens owed their freedom to her. She had married a promising young lawyer, a friend and classmate of Louis Brandeis at the Harvard Law School, who died a few years after graduating. During the whole period of the Sacco-Vanzetti case she lived in the Brandeis household, where the children called her Auntie Bee. When Eugene Lyons and his young wife first came to Boston, Mrs. Evans furnished their apartment for them simply by opening the cellar where Justice Brandeis had stored some of his furniture. She seemed to know everyone, not only in Boston but throughout the country, and she had the key to people as well as buildings. When she was drawn into the Sacco-Vanzetti case, she saw it as just one more worthy cause, but as the months passed she developed a preoccupying attachment for the two men that would last through the years to their execution.

Moore soon brought the case to the attention of the American Civil Liberties Union in New York, and the organization did much to interest native Americans in the predicament of the two Italians. The minutes of its meeting on November 22, 1920, read:

Mary Heaton Vorse reported on the cases of Sacco and Vanzetti, two young Italian anarchists on trial in Boston for highway robbery and murder, stating that they had been indicted on questionable circumstances and because of their activity on behalf of Andrea Salsedo, a political prisoner who committed suicide by throwing himself from the Park Row Building, New York, while being held for deportation. It was agreed that the Union should do everything possible to secure publicity for this case.

Mary Heaton Vorse was a writer with one foot in Greenwich Village and the other in the radical labor movement, the prototype of a number of women who would eventually become concerned in the Sacco-Vanzetti case. Brought up in the cultivated restriction of Emily Dickinson's Amherst, educated abroad, her experiences in the 1912 Lawrence strike turned her sympathies and her writings to the workers and the dispossessed. One can trace her career by the titles of her many books, from *The Breaking in of a Yachtsman's Wife* to *Strike —A Novel of Gastonia*.

After Tresca told her of Sacco and Vanzetti, calling their case a frame-up as bad as the Mooney case, Mrs. Vorse went to Dedham to visit Sacco. In the outline of the case she wrote for Norman Thomas' magazine, *The World Tomorrow*, she described Sacco in his gray prison trousers and striped blue cotton shirt as

a little fellow so life-loving that even six months of inaction in jail had not effaced his vividness. Short, clean-cut as a Roman coin, eyes that looked at you straight, and above all a friendly way with him almost like that of a child who had never known anything but affection. There was something about Sacco that made you think of swift happy things—a jumping fish, a bird on the wing.

She concluded with a paraphrase of Moore:

Active labor men have all the dice loaded against them. All labor is on trial with Nichola Sacco and Bartolomeo Vanzetti. It is bound up with all the fight that is going on for the closed shop and the determinations of the employers to smash the worker's organizations.

The *New Republic* in its December 29 issue carried John Beffel's article, "Eels and the Electric Chair." This account of the Plymouth trial asked for a reversal of Vanzetti's conviction lest there be "another conviction which will send him through a little green door into a wired chamber of death."

Thus, by the New Year, with the trial scheduled to begin in Dedham on March 7, 1921, one of the left-liberal magazines most widely circulated among the intelligentsia of the United States had made the names of Sacco and Vanzetti at least fleetingly familiar to its readers. Moore's case was beginning to gather momentum. Art Shields' pamphlet "Are They Doomed? The Sacco-Vanzetti Case and the Grim Forces Behind It" (actually, Beffel wrote most of it) appeared early in the year as the first general statement of the defense position. Elizabeth Gurley Flynn's Workers' Defense Union distributed fifty thousand copies before the trial. The cover had a sensational drawing by Robert Minor showing Salsedo hurtling from a skyscraper window. Shields described the Brockton arrest as a frame-up from beginning to end, the murder charge against the two men "a mere device to get them out of the way," and stated that they were practically the last of the Italian radicals in New England who had not already been jailed or deported.*

The New York office of the Workers' Defense Union sent out weekly Sacco-Vanzetti releases, most of them written by Beffel, to more than five hundred papers. Gurley Flynn went on a speaking tour, explaining the case to college liberal clubs, including those at Pennsylvania and Harvard, as well as to the captive audience of Mrs. Evans' League for Democratic Control.

After his sentencing at Plymouth, Vanzetti was taken to the Charlestown State Prison, across the river from Boston. That granite fortress, built in 1820, was surrounded by a disintegrating brick slum fouled with the smoke of the Everett chemical plants.

On his arrival Vanzetti went through the usual routine. He was questioned in the interview cell, then given a shower and issued prison clothes, a blanket roll, an enamel slop bucket and a smaller wooden bucket for drinking water, and locked in his cell. Within a few days he was assigned to the shop making auto-license plates, one of the few production tasks allowed convict labor.

The machinery of the law continued to function with bureaucratic regularity. Sacco and Vanzetti were indicted on September 11, 1920, charged with the murder of Alessandro Berardelli and Frederick A.

---

* Shields would end up a Communist. Minor, already one, visualized even that early the propaganda possibilities in Sacco and Vanzetti. He became a cartoonist for the *Daily Worker* and later its editor. By the time of the Bridgewater crime he had written a savage attack on anarchism in which he defended the recent suppression of the Russian anarchists by the Bolsheviks.

Parmenter. Five days afterward a bomb explosion seared New York's Wall Street, killing thirty persons. The crime, never solved, was generally believed to be the work of anarchists. On September 28 Sacco and Vanzetti were arraigned. They pleaded not guilty.

Sacco, as a prisoner still awaiting trial, remained in the Dedham county jail where he had been taken after his preliminary hearing. Unlike the overcrowded Charlestown fortress, the Dedham jail, located on a rural side street, was a relatively pleasant place with fewer than seventy prisoners, most of whom the warden knew by their first name. It was like a well-kept ship, the walls and floors bright with paint, brass shining. The reception room, with its oak benches and bookcases, gave the fugitive impression of a library. There, prisoners could visit with friends and relatives without a guard being present.

What was hardest for Sacco to endure was the idleness. From the time the sun rose until it set, there was a gap of hours marked only by meals and the swing of the shadow from east to west across the recreation-room floor. Except for the few trusties who stoked the boilers or worked in the tailor shop or the laundry or did the cooking, there was no way to kill time except by talking or playing cards.

Inactivity and restraint chafed Sacco's spirit. He missed his wife and son; the baby he had never seen he could not get out of his mind. To this man of abundant energy, for whom the day had never been long enough, the tedium of empty hours became a frenzy of frustration. Yet in this early period he never seemed to doubt that he would be eventually set free.

Sacco and Vanzetti saw each other seldom during the seven years of their imprisonment. Except for the six weeks of the trial and the final period in the death house, they would meet only briefly when some new motion or empty formality brought them into court. Sometimes they would not meet for a year.

Although the interest aroused by the case was still spotty, there was more awareness of the coming trial outside Massachusetts than there was within the state. In Norfolk County it was more or less taken for granted that the suspects were guilty. The Braintree *Observer* of May 8, 1920, had announced that the two South Braintree "yeggs" had been positively identified. It said nothing more about the case till the trial began.

By the time the Thayer Academy boys in their black-and-orange jerseys were holding their autumn football practice behind the Braintree town hall the April robbery was no longer a matter of general conversation. However, Shelley Neal still thought of it each time the payroll came in, delivered now by armed guards, and the girls in the Slater & Morrill offices still liked to gossip about it during the lunch hour.

Two days after the Plymouth trial ended, Katzmann appointed Chief Stewart his official investigator. Stewart's friend Alfred Brouillard, on leave from the State Police, was made his assistant.

Proud of his new status and glad to resign his Bridgewater job, Stewart did most of his sleuthing under the direction of the Assistant District Attorney, Harold Williams. From Katzmann the chief received the four shotgun-shell exhibits of the Plymouth trial. Now, the district attorney told him, it was up to him to dig up the right kind of witnesses. Stewart had little to go on at first. As a starter he went to the Boston Public Library and read the accounts of the South Braintree crime in the back numbers of all the Boston papers, copying down the names of persons mentioned. He and Brouillard were on their own. Chief Gallivan was no help at all. Stewart usually found him sitting on the Braintree town-hall steps with a quid in his cheek.

Not until the new year was the approaching trial mentioned again in the Boston papers. Then a Dedham court interpreter, Angelina DeFalco, spread it briefly across the front pages after Moore had her arrested.

The affair had its origins just before the New Year, when Felicani received a telephone call from Beniamino Cicchetti of Providence, Rhode Island, who introduced himself as a "compatriot of ideas" and said that he had an important letter concerning Sacco and Vanzetti. He agreed to meet Felicani at the Defense Committee headquarters on Sunday morning, January 2.

Like Govoni in Plymouth, Cicchetti was a fixer who followed his special line in the Italian Federal Hill section of Providence, arranging bail and, on a percentage basis, collecting defense funds. For Italians who had run afoul of the law he was useful, almost necessary, to know. An oily, persuasive man, he bustled into the Battery Street office and assured Felicani he knew a woman who could do a great deal for Sacco and Vanzetti. When Felicani showed interest, he bustled out again and returned almost at once with a dumpy near-sighted woman in her early twenties whom he introduced as Mrs. DeFalco.

She explained that she had come from the Dedham court, and that if the Defense Committee would put up a sufficient sum she could guarantee Sacco's freedom. Felicani asked her how it could be done.

"Oh," she told him, "we have a little society of our own, Fred Katz-mann, Mr. Squires, and Percy Katzmann." * When Felicani asked about Vanzetti she said that was something else again, and that she would have to consult Fred. She then tried unsuccessfully to reach the district attorney by telephone. Felicani did not say much. He told her he would have to consult with the rest of the Defense Committee, and she agreed to meet him next day, suggesting at the same time that he bring along five hundred dollars as a deposit.

They met the following morning with Professor Guadagni in a coffee house in North Square. Mrs. DeFalco told them that fifty thousand dollars would be needed to take care of everything. First of all, she said, the committee must appoint Squires and Percy Katz-mann counsel for Sacco and Vanzetti. Money spent on other lawyers would be wasted. When they had paid the fifty thousand dollars, Percy would take charge of the defense. Fred would not prosecute, but the case would be given to Harold Williams or one of the other assistant district attorneys. Guadagni said the committee could not collect so much money quickly, and suggested that Mrs. DeFalco take ten thousand dollars and get the case postponed until September. She said she would see what she could do, and Felicani and Guadagni agreed to meet with her again.

During the week various members of the committee met almost daily with Mrs. DeFalco, though as yet she was paid no money. She made an appointment with Felicani and Guadagni for Friday at the defense headquarters. Following Moore's advice, Felicani concealed a microphone in the room so that a public stenographer in the base-ment could take down the conversation in shorthand.

Mrs. DeFalco said she had come to complete arrangements with them, that Fred Katzmann and Squires had assured her of the free-dom of the two men, but that by Monday the committee must pay fifteen thousand dollars. The money was to be paid to Squires or Percy Katzmann and all the committee's evidence was to be turned over to the latter. After the payment there would be a mock trial with the jury made up so that the foreman would be a member of the county ring. She told them it was a simple matter to fix a jury.

When Guadagni objected that fifteen thousand was still too much, Mrs. DeFalco telephoned the Dedham courthouse and after talking

---

* Francis J. Squires was clerk of the district court in Dedham; Percy, a lawyer, was Fred Katzmann's brother.

briefly with someone not identified, told them that five thousand would be enough for a start; they would also reduce the remainder to thirty-five thousand, which had to be paid as soon as the trial was postponed. She said she had arranged to have the lawyers meet the committee members at her house that evening. Felicani and Guadagni agreed to drive out.

They left Boston about eight o'clock. When they reached the back street in East Dedham where the DeFalcos lived, they hesitated. The small square house was brightly lit and two cars were parked in front of it. Felicani and Guadagni decided not to go in. Before leaving, they copied down the license numbers of the cars. One turned out to be Squires', the other Fred Katzmann's.

The members of the committee were inclined to pay the money. Not so Moore. Suspecting that the defense might be charged with trying to bribe public officials, he—over Felicani's protest—had Cicchetti and Mrs. DeFalco arrested. Cicchetti was released but Mrs. DeFalco was held on the technical charge of attempting to solicit law business, not being an attorney. As no money had changed hands this was all she could be charged with.

On the stand in the Boston municipal court she gave a rambling account of how Cicchetti, a brother-in-law of her brother, had asked her if she could help him see his friend Sacco. He had also asked if she and her brother would go to Boston with him to see Felicani about getting a Norfolk County lawyer to defend Sacco and Vanzetti. She admitted that she had had talks with members of the Defense Committee. One morning she had met Guadagni, who introduced himself as Mr. Giovannetti of New York. He had told her the committee had a lawyer, Moore, whom they were paying three hundred dollars a week although he was not doing much. When Felicani had asked her what lawyer she would recommend she had named Squires, whom she knew because her husband was his gardener. She had arranged a meeting for them with Squires at her home, but Felicani and Guadagni had never showed up.

District Attorney Katzmann then took the stand to deny that he knew Mrs. DeFalco. He had never even heard of her until her arrest. Percy Katzmann said he had known her for about seven years and had employed her as an interpreter in his Italian cases. Mrs. DeFalco had asked him several times if he would take on the Sacco-Vanzetti case, and though he first told her he would not, out of friendship for her he had agreed to meet Felicani and Guadagni at her house.

Inspector Flaherty, who had arrested Mrs. DeFalco, testified she had said then she would "fix those anarchists." She was found not guilty. Judge Murray called her conduct "imprudent, unwise, but not criminal." *

Whatever Mrs. DeFalco had been up to, the episode and the standing of the men involved gave the Greater Boston community its first inkling of the enlarged dimensions of the Sacco-Vanzetti case. Moore's propaganda efforts were getting not only action but reaction.

Even before Sacco and Vanzetti were arrested, their names were in the files of the Department of Justice. After the Plymouth trial the Boston office began to take a more active interest in them. Agents were assigned to attend the various Sacco-Vanzetti defense meetings. One of them, Harold Zorian, even managed to become a collector for the Defense Committee, although, as he admitted afterward, he kept most of the money for himself.

William J. West, the agent in charge of the Boston office's Radical Division, furnished memoranda regularly to District Attorney Katzmann about Sacco and Vanzetti's anarchist activities. As Fred Weyand, one of the Department's Boston agents explained it:

The understanding in this case between the agents of the Department of Justice in Boston and the District Attorney followed the usual custom, that the Department of Justice would help the District Attorney to secure a conviction, and that he in turn would help the agents of the Department of Justice to secure information that they might desire.

Weyand, West, and other agents attended the Dedham trial in the expectation of finding sufficient evidence against Sacco and Vanzetti to deport them as anarchists in case they were acquitted of murder.

In the autumn of 1920, either West or Katzmann conceived the idea of planting an informer in the cell next to Sacco. West hoped to find out something about the Wall Street bomb explosion of September 16. Although all the clues in that bombing had come to nothing, the Justice Department held to its theory that the explosion was the work of anarchists. West and Katzmann talked the matter

---

* Four years after the execution of Sacco and Vanzetti, Angelina DeFalco appeared in the Suffolk Superior Court in Boston, accused of the theft of fifteen hundred fifty dollars from Mrs. Giovanino Voce on the promise of bringing about the release of the latter's brother, then serving a ten-year sentence in state prison. Found guilty of grand larceny, Mrs. DeFalco received a six-month jail sentence. She was still living in Dedham in 1961. When I telephoned her and mentioned the Sacco-Vanzetti case, she hung up. A few weeks before Francis Squires died in 1960, I found him unwilling to discuss the DeFalco incident.

over with Feri Felix Weiss, formerly one of West's agents. Weiss operated his own "Scientific-Secret-Service," but still did occasional work for the Department's Bureau of Investigation. He sent a letter to an informer, John Ruzzamenti, in Reddington, Pennsylvania, asking if he would be willing to help in getting evidence against two probable criminals. He might have to stay in jail for a few days, but success in this job might lead to bigger investigations, like the Wall Street explosion, with juicier expense accounts. The eager Ruzzamenti arrived on Weiss's doorstep two days after Christmas.

Katzmann, on meeting Ruzzamenti in his courthouse office, appeared bluffly cordial, helping him off with his overcoat and calling him John. He then explained his plan. Ruzzamenti would be arrested with burglar tools in the act of breaking into a house. The sheriff would see that he was placed in the cell adjoining Sacco's. Ruzzamenti would act depressed for the first few days and say nothing, then try to strike up a conversation.

Ruzzamenti objected to being tagged with a police record and when Katzmann could not change his mind, he suggested that Ruzzamenti go to Stoughton and see what he could ferret out there. They would arrange that he got some sort of job in the town, perhaps in a shoe factory. As an Italian he might even manage to rent a room from Rosina Sacco. Katzmann said he had reports that she was in an upset state. It should be easy to establish friendly relations with her.

To this proposal Ruzzamenti agreed. Whether or not Katzmann was serious about it or was just thinking aloud, he soon afterward dropped the idea as well as any connection with Ruzzamenti. He and West and Weiss managed to place a more amenable informer near Sacco. The man, Antony Carbone, spent several days in the jail and managed to talk with Sacco at intervals but could find out nothing.

The guilt or innocence of Sacco and Vanzetti in regard to the South Braintree murders was of no direct concern to the Department of Justice. Most of the Boston agents who knew anything about the case felt that Sacco and Vanzetti were not guilty. This was the opinion of Fred Weyand, who later deposed:

From my investigation, combined with the investigation made by the other agents of the Department in Boston, I am convinced not only that these men had violated the Selective Service rules and regulations and evaded the draft, but that they were anarchists, and that they ought to have been deported. By calling these men anarchists, I do not mean necessarily that they were inclined to violence, nor do I understand all the different meanings that different people would attach to the word "anarchist." What I mean is that I think they did not believe in organized government or in private property. But I am also thoroughly convinced, and always have been, and I believe that it is and always has been the opinion of such Boston agents of the Department of Justice as had any knowledge on the subject, that these men had nothing whatever to do with the South Braintree murders, and that their conviction was the result of co-operation between the Boston agents of the Department of Justice and the District Attorney. It was the general opinion of the Boston agents of the Department of Justice having knowledge of the affair that the South Braintree crime was committed by a gang of professional highwaymen.

Six months before the trial Moore was reiterating the claim, sensationally and vociferously, that Sacco and Vanzetti would not and could not get a fair hearing in the biased atmosphere of Norfolk County. In his experience rigged trials were common enough, but beyond this it was part of his tactics to claim unfairness in advance.

Many earnest defenders of Sacco and Vanzetti have maintained, as did Moore, that in the postwar period of xenophobia no alien holding extreme political beliefs could possibly have found justice in conservative Dedham at the hands of a local jury. As early as January 1921, a Defense Committee pamphlet claimed that "a Northern jury does not examine the law and the evidence impartially when a murder accusation is leveled against a member of the Mediterranean race whose reputation is colored with the fanciful versions of the Mafia that furnished Sunday-Magazine readers mental diet for so many years."

Yet, in contrast to these a priori beliefs, a case tried in Dedham in April 1920 demonstrated that the citizens of Norfolk had lost neither their sense of justice nor their common sense. The very week Attorney General Palmer was curling the hair of the credulous by announcing that on May Day the Reds planned to make the national capital "the scene of the slaughter of high officials" an alien anarchist with the outlandish name of Segris Zagroff was brought before Judge Thayer, charged with advocating the overthrow of the government by violence. Zagroff had been picked up in a foreign radical club in Norwood, the walls of which were hung with pictures of the new Bolshevik Russian leaders. He freely and volubly admitted to the police that he was an anarchist and that he did not approve of the

American form of government. In spite of his statements the Dedham jury freed him.

Judge Thayer was vibrant with anger at the verdict. "Mr. Foreman," he asked testily, "did you take into consideration the testimony that was given us here by the police officers that the defendant told them he believed in the overthrow of the government? Didn't you hear the testimony to the effect that the defendant said in the presence of witnesses and in the conversations he had with officers that he did not like this form of government and that the only true government was the kind run by workingmen? How did you arrive at the verdict that you announce?"

Unintimidated, and with equal testiness, the foreman replied that "the jurors disregarded the testimony of the officers after they understood the definition of 'advocating anarchy,' as given by the court, to be the act of a person who actually used violence in bringing about his aims and not the advocacy of those aims when he talked on the subject."

Although this verdict showed that in Norfolk County ordinary men could still think clearly and act justly, it also showed the bias of Judge Thayer. Curiously enough, the prosecution of Zagroff was conducted by Assistant District Attorney Kane, who would shortly assist Katzmann in the prosecution of Vanzetti at Plymouth. Zagroff was defended by Katzmann's brother Percy.

In February, at Moore's request, the trial was postponed from March until May 31 so that he could secure an affidavit in Italy from Giuseppe Adrower, a former consulate clerk who claimed to have seen Sacco in Boston on the day of the crime. The ninety days that followed were a period of rapid polarization. Moore, the artist, had taken two aliens, neither of whom sympathized or cooperated with the organized labor movement, and fashioned them into generic figures of the workingman. He had made ringingly spectacular claims about the fate of accused anarchists in Norfolk County, and now the community responded by accepting his challenge. During Vanzetti's first trial there had been almost no mention of his social and political beliefs, but long before anarchism became an issue in the Dedham court everyone on the jury, in the courthouse, in the town was aware of it. Moore's class-angling in troubled waters had stirred the depths. While no one can now say for certain that, solely in the light of the evidence presented, Sacco and Vanzetti would have been acquitted if they had been Elks or members of the American Legion, they would certainly have had a much better chance.

It was Moore the artist who painted the affair in broad expressionistic strokes, embellished it and retouched it, spread the panoramic design on a world canvas. But for Moore there would have been no case as it is today remembered, and the Dedham trial—whatever its outcome—would have been as forgotten now as the then-sensational Zimmerman trial.

By the time the formal preparations for the trial were being made, Moore had created the situation he wanted. Nick and Bart, the two Italians at first mentioned so casually, had become symbols of man's injustice to man. No one, whatever his views, could now take the trial casually. If the Defense Committee members already saw the shadow of injustice lying across the path of their imprisoned comrades, the citizens of Dedham had a feeling of sinister forces in the offing. Any morning the mannered inhabitants of the High Street half expected to see the columns of the courthouse collapse under a dynamite charge. Sedate Dedham beside its winding river began to take on the aspect of a besieged town with the courthouse a forward bastion. The blue-coated local police, out in force, were augmented by a detachment of the recently formed paramilitary State Constabulary. The tension was sharp as an east wind.

A week before the trial, Stewart interviewed George Kelley. Kelley still considered himself a friend of Sacco's and said so. The arrest made no difference. He had visited Sacco in jail, and his wife had stayed with Rosina during her confinement. Many a time before this trouble the two men, next-door neighbors, had chatted together at the end of a long summer evening as Sacco was coming in from his garden. Kelley did not think much of Sacco's socialist ideas and had warned him about airing them too freely. But Sacco had just laughed, saying that what was in the heart had to come out of the mouth.

Stewart asked Kelley if he could describe Sacco's cap. Kelley said all he could remember about it was that it was dark. Then Stewart showed him a cap and asked if it was Sacco's. It was the cap found near Berardelli's body. Kelley did not want to say. When Stewart pressed him for a definite opinion, he still declined. "I have an opinion about the cap," he said finally, expressing the prevailing Dedham atmosphere, "but I don't want to get a bomb up my ass."

Moore and the Defense Committee had had differing ideas about how the defense should be managed. Local lawyers might be useful, indeed necessary, but Moore wanted them subordinate, subject to his direction. He was in no hurry. This was, after all, his case. Not until

May did he start looking for any legal assistance. On the nineteenth he wrote to a friend:

The defense committee has agreed to pay the McAnarney brothers who are supposed to be the highest grade porch climbers in the business, $10,000 for their professional ability. They don't care how we get the money. We don't particularly care how they get results.

The McAnarneys, John, Thomas, and Jeremiah, had been practicing law together thirty years in the tide-edged granite city of Quincy, five miles south of Boston. John had been for thirteen years city solicitor as well as president of the county bar association. Thomas was associate justice of the district court. Jeremiah, the youngest, was in general practice, and counsel for the Eastern Massachusetts Street Railway. Second-generation Irish-Americans, piously Catholic, conservative in attitudes and beliefs, they represented the middle class that had moved away from the proletarian South Boston matrix that had first sheltered the beaten immigrant survivors of the Famine years. So far had the McAnarneys evolved in the more open environment of Quincy that they had even become Republican—still an act of apostasy in South Boston, if rewarding elsewhere. Thomas had been appointed to the bench by Governor Calvin Coolidge.

John McAnarney was the head of the family, partly from being the eldest but mostly because of his assimilated dignity. White-haired, formal in speech and sedate in manner, he had in his late middle age come to resemble the Yankee prototypes that the Irish were replacing. He kept a second office in Boston where, as the years passed, he spent the greater part of his time, concerning himself more with banks and investments than actions and torts. He moved familiarly in the Boston legal world that was so much a postgraduate extension of the Harvard Law School; he numbered his acquaintances from the law firms with the triple-barreled names; he became a recognized figure on the well-beaten path from State Street through Pemberton Square to the State House.

Thomas, the judge, was the family wit. Frail and in failing health, his legal work off the bench had become nominal. Jerry was the trial lawyer of the family. He was Jerry to everybody. The priest who baptized him had been the last to call him Jeremiah. Unlike John, he had not conformed to State Street, and his speech still bore traces of the South Boston flats. Short, short-mustached, ruddy-faced, he had a tendency to trip over his grammar if he became excited. When he hurried down the street, as he always did, he seemed to do a little clog dance. He had a habit of buttonholing people, in the literal sense, emphasizing the point he was making with a jab of an index finger toward his auditor's chest. He also had the reputation of winning his cases.

When Moore, prodded by the committee, finally decided to use local reinforcement, he consulted James Sisk, with whom he had worked on the Ettor-Giovannitti case in Lawrence. Sisk, who had since been appointed to the superior court, recommended the McAnarney combination. Moore went to John in his Boston office. McAnarney said he no longer took court cases. His brother Jerry, he felt, would be the one to deal with a case like this, with Tom perhaps helping out. He would talk it over with them, but before doing so he wanted to know more about the two Italians. Like everyone else, he had been shocked by the South Braintree murders. Any man, it was true, was entitled to a defense, but if Sacco and Vanzetti had been in any way concerned with this crime his office wanted nothing to do with keeping them from getting the punishment they deserved. Only if the men were innocent would the McAnarneys consider taking part. Moore was convincing.

The three McAnarneys drove over to Dedham and spent the better part of an afternoon in the jail's reception room talking with Sacco and with his wife, who happened to be there on a visit. Sacco was forthright. The McAnarneys felt satisfied with the answers they received. After leaving the jail John McAnarney met Moore and the two of them walked the back streets of Dedham for an hour, discussing the matter. McAnarney said he had put Sacco through every test he could think of and his answers—in fact everything about him—convinced him that the man was innocent. His brothers felt the same way. His office could work for Sacco's acquittal with a clear conscience. The McAnarneys would accept the brief.

The measure of Moore's success in building up the Sacco-Vanzetti case was sensed by the legal profession some time before the rest of Massachusetts became aware of it. Judge Thayer, stimulated by the prospect (and with a blindness to proprieties that would later become increasingly apparent), wrote to his fellow Dartmouth alumnus, Chief Justice John Aiken, requesting that he be appointed presiding judge at the Dedham trial. Thayer apparently saw nothing improper in the request. In fact he may well have visioned himself as a judicial Peter plugging the American dike against the flooding seas of radicalism. Years later at a Dartmouth reunion, he told a friend that if he knew the Reds were outside the door and he could save his country by walking through it to be shot down by them he would be glad to sacrifice his life.

Apparently the impropriety of Thayer's approach to the chief justice was offset by their Dartmouth kinship. Aiken, too, must have been sniffing the wind when he wrote in reply: "I am assigning you to hear the most important murder case tried in Massachusetts since the last century, if not in all time."

◇◇◇◇◇◇◇◇◇◇◇◇◇◇◇◇◇◇◇◇◇◇◇◇◇◇◇◇◇◇◇◇◇

CHAPTER NINE

The Trial—I

Judge Thayer's voice rasped as he looked down from the bench at the plump venireman from Brookline, the fourth in succession who had asked to be excused because he did not believe in capital punishment. "Do you set your opinion above the law?" the judge asked caustically. "Have you done anything to get the law changed? Have you seen your local representative about it?" The man did not know who his representative was.

From the look of the odd-lot prospective jurors who were passing through the courtroom on this first morning of the trial it seemed as if most of the able men of Norfolk County had managed to sneak their names off the jury list. The apologetic line filed by the bench—fogies long past the statutory age, invalids, men who had been deaf for years, whose wives were dying and who had certificates to prove it, who were just about to sail for Europe, and finally the objectionable objectors.

Of course there were the occasional better prospects, but every time a man came along who looked educated or respectable, as if he might be somebody, Moore seemed bound to challenge him. That was the way it struck Jerry McAnarney. If Jerry had been going on trial for murder he knew he would rather take his chances with a businessman than with some fellow who dug sewers. But not Fred Moore; he wanted the sewer-digger every time. There was a young fellow Jerry had spotted in the line, a good clean-cut college type; as soon as Moore found out he worked for Page & Company, that finished him. Then there was someone McAnarney recognized from the New England Trust Company, the sort of man any defense lawyer ought to get down on his knees to have on a jury. He told Moore so, but Moore would not have him.

For thirty years Jerry McAnarney had been going in and out of the Dedham courthouse, but he had never seen anything like this morning. State troopers in khaki, some mounted, were deployed all around the courthouse. Other troopers with motorcycles and sidecars swept up and down the High Street, the pop of their exhausts sounding like machine-gun fire. And inside there were police and deputies at the doors, parading up and down the corridors, on the stairs.

When Jerry and Tom arrived at the courthouse just before ten they found the front door locked. The side door was also locked. When they knocked, a guard looked through the glass and waved them off. Finally a court officer recognized them and let them in. Inside, a trooper patted them over for weapons. Then a flashy policeman stopped them at the foot of the stairs, and on the landing they were stopped again. The way the place was guarded, Jerry told his brother, it looked as if Sheriff Capen was getting ready to try the Kaiser.

Entering the courtroom, the brothers glimpsed the backs of the defendants in the waist-high prisoners' cage. Rosina Sacco, with seven-month-old Ines in her arms, sat close behind her husband, the only ordinary spectator allowed in the courtroom that day. The others present were either reporters or deputies. Fred Katzmann, tanned and glowing from a long week end at golf, spotted the McAnarneys in the doorway and waved to them with casual friendliness. Moore was behind the bar talking with Judge Thayer. The judge's face seemed frozen. Just before the McAnarneys went in, a deputy sheriff said under his breath: "Tom, I like to see you boys win your cases, but I hope to God you lose this case. These men are no good."

At the opening Moore filed a motion for severance and a separate trial for Sacco on the grounds that his association with Vanzetti would be prejudiced because of the latter's conviction for the Bridgewater crime. Similarly, the McAnarneys requested a separate trial for Vanzetti, since his defense was to be "separate and distinct." Both motions were denied.

During the whole morning not a single juror was picked. By lunchtime it was obvious that the Yankee judge was taking a poor view of the Western lawyer. The McAnarneys could tell that merely by the way Thayer glared at Moore, the lines at each side of his mouth etching into his cheeks before he replied to one of Moore's objections. Even Rosina Sacco, with her imperfect knowledge of English, sensed it. Moore kept on needling Thayer, objecting to each triviality, challenging each likely juror. The class-conscious Westerner demanded that prospective jurors be asked if they were opposed to organized labor, if they belonged to a union, or if they hired union help. These questions Judge Thayer disallowed. At the noon recess he remarked angrily and audibly as he left the courthouse that no long-haired radical from California was going to tell him how to run his court.

It was midafternoon before the first juror, Wallace Hersey, a real estate dealer from Weymouth, was picked. By the end of the afternoon only two more had been selected: John Ganley, a grocer, and a machinist, Frank Waugh. Each defendant was allowed forty-four challenges, and that day the defense used up twenty-one. Judge Thayer, exasperated by the delays, held an evening session until ten, when he had to leave to catch the last train back to Boston. It took ten hours and 175 veniremen to get the initial three jurymen.

There was, as there usually is in even the most ponderously sustained trial, an occasional lighter moment. At one point a plump sugar dealer from Braintree had the idea of getting himself excused by pretending he was deaf. The courtroom echoed with laughter as Judge Thayer pounced on him. Sacco laughed so hard that tears rolled down his cheeks. Then the courtroom settled down again, the hivelike humming broken only by the squeak of Sheriff Capen's boots as he walked gingerly across the floor to the upright mace. Behind the judge's dais the triple-cylindered pendulum of the marble-faced clock ticked away the formal minutes.

From time to time the sallow-faced defendants in the cage whispered to one another. Sacco had aged in the year of his arrest. His hair was thinning. That morning was the first time he and Vanzetti had seen each other in eight months. When they met before court opened, they had kissed each other gravely on the cheek.

The McAnarney brothers, seated inside the bar enclosure, saw the unhappy pattern of the morning repeated all through the afternoon and evening. It was clear by now to Jerry McAnarney that Moore, for all his reputation, was doing nobody any good, least of all the men in the cage. Jerry was as convinced as ever that the two men were innocent. He had even brought his wife to the jail after the Decoration Day parade to let her talk with Sacco and get her opinion, and she had felt the same way he did. But now, even before the jury had been picked, he had the feeling of the sands slipping from under his feet, of being beyond his depth. The Italians were never going to get a square deal with Moore running things. Jerry could hear Thayer's edged voice: "Mr. Moore, that may be the way they practice law out West, but not in the Commonwealth of Massachusetts!"

At the close of the evening session the brothers drove to John McAnarney's house in Quincy and told him of what was blowing up between Moore and Judge Thayer. They wanted John to get rid of Moore and take charge. John thought it over, and then, even though it was midnight, telephoned William G. Thompson. Thompson was an old Yankee, a lawyer's lawyer, a lecturer at the Harvard Law School, and whatever he said carried weight in Massachusetts.

In his Chestnut Hill home, Thompson listened to John McAnarney explain the difficulties his brothers were facing at the beginning of the Sacco-Vanzetti trial. John begged him to come to Dedham in the morning, insisting that the lives of two men were at stake, and that in his opinion the men were innocent. Thompson agreed to look in.

As Thompson got off the train in Dedham and walked up from the station past the spent lilac hedges of the High Street, the brim of his Panama flopping with each step, the Phi Beta Kappa key and the Institute of 1770 charm jingling on his heavy watchchain, he looked the very model of a proper Boston lawyer. Even the loose way he held his pipe in his mouth reinforced his assurance. He found John McAnarney, much upset, waiting for him in front of the closed courthouse gates.

They went in through a side door. In the lower corridor the two lawyers found Moore arguing with Rosina Sacco in the center of a group of gesticulating Italians. Thompson could hear Rosina's voice shrill to the edge of breaking, demanding of Moore by what right he represented her husband. She didn't want him, she shouted, she didn't believe in him. She wanted a good lawyer.

Rosina's outburst was the culmination of months of bitterness. She had neither liked nor approved of Moore from the beginning. Her thrifty peasant nature was affronted by his manner of life, his Beacon Hill house and car with chauffeur—all paid for by poor Italians. Now she was telling him in effect: Get out! And he was refusing.

Thompson and John and Jerry McAnarney talked the matter over in one of the anterooms. "I want either you or John to replace Moore," Jerry told Thompson. Thompson said it was too late. The next day at latest the jury would be empaneled. "You have got to make the best of it," he told the brothers.

When Moore joined them in the anteroom, Jerry McAnarney offered to turn back his first payment of two thousand dollars and go on with the case for nothing if Moore would only retire. Moore refused to consider it. He had hired the McAnarneys as subordinates, not to give him orders. With their narrow conservatism, he considered them incapable of the larger view the case demanded.

During the rest of the morning Thompson sat with the Mc-Anarneys watching the resumed parade of prospective jurors. A new lot of 160 veniremen had been brought in, but the selection was going no faster than it had the day before. Moore was again needling Judge Thayer. He could not seem to help it, even though he must have sensed the tensing of the atmosphere. It was a morning Thompson was to remember in all its immediacy years later. "Katzmann would say something," he recalled to the Lowell Committee in 1927, "and Moore would object to it. He was jumping up all the time. He would make objection after objection. Judge Thayer would sit there and look at Moore with the fiercest expression on his face, moving his head a little. Moore would say 'I object to that' and Judge Thayer . . . would sit back in his chair and say 'Objection overruled.' It wasn't what he said, it was his manner of saying it. It looked perfectly straight on the record; he was too clever to do otherwise. I sat there for a while and I told John McAnarney 'Your goose is cooked. You will never in this world get these men acquitted. The judge is going to convict these two men and see that nothing gets into the record; he is going to keep his records straight and you have no chance.' "

When John Dever, a Filene's clothing salesman, received a post card ordering him to report at the Norfolk county courthouse for jury duty, he had expected he might serve on some civil case. Not until the Decoration Day week end did he learn that his summons might be for the South Braintree murder case. Of that case he had only a blurred recollection, something he had read in the papers the year before. It gave him a queer feeling to think he might find himself on a murder jury. His supervisor at Filene's told him he was lucky—it would be like having time off, with Filene's paying his salary.

Although Dever was twenty-seven, he could have passed for twenty-one. He had been a poor Irish-Catholic boy brought up on the wrong side of the tracks in the quarry city of Barre, Vermont. As he grew up he had played with many of the children of the Italian immigrant stoneworkers. Some of these workers had been anarchists, or at least radicals. Dever, though a pious adolescent, had had no particular feeling against the local anarchists in their clapboard hall. He was used to them.

At fifteen he had left Barre for Boston, where he first worked as a bellboy in the Parker House. He had volunteered for the Army in 1917 but had not been sent overseas. In 1919 he had gone to work at Filene's. Unmarried, he lived in a brick rooming house on upper Beacon Street, Brookline.

Inconspicuous as this slight, fair-haired young man may have seemed when he was shepherded into the courtroom with the other veniremen, he was in one respect unique. In the course of the day he would be one of three accepted for the jury, and of the final twelve he alone would write about the trial. His memoirs, although fragmentary and redundant, remain the sole record of the case as seen from the jury box. As a result of the trial Dever became so interested in the judicial process that he enrolled in an evening course at the Suffolk Law School and eventually passed his bar examinations. During the last ten years of his life he prepared his *Memoirs of the Sacco-Vanzetti Case* and at his death in 1956 the manuscript had reached several thousand pages. Interspersed among the tedious legalities are telling casual incidents, still bright over the years: how the jurors were picked, where they slept, where and what they ate, what they did in their spare time, and how they felt about the case.

This was the first time Dever had ever been to Dedham. As he walked from the railroad station through the square he kept thinking what a pleasant town it was. Above the masking elms he could see a white dome with round windows in it like portholes. That, he supposed, was the courthouse. He wandered up and down several of the side streets before heading for the domed building.

Never before had he been inside a court, and the neoclassic building with its marble-tiled floors and marble stairs and marble-paneled walls awed him. With the other veniremen he was taken to the courthouse, where Judge Thayer first explained the procedure and then exhorted them to perform their disagreeable duties as patriotically as the American soldier boy in France.

"What, gentlemen, does the law seek to accomplish?" he concluded. "It seeks to select twelve jurors who will stand between these parties, the Commonwealth on the one hand and these defendants on the other, with an unyielding impartiality and absolute fairness and unflinching courage in order that truth and justice shall prevail, for, gentlemen, verdicts must rest upon truth and justice in order that the life, the liberties, and the properties of the people of the Commonwealth, including the defendants, shall be secure and protected."

John Dever was impressed not only by the rhetoric but by the whole formalized proceedings. To him Judge Thayer seemed "a sincere, honest, absolutely fair and impartial man." Dever was not called during the morning. At one o'clock he ate a sandwich and a piece of pie at Gilbert's Lunch, a one-arm in the square. When he returned to the courthouse it was still too early for the afternoon session. He sat on the back grass plot with some of the other men. Dever said he hoped he would not be picked, because he might lose his two weeks' vacation. "Don't worry," a man wearing a Red Men's badge told him. "You'll be challenged. You're too young. Besides they don't want any of you fellows on this jury." He pointed to the ex-service-man's pin in Dever's buttonhole. "They'll show you right out the front door," he concluded.

Afterward Dever could not remember much about the afternoon. One by one the names were called, one by one the veniremen disappeared. No jurymen had been picked during the morning and only two after lunch: Frank Marden, a mason from Weymouth; and a slightly deaf, slightly senile retired farmer with a handlebar mustache, Walter Ripley, who raised bulldogs and called himself a stockkeeper. For all his challenging, Moore did not spot the fact that Ripley had once been chief of the police and fire departments in Quincy. It was not until eight o'clock that Dever's name was finally called. He was led into the courtroom. Thayer asked him a few questions and then announced, "The juror stands indifferent."

I looked in front of me [Dever recalled] *and saw a whole battery of attorneys, eight or nine in all, I should say. Before I had a chance to orient myself a man whom I was to know as District Attorney Katzmann stood on his feet and said "the Commonwealth accepts the juror." Well, I thought to myself, the defense will now challenge me. I looked at the defense table and saw four attorneys looking at a very large book. They would look in the book, then look hard at me; and then whisper to each other. That went on for what seemed to be six or seven minutes. I began to feel I was on trial. I turned in the witness stand getting ready to leave. Judge Thayer glanced at me and said, "Stay right where you are, young man, we are waiting for these gentlemen," and looked at the defense table. After about two more looks at me, Mr. Jeremiah McAnarney stood up and said, "If your Honor please, both defendants accept the juror."*

Dever was the sixth juror accepted. A few minutes later the court adjourned. The six jurors were taken to the ground floor room of the Court of Probate and Insolvency, where twelve iron cots from the county jail had been set up. There they were locked in for the night.

When Dever woke the next morning, he thought at first he was in a lecture hall. Then he remembered. He got up, washed, and fixed his hair with the brush and comb the sheriff had given each juror. He was not given a razor. At eight o'clock a deputy appeared and took them to breakfast.

Almost at the beginning of the morning session the seventh juror, Lewis McHardy, an elderly quiet-mannered mill worker from Milton, was selected. Seventeen more veniremen filed past the bench. Then the sheriff informed the judge that his list of five hundred was exhausted.

According to the General Laws of Massachusetts, if such a situation occurs in a murder case after seven jurors have been chosen, "the Court shall cause jurors to be returned from the bystanders or from the county at large to complete the panel." Judge Thayer cited the statute and ordered Sheriff Capen to have two hundred more men present by the ten the next morning. The sheriff was doubtful. "They will jump," he remarked, "when they see me coming." He was right. The news got round, and almost before the afternoon session closed, the streets of Dedham and the adjoining towns were deserted.

Capen spread his deputies that evening through Brookline, Needham, Dedham, Norwood, Millis, Medway, Stoughton, and Quincy. They struck at random, ringing doorbells when they saw lights in windows, sometimes summonsing luckless veniremen from their beds. They consulted assessors' lists, voting lists, any list they could get their hands on. In Needham nine unsuspecting men were picked up coming out of a Masonic meeting. Deputy Allen Loring broke up a band concert at Hollis Field, Braintree. Norman Gardenier of Quincy was whisked away from his wedding supper. In spite of all this, Capen managed to seine in only 175 indignant additions. He hoped they would suffice. The defense still had twenty-nine challenges left.

Judge Thayer decided to remain in session until the jury was finally chosen, no matter what the hour. Not until after midnight was the selection finished. The five additional jurors were Harry King of Millis, a shoemaker; George Gerard, a Stoughton photographer; Alfred Atwood, a Norwood real estate dealer; Frank McNamara, a Stoughton farmer; and Seward Parker, a Quincy machinist. By the time Parker's name was called the defense had used up all its challenges. Katzmann affably offered to challenge Parker if Moore had any objection to him, but Moore declined.

No sooner had the left-over veniremen been excused than Moore objected to the five new jurors of the completed panel on the grounds that none of them were bystanders, according to the meaning of the statute. In the clammy courtroom the attendants and deputies yawned and the district attorney fiddled with a blotter while Moore developed his lengthy quibble. Judge Thayer overruled Moore on every point. At 1:20 A.M. he ordered the jurymen brought in and sworn. "The jury is in bed," a deputy sheriff told him.

Thayer's voice rose two notes. "Who allowed them to go to bed? Bring them in!"

A few minutes later, bleary-eyed and bristly, the twelve trudged in to take their seats in the box. Several of them were collarless, their shirts open. Two wore felt slippers. Thayer gave them the conventional warning. He also advised them to get plenty of exercise. In conclusion he told them that they must "see to it that a trial is held according to American law and according to American justice and nothing must be done by anybody to mar or impair a fair, honest trial." The jurors then took their oath and the court adjourned until Monday morning at ten o'clock.

The jurors slept late on Saturday, June 4, took a walk by the Charles River in the afternoon accompanied by a squad of deputies, and in the evening read the Boston papers. All references to the trial had been snipped out, and they made the unhappy discovery that most of the sports news had been on the back of what was cut.

The twelve soon formed their habit patterns. Dever found himself going to bed at nine and waking at five. He spent a lot of time reading old *National Geographics*. The older jurors usually played cards; Dever preferred listening to the Victrola. There were a lot of records that he liked: Van and Schenk, and the All-Star Trio; songs like "Dardenella," "Whispering," "I'm Forever Blowing Bubbles." After he had cranked the Victrola a few times, though, the card-players would begin to look over at him as if to say "Don't you think you've played enough for tonight?" Then he would go back to the *Geographics*.

On their first Sunday they just sat around their made-over courtroom. Since they all had to stay together and could go only to one church, they decided not to go to any. They had breakfast at the Dedham Inn on Court Street beyond the Episcopal church and dinner at the Haven House just across the way; in the afternoon they went for a bus ride.

Monday was hot, a blue clear prelude to summer. The jury, after being polled in the courtroom, spent the rest of the day viewing the various locations connected with the South Braintree crime. A cavalcade of eight cars drove from place to place, carrying not only the jury but also the judge, the district attorney, and two carloads of newspaper reporters.

The jurors arrived at their first stop, South Braintree, just as the noon whistles were blowing, and at once the cars were surrounded by curious factory workers. Katzmann had to order a retreat to Braintree for lunch. When the cavalcade returned, the factory windows were filled with faces but Pearl Street itself was free. From the railroad crossing the procession followed the route of the bandit car along the side roads through Randolph and Stoughton and Brockton to West Bridgewater. The dust churned, covering the men in the cars, coating their faces like masks. The jurors were shown Simon Johnson's house, the Elm Square Garage, the house where Coacci and Boda had lived, and then the Manley Woods. A motorcycle was parked beside the bridle path, and as the assorted jurors, lawyers, police, and newspapermen made their way to where the Buick had been found, they surprised the cyclist and his girl making love under a bush. Their last stop was the gate-tender's shanty at the Matfield crossing. At the end of the day they had covered ninety-one miles, and Dever thought each of them had absorbed about a pint of dust. There was no place for the jurors to get a bath, either—he noted ruefully—after they got back to the courthouse.

Tuesday morning, June 7, when Assistant District Attorney Williams made the opening statement for the Commonwealth, set the pattern for the month to follow. Sacco and Vanzetti, handcuffed to each other and to a deputy, with three blue-uniformed policemen in front, three to the rear, and two on either side, were marched from the jail down Village Street past the cemetery, then up Court Street to the courthouse. A trooper, with a bandolier of a hundred rounds slung across his shoulder and a rifle in his saddle boot, rode sternly ahead of them, while a second mounted trooper followed as a rear guard. At the midday recess the prisoners were marched back to the jail. This martial procession took place four times a day.

Once in the courtroom the defendants were placed in the cage and their handcuffs removed. Then followed a pause of some minutes until the diminutive judge in his built-up heels strode through the door, his black silk gown billowing behind him. At his appearance Clerk Worthington rapped with his gavel and gave the peremptory command *"Court!"* Everyone stood up. For the first time the public was allowed in the courtroom. Among the spectators were Mrs. Glendower Evans, representing the New League for Democratic Control; Cerise Carman Jack, the wife of a Harvard professor, representing the New England Civil Liberties Committee; and Lois Rantoul of the Federated Churches of Greater Boston, a relative of Harvard's President Lowell. Felicani was present, as were most of the members of the Defense Committee and the Italian consul, the aloof pince-nezed Marquis Ferrante di Ruffano, on instructions from his government.

In informal preliminary discussions the prosecution and the defense had come to an agreement not to bring up the subject of radicalism during the trial. Katzmann had also offered to agree "that no particular bullet came from any particular gun" and refrain with the defense from trying to prove one way or the other whether the murder bullets had been fired from Sacco's automatic or Vanzetti's revolver. Moore had refused, exclaiming melodramatically that he was being asked to turn his sword into a shield, and insisting on being free to have the bullets and guns examined by experts. Officially Moore, assisted by William Callahan—the lawyer engaged for Sacco and Vanzetti in the Brockton police court—represented Sacco, and officially the McAnarney brothers represented Vanzetti, but this was merely a maneuver to give both Jerry McAnarney and Moore the right to argue before the jury and to cross-examine. In reality Moore was as completely in charge as if he had been captain of a ship.

The contention of the Commonwealth, Assistant District Attorney Williams said in his explanatory statement,

is that this crime was committed by five men; that use was made of this stolen Buick car which after its theft from Dr. Murphy of Natick had been kept in the curtained shed of the Coacci house in West Bridgewater; that on the morning of the murder it was taken from the Coacci house and was driven to South Braintree; that they picked up Vanzetti at the East Braintree station; that the men who guided and drove that car were very familiar with the localities of West Bridgewater and the roads leading to and from that section; that they went down to the railroad crossing after the shooting, and made that hairpin turn to throw their pursuers off the scent . . . that they proceeded by those back roads, Oak Street and Chestnut Street, until they got to the old turnpike, which, though a rough road, furnished a direct means of access to the West Bridgewater locality; and they tore down there and either started to take Vanzetti over to Plymouth and for that

*reason went over the Matfield crossing or went over there with the
idea of perhaps disposing of something in the Matfield River . . .
found it inadvisable to do that which they intended to do, came back
over the Matfield crossing and subsequently abandoned their car in
the region adjacent to the Coacci house.*

Williams claimed he would later show that Mike Boda was seen
driving a Buick touring car during the winter of 1920. Reminding the
jurymen of Puffer's Place, the house they had seen the day before,
he gave an unsubstantiated account of the police visiting the shed
and finding traces of a hole recently dug in the dirt floor as well as
tire marks to the left of the boards on which Boda had kept his
Overland.

Although Judge Thayer later excluded references to the shed, and
although no evidence was brought forward connecting Coacci, Boda,
or Orciani with the South Braintree crime, Williams in his opening
nevertheless managed to link them with it by innuendo.

The first witness to take the stand was Boston photographer John
Farley, who had photographed the various buildings, places, and
objects covered in the case and whose pictures were now offered to
the jury as exhibits. Moore objected to the angles at which several
of the pictures had been taken and there followed an inconclusive
wrangle with the prosecution, to the visible annoyance of Judge
Thayer.

During the noon recess, while Sacco and Vanzetti were marched
back to the jail for their meal, Judge Thayer walked down the street
to the Dedham Inn. Whenever he was in Dedham he took his midday
meal there, as did the newspapermen and most of those connected
with the courthouse. Returning from the inn, Thayer could not conceal his scorn at the sight of the coatless Moore taking a nap on the
grass plot in front of the courthouse. Moore was always doing things
like that, offending the New England sense of decorum without even
realizing he had offended. Once in court on a hot afternoon he took
off his shoes and stepped before the bench to make an exception in
his stocking feet. Jerry McAnarney, watching Judge Thayer's bottled-
up indignation as it approached the uncorking point, was fearful as
well as dismayed. "For God's sake," he warned Moore, "keep your
coat and vest on in the courtroom, can't you?"

Ripley, the dodderer with the tobacco-stained mustache, had been
appointed foreman of the jury, possibly because at sixty-nine he was
the oldest of the twelve. When on that first day he returned to the

courtroom from lunch, he paused with self-conscious rectitude and—
to the embarrassment of the others—saluted the American flag that
stood beside the jury box.

The photographer was followed by Edward Hayward, the surveyor
who had made the large-scale map of the South Braintree scene that
hung to the right of the flag. Then the medical testimony began, the
reiterative technicalities that the law requires to prove the indisputa-
ble fact that a man is dead. Indifferently the jury followed the course
of the bullets through the bodies, listened to Dr. Hunting, who had
operated on the dying Parmenter; Dr. Jones, who had picked up the
bullet shaken out of Parmenter's jacket; Dr. Frazer, who had examined
Berardelli's body in the front room of the Colbert house. The medical
evidence was summed up and concluded by Dr. Magrath, whose boast
was that he had performed more autopsies and attended more symphony concerts than any other medical examiner in New England.
His toupee, the most obviously artificial in Massachusetts, was equally
familiar to Symphony Hall, city morgues, and the Harvard Medical
School. Dr. Magrath was a character. There was an iron quality about
him that did not brook contradiction. Even Moore had no questions
to ask him.

Such preliminaries took up the first week. Meanwhile Judge Thayer,
irritated enough by the sight of the squint-eyed California lawyer
bobbing up in front of him, found a more pervasive irritant in the
printed broadsides of the Defense Committee denouncing the unfairness of the trial even before it started. "I am here to see the defendants get a fair trial," he announced from the bench. And one day he
asked a group of reporters at the Dedham Inn if they had ever seen a
case in which so many leaflets had been spread around saying that
people could not get a fair trial in the State of Massachusetts. As
he went out onto the porch his face was flushed and his voice rose.
"You wait till I give my charge to the jury," he told the reporters,
shaking his fist. "I'll show 'em!" Even the monarchist Ferrante, whose
chief regret was that Sacco and Vanzetti had not become American
citizens so that he could have washed his hands of them, sensed
within the first few days that Thayer was sure they were guilty.

Not until Wednesday morning, June 8, did the South Braintree
express agent, the Commonwealth's first important witness, take the
stand. Considerably embellishing the story he had told in the Quincy
court the year before, Shelley Neal again described his payroll delivery,
the pale man in the doorway of the Hampton House, his brief view
of the car that he was again to see jolting over the railroad crossing

after the holdup. But Neal did not attempt to identify Sacco or Van-zetti as anyone he had seen that day. Margaret Mahoney, the pay-mistress, followed Neal; she told of making up the payroll boxes and handing them over to Parmenter and Berardelli just before three o'clock.

Mark Carrigan, the shoe-cutter, was next. From his window on the third floor of the Hampton House he had watched the paymaster and the guard go down the street; then he had heard the shots and seen the car cross the tracks with the gunman crouched in the front seat. But from that glimpse Carrigan had not been able to identify the defendants in the Brockton police station and he was not now able to identify them in the courtroom.

So far the trial was going in the routine manner that Katzmann had planned. These early witnesses were not expected to identify any-one. They were there merely to set the scene. Something more, how-ever, was expected of Jimmy Bostock, the repairman, who had talked with Parmenter and Berardelli at the crossing, had seen the two men fall, and afterward had held the dying guard in his arms. The getaway car with the Italian-looking man who was leaning out shouting had passed so close to Bostock on Pearl Street that he could have reached out and touched it. Nevertheless, when asked in the Brockton station if he could tell whether Sacco and Vanzetti were the bandits he had answered, "No sir, I could not tell whether or not they was, no sir." On the stand Bostock testified that Berardelli usually carried a 38-caliber revolver. He had seen it several times, the last time the Satur-day before the murder. He had joked with Berardelli about it and asked him if he carried it to shoot rats. The mention of the revolver seemed irrelevant—especially as nobody had seen it on April 15—and Moore objected. Judge Thayer held a conference at the bench. There Assistant District Attorney Williams revealed for the first time the Commonwealth's contention that the revolver found on Vanzetti had been taken from Berardelli's body by the man who shot him.

When Lewis Wade was taken by Katzmann to the Brockton sta-tion he had pointed out Sacco as the wavy-haired man he had seen standing over Berardelli. At the preliminary hearing in the Quincy court three weeks later he was not quite as certain. "I don't want to make a mistake," he had said, looking at Sacco. "This is too damn serious, but he looks like the man." Since then Katzmann had given Wade a pep talk and was now counting on him for a positive identi-fication. Williams, leading the witness along, became stutteringly dis-concerted when Wade balked, maintaining that although Sacco looked to him somewhat like the man who did the shooting, he "had a doubt." Several weeks ago, Wade explained, he had seen a man in Damato's barbershop who looked just like the man who had shot Berardelli. Since that time he had decided that Sacco was not the man. Williams managed to recover his composure, but though he did his forensic best, he could get no further in persuading the intractable Wade.

As Wade left the stand one of the police officers at the door called him a piker and another muttered: "We're not through with you yet." It was a remark borne out a few weeks later when Wade was dismissed from his job at Slater & Morrill. He had it coming to him. That was the way people felt in South Braintree.

John Dever, in the first row of the jury box, glancing from time to time at the defendants in the cage, was so far not impressed by the Commonwealth's case. Sometimes he felt frightened at having to decide whether two men should live or die. Sacco and Vanzetti, he thought,

did not look like criminals. Sacco appeared to be an alert, bright, and rather clean-cut young fellow. Every time I looked at Vanzetti he seemed to be thinking with an impassive look on his face or listening intently to whatever was taking place at the time. . . . My sympathies were with the men on trial and I was hoping that the evidence would not be sufficient to establish their guilt "beyond a reasonable doubt."

The reasonable doubt became more shadowy after the spinsterish Hampton House bookkeepers, Mary Splaine and Frances Devlin, appeared. Both pointed to Sacco as the man they had seen leaning out of the murder car. Mary Splaine told how, after they had heard the shots, she and Frances Devlin had gone first to the front window, then to the one looking out on Pearl Street, just in time to catch the car as it careered across the railroad tracks. From sixty feet away she had watched the bareheaded bandit for the three seconds the car took to pass. "He had a gray, what I thought was a shirt—had a grayish, like navy color, and the face was what we would call clear-cut, clean-cut face . . . a little narrow, just a little narrow. The forehead was high. The hair was brushed back and it was between, I should think, two inches and two and one-half inches in length and had dark eyebrows, but the complexion was white, peculiar white that looked greenish." She had particularly noticed his left hand resting on the back of the front seat. It was "a good-sized hand that denoted strength."

Dever thought Mary Splaine seemed honest, but he did not see how anyone could have remembered all those details from such a distant glimpse, and he decided that she must have refreshed her memory on her visits to the Brockton police station. At the Quincy hearing the year before, when her memory was greener, Mary Splaine had not been so certain of her identification. There she had said of Sacco: "I am almost sure I saw him at Braintree, but I saw him at the Brockton police station afterward." When Moore, with the Quincy transcript in his hand, pressed her about her negative answers then, she belligerently denied making them but was finally forced to admit that she had said: "I don't think my opportunity afforded me the right to say he is the man." This she now qualified by saying that her observation of him for several hours in the Quincy court had convinced her that Sacco was the man in the car. "I am positive, certain he is the man," she concluded, her voice ringing and determined. "I admit the possibility of an error, but I am certain I am not making a mistake." As she said this Sacco thrust his head forward, smiling at her with fixed bitterness.

Frances Devlin's story was almost the same as her friend's, although not so detailed. She had seen the car spurt over the hill with a man leaning out firing at the crowd. She described him as "a dark man, and his forehead, the hair seemed to be grown away from the temple, and it was blown back and he had clear features, and rather good looking, and he had a white complexion and a fairly thick-set man, I should say." Sacco was that man. She was positive. Like Mary Splaine, in the Quincy court she had been less positive. There, the most she had said of Sacco was: "He looks very much like the man that stood up in the back seat shooting."

McGlone, the young teamster who had caught the staggering Parmenter, was another disappointing witness for the Commonwealth. A ferret-faced, stubborn man, he said that the two bandits he had seen were Italians, but that was all he would say about them. Assistant District Attorney Williams could not bring him to say that Sacco and Vanzetti were the gunmen, any more than Moore could bring him to say that they were not. "Well," McGlone kept on telling them, "I did not get a good look at them to see what they did look like."

Edgar Langlois, the Rice & Hutchins foreman who had looked down from the second-floor window at the two gunmen below him, described them in court as short and dark-complexioned, full-chested, clean-shaven, with curly or wavy hair. He had not been able to identify either Sacco or Vanzetti at Brockton as the men he had seen from the window, nor was he now willing to identify them in court.

The only witness of the actual shooting to make any such identification was the young Jewish shoe-cutter Louis Pelser, who had been working on the first floor of Rice & Hutchins. After hearing shots outside, he said, he had opened the middle window and looked out at a bareheaded man with a gun, only seven feet away, shooting at Berardelli. "I seen this fellow shoot this fellow," he told the court. "It was the last shot. He put four bullets in him." The gunman had "wavy-hair—pushed back . . . dark complexion," and was wearing dark green pants and an army shirt. He had then seen the gunman climb into the car. Pelser pointed to Sacco as the man. Katzmann twice asked him, over Moore's objections, if he had any question in his mind but that Sacco was the man. Pelser hesitated. In the heat of the day, in his blue serge suit, he was an abject sight. John Dever thought he "looked and acted like a man who was doing something he didn't want or like to do." Looking at Sacco, pressed by the district attorney, Pelser reluctantly came out with it: "I wouldn't say he is the man, but he is the dead image of the man I seen." He added that he had thrown open the factory window and watched there from the time the gunman shot Berardelli until the car disappeared up Pearl Street.

The day that Pelser testified, June 10, was the hottest of the year. Outside the sun was molten and inside the air had become so humid that the walls and marble floor were beaded. Judge Thayer allowed the jurors to take off their coats, and finally ordered the sheriff to bring them fans.

Moore, beginning his cross-examination, was like a cat with a not overly nimble mouse. Pelser sweated so that the drops fell. Some months earlier, when interviewed by Robert Reid, a white-bearded Boston constable who had become a defense investigator, Pelser had denied seeing any of the shooting. "They were shooting while I was at the window," he had told Reid, "and I got under the bench, and that is all I seen of them." Now he claimed that he had lied to Reid because he did not want to be called as a witness. Moore, driving him into a corner, made him admit that he had, after all, ducked under the bench. He also admitted that he had avoided going to the Brockton station with the other witnesses by telling the police he had not seen enough to identify anyone. However, Moore could not shake Pelser's insistence that he had seen the gunman and the get-away car—and it was a fact that Pelser was the only person in South Braintree who had written down the car's license number.

William Brenner, Peter McCullum, and Dominic Constantino, all of whom worked at the front benches with Pelser, were brought in as defense witnesses to contradict Pelser's story, but their effect was lessened by the tidy mechanics of legal procedure that postpones the appearance of rebuttal witnesses until the prosecution has finished its case. So it was not until two weeks later, when the details of Pelser's testimony were overlaid by that of a score of other witnesses, that Brenner took the stand. He too, after he had heard shots, looked through the partially opened center window and saw a man "sink-ing—sinking." Pelser had not been near the window. After McCullum had raised the sash he had slammed it down again and yelled "Duck!" and they had all got down behind the benches. Under cross-examina-tion Brenner admitted he really did not know where Pelser was when he himself was looking through the window.

McCullum, following Brenner, was not sure where Pelser was either, but Constantino was certain that when the shooting started Pelser was "right down under the bench." Afterward Pelser had told them: "I did not see any of the men but I got the number of the car." Constantino admitted he had not given any thought to where Pelser was until he had read the latter's testimony in the newspaper two weeks before. Then he had gone to the Sacco-Vanzetti Defense Committee and volunteered his information. At first he maintained that Pelser was at his workbench three windows down when McCul-lum had thrown up the sash, but Katzmann finally forced him to admit that he really did not know where Pelser was or whether he might have opened another window.

The appearance of Hans Behrsin, the Slater chauffeur, was unsatis-factory to the prosecution. All he could say was that the two men he had seen sitting on the Rice & Hutchins fence as he drove past in the Marmon "seemed to be pretty well light-complexioned fellows." He had not noticed their features, and the district attorney did not even bother to ask him to identify the defendants.

It was generally agreed by the newspapermen covering the trial that Lola Andrews was the prosecution's star witness, since she was the only one who had actually talked with any of the gunmen. She was an unpredictable woman. When Moore and two assistants had gone to Quincy on January 14 with a stenographer to interview her as a prospective defense witness, he found her calm and pleasant.

According to the stenographer's record she told Moore that she could not identify the two men she had seen near the car in front of the Rice & Hutchins factory. When she was shown pictures of Sacco and Vanzetti, she said they were not the men. Although she did not mention it to Moore on January 14, she later claimed that two evenings before, a dark one-eyed man in a sailor's reefer had appeared at her door, spoken incomprehensibly about the South Braintree crime, and then, when she refused to listen to him, followed her into the hall toilet and assaulted her.

The evening before Lola appeared in court, Jerry McAnarney had gone to see her in Quincy, and she had told him that she could not and would not identify Sacco or Vanzetti as the men she had seen near the automobile in front of Slater & Morrill. Moore had even considered using her as one of his own witnesses and was surprised when she took the stand for the Commonwealth. She wore a stiff-crowned hat with a flat brim that shadowed her face. It was a coarse apprehensive face which, though faded, still managed to preserve a physical appeal.

Again she told her story of walking down Pearl Street to the Slater & Morrill factory, of seeing the pale man and the dark man by the touring car, of asking directions from the dark man on the way back. "He told me—he asked me," she said, looking at the defendants in the cage, "which factory I wanted, the Slater? I said 'No, sir, the Rice and Hutchins.' He said to go in the driveway and told me which door to go in, it would lead me to the factory office."

Williams then asked her dramatically if she had seen the man since. She replied that she had seen him in the courtroom. It was the climax to which the assistant district attorney had been building. "Do you see him in the courtroom now?" he asked. She paused, raised a bare, fleshy forearm, and pointed to Sacco. "I think I do. Yes, sir. That man, there." Sacco jumped to his feet in the cage, his eyes flashing. "I am the man?" he demanded in his thick accent. "Do you mean me? Take a good look!"

Moore in his cross-examination went back at once to the January evening when he had shown her a selection of photographs including one of Sacco holding a derby in his hand. According to the stenographer's record she had said that the man with the derby was not the one she had talked with in South Braintree. Now, on the stand, she denied that she had said any such thing, claiming on the contrary that she had then identified the man in Moore's picture as the man who had got up from under the car.

Though Moore could not shake her story he brought out that in February Stewart and Brouillard had taken her to the Dedham jail. There she had looked through a grating at a cell tier on a lower level. For about ten minutes she had watched a dark muscular man pacing up and down, the man—she finally decided—whom she had talked with in front of the factory on the day of the murder. That man, she was told, was Nicola Sacco.

At one o'clock Judge Thayer suspended the session for the week end. Lola Andrews' cross-examination would continue Monday and into Tuesday. Moore was determined to drive her to the wall. But in his determination he overlooked the one question that should have occurred to any trained legal mind. Lola Andrews had been given detailed directions to Rice & Hutchins by a man who spoke English easily. Sacco's command of English was so slight that he would not have been capable of such fluent talk. His heavy accent was at times almost incomprehensible. Yet Moore in his two days of hammering at Lola Andrews never once brought up the question of the speech and accent of the man who had directed her.

Judge Thayer's week-end instructions to the jury seem, at least from the record, judicious and temperate. "Drop this case now," he told them, "to be taken up Monday morning at ten o'clock. Don't discuss this case among yourselves. You haven't heard all the evidence; you haven't heard any of the evidence of the defense. You haven't heard the argument; you haven't heard the charge. Just keep your minds open, absolutely open, fair and impartial, so that when you finally cross the threshold of the jury room for your final determination of this case your mind will be as impartial and as open as it is humanly possible for any man's mind to be."

The trial was now beginning to look like a long one, and most of the jurors were concerned about getting back to their families. They talked about asking the judge to hold longer sessions. Dever was worried that Filene's might cancel his summer vacation after he had been away so long. Saturday morning he had just opened a *Geographic* when Sheriff Capen stuck his head in the door and asked if anyone wanted to take a bath. At first they thought it was his idea of a joke, but the sheriff marched them up to the jail and there in the basement they found twelve bathtubs all set up and waiting. For over an hour they soaked and splashed and tossed cakes of soap back and forth. Dever could see a rim of dirt forming all along the edge of his tub. The water felt great. So did the clean clothes his sister had sent him.

Monday morning brought Lola Andrews back to the stand. Moore repeatedly tried to force the witness into admitting that she had spoken to the pale sickly man, not the squat dark one. Over and over he asked about the location of the car, the position of the two men, the distance from the factory. Katzmann objected to the repetitions. So did Judge Thayer. "I thought we had been all through this before," the judge exclaimed caustically. Moore explained that he was trying to show that "much of the testimony of the witness . . . is one of rather hopeless confusion." Katzmann objected and Thayer turned on Moore. "That is an unfair criticism of any witness," he told the Westerner. "Kindly refrain from taking up a subject that has already been exhausted."

Moore's tactics were apparently to wear the witness down. All morning he kept hammering at her, going back again and again to what she had told him in January, making her retrace each step along Pearl Street on the morning of the crime. He could not, however, change her identification of Sacco.

Much of the testimony was irrelevant. Moore wanted to know how long the witness and Julia Campbell had worked at Rice & Hutchins, what they did there, and whether they had worked on men's or women's shoes. He became visibly embarrassed when the subject of Julia Campbell's present address in Maine came up and Lola Andrews said he had asked her how she herself would like a little vacation down there. When she had told Moore she was afraid she would lose her job, he had promised her a job in Maine "as good or better." Katzmann and Williams, sitting at the side of the enclosure, grinned at Moore's efforts to defend himself.

At the beginning of the afternoon session Jerry McAnarney took over the questioning, leading back to the matter of the photographs that Mrs. Andrews had or had not identified for Moore in January. Then there was a conference between Thayer and the lawyers as to how far the defense might go into the witness' past history. On overhearing this, she complained that she felt faint. A few seconds later she fell forward. Katzmann and Williams caught her as she slumped. She did not take the stand again until the following morning.

In the anteroom she told the district attorney that she had fainted because she had suddenly seen in the courtroom the man who had assaulted her. During the short recess it was whispered in the corridors that one of the spectators had been caught with a revolver. Unlike most courtroom rumors, it happened to be true. The man had a permit and was released, but on the morning following Lola Andrews' fainting fit those who arrived early found the courthouse gates closed and guarded. Only five minutes before the session were they opened, and then each entering spectator was patted. There was another flurry when the police thought they had discovered a man in possession of three small bombs. They turned out to be hard-boiled eggs that he had brought for his lunch.

When John Dever thought of Lola Andrews being overborne in Quincy by Moore, with a stenographer taking down every word she said, he felt sorry for her. Moore's harsh cross-examination backfired, causing Dever and the other jurymen to feel sympathetic enough to believe her.

Although Lola's testimony dragged on for another day, little more was added. There was an involved and lengthy discussion as to whether the photograph she had identified for Moore had been of Sacco—as she now maintained—or of an unidentified mustached man in a straw hat holding a cigar. Indirectly Williams brought up the matter of the one-eyed stranger who had assaulted her. The assistant district attorney claimed that she had been in a frightened state of mind at the time of her interview with Moore and could not be held to what she had said. Although the jury was sympathetic, the newspapermen were less so. One of the Hearst reporters nicknamed her "Fainting Lola."

Moore was sensitive enough to a jury's mood to realize the impression her identification had made. To help repair the damage he brought in five refuting witnesses. Alfred LaBrecque, a young Quincy reporter, had gone to Lola Andrews' room shortly after the assault, and she had told him that she could not say if the man who forced her into the toilet resembled the man at South Braintree because she had not seen the face of the man in South Braintree. George Fay, a Quincy policeman, testified that Lola had told him much the same thing. Harry Kurlansky, a tailor, who had known Lola for eight years, told of her passing his shop in February and his saying " 'You look kind of tired.' She says 'Yes.' She says 'They're bothering the life out of me.' I says, 'What?' She says, 'I just came from jail.' I says, 'What have you done in jail?' She says, 'The Government took me down and want me to recognize those men,' she says, 'and I don't know a thing about them. I have never seen them and I can't recognize them'."

Judge Thayer looked down sourly at the little Polish Jew. "Mr. Witness," he rasped, "I would like to ask one question. Did you attempt to find out who this person was who represented the Government who was trying to get her to take and state that which was false?" Kurlansky, already bewildered by the courtroom atmosphere, was almost speechless at the thought of turning himself into a private detective. "Well," he said, "it didn't come into my mind. I wasn't sure, you know. It didn't——" Only later, with Jerry McAnarney to encourage him, was he finally able to say that he didn't see why he should bother about it.

Moore sprang a surprise on Katzmann when he produced the aged but peppery Julia Campbell, whom he had brought down from Maine. Mrs. Campbell addressed Katzmann as "dear man," and when he tried to confuse her with a litany of dates, she sent a titter round the courtroom by exclaiming "Oh, chestnuts!" She swore that Lola Andrews had never spoken to the man under the car but to the man standing by it. As for the two defendants in the cage, she did not think she "ever saw them men in the world."

Lena Allen, who ran a lodging house in Quincy, was the last refuting witness. She said that Lola Andrews had roomed at her house until the other roomers had threatened to leave if she didn't get rid of her. Lola Andrews had a bad reputation and was untruthful, according to Lena Allen—who admitted she disliked her.

Five witnesses identified Vanzetti in one way or another, but only one of them, Mike Levangie, the Pearl Street gate-tender, placed him at the scene of the murders. Almost all the other witnesses had described the driver of the getaway car as pale, fair, sickly. Levangie, at the inquest two days after the crime, had asserted the man was dark, with a dark brown mustache. Now he pointed to Vanzetti in the cage as the man, the only man he had seen.

Katzmann in his summing-up admitted that the driver of the car was indisputably a pale blond man, but he explained that Levangie's identification was still valid as he must have glimpsed Vanzetti leaning over from the back seat and in the excitement thought he was the driver.

Although Levangie was the only witness to place Vanzetti in the Buick, two others placed him in South Braintree on that day. Harry Dolbeare, the piano tuner, had been summoned to Dedham as a prospective juror. While waiting in the courtroom he had seen the defendants being led by. Suddenly he had recalled the carload of tough tickets he had seen on Hancock Street the morning of the South Braintree crime. The man with the mustache, handcuffed to the sheriff, looked just like one of those men in the back seat. Having gone to the district attorney's office with his story, he now found himself appearing as a witness. Dolbeare had no particular recollection of the other four men in the car except for the general impression of their toughness, but the middle man in the back seat was Vanzetti. "I had the same view of him in the courtroom as I had in the car, a profile view," he told the court. He had "not a particle of doubt" about Vanzetti being the man.

John Faulkner, another surprise witness, picked out Vanzetti as a man who had ridden with him in the smoking car of the train from Plymouth to Boston on the morning of April 15. Faulkner, a pattern-maker at the Watertown Arsenal, was an unhesitating witness. Each day he was accustomed to take the train from Cohasset and he always rode in the smoking car. On the morning of the fifteenth as the train was pulling into East Weymouth a man across the aisle had said someone in back wanted to know if the stop was East Braintree. Faulkner turned and saw a foreign-looking man sitting in the single seat next to the toilet. He had a black mustache, high cheekbones, and was wearing old clothes. At Weymouth Heights the man again leaned forward and asked if the stop was East Braintree. When the train stopped at East Braintree the man had picked up an old leather Boston bag and got off. "That is the man," Faulkner said, identifying Vanzetti. He was sure. However, when asked by Moore if he could remember the man across the aisle who had first spoken to him, Faulkner had no recollection of him at all. He remembered the date because it was the time when he had been injured and had gone in on the late train to the hospital. The next day he read about the murders and wondered if the foreigner he had seen had had anything to do with them.

In refutation Moore brought in Henry McNaught, the conductor of the train, who said that no cash fares had been collected that day from Plymouth to Braintree. The station agents of Plymouth, North Plymouth, and Kingston testified in addition that no tickets had been sold from their stations to the Braintrees. However, Katzmann made them admit that they did not know if any such tickets had been sold the day before or how many might have been sold to Quincy or Boston. Edward Brooks, the ticket agent at East Braintree, recalled that about the time of the murders and several times since he had seen a tall dark man carrying a black bag get off the morning train and walk from the station toward Quincy Avenue. He had seen the man perhaps half a dozen times. Vanzetti was not the man.

The other two who identified Vanzetti were Austin Cole, the streetcar conductor, and Austin Reed, the gate-tender at the Matfield crossing. Cole told the same story he had told at the Plymouth trial. The two men who boarded his car at Sunset Avenue on May 5 and had been taken off by the police in Brockton had also got on at the same stop the night of April 14 or 15. Sacco and Vanzetti were the men. Reed, a man in his early twenties, told of the car that had swirled up to his crossing just as the train was coming and how he had gone out into the road with the stop sign in his hand. A man with a "stubbed" mustache and high cheekbones had leaned out of the car and asked loudly what the hell he was holding him up for. When Reed read of the South Braintree holdup the next day he had been sure those men were the bandits, and after he heard of the arrests on May 5 he had gone of his own accord to the Brockton police station to have a look at the suspects. The man with the mustache, Vanzetti, was the same man who had shouted at him from the car. He was sure of it in Brockton, he was sure of it now. There was no doubt in his mind.

Jerry McAnarney cross-examined Reed at random, asking what he was doing before the car appeared, how often the trains ran, where he now worked, how much dust was on the faces of the men in the car, what sort of hats they were wearing. Then Moore took over and at the last came close to the vital question when he asked if the man had spoken "in a loud bold voice." Reed admitted that he had and that the quality of the English was "unmistakable and clear." But Moore did not pursue the matter. As with Faulkner's and Lola Andrews' testimony, Moore overlooked the matter of the defendants' accents. His jibes at Reed's youth and at his going on his own to the police station aroused John Dever's sympathy for the witness.

The weather continued oppressive; the motionless air bore down damply on the marble wainscotting. The routine of the court so enveloped the jurymen, the spectators, and even the lawyers and the sheriff's men, that the outside world became unreal. Though the enlarged map of South Braintree still hung on the wall to the right of the jury box, there seemed no organic connection between the act of violence that had taken place there fifteen months before and this decorous legal game with its inherited rules.

For the newspapers the case lost its novelty, and the accounts of the trial often slipped to an inside page. What blackened the front pages now was the scandal of Mishawum Manor, a roadhouse north of Boston where, at a booze party a few years before, Adolph Zukor and several other film executives had been framed with naked call girls and shaken down for a hundred thousand dollars. The affair had been arranged through the office of District Attorney Nathan Tufts of Middlesex County. Only now was it coming to light, with Tufts, an old Yankee, and District Attorney Joseph Pelletier, an Irishman with a French name, facing disbarment.

It is almost impossible for anyone to sit through a murder trial without taking sides emotionally. With respect to Sacco and Vanzetti the sides had for the most part been taken before the defendants ever appeared in court. In the eyes of the court officers, sheriffs, police, janitors, stenographers, and the rest the two Italians were guilty, otherwise they would not be sitting in the cage. The feeling pervaded Dedham, and Frank Sibley, the dean of the local reporters, covering the trial for the Boston *Globe*, did not like it.

As the weeks passed there were other things Sibley did not like. He had not liked the squads of state troopers. He could not help but notice the antagonism between Moore and Thayer. Perhaps it was not so obvious to the jury, but as an old crime reporter he had been aware of it at once. Thanks to Moore's objections, there was a succession of lawyers' conferences at the bench with the jury sent from the room. Once when the stenographer went up to record what was being said in the buzzing cluster, Sibley heard Thayer snap, "Get the hell out of here! Who called you up here?"

Sibley, who remembered that old Chief Justice Lemuel Shaw would not discuss a current case even with his own family, was shocked by Thayer's fondness for talking about the case to newspapermen. Several times on his way to lunch at the Dedham Inn Sibley had heard Thayer announce explosively that the defendants' counsel were damn fools.

A gauntly impressive figure who wore a Windsor tie and a Latin Quarter hat and could be recognized on any Boston street a quarter-mile away, Sibley decided early that Sacco and Vanzetti were not getting a fair trial.

The last three witnesses to identify Sacco were William Tracey, the owner of the Tracey Building, the railroad detective William Heron, and Carlos Goodridge, who had heard the shooting as he was playing pool with Peter Magazu. Of the two men Tracey had noticed standing by the drugstore on the morning of the murders, one, he felt, was Sacco. "While I wouldn't be positive, I would say to the best of my recollection that was the man," was the most Katzmann could get out of him. When he was cross-examined he maintained that he felt quite sure he was right, but "would not positively say Sacco was the man."

Heron recalled the two Dagos he had seen in the South Braintree station the morning he had collared the McNamara kid. He remembered them particularly because they were smoking under the NO SMOKING sign. There was no question in his mind but that Sacco was one of the men he had seen.

Goodridge, a middle-aged man of uneasy appearance, picked out the bandit who had leaned from the car and pointed a gun at him. He was "the gentleman on the right in the cage"—Sacco.

"Are you not," Jerry McAnarney asked Goodridge "a defendant in a criminal case in this court?" Goodridge denied it, and Judge Thayer broke off the line of questioning by reminding McAnarney that a man's record as a defendant could not be brought up unless he had been convicted. There was another conference at the bench, with the jury sent out. Jerry McAnarney handed Judge Thayer a document from the clerk's office showing that on the same day Sacco and Vanzetti were arraigned Goodridge had pleaded guilty to stealing money from his employer and a week later had been placed on probation. Thayer ruled against the jury being allowed to hear this because the case had been filed. John Dever sensed that something was wrong about Goodridge, even if McAnarney could not bring out the details.

Goodridge was contradicted by four defense witnesses who, unhappily for the defense, also contradicted each other. Harry Arrogni, a barber in Damato's shop, said that when Goodridge had had his hair cut a few days after the holdup, he had told of seeing the man in the car, adding, "if I have got to say who that man was I can't say." Katzmann forced Arrogni to admit that this was the only customer's conversation he could remember from a period of fourteen months. Damato himself claimed that Goodridge had said he was inside the poolroom and did not see any of the men in the automobile.

Just before the shooting Peter Magazu had left his poolroom to wait on a customer in the shoe shop on the other side of the partition. After the car had swung by he asked Goodridge if he had seen anything. Goodridge told him, " 'I seen the men, they pointed with a gun.' I says, 'How do the men look like?' He says, 'Young man with light hair, light complexion and wore an army shirt. This job wasn't pulled off by any foreign people.' "

Andrew Manganaro, Goodridge's disgruntled employer, related that

Goodridge had told him he "saw this automobile going by and as he did one of the men pointed a gun at him and he run in. When he saw the gun he was so scared he run right in from where he was. He could not possibly remember faces." As for Goodridge's reputation for veracity, Manganaro announced with emphatic satisfaction that it was bad.

After the identifications there followed a string of residual witnesses to establish at length for the bored jury facts that were for the most part apparent at a glance. Charles Fuller and Max Wind told of finding the Buick in the Manley Woods, whereupon Moore engaged in a lengthy dispute with Judge Thayer as to whether or not the Buick should be admitted as evidence. Francis Murphy, the owner, testified that the car was his. Warren Ellis identified his stolen license plates. There was more interest in the story of William Hill, the police officer who had driven the Buick to Brockton. He had spent fifteen or twenty minutes looking the car over in the police garage and found it undamaged, yet the next morning he had noticed a bullet hole in the right rear door.

Assistant District Attorney Williams, putting Napoleon Ensher on the stand, announced that the Commonwealth would "show that this man Boda . . . was seen driving a car of the type which is of interest to us in this case; that he was associated with one Orciani, that he was associated with Sacco, and we shall ask the jury . . . to draw the inference that the car which Boda was then driving was the car concerned in this murder, and we shall tie up the car and Boda, by evidence of other association between these four men, Sacco, Vanzetti, Orciani and Boda."

Unfortunately for this theory, there was no link for Williams to connect the murder car with the one Ensher claimed to have seen Boda driving. The assistant district attorney admitted that all he could hope to show was that it was the same kind of car; he could not, however, "place the four men together at any time in this particular Buick car." For lack of such a connection, Judge Thayer excluded Ensher's testimony.

Officers Vaughn and Connolly again told their tale of arresting the two Italians, Connolly elaborating on the story he had told at the Plymouth trial. Vanzetti had so far controlled his feelings, but as Connolly told of Vanzetti's reaching for his revolver the Italian jumped up in the cage and shouted "You are a liar!" The deputies forced him down, his eyes sparkling with anger, as Connolly continued.

Following Connolly, Parmenter's widow gave brief, pathetic, and largely inconsequent testimony. Fred Loring told of picking up the cap near Berardelli's body. George Kelley, Sacco's neighbor, refused to identify the cap as Sacco's. The most Williams could get him to say was that the cap was similar in color to the cap Sacco wore and that at the Three-K factory Sacco hung his cap' on a nail each morning. Williams asked whether he knew of anything happening to the cap because it was hung on a nail. Kelley said he did not. Then Williams asked what he noticed about the condition of the cap lining he was examining on the stand. "Torn," Kelley replied. As he went on, he did his best to put in a good word for Sacco. His feeling of friendship was obvious. However, he was obliged to admit that Sacco had not worked during the Christmas week of 1919—an admission later corroborated by his sister Margaret, the Three-K paymistress.

Mrs. Glendower Evans had become such an assiduous note-taker that the sheriff finally provided a small table for her. Even from behind the table she managed to display a vast assurance and a well-bred disapproval of the proceedings. Judge Thayer took for granted the enmity of radicals and of anarchists (*arnuchists*, he pronounced it) but he expected something different from these Boston women of old families who seemed to form a phalanx at the trial and who, he felt, were people of his own class. One day, as the court adjourned, he asked Mrs. Rantoul to step into his chambers. She found him alone, waiting in his black robe. At once he asked her how she thought the trial was going. "I told him," she said later in an affidavit, "that I had not yet heard sufficient evidence to convince me that the defendants were guilty. He expressed dissatisfaction both by words, gestures, tone of voice, and manner. He said that after hearing both arguments and his charge I would certainly feel differently."

The Commonwealth rested its case on the first day of summer.

CHAPTER TEN

The Trial—II

Of the four bullets taken from Berardelli's body, plus the one removed from Parmenter in the Quincy hospital and the one found in his jacket, five had been fired from a 32-caliber pistol or pistols. The type was determined by measuring the lands (ridges) and the grooves impressed on the bullets by their passage through the barrel. In addition, the rifling had a right-hand twist that also left its mark.

The sixth bullet—the mortal one that Dr. Magrath had cut from Berardelli and marked with three needle scratches—had been fired from a 32-caliber automatic with a left-hand twist. Only the Colt among American automatics had such a twist. The question that four experts debated for several days was simply whether or not this bullet had been fired from the Colt found on Sacco.

For the jury, the experts' testimony was the most tedious part of the trial—"a wilderness of lands and grooves," as the Boston *Post* put it. Through the long sticky days the jurymen fidgeted, fanning themselves as the voices droned on.

Captain Proctor of the State Police led off for the prosecution. From the time he had arrived at South Braintree the night of the murders until Katzmann appointed Chief Stewart, he had been in charge of the investigation. At the very beginning he felt that the holdup with its careful timing was a professional job, and after the arrest of Sacco and Vanzetti he told Katzmann that Stewart had got hold of the wrong men. He still felt so. It was not, however, about his theories but as a ballistics expert that the white-haired Proctor now testified. Only three days before taking the stand he and his colleague Charles Van Amburgh and the defense expert James Burns had fired fourteen test bullets through Sacco's automatic into a box of oiled sawdust. The recovered bullets were compared with the mortal Bullet III. That bullet had a milled groove around it (known as a cannelure) that had been discontinued in more recent Winchester bullets of the same caliber. Burns was unable to obtain any of the older Winchesters corresponding to Bullet III, so used U.S. bullets as most closely resembling the obsolete type.*

To John Dever, Proctor seemed a reluctant witness. The captain first explained that he was accustomed to testing 38- and 32-caliber revolvers by pushing bullets through the barrel manually. When in his demonstration he showed himself unable to strip the Sacco pistol, Dever was not impressed. Proctor then told the jury that the five right-twist bullets had come from a Savage automatic. When the assistant district attorney asked him if he was sure, he replied: "I can be as certain of that as I can of anything." However, when Williams asked his opinion as to whether Bullet III had been fired from Sacco's Colt, Proctor phrased his answer in a much more measured manner. "My opinion is," he told Williams, "that it is consistent with being fired by that pistol." In the casual moment the ambiguity of the answer escaped Moore. Thomas McAnarney spotted it at once and nudged his brother, but wise in the ways of the police, he feared a trap. If he should now ask Proctor what he meant by consistent, Proctor might reply that he meant that the bullet had gone through the gun—and this would be so much the worse for the defendants. Thomas therefore said nothing.

As for the four shells Bostock had picked up from the gravel walk, Proctor explained that Shell W—with the identifying Winchester W on it—had been fired in one pistol, the other three in another. He compared the indentation made by the firing pin on Shell W with the indentations on the test shells fired in Sacco's pistol. The marks on both, he said, were consistent—again he used the word—with their being fired in the same weapon.

The Commonwealth's second expert was Charles Van Amburgh of the Remington Union Metallic Cartridge Company of Bridgeport, Connecticut. Before going to Remington, he had spent nine years at the Springfield Arsenal, and then periods at the Westinghouse and Colt Firearms companies. His evidence was a corroboration of Proctor's. He, too, had compared Bullet III with those recovered from the

---

* The six Winchester shells found on Sacco in the police station were of this same obsolete type, a parallel overlooked by the prosecution and barely hinted at by the defense during the trial but emphasized later.

sawdust. By measuring the lands, he had determined that the bullet had been fired from a 32-caliber Colt. As to whether he thought it had been fired from Sacco's Colt, he replied circumspectly, "I am inclined to believe that it was fired, Number III bullet was fired, from this Colt automatic pistol." He went on to say that there was a rough rust track at the bottom of the pistol barrel, and that corresponding marks could be traced on the bullet. Under cross-examination he admitted that it was common for Colts to rust at that particular place. Like Proctor, he thought that the other five bullets had come from a Savage and had been fired from the same weapon.

Burns, the first of the defense's experts to testify, had spent thirty years as a ballistics engineer with the U.S. Cartridge Company. He agreed that Bullet III could have been fired from a Colt but felt that it could also have been fired from a Bayard, a foreign make. Whatever pistol it had come from, the rifling had been fouled and corroded. The other bullets, he testified, could have been fired from a Savage, a Steyr, or a Walther. Burns produced six of the eight bullets he had fired from Sacco's Colt—the other two, he explained, he had lost. He pointed out that the lands and grooves were regular and clean. To the question whether Bullet III had been fired from Sacco's pistol his answer was: "In my opinion, no. It doesn't compare at all."

J. Henry Fitzgerald, the second defense expert, backed him up. Fitzgerald had been twenty-eight years in the weapon business and was now in charge of the testing room at the Colt Patent Firearms Company. "Number III bullet was not fired from the Sacco pistol," he told the court. "I can see no pitting or marks on bullet Number III that would correspond with a bullet coming from this gun."

With these paired contradictions the bullet testimony ended.

Berardelli had owned a 38-caliber Harrison & Richardson revolver. After his death it could not be found. It was Katzmann's contention, underlined in his summing-up, that the revolver found on Vanzetti the night of his arrest had been lifted by Sacco from the dying detective.

In Dedham Vanzetti was to tell a different story about his revolver than he had told at the Brockton police station. When he took the stand he admitted he had lied before, claiming that he had wanted to protect the friends from whom he had bought the gun. His first story—that he had bought it five years before his arrest for eighteen dollars was false; he had really owned it only two or three months, and he had bought it from Luigi Falzini, an East Boston marble cutter, who in turn had bought it not long before from Ricardo

Orciani. Instead of paying eighteen dollars for it, Vanzetti had paid five; he had never fired it; the bullets now in the revolver were there when he bought it. The reason he had bought it was to protect himself, for often when he went to buy fish he carried eighty or a hundred dollars in his pocket, and it was "a bad time, it was many crimes, many holdups, many robberies." He did not remember telling Katzmann in Brockton that he had bought a box of cartridges or that he had shot off all but six on the beach at Plymouth. If he had said this, it was not so.

Falzini took the stand after Vanzetti and recognized the revolver as his because of rust spots and a deep scratch behind the trigger guard that he had noticed when he bought it. In the time he owned it, he had never fired it or taken it apart.

For his next corroborating witness Moore brought Rexford Slater from Dexter, Maine. Before settling in Maine, Slater had worked in the same Norwood foundry as Orciani. He had bought a Harrington & Richardson revolver from his mother-in-law, a Mrs. Mogridge, who happened to bring it with her when she came from Maine on a visit. He had fired it several times, once killing a cat, and in 1919 had sold it to Orciani. He recognized it on the stand by the way the nickel plating had worn off the end of the barrel and over the cylinder. The holster—picked up by the police in searching Vanzetti's room— he also recognized from the brass knob on it, a tear in the back, and a small side-strap.

Slater was at first an argumentative witness. When Katzmann asked if another revolver of the same kind fired under the same conditions might not show the same wear, he denied that any conditions could ever be the same. As Katzmann kept pressing him, Slater's confidence began to wilt. The district attorney asked him if he was not just guessing, if he was sure that Vanzetti's revolver was the one that had belonged to him. "I am sure the same scars as on the gun I sold, and exactly the same," Slater answered in syntactical confusion. Katzmann persisted. "I did not ask you that. Are you sure that is the same gun?" Slater delayed his answer so long that Judge Thayer finally rapped out: "Answer the question!"

"I am not," he admitted.

Eldridge Atwater, Slater's brother-in-law, took the stand to say that eight years before he had often borrowed his father-in-law's Harrington & Richardson to shoot at bottles and cans. After Mogridge's death, his widow had taken the revolver with her when she went to Norwood to visit her daughter and that was the last Atwater had ever seen of it. He could not quite bring himself to say that the revolver exhibited in court was the same one he had fired seventy-five or a hundred times in Maine. The closest he would come to it was to say that "as far as those two markings, that is the revolver Mr. Mogridge had eight years ago." He had never paid any attention to the revolver's serial number.

The missing link in the ownership chain was Orciani. Some months before the trial he had given up his foundry job to become Moore's chauffeur. The fact that he was never called as a witness was not missed by the jurors. Katzmann in his summing-up made the most of it. "Why didn't you bring Orciani into this courtroom?" he demanded rhetorically. "He has been within the control of this defense. He has been outside the courtroom, and he is not produced. What is the reason?"

While there was no one in South Braintree who could say with certainty that Berardelli had his revolver with him on the day of his death, his widow testified that he generally carried it. Margaret Mahoney and the other girls in the Slater & Morrill office had seen the revolver at various times, and he had even showed it to Jimmy Bostock the Saturday before the robbery. Bostock knew that it was nickel-plated and that the guard carried it in his hip pocket, but what kind it was he did not know. No one had seen the bandits take anything from Berardelli's body. Lewis Wade saw the guard reach for his hip pocket as he was falling, and Peter McCullum saw one of the bandits holding a "white" revolver in his left hand.

Sarah Berardelli, a sad, illiterate Jewish woman, told what she knew of her husband's revolver. It was like Vanzetti's. Three weeks before the murder her husband had taken it to Boston to be repaired —it had a "spring broke." Sarah had accompanied her husband and they had gone to a store on Washington Street which—with prompting from the district attorney—she remembered: the Iver Johnson Company. Berardelli had been given a claim check. This he turned over to Parmenter, who then let him take another gun that looked just like the first. Whether anyone had picked up the gun at Iver Johnson's, whether it had come back into her husband's possession, Sarah Berardelli did not know.

Lincoln Wadsworth, the clerk in charge of repairs at Iver Johnson's, said that according to his records he had received a 38 Harrington & Richardson, the property of Alex Berardelli, on March 20, 1920, to which he had given the repair number 94765. George Fitzemeyer, the gunsmith on the fifth floor, testified that he had been given a revolver with that repair number sometime between the nineteenth and the twenty-second of March. He had repaired it and marked it "H. & R., revolver 32, new hammer, half an hour." Since he repaired twenty-five or thirty revolvers a day, he could not be sure of the caliber of this particular one. On inspecting Vanzetti's revolver he said that it had a new hammer. "The firing pin," he said, "does not show of ever being struck." Williams, conducting the questioning, neglected to ask him whether the Vanzetti revolver was the one he had repaired.

Fitzemeyer's testimony about the hammer contradicted that of the defense ballistics experts, Burns and Fitzgerald. Burns stated that to the best of his knowledge the hammer was no newer than the rest of the weapon, but admitted that the revolver "bore little indication of being fired much." Fitzgerald maintained that "the hammer in this revolver has every indication of being as old and used as much as any other part of the pistol." Thinking it over, John Dever felt that Fitzemeyer, with thirty years' experience taking revolvers apart, ought to know what he was talking about.

According to James Jones, the manager of the Iver Johnson firearms department, the gun with repair number 94765 must have been delivered because it was no longer in the store. When a repaired gun was not called for in a reasonable time the firm's policy was to lock it away until after stocktaking time in January. If still unclaimed, it was then sold. Iver Johnson kept a record of every sale. There was no record of Berardelli's revolver being sold. Unfortunately, records of delivery were not made, and there seemed to be no written record that this revolver had been delivered.

If the serial number of the missing revolver had been recorded when it was left for repair, it could have been determined at once whether or not Berardelli's was the one found on Vanzetti—but at this point, as at so many in the case, the direct proof turned as elusive as a will-o'-the-wisp.

To Ripley, the jury foreman, Vanzetti's revolver looked just like the Harrington & Richardson he himself owned. The last time he had used it—to fire some blanks at the Quincy firemen's muster—he had found three bullets in the cylinder. These he had extracted, putting them in the vest of the suit he had worn to court. At the next recess, when he was downstairs in the dormitory, he searched his vest pockets and found the bullets still there. He later showed them to Hersey and McNamara, and Dever also had a glimpse of them.

While Ripley was downstairs examining his bullets, Thomas

McAnarney in the upstairs corridor happened to run into Captain Proctor and the Commissioner of Public Safety, Colonel Alfred Foote, and they chatted together before court resumed. McAnarney never forgot Proctor's parting remark to the commissioner: "These are not the right men. Oh, no, you haven't got the right men."

On Wednesday, June 22, the short opening statement for the defense was made by William Callahan, who, although he had been dropped as Vanzetti's counsel in the Plymouth trial, still remained associated with Sacco's defense. Whatever his capacities, he kept the confidence of both defendants to the end. Moore wanted him, as a local lawyer, to present the case, and this was one of the few times he emerged from his background role. Callahan first reminded the jurors that the defendants were presumed innocent. Then he promised that the defense would show what Vanzetti was doing on April 15 and would prove that Sacco was in Boston getting a passport. In addition, the defense would offer witnesses to show that the men in the South Braintree bandit car were not Sacco and Vanzetti.

Moore intended to swamp the prosecution with witnesses. After a protracted exposition by Charles Breed, a civil engineer who had made maps and photographs of the Pearl Street area for the defense, Moore produced Edward Carter, a cutter at the lower Slater & Morrill factory. As the first shots were fired Carter had looked out a window and up the street to what, until he saw a man drop, he thought was a bunch of boys fooling. From his distance of eighty yards and with the sun in his eyes the men had been indistinct. He was unable to say whether or not the defendants were the men he had seen.

Frank Burke remembered the man in the front seat who had thrust a pistol in his face as the Buick passed the cobbler's shop. That man was "very dark complected and needed a shave very badly." Burke also noticed a man with a "short cropped mustache" in the back seat. But when Callahan asked him if the defendants were the men he had seen ten feet away in the car, the most he could get Burke to say was: "I would say they were not." John Dever was not favorably impressed. Burke seemed to him to be "altogether too anxious at times to volunteer information and at other times evasive and vacillating."

Katzmann wanted to know how Burke knew the car was a Buick. Because, Burke said, it was like the car belonging to lawyer Callahan in which he had ridden to court this morning. His powers of observation were at a discount when it turned out that Callahan's car was a Hudson.

Albert Frantello, who had run into Parmenter and Berardelli as they left the Hampton House, recalled that on his way up from the lower factory he had met two men leaning against the Rice & Hutchins pipe fence. He particularly remembered the dark one in a dark cap who needed a shave, for he had passed so close he could have touched him. The other man had a lighter complexion. They were talking to each other in "the American language," and he was sure that neither of them was either of the men in the cage.

As part of his cross-examination Katzmann led Frantello to the jury box, asked him to observe two jurors, then turn away and describe them. Although both jurors were clean-shaven, Frantello described one of them as having a mustache as well as a nonexistent watch-chain. Immediately after the murders he had told Brouillard that the dark man by the fence was "a regular wop"; now he denied that the man was an Italian. Whether or not he had told Brouillard that he did not know the language the men were speaking he could not recall, but whatever he might have said then, he now insisted that they were speaking "American."

Wilfred Pierce and Lawrence Ferguson, shoe-cutters who had been working with Mark Carrigan on the third floor of the Hampton House, were no more satisfactory witnesses for the defense than Carrigan had been for the prosecution. Both had heard the shots and looked out the window as the touring car crossed the tracks. Both had seen a dark man climb from the rear seat to the front. Pierce saw him fire a shot. When asked if the man was either of the defendants, he would say no more than "I don't think it was, but I am not positive." Ferguson was equally uncertain: "It may or it may not have been. I don't know positively." The most that their testimony seemed to show—and this by contrast—was the extraordinary vision and tenacious memory of Frances Devlin and Mary Splaine.

Through the last of June the hot spell was unrelenting. To speed up the trial Judge Thayer agreed to extend the session from 9 A.M. until 6 P.M., but he rejected the jurors' suggestion for evening sessions. The days followed each other torpidly. Sacco and Vanzetti sat upright in the cage, occasionally whispering to one another; the jurymen sat fanning themselves. The succession of witnesses accelerated and the spectators thinned out. Mrs. Evans, the "angel for the radicals" as the *Post* called her, continued to write voluminously at her desk. Her hats changed frequently, her attitude did not.

With June fading, Moore found the defense again in the familiar position of running short of money. The fifty thousand dollars collected over the past year was gone, used up in investigations and fees and a hundred other unavoidable expenses. Judge Thayer offered to allow the defense to proceed *in forma pauperis* with some of their costs borne by the Commonwealth, but this humiliation Moore refused to accept. On June 29 with the defense lacking funds even to pay witnesses, Mrs. Evans produced $1500 to tide them over for the week. At the end of the week she added to this all her available income, $2950, plus $600 contributed by her friends. Mrs. Cerise Jack handed over $100.

The sixteen-man crew that had been digging the excavation across the street from Rice & Hutchins and that Mrs. Nichols saw cut and run when the shooting started could scarcely be considered the most reliable of witnesses, but Moore with his weight-of-numbers tactics now brought in five of them, of whom only one could speak English.

William Foley, the driver of a dump truck, had just left the excavation with a load when the shots rang out and the Buick swayed up Pearl Street. Foley, headed in the other direction, saw only the driver clearly and his description of him was unique: "eyeglasses, short mustache, soft hat, high cheek-bones, sallow complexion." He also had a glimpse of another man in a cap sitting in the rear seat. At this point he could not recall the men's faces, but they were not the men in the cage. Katzmann, weaving back to Boda, asked Foley several times if the driver was not wearing a velour hat. Foley remembered it as a soft hat, but was positive it was not velour. He admitted that he could not tell whether or not the man in the back seat was one of the defendants.

Emilio Falcone, who had been shoveling dirt into Foley's truck just before the shooting, testified through the court interpreter, Joseph Ross, who also acted as Judge Thayer's chauffeur. Falcone thought that he had been forty or fifty feet away from the shooting, near enough at least so that he heard Parmenter groan as he dropped. The man who shot him was "kind of pale, light, pale." Another man had picked up the money-box. Under Callahan's rather fussy questioning as to whether the two men in the cage resembled the men in the car, Falcone said they did not. Callahan's reiterations, doubly tedious through translation, made Falcone lose his temper. "Well, for God's sake," he replied, "why do you ask me again?"

Three Spaniards who had been working next to Falcone testified through an interpreter of their own. Pedro Iscorla, on his way to get a drink of water, had seen a "high, thin, slim, light fellow" shoot

Parmenter and a dark man shoot Berardelli. These men were not the defendants. Henry Cerro had seen a light gunman who resembled neither of the defendants. Like Iscorla, Sibriano Guidierris had seen a light man and a little dark man with a dark cap. Each shot a different man. Neither gunman resembled the men in the cage.

Moore now brought in eight of the railroad workers who had seen the Buick pass. They had all noticed the meager light-complexioned driver and four of them had seen the dark man next to him. All were positive that the defendants had not been in the car. Nicola Gatti, one of the workers, had known Sacco in Milford eight years earlier— the only witness of the crime who had previously known either of the defendants. In spite of the remonstrances of the foreman, he had pushed ahead of the others when he heard the shots until as the Buick passed he was standing just behind the gate-tender. He had been that close, and he had seen three men distinctly: the pale driver, the dark man beside him, and a man in the back who was firing a gun. Sacco was none of these men—nor was Vanzetti.

One of the track workers, Joseph Cellucci, testified in English. He had recently joined the Navy and appeared on the stand in uniform. As soon as he had heard the shots he had thrown down his shovel. Ricci, the foreman, had tried to stop him, but he had ducked away and was only about five feet from the Buick as it passed. A dark bristly man half-kneeling between the front and back seats had leveled a revolver and fired at him, the shot winging so close to his ear that he was deaf for three days. Cellucci had only a glimpse of the driver but it was enough to convince him that neither of the prisoners had been in the getaway car.

Barbara Liscomb, who had looked directly down at the bareheaded gunman, was considered the star witness for the defense. The contorted face of the dark man with the pistol who stared up at her as she stood at a second-floor window of Rice & Hutchins, had made an imprint in her mind she could never forget. "I would always remember that face," she told the court. She was "positively sure" it was not the face of Sacco or Vanzetti.

Jenny Novelli described the man she had seen in the car who looked so much like her friend as having "dark hair and a dark complexion, like a man that has to shave every day." Neither prisoner was that man. Just after the arrest of Sacco and Vanzetti, Hellyer, the Pinkerton operative, had shown Mrs. Novelli a photograph of Sacco and she said it greatly resembled the man next to the driver. She now denied ever making such a tentative identification. Sacco was not the man.

Hellyer himself would take the stand almost at the end of the trial and testify that when he interviewed Mrs. Novelli on April 17, 1920, she had described the man beside the driver as "twenty-seven years, five feet seven inches tall, slim build, black hair, black eyes, dark complexion, thin features, wide mouth, smooth-shaven, but appeared to be a man who could grow a heavy beard from the dark stubble on his face." Hellyer's Pinkerton report, which was not produced in evidence, recorded a markedly different description of the man: "27 years, 5 feet eight inches, medium build, light brown hair, fair complexion and smooth shaven, wore a cap but cannot recollect what else he wore."

Mrs. Novelli was followed by minor witnesses whose fleeting glimpses, although not enough to establish much about the other passengers in the Buick, at least corroborated the now-undisputed fact that the driver was a pale, fair man. Elmer Chase, who had been loading his truck in front of the Co-operative Society as the Buick passed, had looked down at the driver and the bareheaded man next to him. He was positive that neither of the men he saw that day were the men in the cage. Walter Desmond, the tobacco salesman who had met and passed the Buick on his way from Randolph, had seen the pale-faced driver but scarcely noticed the man next to him. All he could say in court was that the driver was not one of the defendants. Wilson Dorr, working in the sandpit with John Lloyd on the Stoughton Post Road, had seen four "light complected," men in the Buick as it passed within twenty-five feet of him. All had looked directly at him. None of them resembled Sacco or Vanzetti.

It was to be Vanzetti's claim that he had spent April 15 in North Plymouth going his usual rounds with his pushcart. Before he himself took the stand to make this claim, the defense introduced witnesses to corroborate it. The first was Joseph Rosen, a thirty-three-year-old cloth peddler from Dorchester.

On the fifteenth Rosen arrived in Plymouth at ten minutes to eight. After eating breakfast at Ventura's Restaurant on Court Street, he had taken the streetcar to North Plymouth, carrying a valise of men's suiting and some swatches. He met Vanzetti near Cherry Street and showed him a piece of blue serge that was enough for a suit. He offered it cheap because it had a couple of small holes in it. Vanzetti wanted to let Alfonsina Brini see the cloth. Together Rosen and Vanzetti walked several blocks to Cherry Court, where the Brinis had recently moved. Alfonsina knew cloth because she had once worked in a woolen mill. She felt the material and said it was a good buy. Vanzetti paid Rosen $12.25, then gave him another fifty cents when he complained he was losing money. It must have been about twelve o'clock when they left the Brinis', for as they came out the whistles were blowing and people were hurrying home from the Cordage for lunch.

That afternoon Rosen had gone back to the center of Plymouth, peddled more cloth, stopped in again at Ventura's, and finally left on the last train at 6:10. He had got off at Whitman, about halfway between Plymouth and Braintree, and spent the night in a dollar room at Littlefield's Rooming House. The next day he had continued to peddle his goods in Whitman.

Katzmann spent an afternoon cross-examining Rosen, using the old legal trick known as taking the witness over the hurdles. Where, the district attorney asked Rosen, had he been on May 15, 1920; June 15, 1920; April 15, 1921; May 15, 1921, June 15, 1921?

Rosen could not say, but he maintained he had particular reasons for remembering April 15, 1920. In the morning his wife had paid his delinquent 1918 poll tax and when he returned home next day she had given him the dated and receipted bill he now produced in court. Also, the evening of the fifteenth "it was all boiling" in Whitman about the South Braintree murders. Lillian Shuler, who ran Littlefield's Rooming House, later corroborated Rosen by producing a record of having rented him a room the night of the fifteenth.

When Vanzetti's picture was published in the papers after his arrest and Rosen saw it and the words "fish peddler," it reminded him of the day he sold the piece of blue cloth to the Italian in North Plymouth. He went to ask Alfonsina Brini about the matter the next time he happened to be in Plymouth, and it was through her that he came into the case.

Alfonsina herself again appeared to testify for her old friend. Katzman had agreed not to refer to the Plymouth trial in return for the defense's renouncing any evidence as to the peaceful and law-abiding reputation of the defendants. Regardless, in his summing-up he called Alfonsina "a stock, convenient and ready witness as well as friend who . . . in another case when another date was alleged, testified to the whereabouts of this same Vanzetti on that other date there involved."

Alfonsina told much the same story that Rosen had told of the two men coming in to show her the damaged cloth. She recalled the date as the fifteenth because she had been ailing at the time and Dr. Shurtleff had come from Plymouth to see her on the fourteenth and sixteenth. In between those visits the Cordage nurse had called.

Gertrude Matthews, a nurse at the Plymouth Cordage Company, said she had visited Alfonsina between the fifteenth and the twenty-fifth but could not recall the exact dates. LeFavre Brini, Alfonsina's daughter, told of Vanzetti's coming to their house at about ten o'clock the morning of the fifteenth with some fish which he had left in the sink. He had come back about noon with a peddler and she saw him hand a length of cloth to her mother. She recalled the date because her mother had been in the hospital and it was just a week after she had had to quit her own job at the Gorton-Pew Fisheries to care for her.

Angelo Guidobone, a rug-weaver who lived in Suosso's Lane, told through an interpreter of buying some codfish from Vanzetti during the lunch hour. He remembered it was Thursday the fifteenth because on the nineteenth he had had his appendix removed. When Katzmann asked him if he could not have bought his fish on the thirteenth or the fourteenth, Guidobone said that he bought fish fresh on Thursday to eat on Friday. "Do you think I keep fish in the house for a week?" he asked the district attorney indignantly.

Melvin Corl, a Plymouth fisherman from whom Vanzetti some times bought his supplies, recalled April 15 as the day he had been painting his boat at Jesse's Boatyard. About two o'clock Vanzetti had come down to the water's edge and stopped to talk with him, saying that the fish business was so bad he was thinking of looking for another job. Corl remembered the date because he had planned to put his boat in the water the next day; however, he had not managed to finish it until two days later—the seventeenth, his wife's birthday. On that same day, the seventeenth, he had towed a boat belonging to Joseph Morey from Duxbury to Plymouth.

Frank Jesse, the boatyard owner, remembered seeing Corl painting his boat and Vanzetti standing talking to him, but he could not recall the date. Joseph Morey testified that Corl had towed his boat on the seventeenth; he remembered the date because it was two days before Patriot's Day. Under cross-examination he admitted that he and Mrs. Corl had talked it over and finally decided that the seventeenth must have been the date. Katzmann finally edged him into admitting that neither he nor Corl was completely sure.

John Dever was not sure either. Corl at first had seemed convincing, but Dever now felt that if these people could not be certain about a date, they could not be certain about anything.

For several days Jerry McAnarney had noticed among the courtroom spectators a man with a high forehead, long nose, and drooping mustache so combined that he could have served as Vanzetti's double. He turned out to be an unemployed Italian named Joseph Scavitto who had known Sacco slightly, and who, having nothing else to do, was spending his days at the trial. Jerry sent him, with a borrowed hat that intensified his resemblance to Vanzetti, to have some photographs made. If witnesses like Austin Cole could be persuaded to identify Scavitto from a photograph as the man they had seen, it might do much to establish Vanzetti's alibi.

Nothing came of the idea, but Scavitto's appearance in court resulted in a comic interlude. Asked on the stand what his business was, he replied that he was in the mosaic business. Asked where his place of business was, he answered: "I ain't got no business." From the flat pages of the record it is hard to determine just why his appearance and his explanation caused so much amusement, but according to the *Herald*, when he told of picking up someone else's hat "the court filled with laughter."

It would have been logical for Vanzetti to have followed his alibi witnesses to the stand. However, they had concluded on Friday, July 1, and with the Fourth coming on Monday, Moore did not want to have Vanzetti's testimony interrupted by the holiday week end. In his place several witnesses were introduced to account for Sacco's whereabouts on the day of the murders.

The first, John Williams, a mild-looking advertising agent, said that he had met Sacco in Boston on April 15 between 1:15 and 1:30 at Boni's Restaurant in North Square. He had gone into Boni's for lunch and had seen an acquaintance, Professor Guadagni, sitting at a table with a stranger whom he introduced as Nick Sacco. Guadagni had finished his meal and was smoking a cigar. As the three talked together, Sacco said he planned to go back to Italy and was going to get his passport that afternoon.

Williams, who sold advertising space in several foreign-language newspapers, including *La Notizia*, was well known in Boston. It was not so well known that he was a left-wing socialist and had been an associate of Trotsky and Bukharin in New York in 1917. Every Thursday he made the rounds of the small North End factories soliciting help-wanted ads for the Saturday editions. On April 15, according to his advertising book, he had taken an order from the Washington Knitting Mills. Later in the afternoon he had gone uptown to see his doctor, Howard Gibbs, who was treating him for asthma.

After the arrest of Sacco and Vanzetti, Felicani asked Williams if he remembered seeing Professor Guadagni and Sacco at Boni's. Williams said he did. Felicani than asked him if he realized this was the date of the South Braintree crime. Williams had not thought of it, but checking back in his advertising book to the Washington Knitting Mills order, he found it was so. Felicani and Williams felt that this fixed Sacco in Boston instead of in South Braintree. As Williams explained it in court: "The fact that I secured this order and the fact that I met this young man down there, and the fact that he was said to be going for his passport; all of those things brought a sequence of events back to me, and I recalled the incident very easily."

Under Katzmann's cross-examination Williams could not remember the dates of other visits to his doctor, or any advertisements he had taken on April 14, or any other occasions when he had met Guadagni. However, Dr. Gibbs testified that although he treated Williams regularly, he had seen him only once in April and that was on the fifteenth.

Albert Bosco, one of the editors of *La Notizia*, was another witness who claimed to have seen Sacco in the restaurant. Bosco was already at Boni's with a man named Reffi when Guadagni came in with Sacco and introduced him as "the man that is going to Italy." Then Guadagni talked about the banquet that the Franciscan Fathers of North Bennett Street were giving at their priory that same day in honor of James T. Williams, Jr., editor of the Boston *Transcript*, whom the Italian government had just made a *Commendatore* in recognition of his war work. The next day Bosco published an account of the banquet in *La Notizia*—and also ran a story about the South Braintree killings. When Guadagni spoke to him after the arrests about his meeting with Sacco, Bosco went to the newspaper files and found that the banquet they had discussed in Boni's restaurant had been held on April 15.

Another witness, a contractor named Angelo Monello, had known Sacco for several months before his arrest. On April 15, just before noon, they had run into each other on Hanover Street. Monello had the date fixed in his mind because on Sunday the eighteenth he had tickets for *Madame X*, playing at the Tremont Theatre with the great Italian artist Mimi Aguglia. Both he and Sacco were amateur actors and belonged to dramatic clubs, and they had talked about the play. Katzmann at once took Monello over the hurdles, asking if he had talked with anyone about the play on April 16, 17, 13, 12, 19, 21, 28. All Monello could say was that he did not remember.

Michael Kelley and his son Leon appeared willingly as witnesses for Sacco, but because of the agreement of counsel they were not allowed—as they had intended—to testify as to his character. Katzmann hovered over any such mention with an instant objection. Michael Kelley managed to say, however, that he trusted Sacco with the keys to the Three-K factory and that every night the place had been in his hands. Early in the spring Sacco had shown Michael Kelley a black-bordered letter saying that his mother had died. The letter, from Sacco's father, begging him to come home, was then translated to the jury.

District Attorney Williams now read a deposition by Giuseppe Adrower, made in Rome. In April 1920, Adrower was a clerk in the Italian consulate in Boston. Sacco, he deposed, had appeared early in April about a passport and had been told to come back with two photographs. On April 15 he had returned with an oversize family photograph. Adrower remembered the date because it was "a very quiet day in the Royal Italian Consulate and since such a large photograph had never before been presented for use on a passport I took it in and showed it to the Secretary of the Consulate. We laughed and talked over the incident. I remember observing the date in the office of the Secretary on a large pad calendar while we were discussing the photograph. The hour was around two or a quarter after two, as I remember about a half an hour later I locked the door of the office for the day." When Professor Guadagni came to the consulate the week after the arrests to ask about the incident, Adrower could not remember Sacco, but after Guadagni showed him the oversize photograph he remembered both it and the date and had no doubt about either.

The written cross-interrogatory contained the by-now-familiar Katzmann hurdles. Adrower had stated that between a hundred fifty and two hundred people a day came to the consulate to inquire about passports. He was asked to give the name of each person he talked with on April 17, 19, 21, 24, 29, and May 2, 3, and 4. He could not remember their names. He was then asked to describe every person with whom he talked on those days. "I cannot describe them in detail," he admitted. In the defense's redirect interrogatory, Adrower stated that although many people appeared at the consulate with family group photographs, none had ever brought in such a large one as Sacco produced.

Friday's last new witness was Dominic Ricci, a carpenter living in a boarding house in South Stoughton, not far from Sacco's bungalow. He had known Sacco several years. The morning of April 15, he said, he had seen Sacco on the Stoughton railroad platform at about half-past seven and Sacco had told him he was going to Boston to get a passport. Next day, seeing Sacco in the Three-K factory at eight o'clock, Ricci had talked with him about the newspaper accounts of the South Braintree murders.

Katzmann, with deceiving gentleness, asked Ricci if he had worked on the eighteenth. Ricci said he had. Katzmann asked him about the twenty-fifth, May 2, May 9, 16, 23, 30, and June 6, consulting a pocket diary each time he asked. A titter spread through the court-room as the realization came that each of these dates was a Sunday. The realization did not come as quickly to the embarrassed Ricci. Katzmann continued leading him on a trail of Sundays through the rest of the year, finally closing his diary with mock weariness and smiling ironically at the bewildered Italian. "I have got to the end of my calendar. You worked every Sunday, didn't you, from then on? That is all."

George Kelley now reappeared briefly to say that on April 16 he had got to the factory at seven in the morning and Sacco had already been working there three-quarters of an hour.

Friday evening about ten o'clock, long after the courthouse gate had been bolted and the jury locked in for the night, John Drummond, the courthouse janitor, heard a noise in the library and found Jerry McAnarney lying collapsed on the center table. One of the deputy sheriffs drove him back to Quincy. Actually, Jerry was malingering to give Moore an extra day he claimed he needed for tracking down a new witness. Next morning Thomas McAnarney told Judge Thayer that his brother was under a doctor's care and asked for a postponement. Thayer adjourned the court until Tuesday, July 5. The prospect of the long week end dismayed the jurors, most of whom had hoped to be back with their families by the Fourth. However, they felt somewhat more cheerful after Judge Thayer told the sheriff to see that they were taken on an outing over the holiday. When John Dever heard that after a month of sitting still they were going to the beach, he felt the way he used to when the circus came to town.

The rest of Saturday the jurors spent as usual—playing cards, talking, reading the cut-up remains of the newspapers, and going out to meals. Sunday afternoon they went on their usual ride, this time through Wellesley and the Newtons.

Monday morning, after breakfast at the Dedham Inn, they went by bus to the wooden-turreted Cliff House at North Scituate. There they sat in rocking chairs on the wide veranda, looking out over the sea and enjoying the breeze until their shore dinner was ready. Dever long remembered that meal—clams and lobsters and more lobsters. George Gerard, the Stoughton photographer, had a Graflex with him. He had been born in Paris, and the others kidded him at the table, telling him it was too bad he couldn't go down on the beach and take French pictures of the girls. During the afternoon Sheriff Capen produced a fishpole for each man and they sat on the rocks in the sun, joking and fishing.

It was almost dark by the time they got back to the courthouse. Dever felt contented even though his face and arms were red and the skin tingled on the back of his neck. As he went up the courthouse steps he noticed fireflies zigzagging about.

◇◇◇◇◇◇◇◇◇◇◇◇◇◇◇◇◇◇◇◇◇◇◇◇◇◇◇◇◇

CHAPTER ELEVEN

The Trial—III

On July 5 Jerry McAnarney resumed his place within the bar enclosure. Attendance had fallen off in the last week, but on this Tuesday morning every seat was occupied in anticipation of the defendants' taking the stand. The first witness was Aldeah Florence of Quincy, with whom Sarah Berardelli had boarded after her husband's death. Testifying for the defense, she said that Sarah had told her a few days after her husband's funeral that he might still be alive if only he had not left his revolver in the repair shop. Her examination and cross-examination lasted less than ten minutes. Then came a pause, with Moore and the McAnarneys whispering together, while the district attorney stood by, smiling knowingly.

Finally Jerry McAnarney turned toward the cage and asked "Will the defendant Vanzetti be brought forward?" A murmur ran through the courtroom. It was the moment that everyone had been awaiting since the beginning of the trial. A deputy unlocked the metal door. Quietly, Vanzetti stepped forward and raised his hand in oath before Clerk Worthington. The receding hairline of his domed forehead, the wrinkles around his eyes, the slight sag of flesh under his chin, above all his drooping mustache, made him look at least fifteen years older than thirty-three. He was dressed neatly in a dark suit, white shirt, high stiff collar, and black bow tie. On the stand he told his story in an assured manner, using few gestures, answering all questions without hesitation.

Guided by Jerry McAnarney, he told briefly of his early life, then of his years of wandering until he ended up with the Brinis in Plymouth. The rest had by now become a familiar story. On April 15, he said, he had been peddling fish in North Plymouth. Almost at the corner of Castle Street he had met Rosen with his bolt of cloth and they had gone to the Brinis' together. About one o'clock he had sold all his fish and was going down Ocean Street with his empty pushcart when he saw Mr. Corl painting his boat. He stopped to talk with him and while they were talking Mr. Jesse, the boatbuilder, came along, and also a Mr. Holmes from the lumberyard. They chatted a while, and after he left Mr. Corl he had gone home with his pushcart, changed his clothes, and cooked his evening meal. What he had done that evening he did not now remember. The next morning he went to Marvelli's store to buy a Boston *Post* and find out what time the tide would be low so that he could dig clams. He dug clams most of the day and afterward sold them. On April 17 in the morning he tried to get a job at the garage they were building in front of the carbarn. There was no work there, however, so in the afternoon he took the train to Whitman and from there the streetcar to Brockton where he had eaten supper with a friend named Caldera and afterward gone on to Boston.

He stayed overnight with a friend, Vincent Colarossi, and next morning, Sunday, had breakfast with him and Felicani in Scollay Square; later they had dinner at Boni's with a group of friends. They spent the afternoon at the Naturalization Club in East Boston and at the end of the day Vanzetti had gone back to Plymouth.

On Monday he went around Plymouth looking without success for a job. The next day he tried to get fish from Antonio Carbone down on the pier, but fish seemed as scarce as jobs. He was at Carbone's house that evening paying a bill for fish and Carbone had just given him two cigars when Chief of Police Armstrong came in to tell them an Italian fisherman named Pacci had drowned. Two days later Vanzetti happened to visit the dock, and there was a dory near the wharf with Pacci's body in it and the undertaker's car waiting on the siding. He told the men in the dory it would be easier if they brought the body to the shore and took it up the three cement steps to Water Street.

All that week he could find neither work nor fish. On Saturday he went to Boston, again staying with Colarossi. At their Sunday meeting in the Naturalization Club his friends asked him to go to New York on their affairs and he left that night. Three days later he returned, coming back on the Providence boat.

May Day found him again in Boston with Colarossi, and the next day there was the usual get-together at the Naturalization Club. Monday morning he spent at the fish piers; everywhere he went he found the prices too high. In the afternoon he took the train to Stoughton and stayed overnight at Sacco's house. Next day he spent around the house while Sacco went to Boston to pick up his passport. In the evening Sacco came back with Orciani on the latter's motorcycle, and the three of them agreed to meet the following day.

That last day he and Sacco cut wood while Rosina packed. Just by chance he had pocketed four shotgun shells he found on Sacco's kitchen cabinet.* Vanzetti told in detail about the evening of May 5: how Orciani, with Boda, had gone on ahead, and how he had composed a notice for the next Sunday's meeting. Sacco had thought the notice too long, so he had cut out some of it. Although they had agreed to meet Orciani and Boda at Elm Square, there was no sign of them when they arrived. Only when they were walking over the railroad bridge near Simon Johnson's house had they seen the motorcycle coming along from Brockton.

After talking about the license plates with Johnson they had given up their project. Boda had then told Vanzetti: "I and Orciani go with the machine and you take a car and you go home. We will look for a new number. When I am ready I will tell you and we will come here some other day. We will come to take the automobile."

They had needed the automobile "to carry books and newspapers." As Vanzetti vaguely explained it, they planned to collect this unspecified material "from any house and from any house in five or six places, five or six towns. Three, five or six people have plenty of literature, and we went, we intend to take that out and put that in the proper place . . . not subject to policemen go in and call for, see the literature, see the papers, see the books, as in that time they went through in the house of many men who were active in the radical movement and socialist and labor movement, and go then and take letters and take books and take newspapers, and put men in jail and deported many."

Everyone in the courtroom from Judge Thayer to the defendants themselves knew that this was the great divide. In these few sentences the issue of radicalism, moving so long just below the surface, finally emerged. Katzmann at once objected, and his objection was a warning to the defense. The district attorney was perfectly willing to avoid

---

* The two shells that had not been tampered with during the Plymouth trial were admitted in evidence at Dedham after several witnesses claimed to have seen what they thought was a shotgun protruding from the rear of the getaway car.

any reference to the political views of the two anarchists if the defense would agree to do the same. For the latter it was a peculiar dilemma. Moore was aware of the latent syllogism that the jurors no doubt then shared with most native-born Americans. An anarchist is capable of anything; Sacco and Vanzetti are anarchists; Sacco and Vanzetti are capable of anything: Q.E.D. Yet to go along with the district attorney, to gloss over the defendants' political beliefs, would be to destroy any explanation except that of consciousness of guilt for their actions on the night of their arrest.

Before Vanzetti took the stand, Judge Thayer had advised the McAnarneys that they had better consider whether or not they were going to inject the radical issue into the trial. Moore insisted there was no alternative. John McAnarney told his brothers the same thing: that the defendants would have to tell about their connection with the radical movement fully and frankly. Only thus could they account for their equivocal behavior.

When Vanzetti from the stand finally pronounced the words *radical movement*, John McAnarney was just leaving the courtroom. "As I was passing out," he testified six years later before the Lowell Committee, "Judge Thayer looking over to me, well in his peculiar way of laughing or smiling, sort of threw back his head as much as to say, 'Well you see Mr. McAnarney it is coming out.' That is what he was telling me by his facial gesture. That stands out clearly in my mind. The government would have wanted that kept out of the case I am thoroughly satisfied because how could the men explain the facts?"

Vanzetti admitted he had been in West Bridgewater once, six years before his arrest, but said he had never been there again until May 5. He had never been to East Braintree, had never asked directions of a stranger on the South Shore train, and he had not been in South Braintree on April 15, 1920. When Jerry McAnarney asked him why he had lied to Chief Stewart in the Brockton police station he answered: "Because I was scared to give the names and addresses of my friends as I know that almost all of them have some books and some newspapers in their house by which authority take a reason for arresting them and deport them."

The direct examination continued until midafternoon. Then the district attorney took over with a cross-examination that was to last through the following morning. For this climax Katzmann pushed Williams aside and took full command. His first question was barbed.

"So you left Plymouth, Mr. Vanzetti, in May 1917, to dodge the

draft, did you?" All that Vanzetti could answer was "Yes, sir." Katzmann made him admit that he had run away so that he would not
have to be a soldier.

"If I refused to go to war," the nettled Vanzetti told his inter-
rogator, "I don't refuse because I don't like this country or I don't
like the people of this country. I will refuse even if I was in Italy and
you tell me it is a long time I am in this country, and I tell you that
in this country as long time I am, that I found plenty good people
and some bad people, but that I was always working hard as a man
can work, and I have always lived very humble and—" Katzmann,
who had allowed him to go on that far, now demanded that the
answer be stricken out.

Vanzetti's story shaped itself awkwardly through the counterpoint
of questions and answers. Katzmann hinted that when he was working on the railroad at Springfield he had driven a truck. Vanzetti
agreed that there were trucks used, but denied he had ever driven
one—he did not know how to drive, still did not know. The district
attorney then asked him what he had really intended to do the night
he and Sacco had gone to West Bridgewater. To John Dever the
answer did not seem very cohesive: "We want to take the automobile,
and then my intention is to take the automobile with Boda, because
I do not know how to drive the automobile, to go to Bridgewater
and if we will be able to find the party, because I do not remember
the address of the party. I do not know exactly where he lived. We
will tell to Pappi about telling the Italian people of Bridgewater to
come in Brockton next Sunday at the speech, and after I found
Pappi, and speak to Pappi, go toward Plymouth and speak with
my friends if I can find some friends who want to take the responsibility of receiving such books in their house, in his house."

Vanzetti admitted that he had lied to Katzmann in the Brockton
station the morning after his arrest, even after the district attorney
had told him he was not compelled to answer questions. He had lied
about his revolver, about buying the cartridges and firing them, about
knowing Boda, about the motorcycle. "I was scared," he explained.
Admitting that most of these lies would not have helped conceal the
names and addresses of his friends, he still insisted that he had
lied because he had been frightened about his friends' safety and
because Salsedo's death in New York had made him afraid of the
police.

Katzmann hemmed him in, getting him to say there were half a
dozen people in Bridgewater from whom they were planning to

collect literature, forcing him to confess he knew none of their names. The district attorney then questioned him about his stay in Mexico, leading quietly up to the thundering demand: "And are you the man, Mr. Vanzetti, that on May ninth was going to advise in public meeting men who had gone to war? Are you that man?"

"Yes, sir," Vanzetti told him. "I am that man, not the man you want me, but I am that man."

When Vanzetti had first been questioned in Brockton he could not recall anything specific that he had been doing on April 15. Katzmann now wanted to know how he could recall so much of that day fifteen months later. It was, Vanzetti told him, because in Brockton he had no idea he was going to be charged with murder. But "three or four weeks after my arrest I understand enough to see that I have to be very careful to save my life and my liberty and I have to remember."

Thinking back, he was able to reconstruct most of the day by checking with what he had been doing on the following Monday, Patriot's Day, and on other days. As for the night of his arrest, he had planned to go on to Plymouth with Boda in the Overland. Sacco and Orciani were to go back to Stoughton, and he had not expected to see Sacco again. When asked again about the literature they planned to collect, he said there must have been four or five hundred pounds of it, and that he had been told by his friends in New York to get rid of it. In a brief re-examination Vanzetti said again that when he was arrested he had thought it was because of political matters since he was asked "if I am a Socialist, if I am an I.W.W., if I am a Communist, if I am a Radical, if I am a Blackhand."

Through a day and a half the district attorney flashed questions at Vanzetti so fast that his acquired English collapsed. Still, he managed to keep his calm manner. Such self-control would be beyond Sacco's capacities. For a year now he had fretted in the Dedham jail, and a month's submission to the routine of the courtroom had brought him close to the point of explosion—as the experienced Katzmann well realized.

After Vanzetti was released from the stand, Simon Johnson returned to answer a few questions about Boda's Overland. This ended the morning session. At the beginning of the afternoon session, at a word from Moore, Sacco with one quick backward look at his wife stepped to the stand.

In spite of his jail pallor and his thinning hair, Sacco still kept an appearance of youth. Although born only three years after Vanzetti, he seemed a generation younger. He was dressed in a neat dark suit, a white shirt, and a black string tie. The *Post* reporter found his appearance "frank and open." He seemed glad finally to be able to tell his story.

With Moore guiding him, he gave the matter-of-fact details of his childhood in Torremaggiore, then told of his early longing to go to America. "I was crazy to come to this country," he explained, "because I was liked a free country, call a free country." It was a fateful remark.

After Sacco's arrival in America there were the years of odd jobs before he learned a trade, there was his marriage, and finally there was the black-edged letter from his father that made him decide to go back to Italy. Only in passing did Sacco mention that he had left the United States in June 1917 and returned sometime in August. All this was just a preliminary to the history of April 15, 1920. That day, according to his account, he left Stoughton on the 8:56 A.M. train for Boston to go to the Italian consulate and apply for a *foglio di via*, a one-way passport to Italy. He arrived at the South Station and walked from there along Atlantic Avenue to the North End. On Prince Street he bought a copy of *La Notizia* and spent some time reading it. Then he walked down Hanover Street, turned the corner, and ran into his friend Angelo Monello. Together they walked to Washington Street; Sacco continued alone, looking in the store windows and pricing the new suits and straw hats. The morning was getting on, and he thought he might as well have lunch and see about his passport afterward.

As he was going in to Boni's Restaurant he met Professor Guadagni, and they sat down at a table together. Albert Bosco was already there, and later Mr. Williams, the advertising man, joined them. Sacco stayed about an hour and afterward went uptown to the consulate on Berkeley Street. Arriving there at two, he said to the clerk, "I like to get a passport for my whole family. He asked me—he said, 'You bring picture?' I said, 'Yes,' so I gave it to him, see a big picture. He says, 'Well, I am sorry. This picture is too big.' 'Well,' I says, 'can you cut and make him small?' he said, 'the picture we cannot use, because it goes too big.' I says, 'Can you cut?' He says, 'No, no use, because got to make a photograph just for the purpose for the passport, small very small.' "

After a quarter of an hour at the consulate he went back to the North End, dropped in at a café for a cup of coffee, and met Professor Guadagni again with a Professor Dentamore. Then he went over to a store on the other side of North Square to buy some groceries. Some time in the afternoon he met a man named Afa—that was the way he thought the name was spelled—and paid him fifteen dollars he owed him. A little after four he took the train for Stoughton and arrived there about six. On the way home he stopped off at the drugstore and bought some elixir for a physic.

Sacco was interrupted by a wrangle between Moore and Judge Thayer when Moore tried to bring in the details of the April 25 meeting at the Naturalization Club, "to lay a foundation for the explanation of the subsequent acts of the defendants." Thayer ruled that the subsequent acts must be proved before any explanation could be offered, and the two debated noisily. When Sacco was finally allowed to continue, he told how on May 4 he had gone to Boston for the last time to pick up his passport. He had then taken the elevated to Hyde Park to see Orciani. The two met on River Street, went to Orciani's house for the motorcycle, and then drove to Sacco's home.

Sacco was more explicit than Vanzetti about why they had gone to West Bridgewater the following evening. "We decided in the meeting in Boston to get those books and papers," he told the court, "because in New York there was somebody said they were trying to arrest all the socialists and the radicals and we were afraid to get all the people arrested, so we were advised by some friends and we find out and Vanzetti take the responsibility to go over to the friends to get the books out and get no trouble. The literature, I mean, the socialist literature."

The dark cap that had been picked up near Berardelli's body was produced and Sacco tried it on. He said it was too small—and so it seemed in the courtroom sketches made by the *Post* cartoonist, Norman (W. Norman Ritchie). With regard to the Colt taken from him at the Brockton police station, he explained that his wife had found it in a bureau drawer along with some bullets while she was cleaning up, and asked him what he was going to do with it. "I said, 'Well, I go to shoot in the woods, me and Vanzetti.' So I did. I took it in my pocket. I put the revolver over here and the bullets in my pocket, in my pocket back. Well, we started to talk in the afternoon, me and Vanzetti, and half past four Orciani and Boda came over to the house, so we started an argument and I forgot about to go in the woods shooting, so it was still left in my pocket." The bullets he had bought on Hanover Street in 1917 or 1918.

His story of the trip to West Bridgewater and the subsequent arrest and questioning did not differ greatly from Vanzetti's, although Sacco told in more detail of the identification witnesses coming to the Brockton station. In the conclusion of his direct examination he maintained that he had not been in South Braintree on April 15, 1920, and that he had never made an attack on anyone or participated in any crime, then or at any other date.

"Did you say you love a free country?" was Katzmann's first rapier question. And when Sacco answered yes, the district attorney thrust again. "Did you love this country in the month of May 1917?" "I do not say," Sacco told him, "I don't want to say I did not love this country." The other insisted. "Did you love this country in the month of May 1917?" "If you can, Mr. Katzmann, if you give me that—I could explain—" The district attorney had the Italian in the corner. "Do you understand that question? Then you will please answer it." "I can't answer it in one word," Sacco insisted.

Katzmann's voice was crusty with disbelief. "You can't say whether you loved the United States of America one week before the day to enlist for the first draft?" "I can't say in one word, Mr. Katzmann," Sacco replied.

"Did you," the district attorney finally asked him, "go away to Mexico to avoid being a soldier for this country that you loved?"

Sacco breathed deeply before he said "Yes."

"And is that your idea of showing your love for this country?"

The other hesitated. He knew what he wanted to say but there was no way for him to say it, no means to surmount the barrier of this alien tongue. "Is that your idea of showing your love for America?" the contemptuous voice persisted. "Yes," Sacco said, and again he found himself saying what he had not meant, what he did not want to say, to the courtly, smiling district attorney.

It was question and answer, cat and mouse:

"Do you think it is a brave thing to do what you did?"

"Yes."

"Do you think it would be a brave thing to go away from your own wife when she needed you?"

"No."

"Why didn't you stay down in Mexico?"

"Well, first thing, I could not get my trade there. I had to do any other job."

"Why didn't you stay down there, down in that free country, and work with a pick and shovel?"

"I don't think I did sacrifice to learn a job to go pick and shovel in Mexico."

"Is it because—is your love for the United States of America commensurate with the amount of money you can get in this country per week?"

"Better conditions, yes."

"Better country to make money, isn't it?"

"Yes."

"Mr. Sacco, that is the extent of your love for this country, isn't it, measured in dollars and cents?"

Jerry McAnarney kept objecting to such questioning. "You opened up this whole subject," Judge Thayer told him.

When McAnarney continued his objections, Thayer asked, "Is it not your claim that the defendant wanted the automobile to prevent people from being deported and to get this literature all out of the way? Does he not claim that this was done in the interest of the United States, to prevent violation of the law by the distribution of this literature?"

The amazed McAnarney replied that the defense had taken no such position. All they claimed was "that this man and Vanzetti were of the class called socialists, that riot was running a year ago last April, that men were being deported, that twelve to fifteen hundred were seized in Massachusetts."

Thayer returned to the theme. "Are you going to claim that what the defendant did was in the interest of the United States to prevent further crimes from being committed by the authorities?"

"Your Honor please," Jerry McAnarney replied. "I now object to your Honor's statement as prejudicial to the rights of the defendants and ask that this statement be withdrawn from the jury."

Thayer denied any such effect. "There is no prejudicial remark made that I know of, and none were intended. I simply asked you, sir, whether you propose to offer evidence as to what you said to me."

A lengthy dispute ensued, Katzmann defending his cross-examination as "tending to attack the credibility of this man as a witness." Over Moore's loudly voiced objections Judge Thayer decided to let the district attorney question Sacco further as to what he meant by loving a free country.

Frank Sibley, writing with the afternoon deadline only a few minutes away, pricked up his ears at the "interest of the United States." He could scarcely believe it when he heard the judge's caustic voice ask about preventing crimes from being committed "by the authorities." Before he had a chance to think twice, the telegraph boy had taken away the yellow sheet of paper with the phrase on it. The phrase appeared in the evening *Globe*. When Sibley wrote his more extended story for the next morning's edition he omitted it. "I couldn't credit my remembrance, and so did not use the vicious sentence," he wrote Attorney General J. Weston Allen a few months later. His colleague Shea of the *Post* had also picked up the remark and used it.

The next day Judge Thayer summoned Sibley to his chambers and angrily insisted that he said no such thing. Sibley, having consulted with Shea, refused to back down even when shown that the transcript of the court stenographic notes did not contain the phrase. Just then a bailiff appeared to announce the arrival of the jury, and Thayer huffily broke off the conversation.

As the cross-examination continued, Sacco found himself caught in a web of words of which he could see each strand as it formed, from which he knew he could break out if only they would let him. But always it was the *yes* or *no* answer demanded, always the cutting-off of his explanation, that made it seem as if he had come back from Mexico merely to eat better food and to make more money and to be with his wife and speak a more familiar language. "Food, wife, language, industry—that is love of country, is it?" Katzmann asked him, and he found himself answering yes. The rules, the thin threads of questions twisted about him, smothering his replies. He could feel the anger of frustation pulsing through him at the reiterations. Deftly the district attorney led him into the trap.

"What did you mean when you said yesterday you loved a free country?"

"First thing I came to this country—"

"No, pardon me. What did you mean when you said yesterday you loved a free country?"

"Give me a chance to explain."

"I am asking you to explain now."

Suddenly Sacco felt himself clear of the web, standing free at last with his own thoughts. The frustrations of his arrest and imprisonment, the long months in jail, the legal niceties that had sealed his mouth in the courtroom, now found violent relief in a cascade of words. As he talked on, his wiry body seemed to grow tense and his eyes snapped fire. At first some of the jurors smiled, but before he had finished everyone in the courtroom was listening intently.

"When I was in Italy, a boy," he began, "I was a republican, so I always thinking republicans has more chance to manage education, develop, to build some day his family, to raise the child and education, if you could. But that was my opinion; so when I came here to this country I saw there was not what I was thinking before, but there was all the difference, because I been working in Italy not so hard as I been work in this country. I could live free there just as well. . . . Of course, over here there is good food, because it is bigger country, to any those who got money to spend, not for the working and laboring class, and in Italy is more opportunity to laborer to eat vegetable, more fresh. . . . When I been started work here very hard and been work thirteen years, hard worker, I could not put any money in the bank. I could no push my boy some to go to school and other things. . . . I could see the best men, intelligent, education, they been arrested and sent to prison and died in prison for years and years without getting them out, and Debs, one of the great men in his country, he is in prison, still away in prison, because he is a socialist. He wanted the laboring classes to have better conditions and better living, more education, give a push his son if he could have a chance some day, but they put him in prison. Why? Because the capitalist class, they know, they are against that, because the capitalist class, they don't want our child to go to high school or to college or Harvard College. There would not be no chance, there would not be no—they don't want the working class educationed; they want the working class to be a low all the times, be underfoot, and not to be up with the head. So, sometimes, you see, the Rockefellers, Morgans, they give fifty—mean they give five hundred thousand dollars to Harvard College, they give a million dollars for another school. Everybody say, 'Well, D. Rockefeller is a great man, the best in the country.' I want ask him who is going to Harvard College? What benefit the working class they will get by those million dollars they give by Rockefeller, D. Rockefellers? They won't get, the poor class, but I want men to live like men. I like men to get everything that nature will give best, because they belong—we are not the friend of any other place, but we are belong to nations. . . . So that is why I love people who labor and work and see better conditions every day develop, makes no more war. We no want fight by the gun, and we don't want to destroy young men. The mother been suffering for building the young man. Some day need a little more bread, so when the time the mother get some bread or profit out that boy, the Rockefellers, Morgans, and some of the peoples, high class, they send to war. Why? What is war? The war is not shoots like Abraham Lincoln's and Abe Jefferson's, to fight for the free country, for the better education, to give chance to any other peoples, not the white people but the blacks and the others, because they believe and know they are mens like the rest, but they are war for the great millionaire. No war for the civilization of men. They are war for business, million dollars come on the side. What right have we to kill each other? I been work for the Irish, I have been working with the German fellow, with the French, many other peoples. I love them people just as I could love my wife, and my people for that did receive me. Why should I go kill them men? What he done to me? He never done anything, so I don't believe in no war. I want to destroy those guns. . . . I remember in Italy, a long time ago, about sixty years ago, I should say, yes, about sixty years ago, the government they could not control very much these two—devilment went on, and robbery, so one of the government in the cabinet he says, 'If you want to destroy those devilments, if you want to take off all those criminals, you ought to give a chance to socialist literature, education of people, emancipation.' That is why I destroy governments, boys. That is why my idea I love socialists. That is why I like people who want educa- tion and living, building, who is good, just as much as they could. That is all."

Norman's on-the-spot cartoon caught Sacco gesticulating fiercely, his string tie awry, the astonished jurymen leaning forward and Moore and Jerry McAnarney looking blank with dismay, the harassed court stenographer begging for mercy. Katzmann and Judge Thayer were shown with heads spinning. The district attorney's head, how- ever, was perfectly clear. Making no objections to the passionate out- burst, he registered each point in his mind.

When Sacco finally finished and stood there in rumpled exhaustion a ponderous silence followed, broken only by a few muffled coughs among the spectators. Then the district attorney took up the threads of his web again. If, he asked, things were as bad in America as Sacco said, why had he not gone back to Italy where by his own admission the food was better, he could have lived as well, and he would not have had to work as hard? Did he intend to condemn Harvard Col- lege? Did he know how many children were being educated free by the city of Boston? Over the solid objections of the defense, Judge Thayer allowed such questions on the grounds that they referred to statements the defendant himself had made. Jerry McAnarney, losing his temper, announced that he objected both to the questions and the answers.

The South Braintree murders had drifted into the background. Gradually the district attorney's questions led back to them. If Sacco and his friends had been so alarmed by Salsedo's death, why did they wait three days before doing anything about collecting the incriminating papers? Why had Sacco said they were going out to pick up books and papers on the night of their arrest while Vanzetti had testified they were merely going to make arrangements to pick them up? "Probably I mistake or probably Vanzetti is right," Sacco replied. Katzmann quietly asked a few irrelevant questions about the mackinaw Orciani was wearing. Then suddenly Sacco felt the knife at his throat: "Did you take that revolver off the person of Alessandro Berardelli when he lay on the sidewalk in front of the Rice and Hutchins factory?"

"No, sir."

Defendant and prosecutor stared long and silently at each other in the quiet courtroom.

There were, Katzmann reminded Sacco, the lies he had told the night of his arrest. The district attorney led him over them. It was a lie, Sacco admitted, that he had bought his Colt in the North End. He had really bought it at a store in Milford in 1917. He had lied, too, about buying a new box of cartridges. The truth was that cartridges were hard to come by during the war and he had bought an odd lot of them in a partially filled box somewhere on Hanover Street. Katzmann at once wanted to know if the fact that he later learned there were four different kinds of cartridges had anything to do with his changing his story. If he had told the truth about that box, would it have helped to give away the names and addresses of his friends who had radical literature? Following each logical advantage, the district attorney pinned Sacco down to admitting he could give no reason for such lying that had anything to do with the names and addresses of anarchists.

Sacco still insisted that when he had gone out on May 5 with the Colt tucked in his belt he had forgotten about it. He was used to carrying it while on his watchman's rounds, he said, though it was true he had not been a watchman during the winter of 1920. Sometimes when he went into Boston and came back late on the train he carried it.

"Wasn't it a pretty unusual thing for you to carry the gun?" Katzmann thrust at him.

"Well," Sacco parried, "it is, but men have to defend themselves. In the country you don't know what you need." *

* Long after the trial Sacco admitted privately to Thompson, his later counsel, that he was carrying the Colt that night "because we were at war with the government."

As to his other lies, Sacco had lied when he denied knowing Orciani. He had lied about the time he worked in South Braintree because he was afraid if the police found out he had been working there under the name of Mosmacotelli he would be punished as a slacker and they would find the radical literature in his house. He had lied when he said he had known Vanzetti only a year and a half because he did not want to tell about their going to Mexico. He had known Boda for three years; he had lied when he said he never had heard of him; Boda was a radical and he wanted to protect him. He had had no intention of looking up Pappi that night. That was another lie. As for the day of the crime, he had said in the Brockton station he worked all that day because he really thought he had. Katzmann forced him to admit that he had lied to George Kelley, his friend, in telling him he would be gone only half a day. Next morning he had invented a story for Kelley that there was such a crowd in the consulate that he could not get his passport in the morning and so missed the noon train.

Katzmann questioned Sacco minutely about the evening of May 5. Then after a short recess the district attorney appeared with two caps. Sacco objected that the first, a gray one, was too soiled to be his, but then admitted it belonged to him. The hole or tear in the lining he could not account for, although Katzmann pressed him to agree that it came from the nail in the factory wall on which he used to hang it each morning. The second cap, the dark one found next to Berardelli's body, Sacco denied was his.

Mrs. Evans enlivened the courtroom Friday and caused some confusion among the courtroom attendants by appearing with binoculars. Thursday, July 7, was Judge Thayer's sixty-fourth birthday, and he had been sent a bouquet of rambler roses. They now stood in a vase on the great oak desk, nodding cheerfully in the breeze from the electric fan.

When Sacco, his face heavy with fatigue, resumed the stand he asked for an interpreter and Joseph Ross was assigned to him. Katzmann began to hammer at why Sacco had said he was working at the factory the day before he had admittedly read in the paper about the South Braintree murders. Sacco tried to explain that at the time he had not given the date much though. The district attorney insisted. "Why did you tell me a falsehood that on Thursday, the day before you read the account in the paper, you worked all day?"

"Well, I did not remember for certain," Sacco told him. "I said that I had been out two or three days." There were two other days,

Sacco admitted, that he had gone to the consulate, although he could not even now remember just what days they were. But they were half-days; April 15 was the only whole day he had spent in Boston.

As the cross-examination continued, a dispute arose as to the accuracy of Ross' interpreting. Sacco accused him of translating inaccurately. Felix Forte, a young, bilingual lawyer brought in by the defense, debated with Ross as to the translation of *quando*; Ross had translated it as *before* whereas Forte held that it meant *when*. As the argument boiled up, Judge Thayer sent the jury from the room. An arbiter called by Thayer, A. Minini, tried to reconcile his colleagues. A flurry of English and Italian followed. Vanzetti, in the cage, sprang to his feet to object to Ross.*

After the jurors had again taken their seats, Sacco denied that in Brockton he had said he was away from the factory at the beginning of April and that this was the only time he was away for a whole day.

The district attorney turned abruptly from the debate on days: "Did you shave this morning?" When Sacco said yes, he continued, "Have you shaved every day since this trial opened?" Scarcely waiting for the affirmative answer, the district attorney announced: "That is all, sir."

It was Moore's task in the re-examination that followed to patch up the damage done. He brought out that although Sacco might have admitted in Brockton that there was one whole day in April he had not worked, he had given Katzmann no definite date. He had lied to Michael Kelley about being delayed at the consulate because he was ashamed to admit that the reason he had broken his word about getting back in the afternoon was that he had spent the time talking to his friends. The letter that he had received from his father, after Sabino's earlier letter announcing the mother's death, was shown as corroborative evidence to the jury.

Once more Sacco went over the night in the Brockton police station, still maintaining that he thought he had been arrested because he was a radical and a slacker. The first thing Stewart had asked him was whether he was "an anarchist, communist, or socialist." Again

* During the trial Ross's wife gave birth to a son. To the immense delight of the judge, he was named Webster Thayer Ross. Katzmann became the child's godfather. As it did for Mrs. DeFalco, the calling of court interpreter eventually proved too much for Ross: In 1926 he was sentenced to the Middlesex House of Correction after pleading guilty to attempting to bribe a judge.

the dispute welled up about Ross' integrity. As the morning session reached its end Jerry McAnarney asked that the jury be retired. He then presented another motion for a severance, asking for a separate trial for Vanzetti on the grounds of Sacco's outburst:

"At the beginning of these cases," he told Thayer, "I was apprehensive and fearful of what might transpire during this case were it tried in conjunction with the indictment against Nicola Sacco, and meeting that situation we filed a motion for a severance and a separate trial. At that time, in informal discussion before your Honor, mention was made that if at any time during the trial things should occur we could renew the motion. It now seems to me peculiarly fitting in view of all the evidence on this record at the present moment that the motion be granted for a severance of these cases, and I now offer the motion."

Judge Thayer asked if proper instructions to the jury would not take care of the situation. The defense lawyer must have realized that there was no chance of the motion being granted, but he also realized what a damaging effect Sacco's outburst had had on the jury. He felt he must at least make the gesture of dissociating Vanzetti, with the possibility that this might be allowed later by a higher court.

As Sacco resumed the stand on Saturday morning, the books and pamphlets found in his house were admitted as evidence. Then Jerry McAnarney, taking over the re-examination, asked more details about letters Sacco had received from Italy announcing his mother's death. The week had been long, and the morning seemed anticlimactic, as if the trial were now coasting downhill to its conclusion. Suddenly, dramatically, McAnarney revealed that Sacco had recently seen a man sitting in the front row of the court who, he was certain, had ridden back on the train from Boston with him on April 15.

To Judge Thayer's question as to why this was not merely hearsay, McAnarney replied that he proposed to follow the statement by producing the man in question. Sacco said that Moore had often asked if he remembered anyone who had ridden up on the train with him that day. He had never been able to, then all at once he had noticed this man in court and he somehow remembered his face. He did not know his name. He had not spoken to him. The mysterious witness had been subpoenaed by the defense, but with the conclusion of Sacco's testimony he could not at once be found.

His place was taken by a routine witness, a Stoughton photographer, Edward Maertens, who stated that some time in April he had made a passport photograph of the Sacco family, as well as a much larger one several weeks earlier. Next Walter Nelles, a New York lawyer, testified that he talked with Luigi Quintiliano the last week in April 1920 about disposing of socialistic and radical literature. Two Brockton shoe-workers, Rocco Dalesandro and Michael Columbo, then testified that on Monday, May 3, they had talked with Sacco in Brockton about getting rid of their literature. Later, Columbo had bundled up all such papers and pamphlets that he owned.

The last witness of the week was Felice Guadagni, the comrade who had been first to visit Sacco and Vanzetti at the Brockton police station. He confirmed Sacco's April 15 abili, telling how the two of them had met by chance on the steps of Boni's Restaurant at 11:30 A.M. Sacco, he said, was wearing a derby and a dark suit. They had gone in together and were later joined by Bosco and Williams. Guadagni had come out of Boni's with Sacco at 1:30. He had then gone back to his office at the *Gazzetta del Massachusetts* and Sacco had gone uptown to the consulate. About three in the afternoon he had seen Sacco again in Joe Giordano's café. Guadagni recalled the date of his meeting with Sacco as the fifteenth because on that day he had been invited to a banquet given by the Franciscan Fathers of North Bennett Street in honor of Mr. Williams, the *Transcript* editor, who had just been made a *Commendatore*.

Four or five days after Sacco's arrest Guadagni had gone to the consulate with Rosina, taking along a photograph of Sacco. There they had talked with the acting consul and the vice-consul and the clerk Adrower, but by the archaic rule of law—so frustrating to laymen—Guadagni was not allowed to repeat what had been said.

Under cross-examination he admitted that he had seen Sacco in Boston on several other days, always wearing the derby and the dark suit. He could not, however, recall any specific dates. When Sacco came into Giordano's Café, Guadagni was already there talking about the banquet. He had not attended it, but since it was the only banquet to which he had ever been invited, he could not help but remember it. The invitation had come the week before—he could not fix the date.

Court adjourned just before one o'clock and the jurors were left alone in the marble courthouse to face another Saturday afternoon and Sunday. They were almost certain, however, that this would be the last week end they would be kept in Dedham.

Judge Thayer spent his weekends in Worcester. There, at the

familiar golf club, he could join a foursome and forget the incidents and frustations of the past week. In the clubhouse after the game, in the protecting company of his friends, he found a cathartic relief in saying just what he really thought about those Bolsheviki who were trying to intimidate him. Nobody, he told his friend Loring Coes, could intimidate Web Thayer. A bunch of parlor radicals were trying to get those Italian bastards off and trying to bring pressure on the bench. He would show them, he told Coes, his face darkening with accumulated anger. He would see them hanged, and he would also like to hang a few dozen of the radicals.

On Monday morning George Kelley was recalled to explain more details about the caps. He maintained that the lighter-colored of the two, the one Sacco had agreed was his, looked much more like Sacco's. The one found near Berardelli's body was darker than any Sacco had ever owned. Kelley admitted reluctantly that he might have made some remark about "not wanting to get a bomb up my ass" to Stewart and Brouillard. This morning, while he was waiting in the courthouse library to take the stand, he had seen a pepper-and-salt cap on the table that looked much more like Sacco's cap than the other two. "The nearest I have seen yet," Kelley remarked, as the third cap was offered in evidence. When cross-examined by Katzmann, Kelley admitted that he was fond of Sacco. Four or five months before the murders, learning that Sacco's radical activities were being investigated, he had warned him. It was obvious that Kelley, whatever his own political views, had not changed his friendly feelings.

During the recess Judge Thayer again asked Mrs. Rantoul to come to his chambers. She made notes of the interview immediately afterward. Judge Thayer began by asking her what she now thought of the case.

I answered [she said in an affidavit in 1926], that I thought Kelley's statement as to Sacco's character was important. I well remember Judge Thayer's reply and the manner in which he gave it. He expressed scorn and contempt for my view, and told me that Kelley did not mean what he said because he [Judge Thayer] had heard that on the outside Kelley had said that Sacco was an anarchist and that he couldn't do anything with him. I told Judge Thayer that I had never before realized that it was fair to judge a case by what witnesses said outside of court, and that I had supposed that the only proper way to judge a case was by what the witnesses said in open court. Judge

Thayer's manner and expression of face expressed dissent from this view, but he made no definite statement of dissent.

The mysterious spectator Sacco claimed to have seen on the Stoughton train now appeared as a witness. He turned out to be James Hayes, for thirty-three years a mason and contractor in Stoneham, and town highway surveyor until March 1920. A defense investigator had brought him to court in regard to some technical information about the Stoughton street layout. Watching the trial, Hayes had become interested in it, and he and his wife had returned on three other days to follow the proceedings. It was while he was sitting there that Sacco caught a glimpse of him.

Hayes agreed that he had indeed gone to Boston on April 15. He was certain of the date because he had gone through his time-books and found that on that day his brother had paid him fifty dollars. He had used part of the money the same afternoon to buy parts for his Ford in Boston.

April 11, Sunday, he remembered because it was the birthday of one of his children. Monday, working at an excavation, he had sprained his instep. Tuesday and Wednesday and part of Thursday morning he had spent at home taking down the rear end of his Ford. Friday he needed parts, and he had gone to Boston on the train that left a little after twelve. He arrived back in Stoughton between five and six. Next day, Friday, he started working again. He did not know Sacco, never had met him, did not know whether Sacco was on that train or not, but he did know he himself was.

Katzmann now took Hayes over the hurdles. What had he been doing on March 26, 27, 28, 29, 30, and 31? Hayes could not say. He thought he had probably gone in to Boston a dozen or fifteen times, but he could not remember any particular date because he had not had any occasion to look it up.

Sacco, recalled, testified that he had seen Hayes that day in the train from Boston. There was another inconclusive dispute with Ross as to whether Sacco had said "in Boston" or "in the train from Boston." Sacco said he had been sitting in the middle of a coach on the right-hand side, and a man had been sitting opposite him in the aisle seat on the left. There was no particular reason why he should have remembered this man except that they both got off at Stoughton and somehow Sacco was struck by his face.

Hayes corroborated Sacco's statement that he had been sitting

midway in the car on the left next to the aisle. No one had asked him
until that moment where he had been sitting. There was a person
across the aisle from him, but who it was, a man or woman, he could
not say. He had paid no attention.

Following Hayes, Antonio Dentamore of the foreign-exchange
department of the Haymarket National Bank took the stand to
corroborate Professor Guadagni. On April 15, just before three o'clock,
he had been talking with Guadagni in Giordani's Café when Sacco
came in. He had never met Sacco until Guadagni introduced them.
They had talked together for about twenty minutes, mostly about
passports. The reason Dentamore remembered the day was that he
had just come back from the banquet for the *Transcript* editor, and
in fact he and Guadagni were discussing it as Sacco appeared. Katzmann took him over the customary hurdles. Dentamore could not
recall what he had been doing at ten minutes to three the day before
or the day after the banquet, or twenty days ago, or twenty-one days
ago. He could not say where he had had lunch twenty-two days before. "I am not a fortune teller," he told Katzmann.

The defense tried to get the information into the record that
Dentamore and Sacco came from the same district in Italy. Judge
Thayer excluded the references. Thwarted at each turn, Moore tried
to explain that "through this witness the defense offers to prove
that in the conversation that was had between the witness and Mr.
Sacco it became known to the witness that Mr. Sacco and himself
were both from the same section of Italy, that they were both mutual
friends and acquaintances of Mr. Mucci,* and that the witness, after
learning that Sacco was returning to Italy at an early date . . .
asked Mr. Sacco to convey to Mr. Mucci his good wishes and the fact
that they had met one another in Boston." At once the district attorney objected and his objection was sustained.

As Monday drifted into afternoon there was a feeling of the wheels
running down, of impatience for the hour of decision. Everyone in
the court sensed there would be no more surprises, no more climaxes.
Half the reporters' desks were empty. The *Post* sent its cartoonist
over to the Middlesex courthouse to sketch the juicier proceedings in
the Mishawum Manor scandal. The remaining witnesses, including
the handful to be offered by the Commonwealth in rebuttal, were
like odd bits of string, useful only for tying up loose ends. Speaking
through an interpreter, Carlos Affe, a grocer whom some of the

* Leon Mucci, the deputy from the district that included Torremaggiore.

Italians jokingly called the mayor of East Boston, told of selling
$15.67 worth of groceries to Sacco on March 20, 1920. On April 15
he had again seen Sacco, who had paid him $15.50. Affe had made a
record of this in his account book and marked the date. That book
he now produced.

Luigi Quintiliano appeared briefly to say that he had seen Vanzetti in New York on April 27 and 28 and had talked over the
problem of getting rid of radical literature. The Spanish anarchist
Frank Lopez refused to take an oath and affirmed instead that he
had talked to Vanzetti both before and after his New York trip about
getting incriminating literature out of their friends' houses.

Then Rosina Sacco came forward, glancing at her husband with
as much courage as she could muster. She stood there, a slight pathetic, determined figure, her red-gold hair softening her fine, slightly
archaic features so that with her sprinkling of freckles she looked
almost adolescent. Her story was simple. She told of her husband's
receiving the black-bordered envelope containing the news of his
mother's death one noon just after he had eaten. He had gone back
to the factory, but after half an hour came home again. She remembered how on the day of his arrest she had been cleaning out a
closet and found the shotgun shells. Vanzetti had picked them up
and said he would sell them for fifty cents to a friend. Then, going
through the bureau drawers, she had found a pistol and some more
shells. These she placed on top of the bureau and asked her husband
what he was going to do with them. That same day Orciani and
Boda had come to supper. After supper her husband left with Vanzetti to catch the Brockton streetcar. Boda and Orciani started out
later after fixing a tire on the motorcycle. When Vanzetti had said
good-by to her, he had given her a message to take back to Italy.
She did not learn of her husband's arrest until twelve the next day
when officers Connolly and Scott and two or three others arrived at
the house. On April 15 a man from Milford named Iacovelli had
come to see about taking over Sacco's job and stayed a quarter of an
hour.

Jerry McAnarney showed Rosina the caps that had been exhibited
before. The gray cap, she thought, looked like her husband's, like the
cap the police had taken from her house on May 6. As for the dark
one with the earlaps, her husband had never owned such a cap
"because he never liked it . . . he don't look good in them positively."

When Katzmann questioned her, she told him that even before
the death of Sacco's mother they had been planning to return to Italy.

"That's why we were saving our money, because we wanted to go across in the old country, but since the mother died, we hurried more because he was sorry about his mother died without seeing him." Sabino's letter telling of the mother's death had arrived March 23 or 24. Thirteen or fourteen days later Sacco had gone in to the consulate with his photograph. Katzmann wanted to know how thirteen or fourteen days after March 24 could make the date April 15. "Well, you count up from the twenty-third or twenty-fourth of March," she told him, "and going to the fifteenth, I says thirteen or fourteen days, and I don't think it is much different, because it is over a year he is in prison, and I don't remember everything." Katzmann asked her nothing more. Sacco's savings-bank book, introduced as evidence, showed that from December 9, 1918, he had deposited amounts from $30 to $270 for a total of about $1500.

The Milford shoe-worker Henry Iacovelli was the last defense witness. In April 1920 he received a letter from Michael Kelley telling him there was a job open in the Three-K factory. He had gone to Stoughton on April 15, first seen George Kelley, then gone to Sacco's bungalow. Rosina told him that Sacco had gone to Boston, but this hearsay evidence Jerry McAnarney could not bring out in court. On this fading note the defense rested.

Among the residual rebuttal witnesses were Angelo Ricci, the foreman of the railroad gang near the crossing; a Mary Gaines, who knew Lola Andrews and Julia Campbell; Henry Hellyer, the Pinkerton agent; Chief Stewart; Lieutenant Guerin; and a belated identification witness by the name of Frank Hawley.

Ricci maintained that when the getaway car went over the tracks he did not see any of his gang at the crossing, but he admitted under cross-examination: "When you got to control twenty-four men, what to hell, one fly away. I could not tie them up with string and hold them all as one. If they went around, sneaked around the pile of dirt or something like that, I could not hold them."

Mary Gaines of Quincy was brought in to show that "the statement Mrs. Andrews made about making inquiry of the man under the car is not of recent contrivance." She had visited Julia Campbell and her sister and Lola Andrews in the Alhambra Block the week following the shooting. Lola had then told them "she seen this man underneath the automobile, and she taps this man on the shoulder, she asks him to please direct her to the Rice and Hutchins shoe shop, and he got up and directed her to it."

Hellyer gave his altered account of what Jenny Novelli had told him. As the existence of his written report was not then known, his statements passed unchallenged. Lieutenant Guerin told of going to Sacco's house and picking up the gray cap with a rip in the lining from the kitchen table. Moore objected to the cap being admitted as an exhibit on the grounds of unlawful search and seizure. He also objected to the jury's seeing the Buick and demanded that all references to it be struck out. As usual his objections were overruled.

Hawley, a salesman and a former Brockton special police officer, said that on April 1 he was driving his Ford in Brockton. In starting to turn around on School Street to go to Whitman, he had forced a Buick touring car to come to a stop. It was a dirty car with flapping side-curtains and as it stopped the driver stuck his head out and asked the way to Whitman. The man Hawley had seen sitting next to the unidentified driver was Vanzetti.

Chief Stewart resumed the stand briefly to add a few more passages of the Brockton interrogatory that he had previously omitted. There followed a discussion about the admission as evidence of the books found in Sacco's house and whether they should be translated. Finally both sides agreed to let them in as they were, Moore remarking that the titles spoke for themselves. Shortly after lunch both sides rested.

There was a pause, a rustle in the courtroom, as the lawyers gathered up their documents and the spectators eyed Judge Thayer. He cleared his throat, looked dryly at Moore, then turned to the jury.

"Well, gentlemen," he said in his toneless voice, "the book of fate in these cases has been closed. You will undoubtedly get these cases for final determination Thursday forenoon, or Thursday morning. During your absence quite a number of things have been settled between counsel, one of which is that arguments will be made tomorrow, beginning at nine o'clock. It has been agreed that four hours shall be given to each side—that is four hours for the defendants and four hours for the Commonwealth. They may run a little over that time.

"I must again suggest to you to still keep your minds open. The evidence has simply closed now. You have not heard the arguments of both counsel. You have not heard the charge of the Court. You must hear what the law is of the Commonwealth in order that you may apply the law to established facts found by you to be true, and therefore with this request, which is kindly made by the Court, I trust you will do what you can to see to it that it is fully carried into effect."

Edmund Morgan, in his study of the trial published in 1948, considered it an act of incomprehensible folly for the defense to agree to any such four-hour limitation. But in agreeing to the limitation, Moore and the McAnarneys were from long practical experience aware of the dangers of taxing a jury's patience. Jurymen who had already sat through thirty uncomfortable days of testimony might react against an argument running several days. Besides, it was common bar knowledge that by the time the summations were reached, a jury, despite any judge's hortatory injunctions, had pretty well made up its collective mind.

Moore and Jerry McAnarney agreed to divide their alloted morning, with Moore appearing first. But the ingenious and aggressive general counsel of the I.W.W., the victor of so many underdog courtroom battles, was that Wednesday morning like a speaker who has lost rapport with his audience. He rambled. The telling points escaped him. Jerry McAnarney, tripping over his grammar, made a far better follow-up.

Moore opened by remarking wryly that in the six weeks of the trial, he, as a Californian, had felt almost an alien in the Dedham court. He then went on to develop his argument, claiming that the primary—in fact the only—issue was one of identification. Taking the Commonwealth's witnesses in order, he asked why it was that the expressman Neal, when he felt his life was in danger, had not bothered to look at the number of the threatening car directly in front of his door? How was it that Faulkner, on the train, could remember the man he said was Vanzetti leaning over from the rear seat and yet could not remember the man in the seat beside him? Moore recalled to the jury the Italian railroad worker, Nicola Gatti, the one witness who had known Sacco before the crime, and begged them not to be prejudiced by the fact that the man was an Italian. He pointed out that Mary Splaine's elaborate identification must have derived from the times she saw Sacco at the police station and not from the fleeting glimpse she had had from the upper window of the Hampton House, and he brought up again her indecisive statements in Quincy, so opposed to her Dedham positiveness. As for Lola Andrews, "even though we had not offered a single witness against her, she killed herself on the witness stand by her own personality, but Campbell, Fay, La Brecque finished her up." Pelser was unemployed when he told defense investigator Robert Reid that he had seen nothing of the shooting, but a few months after he got a job with Rice & Hutchins he was willing to testify for the Commonwealth. Goodridge, the poolroom man, was in the courtroom for some other purpose when he identified Sacco. Why?

"Gentlemen," Moore summed up, "there isn't a single witness called by the government who had an unqualified opportunity of observation who gives an identification. Bostock had the opportunity and wouldn't. McGlone had the opportunity and wouldn't. So on down the line. But it is the Lola Andrews, the Goodridges, the Pelsers that made the identification. Miss Splaine and Miss Devlin I reject, because their testimony is utterly unreasonable. They did not have the opportunity. They could not. You know it and I know it."

Moore asked the jury to consider again whether or not the defendants believed on the night of May 5 they were in fear of deportation or that they believed their lives or liberties were in danger, and whether Stewart's questions about anarchism had not inflamed Sacco's suspicions. There were, too, Sacco's alibi witnesses for April 15—Bosco, Dentamore, Williams, Affe, Kelley, Hayes. Had all these men committed perjury?

Only in passing did Moore mention the guns and bullets. "If," he said, "the time has come when a microscope must be used to determine whether a human life is going to function or not and when the users of the microscope themselves can't agree, when experts called by the Commonwealth and experts called by the defense are sharply defined in their disagreements, then I take it that ordinary men such as you and I should well hesitate to take a human life. You are the responsible men," he concluded. "You are the judges of the facts." And he stood there a moment staring somberly at the jurors.

"Take a recess of five minutes," Judge Thayer told the courtroom, then nodding curtly to the Californian, added, "You ran over your time twenty minutes, Mr. Moore."

Jerry McAnarney, in his two hours, did not confine himself to his ostensible client, Vanzetti, but proceeded to go over the same ground that Moore had just covered. He criticized the Splaine-Devlin contradictions, he asked why Sacco and Vanzetti had not been shown to witnesses in Brockton in a lineup, he speculated as to what Goodridge had been doing in Dedham when he first identified Sacco. Then he asked why Sacco, already recognizable in South Braintree as Mosmacotelli, would have spent a morning standing in front of the drugstore or hanging around the depot or finally leaning on the fence under the window of the very factory where he had once worked.

The testy little lawyer warned the jurors about Katzmann: "He can stand up to this rail and say to you gentlemen 'What have we been here for six weeks for, for two slackers, for two men who did not think enough of their country but what they would go to Mexico —murderers, slackers, anarchists?' Ring the changes, gentlemen, and you can play any tune you want to on that. And you have got to be very careful that you don't vibrate in unison with those words. They are fearful, they are potent, they are laden to the limit."

McAnarney poked fun at the bravado of the Brockton officer, Connolly, "listening to the sweetest music of his young life, the sound of Connolly's voice when he was telling you what he did." But when McAnarney mentioned Levangie, the man he had interviewed and who two weeks later had denied under oath talking with him, his face reddened. Captain Van Amburgh he referred to as the "circles" man, but he had obviously not grasped the implications of his testimony, for he reminded the jury: "Van Amburgh said that that number three shell, the fatal bullet that killed Berardelli, came from . . . the Colt revolver that was found on Sacco." In the question of Berardelli's revolver McAnarney pointed out that if the defense had planned to falsify evidence, it would not have been too difficult to have the various witnesses memorize the number of Vanzetti's Harrington & Richardson and afterward recite it on the witness stand.

McAnarney asserted, as had Moore, that the primary fact was in the end identification, and that there was not sufficient evidence to prove beyond a reasonable doubt that the two men had been in South Braintree that day. "I want every man on this panel to treat these two defendants as if they were your own individual brother," he concluded with sincere irrelevance. "Take that as the text, not the other that we feel and what this evidence would make them out, treat them as though, as your brother. He came to this world by the same power that created you, and may he go from this world by the same power that takes you. I thank you, gentlemen."

After the lunch hour Katzmann approached the jury box for his final argument. As usual his debonair appearance was unaffected by the heat. Confident of the game he was playing, sure of his arguments, he faced the jury in the floridity of his top form. But though his verbiage was lush, his mind was sharp.

He began with provincial urbanity by complimenting the jury, the defending lawyers, and the judge. Then he covered the case point by point, missing none of the discrepancies of the defense witnesses and not neglecting by innuendo to tie in Orciani. There was Burke who had said that Sacco and Vanzetti were not in the car as it passed him, Burke who had ridden to court in Callahan's Hudson and called it a Buick, who had described the driver of the getaway Buick as a thickset dark man—when both sides now admitted that the driver was pale and fair. There was Chase, on the truck at the Co-operative Society, a man with permanently impaired eyesight. There were Sacco's alibi witnesses in Boston and Vanzetti's in Plymouth. Katzmann agreed that Corl had painted his boat, that Williams had taken his advertising orders, that Dentamore had gone to a banquet for the *Transcript* editor. "But what in logic is the connection between any of these things that they say helps mark the time?"

The district attorney did not miss the fact that Vanzetti claimed that on the night of May 5 they were just going to get the car, whereas Sacco first said they were going to pick up radical literature. In the matter of picking up literature, if it was so urgent to get rid of it, why did Vanzetti do nothing for a week after coming back from New York? Why did he not warn his friends in Plymouth? Why did Sacco, after he heard from Vanzetti, take no steps to get rid of what he himself owned and so protect his home? Why would Sacco be so afraid of deportation when he was leaving the country in two days? What were they afraid of, anyhow, the night of May 5 when they had no incriminating papers with them?

As for the weapons, Katzmann argued: "They had arsenals upon them. Vanzetti had a loaded 38-caliber revolver, this man who ran to Mexico because he did not want to shoot a fellow human being in warfare, a loaded 38-caliber revolver, any one of the cartridges instantly death-dealing. This tender-hearted man who loved this country and who went down to Mexico because he did not believe in shooting a fellow human being, going down to get a decrepit old automobile, had a 38-caliber loaded gun on him.

"And his friend and associate, Nicola Sacco, another lover of peace, another lover of his adopted country who abhorred bloodshed and abhorred it so that he went down to Mexico under the name of Mosmacotelli . . . had with him, this lover of peace, thirty-two death-dealing automatic cartridges, nine of them in the gun ready for action and twenty-two more of them in his pocket—carried it where the ordinary citizen carries it there? No, gentlemen, carried where those who have occasion to use it quickly and want to slip it out and use it quickly would be prone to carry it, that death-dealing instrument.

"But more than that, gentlemen, and ammunition enough to kill thirty-seven men if each shot took effect, they had or Vanzetti had four shells—no weapon in which to fire them at the moment that we found, but you will remember, gentlemen, that sticking out of the back of the bandit's car on April 15 was either a rifle or a shotgun, and in Vanzetti's pocket were four 12-gauge shells loaded with buckshot that they were going out to shoot little birds with. . . . Maybe, gentlemen, you think that is the way men would be armed who were going on an innocent trip, innocent so far as death-dealing matters are concerned at night time after closing hours of the garage and when the man who ran it was in bed, going to make a social trip down to see Pappi, the friend of Vanzetti, and he did not know where he lived, save that it was in East Bridgewater, gentlemen."

The district attorney admitted that Pelser had lied at first both to the defense and the Commonwealth, because he did not want to be a witness, but afterward he was "manly enough to tell you of his prior falsehoods and his reasons for them." On the subject of Splaine and Devlin, Katzmann became almost lyrical: "Gentlemen, do you think that two young women, presumably endowed with Christian instincts, young ladies who could have no enmity against the defendant Sacco, who could have no reason for committing the most damnable of perjuries, would bespeak evidence against a human being that would take his life away? Gentlemen, that passes the bounds of human credulity. You can't believe that. You cannot have looked on Mary Splaine, a smart businesswoman, you cannot have looked on the gentle Frances Devlin and have seen the truth shining like stars out of her young womanly eyes and believe for a moment that either or both of them would dare, before a court of justice or before God their Maker, condemn Sacco to his death with a willful lie. You cannot believe that, gentlemen, having seen those women."

He agreed that Levangie, the gate-tender, was wrong in saying that Vanzetti had driven the car. The probability was that Vanzetti was directly behind the driver, was leaning forward, and Levangie had given just a quick transposing glance. Lola Andrews conjured up a briefer burst of lyricism: "I have been in this office, gentlemen, for now more than eleven years. I cannot recall in that too long service for the Commonwealth that ever before I have laid eye or given ear to so convincing a witness as Lola Andrews." As for Julia Campbell, she was "Aunt Julia, the elderly lady with the cataracts."

The district attorney underlined the fact that the Buick getaway car was found only a mile or so from Elm Square. "You don't find the car in Worcester. You don't find it in Pittsfield. You don't find it in South Boston, nor do you find it in Fall River. You find it in West Bridgewater, and the night these men were arrested, they were arrested within hailing distance of it. Can you put two and two together?"

In contrast to Moore's objection to the microscope's evidence, Katzmann declaimed: "Heaven speed the day when proof in any important case is dependent upon the magnifying glass and the scientist." He marshaled the evidence of the guns and the bullets carefully in the Commonwealth's favor. "What is the reason Captain Van Amburgh gives for saying that bullet number three was fired by the Colt of Sacco?" he asked, thus compounding Jerry McAnarney's error.

It was after six before Katzman, facing a weary jury and a long-since emptying courtroom, made his last points. He asked who knew better about the Harrington & Richardson revolver, the man who had put in a new hammer or an expert who had never seen it before. He questioned the disorder and general lack of dates in Affe's grocery account books. He wondered why the defense had produced no witnesses from Rice & Hutchins, where Sacco had worked, to say he was not the man. He concluded with a flourish: "You are the consultants here, gentlemen, the twelve of you, and the parties come to you and ask you to find out what the truth is on the two issues of guilt or innocence. Men of the jury, do your duty. Do it like men. Stand together, men of Norfolk!"

Nothing was left but the judge's charge and the jury's verdict.

Judge Thayer spent that evening at the University Club in Boston working on his charge. Like most intermediate judges, he tended to make his charges set pieces formed out of the accumulated mosaics of the law, varying in detail according to the particular case, but in general outline the same. The basic function of a charge is to enable the jury to sift the relevant from the irrelevant. In his Sacco-Vanzetti charge of twenty-four pages, only ten were given to the specific aspects of the case. The formula was based on a standard set of legal truisms: that a man is innocent until proved guilty, that reasonable doubt is the doubt of a reasonable man, that no inference of guilt shall be drawn from an indictment, that circumstantial evidence can at times be as weighty as direct evidence, that English common law as adopted by American practice is one of the glories of the world, and so on. Thayer's first childhood memories were of the boys in blue of the Civil War; he had been appointed to the bench the year that the United States entered the World War, and his attitude toward soldiers was that of a sentimental civilian. Ever since his appointment he had peppered his charges and his less formal addresses with references to "our soldier boys." It was a habit that still continued three years after the Armistice, and that could have somewhat sinister connotations in the trial of two draft-dodging anarchists.

With the fervor of a poet Thayer worked at his manuscript late into the night. He was proud of his literary efforts. Like most Americans whose school course included the elocution lessons of the post-Civil War period, his taste ran to the flamboyant. Vague metaphorical phrases blossomed under his hand. "Let the star of a sound judgment and profound wisdom guide your footsteps into that beautiful realm where conscience, obedience to law and to God, reigneth supreme." Such phrases he found reassuring. And his indwelling sense of insecurity made him need assurance, turned him at times garrulous, biased him against foreigners, and drove him to indiscretions that were later to become notorious.

When Judge Thayer went down to breakfast early Thursday morning and looked hopefully around the club's almost empty dining room, his eye fell on the frosty George Crocker at a table by the window and he walked over and sat down opposite him. Crocker, an elderly codfish Bostonian, greeted Thayer with a noticeable lack of cordiality. Several times during the month the judge had waylaid him in the lounge and filled his unwilling ears with news about the Dedham trial, insisting that Americans must now stand together to protect themselves against anarchists and Reds. Conservative lawyer that he was, Crocker felt offended at Thayer's violation of the legal proprieties in even mentioning a current case. Oblivious of the other's disapproval, Thayer would say that it was nonsense that the defendants were being prosecuted as radicals. Just the same, in his opinion, they were anarchists and draft-dodgers, and they had failed to establish alibis.

This morning, before Crocker had finished his grapefruit, Thayer pulled some sheets of paper out of his pocket saying proudly: "I want to read you part of the charge I am going to deliver today." He talked on, quoting part of Moore's argument, and then reading more of his charge, smacking his lips at the end with "That will hold them!" Crocker replied sniffily or not at all. On leaving the dining room he warned the steward, "For Heaven's sake, don't put me with that man again!"

Court opened late. Judge Thayer had again timed it that way for dramatic effect. Every seat was taken and the bar enclosure was filled with lawyers as Sacco and Vanzetti took their place in the cage, for it had been noised about in State Street that the judge's charge would make legal history. The opening, however, had more the air of a graduation ceremony than a murder trial. The judge's desk was buried in flowers—a huge vase of gladioli sent by the sheriff, and large bouquets of pinks from Mrs. Katzmann and the wife of Assistant District Attorney Kane. Among the spectators were the Marquis Ferrante, Rosina Sacco with the boy Dante, and of course Mrs. Evans and her inevitable notebook. In spite of the heat Sheriff Capen had resumed his blue cutaway.

With the clerk's cry, Judge Thayer rustled in and sat down behind the bank of flowers. For the last time the ritual was intoned, the jury was polled, the defendants answered "Present." Jerry McAnarney approached the bench with a motion for a directed verdict on the grounds that the district attorney in his argument had disclaimed that Vanzetti was driving the getaway car as it crossed the railroad track. Moore made the conventional request that the court order the jury upon all the evidence to return a not-guilty verdict for Sacco. Neither motion, they knew, would be granted. There were a few more words added to the record about the Berardelli revolver, then the judge's brittle voice began:

"Mr. Foreman and gentlemen of the jury—you may remain seated —the Commonwealth of Massachusetts called upon you to render a most important service. Although you knew that such service would be arduous, painful and tiresome, yet you, like the true soldier, responded to that call in the spirit of supreme American loyalty. There is no better word in the English language than 'loyalty.' For he who is loyal to God, to country, to his state and to his fellow men, represents the highest and noblest type of true American citizenship, than which there is none grander in the entire world. You gentlemen have been put to the real test, and you have proven to the world, and particularly to the people of Norfolk County, that you truly represent such citizenship. For this loyalty, gentlemen, and for this magnificent service that you have rendered to your State and to your fellow men, I desire, however, in behalf of both to extend to each of you their profoundest thanks, gratitude and appreciation."

It was of course conventional to butter up a jury at the end of a long trial, but Thayer enjoyed the convention. His mind slipped easily among the sententious moralizings, the hortatory appeals to truth, the assurances of equality before the law:

"Let your eyes be blinded to every ray of sympathy or prejudice but let them ever be willing to receive the beautiful sunshine of truth, of reason and sound judgment, and let your ears be deaf to every sound of public opinion or public clamor, if there be any, either in favor of or against these defendants. Let them always be listening for the sweet voices of conscience and of sacred and solemn duty efficiently and fearlessly performed."

Warning the jury not to be influenced or prejudiced by the fact that the defendants were Italians, he went on to a brief history of murder in common law, the development of degrees of murder, the definition of malice aforethought. He pointed out that there was no vital distinction between circumstantial and other evidence, that the important thing was the degree of proof. He must have puzzled the jurors with his remark that "over-positiveness in identification might under some circumstances and conditions be evidence of weakness in the testimony rather than strength."

There was the expected truism—none the less true—that "guilt or innocence of crime do not depend upon the place of one's birth; neither should the place of one's birth, the proportion of his wealth, his station in life, social or political, or his views on public questions prevent an honest judgment and impartial administration and enforcement of the law, for when the time comes that these conditions exist to an extent that men, because of these conditions, cannot be indicted, tried, acquitted or convicted according to the laws of the Commonwealth in a court of justice, the doors to our courthouses should then be closed and we should announce to the world the impotency of our courts and the utter failure of constitutional or organized government."

Not until he had passed the halfway mark did Judge Thayer abandon generalities for facts. Then he summed up the case adequately enough: "The Commonwealth claims that these defendants were two of a party of five who killed the deceased. The defendants deny it. What is the fact? As I have told you, the Commonwealth must satisfy you of that fact beyond reasonable doubt. The defendants are under no obligation to satisfy you who did commit the murders, but the Commonwealth must satisfy you beyond reasonable doubt that the defendants did. If the Commonwealth has failed to so satisfy you, that is the end of these cases and you will return verdicts of not guilty. This is so because the identity of the defendants is one of the essential facts to be established by the Commonwealth. On the other hand, if the Commonwealth has so satisfied, you will return a verdict of guilty against both defendants or either of them that you so find to be guilty."

In weighing the testimony of the identifying witnesses, the jurors would have to consider the latter's intelligence, "their opportunity for observations, their reasons for making such observations, the duration of such observations, and the mental or nervous condition of the witness at the time." Turning to the ballistics testimony, Thayer fell into the crucial error of McAnarney and Katzmann, for he, too, accepted Van Amburgh's "I am inclined to believe" as a direct assertion that the Berardelli death bullet had come from Sacco's automatic. "You must determine this question of fact," he told them. In speaking of the Vanzetti revolver, he first said that it had had a new hammer and spring, then later corrected himself.

The emphasis of the latter part of the charge was on the question of consciousness of guilt, to which Judge Thayer gave much more space than he did to the other testimony. "If the defendants were only consciously guilty of being slackers," he informed the jurors, "liable to be deported, fearing punishment therefore, and were not consciously guilty of the murder of Berardelli and Parmenter, then there is no consciousness of guilt during the time they were at the Johnson house, because the defendants were solely being tried for the murder of Berardelli and Parmenter, and for nothing else."

This was a question of fact for the jurors to decide, just as it was for them to decide whether or not the defendants had "the desire and purpose and intention" of drawing their weapons when they were arrested on the streetcar. The court decided questions of law, but only the jury could decide on the facts. Alibis were always questions of fact. "Therefore," he instructed them finally, "all testimony which tends to show that the defendants were in another place at the time the murders were committed tends also to rebut the evidence that they were present at the time and place the murders were committed. If the evidence of an alibi rebuts evidence of the Commonwealth to such an extent that it leaves reasonable doubt in your minds as to the commission of the murders charged against these defendants then you will return a verdict of not guilty. On the other hand, if you find that the defendants or either of them committed the murders and the Commonwealth has satisfied you of such fact beyond a reasonable doubt from all the evidence in these cases, you will return a verdict of guilty."

Thayer had been talking for several hours. He shifted a vase of pinks slightly to his right so that he could eye the jury more emphatically before beginning his peroration, his particular pride:

"My duties, gentlemen, have now closed and yours begun. From this mass of testimony introduced you must determine the facts. The law, as I have told you, places the entire responsibility in your hands. I therefore call upon you to constantly bear in mind these parting words of the Court that here, in this temple of justice, before God and man, you made oath that you would 'well and truly try the issue between the Commonwealth and the defendants according to your evidence. So help you God.'

"I have now finished my charge. My duties are now at an end. I have tried to preside over the trial of these cases in a spirit of absolute fairness and impartiality to both sides. If I have failed in any respect you must not, gentlemen, in any manner fail yours. I therefore now commit into your sacred keeping the decision of these cases. You will therefore take them with you into yonder jury room, the silent sanctuary where may the Great Dispenser of justice, wisdom and sound judgment preside over all your deliberations. Reflect long and well so that when you return, your verdict shall stand forth before the world as your judgment of truth and justice. Gentlemen, be just and fear not. Let all the end thou aimest at be thy country's, thy God's and truth's."

There was a moment's silence, then a murmur went through the courtroom like a collective sigh, followed by a shuffle of feet as spectators and jury began to file from the room, while the lawyers worked their way to the back for another consultation. Vanzetti bent over and whispered to Sacco as a deputy with handcuffs opened the cage door.

Moore, observing legal etiquette, remarked formally to the Court that whatever the jury's verdict no one could say that the defendants had not had a fair trial.

Judge Thayer was in a good mood as he walked briskly to the Dedham Inn for lunch. The trial that had cut so deep into his summer was over. He would no longer have to endure the daily sight of that long-haired California radical. His charge had gone off well.

Inside the dining room he stopped at the reporters' table where

Frank Sibley, with his Windsor tie, sat at the head. "Did you see that jury when I finished my charge?" Thayer asked of no one in particular. "Three of them in tears!" Sibley and the others said nothing. The silence nettled the judge. He looked them up and down and then said pettishly, "I think I am entitled to have a statement printed in the newspapers that this trial was fairly and impartially conducted." Again there was silence. Sibley looked down at the table-cloth in embarrassment.

Finally Thayer spoke to him directly. "Sibley, you are the oldest. Don't you think this trial was fairly and impartially conducted?"

Sibley stared at him above his wilted tie. "Well," he said quietly, "I don't know whether to express their opinion, but of course we have talked it over, and I think I can say I have never seen anything like it."

Thayer looked down scornfully, turned on his heel, and walked away.

As the defendants arrived for the afternoon session and the court-room filled, Rosina and Dante were allowed briefly inside the cage. While Sacco talked to his wife, Vanzetti rumpled the boy's hair playfully, his deep eyes glowing, a smile wrinkling across his face. The jury was brought in, polled, and then retired. The defendants were again led away. Lawyers, reporters, and most of the spectators went outside. Those wise in the ways of juries did not expect a verdict until after the evening meal. Sheriff Capen predicted five hours. It was then three o'clock.

Much in the preceding weeks had seemed a legal game, but now the verbiage had been swept away, leaving nothing but the bone-bare interlude like time suspended, a feeling somehow intensified by the paper-littered courtroom and the ticking marble-faced clock and the summer brightness filtering through the maple trees.

From the courtroom the sheriff led the jurymen down the corridor to a room on the left with the word JURY stenciled on the frosted glass of the door. He closed the door behind them and locked it. They found themselves alone in a room containing nothing but a long table and twelve leather-cushioned chairs. Another door at the side led to the lavatory. John Dever noticed that all the doorknobs had the county seal embossed on them.

In their six weeks of close association the twelve men had developed a sense of camaraderie that would bind them together for the rest of their lives. Over thirty years later, Dever, destitute in a veteran's hospital, would find himself visited by Atwood and Gerard, and there again they would talk over the case. But in this first moment of being alone no one quite knew how to begin.

Dever finally suggested that first of all they take an informal ballot, nothing binding, just to get an idea how they felt. Sitting around the table, each marked a slip of paper and handed it down to Ripley who, as foreman, occupied the end seat. Dever believed the defendants guilty but he voted for acquittal on the first ballot to open up a discussion. The vote was ten to two for conviction. "Then," Dever told a reporter long afterward, "we started discussing things, reviewed the very important evidence about the bullets, and everybody had a chance to speak his piece. There never was any argument, though. We just were convinced Sacco and Vanzetti had done what the prosecution had charged them with." The Winchester bullet taken from Berardelli's body had, they felt, been fired from Sacco's pistol. And the same three kinds of shells that Thomas Fraher had picked up in front of Rice & Hutchins had been found in Sacco's pocket. Seward Parker remarked that you couldn't depend on the witnesses—"but the bullets, there's no way of getting round that." Alfred Atwood agreed with him. John Ganley was impressed by what Reed, the Matfield gate-tender, said about seeing Vanzetti at the crossing. The twelve did not even bother to ballot again. They talked over various aspects of the case but no longer debated guilt or innocence. Someone suggested that they ask for a reading glass to examine the bullets. A deputy brought them one. It would have been possible for them to bring in their verdict at the end of the afternoon. They decided, however, that it would look better if they waited until after supper. Shortly after six Judge Thayer sent them out to eat. By half-past seven they were back.

The shadows of the trees and the buildings were long across the High Street, but the setting sun brought no relief from the heat. A scattering of spectators waited in the courtroom. There were groups of white-shirted figures on the steps, on the grass, on the sidewalk across the street, restless groups that joined together, broke apart, or receded in the direction of Dedham Square. Always there was a corporal's guard of newspapermen to keep a careful eye on the upper rear window where, behind the plate glass, the overhead light had now been turned on.

At 7:55 Deputy Sheriff Fales heard a triple knock on the jury-room door. It was sharp, final, not the tentative knock meaning that a reading glass or some such thing was wanted. He unlocked the door and Ripley told him the verdict was ready. Fales' face kept its professional impassivity. He took the message, locked the door again, then went downstairs to telephone the warden at the jail. To the newsmen who looked at him questioningly as he passed, he nodded.

A few minutes before, a slight breeze had sprung up. Harold Williams, the McAnarneys, several state troopers, and deputy sheriffs were standing near the columns enjoying the coolness when someone came out and whispered the news. An invisible telegraph seemed to flash the word through Dedham. The white-shirted groups on the grass dissolved, the loungers vanished, from all directions running figures converged on the courthouse. The High Street echoed with footsteps. Upstairs the courtroom windows suddenly blazed with light.

In the ten minutes that it took to bring the defendants over from the jail the gates had been closed and a guard of troopers thrown around the courthouse. On the steps a crowd that by now stretched across the street forced its way up to the iron barrier. Those who had gone up to the courtroom earlier were allowed to stay, but, except for the lawyers and the newspapermen, no one else was admitted.

Sacco and Vanzetti were brought in through the side entrance, taken up the back stairs, their handcuffs removed, and the door of the cage closed behind them. Sacco looked pale, almost ill. Vanzetti spoke a few words to him, a frown scoring his forehead. Rosina sat close by, making quick birdlike movements, managing to smile each time her husband glanced at her.

The pause before the jury entered the room was so oppressive that it became almost tangible. Inside the bar enclosure the lawyers waited, Moore fiddling with a pencil, his hair dank. The deputies stood at the entrances, the stenographers had their notebooks open, Judge Thayer sat in his place. From time to time everyone in the courtroom glanced at the twelve empty seats flanked by the American flag. Then the door opened.

The jurors filed in, their eyes fixed on the floor. Seeing their mood, Tom McAnarney raised his arm in a gesture of despair. The lines between Vanzetti's eyes were like cords. Sacco glanced from one face to another as the jury passed.

The jurors settled in their seats. Judge Thayer nodded obliquely at Clerk Worthington who, precise and impersonal, asked them if they had agreed on a verdict. Then, scarcely waiting for the foreman's reply, he called out "Nicola Sacco." Sacco rose to his feet as if he were in a trance, and Worthington's singsong voice continued:

"Hold up your right hand, Mr. Foreman; look upon the prisoner. Prisoner, look upon the foreman. What say you, Mr. Foreman, is the prisoner at the bar guilty or not guilty?"

Ripley's voice was like a croak as he spoke the one word. "Guilty."

"Guilty of murder?" Worthington went on.

"Murder," Ripley answered him.

"In the first degree?"

"In the first degree."

While the impact of the verdict was still in transit, Worthington rapidly repeated the formula for Vanzetti.

"What say you, Mr. Foreman; is Bartolomeo Vanzetti guilty or not guilty of murder?"

"Guilty," Ripley croaked again.

"In the first degree, upon each indictment?"

"In the first degree."

"Hearken to your verdicts as the Court has recorded them," Worthington hurried on, his words falling limply in the hush. "You, gentlemen, upon your oath, say that Nicola Sacco and Bartolomeo Vanzetti is each guilty of murder in the first degree upon each indictment. So say you, Mr. Foreman? So, gentlemen, you all say?"

There were murmurs of "We do, we do," from the jury box. Vanzetti stood in the cage, his arm still raised in the air. Then suddenly Sacco's voice rang through the courtroom: *Sono innocente!*

"*Sono innocente!*" he shouted again, and behind the cage Rosina cried loudly, ran to him breaking through the ring of guards and throwing her arms around his neck. Her hat fell off and her copper-red hair tumbled about her neck. "You bet your life," she babbled. Then she cried out as if overwhelmed, "What am I going to do? I've got two children. Oh, Nick. They kill my man." She clung to him sobbing, burying her face in his neck, the torrent of her words unintelligible. Sacco stood upright, paler than ever, stroking her head and occasionally whispering to her. Vanzetti, next to them, said nothing, but his face was drawn with sympathy. Moore tried gently to disengage her. Finally a policeman removed her from Sacco's shoulder and led her away.

Judge Thayer nodded to the clerk for adjournment. No one was even aware of his few words of thanks to the jury.

"They kill an innocent men!" Sacco called out in a shaken voice as judge and jury were leaving. Several of the jurymen looked back at him but none of them paused. "Don't forget. Two innocent men they kill!" he shouted at them.

Within ten minutes the police and deputies had delivered the defendants back to the jail. On their way there the loiterers on the courthouse steps pushed forward and Sheriff Capen threatened to draw his gun if they came any closer.

Now the darkened streets were as empty as the courtroom. Lawyers, deputies, public, all had gone except Tom McAnarney, who was rummaging among some papers on the oak table. As he closed his brief case he noticed Assistant District Attorney Williams in the doorway, and observing the customary legal etiquette he stepped toward him with extended hand.

"Congratulations," he said, "on a brilliant victory." Then he noticed that the other's face was wet with tears.

"For God's sake, don't rub it in," said Williams, without taking his hand. "This is the saddest thing that ever happened to me in my life." And with the tears still streaming down his cheeks he walked on through the courtroom.

◇◇◇◇◇◇◇◇◇◇◇◇◇◇◇◇◇◇◇◇◇◇◇◇◇◇◇◇◇◇◇

CHAPTER TWELVE

Post-Trial—I

The convictions made the Friday headlines of all the Boston papers, but by mid-August references to Sacco and Vanzetti had disappeared from even the back pages. Theirs had been just another Massachusetts murder trial, longer than most, but finished now in every sense. So it seemed to J. Weston Allen, the Attorney General, when he sent a letter of congratulation to District Attorney Katzmann. So it seemed to Chief Justice Aiken, who wrote to his colleague and fellow Dartmouth alumnus Webster Thayer that "Your management of the trial of Sacco and Vanzetti entitles you to the highest degree *summa cum laude.*" Whatever undercurrents of radical protest might still persist, they remained well below the surface of middle-class complacency.

But while in the United States the storm centered in Massachusetts subsided, overseas there were increasing rumblings broken by occasional flashes of lightning. As early as August 6, 1921, the Executive Committee of the Chamber of Labor Unions in Rome sent a telegram to President Harding expressing the hope that "the crime of the execution of Sacco and Vanzetti will not be recorded." Eugene Lyons in his six months in Italy had done a skillful publicity job, for by the time of the trial, Italians were generally convinced that Sacco and Vanzetti were innocent. The Latin anarchists in the United States had written voluminously to their comrades in Italy, Spain and Portugal, laying the groundwork for the later agitation. Frank Lopez, through his contacts with the more important South American newspapers, had managed to appeal to the widespread anti-gringo feeling there.

Although American consulates and embassies overseas had begun to receive letters of protest in September, the real force of the agitation did not strike until October, when large Communist-organized demonstrations took place in many cities. For all their tenacity, the anarchists were no longer a mass organization and, so far as European developments were concerned, the East German historian Johannes Zelt is undoubtedly right in claiming that "from the beginning the Communists stood at the head of the Sacco-Vanzetti campaign." In a tactic foreshadowing the Popular Front of the thirties, the Communist International called on all Communists, socialists, anarchists, and trade unionists to unite for the rescue of Sacco and Vanzetti—while, at the same time, the anarchists in the Soviet Union were being liquidated en masse. The organized protest, as it spread across Europe, would include men of good will of all beliefs and persuasions, but control of the movement stayed in the hands of the Communist International and, later, the subsidiary International Red Aid, founded by the Cheka chief, Dzerzhinsky.

For the Communists, Sacco and Vanzetti were pawns in the class struggle, convenient symbols to be exploited in a drive for power where the blood of even anarchist martyrs might become the seed of the Party. However the anarchists were to feel about the Communists taking over—and in time they would feel bitter indeed—the Party had the tight organization, the mass control, and the finances that made quick action easy. On September 20 the Central Committee for Action of the French Communist Party began making plans for a monster demonstration before the American Embassy. According to the resolution then drawn up, "Only direct and clearly revolutionary action can save the Italian liberators Sacco and Vanzetti from the death penalty to which they have been condemned." The Communist daily L'Humanité opened a subscription fund for the two men and proclaimed: "There is an American Embassy in Paris. We owe it a visit!"

Rank-and-file demonstrators had scarcely heard the names of the two Italians when they received orders to take to the streets, but in their militancy they responded, just as they had for other issues and would again when some central committee pressed a different propaganda button.

The October demonstrations were centered in France and Italy, with echoes in Switzerland, Belgium, Spain, Portugal, and Scandinavia. Concerned for the moment with other matters, the German Communist Party did not participate. In Paris, even before the end of September various committees for action had met. Eight thousand militants filled the Salle Wagram and, on leaving, sang the "Internationale" while from a doorway someone lobbed a grenade at the drawn-up police, wounding several of them. The American Embassy was deluged with letters and telegrams. On October 19 a grenade, wrapped with sinister humor in a copy of the Royalist *Action Française*, was sent through the mail to the new American ambassador, Myron T. Herrick. The valet who opened the package set off the fuse but managed to throw it into a bathroom, where it went off, wounding him slightly and demolishing the room. On the twenty-fourth, ten thousand police and eighteen thousand troops had to be called out to hold back the vast crowd demonstrating before the American Embassy.

The wave spread across Europe. In Switzerland the Communists organized demonstrations in Zurich, Basle, and Geneva. In St. Gall a letter to the American Consulate protesting the judicial murder of "Sachi" and Vanzetti was signed by Communists, syndicalists, socialists, and trade unionists. Amsterdam workers held a protest meeting, as did the Dutch Free Thinkers. Communists marched in the streets of The Hague, Brussels, Liége, Stockholm, and Copenhagen. The American ambassador in Madrid was threatened with assassination. In Lisbon a bomb was exploded in the vestibule of the consulate-general shortly after a letter had been placed under the door demanding the release of the "Brockton anarchists." Medical students of Portugal's National College struck for a day to show their sympathy. Although a demonstration by English Communists before the American Embassy fizzled out in a London rain, the Party's Tooting branch forwarded its objections in a letter to the ambassador. A polite communication was sent to Washington by the Communist Party of Ireland.

When November found the Massachusetts prisoners still alive and no date set for their execution, the Communist International turned off the spigot and the European agitation dried up, but a new wave of agitation now began in Central and South America. The Latin American movement was less well organized, less literate, and, as might be expected, more violent. Anarchists of Guadalajara, Mexico, paraded behind red and black banners reading: "Yankee bourgeoisie, if you assassinate our comrades, Sacco and Vanzetti, your lives and your interests will pay the penalty." La Junta Federal of Santiago, Chile, announced that "the day the Communists of the world learn that Sacco and Vanzetti have been shot, the residences of all American ambassadors which exist in various countries will be destroyed by a tremendous charge of dynamite." In Havana, anarchist circulars warned that "in Cuba, Yankee tyrants are not lacking in whom to let fall the vengeful dagger." A bomb was found in the embassy garden in Rio de Janeiro. The American consul in Mexico City received anonymous threats from "the comrades of Saco and Banzet." There were demonstrations in front of the United States embassies and consulates in Argentina, Brazil, Chile, Mexico, and Panama.

In Massachusetts the overseas disturbances, recorded with increasing frequency in the local papers, stirred up feelings of apprehension. Moore was dismayed, and said so. "I cannot conceive," he wrote, "how any intelligent and sane person sincerely interested in obtaining ultimate justice for these two men could hope that this sort of thing could benefit them." The bombings, he tried to make out, were the work either of enemies or insane people. Prompted by Moore, and aware of the hardening of community opinion, the Defense Committee issued a disclaimer, maintaining that

the lurid plots and threats attributed to mythical individuals referred to as Sacco-Vanzetti sympathizers are so thoroughly harmful to the effort being made to save the two men from the electric chair that they could not have originated in the minds of friends. Either they were planned by persons desirous of putting the case of the two prisoners in disrepute or they are lies pure and simple.

Two days after the trial's end the defense lawyers filed the customary motion for a new trial on the grounds that the verdict was against the weight of the evidence. This motion was scheduled to be argued before Judge Thayer in Dedham on Saturday, October 29. On the twenty-eighth the Boston papers spread a sensational story that groups of Italians were coming to the hearing from New York dressed in army uniforms and carrying automatics. Extra police were at once stationed throughout the city, and the Post Office and the Federal Building placed under guard. At the South Station plain-clothes men watched each incoming train. That night the Dedham jail was surrounded with searchlights.

Saturday morning the courthouse was more heavily guarded than at any time during the trial. State troopers, mounted and on motorcycles, patrolled the streets, and portly Colonel Foote, the Commissioner of Public Safety, came over from the State House in person. Plain-clothes men in all their obviousness tramped up and down the High Street. The Boston riot squad appeared, loaned for the day by the Boston police commissioner. The public was banned from the courthouse. Reporters who were admitted were patted for weapons.

When Sacco and Vanzetti were brought in and their handcuffs taken off, there were fewer than fifty persons in the courtroom. Three months had done much to alter the two men. In July, overwhelmed by the verdict, they had felt isolated. Now the news from overseas had given them the satisfaction of knowing that there were workers the world over who were not going to stand by while the courts of Massachusetts sent their comrades to the electric chair. Newly confident, Sacco and Vanzetti were also full of resentment, particularly against the debonair district attorney whom they once more faced.

Both Moore and Jerry McAnarney well knew there was no chance that Judge Thayer would overrule the jury's verdict, but the motion was a legal step always taken in murder cases. The arguments and counterarguments lasted all that Saturday and the following Saturday, Moore appealing particularly to the fact that the jury had given no consideration to the alibi witnesses. While Katzmann was delivering his arguments defending the verdict, the men in the cage kept interrupting and contradicting him. When he told of taking a witness to the Dedham jail who picked out Sacco from a group of prisoners, Sacco jumped up in the cage and accused the district attorney of having prompted the witness. "Yes," he shouted to Judge Thayer, who motioned to a deputy, "that man he said, 'There's Sacco.' That's the way he know!" The deputy grabbed Sacco by the arm. "Go easy!" Sacco cried out, trying to brush him off. Vanzetti now broke in savagely: "You bring every crook in Massachusetts to testify against us! You and every man of sense know it." Judge Thayer observed acidly that the defendants ought not to interrupt. When they continued to shout and gesticulate, he again signaled to the deputies to quiet them. He too had been hearing of the turmoil in Europe, and had been receiving letters and telegrams daily—some of them threatening—demanding a new trial. His house in Worcester was now under guard, and he was simmeringly aware that last summer's court session and verdict had by no means ended the case. "These cases," he announced with controlled but still obvious anger as he looked sourly at the cage, "seem to have assumed a state, national and international interest. Overseas a statement was published that the presiding justice said to the jury that these men must be convicted because they were Italians and radicals. That statement was absolutely false."

He and Moore continued their verbal dueling, carrying it over to the concluding arguments on Saturday, November 5. When Moore tried to explain how the issue of radicalism had injured his clients, Judge Thayer pointed out his trial ruling that "No evidence of the defendants' radical activities or opinions would be allowed until the defense released such matter themselves." Moore characterized the ruling as a Greek gift, the Virgilian reference escaping Judge Thayer.

Following this formal and predetermined motion the defense filed five supplementary motions for a new trial: the Ripley motion, the Gould-Pelser motion, the Goodridge motion, the Andrews motion, and the Hamilton-Proctor motion.

A month or so after the trial Jerry McAnarney had met the jury foreman, Walter Ripley—whom he had known for years—on the street in Quincy. They stopped on the corner to talk, and Jerry learned for the first time about the three cartridges that Ripley had casually brought to court in his vest pocket and during the trial compared with the five cartridges found in Vanzetti's revolver. Ripley thought nothing of the matter, but for Jerry it was the first crack in the verdict. He now interviewed nine of the other jurors and obtained affidavits from several of them. Wallace Hersey and Frank McNamara admitted they had seen the Ripley bullets, Frank Marden and Seward Parker that they had heard about them. Ripley himself had died of a heart attack on October 10, before McAnarney could get an affidavit from him. His widow signed an affidavit that her husband had had the bullets with him during the trial. This admitted fact was the basis of the first supplementary motion, a lengthy document that claimed in substance that "if during the trial Ripley made a comparison between these three cartridges and the five cartridges taken from Vanzetti's revolver, then the defendants are entitled to a new trial as a matter of right." The Ripley motion with its accompanying affidavits was filed on November 8. Judge Thayer announced that he would set a hearing date satisfactory to both sides.

On the afternoon before Christmas, 1921, exactly two years after the Bridgewater crime, in a gray, nearly empty courtroom, the wintry-faced Thayer denied the October motion for a new trial. "I cannot," he intoned, "as I must if I disturb these verdicts—announce to the world that these twelve jurors violated the sanctity of their oaths, threw to the four winds of bias and prejudice their honor, judgment, reason and conscience, and thereby abused the solemn trust reposed in them by the law as well as by the Court. And all for what purpose? To take away the lives of two human beings created by their own God. The human frailties of man, his tender regard and love for human life and his profound sympathy for his fellow-men, when charged with the gravest offence known to the law, repudiates the suggestion."

Three days after this denial Fred Moore wrote to a friend:

The one hope for these boys now rests in the hope that we may be able to unearth new facts. This means endless investigations. It means that every clue as to the real bandits must be followed up expertly and carefully. As you know this means money.

Thus, briefly, Moore stated his problems for the next three years, and the last problem would always be the most harassing, the one that would seem to be squatting like a dollar sign on the doorstep of Rollins Place each time he returned. For him money was a wretched commodity, something that arrived in the morning and went out in the afternoon, a means merely through which he might obtain more publicity, wider investigations. His restless and inventive mind never stopped thinking of new angles to explore. One week would find him at the federal penitentiary in Atlanta on a tip that two inmates there were connected with the gang that, it was rumored, had really pulled off the Bridgewater job. The next week might find him uncovering the bigamous career of a prosecution witness. Pressed constantly for funds, he wrote countless dunning letters, cajoled his old radical friends and associates from coast to coast, unabashedly appealed to prominent strangers, cultivated sympathetic old women. Given enough money, he was sure he could win.

The trial had been over for half a year; the sentencing of the two men lay somewhere in the months ahead. General interest dwindled. Only the most faithful sympathizers still sent in contributions.

The Defense Committee had moved from Battery Street to the more central Hanover Street, where most of the North End Italian shops were located. Eugene Lyons, returned from Italy, now replaced Art Shields. The new headquarters at number 256 was on the third floor, a large garret anteroom leading into a small inner office. Every Thursday night the committee members would climb the warped, narrow stairs to listen to a repetition of what had been said the week before. Three or four times a year there would be a meeting of several hundred sympathizers at Paine Memorial Hall in the South End, most of them Italian comrades, with a sprinkling of Back Bay dissidents, members of the Civil Liberties Committee, and the more radical trade-union officials.

It was [Lyons wrote] *a motley and colorful and rather high-pitched company that gathered around the defense at this stage. Some were moved by an undiluted urge to save the two innocent men, others were interested primarily in the propagandist value of the case, still others got an emotional kick out of the battle. At one extreme were hot-headed and desperate Italians distrustful of all law, bitterly sarcastic about the hocus-pocus of motions and affidavits, and often refusing in principle to cooperate with their own lawyers. At the other extreme were men and women of old New England stock chiefly concerned with saving the Commonwealth of Massachusetts from the stigma of an ugly miscarriage of justice. I can recall vital meetings in which a snarling, red-headed Italian exponent of direct action argued some question of policy with a benign pacifist like Mrs. Evans. It was Moore's delicate job to reconcile these people and placate their idiosyncrasies.*

The money that Moore needed in floods came in dribbles—$18.30 from an Italian picnic in Connecticut, an anonymous dollar bill posted in Seattle, $38.65 from the Pietro Gori Group of Nokomis, Illinois, the occasional windfall of five hundred dollars collected by the Workers' Defense Union at a New York meeting in Beethoven Hall, a small but steady flow from Moore's friends in the United Mine Workers. Moore knew that what was required was a full-time treasurer to coordinate finances and fund-raising. He wanted Felicani to quit *La Notizia* and devote all his time to the job at a regular salary. Felicani would not hear of it. He was willing to work until midnight each night on the committee accounts, or on propaganda, or whatever else needed doing, but those pathetically small sums that kept dribbling in for the defense of his friends—he could not bear to pay himself from that money. He insisted on keeping a record of every amount received, no matter how small, and of every cent paid out.

Moore did not see the point of such finical accounting. To him it was foolish to waste time on columns of figures when two men's lives were at stake. He and Felicani were always at odds about money. To Felicani it seemed that no matter how much he provided, Moore always needed more. It was as if the lawyer had a hole in his hand. For Moore it was both ridiculous and humiliating that he, the general counsel of the I.W.W., whose name struck sparks from coast to coast, who had taken this case out of the gutter and made it a world issue, should have to appear hat in hand before a printer-nobody to beg for money—and often not get it! Time and again Moore saw what he considered promising investigations shut off by the anarchists. Later he was to ask himself if some deeper motive than a financial one lay behind their refusals. On October 20, 1922, the doctrinaire Frank Lopez, who had become secretary of the Defense Committee, wrote Moore:

I warn you to keep your hands off of many things that in order to obey or please other persons you had been trying to do for many months past.

To supplement such part-time detectives as Robert Reid, Moore hired two permanent investigators, Tommy Doyle and Albert Carpenter. Doyle, a pious Catholic, was still young enough to think of himself as a sleuth, so intrigued at playing Sherlock Holmes that he did not care whether he was investigating thieves, anarchists, or Republicans.

Carpenter was an older man, more self-contained, oriented to radical reform. He and Moore had first meet in San Diego, during the free-speech fight of 1911. Together they had tracked down and exposed the perjurer, Frank Oxman, in the Mooney-Billings case. In Everett, Washington, in 1915, after a dockside clash in which five I.W.W.'s and two sheriffs were killed and seventy-four Wobblies later indicted for first-degree murder—a national record—Carpenter acted as Moore's chief investigator. In Chicago during the 1917 I.W.W. trials, after Moore had been framed by the police and was on the run, it was Carpenter who kept track of him through Lola Darroch, then Moore's secretary. Once Moore had settled down in Rollins Place, it seemed only natural for him to send for his old reliable friend.

Moore had early become convinced that the South Braintree holdup was the work of a gang of professionals. Also, his legal sixth sense warned him there were unexplored depths to such equivocal witnesses as Louis Pelser, Lola Andrews, and Carlos Goodridge. It seemed a pity to him to have the money problem overshadowing all the others.

On May 4, 1922, Moore filed the second supplementary motion, the Gould-Pelser motion. Roy Gould was the razor-paste salesman who on the day of the South Braintree murders had stood near the crossing and been fired at from the getaway car, the bullet passing through his overcoat lapel. No one, not even Jimmy Bostock or Frank Burke, had been so close to the moving car or had such a clear view of its occupants. Immediately after the shooting Gould gave his name and address to a Braintree policemen, John Heaney. Soon afterward he left town to follow the summer carnivals and country fairs across New England with his razor paste.

Moore first learned about Gould and his experience from Frank Burke, who had known him for some time. No one, however, seemed to know what had become of Gould. Moore sent Reid all over New England inquiring at every carnival he could trace, without success. Finally on November 3, while Burke was in Portland, Maine, on business, he noticed Gould's name on the register of his hotel. Burke was almost too astonished to believe his eyes. When the two met, Gould said he had gone to Nova Scotia and Prince Edward Island shortly after the murder, and had not read much about the trial.

Moore came to Portland on the next train and found Gould perfectly willing to tell his story about South Braintree. The man who had fired at him that day, Gould said, was someone he could never forget. Moore paid Gould's way to Boston and there showed him photographs of Sacco and Vanzetti. Gould was positive that neither was the man who had fired at him. Later Moore took him to the Dedham jail where they talked with Sacco. After watching Sacco for about ten minutes Gould said he was certain that this was not the gunman and he was willing to sign an affidavit to that effect.

It was Moore's claim that Gould's affidavit was "new and independent testimony," that the Commonwealth had known about him and yet made no effort to call him as a witness, and that his identification would have been sufficient to warrant a different verdict.

Louis Pelser was the next witness on Moore's retribution list. All Moore could learn of him at first was that after the trial he had lost his job and left his parents' flat in Jamaica Plain. Tommy Doyle finally tracked him to a derelict South End rooming house. Pelser was in an abject alcoholic state, red-eyed and maudlin. When he said he had not eaten anything all day, Doyle bought him a meal, then gave him seventy cents and paid his carfare to Moore's Pemberton Square office.

Doyle had telephoned ahead and Moore was waiting there with Lyons, Reid, and a stenographer. Pelser sobered up when he saw them. As always, when faced with authority, he began to doubt himself, what he had seen, what he had previously said. Moore tried to reassure him, patting him on the back and telling him "You look like a regular fellow." Pelser said that the day he arrived at Dedham

District Attorney Williams had taken him to a little upstairs room in the courthouse and shown him several pictures of Sacco, asking if he was the man he had seen below the factory window. "No," Pelser had told him, "I don't think that's the man I seen. I just got a glance of everything. I could not identify if you brought me a hundred pictures here." Williams insisted that he, Pelser, knew "right well" Sacco was the man.

Now, in the Pemberton Square office, Pelser said he "did not get a good enough view to see any man." How the "dead image stuff" had come up in court he could not tell.

"Now why in God's world did you testify as you did?" Moore bellowed at the cowering sour-breathed Pelser.

"I must have been forced," the other replied lamely. He still maintained that he had seen a man with a gun, but he could in no way describe him. The "dead image," he admitted, had been a mistake.

Moore asked if he would go on the stand again and take back what he had said. Pelser hesitated. Moore bore down on him: "You can tell anything that is the truth. If it's not true that he is the dead image, then you owe it to yourself and your conscience to tell it. If it is the truth, for God's sake stick to your story. It might come to the point when in order to save a couple of men's lives it is going to be necessary—you have got the stuff to come through if it is necessary, that right?"

Pelser gulped out an abject "Yes."

It took the stenographer twenty minutes to prepare the transcript. After Pelser signed it Moore slapped him on the back again, gave him a couple of cigars, and Lyons offered to take him and his girl to the Westminster Winter Garden. Pelser refused. Afterward, when he thought of what he had signed, he felt sick. Two days later, at his parents' flat, he wrote to the district attorney:

> 287 Centre St.
> Jamiaca Plaine
> Feb.6, 1922.

Mr. Katzmann,

Dear Sir:—Saturday afternoon a man called for me in regards the Sacco Case. He did not say which side he represented.

He asked me if I could give a little information on the case.

I was drinking pretty heavy that day. He said I want to show a couple of pictures and got me on the way in town gave me some money bought a dinner cigars & cigaretts we went into some office in

Pemberton Sq. he introduced me to Mr. Moore then he sat me down and locked the door Moore said to me you look like a white man.

He patted me on the back & gave me a Cigar & said give me a little dope on the Sacco Case he handed me a couple of pictures & asked me if I ever saw them. I said "no, he showed me some more. One word led to another, he got around me some way & I didn't know what I was up against. He had 3 or 4 men in his office & a girl stenographer. He asked me one question & other and finaly had my whole story contradicted what I had said at the Dedham Court. I am worried at the way they have framed me & got me in to trouble. When it was over one of the men asked me if I would not have a drink & invited me to a big dinner & dance at the West Minster Hotel. Some how I refused to go because I felt it was another trap to get me to say more.

When I came to my Senses the next day & had a little talk with my folks they told me to get in touch with you as soon as I could I tried to get you on the phone and then decided I had better write you.

Hoping you will give this your immediate attention and favor me with an early reply.

Respectfully,
Louis Pelser

P.S. I forgot to mention that I also signed two papers of some kind.

As soon as Assistant District Attorney Williams read the letter, forwarded to him by Katzmann, he had Pelser up on the courthouse carpet. Williams asked him if he did not remember looking at Sacco's picture and saying "That looks like the man," of seeing Sacco and exclaiming "By George! If he isn't the man he is a dead image for him." Pelser now maintained that what he had said on the stand was the truth as he believed it, and that nothing had since happened to change his mind. The fact was that when he had talked to Moore in Boston he was in no condition to know what he was saying.

However spineless Pelser seemed in other respects, the "dead image" term still troubled him. When Williams asked him again if he had meant those words, he insisted "I didn't mean them in that way. I don't know how I happened to use that word 'dead image.'"

In his new motion Moore claimed that the affidavit Pelser had signed in his office was "tantamount and equivalent to a repudiation of the testimony given by the said Louis Pelser on the trial of this case" and that his testimony was "not entitled to be considered by the jury as trustworthy and reliable."

Eleven weeks later Moore filed the third supplementary motion, based on what he had learned about Carlos Goodridge, the pool-playing Victrola salesman who had so unhesitantly picked out Sacco as the gunman he had seen in the getaway car. During the trial the defense had discovered nothing more about Goodridge than that he was married and lived in Cambridge and that in September 1920 he had pleaded guilty to a charge of grand larceny in the Dedham court and had been placed on probation. What Moore had since learned about Goodridge was enough to destroy him.

Goodridge turned out to be Erastus Corning Whitney, a shiftless bigamist from upper New York State, an arsonist, a passer of bad checks who had served two terms in jail for petty larceny, a man who had passed most of his adult life escaping from old misdemeanors and importunate females. Tommy Doyle spent three months and more than ten thousand dollars collecting documents, pictures, letters, and affidavits that made all this plain.

Armed with the evidence, Moore started off for Vassalboro, Maine, where Goodridge was now living. Stopping in Augusta, he picked up Ethel Lee, a deputy sheriff, and her sister-in-law, Marjorie, a stenographer. It was twilight by the time they reached Goodridge's Vassalboro farm. His third wife, Margaret Rose, said her husband was down the road at a church meeting. Moore found him in the white clapboard building, called him out in the middle of a hymn, and asked him to get into the car. There he displayed Doyle's documents and asked Goodridge if he was not Erastus Corning Whitney, under indictment for larceny in Livingston County, New York. Goodridge admitted that he was. He did not dispute any of the facts that Doyle had dredged up. "Well, the game is up," he said wearily, "and I suppose I will have to go back to New York." He was not aware of the woman in the back seat taking shorthand notes, nor did he recognize his questioner until he said "My name is Moore."

"Glad to meet you," Goodridge said, trying to cover up his fear with cordiality. "I've heard of you from San Francisco to Maine."

Moore said flatly that he was not interested in what Goodridge had or had not done in New York. All he wanted was the full story of how he had come to testify in the Dedham court, and what influence the district attorney's office had brought to bear on him. Of

Dedham, Massachusetts, April 9, 1927, just before sentence was passed.
Bartolomeo Vanzetti, at left, Nicola Sacco, on the right.

(Top) The bullets removed from Berardelli's body. The mortal Bullet III, deformed by impact, is third from left. *(Middle)* The bullets as marked by Dr. Magrath. Note deformation of Bullet III, third from left. *(Bottom)* Composite photograph of Shell W (left) and test shell (right), showing continuous breechblock markings above and below firing pin indentation. *(Following page, top)* The shells Bostock gave to Fraher; Shell W third from left.

Sacco's Colt automatic.

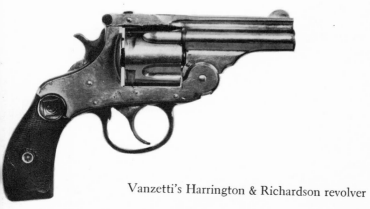

Vanzetti's Harrington & Richardson revolver

The jury's Fourth of July holiday at North Scituate, Massachusetts. Front row: Fales (Sheriff), Capen (Sheriff), Hooper (Sheriff), Ganley, Hersey, Waugh, and Atwood. Back row: Gerard, Ripley, McNamara, King, Parker, Dever, Marden, and McHardy.

(At left) William Thompson, Herbert Ehrmann, Tom O'Connor. (Bottom, left) Judge Webster Thayer. (Bottom, right) District Attorney Frederick Katzmann.

SACCO FLAYS CAPITALISTS IN FIERY SPEECH IN COURT

Holds Courtroom Spellbound by Address---Went to Mexico to Escape War Service, He States--- Proud of Having Been a Slacker

(*At right*) Sacco tries on the cap and addresses the court. Sketches by Norman. (*Bottom, left*) Edna St. Vincent Millay. (*Bottom, right*) Governor Alvan Fuller.

(Top, left) Rosina Sacco and Luigia Vanzetti visiting the death house, August 20. *(Top, right)* Fred Moore and Eugene Debs (front) after visiting Vanzetti in Charlestown Prison. *(Below)* Rosina Sacco and her children leaving Charlestown Prison, August, 1927. BOSTON HERALD

The start of the funeral procession

course if Goodridge did not want to talk, there was the deputy sheriff in the back seat and an indictment waiting in New York.

Goodridge agreed to tell his tale. He had first recognized Sacco's picture, he said, in a newspaper. He had then shown it to a girl he knew, Lottie Packard, who worked at Rice & Hutchins. "I says to Lottie, 'Whose picture is that?' and she called him by name. I had the paper folded so that she couldn't see nothing but the picture. 'I used to work with him in a factory.' I says, 'That's the fellow that was in the gang down here.' I told Lottie never to say anything about it. I never told anyone but my wife."

Williams and Brouillard and Stewart had been after him in the autumn of 1920 to come to the Dedham jail with them, Goodridge continued, but he had always refused, telling them it was no use to take him there, that he had seen nothing and "didn't know anything about the deal." When he himself was arraigned in Dedham he had recognized Sacco as soon as the latter was brought into the courtroom, but he never told anyone about this. He had lied to the district attorney's people and to the police because he did not want to get mixed up in the case.

Moore came back again and again to his central question: Why had Goodridge refused to talk from September to July, and then suddenly gone on the stand and identified Sacco? Goodridge did not have any explanation.

"I think I testified to the truth to the best of my ability," he complained, "and it's a pretty hard proposition."

The lawyer asked him sharply if he thought a man should die on his statement. No, Goodridge did not think so. But when he had testified he thought he had been right. No one had forced him, no inducements had been offered. It was just that Sacco was the man he thought he had seen. "But afterwards a good many times since I have thought that I am not positive," he went on. "I am not positive that if I would have to swear that that man was the one, I could positively identify him as the man." As Moore continued to batter him with questions, Goodridge began to cry.

Moore insisted that the assistant district attorney had badgered Goodridge into taking the stand. Goodridge no longer denied it. "You know just how those things is yourself," he told the lawyer pleadingly. "He talked to me so much I was just about dead, I guess."

The stenographer now interrupted to say she had run out of paper. The four drove back to the farm. On the way Moore urged Goodridge to sign an affidavit. He refused. Finally Moore turned to the sheriff. "I think, Mrs. Lee," he said sternly, "that it is your duty to take this man back to Augusta and notify the New York authorities."

While Goodridge changed his clothes, Moore spent twenty minutes talking with his wife, reducing her, too, to tears. Goodridge then quietly got in the car and they headed for Augusta. Just before they reached the city Moore made a final effort: "Whitney, what I would like to know is what inducement was held out to you to testify at this trial. You did not testify at this trial willingly unless you benefited by it some way or another; that is what I want to know and if you will tell me you will save yourself the trouble of going back to New York." Goodridge still would not say.

Moore took him first to the county jail. There the warden refused to admit him without a warrant. With the help of Deputy Sheriff Lee, Moore managed to have him locked up in police headquarters as a fugitive. "I will come back later," Moore told the police chief, "as I want this fellow to come clean and he is holding back things that he ought to tell us." Mrs. Lee then telegraphed the district attorney of Livingston County that they were holding Erastus Corning Whitney for him. Moore telephoned the clerk of courts in Genesee and asked if Whitney was still wanted. The clerk said he did not think so, but he would ask the sheriff. The sheriff expressed no interest in the eleven-year-old indictment.

Goodridge remained the night at police headquarters. When next day he was brought before Judge Robert Cony and the judge learned that the indictment was dated November 24, 1911, he announced angrily from the bench: "They will never bother you on it, and unless I hear from them tonight I will let you go in the morning, and I do not intend to have his office used by any lawyer to build up any cases for the State of Massachusetts or any other state, and the best thing you can do is not to see Mr. Moore again."

Goodridge was released next morning. There was nothing more Moore could do about him.

On September 11 Moore presented a fourth supplementary motion, requesting a new trial because of additional facts discovered about the witness Lola Andrews, "a person whose testimony should not constitute the basis of a verdict of guilty on a charge of murder."

Six months before the trial, when Moore had interviewed her in the Alhambra Block in Quincy and shown her pictures of Sacco and Vanzetti, she had been unable to identify them and had made a statement exonerating the defendants. On the witness stand she had claimed that this statement had been untruthfully reported. Now Moore, as he wrote to Upton Sinclair, had "wilted" her. She had signed an affidavit for him repudiating her court testimony and admitting that she had lied because the district attorney knew "many chapters of her private life that she could ill afford to have revealed."

Her affidavit stated that some time before the trial Stewart and Brouillard had taken her to the Dedham jail, shown her Sacco, and asked if he was the man she had seen on April 15. She said she did not know. Later Assistant District Attorney Williams put the same question to her. She said she could not be positive. Williams then shook his finger in her face and told her, "You can put it stronger than that. I know you can."

Her testimony in court had been "false and untrue. . . . She had never . . . at any time or place or under any conditions and specifically on April 15, 1920, at South Braintree, seen said Nicola Sacco until she saw him in the Dedham County Jail." Her false statements "were made under the intimidating influences of Michael E. Stewart, Albert L. Brouillard, Harold Williams and Frederick G. Katzmann."

Like Pelser, Lola Andrews found herself overborne by any determined person who talked with her. In addition she had much to conceal. Her life in Quincy was in part known to the police. Recently there had been some business about a naval officer named Landers in her room, hushed up for the time but still rumor-heavy. When Moore found out that she had originally come from Gardiner, Maine, he sent Bert Carpenter there to see what he could learn. What Carpenter learned would have ruined her in any court.

She had been born Rachel Andrews, the by-product of an encounter between a Yankee farmer's daughter and an itinerant Italian. A towpath child brought up in a shanty settlement on the outskirts of the trim Kennebec town, she had scarcely passed adolescence when she married an ex-soldier returned from the Philippines, Mayhew Hassam, an alcoholic who used her cruelly. She had borne him one son. After the marriage ended she had stayed on in Gardiner across the street from the Soldiers' Home, available and accommodating. In Augusta she had been convicted of lewd and lascivious conduct. Moving on to Massachusetts, she had left her son behind, sending money back for his board. At the time she testified in Dedham he was eighteen years old. What her life had been she did not ever want him to know. The boy was her weak spot—a spot Moore did not hesitate to exploit. He had been hard on Pelser, hard on Goodridge, he would be hard on her. A lawyer, to his mind, could not be delicate when men's lives were at stake.

Lola Darroch brought young Hassam from Maine, hired a room for him in the seedy Hotel Essex opposite the South Station, and sent for the mother. The boy, though an unkempt rustic, had proved tractable and intelligent, accepting Moore's version of the case and agreeing to try to persuade his mother to repudiate her courtroom testimony. Lola Andrews, brought in from Quincy, confronted her son while Moore told her that she had lied in Dedham and that it was now up to her to tell the truth. She wilted at once and began to cry. Moore spent the evening drafting an affidavit. When it was handed to her, her son begged her to sign. Moore showed her certain affidavits that Carpenter had collected in Gardiner, without, however, allowing her to read them. She signed.

Moore could indeed browbeat such witnesses as Pelser, Goodridge, and Lola Andrews. The difficulty was that when they were alone again they had second thoughts that generally took the form of a disclaiming letter to the district attorney. On January 9, 1923, Lola signed a counteraffidavit for District Attorney Katzmann and Assistant District Attorney Williams in which she claimed that Moore had used her boy to trap her and that she had not read the nine pages of the affidavit. She had not wanted to sign it.

I told them that if I put my name to that paper that they had already drawn up for me . . . I could see it meant a terrible disgrace for me. They told me no, that I was doing the grandest thing a woman could do, and that by doing what they wanted me to do I would gain the respect and friendship of everyone, and that my boy would not be ashamed to look upon me as his mother, and the evidence they had brought with them from Maine would not be submitted to the court or to the eyes of anyone, not even to my son. . . . Mr. Moore took me over to a small desk and laid the paper in front of me and told me to sign it. I told him I would not, for I did not realize what I was doing. . . . They dipped the pen in the ink and tried to pass it into my hand. . . . All the time I was crying and asking them not to force me to sign it. My son then said, "Mother, I want you to sign that paper, for it means a whole lot to me." I do not seem to remember much what happened after that, only that someone put the pen in my hand and told me to sign it, and asked my boy to come over to me and help me. My boy came over and put his arm around me and said, "Mother, sign this paper and have an end to all this trouble, for

you did not recognize these men"—meaning Sacco and Vanzetti—
"and you will only be doing a terrible wrong if you send those men to
the chair."

"I was like I was in a trance," she later told Katzmann.

Perhaps the most crucial testimony offered in the trial, the deciding factor—if John Dever is to be believed—was the evidence of the
guns and the bullets. If, as Moore was well aware, it could be proved
beyond a doubt that the mortal bullet found in Berardelli's body
had not been fired from Sacco's automatic, the keystone of the Commonwealth's case would be demolished. In February 1923, with this
in mind, he engaged Dr. Albert Hamilton, a New York expert who
had testified in 165 homicide cases, to prepare the fifth supplementary
motion, the Hamilton-Proctor motion.

Hamilton came into the case through Frank Sibley, who happened
to meet him while riding on the train from Portland, Maine, to
Boston. Hamilton, an authoritative little man with a convincing air,
told Sibley that if he had been a witness at Dedham he could have
proved quickly and conclusively whether or not Sacco's pistol had
fired the mortal bullet. Once back in Boston Sibley recommended
Hamilton enthusiastically to Moore. The lawyer immediately wrote
Hamilton to ask what he would charge for coming to Boston. Without bothering to reply, Hamilton confidently took the next train. In
their first interview Moore told Hamilton he was vitally concerned
in learning the answers to four fundamental questions: Had the
hammer of the Vanzetti revolver been replaced by a new hammer?
Were one or more of the shells that Fraher had picked up fired in
the Sacco pistol? Had Bullet III been fired from the Sacco pistol?
Was the mortal bullet discharged from a cartridge of the same date
of manufacture as any of the cartridges found on Sacco when he was
arrested? Hamilton agreed to make the investigation and determine
the four answers.

Hamilton was an unlucky choice. Moore did not suspect that his
doctorate was self-awarded. By trade a druggist and concocter of
patent medicines in Auburn, New York, Hamilton had developed
expertness as a second career, advertising himself as a "micro-chemical
investigator." His avocation became his calling. In 1908, in a publicity
pamphlet entitled "That Man from Auburn," he described himself
as a qualified expert in chemistry, microscopy, handwriting, ink
analysis, typewriting, photography, fingerprints, toxicology, gunshot

wounds, guns and cartridges, bullet identification, gunpowder, nitro-glycerine, dynamite, high explosives, blood and other stains, causes of death, embalming, and anatomy. Unknown to Moore, he had earlier written to Judge Thayer claiming that he knew a method of examining the Sacco-Vanzetti ballistics exhibit that would reveal the truth. He had received no reply. Men who had worked with Hamil-ton in the past did not recommend him. The Auburn coroner said that his reputation for truth was bad. The assistant district attorney of Monroe County considered him "a professional expert . . . whose testimony should not be accepted in any court of record, and should receive no credence at the hands of a judge or jury."

Much of Hamilton's clouded reputation in New York stemmed from the murder trial of Charles Stielow who, in 1915, was accused of shooting Charles Phelps and his housekeeper in West Shelby. Hamilton had appeared for the prosecution. After tests and a minute examination of Stielow's revolver and of the three bullets taken from Phelps' body and the one from that of his housekeeper, he testified that only Stielow's revolver could have fired the bullets. Principally because of this testimony Stielow was found guilty and sentenced to death. Later he was proved to be innocent and pardoned. In a post-trial review of the evidence Max Poser, an expert in applied optics with the Bausch & Lomb Optical Company, demonstrated that the bullets taken from the bodies had not come from the Stielow revolver. "The opinion expressed by the expert Hamilton in his evidence at the trial," Poser concluded, "was worthless." The setback, however, did not seem to hamper Hamilton's career.

It did not take Hamilton long, after inspecting the Sacco-Vanzetti exhibits, to come to his conclusions. In the motion, filed on April 30, 1923, he claimed that by using a Bausch & Lomb compound microscope he was able to ascertain discrepancies between the mark-ings on the test bullets from Sacco's pistol and the markings on Bullet III. According to his measurements the land and groove widths in the barrel of Sacco's Colt agreed with the land and groove widths on the test-bullets but not with the mortal bullet. He also found that a microscopic examination of the Fraher shells eliminated the possi-bility of any one of them having been fired in the Colt. Because of a difference in the cannelures, he contended that Bullet III was not manufactured at the same time as the six Winchester cartridges found on Sacco. Augustus Gill, Professor of Technical Chemical Analysis at the Massachusetts Institute of Technology, had been engaged to assist Hamilton. His tabulations, made under different conditions, varied somewhat from Hamilton's. Nevertheless, he was convinced from his own measurements "that the so-called mortal bullet never passed through the Sacco gun." As for Vanzetti's revolver, Hamilton maintained that it had not been fitted with a new hammer, because an essential screw did not show marks of having been removed.

Captain Van Amburgh, in an affidavit for the Commonwealth, became much more positive than he had been at the trial. He now used a more powerful microscope and in addition he had had comparative photographs taken of Bullet III and one of the test bullets. He offered twelve pictures of each bullet in which the lands and grooves were separately photographed so that the enlarged pictures could be compared. "The facts which I have found from my entire investigation," he asserted, "are so clear that, in my opinion, they amount to proof. I am absolutely certain that the Fraher Shell W was fired in the Sacco pistol. I am also positive that the mortal bullet was fired in the Sacco pistol." His findings were confirmed by Merton Robinson, a ballistics engineer for the Winchester Arms Company. Robinson not only maintained that Bullet III had been fired from Sacco's pistol, but rejected Hamilton's argument that the mortal bullet and those found on Sacco were of a different date of manufacture. As for Hamilton's photographic evidence to prove that the hammer in Vanzetti's revolver had not been replaced, it would have been quite possible, Robinson asserted, for an expert repairman to have inserted a new screw, or to have removed and replaced the old one, without leaving marks on the screw head.

On March 8, 1923, after much persuasion on the part of the McAnarney brothers, William Thompson agreed to enter the case for the limited purpose of arguing the motions for a new trial. He had been hesitant about becoming involved, but, ironically enough, it was Katzmann's attack on the integrity and qualifications of Dr. Hamilton that finally persuaded him.

Thompson knew that his entering this by-now notorious case would arouse a great deal of hostility in State Street legal circles, and he persuaded his friend of many years, Arthur Dehon Hill, to come in with him so that, as he explained, he would have an associate he could talk with more frankly than he could with Moore. Hill, a lawyer who had once been corporation counsel of the City of Boston, was a more integral State Street figure than Thompson, who—like Judge Thayer—had been brought up in Worcester and was a Bostonian merely by attrition. Although fortuitously born in Paris, Hill was an inbred Bostonian whose perspective was limited by the familiar triangle of Beacon Hill, the Harvard Yard, and the North Shore. Like so many Boston lawyers who moved securely in their dimly lit world of irrevocable trusts, he was cadaverous—as if his blood stream had by some subtle osmosis absorbed the dried leather of a century's *Massachusetts Reports*. Even as a Harvard undergraduate he looked as if he had never been young. Yet this secure, aloof lawyer who appeared so typical of his caste was not wholly typical. There was something more to him, a quality of *fiat justitia* that went beyond Beacon Hill. In the 1912 Bull Moose campaign he had come out for Theodore Roosevelt, a rejection of the Boston norm. When Thompson first asked him to enter the Sacco-Vanzetti case, he was reluctant. Although he had a poor opinion of the garrulous Thayer he thought well of Katzmann, whom he had known for a number of years.

Hill joined the defense on March 15 feeling, as he later explained, "What do I care about these draft-dodgers who were skulking in Mexico when their countrymen were fighting for the very life of the land? But I do care for the honor of the Commonwealth of Massachusetts." Thompson would in time come to consider the cause of Sacco and Vanzetti as his own. For Hill, who would appear as counsel in the last tumultuous weeks, it was a case and not a cause, and he the advocate rather than the partisan.

CHAPTER THIRTEEN

Post-Trial—II

Just before Thompson and Hill entered the case Sacco went on a hunger strike. A year and a half had elapsed since his conviction, and he announced that he would continue to fast until the court ruled on his fate. Much of the delay during 1922 had resulted from the additional time granted Moore to follow up clues that he hoped might lead to the real criminals. In the autumn Judge Thayer underwent an operation, causing a further delay.

Sacco chafed under his barred restraint. He was not one to find escape in reading or thinking his thoughts. Even the anarchism that was so fundamental to him attracted him more by its unrelenting code than by its philosophy. He was a man of abounding physical energy for whom work and love were necessary releases. Jail was an exercise in patience that he could never learn. Several times in the course of his years at Dedham he approached and even crossed the borderline of sanity. From his cell, with its rolled blanket and wooden water bucket and tin mug and enamel slop pail, he watched the flaring twilights diminish, the approach of morning along the empty streets, the orbit of the sun as it shifted across the upper windows. Days and weeks and months passed meaninglessly.

In November 1921, Sacco had written to Vanzetti in the grimmer confinement of Charlestown: "I am very sorry that no one comes and see you, no one comes to see me neither, but Rosie." The week before, his wife had brought little Ines to the jail for the first time. Sacco was delighted to hold the plump crowing baby in his arms. Mrs. Evans became a staunch periodic visitor. Sacco, in spite of his theoretical rejection of bourgeois society, developed an intense filial affection for her. From Mrs. Glendower Evans, separated from him by the whole range of the sociological spectrum, she became Auntie Bee. In 1925 he wrote her: "From since the day I have meet you, you have occupied in my heart my mother her place, and so like I been respect you and I been loved you." It was a curious transition from the brown peasant woman of Torremaggiore to the self-contained Bostonian, but Mrs. Evans was only one of the elderly women who were to take an increasingly maternal interest in the Dedham prisoner. Among the earliest was kindly, mousy Mrs. Cerise Carman Jack in her squeaky high-button boots; for a while she took Rosina and the children to her farm in Sharon. There was Mrs. Jessica Henderson, matron of good causes and pillar of the Anti-Vivisection Society. And there were Mrs. Gertrude Winslow and Mrs. Codman, the latter a cousin by marriage of the head of the Civil Liberties Committee. Sacco always took a more trusting attitude toward women than toward men.

Evenings were the most difficult for "thes sad reclus," as he whimsically termed himself. He kept thinking of the bungalow in South Stoughton, how he would sometimes visit friends after supper and come back with the sleeping Dante in his arms and Rosina beside him. "Those day," he wrote Mrs. Jack, "they was a some happy day."

The jail rule that unsentenced prisoners might not work kept Sacco in idleness, intensifying the feelings of persecution that he had developed after the trial. On February 14, 1923, he began his hunger strike. Sheriff Capen made no attempt to force him to eat, and by the middle of March he had grown noticeably weaker. On the afternoon of the sixteenth, at Judge Thayer's request, he was examined by Charles Cahoon, superintendent of the Medfield State Hospital; Albert Thomas, superintendent of the Foxboro State Hospital; and a Boston psychiatrist, Abraham Meyerson.

Sacco, lying on his cot, calmly explained to the doctors that the state was trying to kill him. Poison was being put into his food—even into the food his wife brought him; poisonous vapors were being blown into his cell and electric currents circulated under his bed. His suffering had become so intense, he explained, that he could not permit it to go much further. When Dr. Cahoon asked him why he drank water, which would prolong his life, he "stated that he did not want to die too quickly because, on account of a hearing for a new trial he felt that he should allow his counsel some opportunity to plead. He had no confidence, however, that he would get a new trial; he did not expect any justice from the state or the government."

The doctors found that Sacco was mentally disturbed, and Judge

Thayer ordered him to the Boston Psychopathic Hospital for observation. On his arrival he was warned by Dr. Meyerson, "Nick, they have sent you here to eat, and if you don't, we will feed you with a tube." According to the newspaper reports he was then forcibly fed by an attendant in the doctor's presence, although Sacco later claimed that he broke his strike voluntarily. "You know," he told another doctor some months afterward, "I have read in an Italian magazine that you can live a long time if they feed you with a tube; I knew this, and then I was too weak and could not fight them, so I said, I go ahead and eat. I was against going because I wanted justice."

For the first two days in the hospital he lay on his cot and was fed broth and gruel every hour. Then he began to eat regularly, gaining ten pounds within a week. His Dedham delusions vanished and he spoke of them as "all a mistake" and "prejudices." Although he identified the hospital with the state that was persecuting him, he was friendly with the doctors, sometimes speaking of his love for his wife and children and his feeling for the out-of-doors, joking about his hairiness that "proved the correctness of Darwin's theory," or talking about his work as sole-trimmer.

On March 22, a few hours after Sacco had gone to bed, he complained of a headache and asked the ward attendant for a wet towel to place across his forehead. When the attendant left, Sacco sprang out of bed and struck his head several times against a chair, lacerating his scalp. Wardmen rushed in and seized him, and as they struggled he cried out, "I am innocent! There is no justice!" It took four men to restrain him and put him in a dry pack. Next morning he was again calm and cooperative, and when the director, Dr. C. MacFie Campbell arrived, he said with some embarrassment, "I am ashamed of what I done." He told the director that he was tired of life and wished to kill himself. Dr. Campbell considered the incident "a transitory condition of emotional tension which was intelligible in view of the emotional strain to which the patient has been subject." There was no recurrence of any such episode or of the Dedham delusions. At the end of the observation period Dr. Campbell wrote to Judge Thayer that with the exception of that one night Sacco's "behavior has been that of the ordinary hospital patient. There has been no difficulty in caring for him . . . his mood has, on the whole, been equable." He concluded: "The result of the observation of the patient in the Boston Psychopathic Hospital has been that we have found no evidence of insanity of any type."

Nevertheless, Thayer extended Sacco's observation period for another month, and the early days of April presented quite a different picture. Mrs. Evans, visiting Sacco on April 2, was much disturbed by his mental state. She told the doctor in charge "that she knew nothing about medicine but that in her opinion [the] patient was talking like a crazy man."

She said [the hospital report continued] that the patient insisted he would kill himself. . . . He said that he had suffered long enough, that he wanted it over with one way or another, that when he went back to jail he would give the judge twenty-four hours to decide the case and that if he did not set him free patient would "take things in my own hands."

Five days later when Rosina was visiting, Sacco told her that he was going crazy. After she left, according to the report, he

suddenly jumped out of his bed and rushed toward the edge of the open door, with his head lowered in a blind, impulsive manner. . . . Thereafter, he became excited, somewhat noisy, and struck out violently, requiring considerable restraint. He was given treatment in the form of a dry pack with cold compresses to his head. He was talking and shouting in an excited tone, maintaining that his wife was confined in the ward above him, whence he had been hearing (as a matter of fact), the voices and cries of the women patients, which he believed were those of his wife.

By evening he had calmed down and now said "that he must be going crazy in this place, that his ideas about his wife were all a mistake." Early next morning he spoke of voices telling him that a bunch of roses had been left for him in the hospital lobby.

On the morning of April 12 he suddenly lunged forward as if he were going to dart out of the room. To Dr. Campbell he later explained that he had thought he heard his wife's voice call "D-a-a-n-t-e."

For about a week he seemed calm. Then, on April 19, he became unmanageable. Seven times in the next four days he had to be placed in wet packs.

During these attacks [the ward doctor reported] he shouts and screams that he wants his freedom; he wants to go home to his family. Between the attacks and often during the attack, when he can for a moment be made to control himself, he is rational, clear and oriented, knows the time and the date and the place, and clearly recognizes those about him. During the attacks he at times strikes viciously at those about him, or those who attempt to restrain him, and also hurls all manner of abusive and profane imprecations upon others.

According to Dr. Ralph Colp, in a psychiatric study published in 1958, Sacco was suffering

sensory deprivation, which in its strictest sense, involves the isolation of an individual from everyday sights, sounds and actions. Nick Sacco had been exposed to a somewhat analogous situation for nearly thirty-six months. Although he had contact with people, he had been deprived of the three most important things in his life: wife and children, job, and his exercise and contact with nature. The daily visits of Rosina—in Dedham she had not visited as frequently—aggravated the patient instead of assuaging him, and were the direct cause of his most powerful delusions and hallucinations. It was as if every visit—however much her husband desired it—could only be unbearable to him. No one understood this better than the bachelor Vanzetti, who later wrote: "Has Nick a wife? Yes, and a good one; but, not being free, he most either thinks that she is consoling herself with somebody else, or that she is suffering the unspeakable agony of a loving woman compelled to mourn is living lover."

Sacco was diagnosed as suffering from psychosis of a paranoid character. The court committed him on April 23 to the Bridgewater State Hospital for the Criminally Insane.

Moore was greatly troubled by Sacco's suicide attempts. As one way of saving his client he had agreed to Sacco's examination by alienists and—even though he objected to the Bridgewater institution —signed the commitment papers. Sacco and his wife never forgave him for it, and the differences of opinion that had troubled the two men now began to harden into enmity.

Sacco spent five months at Bridgewater. His mood on entering seemed cooperative. He was not isolated but given a bed in a ward; within two days he began chatting with the other prisoners. Soon he was at work polishing floors and before long he had a chance to work mornings on the prison farm, where he tended a small vegetable garden. His appetite was good—in a month he gained twenty-six pounds. Throughout his stay he remained quiet, cautious, but agreeable. When a doctor asked him whether he was insane, he replied, "I am not one of that kind. My mind is clear. I am not crazy." Although Sacco was at times hopeful about his chances for a new trial, Dr. Mountford, the Bridgewater physician, noted that he occasionally presented a worried look "which he explains by saying that it is all caused by the long procedure of the court which keeps his case from being settled one way or the other." Thought of suicide still ran through his mind. On July 9 Dr. Mountford noted that Sacco

says he has not given the suicide idea up, and regrets that he did not die in his former attempt. In explaining this statement, says he does not wish to commit suicide now, but says he wants to get justice, and insists if ever confronted by similar conditions of those before he came here, he would not hesitate to commit suicide.

After saying this, Sacco looked out the window into the prison yard, and with great interest watched some prisoners playing baseball.

On September 29 he was discharged from Bridgewater with the diagnosis "not insane" and returned to Dedham in time for the arguments on the five supplementary motions, postponed because of his condition.

Some time during the previous summer Elias Field, a lawyer of the modest firm of Brown, Field and McCarthy, and the defending counsel in a Middlesex County murder case, learned that the famous Dr. Hamilton was in Boston. Hamilton seemed to him just the man to examine some bullets, then in the custody of the State Police, that were to be introduced as evidence. Hamilton was willing. On August 7 he and Field went to Captain Proctor's office in the State House to find out about the bullets. Proctor told them that they happened to be at his house in Swampscott, twelve miles away. However, if Field wanted to drive him there, they could look at them. Field agreed. While he drove, Hamilton and Proctor began to discuss the Sacco-Vanzetti case.

"I suppose you know," Hamilton said, "that I have been retained by the defense to study some of the exhibits in connection with the pending motion for a new trial."

"I don't care," Proctor told the other two. "I have been too long in the game, and I'm getting to be too old to want to see a couple of fellows go to the chair for something I don't think they did."

Hamilton asked Proctor why he had not said more in his testimony about whether Bullet III had gone through Sacco's gun. "If the defense had asked me any more particularly," Proctor replied, "then

I should have told them I didn't think it went through that gun, and I did tell the district attorney before the trial I thought it was consistent with going through that kind of a gun, but I don't think it went through that gun."

Hamilton wondered why the defense had not taken up "consistent with."

"I wondered too," Proctor said. "I suppose they were afraid to."

The conversation made such an impression on Field that he noted it in his diary. Some weeks later he talked the matter over with his old Harvard classmate and partner, H. LaRue Brown. Brown, a Kentuckian whose liberalism had become in Boston almost a second career, knew all about the Sacco-Vanzetti case through his connection with the New England Civil Liberties Committee. He relayed the conversation to Thompson.

Thompson felt that this story—if it could be confirmed—would shatter the prosecution's case. But whether Captain Proctor would be as frank with a defense lawyer as he had been on that casual ride to Swampscott was doubtful. However, when Thompson visited him at the State House, Proctor was surprisingly open. He admitted that before he testified in Dedham Katzmann and Williams had repeatedly asked him if Bullet III had come from Sacco's pistol, and each time he told them he had found no convincing evidence in the tests. The captain was obviously distressed in this interview with Thompson, his mind haunted by the role he had played at Dedham. When Thompson asked him if he would sign an affidavit, he at once agreed.

In the affidavit, dated October 20, 1923, he stated that

at the trial the District Attorney did not ask me whether I had found any evidence that the so-called mortal bullet passed through Sacco's pistol, nor was I asked that question on cross-examination. The District Attorney desired to ask me that question, but I had repeatedly told him that if he did I should be obliged to answer in the negative. . . . Bullet Number III, in my judgment, passed through some Colt automatic pistol, but I do not intend to imply that I had found any evidence that the so-called mortal bullet had passed through this particular Colt automatic pistol and the District Attorney well knew that I did not so intend and framed his question accordingly. Had I been asked the direct question: whether I had found any affirmative evidence whatever that this so-called mortal bullet had passed through this particular Sacco's pistol, I should have answered then, as I do now without hesitation, in the negative.

Although this affidavit stood as an entity in itself, Thompson filed it as a subsection of the Hamilton motion. In a counteraffidavit, Katzmann swore that he had not "repeatedly" asked Proctor "whether he had found any evidence that the mortal bullet had passed through the Sacco pistol," but he did not deny having asked the question, nor did he deny Proctor's answer. Proctor died in March 1924, before Judge Thayer could rule on any of the supplementary motions.

Early in September 1923 Thompson had picked up a story about Ripley, the jury foreman, that he considered important enough, even though it was hearsay, to include in the first motion. William Daley, a Quincy contractor who said he had known Ripley intimately for thirty-eight years, willingly signed an affidavit about an occurrence at the Adams railroad station during the last week of May 1921. Daley had met Ripley on the platform there while waiting for a train, and Ripley had told him that he was going away for a couple of weeks to be a juror in the case of the two South Braintree Guineas.

Daley said he did not believe the Guineas were guilty, and that it was not reasonable to suppose a man would go and rob a factory where he had worked and was well known, and in broad daylight.

"Damn them, they ought to hang them anyway!" Ripley had replied.

Of course there could be no corroboration of Daley's statement, for Ripley had been dead now for over two years.

On October 1 Thompson, Hill, Moore, and the McAnarney brothers appeared in an almost empty courtroom to argue the supplementary motions. Again the defendants were brought in and placed in the cage. Sacco was still tanned from his outdoor work at the Bridgewater hospital. Vanzetti looked waxen, his eyes more deeply sunk than ever. Rosina was there with Ines, as was the indefatigable Mrs. Evans. Ines had on a pink dress and bonnet, and both defendants' faces lighted up as Sacco held her for a moment in the cage. When Rosina started to walk away toward Mrs. Evans, Ines became frightened at being left alone with two strangers. She howled until her mother took her away.

Judge Thayer's step lacked none of its briskness as he strode into the room, and his face had lost none of its masklike quality, even though this prolonged case impinged on him now like a recurring bad dream. "There seems to be no justification or excuse for the delays in filing affidavits," he announced in pettish protest. "The court has several times set dates for the completion of filing affidavits on both sides. Apparently no attention has been paid to these orders."

When the report that Sacco was not insane was read to the court, Sacco smiled ironically. Thompson, his self-assurance unruffled, urbanely at home where Moore had appeared the bumptious stranger, nevertheless seemed to feel it necessary to explain his presence in the radical galley. "It is supposed that these defendants have radical opinions," he announced, in opening the argument for the Ripley motion. "Mr. Hill and I do not hold such opinions," he went on, refraining from glancing at Moore, "and we are not here supporting such opinions. I think I shall be believed also when I say that we are not here for pecuniary reasons. We think we are rendering humble service to the institutions of law and order by coming here to argue that an error has been committed.

"I have no reason to believe that either one of these two defendants has ever endeavored by threats or in any other improper way to obtain undue influence in the court. Some of their enthusiastic friends may have done so, but this fact ought not to weigh against the defendants.

"That's why Mr. Hill and I are here," he concluded. "It's because some of our friends have talked in the way Daley says Ripley talked."

Thompson then spent the morning arguing the Ripley motion. In the afternoon Hill took over. "From the time I had been in the courtroom fifteen minutes," he later told the Lowell Committee, "and had my first talk with the judge I did not have any doubt as to what the result of the case would be, independent of its actual merit, and that was not because I felt that there was anybody who was consciously trying to do wrong, but I thought everybody connected with the case had got themselves into a state of mind, a mental condition where reason had practically ceased to operate and prejudice and emotion had taken its place."

The session saw a prolonged altercation between Judge Thayer and the usually quiet-spoken Thomas McAnarney.

"I understand Your Honor to say that after a night of discussion we decided not to open up the issue of radicalism," Judge McAnarney challenged Judge Thayer, his voice hard. "That is not so."

"It is so," Thayer announced bluntly, a tawnier shade creeping into his parchment cheeks.

McAnarney struck back. "All I ever said to my client was to tell the truth and tell all the truth at all times. It didn't take me five minutes to decide that." He turned away from the bench and walked toward his chair, wiping his forehead with his handkerchief.

Thayer's voice pursued him. "Mr. McAnarney! Three times you opened up this subject, and three times it was stricken out."

McAnarney's voice trembled a little. "Three times it had to be opened up. There was no safe course for the defendants to pursue excepting to tell the truth and all the truth."

"I know what took place here," Thayer insisted.

At the end of the session he reluctantly postponed the hearing until October 25 to allow both sides to file additional affidavits. On that day the Andrews and Pelser affidavits and counteraffidavits were read. The next day Moore took over with his old vitality and argued all day on the Goodridge motion, insisting again and again that the district attorney had intimidated the man and shaped his evidence by the threat of revoking his Massachusetts probation.

Judge Thayer was once more living at the University Club. Each morning he and a group of reporters took the same train from the Back Bay Station. Among them was a pretty young woman, Mrs. Elizabeth Bernkopf, from the International News Service, to whom the senescent but still gallant judge took a particular fancy. At first he merely waited until she had taken her place in the car and then asked if he might sit with her. Later he took to joining her on the platform before the train arrived.

Sitting beside her in the train, he would unburden himself of his incubus case while she kept inviolably silent. As the city slums receded, replaced beyond Forest Hills by the trim rectangles of the suburbs and the autumn outline of Great Blue Hill, he talked on and on, boasting that he "could not be intimidated by anybody or anything." The defense "would find that they could not hoodwink him." He represented the integrity of the courts of Massachusetts, he told her, and he was going to maintain that integrity.

One morning Judge Thayer gave Mrs. Bernkopf his autographed picture. Occasionally she would get a knowing look from the other reporters as they passed down the aisle. The judge said he had long been put out by the kind of people who were supporting the defense, but what really stirred him so that even the recollection stepped up his pulse was "that long-haired anarchist lawyer from California." The old man would lean forward confidentially, assuring the young woman that if Moore thought he could outwit the courts of Massachusetts he had another think coming. Maybe Moore could play that game successfully in California, but those tricks and threats just would not work in Dedham. He, Judge Thayer, was not going to be imposed on!

As the train pulled into the Dedham Station, Thayer with avuncular gallantry would guide Mrs. Bernkopf's elbow down the aisle, tip his hat to her on the platform, and say that he hoped he would have the pleasure of her company again. Three years later she recorded the substance of his conversations in an affidavit.

The hearings seemed to fall into the pattern of being argued for a day and postponed for a week. Not until November 8 were they concluded. When Thompson argued the Hamilton-Proctor motion and mentioned the police captain, sparks flew between him and District Attorney Harold Williams.* The district attorney insinuated that the reason Proctor had turned on the Commonwealth was that Katzmann had refused to approve his claim of five hundred dollars for his expert testimony, although it had later been approved by the court and paid.

"I don't want to make this a personal matter," Thompson reminded Williams after the gust of angry words had died down. "I don't want to go off on an attack upon any person. But here are these men, assured by the State of fair treatment here if nowhere else— and then a prearranged question and answer made to appear the exact opposite of what the witness really thought."

"Are you sure there was a prearranged question?" Thayer interrupted.

"They knew and don't deny it that Captain Proctor didn't believe that bullet went through that gun," Thompson replied. In a passionate summing up he asked Thayer if the court could really say that Sacco and Vanzetti had had a fair trial in the face of the failure of the government attorneys to bring out Proctor's real opinion.

Toward the close of the hearing Thompson reserved the right to be heard in a request to fire one hundred cartridges through Sacco's pistol with a view of making further ballistic comparisons. At this point there began one of the equivocal episodes in the post-trial proceedings. Dr. Hamilton appeared with two new 32-caliber Colt automatics and offered to compare them with Sacco's pistol. Before Judge

---

* Katzmann's successor. Katzmann was retained as special assistant in the Sacco-Vanzetti case.

Thayer and the lawyers for both sides he disassembled all three pistols and placed the parts in three piles on a table. Then, picking up various parts one by one, he explained their function and pointed out their interchangeability. After reassembling the pistols, he slipped his two in his pocket and handed Sacco's to the assistant clerk. Hill and Thompson were already leaving the courtroom when Hamilton started after them. "Just a minute, gentlemen!" Thayer called out as they reached the door.

Years afterward, not long before his death, Thayer related the sequel to Captain Van Amburgh: "They stopped, turned and looked at me. I said, 'Come here, Mr. Hamilton.' Hamilton advanced towards me. I said: 'Hand me your pistols.' He did so and I said: 'They shall be impounded.' I don't know why I impounded those pistols. It merely seemed like the proper and thorough thing to do. I have thanked God many times since that I did so. And then the astounding discovery made later that the original barrel in the Sacco pistol was missing and an entirely different barrel substituted for it!"

On November 2, at Judge Thayer's request, District Attorney Williams borrowed from Van Amburgh a plug gauge, a device for measuring the diameter of a gun barrel. He found Sacco's pistol barrel to measure .3045 inches. Hamilton's measurement had given the diameter as .2924 inches, but Williams thought little of the discrepancy since he himself had never seen a plug gauge before and felt he might easily have made a mistake. However, when Hamilton, on December 4, in the presence of the clerk of court, checked Sacco's pistol with the gauge, he confirmed Williams' measurement. Hamilton now observed that the fouled rusty barrel was shiny and, according to his later testimony in a special hearing before Judge Thayer, his first thought was that the court had been cleaning it. "I could not conceive in my mind why you would do it," he told Thayer, "but I said to myself no one else could have done it. . . . I immediately dispelled it because I said, no court would alter an exhibit."

Whatever Hamilton's opinion of the altered condition of the barrel and the variations in his first and second measurements, he afterward maintained that when he examined Sacco's automatic on December 4 it never occurred to him that the barrel was anything but the original.

Acting on Thompson's request to make fresh firing tests, Judge Thayer on February 11 called in Van Amburgh to inspect Sacco's Colt and determine its condition. With the district attorney present, Van Amburgh took the gun from the clerk of court and prepared to disassemble it. No sooner had he drawn back the slide than he saw that the barrel was not the barrel he had last examined. It looked brand-new. There was even a film of cosmoline on it.

"Someone has switched barrels," he at once told Williams.

The two hurried to Judge Thayer. Thayer, after listening to them, announced that he would hold an investigation.

Two days later he began hearings in his chambers with only Moore, Williams, Hamilton, Van Amburgh, and a stenographer present. Press and public were barred, unaware even that such hearings were taking place. They lasted just over three weeks. At the opening Clerk Worthington brought in the three pistols. The briefest examination made it clear to everyone that Sacco's Colt had acquired a new barrel. Hamilton, not at all abashed that every finger seemed to point to him, admitted that the new barrel must have come from one of his pistols, but insisted that he had not made the switch. In his opinion this had been done by someone connected with the prosecution. After examining the fouled barrel in one of his own new guns under a microscope, Hamilton stated that he was unqualifiedly of the opinion it was not the Sacco barrel.

Williams accused Hamilton of working the substitution with the idea of later making the discovery himself so that he could then demand a new trial. Repetitious and acrimonious, the arguments went on each day until five o'clock, but no one in the closed chambers had any real doubt as to who had switched the barrels. Even Moore, arguing bravely that this was more dirty work on the part of the district attorney's staff, knew that Hamilton's deft fingers had done it.

At the conclusion of the hearings Thayer reserved judgment as to who had made the substitution and whether or not it had been accidental. He ruled merely that the barrel in the new pistol had come from Sacco's Colt and he ordered the fouled barrel replaced and the three pistols delivered into the clerk's custody "without prejudice to either side." The prejudice, however, was not so easily obliterated. Hamilton's chicanery had undermined his value as a witness, past or future. Although he was to continue his association with the defense almost to the end, he would prove only a detriment—expensive, untrustworthy, and untrusted.

Almost at the very time Hamilton was discrediting himself in Dedham, Van Amburgh, in Bridgeport, Connecticut, was demolishing his own ethical and technical reputation in the Harold Israel case. Israel was a young ex-soldier of small intelligence who had been charged with the murder of Father Hubert Dahme, pastor of St. Joseph's Catholic Church. On the evening of February 4, 1924, Father Dahme was strolling along Bridgeport's Main Street when a man approached him from the rear, placed the muzzle of a revolver close to his head, and fired. Several witnesses saw the murderer run from the scene.

A week later the police of Norwalk, a dozen miles away, picked up a man who was wandering the streets at midnight in a suspicious manner. He was found to have a 32-caliber revolver in his pocket with four of the five chambers loaded and the other empty. He said his name was Harold Israel, that he had just come from Bridgeport, and that he was on his way to see his father in Philadelphia. Next morning he was given thirty days in the Bridgeport county jail for carrying a concealed weapon. Once there he was interrogated about the priest's death, and several witnesses of the shooting were brought in to look him over.

The crucial evidence against Israel was the 32-caliber bullet removed from Father Dahme's brain. Captain Van Amburgh, called in from the Remington Company, compared it with a test bullet fired through Israel's gun and announced that both had been fired from the same weapon. This he said he had determined not only by his measurements but by the similarity of the bullets after he had made a strip photograph of each and superimposed one upon the other.

After a prolonged interrogation, Israel tangled himself in a web of conflicting statements and confessed that he had killed Father Dahme. When a detective asked what had become of the cartridge of the mortal bullet, Israel said it was in the toilet of his boarding house. The police found it there. With this evidence added to the confession, Israel's trial and conviction seemed only a formality.

Homer S. Cummings, later Attorney General of the United States and then state's attorney for Fairfield County, at first had no doubt of Israel's guilt but gradually noticed flaws in the state's case. First of all, Israel soon repudiated his confession, claiming that when he made it he had been questioned for so long that he was willing to confess anything to get a rest. Then Cummings discovered that after the police had left the boarding house, the landlady had found still another empty cartridge in the toilet. Both shells had been exploded by a dull firing pin. The pin of Israel's revolver was sharp, and it turned out that a friend of his had sharpened it at his shop several weeks before the murder.

Cummings now spent some time with Van Amburgh examining the strip photographs of the bullets. As he testified at the preliminary hearing, Van Amburgh, in order to develop his argument, cut a slit in the photograph of the Dahme bullet. "Then," said Cummings, "he inserts through that slit the strip picture of the recovered bullet, and pushing this up and down, finally reaches a place where he says the lines coincide. Well, I worked at that for two hours one day, and yesterday, in the presence of Captain Van Amburgh worked on it for more than an hour. It took Captain Van Amburgh fifteen minutes to find the point of juncture himself—well, say five minutes, it will be more conservative. Then a peculiar thing developed. I called his attention to it, and he had absolutely, so far as I could see, no answer to it. I asked him to put the photographs in the position which he claimed demonstrated his point, and he got them into that position. Then I said, 'Now, lift up the flap and look and see what is under it,' and I thought, somewhat reluctantly, the flap was lifted and on the under picture we saw a scene totally different from that which we saw on the upper picture. I asked him whether it was not perfectly logical to assume that if the two pictures had been superimposed— that is, if the other picture was transparent and placed over the other —that there ought not to be a continuous similarity in the surface appearance. He admitted that was logical, and I never could get a satisfactory explanation for the discrepancy."

Cummings turned over the bullets and the photographs to five other experts from the Remington Company plus another from the New York Police Department. Their unanimous opinion was that there was no continuous similarity, that the mortal bullet had perceptible land and groove marks lacking in the test bullets, and that it could not have been fired through Israel's gun. Following this testimony, Israel was released.

Van Amburgh's Connecticut record apparently did not follow him north, for not long afterward he was appointed head of the newly formed ballistics laboratory of the Massachusetts Department of Public Safety.

Thompson had a way of striding into a courtroom with a confident ring of leather heels, as if he were taking over command on a parade square. That was how he struck Moore during the arguments on the supplementary motions. Moore, underneath his class-angled exterior, retained a sensitive—at times almost a sentimental—nature. He was hurt by being thrust aside by this corporation lawyer and by the supercilious Hill, who, even as he prided himself on doing his duty to his native state by defending two unpopular radicals, could remark "I do not like these people."

In fact, Moore felt put upon. From his arrival in Boston he had transformed the case. At least a third of the defense money had come from sources he had tapped. He had brought in the American Civil Liberties Union, the International Labor Defense, the phalanx of Back Bay women headed by Mrs. Evans. Thanks to him the Cincinnati convention of the American Federation of Labor had passed a resolution demanding a new trial for Sacco and Vanzetti, "convicted by a biased jury under the instructions of a prejudiced judge." And before the convention the delegates had never heard of the two Italians! At the next convention he would take care that they passed a stronger resolution. These things were his doing. If he had not managed to free the two men, he had at least managed to keep them alive for almost three years. He had brought them visitors, arranged for their English lessons, and encouraged them by letters and by visits, disregarding and excusing Sacco's latent hostility. The reward for his efforts had been the sullen suspicions of the doctrinaire anarchists. They were always a problem to him. "The practical difficulty with such men as Felicani, Lopez and some of the others," he complained in a letter, "is not that they do not want to help, but that in many cases they do not know how to help. They are not affiliated with either the American organized labor nor with the Italian labor movement."

To Moore the Defense Committee seemed to have become more and more impotent. For lack of funds he had had to give up his Pemberton Square office and work from the crowded confusion of Rollins Place. He, who liked good clothes, was now too hard up to buy a suit off the gaspipe racks at Raymond's. His cuffs had frayed, the seat of his trousers showed patches. If he was to continue with the case, *his* case—and the "if" was beginning to take shape in his mind— he did not want to have his efforts diverted any longer by fund-raising and publicity and stubborn anarchists. Now was the time for him to bring his own friends together—those he had personally interested in the fate of the two obscure Italians—in a common unimpeded effort.

Early in April 1924, Moore arranged a meeting at Tremont Temple to organize the New Trial League, with the support of Mrs. Evans, Mrs. Anna Hallowell Davis (who directed the Garland Fund's legal assistance for radicals), John Van Vaerenewyck of the Cigar Makers' Union, and Alice Stone Blackwell. Alice Blackwell, who was to become Vanzetti's most frequent and voluminous correspondent, whom he would address as Comrade, was the daughter of Lucy Stone, the pioneer women's-rights crusader. Old beyond her sixty-seven years, wrinkled and determined, she followed in the tradition of the previous century's indomitable female eccentrics. She belonged to the International League for Peace and Freedom, the Women's Municipal League, and would later lend her name to the Communist-directed International Labor Defense. A member of the belligerently liberal Twentieth Century Club, she used to carry her lunch there in a brown paper bag and eat it in the library, holding the bag close to her face to avoid spilling any crumbs. It was understood that she was to nap undisturbed in a corner afterward.

Moore chose to remain in the background of the new organization. John Codman of the New England Civil Liberties Committee was appointed treasurer. Professor Guadagni, Albert Carpenter, and Harry Canter, secretary of the Communist Party of Boston, accepted appointment on the editorial board. The board got out its one bulletin in May and published a pamphlet containing Eugene Lyons' translation of Vanzetti's "The Story of a Proletarian Life."

From the New Trial League's office Moore proceeded to raise money and make plans independently of the Defense Committee. Felicani questioned Moore's judgment rather than his honesty, but other members of the Defense Committee were unyielding in their resentment of this independent step. Lola Darroch, no doubt glad to escape the ambivalences of Rollins Place, went to New York to raise funds. Much to the resentment of the anarchists, more money began to flow into the New Trial League's Tremont Street office than to the Hanover Street headquarters. But the league was only an expedient, without roots. Even the conciliatory Felicani realized the impossibility of the dual situation. Scarcely had the league been formed than it began to disintegrate. With the intransigent Lopez gone—he had been deported at last in February 1924—Codman and Mrs. Evans were willing to discuss merging with the committee. Only Moore remained purblind in his good intentions.

Since his return to the Dedham jail Sacco had grown increasingly bitter, and though his sanity was no longer in question he became so dominated by feelings of resentment and persecution that he refused to see Mrs. Evans and his other American visitors. He even turned his back on Mrs. Jack, who had been coming weekly during the winter to give him English lessons. Vanzetti, in Charlestown, was much distressed by the news and sent Mrs. Jack a letter of apology assuring her that Sacco's action was caused not by "adverse feelings, sentiments or thought" but by his misfortune. "And, oh, how worth of shympaty and forgiveness the poor Nick is, even in his herrors," he wrote commiseratingly.

Sacco found the ultimate outlet to his anger in Moore and the New Trial League. The latter had sent him several pamphlets and flyers from the new organization. Reading them, Sacco—as on that July day in court three years before—erupted. He had never liked the Westerner, but this was the last straw. On August 18 he spent the afternoon in his cell penning a letter that was a distillation of his bitterness.

Sir:—Saturday I received your letter with enclose the post card that Mrs. Mateola Robbins sent to me—and the little pamphlet that you use to send to me it just to insult my soul. Yes, it is true, because you would not forget when you came here two or three times between last month with a groups people—that you know that I did not like to see them any more; but you broad them just seem to make my soul feel just sad as it could be. And I can see how clever and cynic you are, because after all my protest, after I have been chase you and all yours philanthropist freinds, you are still continue the infamous speculation on the shoulder of Sacco-Vanzetti case. So this morning before these things going any more long, I thought to send you these few line to advise you and all yours philanthropist freinds of the "New Trial League Committee" not to print any more these letters with my picture and name on, and to be sure to take my name out if they should print any more of these little pamphlets, because you and yours philanthropist has been use it from last three years like a instrument of infamous speculation. It is som thing to carry any man insane or tuberculous when I thing that after all my protest to have my case finish you and all yours legione of freinds still play the infame game. But, I would like to know if yours all are the boss of my life! I would like to know who his this men that ar abuse to take all the authority to do every thing that he does feel like without my responsiblity, and carry my case always more long, against all my wish. I would like to know who his this—generous—man!! Mr.—Moore—! I am telling you that you goin to stop this dirty game! Your heare me?

I mean every them word I said here, because I do not want have anything to do any more with "New Trail League Committee," because it does repugnant my conscience.

Maney time you have been deluder and abuse on weakness of my comrades good faith, but I want you to stop no and if you please get out of my case, because you know that you are the obstacle of the case; and say! I been told you that from last May twenty fifth—that was the last time you came see me, and with you came comrade Felicani and the Proffess Guadagni. Do you remember? Well, from that day I told you to get out of my case, and you promised me that you was goin to get out, but my—dear—Mr. Moore! I see that you are still in my case, and you are still continued to play your famous gam. Of course it is pretty hard to refuse a such sweet pay that as been come to you right long—in—this big—game. It is no true what I said? If it is not the truth, why did you not finish my case then? Another word, if this was not the truth you would quit this job for long time. It has been past one year last June when you and Mr. Grilla from New York came to see me into Bridgewater Hospital and that day between you and I we had another fight—and you will remember when I told you this Mr. Moore! I want you to finish my case and I do not want to have anything to do with this politics in my case because it does repugnant my conscience—and you answer to me was this: Nick, if you don't want, Vanzetti does want! Do you remember when you said that? Well, do you think I believe you when you said that to me? No, because I know that you are the one that brings in always in these mud in Sacco-Vanzetti case. Otherwise, how I could believe you when you been deluder me maney times with your false promise? Well—! anyhow, wherever you do if you do not intent to get out of my case, remember this, that per September I want my case finish. But remember that we are right near September now and I don't see anything and any move yet. So tell me please, why you waiting now for? Do you wait till I hang myself. That's what you wish? Lett me tal you right now don't be illuse yourself because I would not be suprise if somebody will find you some morning hang on lamppost.

Your implacable enemy, now and forever,
Nick Sacco

How hurt Moore was by this he showed only indirectly in the courtesy of his reply:

Dear Mr. Sacco

Enclosed you will find a copy of my Withdrawal as your counsel, filed today.

I wish you every possible success in your battle for justice.

Very truly, yours,
Fred. H. Moore

Although Moore continued officially as counsel until November, he took no further part in the defense. On November 8 he left Boston for good in the old Dodge touring car that was his sole permanent acquisition from the case, alone, in his frayed suit and cracked boots, and with three hundred borrowed dollars in his pocket. His immediate wish was to get back to California, to that land of brighter sunshine and wider horizons, three thousand good miles away from the mongrel English city where even the anarchists seemed affected by the constrictions of the Puritan heritage. Stacked behind him in the Dodge were several dozen packages of little tin signs, for attaching to rear license plates, that read: IF YOU CAN READ THIS YOU'RE TOO DAMN CLOSE. By selling these at filling stations and garages he hoped to cover his expenses on the way back.

As he drove down the slum side of Beacon Hill on a lowering afternoon with the taste of winter in the air, he could see the obelisk of the Bunker Hill Monument and squat beyond it the granite pile of the prison that held Vanzetti. "Chill and dreary, the three-hilled city of the Puritans," Francis Parkman had described an earlier Boston. For Moore it was the dreary three-hilled city of his failure. He had failed as a lawyer, as a propagandist, as a husband, as a man, even as a money-changer. Most of all, he had failed himself. For his last glimpse of Boston left him with the racking uncertainty of his own cause, the nebulous doubt that would feed on disappointment until he could reveal to his friend Upton Sinclair three years later that he no longer believed in the innocence of Sacco and Vanzetti.

Sinclair was aghast. A quarter of a century later he recorded his conversation with Moore:

I questioned Fred for many hours, deep into the night. Sacco and Vanzetti were anarchists, and Fred told me that some of the anarchists were then raising funds for their movement by robbery. It was strictly honest from the group's point of view—that is to say, they kept none of the money for themselves. . . . I pressed him with questions: "Did Sacco or Vanzetti ever admit to you by the slightest hint that they were guilty?" He answered, "No." I asked him: "Did any of their friends ever admit it?" Again he answered, "No.". . . I went home with my mind in confusion. The first person I went to see was Fred's former wife, who had divorced him and was employed in Hollywood. Lola Moore said, "I am astounded that Fred should have made such a statement. I worked on the case with him all through the years, and I knew about it as intimately as he did. He never gave me a hint of such an idea, and neither did anyone else. I feel Fred is embittered because he was dropped from the case, and it has poisoned his mind."

Where Sacco's sense of outrage at being imprisoned so permeated him that it could at times cloud his mind, Vanzetti endured his imprisonment in Charlestown with a stoic objectivity. Sacco saw himself as the predestined victim of a predatory class; Vanzetti remained hopeful, willing to admit that he might be wrong in his judgments. His relations with Moore remained amiable, even though he instinctively had more confidence in the caste-formed Thompson than in the class-conscious Westerner.

Yet, although his studious celibate nature was more adaptable to constraint, in his own way he found jail as constraining as did Sacco. He, too, would face a period when his mind failed him. Unlike Sacco, he had never experienced an emotional outlet in his work. Sacco was the *good* shoeworker, he the *poor* fish peddler. It was not a garden or a wife or the starting hum of a factory at eight in the morning that he missed, but the days of sun and wind when he ambled along the lanes of Plymouth with his cart, the salt odor of the flats where he dug clams.

To Mrs. Evans he expressed his longing for the earth in phrases that suggest Whitman:

O the blissing green of the wilderness and of the open land—O the blue vastness of the Oceans—the fragrances of the flowers and the sweetness of the fruits—The sky reflecting lakes—the singing turrents —the telling brooks—O the valleys, the hills—the awful Alps! O the mistic dawn—the roses of the Aurora, the glory of the moon—O the sunset—the twilight—O the supreme extasies and mistery of the starry nights, heavenly creature of the eternity.

Yes, Yes, all this is real actuallity but not to us, not to us chained— and just and simple because we, being chained, have not the freedom to use our natural faculty of locomotion to carry us from our cells to the open orizon—under the Sun at daytime—under the visible stars, at night.

During his first year in Charlestown, preoccupied with the approaching Dedham trial and learning to accustom himself to the regimen of prison life, Vanzetti came for the first time in his thirteen years in the United States to know Americans—the various assorted liberals and radicals whose interests and emotions drew them to the case. Moore, through his contacts with the New England Civil Liberties Committee, had brought Mrs. Evans, Mrs. Jack, and a number of other Back Bay women as visitors to Charlestown. With Vanzetti, if not so directly as with Sacco, they developed a maternal relationship as engrossing to them as to him. He for the first time in his life discovered people with whom he could share his profounder feelings.

The week after the Dedham trial, writing to Mrs. Evans, he composed his first letter in English, struggling with the language.

I was just thinging what I would do for past the long days jail. I was saying to mysefl: Do some work. But what? Write. A gentle motherly figure came to my mind and I rehear the voice: Why don't you write something now? It will be useful to you now when you will be free. Just at that time I received your letter.

Tank to you from the bottom of my earth for your confidence in my innocence; I am so. I did not splittel a drop of blood, or still a cent in all my life. A little knowlege of the past; a sorrowful experience of the life itself had given to me some ideas very different from those of many other umane beings. But I wish to convince my fellow men that only with virtue and honesty is possible for us to find a little happyness in this world. I preached; I worked. I wished with all my faculties that the social whealth should belong to every umane cretures, so well as it was the fruit of the work of all. But this do not mean robbery for insurrection.

During his prison years Vanzetti studied English with Mrs. Virginia MacMechan, a friend of Mrs. Jack. About his uneven progress he could write wryly to Mrs. Evans, "One Friend tells me that my English is not perfect. I am still laughing for such a pious euphension. Why not say horrible?" Vanzetti always had this capacity for laughing at himself, for seeing the humorous side of even the jail world— a quality lacking in Sacco. His difficulties in English, as he explained, did not come from the big words derived from Latin and Greek and familiar to Italian, but from the tricky monosyllables of Nordic origin. In the solitude of Charlestown he felt the renewed lust for learning that had enveloped him so long ago when he had read Dante,

Renan, and Malatesta in his squalid room by the flickering gaslight until the stars faded. Now, however, he would read Longfellow and Franklin and Paine and Jefferson. By 1923 he was reading James Harvey Robinson's *The Mind in the Making;* William James' *Psychology;* books by Jack London, Sinclair Lewis, and Upton Sinclair; and such periodicals as the *Survey Graphic,* the *New Republic,* the *Nation,* and the *Daily Worker.* He felt himself carried away by a Faustian longing to know mathematics, physics, history.

For all its galling restraints, imprisonment was to provide the key that would unlock his personality. His tragedy was to be, as he said himself, his triumph. Earlier than Sacco he sensed that the two of them had become symbols such as Moore had foreseen at the very beginning. The week before the Dedham trial he had written to Alice Blackwell:

What has been done for us by the people of the world, the laborers (I mean workers) and the greatest minds and hearts proves beyond any possible doubt that a new conception of justice is planing its way in the soul of mankind: a justice centered on man as man. For as I have already said, you, they are doing for us what once could only have been done for saints and kings.

Somehow in the years at Charlestown, Vanzetti—the misfit, the wanderer—became the master of language. Even in his early fumblings with grammar he was always eloquent. As early as December 1921, after a brief glimpse of the close-ranged Roxbury streets on the way to his Dedham hearing he could write: "O, funny, humble, old, little houses that I love; little house always big enough for the greatest loves, and most saint affects."

In his letters, in his speech to the court, one can trace the developing cadences of English, the tone-giving rhythm of the Anglo-Saxon that runs below the surface of the modern tongue. This moving eloquence—where did it come from? It was as if the man grew as his prospect of life shortened. After raging to Alice Blackwell against those he considered his persecutors, he could apologize in his next letter: "I am yet man enough to look streight in to the eyes, the black gastly reality and the tragedy of my life."

As he came face to face with that reality, he had no room for accretions and superficialities. What was left to him was acceptance. "I neither boast nor exalt, nor pity myself," he wrote Mrs. Mac-Mechan. "I followed my call, I have my conscience serene." He understood that the most one could hope for was "the little knowledge of the enormous mystery surrounding us and from which we sprang." His freedom taken from him, he became a free man.

Anarchism remained the core of his beliefs: a vision of the peaceable kingdom where the wolves and the lambs of the industrial world would attain their ultimate reconciliation. "Oh, friend," he wrote to his teacher, "the anarchism is as beauty as a women for me, perhaps even more since it include all the rest and me and her. Calm, serene, honest, natural, vivid, muddy and celestial at once, austere, heroic, fearless, fatal, generous and implacable—all these and more it is." He defined the anarchist's creed as

All what is help to me without hurt the others is good; all what help the others without hurting me is good also, all the rest is evil. He look for his liberty in the liberty of all, for his happiness in the happiness of all, for his welfare in the universal welfare.

If the golden age could only come about through violence, he would accept violence—though with deep personal regret:

I would my blood to prevent the sheeding of blood, but neither the abyss nor the heaven's, have a law who condamns the self-defence. . . . The champion of life and of the liberty should not yield before the death.

Sacco's nature had a darker turbulence. The now obsolete term *anarchist-communist* would have applied to him as it would never have applied to Vanzetti. Anarchist though he called himself, he saw life in terms of the Marxist class struggle, in which "as long as this sistem of things, the exploitation of man on other man reign, will remain always the fight between those two opposite class." Unlike Vanzetti, he did not concern himself with anarchism as the rejection of government, but with the immediacy of conflict. In a dream he had at Dedham he described how he found himself in the middle of a strike in a Pennsylvania mining town and how soldiers with guns and bayonets came to put it down:

And so the fite it was to beginning, and while the fite was begin I jump upon a little hill in meddle of the crowd and I begin to say, Friend and comrade and brotherhood, now one of us as going to move a step, and who will try to move it will be vile and coward, here the fite as go to finish. So I turn over towards to the soldiers and I said, Brothers you will not fire on your own brothers just because their tell you to fire, no brothers remember that everyone of us *we have mother and child, and you know that we fite for freedom wich is your freedom. We want one of the fatherland, one sole, one house, and better bread. So while I was finish to say that last work one of the soldiers fire towards me and the ball past throught my heart, and while I was fall on ground with my right hand close to my heart I awake up with sweet dream!*

On a secondary level the dream was Sacco's acceptance of his execution, which he saw as predetermined, inevitable. Vanzetti, on the other hand, was optimistic until almost the end. Even Webster Thayer, in whom all the forces inimical to him and to Sacco seemed concentrated, he could view with the dispassionateness of his note to the Brinis just after the arguments on the supplementary motions: "I dislike to vilify humane being and would be more than glad, happy —if he by one just act, would comples me to change my opinion— but there are no reasons till now."

A few months later, discouraged from any such fugitive hopes, Vanzetti reverted to a more somber picture of the judge:

I have never expected, nor I expect from him other than some then thousand volts divided in a few times; some meters of cheap bord and 4 x 7 x 8 feet hol in the ground.

No matter how much of sympathy I try to bestow upon him, or with how much of understanding I try to judge his actions; I only and alone can see him a self-conceit nerroved mind little tyrent, be-living himself to be just, and beliving his utterly unjust and unneces-sary social office to be a necessity and a good. He is a bigot and, therefore, cruel. At the time of our arrest and trials, his peers were sawing red all around, and he was sawing more red than his peers.

Nineteen twenty-four was the year of indecision when, after Hamilton's discomfiture over the pistol barrels, the legal clockwork seemed to have run down, when Judge Thayer—who alone might have re-wound it—was again ailing, when no one could even guess the date of his decisions on the supplementary motions. Vanzetti, at the time Sacco was turning his back on visitors, became so frustrated by the suspense that for a while he considered going on a hunger strike. "I am tired—tired—tired!" he wrote early in the autumn. "I asked if to live like now for love of life is not, rather than wisdom or heroism, mere cowardness."

From July until September the courts closed for the long recess. In the yard of the Dedham jail during the exercise period the prisoners hung about languidly under the shadow of the wall. At Charlestown the sun beating down on the slate roofs set the air smoldering. In such weather the excremental smell of drains seemed to ooze from the very stones of the old building. Vanzetti noted that it must be equally fetid in the narrow streets of the North End.

Those who could get away fled the heat. Judge Thayer had gone to his cottage at Falmouth, on Cape Cod where, with the breeze cutting in from across Buzzards Bay, he spent the mornings working on his decisions on the five supplementary motions. The close of summer did not see his task at an end. Not until the first of October did he at last file his findings in the clerk's office at Dedham.

The news flashed across the Boston papers in blacker headlines than any that had appeared since the conviction. Thayer had denied all five motions!

With regard to the Ripley motion Thayer found "that said Ripley brought with him innocently and thoughtlessly the said three cartridges . . . that whatever Ripley said or did in relation to said three cartridges, he never intended to prejudice in any manner the rights of the defendants." Hamilton had made an affidavit claiming that the Ripley shells showed signs of having been pushed into Vanzetti's revolver. Thayer pointed out that the other jurors had sworn that Ripley had not exhibited the bullets in the jury room, and there would have been no other opportunity. He considered that any comparison Ripley made between his own cartridges and the exhibits must have been a mental one, since, although jurors had seen the Ripley bullets in the dormitory downstairs, no one had seen them elsewhere.

The basic claim of the defense was that there had been an improper exhibit in the jury room. Certainly Ripley's three bullets were improperly, if accidentally, there. But Thayer's finding seems reasonable: "The mere production of the Ripley cartridges and the talk or discussion about them did not create such disturbing or prejudicial influence that might in any way affect the verdict.

"At any rate," he concluded, in one of the rhetorical flourishes of which he was so proud, "I am not willing to blacken the memory of Mr. Ripley and to pronounce those eleven surviving jurors as falsifiers under oath by claims of counsel that are so weak, so fragile, and so unsatisfactory. If this motion for a new trial based upon hearsay statements made by a deceased juror to a counsel for the defendants under such circumstances as are herein disclosed [were granted], it would result in smirching the honor, integrity, and good name of twelve honorable jurors, by a decision that never could be justified by the simplest rules of sound judgment, reason, truth, and common sense."

As for Daley's affidavit charging Ripley with the remark, "Damn them, they ought to hang them anyway!" Thayer ruled that he "was not bound to believe him," nor was he "required to give the reasons for his action. Furthermore, before being sworn as a juror, it must be assumed that Ripley had answered in the negative . . . whether he had expressed or formed an opinion or was sensible of any bias or prejudice." Even if Daley had no reason for lying, it was still hearsay evidence—and Ripley was long since dead.

In denying the second motion Thayer expressed doubt that the itinerant Gould could "have carried a correct mental photograph in his mind of Sacco for practically eighteen months, when he had only a glance in which to take this photograph on the day of the murder." Gould, however, had merely claimed that the man who had put a bullet through his lapel, the man he had seen in that frozen instant of terror when the gun flashed in his face, was not the stocky Italian he had seen eighteen months later in the Dedham jail.

Thayer held that Gould was just one more witness in the crowd, and that his evidence, if presented, would have had no effect on the jury—"For the evidence that convicted these men was circumstantial and was evidence that is known in law as 'consciousness of guilt.'" For a dozen pages Thayer continued this theme with variations, coming back again to the question of whether the defendants had lied because of their consciousness of being radicals or their consciousness of being murderers. This, Thayer maintained, was a matter of fact that had been settled once and for all by the jurors. In passing, he could not resist an aside at those bothersome dissenters "who ever stand ready, through sympathy, prejudice, or some other unaccountable reason, to criticize and assail the verdicts of juries when, in fact, they never have heard a single word of evidence, nor observed a single witness on the stand."

As far as Louis Pelser was concerned, he had admittedly been drinking on the day he signed Moore's affidavit, and a few days later, when sober, he had retracted it. Thayer accepted the counteraffidavits of Katzmann and Williams that they had not tried to influence Pelser, and ruled that Pelser's statement provided no justification for a new trial.

Often while Judge Thayer sat on his porch at Falmouth preparing his findings he found himself thinking of Moore, and the thought of that "damned anarchist" lawyer was enough to cloud the brightest summer day. There, for example, was the whole Goodridge business. Goodridge had been discredited at the trial. That was obvious to anyone. Yet here was Moore chasing him all over Maine, locking him up in jail, blackmailing him with indictments ten years old. "It is perfectly manifest," Thayer wrote, with a cloud-dispersing mental picture of Moore's discomfort, "that here was another bold and cruel attempt to sandbag Goodridge by threatening actual arrest, to blacken the name of the district attorney's office of Norfolk County, by compelling Goodridge to testify as he did on account of the influence of said district attorney's office. He did not succeed simply because Goodridge would not be intimidated. Was this conduct on the part of Mr. Moore performed in furtherance of public justice, or was it a cruel and unjustifiable attempt to scare Goodridge into swearing to something that was false against the District Attorney's office?" For Thayer the question was rhetorical. "I have tried to look at this conduct of Mr. Moore with a view of finding some justification or excuse of it," he concluded. "I can find none."

He was equally severe with Moore in denying the Andrews motion. Perhaps smiling to himself, he wrote, "My relationship with [Moore] has been very pleasant, although at times it would seem, as was very natural, that he was quite unfamiliar with our trial evidence and practice in this state." Then he let the Californian have both barrels: "Mr. Moore, judging him by his conduct as disclosed under his own motion, signed by him, seems to be laboring under the view that an enthusiastic belief in the innocence of his clients justifies any means in order to accomplish the ends desired." He accused Moore of a "more intense desire to procure a confession of perjury from Mrs. Andrews than a profound desire to seek the truth."

When Thayer came to the Hamilton motion, he was undoubtedly convinced by the episode of the switched gun-barrels that the self-styled doctor from Auburn was a sharper. He did not elaborate, but in each instance he ruled that Hamilton's claim was not sustained.

Captain Proctor's affidavit was more of a problem, for there were no two ways about it. Proctor had signed his name to his own impeachment, and Katzmann and Williams had never denied the substance of it. Nevertheless, it was Thayer's opinion that Proctor had meant what he said in court, and that the jury had so understood it. "If Captain Proctor found no facts to believe that the mortal bullet passed through the Sacco pistol, why, when he had a perfect opportunity so to do, did he not say that his opinion was then, as it is now, that it was not *consistent* with it?" Thayer did not feel there had been any conniving by Katzmann and Williams to shape the question in advance. He did not try to explain why Proctor had afterward made the refuting statement.

"If I have erred in my judgment (and I fully realize I am human)," Thayer concluded with a sense of relief at freeing himself from the burden, "let me express the assurance that the supreme judicial court of this Commonwealth in due time will correct such error."

Neither Moore nor Thompson had expected any other outcome, but the motions had served their purpose. They had postponed the defendants' execution, and they had provided questions of law to be ruled on by a higher court. With the Goodridge, Pelser, Andrews, and Daley affidavits Thompson felt there was nothing more to be gained, that these were to a degree liabilities, but he appealed the denials of the Ripley, Gould, and Hamilton-Proctor motions.

After he had filed his findings with the clerk of court, Thayer felt he deserved a holiday, and for him a holiday in the autumn meant Hanover, New Hampshire. The Dartmouth-McGill football game that Saturday was only an excuse for the trip, since the Big Green was the odds-on favorite. But to get back to Dartmouth gave Thayer a sense of renewing himself, as if when he walked across the campus he was again for one miraculous moment Bobby Thayer, the baseball captain who could not quite make up his mind whether he wanted to be a big-league player or a lawyer. He felt that he belonged in Hanover. There was his familiar table by the window in the dining room of the Hanover Inn, the waiter who knew him, the faces of old friends as they came through the doorway. Much had changed, much had been added, but there were still the white buildings of Dartmouth Row, the Senior Fence where he had carved his initials over forty years ago, the arching elms, still looking just as they had when he arrived as a freshman. Each autumn brought him back, almost as if he had never left.

Thayer was cutting across the College Green in the long-edged sunlight after the game when he saw James Richardson, Dartmouth's Professor of Law and Political Science, walking just ahead of him. Jim Richardson was Class of 1900, twenty years after Thayer, but the two men often met at alumni gatherings. As the judge drew abreast of the professor he nodded and they continued together toward the Inn. "Did you see what I did with those anarchistic bastards the other day?" Thayer asked affably, by way of conversation. He did not notice the shocked look on the other's face as he continued, "I guess that will hold them for a while. Let them go to the Supreme Court now and see what they can get out of them!"

The denial of the supplementary motions was no more than Sacco had expected, but the decision left Vanzetti sunk in discouragement. "While hope is still alive in me," he wrote, "disperation is growing powerful." His fantasies of violence expanded:

My native me is drearing for what it is becoming. I have cut down trees with a sense of sympathy for them, and almost a sort of remorse; while now thinking of my axe, a lust seizes me to get a mad delight and exaltation by using them on the necks of the men men's eaters; on the necks of those who seem to have the evil in their head and on the trunks of those who seem to have the evil in their breast.

In the weeks before Christmas his mental balance began to waver. He told the guards of having feelings in his head and chest that meant earthquakes were coming. He noticed a sensation of electricity in the air. Each night he barricaded the door of his cell with a table for fear that his enemies might overpower the guards and kill him. The day before Christmas he threatened another prisoner who, he said, was laughing at him. Six days later he smashed a chair. Joseph McLaughlin, the prison physician, and Charles Sullivan, the state expert for insane criminals, spent some time questioning him. He told them that everyone had forsaken him; that at his trial "perjurers, fascists and others" had been "out to get him," and that he needed to carry a gun for protection. The doctors diagnosed him as in a dangerous hallucinatory and delusional state of mind, and recommended his committal to the Bridgewater Hospital, where Sacco had been sent twenty-one months before.

Vanzetti arrived manacled the day after New Year's. When the admitting doctor asked him routinely why he was there, he replied, "I don't know, I am not crazy. Perhaps they think I need a rest." Although for the next two months he seemed a model prisoner, quiet and controlled, his inner turbulence persisted. He told the doctors of a fascist plot against him being prepared through certain Italian prisoners in Charlestown who could kill him "any time any day they want to." Even in Bridgewater there were such fascists. "I more than feel it," he told the doctor.

The records of Vanzetti in Bridgewater are scanter than those of Sacco. On February 23 the attendant noted that he spent the day sitting in a chair pretending to have his eyes closed, but watching the other prisoners. At the evening meal he looked at his food suspiciously, then took potatoes from another prisoner's plate and ate them, saying nothing. He was kept in his room except for two periods a day that he could play ball in the yard. When Thompson spoke to the doctors about this, they told him they could not give Vanzetti more freedom because he was dangerous. On the arrival of a new Italian prisoner Vanzetti was removed to a more secluded wing of the hospital, a change he resented deeply. Like most patients in mental institutions, he had the feeling that the doctors were working against him. In April his physical symptoms had begun to abate, and by May he could write, "Yes, my heartburn is gone, and I am quite well—so well that I feel to write a treaty on sociology—wich I have not yet begun, because I wish to hear some friends in its regards." On May 28, 1925, he was certified as not insane and returned to Charlestown.

The disorganization of the Defense Committee that Moore had watched was followed about the time of his departure by a reorganization and an opening up of the membership to non-Italians. Lopez had been inflexible in excluding outsiders, but Amleto Fabbri, the gentle, softspoken shoe-worker who had replaced him as secretary, welcomed them. Many of the new members came over from the dissolved New Trial League, but the influx that really broke through the Latin limitations of the old committee came from the James Connolly Literary Society.

That society was made up of a group of forty or fifty dissidents from the local branch of the Gaelic League. They called themselves a literary society because in Boston they could not say what they really were—Irishmen of the indeterminate left, socialists, associates of the Socialist Labor Party, some of them even Wobblies. Most of them had turned against the church and were anathema to their pious majority compatriots. More concerned with day-to-day problems of economics than with theoretical Marxism, their only literary activity was the distribution of pamphlets. The name Connolly was really a cover—who in such an Irish city could say a word against the martyr of 1916?

The James Connolly Literary Society had become interested in the Sacco-Vanzetti case during the Dedham trial. As it now drew closer to the Italian nucleus of the Defense Committee, three of its members became officers, with John Barry, a quiet, conciliatory Irishman taking over as chairman. Barry, a steelworker, would never play a conspicuous role. His retiring nature made him acceptable to everyone, and in fact he was so accepted as a symbol of intergroup unity.

Michael Flaherty, a painter and member of the Boston Labor Union named vice-chairman, took a much more active part. Flaherty and his associates brought a lighter spirit to the ordained seriousness of the anarchists. An Aran Islander, Flaherty possessed an underlying humor that the darkest situation could never quite down. If he had stayed in Ireland he would undoubtedly have played his part in the Easter Uprising. In America he gravitated naturally to the Sacco-Vanzetti case.

Mary Donovan, who came with him from the Society, was both a more practical and a more pugnacious type, a lank, raw-boned, sharp-featured woman in her thirties. Emotional, opinionated, suspicious, generous, and devoted, she was not an easy person to get along with, but she made the cause of Sacco and Vanzetti so much her own that she became possessed by it. So much of her time did she spend at the Hanover Street headquarters, where she took charge of correspondence and communications, that she soon became the committee's recording secretary and lost her State House job as industrial inspector for the Department of Labor.

With Moore gone, the McAnarneys in turn resigned, leaving the defense temporarily without counsel. Most of the committee by now felt that Moore had been an unfortunate choice, that what was needed was an outstanding local lawyer, someone with authority and position. Elizabeth Gurley Flynn, after consulting with the American Civil Liberties Union and the Workers' Defense Union, came on from New York to talk the matter over with the committee. "I then had long conferences," she wrote with the customary exaggeration of her own role, "in which I interviewed every element—from conservative trade unionists, Socialists, Anarchist, Communists, and Liberals including Professor Frankfurter at Harvard University. The universal opinion was that a new, distinguished local counsel was imperative."

Frankfurter recommended that the committee try to get William Thompson. That had been John McAnarney's idea from the beginning, and many of the committee had come to feel the same way after listening to Thompson's arguments on the supplementary motions. The question was whether he would be willing to take on such an unpopular case.

Elizabeth Gurley Flynn, Mary Donovan, Barry, Felicani, and Mike Flaherty called at the Matthews, Thompson & Spring offices in the

Tremont Building to see what they could do. Thompson received them in his austere office, looked at them through his rimless glasses, and listened noncommittally. Finally he told them, in a tone that suggested he expected to hear no more of the matter, that he would take the case for a fee of twenty-five thousand dollars, paid in advance.

In two days they were back with the money. "I thought sure you couldn't raise it," Thompson told Elizabeth Gurley Flynn. "I can't say that I'm glad." In a quick trip to New York, she had borrowed twenty thousand dollars from the American Fund for Public Service—popularly known as the Garland Fund—on the security of the Amalgamated Clothing Workers and the International Ladies Garment Workers' Union. Felicani, in a stupendous burst of energy, had managed to raise the additional five thousand dollars locally through the harder way of individual contributions.

The moment Thompson received the certified check was, although he did not then know it, the turning point in his life. After that the world of Boston, his incorporated world, would never be the same for him again.

CHAPTER FOURTEEN

The Confessions

It is not unusual for a notable murder case to have several confessions as a by-product. Where these are false, they are either the notoriety-seeking of a psychopathic misfit or the effort of some criminal to obtain a pardon for a crime he has committed in order to stand trial for one he has not. In the latter case he can plan, once safely pardoned, to repudiate his confession.

Such was, no doubt, the motive of Augusto Pasquale, under life imprisonment in New York for kidnaping, when in May 1922 he confessed to being one of the South Braintree gunmen. According to his story he had met two strangers in a Bowery saloon who asked him if he wanted to pull a job with them in a factory in South Braintree. He agreed, and they went from New York to Boston by train to pick up a car. Pasquale did not know the make of car nor did he seem to be familiar with the geography of South Braintree. He said that he and the others held up an auto with the payroll in it. When the paymaster and guard drew their guns, they shot them, took over the auto, drove a quarter of a mile, then hopped a train to New York. His story was so obviously concocted that the police did not even pretend to take it seriously.*

* Certain other leads, neglected at the time, are tantalizing in their possibilities. One such concerns a professional car thief, William Dodson, who worked in a Needham garage from 1917 to 1919 and who in February 1921 was arrested in Providence after stealing Judge Thayer's car in Worcester. When, a year later, Dodson's wife sued him for divorce, she testified that in the spring of 1920 he had given her eight hundred of the thousand dollars he had received for driving the bandit car in South Braintree. Another concerns the Randolph Savings Bank holdup of November 17, 1919. Although the bandits were never identified, the

The confession of Frank "the Winker" Silva to being a member of the gang that staged the Bridgewater holdup was a matter of more substance. Silva did not make his confession until Sacco and Vanzetti were dead—and then only after he was paid for it—but Moore had been aware of some of its details as early as 1922.

Jack Callahan, an ex-bank burglar turned journalist, who still kept his underworld contacts, was the go-between who persuaded Silva to sell his story to the *Outlook and Independent*, where it appeared in 1928.

Silva, at the time of the Bridgewater holdup, was thirty-five years old. He had come to Boston from Italy at the age of ten, and still spoke English with an accent, although his close-set face with its clipped mustache looked more American than Italian. Sensual, indolent, usually down on his luck, as readily a pimp as a mugger, Silva was the petty-criminal type not uncommon in the North End, where the brown, wrinkled-faced old women would draw their shawls tighter in contempt as he passed.

When the police seemed too active Silva would take a job, but never for long. In 1916, he told Callahan, he had worked briefly in the L. Q. White factory in Bridgewater, but soon returned to Hanover Street. His favorite hangout there was Jimmy "Big Chief" Mede's shoeshine parlor and cigar stand, where a few of the boys were always talking about easy money, figuring things out. Jimmy was a dark-eyed, heavy-browed Sicilian who asked questions and let others do the answering.

---

robbery was apparently planned by four men and a woman in a Brockton lodging house. Afterward a phial of cocaine was found in their empty room. The plates of the car they used had been stolen from Hassam's Garage in Needham. According to the Brockton *Enterprise* of five days after the South Braintree holdup, "Thomas Finnegan of Braintree picked up a small bottle said to have been thrown from the murder car as it sped away. This leads police to believe that dope played a part in the crime." Needham again crops up in the suspicion that the never-traced South Braintree payroll money may have been hidden there. Two days after the holdup, Fred Lyons passed a car that had stopped in the middle of an isolated road near the Working Boys' Home. A short, slightly built man was walking up and down beside the car as Lyons drove by. Then, as Lyons continued, the other car started up and followed him a mile to his home. There it turned around and drove away. Next morning Lyons notified the police. They found a freshly dug hole about two feet deep in a clump of brush not far from where the strange car had stopped. After digging down three more feet they struck rock. Several weeks later it was discovered that someone had dug the hole several feet deeper, removing two boulders to uncover a shelf of rock with a pocket scooped out under it large enough to hold a suitcase.

According to Silva, he had told Jimmy it would be easy enough to go down to Bridgewater the day before Christmas and snatch the payroll. He figured it would amount to twenty or thirty thousand dollars.

Several times in the autumn of 1917, Silva said, he and Mede and Joe Sammarco, a nineteen-year-old Italian corner boy known as Joe Nap because he had come from Naples, went to Bridgewater to look over the factory, the bank, and the connecting streets. Then on November 14, 1917, Mede and some of his boys were caught after robbing the paymaster of the American Net & Twine Company in Cambridge, and the Big Chief found himself doing a seven-to-ten-year rap in Charlestown.

Silva, left to himself, joined the Army. After his discharge in 1919 he returned to the North End and ran into Joe Sammarco. They were both broke. Silva remembered the L. Q. White payroll, waiting there in Bridgewater like a Christmas turkey. The job would need two more to pull it off. Sammarco said he knew just the two. Next day he appeared with "Doggy" Bruno, a chunky fellow with a short mustache like Silva's, and "Guinea" Oates, who owned a touring car.

Silva told Callahan that the four of them had driven to Bridgewater several times to check the roads. They had walked around the town, shot a little pool in the parlor under the post office, and taken a long look at the Bridgewater Trust Company, where the White truck picked up the payroll. Because Christmas would fall on Thursday, they knew the delivery would be made on Wednesday.

Monday of Christmas week, Silva told Callahan, Guinea had driven them to Needham and at a garage near the police station Silva asked a man about license plates. When the man walked away for a moment, he spotted an old car that had dealer's plates tied on with string. He untied them, tucked them under his coat, and cleared out to meet the others. From Needham they drove to Bridgewater for another rehearsal.

On Tuesday they made their final dry run. Wednesday morning they arrived in Bridgewater at about half past six and parked on Hale Street, not far from a lunch stand. Silva said, "Boys, let's go down and have something to eat because this is liable to be our last meal."

He and Doggy finished eating ahead of the others and walked up to the square opposite the bank to watch for the truck. Suddenly Silva noticed that it had slipped in from the side street and was parked in front of the bank.

They returned to the car and Doggy got in, leaving Silva outside as look-out man. Guinea Oates was at the wheel. At Silva's signal, he was to back the car into the street and block the truck.

Silva called out "Let's go" and Guinea shoved the car into Broad Street while the other two piled out. What they had not counted on was a trolley car coming down the street right behind the truck. They shouted at the men in the truck, now almost on top of them, and Doggy leveled his shotgun, but, as Silva told it:

When we said, "stick 'em up," instead of the driver sticking up his hands, and the rest of them they kept on going, and all of a sudden shots were fired from both sides. Most of us were behind some trees or posts, a few feet from Hale Street. I seen this man that was sitting on the side seat, I don't know who it was, but it was a big man. He got up from his seat and grabbed the driver's wheel and while he was grabbing the driver's wheel, the street car comes down and cuts us off from seeing the truck. All of a sudden I heard a noise. We heard some glass breaking. We couldn't see the payroll car any more. We all got on our car and we shot straight through Hale Street into Plymouth Street. . . . No cars followed us.

They stopped near a cemetery to change license plates, and Doggy threw the stolen ones into a pond. Back in the North End Silva and Bruno shaved off their mustaches. "I was broke and desperate," Silva told Callahan. "There was some Jew from New York that was hanging around Boston and I got acquainted with him. He was way worst off than I was." The man, a down-and-outer named Jacob Luban, was full of plausible talk about easy money in New York. Calling himself Paul Martini, Silva set out with him. His easy money turned out to be nothing more than working the combinations of post-office boxes and stealing letters that might contain money. In this paltry venture Silva and Luban were joined by another floater, Adolph Witner. Hanging around New York post-office lobbies, they were soon noticed and arrested. Witner turned state's evidence. Luban and Silva received terms in the United States penitentiary in Atlanta.

Doggy Bruno and Guinea Oates vanished. Only Joe Sammarco stayed on in Boston. Three weeks after the Bridgewater failure a policeman was killed during a dance-hall brawl in City Square, Charlestown. Sammarco was convicted for this crime in 1920 and sent to Charlestown State Prison for life. There he found himself with Big Chief Mede.

In August, 1920, Vanzetti was taken to Charlestown. Mede, with an eye to parole, was conducting a weekly English class for those who did not know the language, and Vanzetti became one of his students. Mede never forgot him. Forty years later he was still scornful of the idea that anyone could ever have considered the bookish Vanzetti capable of committing a holdup.

By the end of 1921 Moore's investigators had picked up rumors connecting Mede and Silva with the Bridgewater affair, and in January, February, and March, 1922, Moore visited Mede in Charlestown. The Big Chief would neither deny nor affirm anything, but intimated that if he was given help in getting a parole, plus certain other favors, he would disclose a lot. Moore wrote to Governor Channing Cox, explaining Mede's situation and asking for assurance that no statement Mede made would hurt his chances for parole. Cox replied that inasmuch as Mede was not going to be paroled anyhow, he should feel perfectly free to tell what he knew. The Big Chief did not think much of the governor's answer and refused to talk.

Mede's counsel was James Vahey, the brother of Vanzetti's Plymouth lawyer. As soon as Vahey heard that Moore had been seeing his client, he paid a visit to the Charlestown prison and asked Mede point-blank just what he had said to Moore. When Mede denied that he had told Moore anything, Vahey—according to Mede's sworn statement in 1928—warned him: "Don't you dare say anything in regard to the Sacco-Vanzetti case. You know, my brother defended Vanzetti, and you will only be putting my brother in Dutch."

Mede agreed to say nothing, but shortly afterward he broke with Vahey and on receiving the guarantee of an unrevealed sum of money from Moore told a story of the Bridgewater holdup similar to that later told by Silva. Mede had got together with Sammarco and said the latter would corroborate him, but although Moore talked with Sammarco several times, he could get no admissions out of him.

Meanwhile, Adolph Witner, who had been let off with a token sentence for helping to convict Silva and Luban, found himself extradited to Boston on charges of forgery and mail robbery. Moore ran into him at police headquarters, overwhelmed by his new troubles. He told Moore that he could open up the Sacco-Vanzetti case if Moore, in turn, would help him. Somehow the adroit Moore arranged to get the charges against Witner dropped, and late in April the two men, accompanied by an ex-convict named John Jocomo, then working as an investigator for the Defense Committee, headed for Atlanta to interview Luban and Silva.

Luban, envious of Witner's freedom, decided to turn a little state's evidence on his own and proceeded to write a long, garbled account of these interviews to William J. Burns, the Director of the Bureau of Investigation of the Department of Justice. Burns sent an agent to Atlanta to interview Luban and Silva. Receiving a report of the interview, Lawrence Letherman of the Boston Bureau sent a copy to the attorney general of Massachusetts. A few days later one of the attorney general's assistants, Albert Hurwitz, arrived in Atlanta to take affidavits from the two men.

Luban told Hurwitz that on April 18 he had been called to the warden's office to find Silva and an outsider whom Silva introduced as John Jocomo already there. Jocomo said he had come down from Boston to investigate the Bridgewater holdup "committed by Sacco and Vanzetti." Although he knew that Silva really had had nothing to do with it, Jocomo said he was in Atlanta for two reasons—first because he was being paid; second, to cover himself and his brother, who had deposited some of the money taken in the South Braintree holdup.

The next day Luban and Silva were brought to the office again; this time Moore was there with Jocomo, who asked if they would like to talk to Witner. Moore had Witner brought in. Witner confronted his two former pals as if he were doing them a favor.

During my conversation [Luban explained to Hurwitz] *I was interrupted by Moore who said to me, "There is no use talking, Martini [Silva] don't know the first thing about Bridgewater or about Braintree, but is willing to help along and take the blame providing Mr. Moore will keep the promise that he made him." I forgot to state that when Mr. Moore came to Atlanta he told me he was in Washington, that he seen William J. Burns and Attorney General Dougherty, and that they told him they would be glad if this case would be disposed of in any way at all, as long as Sacco and Vanzetti go free. He also told me he had a conversation with Attorney General Allen of Massachusetts, a man I never heard of or never seen in my life before and that Mr. Allen told him that if he can find a way how to free Sacco and Vanzetti, "we don't care whether legitimate or unlegitimate" that he, Mr. Allen, would help him in any shape or form. . . . He says . . . Mr. Allen wants to dispose of this case in the worst way, and he don't care how it is disposed of as long as these two men are free, because the Governor and everybody else is sick and tired of it.*

The promises made to me were these, first that Mr. Moore will use *his influence to get Martini and myself out of prison, and second that Witner would go to New York and confess to his part of the perjury which would show my innocence automatically. Third, that we would receive $5,000 apiece before Martini takes the stand, $5,000 apiece after he goes off the stand; fourth, that Martini will get a good lawyer who will instruct him while Martini is on the stand testifying, this lawyer will instruct him to refuse to answer questions on the grounds of incriminating and degrading himself, that will create an impression with the judge that he did not want to commit himself, but it is true that he is the one and not Sacco who committed the holdup in Bridgewater, and he believes on these grounds Sacco and Vanzetti will get a new trial. Later on Martini will be able to defend himself by telling the truth and showing that really while this murder and attempted murder was committed Martini was in New York.*

When Hurwitz asked Luban what Moore wanted Martini-Silva to do, Luban replied: "He wanted Martini to confess that he together with another man named Joe Napp and Jas Meade committed the attempted robbery at Bridgewater. He said these two men were willing to take the blame for it, and was also willing to testify that Martini was along with them, providing Martini will consent to it, not otherwise."

Witner, according to Luban, said that he was working as an investigator for Moore and being paid fifty dollars a week and expenses by the Amalgamated Garment Workers' Union. He suggested that Silva also should admit that he and two other convicts now dead committed the Braintree murders. Later it would be easy to prove that he was in New York on both days.

He also stated they had two witnesses [Luban continued], one by the name of Louis Pelser has already been fixed up to change his testimony so it will be in favor of the defendants.

He said they had another witness by the name of Roy Gould who previously did not testify, but will testify now and will identify Martini, but should they want to prosecute Martini for murder Gould will retract his original testimony against Martini.

One of the man's witnesses, a certain woman whose name I don't remember, has already changed her testimony. From Mr. Moore's statement to me I first understood she first testified in favor of the prosecution, and now she is ready to testify for the defense, that the prosecuting attorney had coached her and induced her when she identified Sacco, but she will switch over to Martini if necessary, because they look so much alike, and Witner told me in Jewish that it cost a good many thousand dollars to get the woman to change her testimony, and they are ready to spend a good many thousand more.

Luban gave a complicated account of Witner's going to Moore's office and seeing a picture he recognized as Silva's only to have Moore tell him it was Sacco's.

Then Moore thought for a minute that maybe Martini is the one who committed the crime in Bridgewater and Braintree and they mistook Sacco for Martini. Witner in his heart knew that Martini had nothing to do with it, because Martini was with Witner together in New York at the time these robberies and murders were committed.

Luban's rambling affidavit was of course as suspect as his character. Sacco was never accused of participating in the Bridgewater attempt, although Luban seems to have got it into his head that he was the leader. Nor did Sacco in the least resemble Silva. Luban called Sacco and Vanzetti good union men, but the two had never belonged to a trade-union and as anarchists were opposed to them. Nor, of course, was there ever any indication that Massachusetts officials were interested in finding a way to free Sacco and Vanzetti.

Witner, safe behind the shield of language, undoubtedly told Luban some story about Silva in Yiddish, and it is apparent from Luban's confused accounts of Pelser, Gould, and Lola Andrews that he had heard something about the witnesses. Moore made no further attempts to get in touch with Luban.

Silva, too, made an affidavit for Hurwitz in which he admitted he had known Jocomo for sixteen years and claimed that the latter's brother Joe, who lived in Mattapan, "had come in possession of $12,000 of the money that was stolen at Braintree holdup, and an investigation was started to find from where he got that money."

He stated that he told Moore he had nothing to do with either the Bridgewater or the Braintree holdups and knew nothing about them since on both dates he was living in a house belonging to Luban on West 46th Street in New York. It was on Luban's advice that he had agreed to play along with Moore and pretend he had taken part in the Bridgewater business. Moore, Witner, and Jocomo had coached him on the dates of the holdups, and Moore had promised to show him maps of Bridgewater and Braintree.

Nothing more was to be heard from Silva until after Sacco and Vanzetti were dead. As soon as Mede was let out of Charlestown in

1923, Moore tried to persuade him to make a statement about the Bridgewater attempt. Mede, with the shadow of Charlestown still large behind him, refused, but agreed for a salary to go to New York and see what he could find out about the Braintree affair from the underworld there. A few weeks later Moore's investigator Tommy Doyle had a talk with him in the Hotel McAlpin, and Mede agreed again that he had planned the Bridgewater job and that Sammarco and Silva had miscarried it.

Doyle made notes of this conversation. They remained among Moore's papers until Thompson dug them out in the desperate spring days of 1927 and decided to ask Mede for an affidavit. Mede was then a boxing promoter in Massachusetts, doing a little bootlegging on the side. He still hesitated to say anything, for fear that his athletic license might be revoked, but finally agreed to tell what he knew to Governor Fuller if the governor would promise not to pass the information on to the State Police or take away his license. Six weeks before the executions the Big Chief, accompanied by Tommy Doyle, told the disbelieving governor his story of the Bridgewater holdup; of how he had planned it originally with Silva and later learned the outcome from Sammarco at State Prison. At the end of the interview Fuller called in Captain Blye of the State Police and told Mede to repeat his story. Mede refused.

As August arrived, with the execution date set for the tenth, a Hanover Street lawyer of clouded reputation, Joseph Santosuosso, urged Mede to make one more attempt to save the two men's lives. Mede finally agreed to make a sworn statement about the Bridgewater affair to the State Police. With Santosuosso he went to Captain Blye's office. Blye now refused to listen to him. And Mede's earlier apprehensions turned out to be only too well justified, for his license was revoked soon after he talked with Fuller.

There were other echoes from Moore's visit to Atlanta. On November 1, 1923, an envelope arrived in Boston addressed "The Sacco-Vanzetti Case." It was delivered to the Boston Bar Association and turned over to Moore. Inside was a to-whom-it-may-concern letter from Emil Moller, a Dane awaiting deportation in a Washington, D.C., jail. "I have information about the Sacco-Vanzetti Case," Moller wrote. Through his friendship with Senator Thomas Walsh of Montana, Moore managed to get Moller's deportation postponed, and sent Carpenter, his investigator, to talk with him.

A petty criminal, Moller had made the tactical mistake of breaking into a house within the District of Columbia, thus making a minor crime a federal offense that sent him to the penitentiary in Atlanta. There he had shared a cell with one Joe Morelli, the leader of a Providence, Rhode Island, gang who was serving twelve years for robbing interstate shipments from freight cars. Moller had a typewriter in his cell and used to write letters and appeals for Morelli as well as for two other acquaintances, Luban and Silva.

Sometimes in the long evenings after the lights were out Morelli would tell Moller of the things he had done "that would make your hair stand on end." Once, according to Moller, he boasted that his gang had pulled off the South Braintree robbery. Morelli told about it in detail: how the gang had started out before sunrise from a Providence saloon, how they had driven up Pearl Street in a stolen Buick, how afterward as they were changing cars in the woods they had almost been caught when the wheels of the second car got stuck in the mud. Looking for an alibi in case any of this ever came to light, Morelli asked Moller to swear that during April 1920 he had been living at the American Lodging House in East Side New York—a place run by Luban's wife—and that on the night of the fifteenth he had been playing poker with Morelli, Silva, and Luban. Moller had pretended to go along.

Telling this story to Carpenter and later to Moore, Moller was the first to mention the name—Morelli—that would run like a dark thread through the fabric of the Sacco-Vanzetti case. Moore considered that much of what Moller had to say was hearsay. Not for another two years would his story receive any corroboration, and by that time Moore would no longer be connected with the case, and Moller himself would have been deported.

On November 18, 1925, Edward Miller, a trusty in the Dedham jail, stopped at Sacco's cell, handed him a magazine, and told him to look inside it. A few minutes later Miller passed Sacco's cell again and found him leaning against the wall trembling, a slip of paper in his hands, his eyes full of tears. "What is this?" he asked, his voice barely under control.

"Can't you read English?" Miller returned.

The note read:

I hear by confess to being in the south Braintree shoe company crime and Sacco and Vanzetti was not in said crime.

Celestino Madeiros

The writer was a sallow, stoop-shouldered twenty-three-year-old Portuguese who had shot and killed the cashier of a Wrentham bank during a gang holdup in November 1924. He was being kept in the Dedham jail while his conviction for murder was appealed. Several times Madeiros had sidled up to Sacco in the washroom and said under his breath: "Nick, I know who did the South Braintree job." Once he had sent Sacco a crude map of Oak Street in Randolph, with a house marked "Thomas" and the scrawled notation that Sacco should look up this Thomas.

Sacco had thrown the paper away, deciding that Madeiros was cracked or else another spy, like that Carbone they had put next to him four years ago. But this note in the magazine seemed to be another matter.

Sacco sent it to Thompson, who came at once to the jail to talk with Madeiros. The three men talked together in the reception room for an hour, Madeiros answering Thompson's questions while the lawyer made notes on the back of an envelope. The Portuguese was quite willing to tell about what he claimed was his part in the South Braintree holdup, but he said he would not identify any of his companions. Sacco, sitting beside him, shaking with excitement, kept interjecting: "For Jesus's sake, tell the truth!"

Madeiros' story was that on April 15, 1920, he was picked up at 4 A.M. at Zack's Hotel in Providence, Rhode Island, by four Italians who arrived in a five-passenger Hudson touring car. They drove to some woods near Oak Street in Randolph, Massachusetts, where they found another Italian waiting with a Buick. Changing cars, they drove to South Boston, where they stopped at a saloon in Andrews Square. Then, after returning to Providence, they headed for South Braintree, where they arrived about noon. They killed a few more hours in a speakeasy a few miles from the shoe factories and then, just before three, left for South Braintree.

During the holdup Madeiros said he sat in the back seat "scared to death" with a Colt .38, which he did not use, in his hand. The payroll money, he said, had been in a large black bag.

"These four men," he told Thompson, "persuaded me to go with them two or three nights before when I was talking with them in a saloon in Providence. They talked like professionals. They said they had done lots of jobs of this kind. They had been engaged in robbing freight cars in Providence. Two were young men from twenty to twenty-five-years old, one was about forty the other thirty-five. All wore caps. I was then eighteen years old. I do not remember whether they were shaved or not. Two of them did the shooting—the oldest one and another. They were left on the street. The arrangement was that they should meet me in a Providence saloon the next night to divide the money. I went there but they did not come.

"They had been stealing silk, shoes, cotton from freight cars and sending it to New York. Two of them lived on North Main Street, in lodging houses. I had known them three or four months. The old man was named Mike. Another was called Williams or Bill. I don't remember what the others were called."

Madeiros said that he knew their last names but he refused to give them. After Thompson had his notes typed up into an affidavit, Madeiros signed it without hesitation. A year and a half later he elaborated on this story when he was examined jointly by Thompson and an assistant district attorney, Dudley Ranney. In this dual examination Madeiros said that one of the men in the South Braintree murder car was not Italian but "Polish or Finland." He still claimed that the payroll money had been in a black bag that had been tossed in the back of the car and a blanket thrown over it. As to how South Braintree had looked on that spring afternoon, he could not remember. He had been drinking and, huddled half-drunk in the back seat with shots echoing round him, he noticed no landmarks. However, he remembered that just before they got to the Stoughton turnpike they came to a fork in the road and stopped at a house where there was a woman in the yard. They asked her how to get on the Providence road. From the back seat Madeiros could not see her. At the Randolph Woods hideout they had changed back to the Hudson, and the Italian who had been waiting there had driven away alone in the Buick. They drove very fast in the Hudson through Randolph, where they were seen by a boy named Thomas who lived on Oak Street. Madeiros became acquainted with the boy four years later when he went to live on the same street. Thomas told him then that he had seen the South Braintree car go whizzing by.

There were parallels between the Wrentham and South Braintree holdups, as Thompson soon learned, that made it seem as if the Wrentham gang had used the earlier holdup as a model. Two stolen cars had again been used at Wrentham, a Buick and then a Hudson. The rear window of the getaway car had been removed and the bandits had carried a shotgun in the rear seat to discourage pursuit.

Madeiros was captured a few days after the Wrentham crime, and shortly afterward two of his associates were picked up—Jimmy Croft, usually known as Weeks, and Alfred Bedard, the driver of the car. The fourth bandit, Harry Goldenberg, got away.

Bedard, on arraignment, was represented by Katzmann—now in a law partnership with John Vahey—while Madeiros' counsel was the same Francis Squires who had been involved with Angelina DeFalco in the bribery trial.

Katzmann went to District Attorney Winfield Wilbar, who had succeeded Harold Williams, to see if he could make a deal. Bedard had been waiting in the car when the holdup killing took place, and Katzmann argued that his client should be allowed to plead guilty to manslaughter. Wilbar refused. "Second degree murder or go to bat" was his ultimatum.

Bedard and Weeks pleaded guilty to second-degree murder and received life sentences. Madeiros, who had done the actual shooting, always maintained that Detective Lieutenant Joseph Ferrari of the State Police had promised him a second-degree murder sentence if he confessed. Left alone to stand trial for his life, he felt double-crossed.

His trial began on May 11, 1925, before Judge Henry Lummus, a waddling three-hundred-pounder with a black Van Dyke beard. Scarcely more than a formality, it lasted only a few days. The car used in the holdup, a conspicuous blue Hudson speedster, was traced to Bedard in Providence. Madeiros himself had been picked up in Providence at Zack's Hotel, where he was found in bed with two other Portuguese floaters, Mingo and Pacheco. Under his pillow was the gun he had used at Wrentham. The most that Squires could do for his doomed client was to question his sanity. It took the jury less than an hour to decide that Madeiros was sane and to bring in a verdict of guilty. There the case would have ended with a short walk to the electric chair except for a crotchet of Judge Lummus'. The bulky judge had long wondered why it was considered necessary at the outset of any criminal trial to instruct the jury that a defendant was presumed to be innocent. Deliberately he omitted the banal phrase, and because he did so Squires appealed the verdict. It was while this appeal was pending that Madeiros had written his note to Sacco.

The question was soon raised as to whether Madeiros had done this because, in his version, "I seen Sacco's wife come up here with the kids and I felt sorry for the kids," or whether he thought that the confession might be of help to him in his second trial. He already knew that the Defense Committee had spent a quarter of a million dollars defending Sacco and Vanzetti. According to Oliver Curtis, the deputy jail master, Miller, the trusty, had come to him one afternoon to ask if Madeiros might borrow a pamphlet from Sacco containing the committee's financial report. Thirty or forty minutes later Miller returned it to Curtis with a scrawled note:

I hear by confess to being in the shoe company crime at south Braintree on April 15 1920 and that Sacco and Vanzetti was not there
Celestino F. Madeiros

Curtis kept the note but did nothing about it. After waiting three days Madeiros sent the second note to Sacco. The Portuguese did not deny he had read the financial report but claimed he had read it after he had written the two notes, not before.

A liar, thief, murderer, Madeiros was a man whose uncorroborated word would be worth nothing. His sister and friends testified that he had the mind of a child of ten, and like his parents was subject to epileptic fits. Even before he had quit school at age fifteen he had been arrested a dozen times. In Providence, Rhode Island, in January 1920, he emerged resplendent in the blue-gray uniform of a lieutenant in the American Rescue League and proceeded to solicit money. The League existed mostly in the imagination of one Arthur Tatro, who wore more elaborate insignia on his Salvation-Army style uniform and called himself captain. He and Madeiros bivouacked in the four-story, bathless, threadbare Zack's Hotel—its ground floor conveniently a saloon—Tatro sharing a room with Madeiros' sister Mary, who was given the rank of second lieutenant for her services, while Madeiros bedded in with a young red-headed girl, the sole private of their little army. For some months they drummed the streets in Fox Point—the Portuguese section of Providence—and in neighboring Fall River, Taunton, and New Bedford. On May 1 Tatro's private army was outflanked by the police and arrested for fraud and impersonation. Madeiros was picked up at his rescue work in New Bedford's Bristol House, a combination cabaret and brothel. While he was out on bail the Providence police caught him breaking into a shop on May 25.

In July, beginning his term in the House of Correction, he apparently had no money. Yet five months later he left Providence **with** twenty-eight hundred dollars of unknown origin in his pocket. Not until 1923 did he return. Then for a time he set himself up as a contractor and built several garages, none of which made him a profit. However, with a little hijacking on the side he managed to keep himself in funds. In March 1924, he went to work for Barney Monterios, a Cape Verde Island Brava, who ran the Bluebird Inn at Seekonk, about four miles from Providence.

Conveniently just over the Massachusetts line, this rural haven combined the features of a roadhouse, dance hall, and speakeasy, in which Providence gangsters could relax undisturbed by thoughts of the police. Upstairs there were always a few girls available. Barney ran the place with the help of a brass-blonde companion, Mae Boice, who was sometimes thought to be his wife.

Madeiros helped build a dining annex at the end of the dance floor, drove Mae around on errands, acted as bouncer in the evenings when the boys got a little too steamed, and spent much of his spare time upstairs with a new girl, Tessie, a plum-smooth little Italian. He had two revolvers with him, a .38 and a .45, and sometimes as he lay on the bed he used to scare Tessie by shooting the flies off the ceiling. Once when he was in the yard amusing himself by shooting at trees, he picked off Mae's cat as it passed with its three kittens. Mae was furious, although she later forgave him and with time developed a certain affection for him.

One July evening, Bibber Barone, a trigger man associated with the Morelli gang of Providence, pulled up in front of the inn with a Cadillac full of his pals and announced loudly that he had come for Tessie. Madeiros went out on the porch with his revolver and Bibber stood on the grass, his hand in his pocket, staring at him. Mae Boice and Jimmy Weeks, who often used to drop in at the Bluebird, watched them through the open window. Weeks heard Madeiros tell Bibber "that he and his gang had double-crossed him once on the job, and that he might forgive them for that, but if they took the girl he would bump them all, and that it would be sure death." Bibber wilted back to the Cadillac.

By autumn Madeiros had grown tired of Tessie's olive plumpness and more attentive to the blonde Mae. Once he flashed a roll of thirty hundred-dollar bills in Mae's face and tried to persuade her to run off with him. This was too much for Barney, who fired his carpenter-bouncer at the point of a revolver. Some time after Madeiros had left the inn he drove back with Weeks and picked a gunfight with Barney in the front yard. Madeiros hit nothing except the house, but as he and Weeks drove off Barney managed to shoot out the taillight of their car.

Although the Madeiros confession was signed and ready in November 1925, Thompson did not make it public while his death-sentence appeal was pending, since both he and the district attorney felt that if it became known that Madeiros had admitted to a second murder the fact would damage him in any new trial. Then, too, Thompson was optimistic about the Massachusetts Supreme Court's pending decision on the defense's appeal from Judge Thayer's denial of the supplementary motions—he had argued the appeal before Chief Justice Arthur Rugg in the Pemberton Square Court House through three bleak January days. Four months later, on May 12, 1926, the court ruled against the defense on all points.

Madeiros had better, if brief, luck. His conviction was reversed by the Supreme Court in March 1926, thus demonstrating to Judge Lummus and other whimsically inclined judges that the formula must not be tampered with. Madeiros went on trial again in May. During most of the proceedings he slumped in his chair with his feet on the rail and his eyes shut as if he were asleep. The jury took less than two hours to find him guilty.

On the second day of the Madeiros trial, Thompson drove down to Oak Street in Randolph to locate the house Madeiros had marked on his crude map and see if there was any trace of the boy called Thomas. He found the house more easily than he had expected. It was occupied by a Thomas Driver, who regretfully admitted knowing both Weeks and Madeiros. Weeks, in fact, had been arrested in the house, and the publicity that followed had caused the Drivers much humiliation.

For six months before the Wrentham holdup, Weeks with his wife and children had lived in a shack on Cedar Street a half-mile down the road. A friendly neighbor, he used to run small errands for the Drivers in his Ford, often gave a lift to young Tom, then in high school, and even promised to teach the boy how to drive.

Driver scarcely knew Madeiros in the brief time that the latter lived with Weeks, but shortly before their arrest he had begun to wonder if the pair might not be bootleggers. He could not say whether his son had seen the holdup car on the day of the South Braintree murders.

The boy himself was away at sea, working for the United Fruit Company. Thompson saw him later when he returned from his voyage. Young Driver told him that he had not personally seen the car go past but that his mother had, and that after she had read about the crime in the paper she thought the men must have been the South Braintree bandits.*

Thompson, faced with increasing demands on his time, found the added complications of the Madeiros confession too much for him. He needed an energetic young lawyer to devote all his time to investigating Madeiros' story. In search of one he turned to Dean Roscoe Pound of the Harvard Law School. Pound mentioned Herbert Ehrmann, then in his thirties, a lawyer who had come to Boston from Louisville, Kentucky, via Harvard College and the Law School. Four years before, Pound and Felix Frankfurter had edited a survey, *Criminal Justice in Cleveland,* and Ehrmann had contributed a chapter on the city's courts. It seemed to Pound that Ehrmann, with his Cleveland experience in investigating civic scandals, would be just the man to track down the intricacies of Madeiros and the Providence gang.

At the outset Ehrmann did not have the conviction he came to share later so burningly with Thompson that Sacco and Vanzetti were innocent. When, on May 22, 1926, two days after Madeiros had been found guilty for the second time, he set out for Seekonk and Providence, he did not expect much.

The Bluebird Inn, on the shabby outskirts of Seekonk, had been closed by the police. It looked a traditional New England farmhouse gone to seed. A few chickens were wandering about the dusty front yard, and at the side an open kitchen door sagged on its hinges. Going up to the door, Ehrmann found a wrinkled Brava woman in a red bandana sitting just inside, plucking a fowl. She said she was Barney Monterios' mother. When Ehrmann asked about her son, she slipped into the next room and returned with Mae Boice, who told him curtly that her husband was not at home. Ehrmann got nowhere with her until he mentioned that he had just talked with Madeiros. At the name the hard face beneath the brass hair softened and the voice was full of concern as she asked about the surly Portuguese. Did Ehrmann think it fair to execute a man who was not really sane? As she talked she led him out of the kitchen, across the dance floor, and past the piano to the dining alcove. He told her of

---

* It may have been the mother rather than the son who saw the car go by, but Driver then had a good position with United Fruit Company and obviously did not want to become involved in a notorious case, especially after his family's embarrassing experience with Weeks.

Madeiros' confession. At first she said it could not be true because on April 15, 1920, he had been in Mexico, but after thinking it over she agreed that he had not left New England until the following January. Mae remembered that he had said he had twenty-eight hundred dollars with him. Ehrmann knew that when Madeiros was arrested in June 1920 he had no money at all. Yet six months later and just out of the house of correction he had acquired a sum, it struck Ehrmann at once, equal to just about a fifth of the South Braintree payroll. That was all the Boston lawyer found out at the Bluebird Inn. Nevertheless, he felt he was on the track of something tangible.

Turning south from the inn, he drove to the dingy Providence police headquarters on Fountain Street. What he now needed to know was whether there had been, as Madeiros said, a local gang of Italians engaged in robbing freight cars.

Ehrmann put his questions to Chief Inspector Henry Connors. The answers were more of a corroboration than he would have dared hope. Yes, there had been a gang in Providence robbing freight cars who had finally been arrested on October 18, 1919. They were American-born Italians, known as the Morell or Morelli gang from the five brothers who formed its nucleus. Joe, Fred, and Pasquale Morelli had been tried in May 1920, but during April they had been out on bail. Connors had no tangible reason for suspecting that the Morellis had been in on the South Braintree holdup, but he suggested that Ehrmann see Captain Ralph Pieraccini of the New Bedford police, who might know something of the doings of Frank and Mike Morelli in that city, and John Richards, who had been a United States marshal at the time the Morellis went on trial.

On the way back to Boston Ehrmann reflected on the South Braintree robbery. It was apparent to him that someone must have scouted the factories in advance and learned all about the day and time of the payroll deliveries.* If he could now find some connection between the Morellis and South Braintree, that would show too much coincidence for Madeiros to have invented his story.

Three days later, Ehrmann drove the fifty miles down to Providence again with his wife Sarah. While he interviewed the Morellis' former

---

*In his book *The Untried Case* Ehrmann maintained that there was no link between Sacco and Vanzetti and the South Braintree holdup except for the negligible one that Sacco had worked a week at Rice & Hutchins in 1917. He was apparently not aware that their friend Coacci was working at Slater & Morrill until early in April 1920.

defense lawyer, Daniel Geary, she spent the afternoon looking up the indictments of the Morellis in the clerk's office of the United States District Court. Geary reminded Ehrmann that he could not ethically disclose confidential communications from his clients, nor would he in any way implicate the Morellis in the South Braintree murders, but he would be glad to help in collecting any information that had been made public during their trial.

The Morellis had been systematic in their freight-yard robberies, confining their thefts to shoes and textiles which they disposed of through fences in New York. Ehrmann wanted to know how the gang received information on the shipments of merchandise. Geary thought that they sent spotters to adjacent industrial towns to watch shipments being loaded and get the numbers of the cars. Joe Morelli had taken a railroad detective, Robert Karnes, who had been gathering evidence against the gang, to various towns in Massachusetts and shown him where the shipments were spotted. Probably this was a maneuver of Joe's to divert suspicion from himself, for the individualistic Joe did not follow the gangster's code of loyalty.

Ehrmann asked whether Karnes had mentioned any specific places, and Geary recalled his having said something about Rice & Hutchins. The name had no particular significance for him until Ehrmann exclaimed: "That's in South Braintree where the murders occurred."

Geary whistled. "That brings it home, doesn't it!" he said.

Geary could not find the portion of the trial record containing the detective's testimony—although the court stenographer remembered the reference—and later when he signed an affidavit he referred less specifically to "Taunton, Attleboro and other places in Massachusetts." In the battle of affidavits that followed, Assistant District Attorney Ranney got Karnes to deny that he had ever gone or said he had gone with Joe Morelli to South Braintree. He did not deny, however, having gone with Joe to towns in that general vicinity.

When, after the interview with Geary, Ehrmann met his wife in the lobby of the Providence-Biltmore he found her as full of information and as excited about it as he was about what he had discovered. She had learned in the clerks' office that the first four counts of the Morelli indictment covered the theft of 611 pairs of ladies' shoes from Rice & Hutchins, while the eighth count was for 78 pairs of men's shoes from Slater & Morrill. For Ehrmann that was proof enough. There must have been a spotter for the Morellis in South Braintree who had studied the two factories and noted when the payroll arrived and how it was delivered. He was certain that when he told this to his Harvard classmate, Dudley Ranney, the district attorney's office would want to investigate the whole matter of the Morellis and probably arrange a new trial. But when Ehrmann telephoned the next day, Ranney was not at all interested in the discovery and his voice had an edge to it as he told Ehrmann so.*

While Ehrmann was in Providence on Tuesday, May 25, Thompson was interviewing Jimmy Weeks in Charlestown. He had talked with him five days before, but Weeks had then said no more than that Madeiros' confession was true. Thompson asked Deputy Warden Hoggsett to try to persuade him to make a statement, and several days later he learned that Weeks was willing to talk.

Weeks, a deceptively mild-mannered man, gave Thompson much the same information about the Morellis that Ehrmann was to bring back from Providence. He had been familiar with that large and notorious family when the brothers were living near Eagle Park, Providence. Once he had helped Joe steal a load of whisky out of a warehouse on Smith Hill, but Joe had claimed that the whisky was vinegar and refused to pay him off. It was true, Weeks said, that the Morellis worked on tips. They always had plenty of money and they liked to flash it at the races and at ball games.

Weeks said he had known Madeiros for six years. A short while before the Wrentham holdup, the two of them had talked over their plans in a barroom in Andrews Square, South Boston, Madeiros remarking that it was strange he should be in the very same bar he had been in four years before on the way to South Braintree. The men concerned in that job, whom Madeiros in his first confession had called Mike and Bill, he had called by their real names in talking to Weeks. They were, according to Weeks, the Morellis of Providence. Madeiros had often talked about the South Braintree crime. The four who had been with him there were Joe, Mike, Bill, and Butsy Morelli.

In the Wrentham job Madeiros had used a Hudson as a getaway car. He told Weeks he had enough of Buicks after South Braintree, where they had used a Buick and switched to a Hudson afterward. Joe Morelli, he said, had double-crossed him on his cut of the payroll.

As soon as Weeks had signed the statement, Thompson drove to

---

* Years later Ehrmann happened to meet his old classmate in the Pemberton Square Courthouse, and for some reason Ranney began to talk about the Sacco-Vanzetti case, speculating as to how he would have felt if he had been on the jury. "I think," he told Ehrmann finally, "I should have considered the Commonwealth's case not proven."

the Dedham jail to see Madeiros. Sheriff Capen telephoned Assistant District Attorney William Kelley to ask permission for the interview. Then Thompson himself took the telephone and explained to Kelley that he hoped to clear up the Sacco-Vanzetti case in a few days and that he wanted to question Madeiros about the confession that Weeks had just made to the South Braintree holdup.

Kelley gave his permission, then left at once for Charlestown with State Detective Michael Fleming, who knew Weeks, and Lieutenant Henry Plett of the State Police to act as a stenographer. They met Weeks in the rotunda and moved to a small side room where they sat around a table.

"Jimmy, did you make a full confession in regard to the holdup in South Braintree?" Fleming asked him with professional sternness.

"Jesus, no," Weeks answered fearfully. "I didn't make any confession like that."

Fleming said he heard otherwise. "Well, I did not!" the other insisted. The detective warned him that he would be very foolish to try to help someone else out of a scrape by making statements like that. Kelley then asked Weeks what he had told Thompson.

Weeks said that Madeiros had told him in 1924 "that Sacco was not in the stick-up at South Braintree." Madeiros admitted that he himself had been in on the South Braintree job but never went into details or said how much of the money he received.

Fleming at this point turned paternally reproachful: "Now all the time we used to ride up to see you here you told us nothing about this. If a man is innocent I want to get him out of it. Joe and I are the first fellows you should have told. You don't know whether you believe Madeiros?"

Weeks did not know. He had seen Bibber Barone at the Bluebird Inn, he said, and he knew Frank Morelli, and he remembered Joe Morelli's name as well as the others in his gang: "Joe, Butsy, Patsy and a fellow called Gyp the Blood."

With further questioning Weeks grew confused, talking in the same sentence about the shooting in South Braintree and the gunfight with Barney Monteiros at the Bluebird Inn, speaking also of an unidentified holdup where Madeiros had been double-crossed and that "he told me many times that it was the one that Sacco was in on."

Kelley left Weeks to his confusion, warning him he was at liberty to talk all he wanted but if "anyone comes here to see you and wants information, you have to look out for yourself. If they write out what you say and want you to sign papers, you yourself have to decide what you want to do."

With the salvo of Weeks' counterconfession, accompanied by a triple volley of sworn statements from Kelley, Fleming, and Plett, there began the battle of the affidavits. Relations between Assistant District Attorney Ranney—now in charge of the post-trial developments in the Sacco-Vanzetti case—and the defense lawyers remained alertly decorous. Any asperity was after all tempered by the fact that they were all Harvard men as well as lawyers in the same city.

As soon as Ehrmann or Thompson produced an affidavit, Ranney felt obligated to come up with a counteraffidavit. Thompson suggested to Attorney General Jay Benton that all important witnesses connected with Madeiros should be interviewed jointly by representatives of the defense and the Commonwealth in order that the case "not degenerate into a contest of affidavits in which each party's trying to offset the affidavits of the other party, or to contradict affidavits already obtained." District Attorney Wilbar would not agree to any such combined operation, and the battle was on. During June and July eighty-seven affidavits were filed—in addition to forty-six miscellaneous statements, depositions, and letters—the engagement reaching the ultimate point where affidavits were being filed about affidavits.

During the afternoon of May 25 Thompson returned to Weeks with a typewritten affidavit based on the notes he had made of their morning conversation. Weeks signed it without saying anything of the assistant district attorney's noontime visit. The next day Thompson assembled the affidavits he and Ehrmann had ready and filed a motion with the clerk at Dedham for a new trial based on Madeiros' statement. Not until two days later did he learn of Weeks' maunderings. He went at once to Charlestown.

Weeks, shuffling into the rotunda in his prison denims, quivered when he saw Thompson's set face. Thompson asked about his conversation with Fleming and Kelley. Weeks said that they threatened him about what might happen to him if he signed an affidavit for Thompson. Kelley had taken out a package of Camels and given him one, asking him if anything had been offered him to make a statement in the Sacco-Vanzetti case. Weeks told Thompson he had replied, "No, Mr. Kelley, you have just offered me this cigarette, and not so much as this cigarette had been offered to me by anyone concerned in the Sacco-Vanzetti case."*

* Kelley, in his affidavit, denied that any such conversation had taken place.

He had admitted to Kelley that Madeiros told him and a since-murdered gangster named Steve Benkosky about taking part in the South Braintree holdup. For Thompson he now added several new details. Joe Morelli before his arrest had owned a Cole touring car and had given him rides in it several times. There was a second Mike, called Mike the Rug, in the Morelli gang; his real name was Cameron O'Connor. Weeks knew him as well as he knew Gyp the Blood, Fred Morelli, and Bibber Barone. They would sometimes come to the Bluebird Inn in an open Cadillac. Weeks claimed that some of his conversation with Kelley and Fleming had not been taken down by the stenographer. Both men had warned him about talking too much if he ever hoped to have his sentence commuted, adding that Madeiros was only eighteen at the time of the South Braintree affair and they knew he had nothing to do with it.

When Assistant District Attorney Ranney read the copy of the Madeiros confession that Thompson sent him, he arranged to have the Portuguese examined as to his sanity. Madeiros, sullen and challenging, stuck to his statement about having taken part in the South Braintree crime. He had admitted being in on it "because it was true," although he had "done no shooting." Beyond this he would say little. Whatever the doctors who examined him may have thought of his story, they at least concluded that he was sane.

While the battle of affidavits grew warmer in Boston, Ehrmann was making daily shuttle runs across the placid countryside to Providence and New Bedford. He had become convinced that the Morelli gang alone was at the bottom of the South Braintree crime, and each trip he made seemed to him to make this more certain.

The same day that Thompson was having his second session with Jimmy Weeks, Ehrmann questioned the New Bedford police captain, Ralph Pieraccini. The captain listened quietly to the lawyer's request for information about Mike Morelli, but came to life when Madeiros' confession was mentioned. "We'd better have Jake in," he said.

Jake turned out to be Sergeant Ellsworth Jacobs, who in 1920 had been a department inspector. When he heard Ehrmann's request he slipped out and came back with his 1920 notebook which he opened to the entry: "R.I. 154E, Buick touring car, Mike Morell." This, he explained, meant that a few day before April 15, 1920, he had seen Morelli driving what looked to be a new Buick touring car. Knowing Mike, he suspected the car was stolen and wrote down the license number. On the afternoon of April 15 he caught a glimpse of the same car sometime between five and five-thirty. The license plate was the same, *R.I. 154E.*

On the afternoon of April 12 he saw a Cole Eight touring car with the license plate *R.I. 154E* parked in front of Joe Fiore's restaurant at the corner of Kempton and Purchase streets. "The whole thing looked fishy," Jacobs told Ehrmann, "so I went into the restaurant to inquire, although I was not on duty at the time. At a table inside I saw four men who looked like Italians, one of whom was Frank Morell. The men at the table were extremely nervous when they saw me come in. I can't say just what it was, but they acted apprehensive of something. One of the Italians whom I remember distinctly was a short heavy-set man with a wide, square face, high cheekbones, smooth shaven and dark brown hair. I can never forget that man's face. As I approached the group, this man made a movement with his hand towards his pocket and I thought he was going to draw a gun. As I was unarmed at the time I was badly scared, but tried not to show it. Fortunately, Frank spoke up and relieved the situation somewhat.

" 'What's the matter, Jake?' he said quickly. 'What do you want with me? Why are you picking on me all the time?'

" 'Look here, Frank,' I said, 'there's a Cole car downstairs with a number-plate that I've seen on your Buick car that Mike's been driving. How did that happen?' " At that the bunch eased up somewhat.

" 'Oh,' said Frank, 'that's a dealer's plate. You see, I'm in the automobile business and we just transfer plates from one car to another.'

"At that time I had no way of contradicting Frank, so I left the restaurant and talked the matter over later with Ralph Pieraccini. At the time of the South Braintree murders and payroll robbery he and I had suspected the Morells, especially on account of Mike and the Buick car so that the actions of that bunch at Fiore's made us more suspicious. Shortly after that, however, Sacco and Vanzetti were arrested and as I had no definite evidence, I dropped the matter. I never saw Frank again since approximately that time, but Mike hung around New Bedford for possibly a year afterwards."

Ehrmann fitted another piece to his puzzle when he visited John Richards, now adjutant general of Rhode Island. Richards, a big-boned solid man with slate-colored eyes and a yellow mustache, had been in his youth a soldier of fortune, and even as a middle-aged

United States marshal he had not lost his taste for excitement. Several times he had shot it out with the Morelli gang in the shadows of the Providence freight yards.

Listening to Ehrmann, Richards became instantly sympathetic to this young, dark-eyed lawyer, so different from him in temperament and physique and racial background. Ehrmann showed him Weeks' affidavit and Richards agreed that the composition of the gang was as Weeks had made out: Joe, the oldest and the leader; Pasquale or Patsy; Frank; Fred or Butsy; Bibber Barone; Gyp the Blood. They had owned a Cole touring car and also a Reo truck. In a later affidavit Richards admitted that, like Weeks, he had confused Fred Morelli with Frank and that it was the latter who had been nicknamed Butsy. Richards recalled two other gang members, Paulo Rosso and Tony Mancini. There had also been a pair of young hijackers who were handy with cars: a light-complexioned man named Raymond McDevitt and another known as Steve the Pole. Both had since been killed in gunfights.

From the stories of Weeks and Sergeant Jacobs and Richards, and from the various court, police, and jail records, from his pokings about in Providence and New Bedford, Ehrmann now began to assemble a hypothetical cast of characters for the South Braintree affair. Madeiros had admitted to Ranney that he had shaped his story to Thompson to shield a gang. For Ehrmann, Madeiros' Mike was an obvious transplant. The leader, "the oldest of the Italians," must, in Ehrmann's opinion, have been Joe, a gangster capable of just such careful planning as had gone into the South Braintree holdup. Butsy, the most dangerous of the brothers, was another who seemed to qualify for South Braintree. When Gyp the Blood showed signs of informing, Butsy in open court had threatened to kill him. The milder-mannered Mike was, as Sergeant Jacobs had noted, merely a car thief to whom would probably have fallen the job of guarding the second car in the woods. Madeiros crouched in the rear fitted the assistant district attorney's trial reference to the "man we cannot describe in the back seat." As for the gunman called Bill who, Madeiros said, had got out of the car with the leader to do the actual shooting, Ehrmann thought at first he might have been Bibber Barone, until it turned out that Bibber had provided himself with the perfect alibi of being already in jail. Gyp the Blood, though out of jail, was not the shooting type. Richards had mentioned two other members of the gang, Paulo Rosso and Tony Mancini, but soon advised Ehrmann later to eliminate Rosso. That left Mancini, and the more Ehrmann learned about him the more he seemed to fill the bill.

Mancini, besides being Joe Morelli's close friend, was a nerveless killer. In February 1921, in New York City, he had shot down Alberto Alterio on Broome Street, almost across the street from police headquarters. When the police captured him they found in his pocket a Star 7.65-millimeter automatic—a type of gun that takes American 32-caliber cartridges. James Burns, Moore's ballistics expert, had testified at Dedham that five of the South Braintree bullets could have been fired from a Steyr, and one of the few things that Dr. Hamilton had been able to demonstrate to Van Amburgh's satisfaction was that three of the shells Bostock had picked up from the gravel bore the marks of a foreign-make ejector claw. A Steyr was an Austrian gun, a Star Spanish, but both were of the same caliber and both were common in the United States in 1920.*

Ehrmann at once sensed the possibility that Mancini's gun might have been used at South Braintree. If Mancini himself could be set down tentatively as Berardelli's killer, that left only the driver to be accounted for—the man who (even Katzmann finally admitted) had been pale and fair-haired.

Both McDevitt and Benkosky, the dead hijackers, answered the description, but Ehrmann found no witnesses who would identify McDevitt's picture. However, when he confronted the two Slater & Morrill workers, Minnie Kennedy and Louise Hayes, with a rogues'-gallery photograph of Benkosky, Minnie felt it "looked more like the driver of the car than any photograph I have ever seen," and Louise found that "the picture very much resembles him."

It seemed to Ehrmann that an encompassing pattern was beginning to emerge. Still, he realized, his hypothesis could be destroyed by a single granite fact. Joe Morelli could provide the key piece—if he could be induced to tell the truth.

Truth and Joe Morelli, however, were scarcely on intimate terms. Joe's one steadfast quality was an exclusive loyalty to himself. At the Providence trial he had been quite willing to let his brothers take the rap for him. In fact, the day after he and his gang had been robbing freight cars he had tipped off Marshal Richards, with the idea of diverting suspicion from himself, that the same thieves would be at it the following night. When the Morellis, minus Joe, returned to the yard that evening they walked into a trap.

* Boda's gun, examined by Chief Stewart at Coacci's house, was a Spanish-type automatic. Stewart did not report the make.

Joe liked to maintain whimsically that he was in the piano business. He lived with Pauline Gray, who appeared in the police court records as "a common night walker," and used his house as a depot in supplying girls for out-of-town roadhouses and as a distribution center for drugs and counterfeit money. A few months before his arrest he had persuaded his invalid widowed mother to deed over her house to him, then had her confined as a pauper in the state almshouse. Even gangsters tended to disapprove of Joe's morals. He liked to drop the names of big New York gangsters and boast that he had been mixed up in such headline events as the 1912 Herman Rosenthal murder. Years later he was to come forward to offer his services for making contact with the kidnapers of the Lindbergh baby.

This was the man from whom the young Boston lawyer hoped to extract the truth about the South Braintree crime when, on June 1, 1926, he and Richards went to the federal penitentiary at Fort Leavenworth, Kansas.* What struck Ehrmann at once, what would have struck anyone who saw both men, was Joe Morelli's singular resemblance to Sacco—the identical cheekbones, thin hairline, jutting chin, heavy eyebrows, and nose almost the same except that Joe's had a Cyrano tip.

To all explanatory statements and questions Joe replied with denials. He had never heard of South Braintree or Rice & Hutchins or Slater & Morrill. He had never known Madeiros or any other Portuguese. Weeks' name meant nothing to him. As for Mancini, which Mancini did they mean? There were a lot of Mancinis. When Richards countered with references to the Morellis' activities in Providence, Joe cut him off with the whine: "You are trying to spoil my record with my warden, my good warden!" As for Sacco and Vanzetti, Joe had read something about their case in the paper. He repeated the name Sacco several times, then, as if he were thinking aloud, said "See Mancini about that." Then he wound up in a flurry of indignation. If the Massachusetts people thought he committed the South Braintree crime, let them prove the charges against him and send him to the electric chair!

On returning to Boston, Ehrmann provided himself with a rogues'-gallery photograph of Joe Morelli and tried it on several of the witnesses. Some of the Italian laborers who had been digging in the excavation exclaimed "Sacco!" when they saw the likeness. Mary

* Joe had been moved from the Atlanta penitentiary after tipping off the Atlanta warden to an inmates' drug-smuggling ring—for which he received a letter of commendation.

Splaine also thought it was Sacco. Lewis Wade, after reluctantly examining it, admitted that it was "strikingly like" the man he had seen. Frank Burke took one look, slapped the face of the photograph, and exclaimed: "That's the fellow who snapped his pistol at me and yelled 'Get out of the way, you son of a bitch!' "

Each step Ehrmann took reinforced his feeling that he was on the right path. Joe Morelli's giveaway remark, "See Mancini," sent Ehrmann to the penitentiary at Auburn, New York, where Mancini was serving his life sentence. Mancini had none of Morelli's Uriah Heep quality. He seemed much more the big-time gangster: a square-set impervious face, an on-and-off smile, glazed gray eyes that looked through rather than at anyone. Ehrmann told him that Joe Morelli had said to see him about Sacco and Vanzetti. "He must have been eating something," was Mancini's noncommittal reply. Ehrmann pointed out that Joe was a coward at heart who might be able to plan a big job but would need someone like Mancini along to give him courage.

At this point [Ehrmann wrote later], Mancini gave his estimate of Joe Morelli, deliberately, his gaze turned toward the window and the scene beyond.

"Unless you know that a man has killed, you can't judge what he is capable of doing." There was a long pause. "Take me for instance. If I hadn't been caught, I would not be known as a murderer. At that, they gave me too stiff a sentence. The cops disappointed me, for I relieved them of a man who was worse than I am. The man I killed had killed others." Mancini paused, then added, "It was his life or mine."

Then very quietly, almost gently, he condemned people who tell on others. "I have first-hand knowledge of Joe's trial in Providence. Gyp and Joe got nothing by blaming each other. They'd have been better off, or just as well off if they hadn't given each other up. But if you're going to tell, why not tell the whole truth? Why didn't Madeiros tell a whole-story instead of a half-story? He might as well come clean if he started. If Madeiros wanted to tell a half-truth he might have named as his confederates men who had died and then let the State believe it or not."

Mancini claimed not to have heard of Benkosky or Weeks. He studied the photographs of Sacco and Vanzetti that Ehrmann handed him, then pointed to Vanzetti's and announced: "They're not stick-up men. That's not a stick-up man. Of course, you can't judge only by a man's appearance—you can't be always right on that. But the type of Sacco and Vanzetti—they're radicals, not stick-up men." He could see no resemblance, though, between Joe Morelli and Sacco. As the interview came to an end he shook hands, saying he was sorry he could not be more helpful. "I hope they won't execute Sacco and Vanzetti," he concluded. "Killing them won't bring the dead to life."

Whether Mancini had anything more to tell remained his own secret. There was, however, something else that might tell Ehrmann much—the 7.65-millimeter gun Mancini had used to kill Alterio. Tests could soon show if it had fired the five unclassified South Braintree bullets. Ehrmann went straight to New York City to his old friends Henry Epstein, the assistant attorney general. Epstein was able to locate the report on the gun in the files without any trouble. But the weapon itself, like a tantalizing mirage, had vanished.

Everywhere that Ehrmann went, the Commonwealth investigators went too. Lieutenant Ferrari was dispatched to Leavenworth to see Joe Morelli. Joe swore that he had never seen Jimmy Weeks in his life and accused Ehrmann of trying to bully him into signing a confession for the South Braintree crime. Wilbar and Ranney followed up in Providence with an interrogation of the Morelli trio of Patsy, Fred, and Butsy. Fred had an alibi similar to Bibber Barone's—he had been in jail on April 15, 1920—and tried to maintain that Joe had shared the same accommodations, although Joe was actually out on bail. The other two swore that they had been living in quiet innocence in Providence all that April, that they had never known either Weeks or Madeiros, and that they had never been to the Bluebird Inn. After their remarks had been taken down and transcribed the three were seized with scruples and declined to sign on the grounds that they feared for their personal safety.

The clerk's office at Dedham became inundated with affidavits and counteraffidavits from Georgia, Kansas, New York, New Bedford, Providence, Fall River, Charlestown; from police officials, wardens, jailbirds, streetwalkers, and citizens interested, disinterested, and uninterested.

Manuel Pacheco, one of the floaters found in bed with Madeiros at his arrest, signed an affidavit in the Charlestown prison, where he was serving eight to ten years for a holdup, stating that Madeiros and he had known each other from 1919 to 1921 and that Madeiros had once told him he was "working with a good mob in Providence," which to Pacheco meant the Morellis.

Even Barney Monterios managed to forget his old grudge long enough to visit Madeiros at Dedham, bringing Mae with him. Madeiros again complained to them that he had been double-crossed on the South Braintree job, and insisted that Sacco and Vanzetti had had nothing to do with it. As Mae later related in an affidavit, she asked Madeiros:

"Is it really true, the statement you made about the South Braintree murders, and were you really in it?" and he said, "Yes, it is the truth, I was in it." He didn't give me any more particulars. He said that he would like to save Sacco and Vanzetti because he knew they were perfectly innocent, and he felt sorry for Sacco because he had seen his wife and two children go by, but he said he hated to bring others into it where there were more than two; and he said "If I cannot save Sacco and Vanzetti by my own confession, why should I bring four or five others into it?" I said "It is an awful thing to see two innocent men lose their lives and the guilty escape." He said, "Yes I know it."

Each side in this battle of paper used its affidavits like pieces on a chessboard. On the whole, Thompson played a more skillful game. But it was a game, as he realized, in which a checkmate was not possible. Finally a measure of sense was brought into the proceedings when Ranney proposed that they take a joint deposition from Madeiros.

On June 28 Thompson, Ehrmann, Ranney, and Ferrari and Fleming of the state police spent the day at Dedham interviewing the convicted Portuguese. Madeiros was brought to the sheriff's office in his blue prison denims, his rheumy eyes full of challenge.

As he had before, but in more detail, he told of taking part in the South Braintree holdup. He still declined to give the real names of the men who had been in the car with him, but he admitted that he had known them in Providence and said they had been in a lot of jobs there robbing freight cars. When Thompson showed him photographs of Joe, Patsy, and Fred Morelli he refused "for private reasons" to say whether he recognized them. He also refused to identify Bibber Barone and Jimmy Weeks, although finally he picked out the latter, saying "It doesn't make much difference. It is Weeks, I guess."

He stuck to his story that the payroll money had been in a black bag. There should, he thought, have been over four thousand dollars apiece in the division of the payroll, but he would not say directly whether he had considered himself double-crossed. Indirectly, he agreed that he did not feel he had been used right. He admitted that he had known Steve the Pole, but would not say whether he had ever mentioned the South Braintree holdup to him. He also admitted that he had confronted Bibber Barone in the yard of the Bluebird Inn when they quarreled about Tessie. However, he refused to tell where he had met Bibber or if Bibber had ever double-crossed him.

Ranney, cross-examining, asked Madeiros if it was true, as his mother had sworn, that when she visited him he had told her: "You think I am tough because I am in this case, but there is a man in here for five years who killed two men." Madeiros could not remember saying any such thing. It was Ranney's contention that Madeiros had made up his confession out of whole cloth after reading the Defense Committee's financial report, that he was hoping to tap some of this money for his own defense and that he knew nothing about the South Braintree crime beyond the casual gossip he had picked up. The assistant district attorney kept trying to pin Madeiros down. What kind of a place was South Braintree? Had he seen any factories? Was there a water tank? A railroad crossing? Madeiros did not recall any of these things, nor any stores or excavations. All he remembered was the car going up the slope after the shooting and that "there were houses there. I don't know how thickly populated it was. It was not country." He did not deny that the money he used on his Mexican jaunt came from the South Braintree loot, but to any queries about the details he gave the set reply: "I ain't saying anything about it."

After the holdup, he said, he and his gang had changed from the Buick to the Hudson in the Randolph Woods and from there driven over the back roads to Providence. Yet an hour and a quarter had elapsed from the time the getaway car left South Braintree until Reed saw it at the Matfield crossing. Desperate men in a high-powered car would certainly not have taken so long to cover twenty-two miles. Even allowing the car a modest average speed of twenty-five miles an hour, there was still a time-lag of nineteen minutes. The question remained whether the lag occurred in the Randolph Woods, as in Madeiros' story, or in the Manley Woods a dozen miles south where the Buick was found.

The getaway car was seen at 3:12, before it reached the Randolph Woods, by the tobacco salesman, Walter Desmond. Seven or eight minutes later the Farmers spotted it on the other side of the woods moving at about twenty miles an hour. Although the distance between these points was less than two miles, there would not have been time enough for the bandits to drive a hundred yards into the underbrush, change cars and license plates, transfer the payroll boxes, and drive out again.

When the car passed Clark, the bakeryman, twenty minutes after the Farmers had seen it, he noticed the first two digits of the license plate 49783 that had been identified at South Braintree. Julia Kelliher, going home from school at Brockton Heights, had missed the first digit but scratched the last four in the sand by the road. If, as Madeiros claimed, the bandits had switched cars in Randolph, then they must have taken the license plates from the holdup car and attached them to the second car that Clark and Julia Kelliher noted.

From Brockton Heights to where the abandoned Buick was found is 3.2 miles, and it is 5.3 miles further to the Matfield crossing. When the Kelliher girl saw the oncoming car at 3:45, its speed of fifty miles an hour scared her. Half an hour later it arrived at the crossing. Yet even if the driver had slowed down to forty he should have made the distance in twelve minutes or less. By any reckoning there was a lag of almost twenty minutes in the running time of the getaway car between Brockton Heights and the Matfield crossing. It was a lag easily accounted for if the car shift had taken place in the Manley Woods. Nor was it merely a matter of time. Even the trail to the woods ran directly off the route that the driver must have taken to get to Matfield.

Madeiros' confession just did not fit into the time sequence. His claim that the gang had driven back and forth twice from Providence to Boston before the holdup seemed as unlikely as his account of the getaway, for if the gang had spent so much time driving, no one in South Braintree would have had a glimpse of them or their cars that morning.

CHAPTER FIFTEEN

More History,
Written and Otherwise

The sea-change decades of depression and war did little to alter the pattern of Joe Morelli's life. On his return from Leavenworth he moved from Providence to the scarcely more scenic environment of adjacent Pawtucket. In that gray three-decker jungle city he was to spend the rest of his days—when not in prison—in a house at 70 Toledo Avenue, a convenient half-mile beyond the attentions of the Providence police.

In 1928 he was picked up by the Pawtucket police in connection with a clothing theft, the next year for smuggling liquor into the Providence county jail. In 1932 Secret Service agents arrested him for possessing counterfeit bills and engaging juveniles, including a thirteen-year-old female state ward, to pass them. He managed to get himself acquitted. Later that year the Secret Service raided his house and uncovered a cache of bogus five-dollar bills. The agents also found parts of a book he was writing about his gangland career.

At his trial Joe tried but failed to put the blame for the counterfeit money on his son, John. Sentenced to five years in the new federal prison at Lewisburg, Pennsylvania, Joe had the distinction of being the first Rhode Islander to arrive there.

In 1941, he was arrested for keeping a house of prostitution in his home, setting up slot machines, and selling liquor without a license. A neighbor, James Prete, who had complained to the police about the goings-on at 70 Toledo Avenue had his house wrecked by dynamite.

While Joe was out on bail he was again arrested for counterfeiting. Not until March 1946 was he paroled. Nine months later he was picked up for running a house of prostitution. In March 1947, he was seized for violating his parole and sent to the Danbury Federal Penitentiary.

The following year he was released, only to be arrested on the old prostitution charge. In moments of self-pity Joe liked to predict that he would one day die in jail.

In 1931 Joe boasted to Morris Ernst, a New York lawyer connected with various civil liberties committees, that he and his gang had staged the South Braintree holdup and that he had ridden in the murder car. Ernst had taken no part in the Sacco-Vanzetti defense nor until the execution of the two men had he formed any fixed opinion as to their guilt or innocence, although he had concluded that there had been a lack of due process. Reading the six volumes of the case record as they were published in 1928 and 1929, he was struck by the amorphous Morelli hypothesis appearing in Volume V. "Being what I am," he explained at the Massachusetts Judiciary Committee hearing in 1959, "and for no sensible reason probably, I went on the trail of Joe Morelli. I have had talks with Joe Morelli. I have had letters with him. I have seen him with his counsel. I am told that I am the only person who had examined the man who really did the job for which Sacco and Vanzetti went to the chair."

Ernst started his private investigation by arranging a meeting in the Providence office of Joe Morelli's lawyer, Louis Jackvony, a former Rhode Island attorney general whom Joe had known as a boy. After being introduced to Ernst Joe did not sit down, but stood for several minutes by the window while the latter talked. Finally he gave a signal to someone in the street, explaining then that he had decided Ernst was "jake."

Ernst had prepared a list of detailed questions about the South Braintree holdup: Were there two cars or one? Were they open or closed, and where did they go? Where did the license plates come from? Who was in the car? Were the payroll boxes metal or wood? Who picked them up? How much money was in them and how many people divided it? Was there anyone leaning against the fence? Was there a team of horses? An excavation? A water tower? Why did they double back at the Matfield crossing? For two hours Joe answered all questions affably and correctly.

No person of this man's make-up [Ernst wrote later] *would have read the minutes of the trial with enough precision to fit all his* answers into the known facts, down to the description of the flapping of the side curtains on the murder car. Nor could any human being have guessed the answers as to time and place of the many details of the shooting day about which I confronted him. I left completely satisfied that the gang chieftain was in the murder car and knew all the details of the planning of the robbery, the details of the shooting, and the technique of escape.

Joe was even willing to sign a statement—for a price—but he became angry when Ernst let slip that an underworld intermediary had been promised fifteen hundred dollars for his assistance in the case. Joe hinted that his price would be ten times that. Ernst finally offered him twenty-five hundred if he would produce the metal payroll boxes. "You couldn't get them out of Canapa Pond," Joe told him.

Later, while Morelli was doing his stretch at Lewisburg, Ernst said he learned that Canapa Pond was the local name for a body of water on the route of the escaping murder car, but he made no effort to recover the boxes.

During his three years at Lewisburg Joe continued writing his life history, accumulating almost six hundred pages by the time of his 1936 parole. Back at Toledo Avenue, he made various attempts to cash in on the manuscript. For some time he corresponded with Silas Bent, a friend of Jack Callahan, the journalist who had brought Frank Silva's confession to the *Outlook* in 1928. Bent was impressed enough to get in touch with the *Outlook* and with Upton Sinclair, to whom he wrote:

Joe Morelli has asked me to write you about his autobiography, which he has completed. I have not seen it, and do not know whether he goes fully into the South Braintree holdup; but I have talked to him more than once about it, and if he is free to tell the whole story, the book should be a smash.

When Bent asked Joe's price for a sworn confession that he had organized and committed the South Braintree holdup, Joe, apparently with an author's vanity, insisted that his whole book appear, not just a chapter. After some further dickering, the deal fell through.

Meantime Joe had been angling Ernst, promising him "the real truth and not baloney" about the Sacco-Vanzetti case, and when Ernst again met him in Jackvony's office, Joe had the manuscript with him. His price was twenty-five thousand dollars, and he would not allow the pages to be inspected even briefly. All Ernst managed to see was the cover. Subsequently, with the help of Oswald Garrison Villard, Ernst raised an initial five thousand dollars. Joe still held out for his twenty-five thousand, which in Ernst's court-hardened mind meant he would settle for ten thousand.

Some time in 1939 Ernst took Joe to lunch in Boston with Robert Lemond, an editor of Little, Brown & Co., to discuss publishing the confession-autobiography. Joe had his sealed manuscript with him, but he still refused to turn it over for less than his price. He and Ernst were not to meet again.

With the shadow of World War II moving across the landscape, interest in the Morellis faded. The only person still concerned with them was Ben Bagdikian, a reporter on the Providence *Journal*. In August 1950, he learned that Joe was dying of cancer. Hopeful of getting some last statement from him, Bagdikian went to Jackvony, one of the few men Joe trusted. Jackvony in turn went to Joe's bed-side and told him that a friend wanted to see him about the Sacco-Vanzetti case.

At first Joe refused to see anyone, but a few days later he whispered to the lawyer: "All right, tell him to come. I'll tell him the whole story." Jackvony reminded Joe that he did not have to say anything, but if he had something to get off his chest, this was the time. "Tell him to come," Joe said again.

On August 25 Jackvony and Bagdikian drove to the house on Toledo Avenue. Jackvony went in alone, arranging to signal from the porch when Joe was ready. Bagdikian waited in the car for twenty-five minutes. A man in a large yellow convertible pulled up behind him, watched him suspiciously for fifteen minutes, then drove away. Bagdikian learned later that he was Joe's brother Frank.

As soon as Jackvony entered Joe's bedroom he was aware of the death smell. The white face on the pillow gave him one frightened appealing glance of recognition, the blue lips moved slightly, then Joe slipped into a coma. Jackvony stepped to the bed, tapped Joe's knee, and called out his name, but there was no reply. He bent down, put his mouth to Joe's ear, and shouted, "Sacco and Vanzetti!" There was no response. The secret still hovered inside Joe's skull, but it was to remain there. Early next morning he died.

On a summer morning in South Braintree, just forty years after the holdup, I started off with Bob McLean of the Boston *Globe* to retrace the route of the 1920 getaway car. The day was heavy even at nine o'clock. Bob just managed to squeeze his amiable bulk into the driver's seat of his ten-year-old Buick. I sat beside him as navigator, with map board, green and red pencils, and the topographic sheets of the U.S. Geological Survey—as I used to do with the survey maps in the Army in what we called *tewts*—tactical exercises without troops.

Suburban developments were sprouting up all round the Braintrees. The hard little core of industrial South Braintree had also seen changes. Opposite the station the mansarded Hampton House had been torn down and the space was now a parking lot. The Romanesque granite-and-sandstone station itself was boarded up and year-old signs in the windows of the empty waiting room announced the suspension of passenger service on the Old Colony Line. Rice & Hutchins' brick building was still standing, as was the wooden Slater & Morrill factory, but both had been taken over by the Atlantic Abrasive Corporation, whatever that was. South Braintree's shoe industry had long since disappeared. Where the Italians had been excavating on April 15, 1920, there stood a brick building, no longer a restaurant, occupied by a lamp firm and the Braintree *Observer*.

One afternoon in February I had dropped in at the *Observer* office to ask what Sacco-Vanzetti material they might have in their files. The woman at the desk did not know, but she went in back to the presses and returned with a man in his sixties wearing a printer's apron. As soon as he heard the words *Sacco and Vanzetti* his face mottled. "Why do you people still come round writing sweet stuff about those two gangsters?" he shouted at me. "Why are you wasting your sympathy on them when you got none at all for that poor Mrs. Parmenter that lost her husband? They raised thousands of dollars for those two Eyetalians, and she got nothing. Afterward she had no money, she lost her house. No one ever gave her a thought. Why don't you write about her? Why don't you?" There was no arguing with him, but I was surprised, as I was to be on other visits, that the old emotions could still smolder beneath the small-town tranquillity and be brought suddenly to a flame by some casual word.

Almost every inhabitant of South Braintree over fifty seemed to have his own pet bit of gossip about the case. One story is that Mrs. Sacco was seen early on the morning of the murders at a South Braintree filling station. Another has it that Sacco and Vanzetti were observed wandering about town several days before April 15. The retired express agent tells of a local Italian who knew Sacco before the crime and saw him do the shooting, but was too scared to go to court to testify. Sacco is said to have confessed to one of his lawyers, and Jerry McAnarney is said just before his death, to have told a friend they were guilty. Amid the distortions of gossip there is the more coldly remembered fact that those who testified for the defense lost their jobs. Among others, Brenner and McCullum, who contradicted Pelser in court, were discharged soon afterward, as was Lewis Wade, who disappointed the prosecution by not identifying Sacco positively. All South Braintree still firmly believes that Sacco and Vanzetti were guilty.

"Criminal exercise without criminals," McLean announced as we pulled away from the curb where Berardelli's body had lain. Pearl Street still kept its underlying pattern even though the spindle-legged water tower had gone, along with the gatetender and his shack. Cain's livery stable had been replaced by the Pearl Street Ramblertorium, and Schrout's Bakery was now Adel's Pizza Parlor. But the outline was the same, the wooden two- and three-decker workers' houses still kept their old gray ranks, the barber shop was still there, and Torrey's Drugstore—duly modernized—still hugged the corner.

"Here's where they threw out the tacks," McLean said as we turned left into Washington Street. At the Plain Street railroad crossing we made the sharp right turn and went up the hill past the white wooden grotesqueries of the South Congregational Church, then dipped down, skirting the edge of Sunset Lake.

Joe-pye weed spread in mauve masses along the roadside. There were smaller white patches of boneset, and the first spatterings of goldenrod. Most of the elms we passed were dying of the Dutch elm disease, and even the leaves of the other trees looked frayed and weary. I sensed the pause of the season, like the turn of the tide—that short breathing space between summer and autumn. Somehow it seemed more apparent in this flat browning landscape. Before World War II such sandy outlying acres had been scarcely more than squatters' land. Now they had become dear to the heart of the developer, with his flat-topped regular rows of pastel ranch houses. The Randolph Woods were flat as a punctured tire.

We missed the right turn at Oak Street and drove almost to Randolph before we realized our mistake. One thing was already clear to us: The getaway driver and his crew must have been familiar with the back roads. I had a hard enough time keeping on course even with my map. And from the map it was plain how well they had known how to avoid every center of population. The reason they had gone astray on Orchard Street was apparent enough when we arrived there, for we made the same mistaken left turn ourselves.

Down Chestnut Street and along the old turnpike the way still runs straight and empty, the old pastoral landscape emerging as the ranch houses recede. We found the lane into the Manley Woods where the Buick had turned off, a scarcely visible dirt path branching to the right between an empty shingled cabin and a derelict cemetery. Two hundred yards from the highway we came to a field of stumps surrounded by speckled alders, the earth bulldozed away at one corner as if preparations were being made for another clutch of ranch houses, but still empty and deserted enough to hide a car there all day long without anyone being the wiser. It looked, in its accessible isolation, much the most logical place on the escape route to shift cars.

Ehrmann's version seemed scarcely plausible—that Mike Morelli had driven back from New Bedford that same night in a car with the telltale missing rear window, a car for which by this time all the local police had been alerted, just to leave it in the Manley Woods when there were thirty-four miles of barren country lying between. As we looked at the opening of the lane, it seemed to us it would have been impossible to find it in the dark on the way north. McLean and I agreed that the car must have been abandoned in the Manley Woods on the way down and that the time lag had taken place there.

Why the escape car had returned after going over the Matfield crossing became clear to us only when we had gone over the route ourselves. Obviously the car had headed that way to avoid the five-cornered traffic center of West Bridgewater, half a mile to the south. But then, once beyond the railroad crossing, the driver had found himself on the road to thickly populated East Bridgewater, and had circled back.

Morris Ernst had said at the State House hearing in 1959 that Joe Morelli told him he had thrown the empty cash-boxes into Canapa Pond and had even pointed out the spot. But when I had written to ask Ernst about the location, he replied that he had no idea where Canapa Pond was. As we traced our way from South Braintree I could find no appropriate body of water, large or small. Sunset Lake would have been too near, and anyhow I knew its original name had been Little Pond.

After the Matfield crossing, the last point where the getaway car was seen, we were on our own. We drove toward Providence, through Bridgewater and over Route 44 by way of Taunton. Just before Providence we stopped at Seekonk for whatever trace might remain of the

bullet-scarred Bluebird Inn. We found that unappreciated landmark had long since been torn down. There were only the barest traces
of its foundations in an empty corner lot overgrown with ragweed and
tansy. Next to the corner was a white bungalow with children swarm-
ing on the front steps and a zinc mailbox lettered B. *Monterios.*

The air seemed to get heavier as we approached Providence, or
perhaps it was just the sad wooden decay of those submerged streets
below the anachronistic graciousness of Brown University's island-hill.

I had pictured Ben Bagdikian as the dean of Providence reporters,
a Rhode Island Frank Sibley, perhaps wearing old-fashioned spectacles on a ribbon, but when we met him in the city room of the
Journal he turned out to be a small gray-haired man in his forties,
with the long nose and dark animated eyes of his Armenian inherit-
ance. He had come to the *Journal* from Stoneham, Massachusetts,
after World War II. Before he began writing his pieces on them, he
had never heard of the Morellis. I asked him if he knew anything
about Canapa Pond and told him of the uncommunicative Morris
Ernst.

"That sounds like Ernst," Bagdikian said, at the same time making
a note on a scratch pad. "I worked with him on the Morelli angle,
and I never could get anything really definite out of him. As for
Canapa, he mentioned it in a book and I asked him about it, too,
and got about the same answer you did. There isn't any Canapa
Pond. What I think Joe said was *Canada* Pond—and Ernst may
just have changed a letter to throw us off the track. Canada Pond's
only a couple of miles north of here, half in Providence, half in Pawtucket. You can see it from the new Woonsocket highway. It's in an
Italian district, not very far from Joe's old house. As I remember
there aren't many houses right near it; lot of bushes and things, just
the place to throw old boxes. As a matter of fact they tossed a couple
of gangsters in there a few years back. But whether Joe threw any
boxes in there or not, Canada would probably be the first name that
would come into his mind."

I asked Bagdikian if he had any idea what had become of Joe's
autobiography.

"I never followed it up," he told us. "Perhaps I should have. But
I have the feeling that if you should dig it up you wouldn't find much
in it. It's like Joe and the Lindbergh baby. Joe made contacts with
Jafsie Condon, and he was going to get to the bottom of the kid-
naping, but first of all he needed five thousand dollars. That was Joe.
Cash down!

"I'm not as sold on the Morelli theory as Ehrmann is," he went on, "but I always meant to look up Mancini when I was working on this. He was around here up till a few years ago. He was the toughest and brightest of the gang, and if he decided to talk why he'd talk. But I got off onto something else, and now he's gone. Old Jackvony's gone too. His son could probably tell you a lot, but he won't. The old man was a criminal lawyer, and young Jackvony wants to get away from it all. Once I saw his garage with the back of it all piled up with his father's papers. That autobiography might even be somewhere among them. It would be odd now if you found the key after all these years. Let me know if you get hold of it."

McLean had copied down Frank Morelli's address from the *Journal's* files. It was on Mount Pleasant Avenue, a boulevard cutting through one of Providence's many Italian districts. The house was easy enough to find: a garish cube of red-and-yellow mottled tapestry brick, the largest on the avenue. When we rang the bell a woman in her forties came to the door. Her expression turned sour when we mentioned the Morellis, and she announced with an equally sour voice that she knew nothing about them except that a year or so before her husband had bought the house from Frank. She did not know Frank's address; she did not know who might know it.

Pawtucket is like Providence without the green university enclave, a brooding wooden decay of massed streets. It took us an hour to find Joe Morelli's Toledo Avenue house. This was a different avenue, a still unpaved street on the outskirts, and Joe's was the kind of shapeless wooden house perched on granite foundations common in the early 1900s. The layout would be routine—three rooms downstairs, four smallish bedrooms upstairs, and a room or two on the top floor. I walked up the steps to the long front porch. Everything looked neat, freshly painted. The aluminum combination screen door had a scrolled S on it.

No one answered when I rang, but as I looked over the porch rail I saw a woman by the garage emptying garbage into a can. I waited until she returned. When I mentioned the name Morelli, she winced. She said she knew nothing about the family except Joe's reputation. Some years ago she and her husband had bought the house when it was in bad shape, and since then they had fixed it up. It looked too neat and too mild, really, for the place where Joe had kept his wenches and stored his counterfeit money and hidden his stolen goods and at last uncommunicatively died.

The chief of detectives at the Pawtucket police headquarters shook his head when McLean offered him a cigarette, and picked up a cigar with the end chewed so that it looked as if it were sprouting roots. He was a tanned heavy man in a sport shirt and summer trousers, his hair close-cropped almost to baldness, his only symbol of authority the automatic strapped to his belt. The walls of his office were bare of everything but the daily list of arrests and a safety calendar contributed by Pawtucket firms to warn motorists to look out for children at school crossings.

"Thank God I haven't seen that crowd in a long time," he said when McLean mentioned the Morellis. "That Joe was one of the most troublesome sons of bitches I ever had. I'd keep raiding his place and he'd keep coming back for more. Why, when he was dying he still had a couple of broads hustling upstairs."

That might have ended our conversation if Bob had not somehow mentioned bass fishing. A night light seemed to glow behind the pupils of the chief's smoky eyes. He picked up the cold cigar again and for ten minutes they talked about hula lures with double wiggles, ponds on Cape Cod that nobody knew about, and bluefish in the Canal at Bourne turning the water red when they attacked other fish. The chief had just come back from his vacation and the more he talked about it, the mellower he grew.

"Come to think of it," he said finally, "Joe Morelli's granddaughter was in here just a couple months ago. Her boy was up on some driving charge. She was married to some Italian, then to a fellow named Dunne. She's married again. I don't know his name, but here's her address." He flipped open a file. "On Douglas Avenue, Providence."

Douglas Avenue, when we returned to Providence, proved to be a line of three-decker wooden tenements broken by an occasional barroom. The top floor of the three-decker we were looking for was empty, a FOR RENT sign in the blank center window. The second floor, too, looked empty, though it had Venetian blinds at the windows. We almost turned away, then decided to try the bells. A penciled card over the middle button read *D'Agostino*. I rang, but the rumble of trucks was so heavy anyone could have bawled down through the speaking tube without my hearing it. Finally, through the wavy glass of the door, I had a glimpse of a pair of legs that seemed to be walking by themselves in the shadow of a dim stairway. Then a woman with frizzed metallic hair opened the door. Long-chinned, with bright agate eyes, she seemed to be in her late thirties. When I mentioned Joe Morelli she relaxed and appeared almost amiable.

"Yes," she replied, "I'm Helen Morelli. Joe Morelli was my grandfather." Still expecting that the door might shut in my face, I said there were a few things about Joe I hoped I might talk over with her.

"I guess I got a little time," she said. She turned and led us upstairs to an apartment that was being refinished: the paper off the walls, the floors scraped but not yet varnished. The room had a gypsylike atmosphere, as if everything could and might be moved out in ten minutes flat. We sat on maple chairs with plastic chintz covers.

McLean said we were from the Boston *Globe*. At that she became animated, telling us she had once studied journalism in New York. "I used to know Walter Winchell there," she went on. "My grandfather had a restaurant there for a while and sometimes Winchell would come in for a cup of coffee. My grandfather knew him, knew lots of people—James Michael Curley, the mayor of Boston. You knew him? I used to see him at Danbury. Remember how he got himself re-elected mayor when he was in jail there? I got letters from him."

When I could slip in a word, I told her that what we were really interested in was the whereabouts of her grandfather's autobiography.

She looked at me coldly. "You know, I had a feeling that's what you might of come for. Yes," she went on, her full lips twisting down, "I have it and it's in a good safe place. As a matter of fact I'm rewriting it myself."

"I don't know whether you could let us see it or not"—I tried to make my voice sound matter-of-fact, watching her smile derisively and shake her head—"but could you let us know what's in it in relation to Sacco and Vanzetti?"

I realized suddenly what the cliché about a veiled look coming over someone's face really meant. The derision became vocal. "Do you think you'd get that out of me? A fat chance! But I can tell you this much, the whole secret's there. Why, if it ever came out I guess millions of people would jump. Did you see that TV show? I had to laugh. Making those two ditch-diggers make speeches like that! Maybe people all over the country will fall for that stuff, but I had a good laugh because I know the truth. Silas Bent and Sinclair Lewis offered ten grand for that document. I could get big money for it. I know that, all right. Don't think I'm green.

"Look." Her voice sharpened. "How do you think it felt to be a Morelli when I was a child? When I was at school, any time I wanted to do anything, people would whisper behind my back I was one of them. Now I'm the last one. My Uncle Frank, he's dying of cancer of the throat and he never had kids. My father's in California. So I'm the last of the Morellis, the last legitimate one anyhow. Do you think I'm going to let that come out against my own kids, have all that stuff brought up again? No, sir!"

"Why bother to rewrite it then?" McLean asked her softly. "Why don't you just burn the thing?"

Again her veiled look. "No, I'm going to keep it. Maybe when I'm gone. I don't know. But I'm going to keep it."

While we were talking her husband came into the room, naked to the waist, a dark hairy-chested man, still damp from the shower. He shook hands cordially enough, then turned to his wife.

"They want the document?"

She nodded. "I told them we'd never let it go."

Her husband grinned knowingly.

"But did your grandfather know Sacco and Vanzetti?" I asked.

"Sure he knew them. I'll tell you that much. You'd be surprised. They've made such a big mystery of the whole thing, and underneath it's all very simple. They made them on TV like they had haloes. If I ever told what I know there'd be an explosion."

Bob had his try. "Won't you at least tell us whether your grand-father said they were guilty or not?"

She shook her head. "Sure they were guilty, but I'm not giving away the secret. An eye for an eye, and a tooth for a tooth," she added enigmatically.

"Of course," said Bob quietly, "there's always a court order."

She laughed. "What can they order me? It's my property."

I had a try at persuading her that the Sacco-Vanzetti case was part of the history of our times, that it had all happened too long ago for anyone to be hurt any more, and that if there really was any-thing in her grandfather's autobiography that would settle the un-settled question, she had an obligation to reveal it. That was no good either.

"Maybe you're right," she said. "But I'm not changing my mind. There isn't any money would make me, either. Nobody's going to see it. Some things better stay a secret, I guess, and this is one of them."

Not until a year after this interview did I finally manage to learn the contents of Joe Morelli's document. When he wrote it, Joe was apparently still smarting from the remarks Ehrmann had made about him in *The Untried Case*. Joe's opening pages are full of jeers about "smart Mr. Ehrmann," "Ehrmann who thinks he knows so much."

According to the manuscript the five men in the South Braintree murder car were Sacco, Vanzetti, Coacci, Boda, and Orciani. Coacci was the driver. Joe had known all five for several years, and in fact they had been with him in a Pawtucket holdup in 1918, one never solved by the police. He himself had planned to pull off the South Braintree job with them. Any number of times he had driven over the route to plan the getaway. He was familiar with South Braintree because, with the help of Coacci, who was working in one of the factories, he had occasionally stolen truckloads of shoes from there. Berardelli, the guard, was another of his confederates.

Joe's explanation of the actual holdup was that the others had double-crossed him. He had set the job for April 22. They pulled it themselves a week earlier to cut him out, and they killed Berardelli because he recognized them. During the getaway Coacci had got lost because he did not know the roads as well as Joe did.

Throughout his manuscript Joe refers to Madeiros as the Blind Pig—no doubt a reference to his poor eyesight. Neither Madeiros nor Mancini, according to Joe, had anything to do with the South Braintree affair. Madeiros was just a small-time crook who made a fake confession about South Braintree to try to beat his murder rap. There was not even a house, just a vacant lot, at the place on North Main Street, Providence, where Madeiros said he had started out on the morning of April 15. As for the business of Canada Pond and the money-boxes, that was simply a hoax to take in Morris Ernst, for whom Joe seemed to have as much contempt as he did for Ehrmann.

Such, in its truth or untruth, was the confession of Joe Morelli.

On September 1, 1927, Alfred Foote, the Commissioner of Public Safety, wrote to District Attorney Wilbar:

As a finale to the Sacco-Vanzetti case, it appears to me that it would be well to gather and secure certain of the exhibits, particularly the firearms, bullets, cartridges and fired shells.

I trust you will agree that these important objects should be placed in our vaults for all time where they will be safe from opportunists as well as enemies.

The ample facilities of the State Police Laboratory will be utilized to obtain a photographic record in the most graphic form of each of the exhibits. The work contemplated will constitute an important addition to the record in this great case.

Yet when I asked to examine these "important objects" thirty-three years later, they were nowhere to be found. I tried first at the clerk of court's office in Dedham. The clerk, Willis Neal, a nephew of the South Braintree express agent, said that from time to time someone would drop in to ask about the exhibits, but that he had never been able to locate them. He admitted he had never looked very hard. Together we went down to the storage files in the basement and spent several dusty hours going through the records. Finally he found a 1927 memorandum that the guns and bullets had been forwarded to the Lowell Committee.

I asked about them at the State Police ballistics laboratory on Commonwealth Avenue. Lieutenant John Collins, in charge there, was interested in the case, in fact had a private file on it that he had put together himself, but he had no idea what could have become of the exhibits.

I wrote to Governor Foster Furcolo about the missing exhibits, explaining my belief that they had never been tested properly and might still have much to reveal. After several weeks I received a reply routed from the governor's office to some subordinate of the attorney general, who informed me that "we have no record in this office of ever having had the exhibits or as to any disposition of them after they were viewed by the Lowell Committee." On reading this I again wrote to Governor Furcolo to say that I did not think this was good enough and that someone in the State House should look a little harder. I received no reply.

By chance I came on the trail of the missing exhibits when I happened to be in the Boston police headquarters talking to one of the men in the laboratory there.

"Why," he said, "Van Amburgh's son has those things. I thought everyone round knew. They were in the State Police lab for years, and then one of the Van Amburghs—I don't know whether it was the old man or the son—took them away with him when he retired. That's where they are. Young Van Amburgh has them down at Kingston."

I wrote Van Amburgh twice, received no reply, and finally telephoned him to ask if he had possession of the exhibits in the Sacco-Vanzetti case.

"I have a lot of things around here," he said.

"But do you or do you not have the pistols and the bullets that were examined by the Lowell Committee?"

His voice grew frostier. "I'd have to go through everything to know that."

I did not have a very good hand but I dealt another card. "I have been told that you do have them."

"I might," was all he would answer.

I tried to explain why I wanted to see the bullets. The question had never been settled, I said, as to whether Bullet III might have been substituted for the one found in Berardelli's body.

The voice cut me off. "You and I seem to be working along the same lines. I'm writing a book on the evidence in the case myself. I'm not going to let you see my private material. Why should I?" The telephone clicked at the other end.

Van Amburgh became singularly more communicative when Bob McLean drove down to see him. He told McLean that he regarded himself merely as a custodian of the exhibits "to be kept inviolate." His custodianship lasted until the following week end when the Sunday *Globe* ran McLean's front-page feature story of his discovery. The Commissioner of Public Safety, J. Henry Goguen, was one of the *Globe's* early Sunday readers.

"He hit the roof," McLean told me afterward. "They say he was shouting in his office, 'How did they get out of here? Who let Van Amburgh take them? Send two men down to Kingston with a warrant and if he doesn't give them up, arrest him!' But Van Amburgh turned them over without a bleat. After all, if you're getting a state pension you can't fool around. The stuff was in a big package that looked as if it hadn't been opened in years."

I saw the exhibits on their return in the State Police ballistics laboratory, a room with a grille in the front like a cage and a metal door that opens by an electric button. It is a macabre room, the walls hung with the confiscated evidence of old crimes—a Heinz' variety of pistols, rifles, submachine guns, even a grenade-thrower, dirks, switchblade knives, a Malayan *kris*, brass knuckles with inch-long prongs, blackjacks, homemade zip guns.

Sacco's Colt, Vanzetti's revolver, and the bullets were spread out on Lieutenant Collins' desk next to a china ashtray in the shape of a revolver.

"The way they handled these exhibits from the beginning makes my hair stand on end," Collins said. "The way I do is to impound any exhibits, then call in the defense, the prosecution, make whatever tests I have to make in front of them, and ask them if they're satisfied. I've testified now in over sixty murder trials and nobody on either side has ever disputed my findings. But these things"—he swept his hand toward the display on the desk—"I don't know whether you could prove anything with them now or not. I wouldn't touch them myself. No matter what tests might show, somebody would be bound to accuse me of cooking the results. There ought to be some expert from outside Massachusetts to run the tests. That's the way it should be handled." He picked up one of the bullets. "You think that this Number III might have been switched from the one they cut out of Berardelli?"

"Some of the defense lawyers claimed it was," I told him.

He cupped it in his hand. "The markings on the base do look somewhat different. Those scratches—it's hard even to be sure if there are three of them. There's so much muck on it you can't really tell. They ought to clean them, but first of all they ought to make blood tests. Had you ever thought of that?"

I said I had not. He explained that it might still be possible to detect residual blood with proper tests and even to determine the blood type. Forty years were nothing. They could even blood-type mummies. If bullets I, II, and IV showed traces of blood when tested, while III showed none, it would be fairly conclusive that the mortal bullet was a substitute. If, on the other hand, all four showed blood, then it would be practically certain that all of them came from Berardelli's body.

"Of course it's possible that there won't be any blood traces on any of the bullets," said Collins.

I had thought that once the ballistics exhibits were back in the hands of the State Police, I should have no difficulty in having tests run on the bullets. When I went to see Commissioner Goguen, a gray, diminutive man, sharp-eyed as a chameleon, I soon learned otherwise. Instead of being grateful to me for recovering the material, he seemed aggrieved. "Why don't you just forget the whole thing?" he asked me querulously. "I'm not going to allow any of your tests. No, sir, I don't want any of that Sacco-Vanzetti business stirred up again."

He wore a silver tie-pin engraved with the seal of Massachusetts, and in the buttonhole of his sharkskin suit I noticed the rosette of the Legion of Honor. Someone at the *Globe* told me he had been awarded it ex officio as president of L'Union St. Jean Baptiste d'Amérique, the largest French-Canadian fraternal-insurance association in the United States—from which he still received his salary while serving as Commissioner of Public Safety.

"No tests!" he announced, but a week after I had coaxed an editorial from the *Herald*, "Do Not Let Sleeping Bullets Lie," he said I had quite misunderstood him. He would have no objection to tests made by properly qualified experts; he just did not want amateurs fooling with the exhibits. I thought my difficulties were over when I returned with the names of the honorary curator of the West Point Museum and of an internationally known hematologist. But I still could not get a straight answer from the commissioner. This time he said that before any tests could be made, he must first have permission from the attorney general's office. Undoubtedly he thought this would not be forthcoming, but after a delay of several months I managed to turn up with it.

Goguen's eyes darted at me as if I were a fly on the wall while he explained that he would have to consult with the members of his department. It was a consultation that took two more months. Then he told me that although he personally would be happy to allow such tests, his term of office was coming to a close and he did not want to commit his successor. The governor's council, that archaic colonial survival, delayed month after month confirming the successor, and the gray little commissioner stayed on.

On my last visit to him, a year after the exhibits had been recovered, he had finally evolved what no doubt seemed to him the ideal politician's formula—to say yes and to mean no. He now told me that if the American Academy of Forensic Sciences wanted to appoint a committee of experts to examine all the ballistics evidence, he would allow them to do so; but he could not allow any examination, even by experts, merely at the request of a private individual.

Not until Goguen was out of office did I finally get my permission. His successor, Frank Giles, raised no objections at all. A few weeks later Dr. William Boyd of the Boston University School of Medicine made the blood tests, although he said in advance he doubted whether after so many years and so much handling the bullets would still indicate anything. So it turned out. Dr. Boyd tested the four bullets taken from Berardelli's body and the two taken from Parmenter. The result with all six was negative: no longer any trace of blood on any of them.

Frank Silva was dead, as was Guinea Oates. Of the other two mentioned in Silva's confession of the Bridgewater attempt, Doggy

Bruno had long since vanished, but in 1960 I was surprised to discover that Joe Sammarco was no farther away than Everett, where he was working as a janitor. He had been paroled in 1953 after thirty-three years in prison. At sixty-two, I thought, he should not have much to lose or be afraid of. If I could get him to admit that he had been one of the four in the Bridgewater holdup, that would corroborate Silva and go a long way to proving finally that Sacco and Vanzetti were innocent.

"I don't know about Joe," the parole officer told me in the department offices on Tremont Street, appropriately opposite Brimstone Corner. "Sometimes he comes in here and acts as if I were his uncle. He'd tell me anything. Then the next time he's as cold as a brick. I'll ask him about this Bridgewater business, but I can't promise he'll give out anything."

Two months later I got a call from a Somerville lawyer, Anthony DiCecca, who said Joe might talk to me but that he himself wanted to talk to me first. I drove over the following afternoon. The law office was on Broadway, a lower-middle-class neighborhood, in a remodeled three-story house that had been transformed by plate glass and concrete until it stood out against its drabber surroundings with the glitter of a funeral home.

DiCecca, a bustling, determined man, shook my hand in his paneled office, then sat down behind a vast desk on which a pastel-green telephone kept flashing a warning light. He stared at me for a moment, his eyes calculating in his grave Latin face.

"Now," he said, as if he were satisfied. "I want you to understand I know nothing about the Sacco-Vanzetti case. I have no opinion and don't want to have one. When I was watching that TV show in the spring I began to feel myself getting an opinion so I got up and shut it off. I understand you want to ask Joe about the Bridgewater holdup he was supposed to be in on that they later hung on Vanzetti. I want the details of that."

I gave him a summary of Silva's confession, while he took notes. "Joe can either confirm this or not," I told him finally, "but it will blow a big hole in the Sacco-Vanzetti conviction if he does confirm it."

He sat there, indifferent to the flashing telephone light. "If it's true, Joe could have spoken thirty-five years ago. It's a terrible thing if he kept quiet and let an innocent man die. Maybe he won't want to admit anything because of that, even though there's nothing anyone could do to him now. Let me have a talk with him and then the three of us can get together here Sunday night. Just one thing, though," he went on as I rose to go. "There's no money going to enter into this. I need it like I need a hole in the head. If Joe has any idea that he's going to make a little on a deal, then I want nothing to do with it or with him."

The following Sunday I again drove to Somerville. I kept thinking of Joe Sammarco and his thirty-three years in state prison, all the years back to when I was a schoolboy in corduroy knickerbockers. I felt depressed, half wishing I were not going to see him.

As I walked upstairs and into DiCecca's long anteroom I had my first glimpse of Joe. Squatting on a leather couch before a television set, he was watching the Ed Sullivan show. He was a slight, stooped man with an elongated, almost bald head, cheeks creased against high cheekbones, and eyes that seemed incongruously blue in his wasted face. When we shook hands I could feel his misshapen fingers. He told me DiCecca was out but would be right back. We sat there half an hour in silence. For once I was grateful for the sight of Ed Sullivan's jacked-up shoulders and melon face.

Finally we heard drum-tap footsteps on the stairs. DiCecca brushed in, apologized, and we moved to the inner office, he to his desk, I to the seat I had taken before, and Joe to sit by the window, partly in the shadows.

"Now, Joe," DiCecca began quietly, "I just want you to tell us what you told me here the other night—about Bridgewater, Silva, Jimmy Mede—just as it comes to you."

"Mede is a rat," Sammarco said without anger, his face set like a barrier between himself and the outside world.

"Wait," DiCecca said. "We'll get to that. Now as I read through that article of Silva's—remember, I knew nothing about the case—it seemed pretty convincing. According to that, Silva and you and Doggy Bruno and Guinea Oates drove down to Bridgewater to try to steal the L. Q. White payroll. You'd cased the joint two years before with Jimmy Mede."

Sammarco shook his head, laughed silently, and then spoke again. "It's a pack of lies, every bit of it. Silva got some fellow to write that piece after he got out of jail, and he got paid plenty for it. I know, because he told me." He looked at me quizzically, as if he were wondering whether I believed him. "Not a word of truth in it, not a word."

"Wait a minute!" DiCecca interrupted him. "Let me just ask you these questions in order. Before you went to jail, did you know Jimmy Mede, Frank Silva, Guinea Oates, and Doggy Bruno?"

"Sure I knew them. I was just a kid then and we was all brought up in East Boston together. I knew them since I was that high. We used to hang around Nick's Restaurant just across the street from Jimmy Mede's shoeshine parlor. Frank Silva met this guy Luban in jail or somewheres and cooked up all this story. Why, Silva was too yellow to pull a real holdup. He'd roll some drunk sailor down on Atlantic Avenue, he'd steal when it was safe, but nothing dangerous, not him. Bruno wasn't yellow. He was in dope, robberies, everything, and he got his own living. He never would of worked with Silva or anyone like that. And Guinea Oates, he was younger than the rest of us and never got in no kind of trouble."

Again DiCecca interrupted him. "Did you ever ride in a car with Silva and Mede to plan a holdup?"

"Yes, I did. In 1917 Silva and Mede and me and a guy named Gargalino and someone else went to Braintree. We was going to get a payroll from the factory there when the paymaster come out with it."

"You went down there several times to case it?"

"Yes. Then when we went to pull the job, Mede and Silva got cold feet, so we turned round and come back."

"How do you know it was Braintree?"

"We called it Braintree, where two railroad lines crossed."

"Couldn't it have been Bridgewater?"

"No, it was nearer than that."

I could see the shrug of DiCecca's shoulders. "A matter of a few miles one way or the other. You didn't know any of those places well. It could have been Bridgewater."

"I don't think so," Sammarco said reflectively. "They kept saying it was Braintree. Anyhow, nothing happened. I went into the Navy after that. I was overseas. When I come out they said Jimmy was in jail for holding up a factory in Cambridge. After I took the rap for killing the cop I see Jimmy in Charlestown. He tells me that story about him and Silva. All Jimmy did was take the Braintree trip we made before the war and make it sound like it was Bridgewater afterward. He asked me to string along with his story, so I was dumb enough I says at first I'd go along for a gag. All the Big Chief wanted was to see what he could shake out of Moore. Moore said he'd help him get a pardon and gave him some money. Moore had a lot of money. After he got out Moore was paying him to investigate things in New York until they drove him out of there.

"Ferrari, the state detective, when he heard it, give it to me good. He's still alive, down at the track now. Talk with him and he'll tell you about me and Jimmy Mede. When that piece of Silva's in the *Outlook* come out he come and hit me in the face with it. 'What are you holding out on me for?' he says. 'I never had nothing to do with it,' I told him. Afterward I wrote a letter to Commissioner of Correction Sanford Bates and told him so."

"Now," said DiCecca, steering him back, "were you offered any money by anyone to say you had taken part in the Bridgewater holdup?"

"Yes, Moore come to see me a couple times in Charlestown. He says if I'd confess to the Bridgewater job he'd give me ten thousand and he'd see I got a gun and a getaway car on the way to court."

DiCecca's voice crackled with annoyance. "Look, Joe, a story like this is too stupid for anyone to believe. A sharp lawyer like Moore offering you a gun and a getaway car. That's plain silly. No one would swallow that. Moore wasn't a fool."

"That's what he said," Joe persisted. "I told him I wouldn't. Even if he meant it, what the hell could I have done with a bunch of guards round me with shotguns!"

DiCecca turned to me. "It sounds crazy, all right. But Joe told me exactly the same story the other night when he was here. That's why I say you need a lie detector on this thing."

"All I can think," I told him, "if it's really true—and it certainly sounds fantastic—is that Moore would have said anything, promised anything to get Joe to talk. Moore was a brilliant man, but he thought this whole thing was a frame-up from beginning to end, and he was willing to do or say anything to get his clients off." Then I asked Joe, "Did Thompson ever offer you money?"

"Him? No. He just talked legal. I guess in the end he knew I had nothing to do with it. He never bothered me none. Jimmy brought him in with some other lawyers one day and said in front of them, 'Joe, I want you to give this man the real lowdown on Bridgewater— and then kind of under his breath he says quick, 'No *dice nienta questa no bon paga*'—'Don't say nothing, they won't pay.' I never see Mede again in jail after that. The Big Chief looks tough but he's yellow. After I got out in fifty-three I went to see him in his joint in Revere and I told him what he was to his face. Afterward I see Silva in a bar on Hanover Street and he says 'You should of stuck with us, you could of made ten or fifteen grand! I told him what I thought of him right to his face. He's dead now."

"But why," I asked him, "would Mede go to the governor afterward with his story and lose his boxing license?"

Joe's voice was scornful. "Ah, that's not why he lost it. He lost it for stealing a load of booze. He was never on the level in nothing he done."

"Vanzetti," I said. "You knew him in prison. If Mede and Silva were lying, do you think he was part of the Bridgewater gang?"

"No," said Joe emphatically, "he wasn't any stickup guy. I was in the next cell to him awhile. I used to work in the number plate shop with him. People always coming to see him, old Boston ladies bringing him books and candy and things. He'd give me some. He used to read all the time. I always knew he wasn't guilty."

"The other prisoners, how did they feel about him?"

"They all felt the same way," Joe said in his faded far-off voice. "Most of the guards thought he was innocent too. The night they was executed we made a hell of a row. It used to be the lights went dim at an execution for a couple seconds, but this time they wasn't using Edison current and nothing happened, but we all knew when it was midnight just the same."

His mind groped back to that August night thirty-three years before and he was silent for several seconds before he continued. "I remember Vanzetti come to me once, he was crying. He says, 'You know I'm innocent. Tell them if you had anything to do with Bridgewater.' I told him I would if I had—but I hadn't nothing to do with it. Even my sisters and my cousins come in before the execution and asked me and I says 'I wasn't there, I didn't do it.' Sometimes I used to think, maybe that fellow Weeks had something to do with both the robberies. He was smart, he was. But Vanzetti never had nothing to do with them. He wasn't that kind."

DiCecca swung toward me in his swivel chair as if to call an end to the interview.

"Joe says he's willing to take a lie-detector test along with Mede to see who's telling the truth."

"Or I'll take it all by myself," Joe broke in. "You'll never get the Big Chief to take no test like that. He might try to con some money out of you, but he'd never take the test."

"That's the size of it," said DiCecca. "Whether we believe Joe or not doesn't matter until we give him a lie-detector test."

"I'll take it any time," Joe said. We stood up. Joe and I left

DiCecca there, walking out together through the echoing anteroom and down the stairs. The pinched and hostile face I had first encountered had now become relaxed, softened, the face of a human being.

"I was a dumb kid, no education," said Joe reflectively. "I took that rap for thirty-three years because I didn't know no better." It was the second time he had used the word *rap*. I stopped on the stairs where the arc lamp shone through the doorway. "You're telling me, then, that you didn't kill that policeman?"

His voice was low, quite passionless. "Him or anyone else. I never did. Maybe you won't believe that neither, but I never did. It was my gun all right, but if I'd of said at the trial who pulled the trigger I'd of got a bullet through my head. The one who done it got killed in a gunfight four years later. Back in thirty-one I come up before the parole board and his widow come and told them he done it, but they wouldn't listen to her, just asked her why she didn't tell it before. And she says, 'I got to live too.' "

I remembered that Vanzetti in his speech to the court had said that no human tongue could say what he and Sacco had suffered in seven years' imprisonment. Yet if what Joe had just told me was so, he had suffered over four times as long, unknown, inarticulate, without friends and partisans to speak for him, without the satisfaction of a well-advertised martyrdom, and yet no tongue could truly say— not even his own—what he had suffered.

"Would you be willing to trust that to a lie detector, too, whether or not you killed the policeman?"

"Yes," he said simply. We continued to the bottom of the stairs. Then at the door he held out his maimed hand to me and smiled slightly.

On January 30, 1961, John Conrad, an expert with many years of experience in operating the polygraph lie detector, conducted an examination on Joe Sammarco to verify the truthfulness of the answers to the following questions:

Q. Were you ever in a holdup attempt in Bridgewater with Doggy Bruno, Guinea Oates, and Frank Silva?
A. No.
Q. Were you ever in a car with Bruno and Oates?
A. No.
Q. Did you ever tell Jimmy Mede at Charlestown that you had participated in the Bridgewater holdup?

A. No.

Q. Did Silva tell you that he and Mede received money from Moore to invent a story on the Bridgewater holdup?

A. Yes.

Q. Did Moore offer you ten thousand dollars if you would confess that you had participated in the Bridgewater holdup?

A. Yes.

Q. Have you any knowledge of who did take part in the Bridgewater holdup?

A. No.

Q. Did Frank Silva later admit to you that his confession was false?

A. Yes.

As a result of this examination Conrad certified that in his opinion Sammarco had told the truth.

◇◇◇◇◇◇◇◇◇◇◇◇◇◇◇◇◇◇◇◇◇◇◇◇◇◇◇◇◇◇◇◇

CHAPTER SIXTEEN

1926

After the flare-up in 1921, the Sacco-Vanzetti case smoldered obscurely for five years. Occasional sparks were thrown up, as when Ettor and Giovannitti returned to Boston in 1925 to speak for their imprisoned comrades and Eugene Debs visited Vanzetti in Charlestown, but for the most part the issues seemed lost in a lawyer's maze. Across the Atlantic the case had become overlaid by other events and other conflicts. If the average demonstrator of 1921 had suddenly been asked in 1926 whether Sacco and Vanzetti were still alive, he would probably not have known.

In the United States, except in restricted circles of urban liberals and radicals, the names aroused no more response. The Defense Committee continued its Boston meetings. In December 1925 it published the first number of the *Official Bulletin*, a four-page booklet containing a message from Debs, a review of the ballistics evidence by Mrs. Evans, and an appeal to Governor Cox signed by George Lansbury, Ellen Wilkinson, James Maxton, and other members of the English Labor Party.

Sacco, in Dedham, resumed his English lessons with Mrs. Jack. In Charlestown, Vanzetti's literary activities expanded. He contributed articles to the New Jersey anarchist journal, *L'Adunata dei Rafrattari*, wrote his short autobiography as well as the booklet *Background to the Plymouth Trial*, began to translate Proudhon's *The War and the Peace* into English, and completed a novelette, *Events and Victims*, about his experiences in a factory before the United States entered the war. Both men were much heartened by Thompson's taking over as their counsel. Sacco, in spite of his class-conscious rigidity, trusted the Boston conservative lawyer as he had never trusted Moore, and wrote enthusiastically of the "splendour defense" that Thompson and Hill had made in their first appearance. Vanzetti was even more enthusiastic.

> Permit me to express my gratitude and my appreciation to you [he wrote Thompson in February 1926]. I understand that your work in our behalfe is underpaid; the must difficult test of you; the noble sentiments and impulse by which you were decide to take the side of two underdogs; this I understand. And I also hope to understand a little the brave, learned, beautiful fight that you are fighting in our behalfe, paying of it in peace, rest, interest and other universally desired things.
>
> Ha! to have known you 6 year ago! I would never have been a convict.

Thompson, in turn, as the months went on, found himself drawn closer to the two men he had reluctantly elected to defend. In May 1927 he could write:

> I went into this case as a Harvard man, a man of old American tradition, to help two aliens who had, I thought, been unjustly treated. I have arrived at a humbler attitude. Not since the martyrdoms of the sixteenth century has such steadfastness to a faith, such self-abnegation as that of these two Italians been seen on this earth.
>
> The Harvard graduate, the man of old American traditions, the established lawyer, is now quite ready to say that nowhere in his soul is there to be found the faith, the splendid gentility, which make the man, Bartolomeo Vanzetti.

Thompson later admitted that the case had been something of a catastrophe for his firm: that by taking it he had lost friends, clients, and a great deal of money. But it was a choice he never regretted. He told Felicani that if he had understood the situation better at the beginning, he would not have taken a fee.

While the jail years for Sacco and Vanzetti passed with unrelenting sameness, Rosina moved from the Stoughton bungalow to an old farmhouse near Milford. Here Mrs. Evans and Mrs. Jack aided her, and in addition she received a small monthly allowance from the Defense Committee. Ines was now almost old enough to go to school; Dante had reached the seventh grade. Even before Rosina left Stoughton she had living with her as a companion Susie Valdinoce, the grave, sad-faced sister of the man killed in the dynamiting of Attorney General Palmer's house.

The rejection of Thompson's appeal by the Massachusetts Supreme Judicial Court on May 12, 1926, marked the second stage of the case. With the court's decision, affirming the convictions, came the realization that the affair was now moving toward a foreseeable climax. For the prisoners it was as if they had been walking down a long corridor of months and years, and now at last at the far end they could glimpse the door of the execution chamber.

To those familiar with the formalisms of Massachusetts legal procedure the court's negative decision was expected. According to the statutes of the Commonwealth it was not the function of the higher court to review the facts of a case in an appeal but merely to consider questions of law. That in Madeiros' first trial Judge Lummus had neglected to mention the presumption of innocence was an error sufficient to overthrow an obviously justified verdict. Judge Thayer had committed no such errors. Whatever his feelings, he had kept the written record straight just as Thompson, at the beginning of the trial, had predicted he would. In regard to the denied motions, the Supreme Court ruled that as long as Judge Thayer had given these consideration according to the prescribed legal forms, there would be no review of his decision. These were matters for his discretion, beyond the compass of any higher court.

The Supreme Court's decision was like the tolling of a bell. In the next fifteen months the case would become a passionate issue, the linked Italian names a battle cry in all corners of the globe. Millions of men in dozens of countries, most of them with only a hazy and often erroneous notion of the facts, would identify themselves with the condemned Italians with such binding emotion that the fate of the two men would come to seem the very symbol of man's injustice to man. For many European radicals the case loomed up as the most important occurrence since the Russian Revolution. Stalin, at the 1927 Party Congress, spoke of the recent Sacco-Vanzetti demonstration as evidence that "we are on the threshold of new revolutionary events." The American Communist Max Shachtman asked rhetorically: "Since the Russian Bolshevik revolution, where has there yet been a cause that has drawn into its wake the people, not of this or that land, but of all countries, millions from every part and corner of the world; the workers in the metropolis, the peasant on the land, the people of the half-forgotten islands of the sea, men and women and children in all walks of life?"

That the renewed European agitation was conceived and directed by the Communist International is beyond dispute—a fact proclaimed with equal stridency by both Communists and their enemies. Moscow gave the signal and the International Red Aid set the well-oiled machinery in motion. But the Communists themselves must have been startled by their own quick success. Their calculated gesture loosed an avalanche, elemental and overwhelming, that spread beyond the bounds of any political party or dogma. Men of good will everywhere rose up to challenge the course of Massachusetts justice. There were protests from the Vatican; from ex-Premier Caillaux of France; from Paul Loebe, the president of the Reichstag; from Count Bernstorff, who had been ambassador to the United States in 1917; from John Galsworthy, Fritz Kreisler, Henri Barbusse, Romain Rolland, Thomas Mann, Albert Einstein, and scores of other international figures.

Why was it that in the fifteen months between the Massachusetts Supreme Court's adverse decision and the executions the case of Sacco and Vanzetti became the most widely known and bitterly felt of its generation? They were not conscious martyrs. Nor, if it be assumed that they were innocent, were they uniquely so. It was already a cruel commonplace of the century for innocent men to die ignominiously and obscurely for their beliefs under red, black, white, or varicolored flags. In an era of bloodshed, violence, and injustice, why should the names of these two obscure Italians stand out, enduring over the years in literature, in art, in the theater, and even in that newest of media, television? *

Perhaps it is that when any celebrated or notorious trial becomes encrusted with doubts as to its justice, it becomes a focus for the raging social passions of the moment. Certainly, in the grim weeks before the execution of Sacco and Vanzetti, the hundreds of thousands of militants demonstrating in the world's cities found their own

---

* In June 1960 the National Broadcasting Company presented Reginald Rose's television play, *The Sacco-Vanzetti Story*. For those unfamiliar with the case it may have seemed an entertaining melodrama. As a balanced presentation of facts it was a failure. Eugene Lyons turned off his television set in disgust. Harry King, one of the four surviving jurors, and the only one who saw the presentation, commented: "Well, I laughed. Quite a show. My only reaction is that it is hard to reconcile anything I saw with the actual trial."

resentments and anger objectified in these two comrades whom they considered victims of class justice. Frustration and the envy of America's callous wealth undoubtedly stirred them too, and the hope that through such potent symbols of martyrdom the hated system could be overthrown.

Among many Europeans unswayed by the more primitive emotions of hate and revenge, there was the feeling that, beyond any question of the fairness of the trial, the years under the shadow of death were themselves torture enough to demand the commuting of the death sentences. "We wish to see the lives of these men spared, whether they are innocent or guilty," said *Le Temps* in Paris. The London *Times* felt that it was not the wrongs of the trial that had so stirred the public's imagination but the fact that any man should be kept so long in suspense. The suspense was particularly aggravated by Massachusetts' means of execution: Far more than the traditional noose, the electric chair was a horror symbol to the European.

If—regardless of the question of their guilt or innocence—Sacco and Vanzetti had been executed within a few months of their conviction (as would have happened had they been tried in most European countries), their names today would be almost unknown. To non-Americans the pettifogging byways of American justice, the complications and contradictions and the time entailed in appealing from state to federal courts, the to them astonishing fact that even if injustice is being done by the judicial system of an individual state, so long as it is being done within the limits of the Constitution the national government can do nothing—such things were outrageously incomprehensible. And the years of delay seemed to presume doubt. "It is impossible for us on this side to feel that execution would have been so long deferred," George Bernard Shaw wrote, "if the case were clear enough to justify this infliction."

Anticipating the Massachusetts Supreme Court's adverse decision, the Red Aid's Central European Headquarters in Berlin began in February 1926, to flood Europe with Sacco-Vanzetti propaganda and plans for a united front of artists, writers, actors, scholars, and teachers.

The anarchists had never ceased their sporadic and individualistic action, but international anarchy no longer rivaled Marxism as a world movement, as it had in Bakunin's day, and it persisted mostly in the Latin countries. The Sacco-Vanzetti case contained, among many other things, the last gesture of international anarchism. Yet the anarchists by themselves could have accomplished little. It was the executive committee of the Communist International, with its tight organization and intricate networks, that was able to stir the streets. By the autumn of 1926 the groundwork had been laid for the world-wide agitation to come.

The year 1926 brought a belated stirring of interest in the case throughout the United States, partly as a reaction to the renewed agitation overseas as reported in such mass-circulation journals as the *Literary Digest*, partly because of the Supreme Court's decision in May, and partly from the labors of the Defense Committee. In Massachusetts there was a quickening of emotions lying dormant since 1921, a xenophobic reaction by the community to criticism from outsiders that would rise to hysteria as world agitation rose.*

Robert Lincoln O'Brien, the half-Irish half-old-Yankee editor of the Boston *Herald*, whose reaction to the Sacco-Vanzetti case remained essentially neutral, observed that "a surprising number of groups and elements of the community came to regard leniency for Sacco and Vanzetti as an assault upon the honor of the Commonwealth." That feeling, still amorphous in the spring of 1926, hardened under the impact of hostile gestures from overseas and was suddenly exacerbated in June when the house of Samuel Johnson in West Bridgewater was demolished by a bomb. Whoever planted the bomb apparently mistook Johnson's house for that of his brother Simon, who with his wife had received a reward of several hundred dollars after their court testimony. No one was ever apprehended in this or any other bombings connected with the case, and the Defense Committee at once repudiated the act, but to the community it seemed a confirmation of its worst fears in regard to radicals. Guards were at once placed around the houses of Judge Thayer and of Chief Justice Arthur Rugg. District Attorney Wilbar announced that he would ask for the immediate imposition of the death penalty on Sacco and Vanzetti.

The Commonwealth was coming to feel that reviews enough had been made, the matter had been discussed long enough. Doubts expressed from outside, either in the United States or overseas, merely sharpened the edge of Massachusetts majority opinion. The Boston architect C. Howard Walker, on returning from Europe at the height of the agitation, declared himself "enough of a Machiavellian to re-

* G. B. Shaw understood this xenophobia well. "Americans must decide for themselves," he wrote to Upton Sinclair, "whether they will slaughter their Saccos and Vanzettis and Mooneys; for the moment a foreigner interferes, to yield to him would be an unbearable humiliation; perish a thousand Saccos first."

joice in the electrocutions whether the accused are innocent or guilty."

Stubbornly the Massachusetts community, the articulate, rooted middle-class community, closed ranks. Granville Hicks, teaching at Smith College, helped organize a clemency meeting in Northampton in the spring of 1927. So strong was the feeling of the townspeople against Sacco and Vanzetti that it broke up in bedlam. It was not, Hicks had to admit, just the rich and powerful who were against the two Italians: "It was also the doctors, the lawyers, the shopkeepers, the farmers, the workers. It was practically all my neighbors in Northampton except for the other members of the college faculty. The battle was between the intellectuals and everybody else."

There was, however, a thoughtful minority made uneasy by the slow steamroller of Massachusetts justice. Liberals like Edward Filene, John Moors of the brokerage house of Moors & Cabot, and Professor Felix Frankfurter joined with conservatives like Joseph Walker, a former Republican speaker of the Massachusetts House of Representatives, and Richard Washburn Child, a former ambassador to Italy, in questioning the legal proceedings. Names old and distinguished were added to the list of protesters—the historian Samuel Eliot Morison, the philosopher William Hocking, William Allan Neilson, the president of Smith College, and the Harvard economist Frank Taussig.

In June 1925 the American branch of the International Red Aid was set up in Chicago as the International Labor Defense. For the Communists the Sacco-Vanzetti case was an issue ripe for manipulation. By exploiting it, the Party hoped to confirm its pose as the champion of the oppressed and for the first time develop into an American mass movement. After his expulsion from the Party, James Cannon, the International Labor Defense's executive secretary, was to admit privately—much as Moore did—that he felt Sacco was guilty. But to the Communists guilt or innocence was immaterial. What mattered was the inflammability of the cause.

For Cannon and his lieutenant Max Shachtman, editor of the monthly *Labor Defender*, the efforts of the Boston Defense Committee were naïve, self-defeating, contaminated by "the slow poison of middle-class treachery." Thompson, the aloof upper-class lawyer, had announced that he would not tolerate "pressure from the outside," meaning in Shachtman's view "the mass movement of labor that could surround Sacco and Vanzetti with a wall of iron against the attacks of their enemies." That the Defense Committee could replace a class fighter like Moore with a reactionary like Thompson was merely another demonstration of the liberal fallacy—belief in the law, in justice above class, in all the paraphernalia that concealed the claws of capitalist society. Abstract justice could play no role, in Shachtman's pronouncement as echoed by the *Daily Worker*, since "Sacco and Vanzetti were being legally assassinated because of their political and economic views and activities."

Johnnies-come-lately though they might be, the Communists took the attitude that it was they who were the organizers of the protest movement. The Sacco-Vanzetti case was now theirs by right of Marxist eminent domain. And, here as abroad, they were able to bring about immediate sensational results. The International Labor Defense poured out posters and buttons and press releases, organized meetings all across the country, and collected large sums for what Cannon called "the protection" of Sacco and Vanzetti.

Of the millions collected by the Red Aid in various parts of the world for the defense of the convicted men, less than six thousand dollars ever found its way to the Defense Committee. There was no accounting for the balance. Felicani, who had so scrupulously recorded each dollar he received, was outraged. In July the Defense Committee warned in its *Official Bulletin:* "We are absolutely opposed to the collection of funds and the use of this cause to further special political or economic interests." The *Daily Worker* and the International Labor Defense replied by calling the Defense Committee and its counsel ineffectual liberals who relied on bourgeois legal proceedings rather than the direct action of the workers.

Yet, whatever the Communists might claim, whatever self-advertising actions they might take, the shabby two-room headquarters at Hanover Street still remained the center of the Sacco-Vanzetti defense. The yeast of the Massachusetts Supreme Court decision worked as actively there as outside. Fabbri was succeeded as secretary by Joseph Moro, an Italian shoe-worker with a family, who gave up a job at forty dollars a week to work full time for the committee at ten dollars less. Eugene Lyons had left Boston at the end of 1922 to work for the New York branch of Tass, the Soviet news agency. Until 1926 no one took his place. As long as Moore remained in charge of the defense, Lyons continued to contribute articles and support, but Thompson's advent was too much for him. Still wearing his

Communist heart on his sleeve, still at the beginning of his long arc from left to right, he held to his opinion that the defense of Sacco and Vanzetti should be a class defense.

Through the quiescent years the members of the Defense Committee, working doggedly, had kept both the case and the defendants alive. As the tempo rose in 1926, so did the activity in Hanover Street. The headquarters developed into a small publishing house. Tables and typewriters and filing cabinets were wedged in by bales of pamphlets that served as seats for volunteer workers and visitors.

The moody, indefatigable Mary Donovan seemed always to be at her desk. Mrs. Evans appeared regularly, bringing with her such friends as Mrs. William James, the widow of the philosopher. Professor Frankfurter often trudged up the dark stairway accompanied by one or two of his sympathetic Harvard colleagues. In June a young *Globe* reporter, Gardner Jackson, gave up his newspaper job to take over where Lyons had left off. With the publicity under his enthusiastic control, the *Official Bulletin*—only one issue of which had appeared before this—now came out monthly.

Except for their energetic youth and their devotion to the same cause, the wealthy liberal "Pat" Jackson and the East Side Marxist Morris Gebelow, who wrote under the name of Eugene Lyons, had little in common. Jackson's mother was the third wife of William Jackson, a Colorado banker and railroad owner whose second wife had been Helen Hunt Jackson, the author of *Ramona*. Starting at Amherst College, Pat joined the Army in 1917. After the war he studied at Columbia, took a turn at selling bonds, then worked in a Denver enterprise of his father's before becoming cub reporter on the *Globe*, the paper that was reputed to print the name of every inhabitant of Greater Boston, and, if possible, his picture, at least twice a year.

Jackson had been gathering such neighborhood news for the *Globe* during the Sacco-Vanzetti trial. At the end of many an afternoon he would see Frank Sibley stalking into the city room on his return from Dedham. Sibley's indignation expanded by the day, the more so since he was confined to factual reporting and unable to write his personal reaction to the Dedham goings-on. Sometimes he would stop by the tall, shock-haired young reporter to let off steam.

It was through Sibley that Jackson met Felicani. Never before had the tweedy, rather elegant young man met anyone like this philosophical anarchist. Evening after evening now found Jackson working in the upstairs rooms on Hanover Street. Then, in the summer of 1926, Felicani persuaded him to give his full time to directing the Sacco-Vanzetti publicity.

As it would for many others in the year to come, the cause brought Jackson's being into focus. Independent financially, vaguely liberal, he had never really known what he wanted to do until he found his goal in the struggle for the two Italians' lives. Though later he would become a minor New Deal administrator and a friend of Franklin Roosevelt's, this was to be the high spot of his life. Journalistic talent, energy, honesty, and dedication—these he brought to the cause with the fervency of a convert.

By August 1926 it was clear to James Cannon that the Defense Committee could be neither dislodged nor superseded and that the only other possibility was infiltration. To mark this change in tack the International Labor Defense sent two thousand dollars to the Hanover Street headquarters while the *Labor Defender* announced in conciliatory tones that it was no longer making a general appeal for funds: All future donations for the defense of Sacco and Vanzetti should be sent direct to the Boston committee. In addition, Cannon sent Charles Cline to Boston to try to arrange an amalgamation of the committee with the International Labor Defense.

Cline, one of the Party's so-called Texas martyrs, had just been released from prison after serving thirteen years of a life sentence for murder. In 1911 he had been the sole American among a band of Mexicans who had organized an expedition in Texas to join the Mexican revolutionaries in their fight against the government of Porfirio Díaz. When Texas Rangers found a dead Mexican spy tied to a tree, they pursued and captured Cline and a dozen of the expedition. Cline maintained that he was innocent of the spy's death, and the American Federation of Labor had frequently demanded his liberation. He was finally freed by Governor Miriam "Ma" Ferguson.

Cline's long imprisonment for a revolutionary cause was expected to make him attractive to Sacco and Vanzetti. The real object of his visit was to persuade them to let the International Labor Defense take charge of their fight. Cline explained persuasively that the Boston Defense Committee was run by amateurs who were unable to grasp the class significance of the case. Even so, Cannon would be willing to form a united front organization with certain members of the Defense Committee on condition that the headquarters was moved to Chicago. There the Communist International would be able to bring an overwhelming force into operation that would compel the Massachusetts reactionaries to stay their hand. As a final glittering attraction Cline promised Sacco and Vanzetti that Clarence Darrow would take over from Thompson as their chief counsel.

Running through the letters of Sacco and Vanzetti, unaltered in the alterations of their moods, is their sense of outraged bewilderment at their predicament. What had brought them behind bars? What had taken Sacco from his neat Stoughton bungalow, his red-haired wife, the light-long summer evenings in his vegetable garden? What had taken Vanzetti from the Plymouth streets overlooking the harbor? What had ended the brightness of their years of freedom?

To each man the insistent answer was that they had been radicals, that however small they may have seemed to the men of state, the latter had nevertheless banded together to crush them. The owners of the Cordage works, of the Lawrence mills, those who lived in the big houses on the hill, who controlled the government and the police, who lived at the expense of the workers, this gross capitalistic world, this dying order would kill to preserve its insecure position. District Attorney Katzmann's taunting phrases, the dry words that rustled from Judge Thayer's set lips—these were the voices of executioners.

After the Supreme Court's rejection of Thompson's appeal on May 12, Vanzetti wrote to Alice Stone Blackwell:

Yesterday we got the last struck. It end all. We are doomed beyond any kind of doubts. I am sorry for myself. It is creuil to be insulted, umiliated, wronged, imprisoned, doomned, under infamous charges, for crimes of which I am utterly innocent in the whole sense of the word. But more for myself, I am sorry for my father, my sisters and my brothers, and for poor Rosi and her two children.

Both prisoners had been heartened by the renewed demonstrations in Europe and felt uncritically grateful to the International Labor Defense for its belligerent propaganda. Both felt at times that—as the Communists had said all along—only direct revolutionary action by the masses could save them. Both were divided between the class-struggle interpretation of their dilemma and their attachment to bourgeois partisans like Mrs. Evans. Both were inconsistent in their attitudes—as who might well not be after seven years in the shadow of the electric chair.

Sacco, in particular, with his more dogmatic mentality and limited outlook, tended to distort the possibilities of justice that could transcend class.

Let us tell you sincerely, dear comrade [he wrote a member of the International Labor Defense], that for hereafter I will never fall into another new delusion again, if I don't see first the day of my freedom. Even when Mrs. Elizabeth G. Evans—that through all these struggle years she has been kind to me as kind as good mother can be, come to tell me "Nick! you again." No! No! Six long torment years gives me enough experience because it is a great masterpiece for me and to anybody else not to be disappointed any more. Poor mother! She is so sincere and faithful to the law of the man that she has forgot very early that the history of all the government it were always and everytime the martyrdom of the proletariat. But, however, we will stick like a good Communard soldier to the end of the battle and looking into the eyes of our enemy, face to face, to tell them our last breath—which I had always faith—that you, the comrades and all the workers of the world solidarity, would free Sacco and Vanzetti tomorrow.

Yet in spite of such sentiments he would continue to prefer the conservative Thompson to the radicals.

Vanzetti, in his enthusiasm for the éclat of the International Labor Defense activities, could write to Cannon in an almost similar tone:

The echo of your campaign in our behalf has reached my heart. I repeat, I will repeat to the last, only the people, our comrades, our friends, the world revolutionary proletariat can save us from the powers of the capitalist reactionary hyenas, or vindicate our names and our blood before history.

Nevertheless, Vanzetti was as harsh in his judgments of the new Russia as he was of the old America. To his mind all governments were oppressive, whether they ruled in the name of proletariat, king, or constitution. His frequently expressed disbelief in the progress of the Russian Revolution, his contrary belief that "the Bolsheviki leaders' dictatorship is an increased perfectioned exploitation of the proletariat," constantly embarrassed the editors of the Daily Worker and the Labor Defender. The antirevolutionary, anti-Marxist individualistic anarchist, Proudhon, remained his ideal, and the Frenchman's ringing words: "Liberty of conscience, freedom of the press, freedom of labor, of commerce, and of teaching, the free disposal of the products of labor and industry—liberty, infinite, absolute, everywhere and forever," are often echoed in Vanzetti's letters.

The first reaction of Sacco and Vanzetti to Cline's proposal was to accept it and let the International Labor Defense see what it could do. However they might differ theoretically from the Communists, such potent help was not to be spurned. And for all the Defense Committee's efforts, they were still in jail after six years. Clarence Darrow—the untidy colossus who had slipped the noose from so many necks—appeared as a sudden new hope, a more certain guide than Thompson out of their legal labyrinth. Even though their trust and confidence in the Boston lawyer remained intact, they felt that they had nothing to lose by the change and much to gain.

Felicani, with whom they talked it over, felt otherwise. His distrust of the Communists was innate, and he, as the organizer of the Defense Committee, had a much clearer view of the Party's reasons for taking up the case than did his two comrades. Darrow himself, in Felicani's opinion, could do no more than Thompson had done and would do.*

Sacco and Vanzetti finally agreed to reject Cannon's offer. When Cline reported this to Chicago, the *Labor Defender* struck back at the Defense Committee savagely, accusing it of "trying to represent the martyrdom of Sacco and Vanzetti as an 'unfortunate' error which can be rectified by the 'right' people proceeding in the 'right' way." When Shachtman claimed that it was the Communists' "campaign for international solidarity that has so far saved Sacco and Vanzetti from the death chair," Jackson's *Bulletin* announced angrily that "the Sacco-Vanzetti Defense Committee has no official relationship with the International Labor Defense, the Communist Party, or the Sacco-Vanzetti Conferences, which we understand were organized through the ILD."

During the summer and autumn of 1926 a whole new aspect of the case was opened up by the defense's belated discovery that Pinkerton Detective Agency reports had been filed on both the South Braintree and the Bridgewater holdups. The existence of these primal documents became known largely through the efforts of Tom O'Connor, a State House News Service reporter who had

---

* This was also Darrow's own opinion when some time later he came to Boston and talked with Thompson and Felicani.

first become interested in the case in 1920 after reading about it in the *New Republic*.

O'Connor kept in touch with developments after the trial, dropping in from time to time at Moore's office and at the Hanover Street headquarters. Making his own investigations in Providence and elsewhere, he finally became so engrossed in the case that he gave up his State House job to work for Thompson without pay.

O'Connor was aware—it was common newspaper knowledge—that the Travelers Insurance Company had insured the South Braintree payroll. Searching the back numbers of *Protection*, the Travelers publication, he found what he had assumed—an account of the South Braintree crime and a statement that the company had hired the Pinkerton Agency to investigate it. O'Connor realized that the agents must have made day-by-day reports of what they found, but what interested him even more was the obvious fact that these reports, which would have been submitted long before Sacco and Vanzetti were arrested, would be uncolored by preconceptions. If they could be located, O'Connor was certain they would prove to be the raw material of the case.

A week after the May Supreme Court decision O'Connor went to Thompson, then preoccupied with the Madeiros confession. Just what had occurred, he asked—well aware that Thompson did not have the answer—between the evening the Buick was stolen in Needham and the evening almost six months later when Sacco and Vanzetti were picked up on the streetcar? How did it happen they were arrested? All Thompson could do was to gesture helplessly and answer that he did not know. O'Connor then told him about the South Braintree Pinkerton report. Thompson, who had not heard of it before, banged his desk in his excitement.

Some days later, following Thompson's request, a copy of the report arrived at the Travelers Boston office. Thompson was then away, but O'Connor managed to borrow the report and copy it. As he had hoped, it gave a picture of the case as it appeared before and just after Sacco and Vanzetti were picked up. O'Connor was particularly struck by Henry Hellyer's notes on the fair brown-haired man Jenny Novelli had seen in the murder car who, by the time Hellyer testified at Dedham, had become black-haired with a dark complexion.

After this report came to light, O'Connor, while going through the files of the Bridgewater *Independent*, discovered references to a Pinkerton report on the Bridgewater holdup. But this second report, with its even more glaring discrepancies between the immediate impressions of witnesses and the evidence subsequently offered at the Plymouth trial, was not to come to light until 1927.

It had been common knowledge at the Dedham trial that the United States Department of Justice and District Attorney Katzmann's office had cooperated in getting evidence for the prosecution. What was still not known was the degree of cooperation, for when Thompson raised the issue, the Bureau of Investigation followed its customary policy of refusing to open its files. Thompson increasingly came to feel that there might be evidence in the files indicating that Sacco and Vanzetti were innocent, and in any case he was outraged when he learned that the Bureau had placed spies in the Dedham jail and on the Defense Committee and had even planned to introduce one into Rosina Sacco's house. He wrote to United States Attorney General John Sargent requesting that William West of the Boston office show him whatever documents and correspondence he had covering the investigations made before, during, and after the trial. In indirect answer to this, Thompson received a call from the Boston Bureau asking what information he was after. When he said that he wanted to go through whatever files the department had on Sacco and Vanzetti, West informed him that this would not be allowed.

If one can judge by a memorandum now in the National Archives and prepared by the Department of Justice at the request of the State Department on October 17, 1921, Sacco and Vanzetti, before their trial, were known merely as subscribers to Galleani's *Cronaca Sovversiva* and a New Jersey anarchist paper, *La Jacquerie*. In the files Thompson particularly wanted to see there were of course the reports of the agents attending the trial, as well as the reports of Harold Zorian, who had infiltrated the committee, and Anthony Carbone, who had been planted in the Dedham jail.

Although he was unable to see the files, Thompson discovered that two former Bureau agents, Lawrence Letherman and Fred Weyand, were willing to sign affidavits as to what had taken place in the Boston office in regard to Sacco and Vanzetti during 1920 and 1921. Weyand explained quite frankly that the purpose of the Boston agents in going to the trial was to obtain enough evidence there to deport the accused as anarchists in case they were not convicted of murder.

Letherman, in his affidavit, corroborated Weyand:

The Department of Justice in Boston was anxious to get sufficient evidence against Sacco and Vanzetti to deport them, but never succeeded in getting the kind and amount of evidence required for that purpose. It was the opinion of Department agents here that a conviction of Sacco and Vanzetti for murder would be one way of disposing of these two men. It was also the opinion of such of the agents in Boston as had any actual knowledge of the Sacco-Vanzetti case, that Sacco and Vanzetti, although anarchists and agitators, were not highway robbers, and had nothing to do with the South Braintree crime. My opinion, and the opinion of most of the older men in the Government service, has always been that the South Braintree crime was the work of professionals.

The words are ambiguous. Thompson took them to mean that the Department of Justice, if it could not get Sacco and Vanzetti deported as radicals, would cooperate in getting them executed for a crime they had not committed. As a matter of fact, Sacco and Vanzetti, if they had been acquitted at Dedham, would through their own courtroom testimony have then been subject to deportation as anarchists. West's attitude in cooperating with Katzmann, may have been a callous one, but it seems clear that there was nothing in the Bureau of Investigation files tending to prove either the guilt or the innocence of the two Italians.

On September 13 Thompson again appeared before Judge Thayer in the Dedham courthouse to argue that the verdict against Sacco and Vanzetti should be set aside because of the Madeiros confession and the Weyand and Letherman affidavits. Thayer denied Thompson's request to have Madeiros examined and cross-examined in open court, but aside from this the judge's manner was courteous if impassive. From time to time he would even unbend enough to come out with a small witticism. For five days affidavits were read and Thompson argued for, while Assistant District Attorney Ranney argued against, the motion. Sacco and Vanzetti were not in the courtroom. Rosina was there with Mrs. Evans as well as Mrs. Rantoul, Jerry McAnarney, and Professor Frankfurter.

Thompson maintained that if Sacco and Vanzetti had never come into the case, the evidence he had assembled in Providence would have been sufficient to indict the Morellis. Under these circumstances he felt that Judge Thayer should order a new trial. Thompson's attack on the Department of Justice and his interpretation of its role caused much more of a sensation in Boston than did the twice-told tale of the Madeiros confession. One of his incidental revelations was that a Bureau agent named Shaughnessy who had investigated Sacco and Vanzetti had subsequently been sent to prison for highway robbery.

Assistant District Attorney Ranney admitted that if Madeiros had participated in the South Braintree holdup, Sacco and Vanzetti were innocent, but he considered Madeiros' confession worthless. The district attorney's office would "answer, but not investigate, because we know or believe that the truth has been found." As for Letherman and Weyand, Ranney took the position that the two ex-agents were traitors. "In all police departments, in all detective departments," he told the court, "secrecy is a watchword, a byword—'Do not betray the secrets of your departments.' And if the secrets were broadcast, what would be the result? There would be no crime detected and punished. And yet Letherman and Weyand give their affidavits to these defendants and betray the secrecy of their department. We say on the face of it that there is a breach of loyalty, and we wonder if we cannot conscientiously and logically find that these men, not now in the department, did not leave there with honor but dishonor."

Thompson flared up at Ranney's mention of secrets: "I will say to your Honor that a government which has come to value its own secrets more than it does the lives of its citizens has become a tyranny, whether you call it a republic, a monarchy, or anything else. Secrets! Secrets! And he says you should abstain from touching this verdict of your jury because it is so sacred. Would they not have liked to know something about secrets? The case is admitted by that inadvertent concession. There are then secrets to be admitted!"

After studying the documents and affidavits for five weeks Judge Thayer, on October 23, rejected the motion. He could have done so without giving his reasons, but apparently feeling the need for self-justification, he issued a twenty-five-thousand-word opinion.

Being controlled only by judgment, reason and conscience [he wrote], and after giving as favorable consideration to these defendants as may be consistent with a due regard for the rights of the public and sound principles of law, I am forced to the conclusion that the affidavit of Madeiros is unreliable, untrustworthy and untrue. To set aside a verdict of a jury affirmed by the Supreme Judicial Court of this Commonwealth on such an affidavit would be a mockery upon truth and justice. Therefore, exercising every right vested in this Court in the granting of motions for new trials by the law of the Commonwealth, this motion for a new trial is hereby denied.

In his years on the bench Thayer must have told hundreds of juries that it was for them to determine the facts. Yet here, where his function was merely to determine whether the Madeiros evidence was weighty enough to warrant presentation to a jury, he had taken over the jury's function of determining its truth. But beneath his formalism on the bench and his outward courtesy to Thompson, Judge Thayer was nettled. Why any respectable lawyer should attempt to stretch the law for two properly convicted anarchists was beyond him. He concluded:

Since the trial before the Jury of these cases, a new type of disease would seem to have developed. It might be called "legopsychic neurosis" or "hysteria" which means: "a belief in the existence of something which in fact and truth has no such existence."

This disease would seem to have reached a very dangerous condition, from the argument of counsel, upon the present Motion, when he charges Mr. Sargent, Attorney-General of the United States and his subordinates, and subordinates of former Attorney-General of the United States Mr. Palmer and Mr. Katzmann and the District Attorney of Norfolk County, with being in a conspiracy to send these two defendants to the electric chair, not because they are murderers but because they are radicals. . . . In these cases, from all the developed symptoms, the Court is rather of the opinion that the disease is absolutely without cure.

Until Thayer's decision was published, the only Massachusetts newspaper to take the side of Sacco and Vanzetti was the Springfield *Republican*, a paper that, though conservative in outlook, never altered its outraged opinion that "a dog ought not to be shot on the weight of the evidence brought out in the Dedham Trial." As the waning months of 1926 whetted the issue, the Boston newspapers at first reacted predictably. The independent *Globe* kept to its traditional wary policy of not taking sides on divisive issues. Frank Sibley, in spite of his standing, was taken off the case, and on the day of the executions found himself covering a flower show. Federalist preimmigrant Boston spoke with two voices: the McKinley-minded *Herald*, the breakfast voice of State Street; and the genealogical *Transcript*, the teacup voice of Beacon Hill. The *Transcript* held and would continue to hold that Sacco and Vanzetti had been given a fair trial, that the verdict was just, the defendants had been given every opportunity of appeal, and any further delay was an unworthy concession to foreign radicals, long-haired men, and short-haired women. But doubts had begun to creep into the editorial rooms of the *Herald*. They crystallized in the editorial "We Submit" that appeared three days after Judge Thayer denied the Madeiros motion. It was written by the chief editorial writer, F. Lauriston Bullard, with editor-publisher O'Brien neither suggesting nor objecting, and it is indicative of the national interest the case was now arousing that it was awarded a Pulitzer Prize. The paragraphs that appeared on October 26 must have goggled eyes at many a Back Bay breakfast table:

In our opinion Nicola Sacco and Bartolomeo Vanzetti ought not to be executed on the warrant of the verdict returned by a jury on July 14, 1921. We do not know whether these men are guilty or not. We have no sympathy with the half-baked views which they profess. But as months have merged into years and the great debate over this case has continued, our doubts have solidified slowly into convictions, and reluctantly we have found ourselves compelled to reverse our original judgment. We hope the supreme judicial court will grant a new trial on the basis of new evidence not yet examined in open court. We hope the Governor will grant another reprieve to Celestino Madeiros so that his confession may be canvassed in open court. We hope, in case our supreme bench finds itself unable legally to authorize a new trial, that our Governor will call to his aid a commission of disinterested men of the highest intelligence and character to make an independent investigation in his behalf, and that the Governor himself at first hand will participate in that examination, if, as a last resort, it shall be undertaken. We have read the full decision in which Judge Webster Thayer, who presided at the original trial, renders his decision against the application for a new trial, and we submit that it carries the tone of the advocate rather than the arbitrator. At the outset he refers to "the verdict of a jury approved by the supreme court of this commonwealth" and later he repeats that sentence. We respectfully submit that the supreme court never approved that verdict. What the court did is stated in its own words thus: "We have examined carefully all the exceptions in so far as argued, and finding no error the verdicts are to stand." The court certified that, whether the verdict was right or wrong, the trial judge performed his duty under the law in a legal manner. The supreme court overruled a bill of exceptions but expressed no judgment whatever as to the validity of the verdict or the guilt of the defendants. Judge Thayer knows this.

Bullard went on to object to Thayer's innuendoes, to say that the files of the Department of Justice should be opened, and to charge that Captain Proctor's affidavit stood as a condemnation of the Dedham verdict. He concluded:

If on a new trial the defendants shall again be found guilty we shall be infinitely better off than if we proceed to execution on the basis of the trial already held; the shadow of doubt, which abides in the minds of large numbers of patient investigators of this whole case, will have been removed. And if on second trial Sacco and Vanzetti should be declared guiltless, everybody would rejoice that no monstrous injustice shall have been done. We submit these views with no reference whatever to the personality of the defendants, and without allusion now to that atmosphere of radicalism of which we heard so much in 1921.

Here was the first breach in the Commonwealth's fortifications. The defenders of Sacco and Vanzetti now pressed forward in the paper war that thundered through the correspondence columns of the *Herald* and the *Transcript*.

Bullard's attack received formidable support. Dr. Morton Prince, the internationally famous Harvard professor of psychiatry, wrote to the *Herald* that, after reading the evidence, he "had come to the conclusion that the trial was a miscarriage of justice, that the government had not proved its case and probably Sacco and Vanzetti had not committed the murder charged." Dr. Prince particularly questioned a verdict to which Mary Splaine's evidence had substantially contributed:

I do not hesitate to say that the star witness for the government testified, honestly enough, no doubt, to what was psychologically impossible. Miss Splaine testified, though she had only seen Sacco at the time of the shooting from a distance of about 60 feet for from 1½ to three seconds in a motor car going at an increasing rate of speed at about 15 to 18 miles an hour; that she saw and at the end of a year she remembered and described 16 different details of his person, even to the size of his hand, the length of his hair as being between two and 2½ inches long and the shade of his eyebrows! Such perception and memory under such conditions can easily be proved to be psychologically impossible. Every psychologist knows that—so does Houdini. And what shall we think of the animus and honesty of the state that introduces such testimony to convict, knowing that the jury is too ignorant to disbelieve?

How came Miss Splaine to become acquainted with these personal characteristics of Sacco?

The answer is simple. Sacco had been shown to her on several occasions. She had had an opportunity to study him carefully. More than this, he sat before her in court. At the preliminary hearing in the police court she was not asked to pick Sacco from among a group of other men. Sacco was shown to her alone. Everyone knows that under such circumstances the image of a person later develops, or may develop, in an observer's mind and becomes a false memory. Such a memory is produced by suggestion. Every lawyer knows the unconscious falsification of memory due to later acquired knowledge, though ignorant of the psychology of the phenomenon. And yet Miss Splaine's testimony was offered by the state to the Jury.

Why was not Miss Splaine asked to pick out Sacco from among a group of men? If this had been done, this unconscious falsification of memory would have been avoided.

In Morton Prince the genealogy of the Back Bay combined with the intellectualism of Cambridge across the river, and while the *Herald* editorial might jar Boston, his letter would cause the greater explosion. Even if the Supreme Judicial Court should rule against Thompson's appeal from Thayer's last decision, it was now clear to the more knowing Bostonians that the matter would not rest there. Many felt that Governor Fuller would commute the death sentence to life imprisonment.

When Judge Thayer brushed aside the Madeiros evidence, Sacco felt that nothing could now save him from his fate, neither lawyers nor appeals nor—hardest of all to face—the embattled proletariat. "I don't care how it all ends, if it only ends," he told one of his visitors.

At Christmas Mrs. Jack's daughter Elizabeth brought Sacco apples and candy and—what moved him much—a present for his "dear darling Ines." He wrote to Mrs. Jack in an afterglow of optimism that he hoped from the bottom of his heart "that the new year would bring us a freedom and in the embrace of mine and in the grant human family." But it was something he had given up believing, and he had already requested Thompson to take no more legal steps on his behalf. The two prisoners' joint Christmas message to their supporters sounded much more like Sacco than Vanzetti:

We are convinced that our murderors are determined to burn us within this, 1927, and that it is most probable that they will succeed. And our hearts move is that the new year may give us liberty or death—but menwhile we are ready to bear our cross to the last.

Vanzetti's moods alternated. There was a black period in the autumn when he considered going on a hunger strike. Close to his cell he could hear workmen constructing a new prison electric plant, following the Boston Edison Company's refusal to provide the Commonwealth with current for executions. But even in his darkest moods, when he thought of himself as a vanquished man, the shadow would in a few days be overcome by his basic optimism, just as he could forget the jangle of the electric-plant construction when he learned that Mrs. Corl, the wife of the Plymouth boatbuilder, had kept a vigil lamp lighted before the statue of the Virgin for the last six years for the grace of his liberation. Something in her naïve faith gave strength to his disbelieving heart. At times he would attend the prison's Christian Science services, not out of any belief but merely to be able to sit in the spacious, almost empty chapel and glimpse the sky again through the barred windows and the sunshine reflecting on the gilt dome of the State House. To the chaplains he remained generally hostile. Unlike Sacco, he could still be hopeful of the higher court and of Governor Fuller as an independent-minded man. Even so, he refused to apply for a pardon. "Why should I," he said, "when I am innocent?" Nevertheless he was still willing to cooperate with his lawyers and the Defense Committee. He began to translate Thompson's brief into Italian for distribution in Europe.

In one and the same letter Vanzetti could announce that he was doomed, and then turn with lyric nostalgia to his father's garden at Villafalletto:

It takes a poet of first magnitude to worthly speak of it, so beautiful, unspeakably beautiful it is . . . the singing birds there; black merles of the golden bick, and ever more golden troath; the golden oriols, the gold-finches, the green finches, the chaf-finches, the neck-crooking, the green ficks; the unmachable nightingales, the nightingales over-all. Yet, I think that the wonder of my garden's wonders

*is the banks of its path. Hundreds of grass, leaves of wild flowors
witness there the almighty genios of the universal architecture—reflecting the sky, the Sun, the moon, the stars, all of its lights and
colors. The forgetmenot are nations there, and nation are the wild
daisies.*

Christmas—his seventh behind bars—brought a cold snap, etching
the jail windows with frost. Among Vanzetti's letters and Christmas
cards were a number of books—*The Life of Debs,* Jack London's
Essays on Revolt, and, accompanied by a necktie from Mrs. Evans,
Emerson's *Essays.* Emerson he found "so exquisitely anarchist," de-
lighting "at the lecture of *Politics, Nature and New England
Reformers.*"

Just after Christmas he wrote to Alice Stone Blackwell:

*I know perfectly well that within four month the Massachusetts
will be ready to burn me. . . .*

*So every hope to get reparation and freedom having been killed in
me by each and all the words and deeds of Massachusettes black
gowned, puritanic, cold-blood murderors, on the first day of the 1927,
I formulated the wish, the wove, that I am get out within this year,
no matter if alive or death. And I hope with all my force that this
will come true. By it, I do not mean suicide.*

As the short and frigid days moved toward the final year, the
clamor from overseas echoed more loudly within the United States.
The obscure foreigners who had stood up in court that sultry summer evening of 1921 to hear the foreman, Ripley, pronounce the
verdict against them could at least console themselves that their
names had been blazoned round the world. They who had traveled
on the swaying Brockton trolley talking of a Sunday meeting of a
few dozen immigrants, now could conjure up hundreds of meetings
in dozens of countries. Proudly they accepted the fact that they
had become symbols.

CHAPTER SEVENTEEN

◇◆◇◆◇◆◇◆◇◆◇◆◇◆◇◆◇◆◇◆◇◆◇◆◇◆◇◆◇◆◇◆

1927

The state prison's new electric plant went into use five days after New Year's, when three young men known as the Carbarn Bandits were executed. Following executions the warden customarily served a buffet supper to the witnesses and the press, so when on January 4 Vanzetti noticed three hams being cooked in the kitchen for the warden's house, he knew it was the bandits' turn.

The three—Edward Heinlein, John Devereaux, and John McLaughlin—had held up the night cashier at the Waltham carbarn on October 4, 1925; while escaping, Devereaux had shot and killed an elderly night watchman who tried to stop them. They were caught the same night, and by next day the press had already labeled them the Carbarn Bandits. At their trial Devereaux admitted that he had fired the fatal shot but said he had meant to fire at the ground. He told the court that he did not see why his two friends should suffer for what he had done. Nevertheless, all three were found guilty of first-degree murder and sentenced to death. As faithful if erring Catholics they walked to the chair accompanied by a priest, and their last look was at a crucifix held before their eyes.

In the six months between their conviction and their execution, their fate caused more of a stir locally than did the postponed fate of Sacco and Vanzetti. All three had served in the Army during the war, and Devereaux had been wounded. They were Irish by descent, and whatever their faults, they had remained true to their church. The mothers of the three organized a Massachusetts Clemency Committee and presented the governor, Alvan Fuller, a petition of 120,000 names that included those of three ex-governors. Protest meetings were held all summer and autumn. In a desperate last appeal the mothers visited Fuller in his office and got down on their knees in front of him to pray for their sons' lives. But the governor was adamant. As he had often publicly stated, he believed in the death penalty as a deterrent, in less sentimentality about murders, in modernization of the law, and more religion in life.

If Fuller had been a politician rather than a businessman he would not have hesitated about commuting the sentences, for no Massachusetts politician in his senses would have let three Irish-Catholic ex-servicemen go to the chair. To the astute it had long been clear that the descendants of the Famine immigrants, who had taken over Boston in 1905 with the election of Mayor John F. "Honey" Fitzgerald, would before long take over the Commonwealth. That Fuller's belief in the salutary effects of capital punishment could overrule his concern for this powerful voting bloc would make it that much more difficult for him later to consider clemency for two anarchist atheist alien slackers. The execution of the Carbarn Bandits filled the Boston Irish with resentments that were transferred with accrued bitterness to Sacco and Vanzetti.

Fuller prided himself on not being a politician. His favorite maxim was Calvin Coolidge's "More business in government, less government in business," and he had forty million dollars to prove his point. Never had he bothered to conceal his contempt for the Republican bosses of Massachusetts with their well-established escalator system of advancement that he was rich enough to disregard. In fact, his contempt for them and his successful defiance of their candidates had made him seem outside the Commonwealth something of a La Guardia-type liberal. In 1912 he had broken with the Republican State Committee to support Theodore Roosevelt's Bull Moose party. In 1916, again in disregard of the state committee, he had run for Congress as an independent, defeating the regular Republican candidate.

During two terms in Congress he distinguished himself chiefly by attacking abuses of the franking privilege and the mileage allowance. However, he did not hesitate to defy Masachusetts' senior senator, Henry Cabot Lodge, by supporting the League of Nations. In 1920 he again frustrated the state Republican bosses by taking the nomination for lieutenant governor away from their designated candidate. He served the conventional two terms as lieutenant governor before defeating James Michael Curley for the governorship in 1924. In 1926 he was easily re-elected.

As he approached his fiftieth birthday he could take satisfaction in being both the leader of his state and the richest man in Massachusetts. His granite-faced neo-Renaissance mansion on the water side of Beacon Street occupied the site of two brownstone town houses that had belonged to Mrs. Jack Gardner. Old ladies might shrug their shoulders and whisper behind his back at the Longwood Cricket Club, but no one could deny him entree anywhere. The lean bicycle mechanic had become portly in middle age, his confident asymmetrical face plumping over his stiff collar. His lobeless ears clung close to his head, his thinning hair clung to his scalp, and he had curiously amber-tinted eyes that many found disconcerting. His mouth looked like a dollar sign set sideways. On the stubby little finger of his right hand with its moonless nail he wore a gold signet ring with the resurrected Fuller crest. When in an affable mood he used to say he would like to run a newspaper and teach Sunday school.

The unspoken image that fluttered in his mind during his final term as governor was the Republican National Convention of 1928 with its shimmering prospect of the Vice-Presidential nomination. It was not an impossible thought after all, for mousy Calvin Coolidge had managed it eight years before from the same governor's chair on the strength of one of his copybook maxims pronounced during the Boston police strike: "There is no right to strike against the public safety by anybody, anywhere, any time."

On January 27 and 28, 1927, in Boston's Pemberton Square Courthouse, Thompson, assisted by Ehrmann, appeared before the Massachusetts Supreme Court to argue against Judge Thayer's denial of the Madeiros motion. It was the coldest weather in two years, with a high wind curling up State Street and the fringes of the harbor beginning to freeze. The courtroom was almost empty as Thompson developed his thesis. Not until he mentioned Judge Thayer could one sense the restrained passion behind the quiet voice:

"I must refer to a thing I am almost ashamed to mention. The judge, having spent a page and a half of his decision in vituperation of myself, suggested that my belief in the innocence of these defendants was due to a mental disease. He also suggested that there had been fraud and deceit in the methods used in procuring this evidence."

Thompson then pointed out various misstatements in Thayer's decision—such as that the Supreme Court had approved the jury's verdict, when it had done nothing of the kind—and accused him of being so overwrought by the case that he was not capable of reasoning "with a calm mind free from impartiality." Beyond all the renewed arguments about Madeiros, the Department of Justice, and other points, Thompson's chief contention was that the defendants were entitled to a new trial because there had been an abuse of judicial discretion.

In the thin winter light of the musty echoing courtroom the stiff faces of the five justices looked like Copley portraits of a century and a half earlier. Chief Justice Arthur Prentice Rugg presided, flanked by Henry King Braley, William Cushing Wait, John Crawford Crosby, and Edward Peter Pierce—New England names, bloodless New England features. To Thompson they seemed as chill as the city streets outside.

Vanzetti was pessimistic about the appeal:

We know that in a case of such nature as ours, legallity alone is insufficient. Mr. Thompson has known to place the case in such perfect manner before the Supreme Court, that if the just-ices wish, they can give us justice now. . . . Therefore, if they are going to a refusal, it would unmistakably prove that they have prostituted their consciences, their intellect, and will to a categoric order of an invisible and trascendental master or class.

The appearance of Felix Frankfurter's article, "The Case of Sacco and Vanzetti," in the March issue of the *Atlantic Monthly* initiated the final world-shaking stage of the case. The *Atlantic* still remained the voice of conservative intellectual America. For seventy years its staid ocher cover with the oval intaglio cut of Poseidon and his sea horse had borne the names of Lowell, Longfellow, Whittier, Emerson, Hale, Holmes, James, and Howells. That it should now feature an article by a Harvard Law School professor attacking the trial, the jury, the witnesses, the verdict, and the Massachusetts judiciary, gave the affair at once a national significance. The stirrings in Europe, the mutterings in New England had now become articulate. Frankfurter's article was like a lighted fuse leading to a powder magazine. Sacco and Vanzetti became familiar names in all the forty-eight states, not just among the urban left-liberals but in the suburbs and the small towns and the women's clubs and the little brick Carnegie libraries.

For most of those who read it, Frankfurter's attack was their factual introduction to the background of a case they had heard about only vaguely. Deftly and concisely the law-school professor explained how the two men had come to be arrested, described the method of selecting the jury, Katzmann's harrying cross-examination of Sacco, Judge Thayer's patriotic rhetoric, and the later discrediting of various witnesses. Accepting the hypothesis that the Morelli gang committed the South Braintree murders, he asserted "with deep regret" that Thayer's ruling on the Madeiros motion was "a farrago of misquotations, misrepresentations, suppressions and mutilations."

The weakness in Frankfurter's article was that basically the prosecution had a more formidable case against the two men than readers of the *Atlantic* would have gathered. Of the expanded book version that appeared the same month, Justice Oliver Wendell Holmes wrote to Harold Laski:

My prejudices were all with Felix's book. But after all, it's simply showing, if it was right, that the case was tried in a hostile atmosphere. I doubt if anyone would say there was no evidence warranting a conviction.

With the appearance of the *Atlantic* article, Frankfurter became the moving spirit of the Sacco-Vanzetti defense. Even Thompson turned to him. His were the final decisions as to tactics and action. Lithe, dark, youthful in manner but obviously the professor, the forty-five-year-old Frankfurter was as intense as he was opinionated, the picture of academic intellectualism without its self-deprecatory pose. Whenever he appeared at the Hanover Street headquarters he always managed to look as brisk as if he had just walked over from Cambridge—as he sometimes had. He and Governor Fuller shared a common start from nothing and were both driven by the same fierce will to succeed, but the governor saw success as the power of money while the professor saw it as the power of the mind.

Felix Frankfurter had been sure of himself from the day he arrived in New York from Vienna as a twelve-year-old immigrant, bookish and eager, speaking no English yet shortly afterward leading his classes in the Lower East Side's Public School 25. At the Harvard Law School, which he entered more or less by chance in 1903, he stood for three years first in his class, receiving the highest honor of becoming an editor of the *Law Review*. After graduation he served as assistant to Secretary of War Henry Stimson in the Taft administration, continuing briefly into Wilson's first term. Just ten years after the unknown Frankfurter had entered the Harvard Law School, Professor Edward Warren enticed him back with an invitation to join the faculty.

Frankfurter had not concerned himself with the Sacco-Vanzetti case during the trial or immediately following it. Only when he saw the headlines in the autumn of 1923 that Thompson had accused the prosecution of a frame-up in regard to Captain Proctor's testimony did he begin to take an interest. After he read that Proctor had sworn that when he said "consistent with" he did not really think the bullet had gone through the gun, his neutrality evaporated. And when Katzmann, in reply to Proctor, said he had not "repeatedly" asked the question, that settled it. Frankfurter wrote his *Atlantic* article with, as he himself boasted, the intention of jolting minds.

On April 5, in the Pemberton Square courthouse, the Supreme Court handed down its decision. Guards took their places all through the cavernous building; deputy sheriffs and court officers patrolled the corridors. Guards were also placed in front of the railings of Governor Fuller's Beacon Street mansion and sent to Judge Thayer's home in Worcester.

The decision upheld Judge Thayer at every point. Through the late afternoon the news, first chalked up on the bulletin boards of Newspaper Row on Washington Street, spread through the business district like wildfire. Everyone wanted to know just one thing: What could the two Italians do now?

According to Massachusetts law the court was limited to determining whether the trial judge had committed any errors of law or abuses of discretion. These were the limitations rigidly held to by Justice Wait in his opinion. Could Thayer conscientiously, intelligently, and honestly have reached the result he has reached? the court asked itself collectively, and answered, through Justice Wait, that he could have.

The granting or the denial of a motion for a new trial of an indictment for murder rests in the judicial discretion of the trial judge, and his decision will not be disturbed unless it is vitiated by errors of law or abuse of discretion.

The question of the guilt or innocence of the defendants was not a matter for consideration. Citing a civil case, Davis *v.* Boston Elevated Railway, as precedent, the court ruled:

It is not imperative that a motion for a new trial of an indictment for murder based on newly discovered evidence be granted, even though the evidence is newly discovered, and, if presented to a jury, would justify a different verdict.

The Massachusetts tradition, sternly enforced by Chief Justice Rugg, was that Supreme Judicial Court decisions were unanimous, but that behind the ruling of April 5 there may have been some suppressed stirrings of doubt was indicated by an incident related by Herbert Ehrmann. In 1938, as he was addressing a Boston Bar Association memorial meeting in honor of Thompson, he noticed Justice Pierce in the audience. Pierce had been a member of the Massachusetts Supreme Court during the entire period of the Sacco-Vanzetti case, and Ehrmann felt uneasy over the critical remarks he was about to make. When, however, the meeting was over, the justice came forward with tears pouring down his cheeks, grasped Ehrmann's hand, and said in a broken voice, "Thank you! Thank you! Thank you!"

Following the Supreme Court's decision, District Attorney Wilbar asked for imposition of sentence, and a special session was called at the Dedham courthouse for Saturday, April 9. In Charlestown, meanwhile, Warden Hendry transferred Vanzetti to the state prison's grim and ancient Cherry Hill section "to protect him from the unwelcome attention of curious visitors."

Outside Massachusetts the protests were immediate. A Committee for the Defense of Victims of Fascism and the White Terror sent a wire from France to President Coolidge, signed by Henri Barbusse, Romain Rolland, and Albert Einstein, requesting the liberation of Sacco and Vanzetti. From Berlin the International Red Aid cabled Governor Fuller demanding "pardon and release in the name of half a million members." The Regional Federation of Labor in Buenos Aires called a forty-eight-hour strike to protest the court's decision. Letters, telegrams, and cables poured in on Governor Fuller, at whose ornate wrought-iron gate the problem had now been left. Privately, Fuller considered that the court's word should be the last word, but publicly he announced that the evidence in the case had never been presented to him and that consequently he had not formed any opinion. On April 7, as if to emphasize his detachment, he bought another Gainsborough portrait, "Master Heathcote," from Sir Joseph Duveen.

The day of the sentencing broke cold and damp and gray. At Charlestown, Vanzetti was waked at five o'clock. He ate his breakfast of frankfurts, baked potatoes, bread, and coffee, then—since he would not be returning immediately to the state prison—wrapped his belongings in brown paper. After he had finished he went to the rotunda where he sat calmly smoking his pipe until the car came to take him to Dedham. As he left he waved a friendly good-by to Warden Hendry.

He rejoined Sacco in the library of the Dedham jail. Again they embraced gravely. Shortly before ten a bus took them to court. They left surrounded by a dozen deputies and three policemen with shotguns.

The courthouse was again surrounded by police with rifles. Admission was by ticket, obtainable only by those connected with the defense or the prosecution, plus the curious-minded with political pull. Felicani, Mary Donovan, and Mrs. Evans' secretary Anna Bloom arrived at the courthouse a little after nine only to find the iron gates locked. A janitor refused to let them in until ordered to by a state trooper. Mrs. Evans, who had broken her ankle recently, limped up the steps in the company of Sarah Ehrmann and Mrs. Gertrude Winslow, the secretary of the Community Church. Rosina Sacco did not appear. The prosecution was represented by Albert Brouillard and state detectives Fleming and Ferrari.

When Sacco and Vanzetti stepped from the bus they were handcuffed together, and Vanzetti was handcuffed to Deputy Sheriff Caldwell. Both prisoners wore shabby overcoats with velvet collars. Sacco had on a dark suit, a dark necktie, and a felt hat. Vanzetti was wearing a bow tie and a full light-brown cap that seemed to exaggerate the droop of his mustache. They stood for a few minutes by the granite steps, smiling and self-possessed in spite of the guards. At the request of the photographers and newsreel men they took off their hats and faced in various directions. The two men had aged much in six years.

After several minutes they were marched through the iron gate and upstairs. At the door to the courtroom the jail chaplain, William Beal, chatted with them briefly. Just as their handcuffs were being removed before they entered the cage, Mrs. Evans caught their eye and tried to get to her feet. A deputy ordered her to sit down. The quiet in the waiting courtroom was broken only by the ticking of the marble-faced clock. One of the reporters had the feeling that everyone present was holding his breath.

Judge Thayer got out of his car just as the clock of the First Church across Court Street was striking ten. He was wearing a derby, as was the ham-faced state detective who accompanied him, and though he skipped up the steps briskly enough he looked frail. The years, culminating in this moment, had brought about a curious transposition that was sensed by everybody in the waiting room. For it was as if somehow the defendants had become the prosecutors and the judge the defendant. Thayer himself seemed to sense it as he strode into the courtroom, preceded by a deputy and Clerk Worthington's warning cry. He sat down, smoothed his gown, but did not look at the men in the cage thirty feet in front of him. The preliminaries were so brief that they were over before they could make an impression. District Attorney Wilbar in an almost inaudible voice asked that sentence now be imposed on the two defendants convicted of murder in the first degree, the sentence to be executed during the week of July 10. Clerk Worthington then asked: "Nicola Sacco, have you anything to say why sentence of death should not be passed on you?"

Sacco stood up, stared at Judge Thayer, then began slowly to speak:

"Yes, sir. I am not an orator. It is not very familiar with me the English language, and as I know, as my friend has told me, my comrade Vanzetti will speak more long, so I thought to give him the chance."

After the halting beginning his words began to flow more freely as he felt himself stirred by the impassioned moment. He held a small piece of paper in one hand, and every now and then he slapped the railing of the cage with the other.

"I never know, never heard, even read in history anything so cruel as this Court. After seven years prosecuting they still consider us guilty. And these gentle people are arrayed with us in this court today.

"I know the sentence will be between two class, the oppressed class and the rich class, and there will be always collision between one and the other. We fraternize the people with the books, with the literature. You persecute the people, tyrannize over them and kill them. We try the education of people always. You try to put a path between us and some other nationality that hates each other. That is why I am here today on this bench, for having been the oppressed class. Well, you are the oppressor.

"You know it, Judge Thayer—you know all my life, you know why I have been here, and after seven years that you have been persecuting me and my poor wife, you still today sentence us to death. I would like to tell all my life, but what is the use? You know all about what I say before, and my friend—that is, my comrade—will be talking, because he is more familiar with the language, and I will give him a chance. My comrade, the man kind, the kind man to all children, you sentence him two times, in the Bridgewater case and the Dedham case, connected with me, and you know he is innocent. You forget all the population that has been with us for seven years, to sympathize and give us all their energy and all their kindness. You do not care for them. Among that peoples and the comrades and the working class there is a big legion of intellectual people which have been with us for seven years, but to not commit the iniquitous sentence, but still the Court goes ahead. And I think I thank you all, you peoples, my comrades who have been with me for seven years, with the Sacco-Vanzetti case, and I will give my friend a chance.

"I forgot one thing which my comrade remember me. As I said before, Judge Thayer know all my life, and he know I am never been guilty, never—not yesterday nor today nor forever."

In five minutes it was over, and for an instant the atmosphere of the courtroom loosened with a rustling and shuffle of feet and a few coughs, then tightened as Clerk Worthington called on Vanzetti.

As he stood up, Vanzetti appeared calm, almost cheerful, and his voice at the beginning was deceptively gentle. He held a few penciled notes.

"Yes. What I say is that I am innocent, not only of the Braintree crime, but also of the Bridgewater crime. That I am not only innocent of these two crimes, but in all my life I have never stole and I have never killed and I have never spilled blood. That is what I want to say. And it is not all. Not only am I innocent of these two crimes, not only in all my life I have never stole, never killed, never spilled blood, but I have struggled all my life, since I began to reason, to eliminate crime from the earth.

"Everybody that knows these two arms knows very well that I did not need to go in between the street and kill a man to take money. I can live with my two arms and live well. . . .

"Now, I should say that I am not only innocent of all these things, not only have I never committed a real crime in all my life—though some sins but not crimes—not only have I struggled all my life to eliminate crimes, the crimes that the official law and the official moral condemns, but also the crime that the official moral and the official law sanctions and sanctifies—the exploitation and the oppression of the man by the man, and if there is a reason why I am here as a guilty man, if there is a reason why you in a few minutes can doom me, it is this reason and none else."

Judge Thayer stared at his bench as if he were unaware of the man addressing him. The judge's impassivity nettled Vanzetti and as he continued his voice showed it. His eyes seemed to flash at the bent figure whom he had once called a black-gowned cobra.

"Is it possible that only a few on the jury, only two or three men, who would condemn their mother for worldly honor and for earthly fortune; is it possible that they are right against what the world, the whole world has say it is wrong and that I know that it is wrong? If there is one that I should know it, if it is right or if it is wrong, it is I and this man. You see it is seven years that we are in jail. What we have suffered during these seven years no human tongue can say, and yet you see me before you, not trembling, you see me looking you in your eyes straight, not blushing, not changing color, not ashamed or in fear.

"Eugene Debs say that not even a dog—something like that— not even a dog that kill chickens would have been found guilty by American jury with the evidence that the Commonwealth have produced against us. I say that not even a leprous dog would have his appeal refused two times by the Supreme Court of Massachusetts —not even a leprous dog. . . .

"We know that you have spoke yourself and have spoke your hostility against us, and your despisement against us with friends of yours on the train, at the University Club of Boston, on the Golf Club of Worcester, Massachusetts. I am sure that if the people who know all what you say against us would have the civil courage to take the stand, maybe your Honor—I am sorry to say this because you are an old man, and I have an old father—but maybe you would be beside us in good justice at this time."

The record of Vanzetti's first trial is incomplete, and though the phrase does not appear in the transcript or in the newspaper accounts, Thayer was said by members of the Defense Committee who were in the courtroom to have instructed the jury that the defendant's beliefs were "cognate with the crime." Vanzetti now threw that in Thayer's face, as well as the fact that his sentence for attempted robbery was double that of other prisoners in Charlestown convicted of actual robbery. At the recollection he struck angrily against the rail of the cage with his notes.

"You know if we would have Mr. Thompson, or even the brother McAnarney in the first trial in Plymouth, you know that no jury would have found me guilty. My first lawyer has been a partner of Mr. Katzmann, as he is still now. My first lawyer of the defense, Mr. Vahey, has not defended me, has sold me for thirty golden money like Judas sold Jesus Christ. If that man has not told to you or to Mr. Katzmann that he know I was guilty, it is because he know that I was not guilty. That man has done everything indirectly to hurt us. He has made long speech with the jury about things that do matter nothing, and on the point of essence to the trial he has passed over with few words or with complete silence. This was a premeditation in order to give the jury the impression that my own defender has nothing good to say, has nothing good to urge in defense of myself, and therefore go around the bush on little things that amount to nothing and let pass the essential points either in silence or with a very weakly resistance.

"We were tried during a time that has now passed into history. I mean by that, a time when there was a hysteria of resentment and hate against the people of our principles, against the foreigner, against slackers, and it seems to me—rather, I am positive of it, that both you and Mr. Katzmann has done all what it were in your power in order to work out, in order to agitate still more the passion of the juror, the prejudice of the juror, against us. . . . But the jury were hating us because we were against the war, and the jury don't know that it makes any difference between a man that is against the war because he believes that the war is unjust, because he hate no country, because he is a cosmopolitan, and a man that is against the war because he is in favor of the other country that fights against the country in which he is, and therefore a spy, and he commits any crime in the country in which he is in behalf of the other country in order to serve the other country. We are not men of that kind. Katzmann know very well that. Katzmann know that we were against the war because we did not believe in the purpose for which they say that the war was done. We believe it that the war is wrong, and we believe this more now after ten years that we understood it day by day—the consequences and the result of the after war. We believe more now than ever that the war was wrong, and we are against war more now than ever, and I am glad to be on the doomed scaffold if I can say to mankind: 'Look out; you are in a catacomb of the flower of mankind. For what? All that they say to you, all that they have promised to you—it was a lie, it was an illusion, it was a cheat, it was a fraud, it was a crime. They promised you liberty. Where is liberty? They promised you prosperity. Where is prosperity? They have promised you elevation. Where is elevation?' "

He accused Katzmann of breaking the agreement not to mention the Plymouth trial, he accused the Commonwealth of being more responsible than the defense for the delays, he accused Thayer of deliberately handing down his denial of a new trial motion on Christmas Eve "to poison the heart of our family and of our beloved," for even though they did not believe in "the fable of the evening of Christmas," nevertheless "we are human, and Christmas is sweet to the heart of every man."

The marble-faced clock had ticked off forty minutes. Vanzetti disregarded his notes now. In his long-deliberated conclusion he had no need of them. His deep-set eyes took on the searing quality that Chief Stewart had remarked on seven years before.

"Well, I have already say that I not only am not guilty of these two crimes, but I never commit a crime in my life—I have never steal and I have never kill and I have never spilt blood, and I have fought against the crime, and I have fought and I have sacrificed myself even to eliminate the crimes that the law and the church legitimate and sanctify.

"This is what I say: I would not wish to a dog or to a snake, to the most low and misfortunate creature of the earth—I would not wish to any of them what I have had to suffer for things that I am not guilty of. But my conviction is that I have suffered for things I am guilty of. I am suffering because I am a radical and indeed I am a radical; I have suffered because I was an Italian, and indeed I am an Italian; I have suffered more for my family and for my beloved than for myself; but I am so convinced to be right that if you could execute me two times, and if I could be reborn again two other times, I would live again to do what I have done already.

"I have finished. Thank you."

He stood there, a spare, slightly stooped figure, his face pale behind the screen of the swooping mustache, eyes still glittering with suppressed emotion. Judge Thayer's precise arctic voice broke the silence, moving on in a few phrases to the sentencing. There was a hushed tenseness as everyone leaned forward to catch the ritual words:

"First the Court pronounces sentence of Nicola Sacco. It is considered and ordered by the Court that you, Nicola Sacco, suffer the punishment of death by the passage of a current of electricity through your body within the week beginning on Sunday, the tenth day of July, in the year of our Lord, one thousand nine hundred and twenty-seven."

Except for Thayer's voice there was only the muffled sound of a few women sobbing.

"It is considered and ordered by the Court that you, Bartolomeo Vanzetti—"

Vanzetti's interrupting voice was like a stone shattering thin ice. "Wait a minute, please, your Honor," he called out. "May I speak with my lawyer, Mr. Thompson?"

Thompson, within the bar enclosure, was so taken aback that all he could do was to mutter to the court, "I do not know what he wants to say."

Judge Thayer brushed aside the interruption. "I think I should pronounce the sentence. Bartolomeo Vanzetti, suffer the punishment of death—"

Sacco broke in, shrill and furious, and as he stood he stretched his arm and pointed at Judge Thayer. "You know I am innocent!" he shouted, his facial muscles bunched in fury. "That is the same words I pronounced seven years ago! You condemn two innocent men!"

For a moment it seemed as if the long sustained decorum of the neoclassic room was dissolving, but Thayer's impervious voice continued with the regularity of the ticking clock—"by the passage of a current of electricity through your body within the week beginning on Sunday, the tenth day of July, in the year of our Lord, one thousand nine hundred and twenty-seven. This is the sentence of the law." He paused, gathering his gown about him in a preliminary gesture before he announced: "We will now take a recess." Without a glance at the men he had sentenced he stood up and walked slowly down from the bench and out into the corridor that led to his chambers.

As Sacco and Vanzetti were again being handcuffed, their friends, Italian and American, crowded round them trying to touch them, to clasp their hands. Mrs. Evans hobbled up close enough to call out cheerfully, "There's lots to hope for yet." There were tears in Vanzetti's eyes. Mary Donovan pushed forward, her cheeks wet. "Do not cry, Mary," he told her. "Keep a brave front." Then the guards and deputies intervened.

Vanzetti, brooding in his cell, thought less of the sentence than of the words he had not been allowed to speak. Next day, with the eloquence of death on him, he wrote out his eulogy of Sacco, telling Thompson that it was "the most important thing" he had to say, and that "I would have given half my blood to be allowed to speak again."

I have talk a great deal of myself but I even forgot to name Sacco. Sacco too is a worker from his boyhood, a skilled worker, lover of work, with a good job and pay, a bank account, a good and lovely wife, two beautiful children and a neat little home at the verge of a wood, near a brook. Sacco is a heart, a faith, a character, a man; a man lover of nature and of mankind. A man who gave all, who sacrifice all to the cause of Liberty, and to his love for mankind; money, rest, mundain ambitions, his own wife, his children, himself and his own life. Sacco has never dreamt to steal, never to assassinate. He and I have never brought a morsel of bread to our mouths, from our childhood to today—which has not been gained by the sweat of our brows. Never. His people also are in good position and of good reputation.

Oh yes, I may be more witfull as some have put it. I am a better babbler than he is, but many, many times in hearing his heartful voice ringing a faith sublime, in considering his supreme sacrifice, re-membering his heroism I felt small, small at the presence of his great-ness and found myself compelled to fight back from my eyes the tears, and quanch my heart trobling to my throat to not weep before him—this man called thief and assasin and doomed. But Sacco's name will live in the hearts of the people and in their gratitude when Katzmann's and yours bones will be dispersed by time, when your name, his name, your laws, institutions, and your false god are but a deem rememoring of a cursed past in which man was wolf to the man.

Over the week end Thompson told reporters that he felt Sacco and Vanzetti could derive no benefit from further proceedings in the Massachusetts courts, and that he was not prepared to take steps designed merely to delay their execution. Moore would have acted very differently, would in fact have taken any steps, scrupulous or otherwise, and two at a time, that he thought might prolong the men's lives. But to Moore justice was a class shell game that he was ready to operate as trickily as his opponents. "At least I have kept them alive," he was able to say as he left Boston. Thompson still kept his faith in the traditional impartiality of the law. He would not play tricks with it.

Anticipating the adverse decision of April 5, Thompson, a few days earlier, accompanied by John Moors, Dr. Morton Prince, and Professor Frank Taussig, had called on the Episcopal Bishop of Massachusetts, William Lawrence, to ask his help in persuading Governor Fuller to appoint a commission to review the whole proceedings. It struck none of these Boston-bred men as strange to turn to a bishop in a matter of law. On the contrary, it seemed to them the most obvious step to take, for during a third of a century the voice of Bishop Lawrence had become the ethical voice of Massachusetts.

Bishop Lawrence combined uniquely in his person the dominant strands of the community. Descended from the founders of the Bay Colony, he could walk through Boston along streets named for his ancestors. As successor to Phillips Brooks, who had preached before Queen Victoria, he concluded the reconciliation of upper-class Boston to Episcopalianism after the disestablishment of the Revolution. His income came from the textile industry that his relatives the Lawrences, the Lowells, and the Abbotts had established. Though he was a second-generation Episcopalian, the blood of ancestral Calvinism still coursed in his veins. By and large, he observed to his acquaintances, it had been his experience that the more godly members of the community were the more financially successful. As a young curate in industrial Lawrence he would cheerfully give up an afternoon to visit a crippled spinner of his congregation, yet not think it strange that the man was earning eighty cents a day. As a bishop and member of the Corporation of Harvard University he would undertake to raise five million dollars for the new Harvard Business School and also not think it strange.

A stocky man with a glowing face, Bishop Lawrence looked a cherubic Puritan. He eschewed rings, miter and crozier, pectoral crosses, black suits, and clerical collars, preferring English tweeds and gray felt hats. He received Thompson's delegation, representative of the law, medicine, State Street, and the academy, as a matter of course. He knew at once what his duty was.

Sent to Governor [*he noted in his diary*] *a letter saying that in Sacco-Vanzetti sentence thousands of citizens felt that they had not had a fair trial and asking the Governor to call leading and trusted men to his advice.*

As both the sender and the recipient were aware, the letter, dated April 11, was more nearly a command:

Your Excellency,—

Two men, having been tried by the Courts of Massachusetts for murder, have now been sentenced to death. Upon you falls the heavy and responsible duty of carrying out the sentence unless you are moved to take other action. Confidence in the Courts of Massachusetts, which has justified itself for generations, leads its citizens to assume the sentence given is just and should be carried out.

There are, however, we believe, thousands of citizens of the Commonwealth who, having read or studied such parts of the proceedings in the Superior Court as have appeared in the public press, have serious doubts as to whether these two men have had a fair trial.

They were, as the law requires, tried by a judge and jury and found guilty. Motions for a new trial on grounds of newly discovered evidence were heard by the same judge and denied. Exceptions on points of law were taken to the Supreme Court and unanimously overruled. But the Supreme Court could not under our law reconsider and revise the findings of fact of the trial court or the exercise of the trial judge's discretion. Hence have arisen the doubts of the citizens for whom we venture to speak.

Knowing well your sense of justice, your integrity of purpose, and your courage when assured of the rightness of your position, we ask with great earnestness that you call to your aid several citizens of well known character, experience, ability, and sense of justice to make a study of the trial and advise you. We believe that it is due to the exceptional conditions of the case, to yourself, and to the State that these doubts be allayed and that it be made evident to all citizens that the Commonwealth has done full justice to herself as well as to these men, and also that you may have strong and intelligent support in whatever decision you may make.

Rt. Rev. William A. Lawrence

Additional signatures were superfluous. Nevertheless, as if to underline his position, the Bishop took care to have his letter signed by three most proper Bostonians—fellow Harvard Corporation member Charles Curtis, Jr.; Heman Burr, as well known in the city as a lawyer and financier as he was unknown elsewhere; and Roland Boyden of Ropes, Gray, Boyden and Perkins, a law firm whose name was said to have such magic force that it was seldom mentioned; one only thought it.

The letter was not immediately made public. Meanwhile, on April 12, Representative Roland Sawyer, a Congregational minister who for fourteen years had represented Ware and several other small western Massachusetts towns in the state legislature, drew up a resolution which he presented in the House of Representatives to provide for a special commission "to examine and review the proceedings of the Commonwealth against Nicola Sacco and Bartolomeo Vanzetti." Sawyer realized that the measure had no chance of passing but he felt that a public hearing on it would be the informal equivalent of a trial, and that additional evidence there presented would undermine the prosecution's case to such an extent that it would make the carrying out of the death sentences impossible. Thompson favored Sawyer's plan, but Frankfurter, after meeting with the Defense Committee in a downtown law office, decided against it. He told Sawyer that he had confidence in Fuller. Sawyer's resolution was rejected in the legislature by a rising vote of 146–6.

The next move was Governor Fuller's. He who a few weeks before had announced that he had not formed an opinion had now become the court of last appeal. In a few more weeks a stroke of his pen would have to decide whether it would be freedom for the two men, commutation of their sentences to life imprisonment, or death. To Thompson, who visited him privately, he announced that he could make no investigation unless he was requested to do so by Sacco and Vanzetti. Thompson promised to see that such a request was made.

The written and telegraphed appeals, requests, and suggestions now reaching the governor by the hundreds were signed with such nationally known names as Rabbi Stephen Wise, novelist Gertrude Atherton, President Emeritus David Starr Jordan of Stanford University, and biographer Ida Tarbell. A Massachusetts communication was signed by author and doctor Richard Cabot; John Hays Hammond, the North Shore millionaire industrialist; Harvard philosopher William Ernest Hocking; Harvard teacher and essayist Bliss Perry; and historians Samuel Eliot Morison and Arthur Schlesinger. The name of Dean Pound of the Harvard Law School headed a petition signed by Francis Sayre, the son-in-law of Woodrow Wilson.

The tone of most of these appeals was conciliatory, not to say flattering. That most tirelessly—some thought tiresomely—liberal of clergymen, John Haynes Holmes of New York's Community Church, expressed his strong faith in Governor Fuller's fairness. Fiorello La Guardia, who had served with Fuller in Congress, wrote optimistically to the New York *World* that the governor was "free from bigotry and prejudice and will investigate fairly and fully." The *Nation* believed, in an open letter, that the governor would fearlessly face the great issue that had aroused not only masses of Americans but millions all over the world. Only the Communists, seeing no advantage from their point of view in conciliating anybody, kept up a counterpoint of invective, the *Daily Worker* denouncing Fuller as "that toothless troglodyte and flunky of the mill owners."

Cardinal O'Connell, as urbane and adept a weigher of words as could be found in the Commonwealth, suggested an investigating commission indirectly when he urged that the governor reach his decision "by making use of every human aid that he can possibly gather." Fuller himself, in an unexpected interview with Joseph Lilly of the Brooklyn *Eagle*, said that he did not know whether to appoint a commission or go over the case himself.

There were rumors that Charles Evans Hughes would soon head a Sacco-Vanzetti commission, then contrary rumors that there would be no commission after all. The *Transcript* continued to denounce the substitution of "public opinion in place of judicial conclusions." Nine out of ten of the city's lawyers were agreed that when the courts had spoken, contrary voices should become mute. Robert Goodwin and Joseph Proctor, Jr., of the august firm of Goodwin, Proctor, Field and Hoar, felt it their civic duty to try to offset the unaccountable aberration of Ropes, Gray, Boyden and Perkins by declaring that for Fuller to appoint a fact-finding commission would be an abdication of the powers of his office.

Although the Massachusetts Supreme Court could not reply directly to its critics, it managed to find a semiofficial defense in the pamphlet "Sacco and Vanzetti in the Scales of Justice," written and published by its Reporter of Decisions, Ethelbert Vincent Grabill. For the reporter, the Massachusetts legal structure was a parthenon inherited from the Puritans, and he claimed that he had been moved by the spirit of his ancestors to attempt to "bring a wandering citizenry back to confidence in our courts, in their proceedings, and in our Governor, and fortify and strengthen those who have not wandered." Grabill was untroubled by the proceedings at Dedham. For him it was "doubtful if Judge Thayer's charge was ever equalled for clearness, completeness and fairness." He considered it presumptuous for anyone to ask the governor to appoint a review commission, and complained that "having persons passing around . . . petitions on the subject tends to stir up opposition to our Constitution and laws."

Not until two weeks after the sentencing did Fuller finally ask District Attorney Ranney for the Sacco-Vanzetti records. On May 4 Thompson brought the governor a formal petition in which Vanzetti asked to be set free from his sentence. Carefully Vanzetti avoided the word *pardon* with its connotation of admitted guilt; he emphasized that he was asking for justice, not mercy. He pointed out to the governor that it would be unlikely for robbers to linger near the scene of a crime "in order to address public meetings in behalf of persecuted radicals." Beyond this, the lengthy presentation was mostly a recapitulation of points that had been made in the various motions—Proctor's equivocations, the dubious character of the chief witnesses, Judge Thayer's prejudice, and the issue of radicalism.

The petition came from Vanzetti alone. True to his resolve to take no further part in the defense, Sacco refused to sign it. As a result, he was again examined to determine whether he should be considered mentally responsible. Dr. Abraham Meyerson, who conducted the examination, reported that:

There is no question that the seven years of his incarceration, mainly without employment and entirely preoccupied by his situation, have helped bring about an abnormal state in which his fanaticism has been intensified to an obsession. Though he is not insane, his inaccessibility to all reasoning and his emotional reactions are pathological. His mind has lost the flexibility which enables a man to adjust normally to situations.

Governor Fuller received the petition without comment. On May 8 he tripped going upstairs and tore a tendon in his left leg. While he was confined to his Beacon Street house, reporters noted that among his visitors were the McAnarney brothers and ex-District Attorney Katzmann.

The first real inkling of what was going on behind the wrought iron gates of 150 Beacon Street was provided on May 12 when Will Rogers, the gum-chewing lariat-swinging comedian-philosopher, appeared in Boston for a one-night benefit at the Opera House. Before the performance he had visited Governor Fuller. "I don't know anything about this murder case that is interesting you in Massachusetts," Rogers told his Opera House audience, "but I want to tell you that your governor is working on it. I stopped in on my way here to sit with him for a few moments and I found him in his room with crutches by his side. He had three or four pistols, and he had a big pile of books, the record of the case, and he is working away at it. I don't know what he is going to decide, of course, but I do know that he isn't going to be skeered into deciding it, and I do know that when he makes his decision, it's going to be a decision he believes right down through him. He's terribly anxious about it, but he is going to get all the facts."

It was clear at last that Governor Fuller was going to do his own investigating. Day after day now the newspapers recorded the appearance of witnesses old and new, first at 150 Beacon Street and then at the executive chambers in the State House. Through the late spring weeks the governor interviewed the eleven surviving Dedham jurors and the twelve from Plymouth, Judge Thayer, and as many of the original witnesses as could be located, as well as the "suppressed" witness, Roy Gould. One day it was observed that he took Beltrando Brini to lunch. Another day he spent several hours with Lola Andrews' son, now Corporal Hassam of the U.S. Marine Corps. Assisting him were his sharp, bald, thin-lipped private counsel, Joseph Wiggin, his confidential secretary, Herman MacDonald, and Lieutenant Governor Frank Allen. Reporters could get no information from the gruff MacDonald, whose function was to act as a buffer between the governor and the external world. This function he exercised with a gusto that earned him the nickname of Hard-boiled Herman and the dislike of newspapermen and State House employees generally.

When the Defense Committee protested against the secrecy of the governor's hearings, Fuller began consulting with Thompson and Ehrmann. He refused, however, to allow representatives of the defense to confront witnesses in his presence.

Vanzetti was convinced that the governor must have had him and Sacco in mind when he wrote his article "Why I Believe in Capital Punishment," for the December 1926 issue of *Success Magazine*. He wrote Mrs. Evans not "to expect that Fuller will stand against the judiciary, the middle class, the big money in behalf of two damned dagos and anarchists."

Nevertheless, as the weeks wore away with their succession of witnesses, Fuller appeared uneasy and uncertain. Robert Lincoln O'Brien, sitting next to him at a Boston University commencement dinner, hesitantly brought up the subject of Sacco and Vanzetti. Far from objecting, Fuller seemed eager to talk about it. He said he felt it was abhorrent that one man should have the decision in a capital case, that O'Brien would be surprised at the way much of the trial testimony had collapsed. According to O'Brien's later account, Fuller then told him he was going to settle the case in such a way that he could live with his conscience.

As in Elizabethan tragic drama, there now occurred a clown's interlude, furnished by Edward Holton James, the bearded pipe-smoking son of William and Henry James' black-sheep alcoholic brother, Robertson. James was a dilettante with a town house on Mount Vernon Street and a country estate in Concord that had two houses, one for his wife and one for himself, where he built and repaired musical instruments. He described himself variously as a musician and as a lawyer—though whether he practiced either law or the violin was questionable. "The millionaire pacifist," as the newspapers tagged him, had written a shrill pamphlet on the Sacco-Vanzetti case, a counterblast to Grabill's effort, in which he announced:

You had a crazy judge and jury in Plymouth. You had the same crazy judge with another crazy jury in Dedham. You had a crazy Supreme Court of Massachusetts, sitting in the Court House in Boston, saying it was all right. The whole lot of them ought to be sitting in the insane asylum.

On April 15 James drove to South Braintree to re-enact the crime and demonstrate the innocence of Sacco and Vanzetti. He had planned to recruit his cast from members of the Harvard Liberal Club but at the last minute found himself speeding through the Blue Hills with only a solitary lawyer friend, Abraham Wirin, to play a bandit's part. At South Braintree their efforts to pick up local volunteer actors drew a blank, and Thomas Fraher, the Slater & Morrill superintendent, refused to let them into the factory. They glimpsed a moment of martyrdom when the chairman of the board of selectmen, Edward Avery, tried to stop their two-man show, but the new police chief, John Heaney, waved Avery back and told them to go ahead. A few days later James returned alone to make some pencil sketches and this time, while heads gawked from all the factory windows, Avery gave him fifteen minutes to leave town. After telling Avery to go to hell, James at last had the satisfaction of being arrested and charged with disturbing the peace. He left twenty dollars as bail money—which he later forfeited—and returned triumphantly to Boston in time for lunch.

The pigmy sparrings of Grabill and James were succeeded by a battle of giants when on April 25 Dean John Wigmore of the Northwestern University Law School commandeered the front page of the *Transcript* to answer Frankfurter's *Atlantic* article. Wigmore was one of the great scholars of his day, and his monumental treatise *The Law of Evidence* remains one of the classics of Anglo-American law. A Harvard graduate of the class of 1883, he was furious that Frankfurter should have so influenced intellectual and university opinion. He did not once mention Frankfurter by name but referred to him with surly pedantry as the "plausible pundit."

"To vindicate Massachusetts Justice, I crave the opportunity of your pages to address the lawyers of the Commonwealth," he wrote the *Transcript*, and that paper obliged by giving his article the largest headlines since those announcing the 1918 armistice. Calling the Frankfurter article "neither fair nor accurate nor complete," Wigmore protested that the "insinuation of a 'picked' jury was baseless and worthy only of unscrupulous yellow journalism." He drummed on the fact that it was the defendants who had first brought up the subject of radicalism at the trial, asked why Frankfurter had not mentioned Sacco's cap, accused him of saying nothing about the passport found on Sacco's person the night of his arrest, proof in itself that the latter did not need to lie from fear of deportation. He asserted that if the Supreme Court had had any doubts of the defendants' guilt it would have been "astute enough to lay hold of some point of pure law as a ground for ordering a new trial," and pointed out that the defense at the time had taken no exception to Judge Thayer's charge. Finally, he set off a series of rhetorical questions that streaked like red rockets across the *Transcript*'s staid pages:

Is Massachusetts subject to dictates of international terrorists? Where has the like ever been known in modern history? The thugs of India, the Camorra of Naples, the Black Hand of Sicily, the anarchists of czardom—when did their attempts to impose their will by violence ever equal in range of operations and vicious directness, the organized efficiency of this cabal to which Sacco and Vanzetti belong?

Frankfurter received a copy of the *Transcript* in the early afternoon and sat down at once to write his answer. Frank Buxton, the *Herald*'s editor, held up the presses so that his reply could appear in the next morning's edition. In spite of the speed at which he had to write, Frankfurter had the advantages of a controlled temper and a deeper knowledge of the case. With mock mildness he began by suggesting that Wigmore could not have read the record or the opinions of Judge Thayer with care. He pointed out that the prosecution knew all about Sacco's radicalism before the trial began—that the prosecution's excuse for the cross-examination did not hold. In his *Atlantic* article he had challenged Judge Thayer's statement that the Supreme Court had "approved" the verdict. Wigmore having denied that Thayer had used the word, Frankfurter now pointed to the passage where it occurred in the decision on the Madeiros motion. He also showed that Wigmore had accepted as genuine an erroneous passage about Sacco's passport. He admitted not having mentioned Sacco's cap in his article, adding that he had dealt with it in his book.

Two weeks later Wigmore came charging back with another piece for the *Transcript* in which he accused his opponent—this time referred to as the "contra-canonical critic"—of violating Canon 20 of the American Bar Association's Code of Professional Ethics, which condemns "newspaper publication by a lawyer as to pending or anticipated legislation," and of being behind-the-scenes counsel for Sacco and Vanzetti. He had also determined that while Judge Thayer used the word *approved* once, he had on eight other occasions used *affirmed* or some similar neutral word. Insisting that the real issue was whether the trial had been unfair—"a riot of political passion" through the misconduct of the district attorney and the judge— Wigmore held that it had not been. "If the Bar of Massachusetts should take this body-blow lying down," he concluded, "they would deserve to suffer their profession polluted and their bench bolshevized by agitators financed and led as this case has been."

In writing to William Howard Taft some months after the executions, President Lowell of Harvard commented that "Wigmore's ridiculous article looked as if there was nothing serious to be said on the side of the courts."

Frankfurter was not to be drawn out by Wigmore's name-calling. His second reply in the *Herald* was as detached and temperate as before. He observed that Wigmore had answered nothing at all about Judge Thayer's mistaken interpolation about Sacco's passport. And it was still a fact, however Wigmore might feel about it, that Thayer had used the word *approved*. Frankfurter denied that the Massachusetts Supreme Court had the power the Northwestern dean attributed to it, and he concluded with the statement that "in no sense in which lawyers responsibly use the term have I ever been of counsel for Sacco and Vanzetti."

Through May Governor Fuller continued his investigation to the exclusion of all other state business, sometimes spending twelve to fourteen hours a day interviewing witnesses and reading documents. Since the imposition of the death sentences he had received over 17,000 protesting letters and telegrams. Whatever he decided, he knew there would be an uproar. It was too much for one man.

On June 1, when rumor had all but settled the matter the other way, Secretary MacDonald announced that the governor had named a three-man advisory committee to go over all the aspects of the Sacco-Vanzetti case. The three were President Lowell; Robert Grant, a retired probate judge; and President Samuel Stratton of the Massachusetts Institute of Technology.

Several weeks before this appointment Lowell—possibly at the suggestion of his cousin, Bishop Lawrence—had written Fuller to the effect that men with no sympathy for anarchists were troubled by the charges that the Sacco-Vanzetti trial had been unfair and the verdict unwarranted by the evidence. But even if the president of Harvard had not so written, he would have seemed to the governor the logical first choice for any such committee. Lowell incarnated to Fuller what he most admired: status, family, academic learning, inherited assurance—the things his Packard money could not buy.

Abbott Lawrence Lowell—the Massachusetts spindle cities of Lowell and Lawrence were named for his forbears—was the tenth-generation descendant of the Bristol merchant-trader Percival Lowle who in 1639 at the age of sixty-seven had protested against the ship-money tax by sailing for America with his family of fifteen. Second of the two armigerous families in early New England, the Lowells became one of the few truly dynastic families in America. Abbott Lawrence was a worthy if not extraordinarily distinguished member of his clan. Although in his early middle years he had written the solid, pedestrian *The Government of England* and been appointed Professor of the Science of Government at Harvard, without the prestige of his family name he would never have succeeded Charles W. Eliot in 1907 to the presidency of America's oldest university.

He was born in 1856, but his mind was a throwback to a decade earlier than that—before the Irish invasion—when Boston was still a mellow self-contained brick town to which he and his sisters and his cousins and his aunts belonged, and which in turn belonged to them. To Lowell the mass newcomers—the Famine Irish and the later Italians and Jews—were an intrusion on the Athens of America that Boston might have been. Dismayed at the appearance among his undergraduates of increasing numbers of Polish-born Jewish day students, he at one time planned to limit their admission to Harvard to a small fixed quota.

Yet Lowell, whatever the limitations of his outlook and sympathies, inherited a rectitude impervious to external pressures. When, during the Boston police strike of 1919, Harold Laski—then a temporary lecturer in political science at Harvard—spoke out in favor of the strikers, many local Harvard graduates denounced him as a traitor and a Bolshevik and demanded his dismissal. Lowell himself had opposed the policemen and even helped furnish strikebreakers from the undergraduates, but at the hint that the governing boards were considering getting rid of Laski he announced that if they exercised this undoubted legal right his own resignation would immediately and irrevocably follow. In that same year he took the side of United States entry into the League of Nations in a debate at Boston's Symphony Hall with the irreconcilable Henry Cabot Lodge.

When Lowell agreed to serve on Fuller's committee he did so reluctantly. From what he had read of the case in Frankfurter's *Atlantic* article, he told Judge Grant, he rather expected to find that injustice had been done.

Whatever the criticisms that dogged Lowell afterward, he would always feel that he had done his duty. No man would ever be able to accuse him of temporizing with what he thought was right. The only question centered in that qualifying word *thought*. Ferris Greenslet, the well-disposed chronicler of the Lowell generations, remarked that although President Lowell had shown all his life an open mind, "it was perhaps closed at one point only, against any action or consideration tending to show a flaw in the administration of justice in the Commonwealth of Massachusetts." John Moors, Lowell's Harvard classmate, was blunter; he told Frankfurter that Lowell was "incapable of seeing that two wops could be right and the Yankee judiciary wrong."

At the time Lowell acceded to the governor's request he was in his seventy-second year, still briskly vigorous in walk and manner, although his Lowell features had begun to droop. It has been said that people as they grow older tend to resemble their dogs. Lowell, with his paunched and brooding face, seemed more and more to take on the look of the sad-eyed cocker spaniel that was the companion of his walks.

At the outset of the committee deliberations he assumed, as did everyone else except Judge Grant, that his was to be the controlling voice, and indeed the officially designated Governor's Advisory Committee became known almost at once as the Lowell Committee. Each day when the three men returned together to the State House after lunch, Grant and Stratton would head for the basement elevator while Lowell would spring up the forty-one granite steps leading to the porticoed entrance to the executive chambers. By the time the other two arrived they would find him already seated at the head of the table preparing the agenda.

Grant and Lowell had played together as children on Beacon Hill, and Grant for all his self-effacing manner resented the automatic assumption of authority by his younger playmate. Alphabetically his name had come first on the governor's list and he had, he felt, more right than Abbott Lawrence to head the committee even if the latter had suggested his name to the governor. For thirty years Grant had been Judge of the Suffolk Court of Probate and Insolvency. From the cut of his mustache to the cut of his voice he was a wispy man, with shoe-button eyes and an English accent once removed, part of the genteel desiccated Boston that after its brief literary flowering had been withering away for two generations under the cloud of immigrants. A light versifier and wit, in hours filched from his not-too-arduous judicial duties he had written unreadable novels about Boston that were at one time much read in the city. In 1908, while he was traveling in Italy, some of his luggage was stolen, whereupon he sent outraged appeals not only to the American ambassador but to the State Department in Washington; several years later in his autobiographical *The Convictions of a Grandfather* he was still spluttering about Italian thievery. Before accepting his place on the committee he did have the common sense to ask Fuller what he would do if he got a divided report. The governor replied that he would then consider that there was ground for doubt.

Stratton, chosen by Fuller at Lowell's suggestion so that the committee would not seem too much of a Back Bay family affair, was an Illinois farm boy who had made himself into a mathematician, physicist, and engineer. As president of one of the country's great scientific schools he inhabited a Cambridge divorced from the old literary associations. It was predicted that he would be of great help in evaluating the ballistics evidence and other technical points. So far as can be determined he never opened his mouth during the sixteen days that the committee met.

When it turned to the ballistics evidence, the Lowell Committee was undoubtedly greatly influenced by the findings of Major Calvin Goddard, a New York expert who came to Boston at the end of May on his own initiative, bringing with him a comparison microscope and offering to make what he maintained would be conclusive tests on the shells and bullets offered in evidence at Dedham. He was accompanied by William Crawford, a reporter from the New York *World*, who called on Thompson to ask if he would cooperate in the holding of the tests. Resentful of Crawford's contemptuous remarks about Dr. Hamilton, Thompson declined but said he would put no obstacles in Goddard's way. Ranney, for the district attorney's office, had no objections.

When, in preparation, Goddard demonstrated his double-image microscope to Hamilton's supporting expert, Professor Gill, the latter was so taken with "the simplicity and accuracy of its findings" that he not only recommended its use to the governor but announced that he himself would abide by the results.

With Gill, Ranney, and Ehrmann present, as well as a stenographer and Frank Buxton and Thomas Carens of the *Herald*, Goddard examined the evidence in the clerk of courts' office at Dedham on the afternoon of June 3. Comparing Bullet III with a test bullet fired from Sacco's pistol, he suggested that Gill make the same comparison. "Well, what do you know about that?" Gill muttered to himself as he looked into the microscope. Goddard's conclusion was that the mortal bullet taken from Berardelli's body had been fired through Sacco's pistol and could have been fired through no other. Gill, too, now became convinced of this, despite his earlier findings to the contrary. Ehrmann, examining the identifying scratches on the base of Bullet III, remarked that they were irregular and almost indecipherable compared with the scratches on Bullets I, II, and IV.

Looking at the shells through his microscope, Goddard concluded that Shell W had been fired in Sacco's pistol and could have been fired in no other. Ehrmann, Buxton, and Carens did not find the comparison of the shells conclusive.

Soon after these tests, Gill told Thompson that he now doubted his original findings and wished to sever all connection with the case. His disavowal was followed by one from James Burns, another of the defense experts, who had recently become convinced, after studying certain microphotographs made earlier for Captain Van Amburgh, that the Fraher shell had been fired in Sacco's gun.

Goddard's report was forwarded without comment to Governor Fuller and to the Lowell Committee. Goddard claimed afterward that his tests would have been even more satisfactory if a sticky substance coating the bullets could have been removed. Ranney had been willing to have the bullets cleaned but Thompson refused to approve of this under any circumstances, adding that he believed there had been trickery and that the prosecution had made a substitution of bullets and shells among the exhibits. Goddard in turn said he had no opinion as to the genuineness of the exhibits, although he agreed that the scratches on Bullet III were less clear than on the others.

Before leaving Boston, in a deflating interview with Thompson, Goddard admitted that he had come to town with an adverse opinion about Sacco already formed, the result of studying Van Amburgh's microphotographs. When he went on to express doubts about Hamilton, Thompson produced a letter that the aspiring Goddard had written the druggist-expert in 1924, asking his advice about starting a career in ballistics identification. Goddard's reply was that he knew more about Hamilton now than he had known in 1924, and the interview ended with Thompson angrily defending Hamilton as a man of honor.

The uncertainty that eventually clouded the reputations of all the ballistics experts in the case enveloped Goddard three months after he left Boston. In Cleveland, several weeks after a bootlegger, Ernest Yorkell, was shot to death, the police arrested a Frank Milazzo with a revolver in his possession similar to the murder weapon. Two bullets from Yorkell's body and several test bullets from Milazzo's gun were submitted to Major Goddard in New York. When Goddard reported that one of the murder bullets and one of the test bullets had been fired from the same gun, Milazzo was charged with the murder. Unfortunately for Major Goddard, though not for his comparison microscope, Milazzo was able to prove that he had bought the revolver new a month after the shooting. Goddard attributed his mistake to a bullet mixup by the Cleveland police. Although it was never determined whether the fault was his, he had apparently compared the two murder bullets.

In the unconfessed course of events, Madeiros, following his second trial, would have been electrocuted during the week of September

5, 1926, but the motion and appeal based on his confession brought him a series of reprieves. Not until late in Governor Fuller's Sacco-Vanzetti investigation did he see Madeiros personally and then for only fifteen minutes.

In his testimony to me [the governor reported] he could not recall the details or describe the neighborhood. He furthermore stated that the Government had double crossed him and he proposed to double cross the Government. He feels that the District Attorney's office has treated him unfairly because his two confederates who were associated with him in the commission of the murder for which he was convicted were given life sentences, whereas he was sentenced to death. He confessed the crime for which he was convicted. I am not impressed with his knowledge of the South Braintree murders.

Madeiros gave a different interpretation of the interview to Thompson when the lawyer next visited him. Over a year later in connection with another case Thompson related on the witness stand what Madeiros had told him:

"Madeiros said that Governor Fuller began the interview by saying that he understood that Madeiros said that he thought he had been given—I think the expression was, 'a raw deal,' or something indicating double-dealing or improper dealing by the Government, and that Madeiros said that Officer Ferrari of the State Police had given him a promise of second-degree murder if he confessed the murder. . . . The Governor said if he was satisfied that any such promise had been made he would do something for Madeiros. The Governor then said, before waiting for any reply from Madeiros, according to Madeiros' statement to me, 'You do not know anything about the Sacco-Vanzetti case, do you?' And Madeiros said he did, and the Governor asked him if he was in the car with the other men who committed the murder in South Braintree, the South Braintree murder, and Madeiros said that he was, and the Governor then said, 'So you are a double murderer; I will do nothing for you.' "

Fuller unquestionably said something of the kind to Madeiros, although the meaning remains double-edged. Defenders of Sacco and Vanzetti have interpreted it as an offer to trade Madeiros a commutation for a recantation of his South Braintree confession. Others have maintained that the governor would not have been foolish enough to risk his reputation by making any such offer to an admitted liar like Madeiros.

But there is still another possible explanation. From the governor's attitude to the later witnesses appearing at his investigation, it seems fairly certain that at this stage he had come to believe Sacco and Vanzetti were guilty. And if he felt they were guilty, Madeiros' confession could only have seemed a fraud. When Fuller talked with Madeiros and the latter still stuck to his story, the governor might well have snapped back that he would do nothing for him. If so, it was a remark spoken in anger rather than a premeditated offer.

CHAPTER EIGHTEEN

◇◇◇◇◇◇◇◇◇◇◇◇◇◇◇◇◇◇◇◇◇◇◇◇◇◇◇◇◇◇◇◇◇

The Public and
the Lowell Committee

Not only in Europe but around the world—in Shanghai, Tokyo, Melbourne, Calcutta, Buenos Aires—the names Sacco and Vanzetti were by now familiar syllables and the image had become fixed of two dissenters from the American way of life being done to death for their dissent. Where scores and then hundreds had demonstrated in isolated groups, now in the approaching climax thousands thronged to vast and passionate assemblies that somehow, the participants felt, by their very vastness and passion might force the Massachusetts executioners to stay their hands. There was a fierce joy, too, in such protests, a tensing of muscles, a sense of unity and a feeling among the urban masses that in their increasingly turbulent protests against the fate of Sacco and Vanzetti they were protesting against their own isolation and their own fate.

To Continental intellectuals disillusioned by the collapse of Wilsonian idealism, the Sacco-Vanzetti case was one more devastating example from postwar America, to be set beside Prohibition, Chicago gangsters, the white-sheeted Ku Klux Klan, and the Tennessee monkey trial. The fate of the two men was what one might expect from the heartless materialism of the transatlantic republic that had won a war with its money and the blood of others and now wanted the money back.

In July, Mussolini wrote to the American ambassador in Rome "not as the head of the Italian Government but as a man who is sincerely your friend," asking for a commutation of sentence as an

380

"act of humanity so much more noble as it is less delayed." Shrewdly the Duce pointed out that

> The agitation of the elements of the left throughout the world is increasing in intensity, in these last days, as is shown by the bombs thrown in Buenos Aires against the Ford establishment and the statue of Washington.
>
> Now if the act of clemency is held back still longer it may give the impression that the American authority may have yielded to the pressure of this world-wide subversive activity and this impression can injure the prestige of the United States.
>
> I hope that His Excellency Governor Fuller may give an example of humanity. The example will brilliantly demonstrate the difference between the methods of Bolshevism and those of the great American republic as well as strike from the hands of the subversive elements an instrument of agitation.

In the last pitched months conservatives determined to show that they, no less than the radicals, were concerned with human rights as exemplified by the fate of the two Italians. The royalist *Action Française* now protested the course of Massachusetts justice in as shrill a tone as the Communist *L'Humanité*. The conservative *Frankfurter Zeitung* spoke out with the vehemence of the liberal *Berliner Tageblatt*. Even the shadowy Alfred Dreyfus emerged from his seclusion to announce that he was willing to go to America to plead for Sacco and Vanzetti.

Communist propaganda continued, bizarre and embracing. The day after Judge Thayer pronounced sentence, *Pravda*—remembering Edgar Allan Poe but apparently confusing Charlestown with Charleston —reported that Sacco and Vanzetti had been held for several years in a torture prison in South Carolina where they had been confined "in a specially constructed padded room having a mirrored ceiling on which appeared at intervals a spot which gradually took the form of a terrifying open-jawed creature. Meanwhile, a human voice shouted: 'Tell the names of your accomplices!' "

H. G. Wells, after reading Frankfurter's *Atlantic* article, became so indignant that he proposed the word *Thayerism* to describe "the self-righteous unrighteousness of established people." Millions read his angry statement in the London *Sunday Express* for June 5, 1927:

> I do not see how any clear-headed man, after reading the professor's summary, can have any other conviction than that Sacco

and Vanzetti are as innocent of the Braintree murder, for which they are now awaiting death, as Julius Caesar, or—a better name in this connection—Karl Marx.

Within the United States Italians generally were behind the two prisoners because they were *paesani*. Their anarchism did not matter. The same North Enders who first came to support the Defense Committee would a few years later support Mussolini's African campaign and fill the windows of Hanover Street shops with photographs of Ethiopian atrocities. Other foreign groups, like the Jewish enclaves in New York and Boston, would find themselves drawn sympathetically to the defense of Sacco and Vanzetti out of their socialist tradition and their own bitter experiences of race hate.

American union members never came to identify themselves with the cause of Sacco and Vanzetti as did their counterparts in Europe. Moore had had enough contacts to engineer resolutions asking for a new trial through the American Federation of Labor conventions of 1922 and 1924, but such resolutions would not be presented again until the winter of 1926–1927. In the last months of the case President William Green of the American Federation of Labor added his protest against the impending executions, but in the Indian summer of the Coolidge prosperity the rank and file union members were at best lethargically sympathetic. When, the week before the execution of Sacco and Vanzetti, the Defense Committee sent out an appeal for a hundred thousand trade-union members to come to Boston in protest, less than two hundred showed up. Elsewhere than in the big cities with their heavy foreign populations the American worker was not class-conscious enough to see Sacco and Vanzetti as his representatives. He found the erotic enticements of the New York trial of Ruth Snyder, a suburban housewife, and her corset-salesman lover Henry Judd Gray for the murder of Ruth's husband more enticing than the brief final scene in the Dedham courtroom. He took Lindbergh's solo flight across the Atlantic on May 20, 1927, much more to heart than the erosive progress of Sacco and Vanzetti toward the electric chair. He was more concerned with the second Dempsey-Tunney fight, scheduled for September, than with the Massachusetts executions scheduled for July.

In the six years since John Codman, Mrs. Evans, Mrs. Jack, and other members of the New England Civil Liberties Committee had appealed for defense funds, the New England Committee and the parent American Civil Liberties Union in New York had remained steadfast in their support. Frankfurter's article was in a sense a culmination of their efforts. They had by their prolonged and reiterative publicity made the cause of Sacco and Vanzetti intellectually fashionable. Those whose names rang the changes in the last months of the case, now made their rather flamboyant appearance. Officially the civil-liberties groups kept their distance.

When Moore was in charge of the defense, publicity was oriented toward the radicals, but with the coming of Thompson and Gardner Jackson the appeal was directed much more to what the class-conscious Lyons would have considered "handwringing" liberals. Thompson disapproved of pamphlet wars, of the case being tried in the streets. Both he and Frankfurter wanted to avoid further antagonizing the Massachusetts community. Sometime in July 1927, when the Defense Committee had arranged to hold a protest meeting at Faneuil Hall, Frankfurter discreetly vetoed the idea.

Those who (in that jagged term that had emerged with the Russian Revolution) considered themselves the intelligentsia accepted the innocence of Sacco and Vanzetti and the guilt of Massachusetts as a matter of faith. It became a shibboleth of the liberal academic mind, just as within Boston their guilt had become a conservative shibboleth—in both cases a hotly held nonrational belief. Academic conformity, which—though usually opposed to—is even more rigid than middle-class conformity, belatedly took up the Sacco-Vanzetti cause, in part with sincere deliberateness but more often as a fervent avant-garde gesture. The 381 protesting petitioners from Mount Holyoke, the 326 from Bryn Mawr, the 203 from Wellesley, the faculty and 650 students from the University of California, the 36 Amherst faculty members, the hundreds of bloc names from so many other American colleges and universities, knowing only a smattering of the case, were making a reflex response to an appeal to themselves as an elite. In May, 61 members of assorted law faculties that included Yale, Columbia, Cornell, and the Universities of Kansas, Indiana, Ohio, Illinois, Minnesota, Missouri, Alabama, and Texas, petitioned Governor Fuller for a commutation on grounds of reasonable doubt. Dean Robert Hutchins of the Yale Law School, one of the minority who had read the record, wrote an open appeal in which he castigated Katzmann's cross-examination of Sacco. Three-quarters of the graduating class of the Harvard Law School, in defiant contrast to the State Street alumni majority just across the river, signed a request for a new trial. Professor Glenn Frank of Wisconsin, Dr. Alexander Meiklejohn, former president of Amherst, Mount Holyoke's Professor of English Jeannette Marks, and President Ellen Fitz Pendleton of Wellesley added their academic pleas.

As the New England spring slipped into summer, the roster of those opposing the impending execution and demanding a new trial added names as diverse as Norman Thomas, Jane Addams, Alfred Landon, Senator Robert La Follette, the Right Reverend Chauncey Brewster of Washington Cathedral, Sherwood Eddy, John Dewey, the Reverend Harry Emerson Fosdick, Dean Christian Gauss of Princeton, H. L. Mencken and Dean Edward Devine of the American Catholic University. Congressman Emanuel Celler of Brooklyn announced that he would introduce a measure in the next session of Congress to compel the attorney general to open the Department of Justice files concerned with Sacco and Vanzetti. On June 22 Joseph Moro, Gardner Jackson, and Mary Donovan appeared at the State House on behalf of the Defense Committee with a giant rolled petition for a public investigation, containing 474,842 names from all countries. Two weeks later the committee forwarded 153,000 additional names collected by the Swiss Union of Workers.

Within Massachusetts the reaction of the general public to such high-placed outside criticism was one of embittered, unreasoning hostility. A former district attorney said that it would be better even for two innocent men to be electrocuted than for public confidence in the established order of judicial procedure to be broken down. John C. Hull, the Speaker of the Massachusetts House of Representatives, received prolonged applause when he announced at a banquet that the Commonwealth's demand of outsiders was this: "We would respectfully ask you to mind your own business."

Such was the reaction of the well-born and the well-to-to. The reaction of what William Butler Yeats called "the little streets" was even more savage. In the massed streets of South Boston and Charlestown and Brighton and Ashmont there was a virulent hatred of Sacco and Vanzetti, coupled with a social jealousy of the better-known colleges and universities, a smoldering distrust of the professorial stance, a suspicion of academic attainments as being tainted with subversion. If the wiser-than-thou professors from Harvard and Yale were now taking it on themselves to proclaim that Sacco and Vanzetti should be freed—then so much the worse for Sacco and Vanzetti!

Sans-culotte anti-intellectualism echoed in a speech of Registrar of Motor Vehicles Frank Goodwin to the Lawrence Kiwanis Club:

It is impressive fact that the nearer we get to the scene of this murder the more convinced are the people that these men are guilty. . . . The citizens of Norfolk County know these men are guilty. On the other hand, in those domains where foreign and un-American principles are in vogue, such as Russia, Harvard, Argentine, Wellesley, China and Smith, they are sure these men are innocent. . . . The leader of the movement to set these two murderers free is Felix Frankfurter.

Professor Hocking might announce with urbane indignation from the platform of Boston's Community Church that he believed Sacco and Vanzetti "as innocent of that murder as you or I." Bishop Lawrence and the Dean of Washington Cathedral might entertain refined Episcopal doubts. But for the Reverend Billy Sunday—the preacher of the little streets—hoarsely saving the city from the fate of Sodom at Tremont Temple, no doubts existed. "Give 'em the juice," he rapped out from the pulpit. "Burn them, if they're guilty. That's the way to handle it. I'm tired of hearing these foreigners, these radicals, coming over here and telling us what we should do."

For five weeks after their sentencing Sacco and Vanzetti occupied adjoining cells in the Dedham jail. It was the first time since their arrest that they had been together for any length of time. Those shadowed weeks turned out to be the most serene of their imprisonment. Everyone who met Vanzetti remarked on his composure. Sacco, having decided not to struggle further against the fate he considered inevitable, attained a tranquillity that gave the surface appearance of cheerfulness. "As you know," he wrote with wry unaccustomed humor to Mrs. Henderson, "I am still living at the same hotel, the same room, and also at the same old number 14—but on the first of July probably, they will bring us to the death house, and from there to the —eternity."

A friend had brought Sacco a *boccie* set, and the two prisoners were allowed to bowl in the yard each afternoon for an hour and a half. Vanzetti began to take morning exercises and wrote Mrs. Winslow that he felt a new man. His cell was always filled with flowers from Mrs. Evans and other friends. As he described it:

My window here is peopled of recipients, it is a riot of blissing colors and beauties forms: a giranium plants a tulipan plant from Mrs. Evans. White flowers, pink carnations, roseate peaches, buds, and flowers, bush-yellow flowers from Mrs. Jack, and a boquet of May flowers from Mrs. Wislow.

Flowers he asked for instead of sweets, though as for tobacco—as he himself admitted—he smoked like a Turk. Being under sentence of death, and so exempt from prison work, he now had much more time to read and write. For Mrs. Jack he translated the last stanza of Gori's revolutionary hymn, "May First":

> *Give flowers to the rebels failed*
> *With glances revealed to the aurora*
> *To the gayard that struggles and works,*
> *To the vagrant poet that dies.*

Even the free jail days were too short for him. After nine when the lights went out he would prop himself up with a pillow against the wall, a blanket over his shoulders, using the corridor light coming through the bars to read some book that Mrs. Evans had just given him.

During the visiting periods Rosa came daily with the children for the allowed half-hour, and Sacco noticed lovingly how big Ines was growing and that Dante's face was burned from the spring sun. Mrs. Evans came almost as regularly to see Vanzetti.

On June 11, Vanzetti's thirty-ninth birthday, the two were visited by Georg Branting, a well-known lawyer and son of a former Swedish prime minister, who had crossed the Atlantic to make his own investigation. The Defense Committee had planned a parade to welcome Branting, and even though the police refused permission some fifteen hundred sympathizers met him at the South Station and escorted him to Boston Common. After ten days of on-the-scene study Branting announced that he was persuaded the two men were innocent, and sent a telegram to Sweden informing the press that "according to my best judgment, no conviction would have been pronounced if case tried under normal judicial conditions."

Phil Stong, a young reporter for the North American Newspaper Alliance, was another outsider who came to Boston to develop his opinion of the case. One afternoon he visited the prisoners in the jail library, later writing:

> *Both men expect to die. They say so, and the conviction is written in grave, serene characters on Vanzetti's face. . . . A ferocious mustache covers an expressive, smiling mouth. The stamp of thought is*

in every feature; the marks of the man whom strong intelligence has made an anchorite.

It was at the conclusion of this visit that Vanzetti casually made his utterance that has been so often quoted in anthologies. They sat there with Vanzetti doing most of the talking, Sacco breaking in only occasionally. Yet as these Italians talked in their imperfect English, even joked at times, the effect of their personalities gave Stong an overwhelming conviction of their innocence. He had brought a newspaper with him containing an account of some college students' suicides, a sensational topic of the last few days. "I think Dr. Frood wrong," Vanzetti remarked on glancing at it, "when he says student kill himself to make someone sorry. It is when he cannot make someone sorry, he kills himself in anger at world which pays him not attention—in despair—" Sacco disagreed, maintaining that if he himself were dead it would be the best way to free his wife and children. Vanzetti observed that "only sick mind kill himself." Then he spoke of a Charlestown inmate who had murdered his wife when he had caught her with another man. "You know what he says to me once? 'Vanzetti, you know what I think of all night? My wife—my home. Every night—all time. Now—all gone.'"

A bell rang, a gray line of prisoners began to file past on the way from the workshops to the cells, blank-faced men, their arms folded. Seeing them, Sacco grew bitter about his own enforced idleness. "We're capitalists," Vanzetti jollied him. "We have home, we eat, don't do no work. We're nonproducers—live off other men's work; when Libertarians make speech, they calling Nick and me names."

Sacco's mood changed and he seemed amused. Then a deputy approached as a sign that Stong's time was up. He had managed so far to cover his feelings by a forced cheerfulness but, as he rose to go, Vanzetti spotted the lurking dismay in the other's features. He then began to speak very quietly and simply as if to comfort the young man, and as he spoke Stong jotted down the words in shorthand on the margin of a newspaper:

If it had not been for this thing, I might have live out my life talking at street corners to scorning men. I might have die, unmarked, unknown, a failure. Now we are not a failure. This is our career and our triumph. Never in our full life can we hope to do such work for tolerance, for joostice, for man's onderstanding of man, as now we do by an accident.

*Our words—our lives—our pains—nothing! The taking of our lives
—lives of a good shoemaker and a poor fish peddler—all!
That last moment belong to us—that agony is our triumph.**

Neither Sacco nor Vanzetti had expected Fuller to appoint his
review commission. "That would impose freedom," Vanzetti told
Mrs. Winslow, "and the men of the judiciary and of the executive
want save America by dooming us." As for Governor Fuller's own
private investigation, Vanzetti's conclusion was: "He may give us
justice—I expect nothing."

At times, when he was temporarily overcome by a mood of ob-
sessive frustration, Vanzetti would crudely appropriate the symbolism
of the Passion to express his dilemma. In such a mood he first learned
of Fuller's appointment of the Lowell Committee. "His this double
investigation," he wrote Mrs. Evans, "going to be another mockery?
spitting on our face? sponge of vinager and bitterness on the top of
a lance? the last stubbing between our ribles?" As the sun moved
higher in the sky, as the elms again arched their spring greenery over
the High Street, the two Italians behind the jail walls sensed their
lost freedom in all its urgency. "Oh! that Sea, that sky," Vanzetti
wrote, "those freed and full of life winds of Cape Cod! Maybe I will
never see, never breath, never be at-one with them again."

On June 29 Governor Fuller gave Sacco, Vanzetti, and Madeiros
a stay until August 10, to allow his Advisory Committee time to
review the evidence and examine Madeiros' confession. The Dedham
interlude ended abruptly and finally at midnight on July 1 when the
prisoners were waked, manacled to deputies, packed in a car followed
by a second car with armed guards, and driven along the empty
Dedham streets and across the drab brick outskirts of Boston to
Cherry Hill. In this midnight scurrying Vanzetti lost some of his

---

* An English writer, Edward Shanks, thought that these paragraphs compared
with the *Gettysburg Address* but doubted that Vanzetti had ever uttered them.
Stong defended himself by saying that he could not write that well, that he had
supplied only the exclamation marks, and that these would have been better
left out. "It seems to me," he wrote, "that the internal evidence of that interview
is sufficient to convince any honorably disposed person of its authenticity. The
change of number in the pronoun was beautifully characteristic of Vanzetti.
'I' unmarked, unknown, a failure—but 'Our' career, triumph, work for tolerance
and justice." This version that Stong gave in the New York *World* of May 13,
1927, differs, nevertheless, in several places from the one he printed in 1949 in
his essay on the case in *The Aspirin Age*.

books and papers. Both men saw the hurried transfer as another example of deliberate spitefulness on the part of the authorities. Actually it was a strict following of the rule that a condemned man must be sent to Cherry Hill ten days before the date set for his execution. Sheriff Capen, anxious to get rid of his notorious prisoners, interpreted the rule to the letter. Even though the executions had been deferred, their official date as set by the court was still July 10.

Sacco accepted the transfer with shoulder-shrugging indifference as no more than he had expected. Vanzetti could not get over his depression at the ominous change from the casual Dedham jail with "some air, light, a slice of land and of sky to contemplate, and a daily blass of an hour of sun-shine and free air in the yard" to the "windowless, airless, lightless . . . malebolgic of the State Prison."

The Defense Committee took a more optimistic view of the Lowell Committee than did Sacco and Vanzetti. They were content with Lowell, neutral about Stratton, and objected only to Grant. Not only were the petulant paragraphs of *The Convictions of a Grandfather* exhumed, but Grant was accused of having told John Moors and Samuel Eliot Morison that he disapproved of anyone's taking issue with the trial, the verdict, and the subsequent decisions.

When Fuller questioned him about this, Grant explained with characteristic prissiness that he had not read the evidence in the case and knew nothing of the merits of the subsequent proceedings, but thought it "indecorous and contrary to the bonos mores for a professor at the Harvard Law School to rush into print while the case was *sub judice*."

The *Herald* and that section of State Street less intransigent than the *Transcript* were pleased by the appointment of Fuller's committee. Privately the more sedate Boston legal circles had always been dubious about Webster Thayer, and with the recent disbarment of the district attorneys of Suffolk and Middlesex counties, Democratic Joseph Pelletier and Republican Nathan Tufts, who could say what might not have been going on in neighboring Norfolk? Bishop Lawrence was another who had long been troubled by the thought, but now he too was satisfied. With Cousin Abbott in the State House, all would be well with the world!

Although the Advisory Committee appointment had been announced at the beginning of June, President Lowell was too occupied with his Harvard commencement activities to take any action until the end of the month. Finally, on the thirtieth, the three members met briefly in the governor's council chamber to discuss procedure and to receive typewritten transcripts of the trial record. Two days later they drove to South Braintree to inspect the murder scene. On July 8 they opened their hearings by examining seven of the Dedham jurors. The next day they spent two hours talking with Sacco and Vanzetti. Of that meeting Vanzetti wrote Mrs. Henderson:

From the Commission interview of us I got the impression that President Lowell and President Stratton are honestly intentioned and not hostile to us by predetermination. Yet it seemed to me that in spite of their great scholarship, they had not understood certain most vicious actions of the prosecution and the iniquity of Thayer's conduct. As for Judge Grant he is but another Thayer.

Meanwhile Governor Fuller was continuing his own daily sessions in his high-ceilinged office with the portraits of Sam Adams and John Hancock staring down from the walls. Secretary MacDonald kept his watchdog position at the Governor's right, while the bald quizzical Wiggin sat at his left. In spite of repeated objections by the defense, Fuller insisted on complete secrecy for whatever the witnesses might wish to tell him. Otherwise, he explained, his office would be turned into a bear den. Day by day the reporters noted the parade of faces up the State House steps—the ballistics experts, including the disillusioned Professor Gill; the star witnesses from both trials. There was no way that either the governor or the Lowell Committee could compel anyone to testify. Pelser, Lola Andrews, and Goodridge did not appear, either because they refused to or because they had disappeared.

Philip Cox, the brother of Alfred Cox, the Bridgewater paymaster, wrote to Fuller that his brother "alone had an opportunity to see the man who held him up, and he declined to identify his assailant as Vanzetti." This, it seemed to Philip Cox, "should have afforded good reason for hesitating to accept the verdict of guilty." But what the Bridgewater paymaster had come to think in 1927, and what he said in the private interview he had with the governor, remained a tight secret.

Yet, in spite of the imposed secrecy, signs here and there made it apparent that Fuller's mind was hardening against the two Italians. When John Richards, who, as marshal, had arrested the Morellis for their freight-yard thefts, talked with the governor, he was amazed to hear him say he discounted Madeiros' confession. "I am convinced it was a fair trial," he told Richards finally. When Robert Benchley came from New York to tell of his conversation with Loring Coes in which Coes—according to Benchley—had repeated Thayer's clubhouse remark that he would "get those bastards good and proper," Fuller asked Benchley to point out a single place in the record that indicated the trial was not fair.

"Why didn't Vanzetti take the stand at Plymouth?" It was a question that the governor threw at defense witnesses with increasing frequency. "Why didn't Sacco testify at Plymouth for his friend Vanzetti?" Fuller demanded of Tom O'Connor, who was trying to explain how the case originated in Chief Stewart's mind. Each point that O'Connor made, whether it concerned Proctor's ambiguous testimony or the Department of Justice files, Fuller and his counsel Wiggin brushed aside. O'Connor in a flash-tempered parry accused the governor of prejudging the investigation, and the two men shouted at each other until their voices reached the newspapermen in the corridor. Fuller, red-faced and furious, stood up to indicate the interview was over. Stalking from the room, he snapped at O'Connor, "Why did Boda skip?" Later O'Connor told a friend, "His hand is on the switch.'"

A new volunteer defense lawyer now arrived from Pittsburgh, young Michael Angelo Musmanno, bringing a petition in behalf of the two men from the half million members of the Sons of Italy. Dramatic, impulsive, abounding in cheerful energy, with a bronze ex-serviceman's pin in his buttonhole and wearing a poet's brown tie, Musmanno had quit the promising beginnings of his law practice to offer all his talents to the Defense Committee. Sometimes his zeal would trip him, as when he drove down to the New Haven slum where Berardelli's widow was living. She would not talk about the events at South Braintree and refused to sign an appeal. The most Musmanno could bring her to say was that she did not want to see innocent men punished. That was enough, however, for the poetic-minded Musmanno, who dashed to the telegraph office and sent a telegram to Fuller that echoed across Europe as far as Moscow:

I am one of the two who suffered most from the Braintree murders. I lost my husband and the father of my two children, but I would be sorry to have two innocent men put to death. I have always doubted that Sacco and Vanzetti were guilty and I hope that you will free them and let them go home to their families.

Several days later Sarah Berardelli denied that she had ever written or sent such a telegram. Musmanno had hoped that an appeal by Berardelli's widow would help counteract the recent news that Parmenter's fourteen-year-old son had been caught in South Easton, breaking and entering the railroad station. The newspapers had blamed the poverty and lack of direction of young Parmenter's fatherless household.

Thompson forwarded to the governor a thirty-three-page analysis of the discrepancies between the newly discovered Bridgewater Pinkerton report and the Plymouth trial record. When this was not acknowledged, John Moors finally went to ask Fuller about it. Apparently nothing concerned with either the South Braintree or the Bridgewater Pinkerton reports had ever reached the governor's desk, for he at once turned blankly to MacDonald. The secretary shrugged off Thompson's analysis as "just a lot of stuff about a cropped mustache."

Hard-boiled Herman's job was to cull the governor's Sacco-Vanzetti mail, most of which he threw away. In 1926 the Defense Committee had forwarded a protest signed by a group of English M.P.'s. When no reply came back, Gardner Jackson stormed up to the State House. His complaint got no farther than the anteroom obstacle of the secretary's broad-topped desk. "Oh, those goddam crooks!" Mac-Donald told him. "Do you think we pay any attention to this stuff? It comes in here by the barrelful and we shoot it right into the fire!"

Rosina, when she appeared at Fuller's office on July 11, quickly sensed the hostility behind his superficial politeness. He told her that Vanzetti had been asked by his lawyers to take the stand at the Plymouth trial but had refused. Young Brini, as the chief defense witness, had, he felt, merely learned an alibi by heart. After Rosina left the governor she spent some time with the Lowell Committee in the council chamber next door, then went on to Charlestown where, much troubled, she repeated Fuller's remarks. Only she and Thompson were allowed to see the prisoners now, since according to regulations condemned men in Cherry Hill could have visits only from close relations and counsel.

Sacco brooded over what Rosina told him. On July 17, after deliberating for several days, he began a hunger strike in protest against what the Defense Committee called the "veil of secrecy that encourages the bias—economic, racial, political and religious—which has been shown all through this case." Vanzetti joined with him to protest "the whispers of nameless informers," explaining to Mrs. Evans:

But my hungry strike is progressing because I knew that both the Governor and the commission have ill-treated our witnesses, wrongly, and that they believe nothing of what our witnesses say. They believe, and treat well those handful of criminals, harlots, and degenareted who perjured against us.

His stomach, he complained after a few days, affected his mind and heart. He found difficulty even in writing letters. As he saw his end drawing closer he felt a longing for his own blood, for that far-off family in Villafalletto he had not seen in almost twenty years. The day after he began his strike he asked Felicani to send a telegram to his sister Luigia. Even though it might be too late now, he wanted above all to see her again before he died.

Sacco could at least see his wife, who came daily with Ines and Dante, now grown taller than his mother. The children were not allowed to see their father but waited in the warden's office. Seven-year-old Ines wrote her first large-scrawled letter to her father, and he was so moved that even in the lassitude of his hunger strike he sat down at once to reply:

I will bring with me your little and so dearest letter and carry it right under my heart to the last day of my life. When I die, it will be buried with your father who loves you so much, as I do also your brother Dante and holy dear mother. . . . It is the most golden present that you could have given to me or that I could have wished for in these sad days.

As he wrote he found himself caught up in an imagined idyll:

It was the greatest treasure and sweetness in my struggling life that I could have lived with you and your brother Dante and your mother in a neat little farm, and learn all your sincere words and tender affection. Then in the summer-time to be sitting with you in the home nest under the oak tree shade—beginning to teach you of life and how to read and write, to see you running, laughing, crying and sing-ing through the verdent fields picking the wild flowers here and there from one tree to another, and from the clear, vivid stream to your mother's embrace.

The same I have wished to see for other poor girls, and their brothers, happy with their mother and father as I dreamed for us—

but it was not so and the nightmare of the lower classes saddened very badly your father's soul.*

When Fuller came for the first time to Charlestown to interview the three condemned men he talked only briefly with the sullen Madeiros and not at all with Sacco, who shook hands but told him courteously that they had nothing to say to each other. With Vanzetti Fuller spent over an hour and a half, breaking off only to dash back to a State House reception for Lindbergh, who had arrived in Boston that afternoon on his triumphal tour of the country. Vanzetti and Fuller were open with each other. Fuller pointed out what he considered the most damaging facts against Vanzetti: his failure to take the stand at Plymouth, the revolver found on him, his quick convictions by two juries. Vanzetti gave his interpretations of these things and then quite typically began to talk of other matters unrelated to himself. As they sat together in the warden's office the two men found each other curiously sympathetic. When Fuller broke off the interview he promised to return later. "What an attractive man!" he observed to Warden Hendry as he hurried away. Reporters noticed that the governor appeared nervous as he headed down the walk to his waiting Packard. His nervousness was probably not so much because of the interrupted interview as at the thought of keeping America's hero waiting. Getting into the car he knocked his hat off.

Thompson wanted Vanzetti to break his fast so that he would be better able to talk with Fuller on his next visit. Vanzetti finally agreed to drink a cup of tea, and later took some coffee and milk. Fuller spent most of July 26 in South Braintree inspecting the scene of the shootings and driving over the escape route with Chief Stewart. In the evening he again interviewed Vanzetti, arriving at Charlestown just after nine and staying two hours. It was not time enough for Vanzetti. He asked if he might write Fuller at length, and Fuller, with salesman's affability, agreed. In this second interview Vanzetti felt a growing confidence in the governor that he showed in his letter next day to Alice Stone Blackwell:

He make me the impression of being just as you say of him; an honest man, as he understand it, and sincere, courageous, stubborn man but well intentioned at bottom and in a way, clever. And I like to tell you that he gave me a good heartfull sake hand, as I lef. I may

---

* The original of this letter is not available. The published version has undoubtedly been edited.

be wrong, but I don't believe that a man like that is going to burn us on a case like ours.

A heat wave seared the city. Through two weeks the Lowell Committee interviewed its witnesses. Thompson again and in vain asked for public hearings. The committee agreed, however, that with the exception of Judge Thayer, Chief Justice Hall, the district attorney, and the jurors, all of whom would be examined privately, counsel for both sides might suggest witnesses and be present to question them.

Most of the witnesses the committee examined had already been interviewed by the governor. Sometimes, as Rosina had, they merely stepped from the governor's office to the council chamber.

Day after day the three old men in coats and stiff collars sat at their wedge-shaped mahogany desks while the witnesses filed damply by and Thompson and Assistant District Attorney Ranney struck sparks from each other. Lowell dominated the sessions, with Stratton silent and Grant fretting at his subordination. In the city four people died of the heat. The grass on the Common where the derelicts sprawled in alcoholic stupor—impervious to Prohibition—had turned to cocoa matting. Through the open windows of the council chamber came the summer hum of the city, broken faintly by the yelps of urchins in the Frog Pond. Within that Federalist room dominated by the spaniel-featured autocrat it was hard to realize that the matter of debate was two men's lives.

Katzmann, after testifying privately, voluntarily submitted to being cross-examined by Thompson. Thompson accused the district attorney of having arranged the Plymouth trial first so that Vanzetti would appear in Dedham as a convicted felon. Katzmann said it was merely the chance that there happened to be a June term in Plymouth and none in Dedham. In the matter of Captain Proctor he would not positively deny that the captain thought Sacco and Vanzetti were innocent, but doubted he ever said so.

Katzmann was followed—at Lowell's request—by Professor Guadagni and Bosco, the editor of *La Notizia*. Lowell particularly wanted to ask them about their Dedham testimony that they, along with Dentamore, had met Sacco in Giordani's Café on the day of the crime and had remembered the date afterward because a banquet had been given at the Franciscan Priory for the editor of the *Transcript* that same day. In reading over the trial record Lowell had noticed that although Dentamore had said he had just come from the banquet, Guadagni said it was to be held in the evening. Struck by the discrepancy, Lowell had gone through the files of the *Transcript* and discovered that a group of Italians had given a dinner for Editor Williams at Frascati's on May 13, eight days after Sacco and Vanzetti were arrested. Thinking that there might possibly have been two banquets, Lowell telegraphed Williams, who happened to be in Washington. Williams replied that there had been only one.

With this information concealed like a time bomb, Lowell faced Guadagni while Bosco waited outside. Guadagni now appeared uncertain whether the banquet had been held before or after the talk in Giordani's Café. When Lowell showed him the account of the banquet in the *Transcript*, he concluded that it must have taken place the night before and added ruefully, "I was so sure of that day." Then Lowell set off his bomb, pointing out that the paper was dated May 14. The banquet had taken place May 13! How, then, could Guadagni have discussed it a month before? Lowell felt he had the proof in his hand that the story was a fraud, concocted by Guadagni, Bosco, and Dentamore to create an alibi for a fellow anarchist.

Thompson was shattered in his dismay. Guadagni's lie seemed too flagrant, too utterly exposed. "If it was deliberate I do not think you would see me around here very much longer," he told Lowell. "If I did not think these men were innocent I should not be fooling away my time. And I would not resort to any means to justify an end, just because I was convinced these men were innocent, any more than if I thought they were guilty."

"Of course not, Mr. Thompson," the other assured him urbanely. Guadagni stood there, beaten down, admitting now that the banquet had had nothing to do with his meeting Sacco, that he had accepted the idea from Dentamore, that it was a mistake.

Bosco was of sterner fiber. When he appeared, not only did he insist to the aroused and hostile committee that there had been a banquet for Commandante Williams on April 15 but that he had printed an account of it on the sixteenth in *La Notizia*. Lowell stared at him with contempt. "It is perfectly obvious that is not so," he remarked coldly. Thompson could scarcely control himself as he turned on the still-defiant Italian:

"You can trust Mr. Lowell for that. He has investigated it. He knows there was no banquet on the fifteenth."

When Bosco remained adamant, Lowell ordered him to bring in the files of *La Notizia* for April and May 1920. Next morning Bosco and a revived Guadagni appeared with the paper of April 16, 1920. There on the front page was the vindicating notice:

Yesterday the Franciscan Fathers of North Bennett Street gave a luncheon in honor of the new Commendatore Williams, editor of the Boston Evening Transcript.

Lowell sent the Italians out of the room and put a telephone call through to Williams. This time the *Transcript* editor recalled the earlier luncheon. Lowell turned to the stenographer, who had begun to record the conversation, and told him not to take down "colloquies." He summoned Bosco and Guadagni back, shook hands with them, told them he believed them to be honest, and that he regretted his mistake.*

Thompson tried to impress on the committee that since the alibi had been reestablished, it must again be taken seriously. Lowell did not reply. Grant remarked that "You are just back where you were before."

Lottie Tatillo, though presented to the committee a few days later as a new witness, could scarcely be considered new by either side. Both prosecution and defense had been aware of her and her story since the summer of 1920, when she made a statement to Brouillard and Stewart that on the morning of April 15 she had seen Sacco and Vanzetti in South Braintree.

Everyone in South Braintree knew Lottie by her maiden name of Packard. In 1901, when she was fourteen, she had gone to work in the stitching room of Rice & Hutchins. Pretty and wayward, full of wild stories, she would take the path down behind the millpond evenings with any good-looking young fellow from the factory. "Twelve ounces to the pound," Frank Jackson, the Rice & Hutchins foreman, described her. "A nut. She is crazy and has been for years," was Police Chief Gallivan's opinion.

After Sacco and Vanzetti were arrested, Lottie told Jackson that she had seen Sacco in South Braintree the day of the murders and remembered he used to work in Rice & Hutchins. Later she elaborated on this story to John Shea, the local policeman, who passed her on to Stewart and Brouillard. She claimed she had rec-

---

* The transcript of the committee hearings merely states that Bosco appeared as requested on July 15 with editions of *La Notizia*. The omission from the record of what followed has been much criticized by defenders of Sacco and Vanzetti.

ognized Sacco's picture in the paper after his arrest because she had known him in 1915 when he was working in the finishing room of Rice & Hutchins. On the morning of April 15 on her way to lunch she had passed him on Pearl Street standing near a shiny Buick touring car. She noticed him bite his lip and then all of a sudden it came back to her that he was the fellow named Sacco who used to work in the factory as a laster. She would never forget him because once in a temper he had thrown a last across the room at a boy and it had struck her in the foot.

If Lottie's story was true, she would stand out as the most important witness of the murder day, the only one who had known Sacco previously and had then seen him at the scene of the crime. And if she had told her story to Jackson or Shea the day after the holdup, when no one in South Braintree had even suspected Sacco, that would indeed have made an almost watertight case for the prosecution. But Lottie had said nothing, nothing to Carlos Goodridge or anyone else, until after Sacco and Vanzetti had been arrested and their pictures had appeared in the paper. Stewart could find no record of Sacco's ever having worked at Rice & Hutchins. It is of course possible that Lottie had seen Sacco during the week or so he worked in the factory under the name of Mosmacotelli in October 1917, and if before the arrests she had identified the man she had seen in the stitching room then with the man she claimed she saw standing by the Buick on April 15, 1920, this would have come close to being conclusive. Even after the arrests such an identification from a more stable person might have carried weight. But, as LaBrecque, the Quincy reporter, later explained to the committee, Lottie would tell one story one night and another the next and make so many irresponsible statements there was no use believing her. Stewart and Brouillard had long ago made the same discovery. Whenever they tried to check up on her account, she would take each question as an insult, denouncing both them and Sacco and Vanzetti incoherently. Finally Stewart gave up. "A blister," he decided, as he struck her off his list of witnesses.

In the autumn of 1920 Moore had got wind of Lottie's potentially dangerous testimony and sent down a Joseph Mirra from East Boston to see what he could find out about her. Mirra, under the name of Joseph Meyers, got himself a job as a vamper in the finishing room of Rice & Hutchins and found it easy enough to strike up an acquaintance with the accommodating Lottie. He made several dates with her, taking her to the pictures at Gordon's Olympia in Boston and to the amusement park at Revere Beach. Each time he took her out he tried to pump her about Sacco and Vanzetti. One night when he took her to his house in East Boston for supper and felt he had broken the ice sufficiently, he asked her if she would tell what she knew to a lawyer friend of his. She agreed, and the two of them went to Moore's Tremont Row office.

Moore and several others were waiting with a stenographer when Lottie and Mirra arrived. Lottie was voluble. She again said that she had known Sacco in 1915. The morning of the murders when she passed him on Pearl Street he was standing near the Buick wearing a derby,* and looking as if he were in a hurry. Vanzetti, whom she had never seen before, was standing on the other side of the street and called across to Sacco as she passed: "I wish you would hurry up and get this over. I have an appointment at 3:30 this afternoon in Providence to dig clams." After Sacco was arrested she said she had seen his picture and asked the other girls in the factory: "What has Sacco done?" They told her he was being held for murder.

Lottie told Moore she had informed Shea, the day after the crime, that one of the men by the car was the one who had thrown the last at her. But, she told Moore, she did not want to testify in court. She had not come to ask him for money, but she saw no way of avoiding going on the stand except to leave the state for a while. She continued, according to the stenographic record, "I am pretty sure that Mr. Sacco was the man who done the murder. It is his wife that holds me back. I think she needs him. . . . I'll tell you the truth. I am not a girl crazy for money or anything like that."

"How much are you willing to suggest that you want?" Moore asked her finally.

"I don't know," she told him calculatingly. "I just came to help you on the defense case."

Lottie's story as she presented it to the Lowell Committee had altered singularly since that November evening, seven years earlier, at Tremont Row. Whenever Thompson challenged her, she stormed at him until her voice rang down the corridors. "I don't remember," she replied at one point to a question of Lowell's, "my head is too full of music and things like that, to remember." She now insisted that Sacco had worked for Rice & Hutchins in 1908 at the time of a strike—it was then and only then she had known him. That was

* A photograph of Sacco reproduced in the papers after his arrest showed him wearing a derby.

the time when he had struck her with the last, and she had thought to herself: "That man will do something before he dies." She denied ever having told Moore she had known Sacco in 1915, or that when she saw him on the street in 1920 he was wearing a derby. He was, she told Lowell, bare-headed. When Lowell first asked her whether she had seen Sacco on April 15 she replied: "I don't say I saw him. I will never say I saw him, and I don't think it was him now." A few minutes later, however, she revived her story of seeing him by the car with Vanzetti across the street talking about clams, this time with Parmenter, the paymaster, standing in the background. After she came back from lunch she had told Frank Jackson she had seen Sacco. She did not tell Shea about this until after the men's arrest.

When Thompson produced her 1920 statement that she had told Shea about Sacco the day after the crime, she raged: "No, I did not tell it to John Shea. How many times do you want me to answer that question? I will tell the truth at the Divine bar of Justice, and that has got more power than you have got. You have got a witness here that you cannot make waver."

Judge Grant, trying to calm her, brought her a glass of water and accidentally spilled some down her back. Still trying to be helpful, he suggested she might have lunch now. "I don't want any lunch," she snapped, glaring at Thompson. "I have got enough lunch listening to this man here, he's good enough lunch for anybody."

When Thompson remarked that she had gone to Moore voluntarily, her voice rose to a shriek: "Who came to Moore voluntarily? You lie, I did not; I was brought to Moore, for Sacco and Vanzetti to do a dirty, rotten, nasty thing! I will make you prove your statement."

She now insisted that Moore had offered her five hundred dollars to leave the state, an offer she had indignantly refused. Thompson sent her into another tantrum when he suggested she was trying to get money from Moore. When Lowell finally dismissed her, she left the room still spluttering.

A few days later Jackson, the Rice & Hutchins foreman, made his appearance in the council chamber. He admitted that Lottie had told him of seeing Sacco, but only after Sacco was in jail. Before his arrest she had never mentioned Sacco to anyone. Only afterward had she come out with her story of talking with him on the street the morning of April 15. Jackson had no memory of Sacco's working in the factory, and there was no record of his having worked there.

Lottie, following her turbulent session with Thompson, swung round again a few hours later and told a sympathetic *Post* reporter that she was now convinced that the man she had seen was not Sacco and that she believed Sacco and Vanzetti were innocent.

One of the new discoveries claimed by the defense concerned the cap found by Berardelli's body—the cap that the prosecution had tried to prove belonged to Sacco. Williams had pointed out the tear in the lining, implying that Sacco had made it by hanging his cap on a nail at the factory. It was a corroborative point mentioned several times during the trial and later by Judge Thayer in his ruling on the Madeiros motion.

Not until shortly before the Lowell Committee began its meetings was the point again raised. Then Tom O'Connor, combing South Braintree for new evidence, had the thought that he might pick up something from the now-retired Chief Gallivan. He found him weeding in his garden and quite willing to talk. The first thing they talked about was the cap Loring had picked up.

Gallivan said that the Saturday after the murder Fraher called him from Rice & Hutchins to say he had a cap found on the street after the murders. That evening Gallivan went to pick it up. The autumn before, he had been able to identify the remains of a man who had hanged himself in the Braintree woods by the name inked into the lining of the man's cap. With that identification in mind, he ripped a hole in the lining of the cap Fraher gave him. Finding neither name nor marks, he tossed the cap under the seat of his car. There it stayed for a week or two until John Scott of the State Police asked him for it.

For O'Connor the tear in the cap seemed a tear in the very fabric of the prosecution's case. He gave his information to Thompson, and Gallivan was summoned before the Lowell Committee. The ex-chief readily admitted that there was no hole in the cap's lining before he got his hands on it, and said he told Scott he himself had made the tear. Tampering with evidence was a concept alien to his naïve mind; he still could see nothing wrong in what he had done. Katzmann, when the tear in the cap was brought to his attention, insisted that this was the first time he had ever heard of it—that if he had known about it during the trial, he would have explained it to the jury. Although Thompson argued that an important piece of evidence relied on by the prosecution had now turned out to be false, and that this alone should be sufficient grounds for a new trial or for clemency, the committee members did not appear impressed.

The confidentially verbose Dr. Hamilton again came from Auburn to defend his ballistics theses before the committee and to repeat his conversation with the conscience-stricken Proctor. Whether or not the committee had read the Dedham file on Hamilton, Ranney obviously had, for he ticked off the ex-druggist's extraordinary expertise and ended with a reference to the Stielow case that made Hamilton jump. Major Goddard's apparently definitive report had been read, and the committee was also much more aware than the jury had been that the six obsolete Winchester bullets found on Sacco were similar to Bullet III.

Thompson now produced Wilbur Turner, a self-designated criminologist, who had just examined the four Berardelli bullets at Dedham and found "a tremendous difference" between the markings on the base of Bullet III and the others, "as though they were made with a different tool or scratched with a different instrument." And Thompson spelled out for the record his bitter conviction that Captain Proctor had substituted a fake bullet test-fired from Sacco's gun for the genuine bullet taken by Dr. Magrath from Berardelli's body.

The hot days slipped by, the old autocrat met his two colleagues with austere condescension each morning, and the parade of witnesses continued. Lowell felt—he would feel this way for the rest of his life—that he was performing a disagreeable civic duty because such was the obligation of a Lowell. In essence the committee bearing his name was conducting a second trial, but it had without his conscious awareness become a trial in which the Commonwealth was the defendant. What the Lowell Committee was taking on itself to decide was not whether Sacco and Vanzetti had had a fair trial and were guilty beyond a reasonable doubt, but whether the presumably innocent Commonwealth had beyond a reasonable doubt erred. In the beginning Thompson and Ehrmann, as Harvard graduates, had pinned their hopes on Lowell, but after the Guadagni-Bosco episode Lowell began to seem more the challenger than the judge. The two lawyers had the uneasy feeling that evidence and argument were becoming useless, and even considered whether or not they should boycott the hearings.

The doom of our clients seemed as inevitable as that of Socrates [Ehrmann wrote afterward], and we were unwilling to continue in the farce of fair treatment. We were diverted from this course, however, by two outstanding jurists [Dean Pound and Professor Frankfurter], who inspired us with some semblance of hope. Theirs was perhaps

*the greater wisdom, since, had we withdrawn, it would have been said
that we had lost faith in the cause of our clients.*

By Saturday, July 23, the committee members had run through
their witnesses, from Cox the paymaster to Rosen the peddler, Gould,
the Hayes and Kennedy girls—everyone they thought might add anything new to the case. Lincoln Wadsworth, still working for Iver
Johnson, and afraid that his Dedham testimony had been misinter-
preted, told the committee that although the revolver found on
Vanzetti might have been Berardelli's, "there are thousands of times
more chances that it was not than that it was."

Lowell spent the week end writing a report of the proceedings,
which in token deference to his colleagues he referred to as an
abstract. Monday the committee spent listening to the closing arguments of Thompson and Ehrmann, followed by Ranney for the
Commonwealth. Then, when the humid council chamber was at
last empty, Lowell handed typewritten copies of his abstract to his
colleagues, saying off-handedly that it was just a suggestion, of course,
but would they look it over?

The next day the three met privately in the Faculty Room of
Harvard's University Hall. The autocrat of the faculty table having
made up his mind in writing, all he wanted from the silent physicist
and the garrulous poetaster was confirmation. They spent that day
and the next discussing minor details of the abstract. "So fully did
we find ourselves in agreement," Grant admitted later, "that though
many alterations were made in it, they were chiefly of phraseology
and shades of expression rather than the substantive point of view."

On the afternoon of July 27 at ten minutes past five Lowell, Stratton, and Grant, sphinx-faced, entered the executive offices of the
State House, each carrying a brown manila folder with a signed copy
of the revised abstract-report.

◇◇◇◇◇◇◇◇◇◇◇◇◇◇◇◇◇◇◇◇◇◇◇◇◇◇

CHAPTER NINETEEN

August 1927

Governor Fuller continued hearing witnesses until the end of July. Obviously he was not going to draw his own conclusions or even appear to have drawn them before taking his cue from the Lowell Committee. In an interview with Jackson and Felicani he asked them flatly how he could be expected to believe Vanzetti's alibi that he was selling eels on December 24. "I am a businessman," he told them. "I am used to proof before I decide anything. There isn't a single document in the case proving that Vanzetti sold eels. There's only the word of his Italian friends."

Spurred by the governor's disbelief and furnished with a sketch map by Vanzetti, Felicani and Ehrmann made the rounds of the waterfront wholesale fish dealers. Finally, at 112 Atlantic Avenue, they found that one of the partners of Corso & Gambino remembered shipping fish to Vanzetti in 1919. The firm had then been Corso & Cannizzo. Ehrmann and Felicani dug away for hours among Corso's dusty account books until at last they uncovered what they had almost given up hope of finding, an American Express Company receipt showing that on Saturday, December 20, 1919, a forty-pound barrel of eels had been shipped with C.O.D. charges of $21.79 to B. Vanzetti, Plymouth.

The eels must have been delivered either on Monday or Tuesday. Mary Fortini, Vanzetti's landlady, had testified they arrived "either the twenty-second or the twenty-third, I do not remember exactly." She said the expressman had brought the barrel at about half-past nine in the morning, when Vanzetti was out, and as she had no money to pay him he had taken it away and come back later. "After one Monday Vanzetti and the express came back" was the awkward way the interpreter translated her explanation. Ehrmann took "after one Monday" to mean "the following day." Vanzetti would have received his eels on Tuesday, spent Tuesday night cleaning them, and on Wednesday—the morning of the Bridgewater holdup attempt —he would have been busy making his deliveries. Ehrmann thought at last he had found the key to unlock the doors of the state prison. He and Felicani took the yellowed express receipt to Thompson who, in Fuller's absence, handed it over to the governor's secretary—and that was the last they heard of it.

Sunday, the last day of July, the heat wave broke in drizzling rain. A crowd of three thousand, divided between sympathizers and the usual Sunday afternoon floaters, attended a Sacco-Vanzetti protest meeting on the Charles Street Mall of Boston Common. Alfred Baker Lewis, the wealthy pince-nezed perennial Socialist candidate for governor, introduced the speakers: Gardner Jackson, Harry Canter, Mary Donovan, and Professor Guadagni. Canter called for a general strike, and Mary Donovan shouted in a trembling voice that if they executed those two innocent men they could execute her too. The fiery words spluttered out damply in the rain; the crowd remained inert.

Fuller spent the week end at his summer estate at Little Boar's Head, Rye Beach, New Hampshire. Two days before, his son Alvan, Jr., had to be operated on suddenly for appendicitis, and for a day or so the governor thought he might have to delay his decision. However, just before leaving the city he promised reporters that he would make it known Wednesday evening. The feeling in the corridors of the State House, in State Street, on Newspaper Row, among those in the know was that the governor would end up by granting a new trial. Louis Stark's dispatch to the New York *Times* concluded:

Nicola Sacco and Bartolomeo Vanzetti will not die in the chair on the date set. Neither will they be pardoned. Further reprieve pending steps by the Massachusetts Legislature looking to a new trial was indicated as the solution which Governor Fuller will place before the Executive Council when it meets tomorrow night.

Whatever the rumors of a reprieve, there was no sign of it as August began. Imperturbably the clockwork mechanism of the law advanced another notch as, on the night of August 2, Sacco, Vanzetti, and Madeiros were moved to the isolation of the death house. The day before that move, Vanzetti had tried to persuade Sacco to give up his hunger strike, but the other refused, saying there was no use in making himself fat to be killed.

The transfer was made secretly, the guards waiting until ten minutes after lights out before coming to the cells to take the condemned men away. Down the short flight of iron stairs guards and prisoners clattered to the darkness of the outer yard and then diagonally across the inlaid brick to the narrow passage between the north wing extension and the license-plate shop. "In coming, I got a glance to the nighty, starry sky," Vanzetti wrote. "Hit was so long I did seen it before—and thought it was my last glance to the stars."

There were only three cells in the blank-walled death house. The white-tiled floors had a black line painted six feet in front of each cell beyond which no visitor might step. Sacco and Vanzetti, locked up there, could not see each other, but they could talk back and forth. Each cell was lit by a lamp outside the bars and contained a cot, a chair, a table, and a toilet. The perspective of the antiseptic room concluded in a small gray door leading to the execution chamber.

Sacco's reaction to the death house was to pace up and down, his energy undiminished even though he had not eaten for over two weeks. Vanzetti, who again refused food, tried to immerse himself in *The Rise of American Civilization*. Only Madeiros seemed unaffected by the change. Torpid, outwardly indifferent, he ate enormously but gave scarcely any other sign of life. When Warden Hendry offered to pay his mother's way to Boston, he said he did not want to see her.

Sunday's rain continued into Monday, leaving the city and the State House streaked with fog. Fuller returned from New Hampshire early in the morning and again told the waiting reporters his decision would be ready on Wednesday. During the morning he talked with Jackson, Moro, and other members of the Defense Committee. In the afternoon he spent several hours with the Brockton policemen, Connolly and Vaughn, and after they left he conferred with John McAnarney. During the day he sent for Judge Thayer, who was spending his vacation at Ogunquit, Maine. Thayer arrived at the State House a little after six. The reporters noted that the governor's mood seemed genial. They thought it a good omen for the prisoners.

Tuesday morning the governor was closeted with Assistant District Attorney Ranney. At lunch time he informed reporters that he had seen 102 witnesses besides those from the Plymouth trial. That day, however, the fate of Sacco and Vanzetti was overshadowed by the noontime news from the Summer White House in the Black Hills of South Dakota where Calvin Coolidge had just announced: "I do not choose to run for President in nineteen twenty-eight." Boston political gossips at once recalled how the vacillating governor had made himself nationally known as Law and Order Coolidge by what seemed, at least outside Massachusetts, to have been his firmness in handling the 1919 police strike. Perhaps there would be a Law and Order Fuller now, another President from the Bay State.*

The week between the submission of the Lowell Committee's report and the governor's decision was one of vexing suspense that added to the growth of Sacco-Vanzetti militancy all over the world. Even the apolitical sports-minded newspaper readers in America, who had remained so far indifferent, could no longer restrain their curiosity as to the outcome of this mortal contest. Life and death, the seven-year issue with all its implications, now lay in the stubby hands of the ex-bicycle mechanic.

Correspondents from the various newspaper services had come to Boston and set up their headquarters in the State House press gallery next to the balcony entrance of the House of Representatives. For the first time in Massachusetts history permission was given to run in telegraph wires from outside. The news for the first three days, however, was scant: the names of a few last witnesses, the rare glimpse of the governor, a brush-off remark from Hard-boiled Herman. Time seemed out of focus. The newsmen waited in the corridor outside the executive chambers, wandered through the Hall of Flags, made notes in the House balcony under the suspended Sacred Cod totem.

Wednesday, August 3, broke fair in Boston, with the fog bank receding along the line of harbor islands. Fuller put in a brief appearance at the State House, told the reporters he would give them the news at 8:30 that night, then announced he was leaving town to put the last touches on his decision. Actually he went no farther than a suite at the Ritz-Carlton at the other end of the Public Gardens, where he shut himself up with a Boston newspaperman, Edward Whiting, who did the actual writing, since the self-made governor was not capable of such sustained literary effort.

Just after dusk a crowd of several hundred gathered across the street from the State House, looking up at the five lighted windows in the left wing of the otherwise darkened building until dispersed by

---

* Fuller has been accused of altering his decision following Coolidge's announcement, but he had undoubtedly made up his mind the week before, after reading the Lowell Report.

the police. At the Hanover Street defense headquarters the two littered rooms were filled with tense silent figures. Mary Donovan sat by the telephone to answer calls in English, Moro took over when the caller was Italian. Frankfurter, in his shirtsleeves, squatted on a bale of papers. Gardner Jackson kept dashing to and from the State House. Most of the others were Italians from the North End. The thin light from an unshaded fixture drew out the lettering on the wall posters in bas-relief: JUSTICE IS DEAD in German; CALVARY OF SACCO AND VANZETTI in Italian; a Mexican poster demanding LIBERTY AND JUSTICE.

At the State House a score of reporters were waiting at the double-doored entrance to the executive chambers when Fuller finally reappeared at 8:26, his plump face set and unsmiling above his starched collar. He brushed past, impervious to questions. At 8:50 he reappeared, and read out a statement he had scribbled on the back of an envelope:

"I am very sorry not to oblige you with an interview. I can truthfully say that I am very tired and I trust the report will speak for itself. I would prefer not to indulge in any supplementary statement at this time." He promised that copies of the decision would be distributed at 9:30.

Nine-thirty passed into ten, with still no sign from behind the closed doors. There was the same impersonal sense of tension as when a jury is out, the same unreality of the immediate moment. The reporters walked up and down the darkened echoing corridors, talking and smoking. Most of the crowd driven away from the State House had drifted downtown to Newspaper Row. Hundreds gathered in front of the *Globe* and *Post* buildings to watch the blackboard bulletins. It was a strangely quiet crowd. A *Globe* reporter looking down from the second floor at the upturned heads wondered how anyone could tell what they were thinking. The director of Station WEEI had held an announcer ready all evening to go on the air with a special bulletin; now that the closing hour of eleven was approaching, he debated whether he should shut down. Mary Donovan and Moro at defense headquarters kept repeating over the telephone, "No news, Nothing yet." Louis Stark, pacing the State House corridor, began to doubt whether he would be able to meet the *Times'* 11:30 deadline.

Finally at 11:25 the double doors opened and Hard-boiled Herman appeared with several clerks who carried copies of the decision in sealed envelopes, each addressed with the name of a newspaper. Stark

sprinted for the marble stairs, ripping open his envelope and flipping
through the pages:

I believe . . . Sacco and Vanzetti . . . had a fair trial.

The telegraph operator was still holding the wire open to the *Times*
city room. "*Bulletin,*" Stark shouted as he reached the door of the
press gallery. "They die!"

The words flashed across the world from the ten telegraph wires.
Within minutes they were chalked up on the *Globe* bulletin board,
broadcast to New England by the waiting WEEI announcer, head-
lined on the morning editions that would shortly whip off the presses.

The morning papers carried the full text of the decision. Fuller
announced that he had set himself three tasks: to see whether the
jury trial was fair, whether the accused were entitled to a new trial,
and whether they were guilty or not guilty. Of Thayer he wrote:

*I see no evidence of prejudice in his conduct of the trial. That he
had an opinion as to the guilt or innocence of the accused after hearing the evidence is natural and inevitable.*

The governor did not consider that any of the supplementary
motions presented valid reasons for granting a new trial. He gave
no weight to Madeiros' confession, nor was he impressed with the
latter's knowledge of the South Braintree crime. His conclusion
and, he added, the unanimous conclusion of his advisory committee
was that Sacco and Vanzetti were guilty.

Warden Hendry kept the news from the prisoners until the next
morning when Thompson arrived with Rosina and Felicani. While
the other two stood behind him with bent heads, Thompson quietly
told the prisoners that they must die. Sacco appeared unruffled. "I
told you so," he called to Vanzetti in the next cell. Vanzetti seemed
stunned. "I just can't believe it," was all he said. Madeiros said
nothing at all.

After Rosina had left, Sacco sat down and wrote an open letter
to his "Friends and Comrades." Over the years his neat script had
become increasingly stylized, and in this moment the copperplate
regularity of his lines could have served for a formal invitation:

*From the death cell we are just inform from the defense committee
that the governor Fuller he has desede to kill us Ag. the 10th we
our not suprised for this news because we know the capitalist class
hard without any mercy the good soldiers of the rivolutions. We are*

proud for death and fall as all the good anarchist can fall. It is up to
you know o, brothers comrades! as I have tell you yesterday that your
only that can save us because we have never had faith at the governor
for we have always know that the gov. Fuller—Thayer and Katzmann
are the murders.

Vanzetti's blasting reaction found its outlet in a scarcely legible
scrawl, the direct opposite of Sacco's passive acceptance:

Governor Alvan T. Fuller is a murderor as Thayer, Katzmann, the
State perjurors and all the other. He sake hand with me like a
brother, make me believe he was honestly intentioned and that he
had not sent the three carbarn-boy to have no escuse to save us.
Now, igoring and denia all the proofs of or innocence and insult
us and murder us we are innocent.
This is the way of plutocracy against liberty, against the people.
Revenge our blood. We die for Anarcy. Long life Anarcy.

Yet by afternoon Vanzetti had so recovered himself that he was
able to give Mrs. Evans a remarkably detached view of Fuller.

We are his opposite all at all and all in all, while our enemies are
affines to him in all-most everything. Consciousely, subconsciousely
and unconsciousely he cannot escape to be tremendously influenced
and predisposed against us. But he gave me the impression he is
sincere; had made great efforts to learn the truth and was not settled,
at least deliberately, against us, before to begin his inquiry.
If he is sending us to death, it does not matter how honestly the
Governor can be convinced of our guiltiness, his conviction will not
make us guilty—we are and will remain innocent.

Fuller's adverse decision was for Thompson the end of the road.
There might be hasty appeals to the state and federal supreme courts,
all the delaying paraphernalia of certiorari and habeas corpus, with
at best the addition of a few extra weeks to lives he was convinced
were forfeit. Thompson felt a profounder sense of failure than
Moore's, for his world had failed—that pleasantly circumscribed
world of Boston into which he had fitted so easily. He had believed
that the venerable institutions of Massachusetts to which he gave his
allegiance would render justice even to two obscure foreigners, would
rectify the aberrations of a prejudiced trial and the blind partisan-
ship of a bigoted judge. Instead, the institutions had savaged these

men, and now were preparing to annihilate them. In these institutions and in the comfortable society they guarded he could no longer believe. A Harvard class day would never seem the same to him again, a Sunday sermon at the sedately familiar Church of the Redeemer would never sound the same. The brick fronts of Beacon Hill would have lost their mellowness. A traditionalist still, in the years that followed he faced Boston and complained of the lack of a responsible aristocracy that could restrain what he called "the shopkeeper's mentality." He tried to compensate for his disbelief in his class by participating in liberal causes, taking the stump at elections, speaking at legislative hearings and in the Massachusetts Judicial Council. But the gesture had lost its meaning, the spark had gone from his life.

He had already told Frankfurter that he would not continue. On receiving the news of the governor's decision, he and Ehrmann sent the Defense Committee their formal resignation, explaining:

We feel that the defendants are now entitled to have the benefit of the judgment of counsel who can take up the case untrammelled by the commitments of the past and less disturbed than we are by a sense of injustice.

Frankfurter at once telephoned Arthur Hill to say that he had a most serious matter to discuss with him. They lunched at the Somerset Club, then crossed Beacon Street and sat on a bench on the Common overlooking the Frog Pond. Frankfurter asked Hill if he would undertake the final appeal of the Sacco-Vanzetti case to the Supreme Court. Hill did not share Thompson's belief in the men's innocence, but he did believe they had not had a fair trial. He felt he could not refuse to make the effort on their behalf.

First of all he persuaded Elias Field and Richard Evarts to join him as junior counsel. Then on the morning of August 5 he called a conference in his office of Frankfurter, Ehrmann, and Musmanno. It was a conference of desperation, as Hill, beneath his assured, impervious exterior, was well aware. So it was felt by everyone present except for the buoyant Musmanno. There were only a few legal maneuvers left, and time was running out like quicksilver from a broken thermometer. Hastily they evolved a program. They would file a motion in Dedham for a new trial and revocation of sentence on the grounds of Judge Thayer's prejudice. They would request Chief Justice Hall of the Superior Court to assign a judge other than

Thayer to hear the motion. They would petition Governor Fuller for a stay of execution. They would file a motion in the Supreme Court for a writ of error, a writ of habeas corpus, and a stay of execution.

Musmanno arrived next morning at the clerk of court's office with a sheaf of affidavits from Mrs. Bernkopf, Mrs. Rantoul, Frank Sibley, George Crocker, Robert Benchley, Professor Richardson, and Chief Gallivan. He had also dug up a new witness of the South Braintree crime, Candido Di Bona, whose peculiar version of the event was that the driver of the Buick had been a gray-haired man, the two men leaning against the Rice & Hutchins fence had been about eighteen years old, and that there had been a fourth man wearing a soldier's uniform and carrying a rifle. Hill and Field, arguing on Thayer's unsuitability, got nowhere at all with Chief Justice Hall, who retired into legal phraseology to observe that "precedent and established practice require that the said motions in the said cause should be heard by the judge who had presided at the original trial thereof." He then directed that the motions should be heard before Judge Thayer on Monday, August 8.

Musmanno had more to think of than his affidavits as he drove to Dedham on that August Saturday, for the morning papers were splashed with accounts of a series of bombings that had wrecked four New York subway and elevated stations the night before. Between 11:17 and 11:37 tremendous explosions had occurred at Times Square, and on Fourth Avenue at Thirty-third, at Twenty-eighth and at Twenty-third streets, destroying surface kiosks, blowing sidewalks into the air, and shattering windows a hundred yards away. Only one person was killed, but numbers were injured. The same night the Emmanuel Presbyterian Church in Philadelphia was bombed, as was the house of the mayor of Baltimore. None of the bombers was ever discovered—in that respect the police kept their record unblemished.

Two days later bombs did heavy damage in Utica, New York. News came—undoubtedly exaggerated—of a wave of bombing overseas. Whether or not the bombings were the result of Governor Fuller's decision, a renewal of the anarchist propaganda of the deed, most Americans thought that they were. That week Massachusetts businessmen took out two hundred million dollars' worth of bomb and riot insurance. Boston police were placed on a bomb alert, all leaves and vacations were canceled, and the police commissioner ordered three hundred rapid-fire guns for the riot squad. Filene's sent John Dever away on an indefinite paid vacation.

The full text of the Lowell Committee report was published in the Sunday papers of August 7. Those concerned with the case spent the better part of the day analyzing it. It was a curiously ambiguous document. In regard to Sacco it concluded:

The Committee are of the opinion that Sacco was guilty beyond a reasonable doubt. In reaching this conclusion they are aware that it involves a disbelief in the evidence of his alibi at Boston, but in view of all the evidence they do not believe he was there that day.

As for Vanzetti:

The alibi . . . is decidedly weak. One of the witnesses, Rosen, seems to the Committee to have been shown by the cross-examination to be lying at the trial; another, Mrs. Brini, had sworn to an alibi for him in the Bridgewater case, and two more witnesses did not seem certain of the date until they had talked it over. . . . Four persons testified that they had seen him. . . . His face is much more unusual and more easily remembered, than that of Sacco. On the whole, we are of the opinion that Vanzetti also was guilty beyond a reasonable doubt.

What had the Committee meant by the phrase "on the whole" which seemed in itself to imply reservations about "reasonable doubt"? Did the Committee still feel some residual doubt in regard to Vanzetti? That was just one of the enigmas of the report. As for Madeiros:

His ignorance of what happened is extraordinary, and much of it cannot be attributed to a desire to shield his associates, for it had no connection therewith. . . . Indeed, in his whole testimony there is only one fact that can be checked . . . his statement that after the murder the car stopped to ask the way at the house of Mrs. Hewins. As this house was not far from . . . where Madeiros subsequently lived, he might very well have heard the fact mentioned.

With Grant a judge and Lowell a historian, the committee's ignorance of the law was at times astonishing:

The impression has gone abroad that Madeiros confessed committing the murder at South Braintree. Strangely enough, this is not really

the case. He confesses to being present, but not to being guilty of
murder. . . . If he were tried, his own confession, if wholly believed,
would not be sufficient for a verdict of murder in the first degree.

According to the law, of course, an accessory to a murder is equally
guilty.

As for the trial:

The Committee have seen no evidence sufficient to make them believe
that the trial was unfair. On the contrary, they are of the opinion that
the Judge endeavored, and endeavored successfully, to secure for the
defendants a fair trial; that the District Attorney was not in any way
guilty of unprofessional behavior, that he conducted the prosecution
vigorously but not improperly; and that the jury, a capable, impartial
and unprejudiced body, did, as they were instructed, "well and truly
try and true deliverance make."

However, in a measured way, the committee censured Judge
Thayer:

From all that has come to us we are forced to conclude that the Judge
was indiscreet in conversation with outsiders during the trial. He ought
not to have talked about the case off the bench, and doing so was a
grave break of official decorum. But we do not believe that he used
some of the expressions attributed to him, and we think that there
is exaggeration in what the persons to whom he spoke remember.
Furthermore, we believe that such indiscretions in conversation did
not affect his conduct at the trial or the opinions of the jury, who
indeed, so stated to the Committee.

Judge Grant felt more troubled than his colleagues, as he indicated
later in his autobiography:

It had fallen to me, at the request of my two associates, to examine
Judge Webster Thayer when he appeared before us at the State House.
The evidence that he had been grossly indiscreet in his remarks off
the bench was cumulative. I was amazed and incensed that any
Massachusetts Judge could have been so garrulous. That he had
talked he did not deny, but he declared under oath with convincing
emotion that several of the accusations against him—notably that of
having rehearsed a part of his charge to the jury—were untrue. When
we came to consider the language of our Report, I was asked, as the
one who ought to know how a judge should conduct himself, to

suggest the words of censure. They were used, and if my associates felt a shade less outraged than I by his unseemly conduct, it was from a due sense of perspective.

Most of the new evidence that the defense had unearthed appeared to the committee inconsequential. The cap with the lining Gallivan had torn was dismissed as a trivial matter. Gould's evidence added nothing new. Whatever affidavits Proctor may have signed later, "It must be assumed that the jury understood the meaning of plain English words, that if Captain Proctor was of the opinion that the bullet had been fired through Sacco's pistol he would have said so, instead of using the language which meant that it might have been fired through that pistol." This, of course, was an assumption Judge Thayer himself failed to make in his charge to the jury.

The committee did not mention Major Goddard's report, but from an inspection of the Van Amburgh parallel photographs they were "inclined to believe" that Bullet III had come from Sacco's pistol. They were impressed by its similarity to the obsolete cartridges found on Sacco. Thompson's contention that this bullet was a substitute they considered preposterous:

Such an accusation, devoid of proof, may be dismissed without further comment, save that the case of the defendants must be rather desperate on its merits when counsel feel it necessary to resort to a charge of this kind.

They found it a telling fact that the two men were armed when they were arrested. "Carrying fully loaded firearms, where they can be most quickly drawn," they observed, "can hardly be common among people whose views are pacifist and opposed to all violence." That Sacco could have put his pistol in his belt and forgotten about it they found incredible.* Nor did they feel that the defendants' radicalism explained all their lies. Lottie Packard's whirlwind remarks, for all their flights, impressed them. "The woman is eccentric, not unimpeachable in conduct," they concluded, "but the Committee believe that in this case her testimony is well worth consideration."

To the militants in Europe the reports of Governor Fuller and of the Lowell Committee set the official seal on what even the *Frankfurter*

---

* In 1960, at the State Police ballistic laboratory, I tried carrying Sacco's pistol in my belt. I found it impossible to move without being aware of both its weight and bulk.

Zeitung now referred to as a "political judicial murder." Letters and cables to Fuller, to the Secretary of State, to the White House, poured in from overseas, a certain lack of information and spontaneity apparent in the fact that some of them were addressed to President Harding, four years dead. The Vatican expressed its hope that an appeal to the United States Supreme Court "may open the way to justice or clemency." Former French Premier Edouard Herriot asked for a "measure of clemency." *Le Soir* reacted to the decisions "with a sentiment of profound horror." A past era echoed dimly when the Veterans of the Commune forwarded their protest. In Paris the police had forbidden all meetings, but in the Bois de Vincennes just outside the city a group of five thousand bannered militants paraded with linked arms behind Luigia Vanzetti. Luigia, passing through on her way to America, carried a banner reading: PARISIAN PEOPLE, SAVE MY BROTHER AND SACCO. THANKS.

The new wave of explosions caused alarm all over the United States. Extra guards were dispatched to the Summer White House in the Dakota hills. Federal buildings were placed under guard. The Army announced plans to move troops from Fort Meyer, Virginia, to Washington. Machine guns were posted around Fuller's summer home at Little Boar's Head. Harvard's buildings were guarded. Yet Boston, on the Sunday the Lowell Report was made public, seemed calm, almost indifferent. Alfred Baker Lewis for the Defense Committee and Harry Canter for the Communists had each obtained a permit to hold a meeting at designated trees on the Charles Street Mall. On the Tremont Street side a band in the Parkman Bandstand offered rival attractions. Between five and ten thousand persons gathered on the Common that afternoon, no great number for a city with a surrounding population of over two million. Some were there who made a habit of sauntering on a summer Sunday afternoon, others came from curiosity or to listen to the band. The genuine sympathizers, mostly from the North End, were probably in a minority. Nevertheless Superintendent of Police Michael Crowley disapproved of any such meetings, and his feelings were reinforced by the bombings of two days before. A plump set-faced man in a panama with a turned-down brim, he waddled up the Mall to warn both Baker and Canter that if any disparaging remarks were made about Governor Fuller or the Lowell Committee, that would end the meetings.

In no time at all, Mary Donovan, standing on a platform with a banner reading "DID YOU SEE WHAT I DID TO THOSE ANARCHIST

BASTARDS?"—JUDGE THAYER, proclaimed that Governor Fuller was a murderer. Crowley, raising his fat hand, announced that the meeting was suspended. Four mounted police edged their horses in and began scattering the crowd. Mary Donovan protested wildly: "This meeting must go on. I will speak for Sacco and Vanzetti. They are innocent men! They must not be murdered!" Crowley, in an attempt to be fatherly to a fellow Celt, observed that *bastard* was no word for a lady to use. It was no word for a judge to use either, Mary Donovan snapped.

As the core of the crowd began to mill about the speakers' stands, while the others moved away, the bearded Edward James bobbed up, scarlet with indignation, to stutter: "Down with the police! Get at them, men!" After a scuffle four men were arrested, including Canter and a bloody-nosed James. Next day in police court James, in the true revolutionary tradition, refused to recognize the judge or reply to charges. He was fined seventy-five dollars, which he refused to pay until the judge offered him the alternative of ninety days on Deer Island. At first James announced that he was going to be a martyr. Then, as the glow of the barricades faded, he paid up.

With the executions only three days off, the Defense Committee now appealed for a hundred thousand Americans to march on Boston and take part in a death watch at the State House and at the State Prison:

We call the leaders of American letters, science, art, education and social reform to lead the peaceful demonstration at the Charlestown jail. Come by train and boat, come on foot or in your car! Come to Boston! Let all the roads of the nation converge on Beacon Hill! Come armed with a black band on your sleeve, come armed with inextinguishable faith that Sacco and Vanzetti must and shall live.

Few people in Massachusetts failed to read the Lowell Report the Sunday of its appearance. The Defense Committee denounced it at once, the Communists derided it, but its effect—with the potency of the Lowell name behind it—was to settle the matter for a large number of Back Bay and Cambridge middle-of-the-roaders. "Most of the serious and earnest-minded people who had misgivings as to the original verdict in Judge Thayer's court," the *Herald* editorialized, "have had these dissipated by the calm and dispassionate recital of the evidence by President Lowell and his associates." Dr. Morton Prince said he could see no escape from the report's conclusions. Bishop

Lawrence, who was not bashful about treading with angels, wrote to Fuller:

You will, I am sure, allow me to express to you my admiration of the way in which you have done your duty in the Sacco-Vanzetti case.

You have been wise, patient, dignified and courageous, worthy of the highest traditions of the Commonwealth.

Medical Examiner Magrath announced that he was now "morally certain" of the two men's guilt, an opinion he had undoubtedly held from the beginning.*

Chief Justice of the United States William Howard Taft, whose knowledge of the case was slight but whose Wigmorish opinion was that the propaganda "had been created by large contributions of female and male fools and had been circulated through all the communistic and criminal classes the world over," sent congratulatory notes to Lowell and Grant later in the year, writing to the latter:

Now that all is over I can properly . . . thank you for accepting the task of serving on the Governor's committee of advisors in that case. It was a thankless task and required courage and sacrifice to do it. You and your colleagues did it and did it well. It concerned the welfare of society and the world in an unusual way. It is remarkable how Frankfürter with his article was able to present to so large a body of readers a perverted view of the facts and then through the world-wide conspiracy of communism spread it to so many, many countries. Our law schools lent themselves to the vicious propaganda. The utter lack of substance in it all is shown by the event. It was a bubble and was burst by the courage of the Governor and his advisors.

Robert Lincoln O'Brien regarded the Lowell report in the light of an umpire's decision at a Longwood Cricket Club tennis match:

---

* In his book *Sacco-Vanzetti: The Murder and the Myth*, Robert Montgomery attributes the following story about Magrath to Chief Stewart and G. Andrews Moriarty, a friend of Magrath's:

"During the trial Stewart . . . obtained for Magrath several hairs from Sacco's cap and several hairs from the comb Sacco was using in the jail. Magrath put these hairs on slides and looked at them through a microscope. They were identical, and both Stewart and Magrath suggested to Katzmann that he use the evidence, which certainly would have been conclusive so far as the cap was concerned.

"Katzmann was tempted, but he finally decided against it, because he believed that the defense and the newspapers might ridicule an attempt to hang the defendants by a hair or make some other pun on this much-punished word."

To those of us who felt that the need of some further inquiry existed, even after the Supreme Judicial Court had ruled that the case had been properly concluded, it seemed the part of good sportsmanship to accept the findings of Mr. Lowell and his associates, particularly since we could find no three men in all the world—were we to select them ourselves—in whose findings we would have more complete confidence.

But there were others, conservatives like Waldo Cook, the editor of the Springfield *Republican*, who found the report staggering. Speaking of its mention of Thayer's grave breach of judicial decorum, Cook wrote: "If it was grave, it must taint irretrievably in the record the Sacco-Vanzetti case for all time." The New York *Times* questioned the phrase "on the whole" and wondered "whether the ends of justice could not better have been obtained in some other way." Pulitzer's New York *World*, which under its chief editorial writer, Walter Lippmann, had consistently taken the side of Sacco and Vanzetti, gave its entire editorial page to an editorial "Doubts That Will Not Down." Heywood Broun, as columnist for the *World*, announced bitterly that "if all the venerable college presidents in the country tottered forward and pronounced the men guilty they would still be innocent." Broun—reacting to what he considered the general apathy about the case in the United States—became so violent in his comments on President Lowell's throwing the switch and Harvard as Hangman's House that Pulitzer finally suspended his columns.

On opinion overseas, even conservative opinion, the Lowell Report had almost no effect.

On Monday morning, August 8, in the Pemberton Square Courthouse, Supreme Court Justice Sanderson listened to Thompson—now merely a witness—testify that the right of the defendants had been violated by Judge Thayer's prejudice. The justice denied the application for a writ of error and stay of execution. At Dedham in the afternoon, when Judge Thayer opened his special session he found himself in the anomalous position of ruling on his own prejudice. The courthouse was again heavily guarded and the public barred from the courtroom, although Sheriff Capen made no difficulties about admitting Rosina, Mrs. Evans, Mrs. Henderson, and other friends. The prisoners themselves were not present.

Thayer remained stubbornly vulnerable and Hill did not spare him. To the latter's passionate request that he step down from the bench he observed impassively that the chief justice had assigned him and he was there to hear the motion.

Hill's anger vibrated through the open-windowed courtroom: "Do you think you can sit on the case and consider the issues? It is beyond human power to do. No man is so wise, clear-headed and dispassionate that he can sit on the question whether he was actuated by prejudice, and it is not fair to ask him. It should be before some other man, not only because of the welfare of the defendants, the welfare of the bench, the welfare of the administration of justice, but the welfare of Your Honor himself."

In answer to the motions for a new trial, Thayer ruled that according to Massachusetts law he had no jurisdiction to grant one, once sentence had been passed. As to the motion for a revocation of sentence and stay of execution, he agreed to accept Hill's affidavits and listen to his arguments. With chill and condescending politeness Hill, enumerating the affidavits, pointed out that Judge Thayer's state of mind at the trial and afterward disqualified him from acting as a judge. Hill insisted that in all the judge's rulings as well as in his actions off the bench he had shown prejudice.

Thayer stared fixedly at Hill, his eyes hard and bright, a thin glow behind his waxen pallor. When the lawyer had finished he began to speak, his voice more charged with feeling than ever it had been before in that familiar room:

"I agreed and always insisted with the full force of my nature that no matter what race or religion, conservative or radical, conformist or nonconformist was entitled to a fair and impartial trial and as my mind goes back over seven years of lawyers contesting every point, I recall that the case was taken on two occasions to the Supreme Court and the court dealt with two hundred sixty exceptions and . . . did not leave one exception.

"That I am willing to be judged by—but prejudice—there isn't any now and there wasn't at any time. I do this now as it is the only way a judge can plead his own case. For seven years I have been in a position where I could not say a word. This is the only time I could say anything."

The arguments were brief. Attorney General Arthur Reading for the Commonwealth characterized Hill's as "the most preposterous ever heard from a learned lawyer." Thayer at the end of the afternoon announced that he would reserve his decision on the second motion. Then, early Tuesday morning, he telephoned in from his home in Worcester that the revocation of sentence and stay of sentence were denied. From this and from Justice Sanderson's ruling, Hill at once filed exceptions. Privately, however, he admitted he had given up hope. Only the young inexperienced Musmanno could find any encouragement in the further manipulation of the bastard Latin legal phrases. Certiorari, coram nobis—they were like the last moves in a chess game when a player has only a pawn to interpose between his king and his opponent's queen.

That afternoon for the first time pickets appeared before the State House, a half-dozen at the start, men in shirtsleeves and women in work dresses, wearing black armbands and carrying placards denouncing the imminent executions. Defiantly they marched back and forth, their numbers growing to a dozen, a score, and finally to over a hundred, watched with jeering curiosity by a much larger crowd from the other side of the street near the Shaw Memorial. News of the picketing spread through the State House. Governor Fuller stepped into the council chamber briefly to look down from the oval-topped window on the sweaty marchers. The picketing was the beginning of the legend that in the last days of the case the Massachusetts State House was zoned by a constantly replenished line of writers, artists, and intellectuals. Some such did find their places in the line—John Dos Passos, Dorothy Parker, Edna St. Vincent Millay, and others—and were arrested and taken to the Joy Street Station on the other side of Beacon Hill, but most of the picketers were foreign-born men and women from the garment district.

Harry Canter led the pickets the first day, encouraged by Alfred Baker Lewis. The Defense Committee, increasingly angry at the Communists' infiltrating efforts, held aloof. Fred Beal, a young and dedicated Communist whose radicalism dated from the Lawrence strike, was astonished at the coldness of his reception when he turned up at Hanover Street. "Why can't you leave Sacco and Vanzetti alone?" Secretary Moro asked him bitterly. "Why can't you let them die in peace? You people don't care for Sacco and Vanzetti. Let them burn; it will be better for the cause."

As the picketing continued and the watching crowds increased, Police Captain James McDevitt was sent down from the Joy Street station. In the pattern that would be followed in dealing with the subsequent picketings of the State House, he approached the marchers and gave them seven minutes to disperse. When they did not, he carted off thirty-nine of them to the station. Thirty-one of those arrested were named in the Boston papers. So far as their names are any indication, twenty were Jews and three Italians.

The general strike called for that afternoon brought out only a few hundred men and women in Boston, most of whom found their way to the line in front of the State House. In New York almost 100,000 walked out, the majority of them garment workers. Overseas there was an almost hushed expectancy. Sacco and Vanzetti dominated the European headlines. The Atlantic cables continued to be weighted with protests that included such noted names as that of Lafayette's great-grandson. At the Charlestown prison Western Union and Postal Telegraph installed eighteen wires, four for direct communication overseas. The area within half a mile of the prison was declared a dead zone. The streets were barred and Prison Point Bridge closed.

Early in the evening Vanzetti sent for Thompson, who spent two hours in the death house talking with the prisoners. Sacco was now in the twenty-third day of his hunger strike. Vanzetti had not eaten for five days. Thompson, on leaving, met a group of reporters at the prison gate and told them that the prisoners "continue to assert their innocence, do not express any hope, remain courageous, and feel they are dying for a principle."

Would Governor Fuller grant the prisoners an additional respite to give Justice Sanderson and Thayer time to decide on Hill's exceptions? That was the question on the morning of August 10. Fuller reached his State House office at 9:30 and at once summoned the members of his council.

At almost the same time the executioner for New York, New Jersey, and Massachusetts, Robert Elliott, arrived with his famous black bag at the South Station. When Musmanno went to the prison later in the morning with a petition for a writ of habeas corpus, he noticed guards setting up machine guns on the brick ramp running along the top of the prison wall. As he reached the death cells and began to talk to the men through the bars, he could hear the workmen tinkering with the electric chair in the next room, and he sensed the sudden vibration of the floor as they switched on the current. Vanzetti told him not to mind, that the men had been working on it since the day before. Sacco again refused to sign any petition, telling Musmanno: "They are going to crucify me, crucify both of us. They have been driving nails into us for seven years. Let's have it over." Vanzetti signed willingly enough, then inscribed his copy of *The Rise of American Civilization* and offered it to Musmanno, who refused it, saying he would wait until Vanzetti got out. From Charlestown Musmanno drove with Hill—as did Thompson and a Washington lawyer, John Finerty, later in the day—thirty miles north to Beverly where United States Supreme Court Justice Oliver Wendell Holmes had his summer home. All four men knew that if Fuller failed to act, the only other hope for Sacco and Vanzetti was in an appeal to the federal courts. Holmes met his visitors on the porch, listened to them gravely, even regretfully, but held that he had not the legal right to intervene in the internal judicial processes of Masachusetts. "You don't have to convince me that the atmosphere in which these men were tried precluded a fair trial," he told them, "but that is not enough to give me as a Federal judge jurisdiction. If I listened to you any more I would do it," he continued. "I must not do it." With that the old justice turned on his heel and went into the house.

Hill, following his rebuff, went on to hunt out Judge George Anderson of the United States Circuit Court. After the 1920 Palmer raids Judge Anderson had released the Boston aliens rounded up by the Bureau of Investigation and had castigated the Department of Justice. But this time Judge Anderson, like Holmes, held that he could not interfere in state affairs.

Fuller, determined to expand the collective responsibility for his decision, sent for all the Commonwealth's former attorneys general. Seven of them arrived before midday at his office for consultation. His council began its own deliberations after lunch and continued all afternoon. Meanwhile the pickets with their black armbands and placards, chanting their slogans, again marched in front of the State House. Captain McDevitt gave his dispersal warning, and after seven minutes the police moved in. Those pickets who did not scatter were taken to the Joy Street Station. This time the watching crowd showed itself much more hostile. There were mocking shouts of "Hang 'em!" as the pickets were hustled up Joy Street. They were booked at the station, and those who did not have the twenty-five dollars bail money were bailed out by Mrs. Evans and her friends.

A solid blue line of police extended along the cobbled paving in front of the Charlestown prison. Prison police, State Police, Metropolitan Police, Boston and Cambridge police, had all been called out—the largest force ever assembled in Boston's history. On Prison Point Bridge a platoon of firemen uncoiled hoses and stood ready to water down any mob trying to force the barriers. Below the bridge, in the slimy tidal inlet known as the Miller River, the police launch Argus chugged up and down with a machine gun at its bow.

Inside the blank-walled death house Madeiros and Sacco lay on their cots in listless inanition. Some days earlier Sacco had begun a letter to his son, but he no longer felt the strength to continue with it. Vanzetti wrote brief farewell notes to Mrs. Winslow, Mrs. Codman, Mrs. Henderson, and Mrs. Evans, whom he now addressed as "Comrade." His one enduring regret as the hours slipped away was that he would not be able to see his sister Luigia again. Late in the afternoon Madeiros' mother and sister arrived from Providence, but he received them indifferently. The old Portuguese woman collapsed on the threshold of the death house and had to be helped from the building.

At the cluttered Hanover Street rooms there was the same penumbral atmosphere that there had been the night of Fuller's decision, but with the tenseness giving way by almost imperceptible degrees to lassitude. Mary Donovan answered the telephone, the shaggy Jackson scribbled notes, Felicani bent forward under the poster proclaiming JUSTICE IS THE ISSUE, Rosina Sacco sat in a corner, silent except for an occasional dry cough while from time to time she abstractedly crumpled bits of paper. During the evening Frankfurter bustled in and out on obscure errands, his eyes deep and compassionate behind his rimless oval pince-nez. Hill and Joseph Moro appeared briefly and spoke a few encouraging words.

After spending the afternoon with his council, Fuller broke off for a meal, then resumed the sitting at 7:30. An hour later Hill appeared in the Council Chamber and pleaded and argued for two hours, begging the councilors and the governor not to destroy the subject matter of litigation while it was still in the hands of the courts. After he left, the councilors buzzed among themselves. Still the governor could not make up his mind.

Meanwhile the slim, gray-haired, twisted-mouthed executioner arrived at the prison with the official witnesses. As usual, refreshments had been prepared. The prison officers' clubroom now held the largest group of reporters ever assembled in Massachusetts for an execution. By ten o'clock the three prisoners had been notified that they were to die at midnight.

At defense headquarters Rosina suddenly fell forward in a faint. Mary Donovan picked her up, took her away in a taxi, and left her at a friend's house in the neighborhood. When she returned she sat down again by the telephone, and, as if she were thinking aloud, suddenly said: "What if the finger of God should stay this execution tonight!" Then she picked up the receiver and in a broken voice called Thompson to ask what steps should be taken to claim the two men's bodies.

It was 11:24 before Fuller finally made up his official mind. With the concurrence of his council he decided to grant the prisoners a twelve-day respite "to afford the courts an opportunity to complete the consideration of the proceedings." Captain Charles Beaupré of the State Police gave the word to the reporters outside the council chamber. Secretary William Reed telephoned the news to Warden Hendry. Hendry was pleased, and showed it. Despite his meaty butcher's face, he was a good-hearted man who hated executions. With the copied reprieve in his hand he hurried down the long cement corridor to the death house, calling out as he reached the threshold: "It's all off, boys!" The three men rose from their cots. Vanzetti gripped the bars of the cell until his knuckles turned white. "I'm damn glad of that," he said shakily. "I'd like to see my sister before I die."

Back at his office Hendry passed around cigars to the reporters and witnesses while an unheeded assistant read out the formal wording of the respite with all its whereases and know-ye-alls.

Not until a few minutes before midnight was the news of the respite telephoned into the Hanover Street offices, yet when the announcement came it caused no tremor, no babble of voices, only a relieving quiet. Mary Donovan left without saying a word to go to Rosina. Someone, who seemed to speak for everyone in the room, remarked: "We have until the twenty-second. Well, that is something."

Across the ocean it seemed for a moment as if the protesting voices had won. *Pravda* proclaimed:

The mighty roar of protest from the Soviet Union, together with the voice of the working classes the world over, forced even the pluto-cratic American bourgeoisie to hesitate and maneuver.

In Berlin, *Die Rote Fahne* announced triumphantly:

The working millions and only they in the forefront of the battle against class injustice have won the first victory. Sacco and Vanzetti are provisionally rescued.

L'Humanité rallied its readers with militant confidence:

Now let us exact the liberty of the two martyrs.

In the United States there was a feeling that Fuller would now commute the death sentences to life imprisonment, a course recommended by the Springfield *Republican*. The New York *Times* shared this opinion, observing four days after the respite:

Honest and fair-minded people are still disputing about certain aspects of the Sacco-Vanzetti case, but on our part there is virtual unanimity of opinion. This is that the long delay in determining the fate of the two men is a reproach to American justice. It is something that is almost impossible to explain to foreigners.

Outside opposition and criticism had long since contracted the mood of the Massachusetts community beyond reason. With each external attack the community ranks closed in an emotional need—masquerading as justice—to see Sacco and Vanzetti dead. This feeling was reinforced by the bombing on August 15 of the East Milton home of Dedham juror Lewis McHardy. The charge placed on the porch of his two-story frame house at 463 Pleasant Street, exploded at 3:30 in the morning. So great was the blast that little was left of the house but the frame. Windows were shattered a quarter of a mile away. McHardy, his wife, and three grown children were asleep on the second floor. They were hurled out of bed and covered with debris, but somehow managed to escape with only minor bruises.

If before the blowing up of the McHardy house there had been the slightest chance of a commutation of sentence for Sacco and Vanzetti, afterward there was none.*

The twelve days of respite were marked by dramatic defense efforts that filled the world's headlines. The author and journalist Isaac Don Levine came on to Boston, convinced that a legal case could be built around the issue of the Department of Justice files. Perhaps Thompson might have inspected them in 1926 if he had been more tactful in dealing with the tentative offer of the Bureau of Investigation's Boston branch. Since then Attorney General Sargent had refused the defense any access to them. However, he offered to forward them on request to Governor Fuller, the members of the Lowell Committee, or the Commonwealth's attorney general. Such a request

---

* A reward was offered and a few unlikely suspects were questioned, but the police never developed any real clues as to the bomber. The same bombing pattern was followed five years later when Judge Thayer's house in Worcester was partially destroyed. Executioner Elliott's New York house was also bombed some time after the executions.

was never made. Fuller told reporters that the files would be no use to him in forming his opinion inasmuch as he did not know what an anarchist was.*

On August 10 the Defense Committee had sent a long telegram to United States Attorney General Sargent claiming that "evidence exists in the files of the Department of Justice, of the most competent character which would clear Sacco and Vanzetti of the charge of payroll robbery" and demanding that Sargent persuade President Coolidge to intervene. The committee also repeated Thompson's charge of "a conspiracy between the employees of the Department of Justice and Katzmann and Williams to wrongfully convict." For Levine these claims and charges were all very well, but in the unskilled hands of Gardner Jackson and Mary Donovan and the Italians on the committee they would lead to nothing. What was needed was a professional touch, "a fresh corps of attorneys of national reputation," publicity directed like an arrow to the Department of Justice, names that carried weight. For this purpose, and to the impotent fury of Mary Donovan, Levine organized the Citizens National Committee for Sacco and Vanzetti. He himself kept in the background—the figurehead chairman was the *New Republic's* editor, Robert Morss Lovett—but he brought to the new organization his own energy and the names of noted acquaintances. Glenn Frank, Zona Gale, Ida Tarbell, David Starr Jordan, Paul Kellogg of the *Survey*, John Haynes Holmes, Oswald Garrison Villard, Alexander Meiklejohn, Katharine Anne Porter, Jane Addams, William Hocking, Waldo Cook, John Moors, Mary Woolley, and John Dewey were among those endorsing the new committee.

In an open letter the committee announced its purpose, "to induce the Federal Government to intervene in the Sacco and Vanzetti case because of the grave charges which have been made against the Department of Justice and because of the serious international situation which has arisen." During the last feverish week it raked Washington with drumfire demands that the Department of Justice open its files. The committee set up quarters in the Hotel Bellevue just below the State House. There, in a long room on the second floor

---

* Nine years earlier Congressman Fuller had seemed more knowledgeable when he voted to exclude the elected Socialist Victor Berger from Congress and in a jangle of metaphors called for "the crucifixion of disloyalty, the nailing of sedition to the cross of free government, where the whole brood of anarchists, bolsheviks, I.W.W.'s and revolutionaries may see and read the solemn warning."

known as Parlor D, a swarm of volunteer workers moved in with desks and typewriters. For twenty hours a day letters and releases poured out across the United States. Paul Kellogg sent over five hundred telegrams to Americans of note. Almost everyone who arrived in Boston, from Michael Gold to Edna St. Vincent Millay, now stopped off at Parlor D rather than at the Hanover Street rooms. A new cluster of lawyers gathered there: John Finerty of New York, who drew up the final habeas corpus motion; former New York attorney general William Schuyler Jackson; Arthur Garfield Hays, Francis Fisher Kane, and Frank Walsh, who together would take up the matter of the Justice Department files directly with Attorney General Sargent. The new committee, unlike the Communists, managed to remain on speaking terms with the old. Relations remained, in Levine's words, "correct but remote."

The morning after the midnight respite, the three prisoners were taken from the death house back to Cherry Hill. In spite of having gone twenty-six days without food, Sacco was able to walk unaided across the prison yard and up the iron staircase. When Musmanno visited Sacco and Vanzetti in the barber shop later in the morning to tell them that Justice Sanderson had allowed the exceptions to his ruling to be taken to the full bench of the state supreme court, he found them in a cheerful mood. Both seemed to absorb something of the young Italian lawyer's optimism. Although Sacco still refused to eat, Vanzetti broke his five-day fast with a cup of coffee.

During the day the New England manager of the United Press, Henry Minott, visited the prison and asked Vanzetti to write an open letter explaining his side of the case. In his renewed optimism, Vanzetti spent the next two days setting down what he well realized might be his final thoughts. On August 12 his two-page letter to "Friends and Comrades" was sent—in somewhat altered form—all over the world through the wires of the United Press:

There is nowhere, neither in earth nor in heavens, anything that can makes the true untrue and the untrue true. By true I mean the truths which altogether form the Universal truth. By truths I mean the real condictions, faculties, essence of each one of those unnumerable, relative things, all related and all evolving, which total sum forms the Universal truth—which is what it is in itself and not at all what anyone or ones—I, you, or all—believe or may think to know what it is. . . .

II

On Dec. 24, 1919, at 8.20 A.M. a robbery was attempted in Bridge-water, Mass.

In every minutes of the 24 hours of that day I was in Plymouth, Mass., about 30 miles from the place where the above cited attempt to robb occured. Furthermore, I had been never in such place before my arrest on May 5th, 1920. In the very moment I was in the bakery shop of Luigi Bastoni in Plymouth.

On April 15, 1920, at 3 P.M. and high-way robbery was committed in South Braintree and two men were killed.

In every minute of that day's hours I have been in Plymouth, Mass., about 35 mile from the place of the crime; I have not yet been there, that I know, and in the very minute of the crime I was speaking with Mr. Corl, who was preparing his motorboat, on the Plymouth shore, to be put in the water for the new fishing season (1920)

The above said is true and there is nothing that can makes it untrue.

III

At the Plymouth trial my counselor, Joe Vahey has betrayed me like Iscariat betrayed Christ. He not even went to the place of the crime to see how it happened what it was; what people were saying and knowing. Out of hundreds of the eyes-witnesses of the crime who came to look upon me for several consecutive days, on my arrest, in Brockton police station, and all of them, safe one or two posetively denied I was one of the bandit they saw. Mr. Vahey even failed to produce a single one of those eyes-witnesses

Chief Steward, Katzmann, Judge Thayer succeeded to form a jury out of a dozen hating, prejudiced, jelous, fearing, narrow-minded, vain, excited and ferociouse provincial bigits, real lyncher in vest of jurors.

These our jurors may believe or feign to believe the most apparently false Governament witnesses; they can disbelieve or feingn so, the truthful 18 defence; witnesses and they can bring out a verdict of guiltness against me.

Judge Thayer can injoy in given me the most severe and cruel sentence that I knew for such offense as the one of which I was framed. He can insult me. All this may be a great sadisfaction for the Plymouth Cordage Company, for Joe Vahey, Steward, Katzmann, & Thayer.

But I tell you that I am innocent of that crime and there is nothing that can make me guilty of it.

IV

Dedham trial. . . . Again Chief Steward, Persecutor Frederick Katzmann, William, Judge Webster Thayer, Cheriff Copan, a Joshef Ross, Lola Andrew, a Pelzner, twelf Linchers in vest of Jurors, a double verdict of murder in first degree against us. . . .

I tell you that I am innocent of such crime, and no State tools, no perjuring harlots, crooks, criminals, venals, deficients, no Steward, no Copan, no black-guards, no thief as Ross, no Katzmann, no Williams, no sadism of jurors who had been ready to hang us before the beginning of the trial, no verdict of guiltness, no death sentence, no Webster Thayer, no Massachusetts, none of them nothing of this, not even all of this can change an innocent man in a guilty one.

And I tell you that Nicola Sacco is neither a thief nor a high-way murderors and not even all of our enemies and of our case can make this truth untrue.

V

Judge Webster Thayer can denies us as many unrefutable and undenyable appeals and doom us at his heart content.

The Judges of the Massachusetts Supreme Judiciary Court can uphold Thayer's "decision" at their heart content.

The Judges of the Supreme Court of the United State can uphold at their heart content both Thayer and the Massachusetts Justice: we will remain innocent.

Although Sacco had been able to walk from the death house to Cherry Hill, his sturdy peasant body was beginning to give way. On the thirtieth day of his strike Dr. McLaughlin, the prison physician, told him flatly that the time had come when he must eat. To emphasize this McLaughlin showed him a rubber tube three feet long, greased at one end for insertion in the nose and with a rubber bulb for pumping at the other end. Two guards had brought the men to the prison barber shop, where Vanzetti, Musmanno, and Rosina were waiting. Rosina, as she had done all along, begged her husband to eat. The others kept urging him. Sliding the tube between his fingers, Dr. McLaughlin told him: "You must eat. I can make you. I am stronger than you are." Sacco smiled, took a mug of soup that one of the guards had poured out, lifted it, and said ironically, "Good health to all of you,"

The day after McHardy's house was bombed, Hill appeared at the heavily guarded Pemberton Square Courthouse to argue the exceptions before the four available members of the Supreme Court. Impassively the justices listened to the familiar argument that Judge Thayer himself had become a defendant and that to allow him to hear any question concerning Sacco and Vanzetti was to make him a judge in his own case. Attorney General Reading countered that even if Thayer had been privately prejudiced, that would not disqualify him unless his prejudice had been communicated to the jury. The justices reserved their decision.

Three mornings later Court Reporter Grabill walked down the inner steps of the still-guarded courthouse with a copy of the Supreme Court decision. He handed it to Musmanno and Hill, at the same time informing the reporters: "Gentlemen, the exceptions in both cases have been overruled."

The Supreme Court had in effect reaffirmed that it had no jurisdiction, that once sentence had been passed, a motion for a new trial came too late. And a motion for revocation was the same thing as a motion for a new trial. As for the prejudice of Judge Thayer:

The judicial conduct of the trial judge in hearing and deciding the motion based on his own alleged bias or prejudice need not be discussed because neither the judge nor any of his associates had jurisdiction to entertain the motion.

In brief there was nothing more to be expected from the courts of the Commonwealth of Massachusetts. When Hill and Evarts asked Chief Justice Hall for a stay of execution until the United States Supreme Court might decide whether the law of the land had been observed in the case, he coldly refused.

Musmanno went at once to Charlestown to tell the prisoners. Sacco merely said it was what he expected, and continued the letter he was writing to Dante.* But when Vanzetti heard the news the discipline of his mind suddenly snapped. "Get the million men!" he shouted. He demanded a radio transmitter in his cell so that he could tell the whole world his story. All that morning he remained standing behind the bars, calling out for the million men. That night he wrote a letter to Thompson dating it "New Era year I":

My enemies make me to aim their cannons, shoting at me every night to kill me.

---

* Dante had visited his father the day before and Sacco had been much moved, noting proudly that his boy was now taller than he was.

*Please, send this instruction to the Boston Defense Committee—
as quickly as possible.*

Dear Friends of the Committee.

*I hope you have radiocasted at once my order of mobilization to
all the nations of the world. Big corps of men are in march, if I per-
ceived well last night. Take all the protective measure to the crossing
of Rio Grande and Panamal Canal; lent me the coasts most you can.
Renew my notes to the King of Italy and the Pope. I want all my
witnesses as well. Informe me by wireless, and immediately, of each
move and particular. I wait for you and Mr. Thompson as soon as
possible for a general council. Recur to Mr. Thompson for legal
matters.*

In spite of Vanzetti's seizure, the prisoners were taken back to the
death house that afternoon.

At almost the same time Luigia Vanzetti arrived in New York on the
Aquitania. She was met on the dock by Felicani, Rosina, Carlo Tresca,
Mrs. Henderson, Dorothy Parker, Ruth Hale—Heywood Broun's wife
—a corps of newsmen, and several hundred supporters carrying signs
and banners. Rosina embraced her solemnly as a sister in sorrow, then
the reporters pressed in. The crowd made Luigia shrink. She was a
frail, plain, dark woman, plainly dressed, who even at the age of
thirty-six had the withered appearance of an autumn leaf. Her large
eyes were shadowed by a helmet hat, her mouth permanently sad, her
chin receding. She was of that Latin type, sexless and compassionate,
ordained from adolescence either to be a maiden aunt or a nun. As
she talked through an interpreter to reporters, she fingered a gold
medallion of the Sodality of the Blessed Virgin. What she said was
embarrassing to all but Rosina. "I am here," she told them, "to guide
my brother back to the religion from which he has fallen, so that he
may be prepared to meet his Maker. He was brought up in the church
and he used to be a good Catholic. I have prayed continually that
he return to the church and see a priest."

In the last seventeen days before the executions, Hill and the other
defense lawyers appealed to fourteen justices of four courts. The
evening of Vanzetti's seizure Musmanno took the train for Washington to file writs of certiorari with the clerk of the United States

Supreme Court on the grounds that the actions of the Massachusetts courts were a denial of the rights of Sacco and Vanzetti under the Constitution's fourteenth amendment, providing that "no State shall deprive any person of life, liberty, or property without due process of law." Once these writs were filed, once the case had officially reached the Supreme Court, the young lawyer, boundlessly confident, was certain that one justice could be found from among the nine who would grant a stay of execution.

After finding that he could not yet file his papers because he had not brought the record of the proceedings, he went on to the Justice Department to see the acting attorney general, George Farnum, who had once served in Massachusetts as Assistant United States Attorney under Katzmann's former aide, Harold Williams. Musmanno and Farnum afterward gave conflicting versions of what occurred in their interview. To Musmanno's question, Farnum replied there was nothing in the files linking Sacco and Vanzetti with the South Braintree crime but added that there was matter in the files unfavorable to them. What this was he refused to disclose unless Musmanno would agree to keep it secret, and when the latter refused the conversation came to an end. Next day Jackson, Hays, Kane, and Walsh, representing the Citizens' Committee, spent the morning with Farnum, to whom they had been shunted by Attorney General Sargent, then on vacation in Vermont. Farnum, repeating the Department's refusal to make the files available to representatives of unofficial organizations, declared that they "contained no evidence tending to establish the guilt or innocence of Sacco and Vanzetti, or either of them, of the crime for which they were convicted in the Massachusetts courts, nor any evidence whatever of any collusion whatsoever between the State and Federal authorities prior to the arrest of Sacco and Vanzetti or prior, during or subsequent to the trial of these two men."

Meanwhile, the contest of the courtrooms accelerated. At the same time that Musmanno was walking up the steps of the Capitol, Field, in Massachusetts, was presenting another petition for a writ of habeas corpus to Judge James Morton, Jr., of the United States District Court. Morton brusquely denied the petition and refused to allow any appeal. At 2:15 Hill and Evarts conferred with Justice Holmes in Beverly. Holmes listened to them with grave courtesy but said that he did not have the authority to meddle in the affairs of state courts, and that he would not feel justified in granting a stay of execution unless he felt that there was a reasonable chance that the Supreme

Court would ultimately reverse the judgment against Sacco and Vanzetti. This he could not bring himself to believe, but he added that another of his fellow justices might see the matter in a different light.

With each rebuff the defense lawyers frantically sought out another judge, each time to receive again the inevitable answer.

While Hill was arguing vainly with Holmes in Beverly, Luigia, accompanied by Rosina, Felicani, and Mrs. Henderson, went to the prison. Warden Hendry met her at the gate. Although it was quite unprecedented, he had Vanzetti let outside his cell to meet his sister.

Vanzetti had recovered from his seizure of the day before. He was standing a few feet from the door as Luigia, followed by the others, walked down the corridor. Then he stepped forward and took her in his arms. In that moment the stooped, sallow prisoner in the convict's gray shirt and trousers and the fading spinster with her tightly-drawn hair were as they had been in Villafalletto nineteen years before—he the curly-haired young man, she the shy sprouting girl of sixteen. During the hour allotted them they sat in the corner clasping each other's hands as they talked about the old days and of their relatives and friends. Luigia said later that they had not spoken of her brother's predicament nor of religion. At the hour's end they embraced again and Vanzetti returned to his cell. Despondently Luigia walked back along the corridor.

From Charlestown Mrs. Henderson drove her to Marblehead to see Cardinal O'Connell at his summer home. The Cardinal, although surprised by the visit, invited them to tea on the lawn. William Cardinal O'Connell—who wintered in Nassau and was known as Gang-plank Bill by some of the less reverent faithful—modeled himself after a Renaissance prelate. Although a friend of Governor Fuller's, he knew better than to take secular sides as had Bishop Lawrence. Men's ways were not God's way, he assured Luigia over the teacups. Later in the day he amplified his remarks in a neatly ambiguous statement to the Defense Committee:

Human judgment is fallible always at best, but it is the only human method of government which civilized life has developed. But the justice of God is perfect, and in the end He and His way, mysterious as they are, are our hope and our salvation.

Vanzetti had at least had the consolation of seeing his sister once more. But, as he wrote in a note of thanks to Mrs. Henderson,

Since I saw her my heart lost a little of its steadyness. The thought that she will have to take my death to our mother's grave, it is horrible to me—to think of what she will soon have to stand and to bear revolts all my being and upsets my mind.

Sunday the twenty-first broke grayly in a tentative drizzle. Early in the morning Evarts and Hill reached Justice Louis Brandeis at his summer home on Cape Cod, to ask for a stay of execution. Brandeis was sympathetic but felt he was too close to the case personally to take any action, since during the trial his wife had lent Rosina their empty Dedham house and since he had talked the matter over many times with his friend Frankfurter. Hill had counted most on Holmes and Brandeis, the two liberals on the Supreme Court. The only other New England justice, Harlan Stone, was spending the summer at Isle au Haut, Maine, in the middle of Penobscot Bay. With Brandeis' refusal ringing politely in his ears Hill started immediately on the 275-mile drive north.

Musmanno arrived back in Boston on the night train at about the time Hill and Evarts were leaving Chatham. Still undaunted, he telegraphed the Summer White House in South Dakota demanding that President Coolidge intervene. When he received no reply, he telephoned and managed to get hold of a presidential secretary who refused to give his name. The President, the anonymous secretary informed Musmanno, could not be disturbed; there could be no federal action in any case since no federal question was involved. Musmanno offered to fly out to South Dakota in a chartered plane. The secretary told him sharply that if he did he would not be received. In 1917 Woodrow Wilson had asked the governor of California to commute the Billings and Mooney death sentences, but Cautious Cal was—as Musmanno discovered—no Wilson.

Bouncing back from each rebuff, Musmanno telephoned Chief Justice Taft, summering at Point-au-Pic, Quebec, and asked if he might fly to meet him. Taft's rotund voice came over the wire in such distortion that Musmanno could barely make out the irritated reply. Taft said he was outside the jurisdiction of the United States and it was too far for him to cross the border. Finally he told Musmanno to send a telegram explaining just what he wanted. To this telegram, which Musmanno sent off at once, Taft replied at such length that the collect charges came to $19.20. For all its length it merely said "No." Taft referred Musmanno to Holmes, Brandeis, and Stone, all within the First Judicial Circuit. He saw no reason to think that his own opinion would differ from that of Holmes. "The absence of jurisdiction in our court to grant the writ of certiorari in the case seems to me apparent," he concluded.

The numbers of those who heeded the call of the Defense Committee to come to Boston were disappointing, but the individuals who flocked there in the last days gave the case and the cause a permanent coloration. There were the dedicated, the troubled, the bohemian, the self-seeking and the selfless, the lovers of justice and strikers of poses, each wrapped in his own individuality. There was Powers Hapgood, six years out of Harvard and still looking like an undergraduate, from whose lips the word *comrade* tripped more frequently than any other and whose compulsion was to clash with the police. Hapgood had been a fashionable young clubman at Harvard but after graduating turned to romanticizing himself as a proletarian. He had worked in coal mines in Wales, Germany, France, and the Soviet Union; later he was to become Socialist candidate for Vice-President of the United States. In December 1927, his proletarian zeal took the form of marrying Mary Donovan.

There were John Howard Lawson and the young William Patterson, president of the American Negro Labor Conference, whose reaction to the futility of the last efforts would confirm them as Communists. There was the elderly, leather-tongued Ella Reeve Bloor, recipient of the Communist accolade of "Mother," who had hitchhiked from California. There was Paula Holladay, with boyish bob and red slicker, who had trudged a mere 117 miles from Provincetown wearing a sandwich board reading AMERICA CANNOT LOOK THE WORLD IN THE FACE IF SACCO AND VANZETTI ARE MURDERED, subject to the jeering suggestions of passing motorists that she go home and wash the dishes. There was Captain Paxton Hibben, a dapper, martial little man with a clipped imperial, who still clung to his military rank acquired overseas with the 391st Field Artillery of New York. There was Wellesley College's retired professor of astronomy and mathematics, the seventy-six-year-old Ellen Hayes, with white bobbed hair, flat hat, flat heels, and invisible blue stockings. There was the mysterious Louis Bernheimer, a Yale graduate, an aviator in France during the war, a student of philosophy, and a hermit who had already circulated more than thirty thousand pamphlets about the case to clergymen all over the country.

Then of course there was Edward Holton James, now engaged in running daily sightseeing tours to South Braintree for newly arrived sympathizers. Outstanding among the characters drawn to the scene was Zara du Pont, aunt of most of the living du Pont dynasty. Her singularly squashed hats, tweed suits that never wore out, and brass ear trumpet identified her a hundred yards away. She had come from Cambridge to indulge in her passion for picketing, for she made it her habit to join any line she saw, often with no idea of what or why she was picketing and—because of her deafness—with no way of finding out. Less well connected if no less obvious was William Obey of New York, who arrived at Parlor D with a certificate of release from a mental hospital. When his individualism became too flagrant and Tom O'Connor at last had to ask him to leave, he seated himself on the curb at Bowdoin Street with his portable typewriter in his lap, pecking away and telling the bystanders that the rush was so great at headquarters that he had to do his work outside.

On that final Sunday, August 21, Police Superintendent Crowley was taking no chances. For the first time anyone could remember, no permits were given out and no meetings on the Common were allowed. The Defense Committee had held its final meeting the night before at the Scenic Auditorium. By the middle of the overcast afternoon there were about twenty thousand people scattered over the forty-eight acres of Boston Common. Some watched the baseball games being played in the diamonds beyond the old Central Burying-Ground. Others listened to Stone's Band at the Parkman Bandstand playing excerpts from *The Bohemian Girl*. Still others—the flotsam of the city—lay asleep on the grass. Perhaps a third of those wandering on the Common had come there out of a sense of curiosity, a feeling that something exciting was going to happen. For most of the afternoon nothing happened. Then shortly after four o'clock Paula Holladay in her red slicker walked up from Charles Street and across the Common toward the bandstand. On the back of the slicker was lettered: SAVE SACCO AND VANZETTI. IS JUSTICE DEAD? As she walked along the mall a crowd began to fall in behind her. Most of those following her were indifferent if not hostile, but a few sympathizers produced Sacco-Vanzetti placards from under their coats. She continued her Pied Piper walk, gathering several thousand in her wake by the time she reached Tremont Street. The police did not interfere until the crowd spilled over into the roadway and blocked traffic. Then a squad of bluecoats surrounded her and carried her off, along with William Patterson and several other placard-wielders, to the Joy Street Station. Here she was told she might go free if she would promise to take off the slicker and not to return to the Common.

Superintendent Crowley came in person to the station to warn her paternally that Boston was "full of Irish Catholic boys, young hoodlums, who will be sure to try to do you harm if you go on the streets wearing that slicker."

Within the Charlestown prison the customary Sunday afternoon bustle of visits continued, even though the whole area was cordoned off by the police. The prison band played its limited selections in the octagon anteroom, and prisoners sat in their usual rows at the oak tables facing their visitors. So damp was the air that drops of moisture kept dripping from the skylight struts. Because of the humidity Warden Hendry allowed the door of the death house to be left open. Luigia and Rosina came and stayed their hour. Rosina had not brought the children; she did not want them to see their father in his death cell. Sacco had been for some time occupied with a letter to Dante and spent the day, except for the visiting hour, working on it. He told Vanzetti that he did not want it made public for five years. Although Sacco had planned to have its contents kept secret, the Defense Committee persuaded him to allow them to release it immediately for its propaganda effect, to sway every ounce of opinion possible in the last hours.

Facing extinction, Sacco achieved the slow-moving dignity that came, as a rule, more easily to Vanzetti:

Much have we suffered during this long Calvary. We protest today as we protested yesterday. We protest always for our freedom.

If I stopped hunger strike the other day, it was because there was no more sign of life in me. Because I protested with my hunger strike yesterday as today I protest for life and not for death.

I sacrificed because I wanted to come back to the embrace of your dear little sister Ines and your mother and all the beloved friends and comrades of life and not death. So Son, today life begins to revive slow and calm, but yet without horizon and always with sadness and visions of death. . . .

But remember always, Dante, in the play of happiness, don't you use all for yourself only, but down yourself just one step, at your side and help the weak ones that cry for help, help the prosecuted and the victim, because that are your better friends; they are the comrades that fight and fall as your father and Bartolo fought and fell yesterday for the conquest of the joy of freedom for all and the poor workers. In this struggle of life you will find more love and you will be loved. . . .

Much have I thought of you when I was lying in the death house—the singing, the kind tender voices of the children from the playground, where there was all the life and the joy of liberty—just one step from the wall which contains the buried agony of three buried souls. It would remind me so often of you and your sisters Ines, and I wish I could see you every moment. But I feel better that you did not come to the death-house so that you could not see the horrible picture of three lying in agony waiting to be electrocuted, because I do not know what effect it would have on your young age. . . .

Dante, I say once more to love and be nearest to your mother and the beloved ones in these sad days, and I am sure that with your brave heart and kind goodness they will feel less discomfort. And you will also not forget to love me a little for I do—O, Sonny! thinking so much and so often of you.

Best fraternal greetings to all the beloved ones, love and kisses to your little Ines and mother. Most hearty affectionate embrace.*

Vanzetti also wrote a long letter to Dante. Like Sacco's, it was more a testament than a farewell to a thirteen-year-old boy. Even more explicitly than Sacco, Vanzetti reaffirmed his revolutionary faith:

I still hope, and we will fight until the last moment, to rivendicate our right to live and be free, but all the forces of the State and of the Money and reaction are deadly against us because we are libertarian or anarchist.

I write little of this because you are now a yet to little-boy to understand this things and other things of which I would like to reason with you.

But if you do well, you will grow and understand your father's and my case and your father's and my principles, for which we will soon be put to death.

I tell you that for and of all I know of your father, he is not a criminal, but one of the bravest men I ever knew. One day you will understand what I am about to tell you: That your father has sacrificed everything dear and sacred to the human heart and soul for his fate in liberty and justice for all. That day you will be proud of your father; and if you come brave enough, you will take his place in the struggle between tyranny and liberty and you will vindicate his (our) names and our blood.

* The original of this letter is not available for comparison, but undoubtedly the published version has been edited.

If we have to die now, you shall know, when you will be able to understand this tragedy in its fullness, how good and brave your mother has been with you, your father and I, during these eight years of struggle, sorrow, passion, anguish and agony.

Even from now you shall be good, brave with your mother, with Ines, and with Suzy*—brave, good Suzy—and do all you can to console and help them.

I would like you will also remember me as a comrade and friend of your father, your mother, Ines, Suzy and you, and I secure you that neither I have been a criminal, that I have committed no robbery and no murder, but only fought modestily to abolish crimes from among mankind and for the liberty of all.

Remember Dante, each one who will say otherwise of your father and I, is a lier, insulting innocent death men who have been brave in their life.

Remember and know also, Dante, that of your father and I would have been cowards and hypocrits and rinnegetors of our faith, we would have not have been put to death. They would not even have convicted a lebbrous dogs; not even executed a deadly poisoned scorpion on such evidence as that they framed against us. They would have given a new trial to a matricide and abitual felon on the evidence we presented for a new trial.

Remember, Dante, remember always these things; we are not criminals; they convicted us on a frame-up; they denied us a new trial; and if we will be executed after seven years, four months and 17 days of unspeakable tortures and wrongs, it is for what I have already told you; because we were for the poor and against the exploitation and oppression of the man by the man.

The documents of our case, which you and other ones will collect and preserve, will proof you that your father, your mother, yourself, Inez, I and my family are sacrificed by and to a State Reason of the American Plutocratic reaction.

The day will come when you will understand the atrocious sense of the above-written words, in all its fullness. Then you will honor us.

Now Dante, be brave and good always. I embrace you.

Not until Monday morning did Hill reach Rockland, Maine, and board the leisurely excursion steamer that finally brought him through the shredding fog to the granite-edged Isle au Haut. Justice

---

* Susie Valdinoce.

Stone, sitting on his front porch in his shirtsleeves, received him curtly. He said he would listen to Hill's arguments but he could grant no stay. Another justice might perhaps feel differently.

In Boston, Monday broke sallow and heavy. The still-empty Common looked frayed and untidy. By nine o'clock the first busloads of sympathizers began to arrive from New York. The air was lighter by the time Governor Fuller arrived at his office from Rye Beach a little before eleven. "A beautiful day," he said, smiling and nodding affably to the reporters. One of his first visitors was Edna St. Vincent Millay, whose poem "Justice Denied in Massachusetts" had appeared in the New York *Times* that very morning. Fiorello La Guardia had come by chartered plane from New York to make a last appeal to his old congressional colleague, but when he emerged from the executive chambers he shook his head and told reporters that there was only one chance in a thousand.

On this last day the governor was willing to keep open house for any delegation that chose to visit him. To nearly all who so chose he listened with stiff politeness. Just before lunch the newly installed state commander of the American Legion appeared to assure the governor that the Legion stood four-square behind him. Almost a thousand letters and telegrams arrived at the executive offices during the day, two thirds of them asking for suspension of the death sentence.

Late in the morning Luigia and Rosina arrived at Charlestown for a tear-blurred hour in the death house. Sacco talked to his wife about Ines and Dante; Vanzetti again recalled the old days in Villafalletto. Madeiros, who had been lying indifferently on his cot, chain-smoking, received an unexpected visit from his sister Consuelo. When she told him that their mother was too overcome to make the trip, he for the first time showed emotion.

On Saturday there had been a tentative attempt to renew the State House picketing, and Captain Hibben, Powers Hapgood, James Rorty, and Katherine Anne Porter had been arrested. Now, as the morning advanced, pickets with armbands and banners appeared again. The Scenic Temple served as a supply depot; there pickets assembled, were grouped in dozens, and sent on to the State House with their signs, JUSTICE IS CRUCIFIED TODAY, JUSTICE IS DEAD IN MASSACHUSETTS. All afternoon the line grew, the pickets forming fours as their ranks increased. The line became an endless chain, its links made up of girls and sweaty shirtsleeved men from the garment district, self-conscious intellectuals, a scattering of adolescents welcoming the chance to challenge authority, and a rank and file of friends and sympathizers of every class and description. Mrs. Evans was there. She had aged much since the trial, but with her solid figure and rimless glasses she still looked the transcendental grand-mother. One of the younger policemen on duty complained that there was not a good-looking girl in the bunch.

During the course of the afternoon and evening 156 pickets were arrested. Isaac Don Levine and Mrs. Evans bustled about raising bail money. Edward Holton James showed up at the Joy Street Station with his pockets full and bailed away for several hours until he ran out of both funds and patience, then found himself booed when he returned to the Scenic Temple to announce that he would bail no more.

The garment workers in the station's close-packed guardroom sang the "Internationale," and afterward everyone joined in the more singable "Solidarity Forever." Police Captain McDevitt had long had his eye on Powers Hapgood. The other pickets might with luck be out on bail in an hour or so, but McDevitt made a point of turning Powers over to the State Police, who, instead of arresting him, hurried him off to the Psychopathic Hospital where he was held for four days.

Crowds formed on the Common side of Beacon Street to stare at the picket parade. Occasionally someone would dart across the street to join the line. Superintendent Crowley, with memories of the mob rising in the police strike of 1919, was determined there would be no rising today. Halfway down the mall a police company with rifles was drawn up like a detachment of infantry. Mounted police wove their horses in and out of the gathering throngs. There were more blue uniforms on Boston Common than there had been since the Civil War encampments.

The day wore on. All the public buildings were garrisoned by police. A squad even occupied the roof of Fuller's Packard salesroom. Yet except for the State House picketing and the unusual numbers crowding the Common there were no incidents in the city. None of the anticipated bombs went off.

With Hill delayed in Maine, the last-minute legal efforts became a confusion of volunteer lawyers. Field appealed for a stay to Judge Sisk—most liberal of the Superior Court judges. Sisk, for all his obvious sympathy, maintained that he lacked jurisdiction. Surrounded by the clicking typewriters of Parlor D, Tom O'Connor worked with John Finerty on a new inclusive habeas corpus motion. Finerty, former assistant general counsel for the United States Railroad Administration, was probably the ablest lawyer to take part in the final proceedings. This thin, long-jawed man in a white linen suit, who resembled Woodrow Wilson, had dropped in at Parlor D on his way to spend two weeks by the sea at Cohasset. O'Connor managed to arouse his interest so that he never went on. He and O'Connor were convinced the new motion stood its best chance with Federal Judge Anderson. Unfortunately, Anderson was at Williamstown, in the Berkshires. O'Connor arranged to have a plane waiting at the East Boston airport, and all the afternoon he kept trying vainly to get to Anderson by telephone.

At 2:30 Musmanno brought a copy of the completed Finerty motion to Charlestown. Vanzetti signed it. Sacco again refused. Both condemned men were now convinced that nothing could save them. Vanzetti gave a message to Musmanno for Thompson, whom he asked to see once more. Thompson, worn out physically and mentally, had left Boston shortly after the August 10 reprieve for his summer place in South Tamworth, New Hampshire, but as soon as he received the message he set out at once for Charlestown.

It was six o'clock before he arrived at the prison. As he entered the death house, Vanzetti, who had been sitting at his table writing, stood up at once as if he had been expecting him, smiled warmly, and reached through the bars to shake hands. Then Thompson took a chair from one of the guards and sat down just behind the painted warning line.

They talked tentatively at first. Thompson had heard a rumor that Vahey and Graham knew Vanzetti was guilty of both crimes and could prove it if only they were released from their lawyers' obligation of secrecy. Vanzetti emphatically and without anger said he had never told Graham or Vahey anything that would link him to either crime. Thompson beckoned to a guard to be a witness to their conversation.

For both men it was the most solemn moment of their lives. There was the quality of a Socratic dialogue to their questions and answers. The American lawyer's low, controlled tones were a counterpoint to the more musical voice of the Italian. As Thompson recalled the scene afterward it struck him in its more humble way as a recreation of the *Phaedo*.

I told Vanzetti that although my belief in his innocence had all the time been strengthened, both by my study of the evidence and by my increasing knowledge of his personality, yet there was a chance, however remote, that I might be mistaken; and that I thought he ought for my sake, in this closing hour of his life when nothing could save him, to give me his most solemn reassurance, both with respect to himself and with respect to Sacco. Vanzetti then told me quietly and calmly, and with a sincerity which I could not doubt, that I need have no anxiety about this matter; that both he and Sacco were absolutely innocent of the South Braintree crime, and that he was equally innocent of the Bridgewater crime; that while, looking back, he now realized more clearly than he ever had the grounds of the suspicion against him and Sacco, he felt that no allowance had been made for his ignorance of American points of view and habits of thought, or for his fear as a radical and almost as an outlaw, and that in reality he was convicted on evidence which would not have convicted him had he not been an anarchist, so that he was in a very real sense dying for his cause. He said it was the cause for which he was prepared to die. He said it was the cause of the upward progress of humanity, and the elimination of force from the world. He spoke with calmness, knowledge, and deep feeling. He said he was grateful to me for what I had done for him. He asked to be remembered to my wife and son. He spoke with emotion of his sister and of his family. He asked me to do what I could to clear his name, using the words "clear my name."

Vanzetti, after bringing up the cruelty of his seven years in prison, spoke of the history of movements for human betterment, among them early Christianity. Thompson remarked that the essence of the appeal of Christianity was the supreme confidence shown by Jesus in the truth of his own views by forgiving, even when on the cross, his persecutors and slanderers. Many times in his letters Vanzetti had made comparisons between his own fate and that of Jesus. It was at these words of Thompson's that their dialogue, as he recorded it, reached its climax:

Now, for the first and only time in the conversation, Vanzetti showed a feeling of personal resentment against his enemies. He spoke with eloquence of his sufferings, and asked me whether I thought it possible that he could forgive those who had persecuted and tortured him through seven years of inexpressible misery. I told him he knew how deeply I sympathized with him, and that I had asked him to reflect upon the career of One infinitely superior to myself and to him, and upon a force infinitely greater than the force of hate and revenge. I said that in the long run, the force to which the world would respond was the force of love and not of hate, and that I was suggesting to him to forgive his enemies, not for their sakes, but for his own peace of mind, and also because an example of such forgiveness would in the end be more powerful to win adherence to his cause or to a belief in his innocence than anything else that could be done.

There was another pause in our conversation. I arose and we stood gazing at each other for a minute or two in silence. Vanzetti finally said that he would think of what I had said.

Thompson, the believer, then referred to the possibility of immortality, saying that he understood the difficulties of such a belief, yet that if there was personal immortality Vanzetti might hope to share it. The other did not reply, but spoke briefly of the evils of present-day society—and the two men parted.

In this closing scene [Thompson wrote] the impression . . . which had been gaining in my mind for three years, was deepened and confirmed—that he was a man of powerful mind, and unselfish disposition, of seasoned character, and of devotion to high ideals. There was no sign of breaking down or of terror at approaching death. At parting he gave me a firm clasp of the hand, and a steady glance, which revealed unmistakably the depth of his feeling and the firmness of his self-control.

As he was about to leave, Thompson exchanged a few words with Sacco, who shook hands firmly through the bars, thanked the lawyer for what he had done, and said he hoped their differences of opinion had not affected their personal feelings. Like Vanzetti, he showed no sign of fear.

However darkly anticipated by public officials across the United States, the day passed off lightly with scarcely more than a few token strikes. The underlying fear was of another series of bombings. Police blanketed all the larger cities. In Washington guards with riot guns patrolled the Capitol. Police used clubs to break up a meeting of three thousand sympathizers in Philadelphia. The Communist Sacco-Vanzetti Emergency Committee in New York had called for a general strike and a mass meeting in the afternoon at Union Square. Other organizations, such as the American Federation of Labor, the

Central Trades and Labor Council, and the Defense Committee, refused to participate, and only a few hundred responded to the strike appeal. Late in the afternoon a crowd of ten thousand gathered in Union Square under the eyes of five hundred police, some of whom manned machine guns on the rooftops.

The afternoon and early evening were marked by a frenetic dashing about of volunteer lawyers. Shortly before three Musmanno filed the Finerty motion in the Federal Building, and at five o'clock Judge James Lowell of the United States District Court held a hearing on it. After listening for over an hour to Finerty, William Schuyler Jackson, and Benjamin Spellman, a New York lawyer who had aided in the defense of Harry Thaw, Judge Lowell ruled that nothing had been brought out to justify his issuing a writ or stay of execution. "The only question before this court is whether these men were deprived of their constitutional rights," the judge snapped at Spellman, who seemed to irritate him. "Don't tell me about the public. Stick to the law. I am sorry to see these two men executed, but it is a question of law, and it doesn't make any difference whether ten persons or ten thousand persons are sorry for them."

On leaving the courthouse, Finerty drove at once with Jackson for a third appeal to Justice Holmes. It was twilight by the time they reached Beverly. The old man listened to them for two hours, said he appreciated the force of their arguments, but felt—as he had before—that he had no right to intervene. With this rebuff the legal side of the case ended. From Beverly, Finerty and Jackson drove to East Boston in a last attempt to reach Judge Anderson, only to be told at the airport that the chartered plane could not take off after dark.

Luigia and Rosina had visited the death house again in the afternoon. At seven the warden allowed them a farewell visit of five minutes. Luigia walked up the prison steps, supported by Rosina. The two women had exhausted their tears. Dry-eyed, they kissed the prisoners for the last time through the bars.

Meanwhile the indefatigable Musmanno made his way to the executive chambers where he again argued the case from beginning to end before the unwilling ears of Fuller and Wiggin. Finally the governor put him off by telling him to see Attorney General Reading, promising to accept any recommendations Reading might make. While Musmanno was concluding his arguments Luigia and Rosina arrived and he remained as their interpreter. Luigia, her rosary in her hand, knelt on the floor, imploring the governor to save her innocent brother. Rosina begged passionately for the life of her children's father. Fuller listened to the wildly pleading women for over an hour, his professional courtesy fitting like a mask. "It cannot be expected," he told them finally, in dismissal, "that you would know the case as the lawyers and judges know it, and I can understand the sorrow that overwhelms you. I wish I could do something to lighten that sorrow, but I can do nothing."

Musmanno, after leaving the governor, went down the corridor to the attorney general's office. Reading listened to him with apparent interest while he explained that there were still five United States Supreme Court justices—any one of whom might grant a habeas corpus petition—whom they had not been able to reach. Another respite was necessary to allow the defense the necessary time. Reading said he would let Musmanno know his decision within the hour.

Just before eleven o'clock, the waiting Musmanno was called into the governor's office. Fuller told him that the attorney general had decided not to recommend a stay of execution. Musmanno, his voice trembling, asked the governor if he would stand for all time on that decision. Fuller replied that he would.

Charlestown prison, with eight hundred police surrounding it, was quiet. Mounted troopers, cap straps under their chins, and supplied with gas masks and tear gas, flanked the arched granite entrance. Fire-department squads had connected their hoses. Marine patrol boats chugged up and down the Miller River adjoining the freight yards.

Again the slum streets about the prison had become a dead zone, roped off for a distance of half a mile. Those who lived within the area were told to stay indoors.

The prison walls and catwalks were lined with machine guns and searchlights. As the darkness came on, the purple-white rays began to crisscross the whole moldering Charlestown area—the Boston and Maine freight yards, the tenements, the slime-banked river. On the far side of Rutherford Avenue, beyond the rows of junk shops, the light bands swept across the forgotten cemetery where John Harvard lay buried, flashing beyond to the Bunker Hill obelisk and the spire of the St. Francis de Sales Church. Then, as if in reply, searchlights on the roof of the State House began to probe the darkness. In the middle distance the elevated cars moved across the Charlestown Bridge like illuminated beetles.

Within the dead zone the quiet was broken only by the clip-clop of horse hoofs on the granite paving blocks and by passing motorcycle patrols. Only as the silence resumed did one become aware of the steady cricketlike tapping of a cobbler's hammer from a shop on Rutherford Avenue.

As the twilight faded, the tenseness in the city was so pervading that it seemed to go beyond action. Crowds gathered on the Common across from the State House to gaze up silently at the lighted windows of the executive wing. At ten o'clock the pickets reappeared. Again the police hustled them away. Hundreds stood impassively in Newspaper Row to watch the bulletin boards. The radio stations announced that they would stay on the air until after midnight. In City Square, Charlestown, several thousand men and women milled about beyond the barriers, curious rather than partisan, making no attempt at any sort of demonstration.

From the second-floor headquarters of the Hod Carriers' Union, Mother Bloor, flanked by Fred Beal, attempted to harangue a crowd of several hundred in the street below and was promptly arrested. Beal then set out with a group of fifty militants for Charlestown, placards and banners concealed under their shirts, resolved to break through the barricades and demonstrate in front of the prison itself. As the marchers reached City Square, they brought out their placards and banners, and at once there were cries of "The Reds are coming!" A shot rang out. At the sound the bluecoats stampeded out of the precinct station. The mounted police charged the crowd. A number of people were hurt. Beal and nine others were arrested. "The crowd didn't beat you up," the patrolman who had Beal by the collar told him, "But, O boy, wait until you get to the station!"

Inside the prison walls everything was darkened and quiet except for the smoke-filled press room with its clicking typewriters and clattering telegraph keys. As on all execution nights, few of the prisoners were asleep. At ten the electricians arrived to make a final test of the chair. Shortly after eleven Musmanno arrived, his panama hat flopping as he dashed up the steps, tears streaming down his cheeks. The warden would not allow him to see the condemned men.

At 11:15 Warden Hendry, bearing himself with all the official gravity he could muster, walked up the iron stairs into the death house. Vanzetti had been pacing up and down in his cell. At the warden's approach he stopped. "I am sorry," Hendry informed him in the customary stereotyped phraseology, "but it is my painful duty to inform you that you have to die tonight." Vanzetti stood staring at the floor for a moment, then flung his arms out, his eyes glittering. "We must bow to the inevitable," he whispered.

Sacco was at his desk writing a letter when Hendry repeated the formula. He slumped down in his chair, then in a thin voice asked the warden if he would see that the letter he was writing was mailed to his father in Italy. Hendry promised to mail it himself. In the last cell Madeiros lay on his back with his shoes off and a blanket over him, as if asleep. At the warden's announcement he neither moved nor spoke. Father Michael Murphy followed the warden into the room and asked hopefully if the prisoners would receive the rites of the church. Vanzetti and Sacco refused. Madeiros did not reply. Sacco thanked Father Murphy and told him he had enjoyed his talks with him. The priest looked dejected when he left. "Well, I guess they don't want me now," he told the newspapermen in the press room. The three were the first condemned men in Charlestown's history to refuse a clergyman.

Shortly before midnight Executioner Elliott, with Warden Hendry and Deputy Warden Hoggsett and the official witnesses, entered the death chamber from a side door. The witnesses were Surgeon General Frank Williams of the Massachusetts State Guard, Medical Examiner Magrath, Dr. McLaughlin, Sheriff Capen, Dr. William Faxon from the Dedham jail, and Dr. Howard Lothrop, a surgeon at the Boston City Hospital. Warden Hendry would allow only one reporter to be present. Lots were drawn in the press room and the choice fell to William Playfair of the Associated Press.

The witnesses ranged themselves along the wall, stony-faced, their voices held to a whisper. In the center of the room the chair stood with its unfastened straps hanging down, under the glare of the overhead lights. Executioner Elliott took his place behind the screen that hid the switch but not his head. Another screen concealed three litters.

Somewhere in the middle distance a clock struck midnight. At 12:03 two guards brought Madeiros into the bright silent room. Supported by a guard on each side he shuffled as if he were walking in his sleep. They guided him to the chair and he sat down and waited like an automaton while they strapped his arms and legs in place, adjusted the electrodes and the headpiece that covered the upper part of his skull, and finally placed a black mask over his eyes. At a nod from Warden Hendry, Elliott pulled the switch. The masked body stiffened, the mouth grimaced, and in a few seconds the witnesses noticed the odor of burning hair. Three times Elliott switched on the current, then Dr. McLaughlin stepped forward, applied his stethoscope, and pronounced Madeiros dead. Deftly the guards placed the body on one of the litters.

At 12:11 Sacco was brought in. Although the guards flanked him, he walked the seventeen steps from his cell to the chair unaided. As they began to adjust the straps he sat bolt upright, casting about wildly with his eyes. Then in the iron tradition of his belief, like so many of his comrades on the gallows before him, he called out in Italian: "Long live anarchy!" With that he grew calmer, and added more quietly in English: "Farewell my wife and child and all my friends." Only then did he seem to become aware of the witnesses. "Good evening, gentlemen," he said. The guards had finished with the straps and the headpiece and the electrodes, and one of them now slipped on the mask. In that last second Sacco found himself beyond wife, children, friends, anarchy, bared to the last basic verity. "Farewell!" he cried out in English as Warden Hendry nodded and the executioner's hand moved behind the screen, and then in Italian: "Mother!" Elliott increased the current by 300 volts for that sinewy peasant body.

When the guards came to Vanzetti's cell, he knew that the other two were already dead. With the guards beside him he entered the death chamber, his step firm, his head erect, his gray denim prison trousers flapping slightly from the slits in the sides. Just inside the door he paused near Warden Hendry and said with great precision:

"I wish to say to you that I am innocent. I have never done a crime, some sins, but never any crime. I thank you for everything you have done for me. I am innocent of all crime, not only this one, but of all, of all. I am an innocent man."

With that he shook hands with Hendry, Deputy Warden Hoggsett, Dr. McLaughlin, and two of the four guards, then took his place in the chair.

There was still something more. As the guard on his right knelt to adjust the contact pad to his bare leg Vanzetti spoke again, his eyes covered. "I now wish to forgive some people for what they are doing to me," he said gently. Warden Hendry's eyes were filled with tears as he gave the signal. Afterward he was scarcely able to pronounce the required formula: "Under the law I now pronounce you dead, the sentence of the court having been carried out."

CHAPTER TWENTY

Aftermath

During the last hour before the executions Mary Donovan, Felicani, Gardner Jackson and his sister Edith, Ruth Hale, Jeannette Marks, and Joseph Moro waited in the inner office of the Hanover Street headquarters. "They must be starting now," someone remarked at midnight. "Let us be quiet."

The outer room was full of people, heavy with cigarette smoke, darkly expectant. All evening there had been a constant coming and going, a mixture of North End Italians and strangers from outside Massachusetts. Some minutes before midnight Mother Bloor puffed up the stairs, having been bailed out earlier by Mary Donovan.

The group in the inner office did not move. After twenty minutes the telephone rang twice, the prearranged signal that the executions had taken place. Jackson picked up the receiver, listened, and still holding it to his ear nodded to the others. No one spoke. Felicani's face was a white mask. Then Mary Donovan cried out, "I can't believe it!" After several seconds she stood up, opened the door to the anteroom, and said sternly, "It's all over." Moro bit at a sheaf of papers he held in his hand, then began to sob. Outside there was a babble of voices rising to shouts. Some of the less-restrained Italians threw themselves down on the floor and howled. The rest began to grope their way down the steep stairs. As Mary Donovan turned back to the little office, the telephone bell tinkled again. "Come," she told the others, "let us not answer the telephone any more."

For many, as for those at the defense headquarters, that night was to be the dividing line of their lives. Ferris Greenslet, the biographer of the Lowells, stood with the crowd on Boston Common staring up at the oval windows of the governor's office, "hoping, doubting, despairing." From Parlor D at the Bellevue, a few minutes before midnight, Tom O'Connor telephoned John Vahey at Plymouth. "This is Vanzetti," he announced to the lawyer savagely. "Thanks to you I'll be dead in twenty minutes!" O'Connor would spend the rest of his life trying to vindicate the two dead men.

Helen Peabody, a young artist who had marched across the Charlestown Bridge with Fred Beal's group, somehow managed to slip through the police lines to the gates of the prison, where she was arrested and taken inside to the guardroom. Although offered a chair by one of the guards, she insisted on standing at attention until after the executions.

Beal, his lip gashed from a policeman's blow, was sitting in a cell in the City Square station house when a matronly woman he did not know arrived to post his bail. "They've done it," she told him softly. "Sacco and Vanzetti are dead." In just two years Beal himself, as a textile workers' organizer, would be on trial for his own life on a trumped up murder charge in Gastonia, North Carolina.

Noel and Herta Field, sitting beside the radio in their Washington, D.C., apartment, listened to the last-minute efforts with waning hope. The shock of the executions was for them the beginning of a long journey leftward that would lead them to a Communist prison cell in Hungary. Rockwell Kent withdrew a show of his paintings in Worcester and began a life-long boycott of Massachusetts.

Shortly before midnight Mrs. Evans went with Alice Hamilton to the roof of the Women's City Club on Beacon Street from where they could see the State House dome and across the Charles River basin the illuminated octagon of the prison. While they waited, the Church of the Advent bell tower below them sounded the quarters. At a quarter past twelve Mrs. Evans murmured, "Good-by, Sacco."

In New York John Haynes Holmes, the pastor of the Community Church, held a watch-night service at which La Guardia and others spoke.

Those who spoke said what was right to say [Holmes wrote]. By common consent those present put anger aside, and moved to higher levels of the spirit. Watchers in Boston flashed to New York the fateful moment when the two men died. Something happened in that moment when myriads of hearts, the world around, were cleansed of fear and hate. In them Sacco and Vanzetti were born again, and will surely live.

Others were not able to attain such humanistic serenity. For Eugene Lyons, in the New York Tass office, Sacco and Vanzetti had become like members of his own family. Up until the execution hour he kept cabling the news to Moscow. When the two men died, he recalled,

the case which was integrated with my own existence, intimate as few things in life ever become intimate, was over, finished. Nothing to do but go home to bed. . . . I remember wondering why I could not weep and shriek with the hurt of it, just as I was to wonder seven years later at my father's coffin.

With the news of the executions, Europe seethed. The issues of the case that had confused and divided the United States seemed perfectly clear in transatlantic perspective. The inhabitants of expatriate Elliot Paul's tiny left-bank Rue de la Huchette represented the workers generally in their indignant conviction that Sacco and Vanzetti had been murdered because they were foreign anarchists and leaders of American labor, and that Judge Thayer and Governor Fuller had destroyed them for the good of their own privileged kind. Paul saw the week of rioting that followed as the first of a series of quakes that would jar France's hostile classes apart and lead to the death of the Third Republic. On the day of the executions Paris was like a city under siege. A general strike halted almost all traffic. Soldiers with machine guns took up positions in the principal squares and along the boulevards. Republican Guards were out in their brass helmets. The American Embassy was ringed with tanks. In the working-class districts—which the bourgeois took care to avoid—the metal shutters were closed. Yet there were no demonstrations during the day, and except for the soldiers and the guns and the tanks the city seemed almost empty. Pierre Van Paassen remembered the silence of the streets as so intense it was almost frightening. But early on the following morning, when *L'Humanité* spread the news in an extra sheet with one black-splashed word "*Assassinés!,*" the militants struck out. On the Boulevard Sebastopol they tore the iron lamp posts from the concrete and tossed them through plate-glass windows, then looted the largest grocery store in Paris and pelted the police with canned goods from behind a barricade of tables and carts. With linked arms, fifty abreast, they surged across the Place de l'Opéra while long-aproned café waiters scurried to hide the seltzer siphons. Sixty police were injured in a pistol battle when a mob tried to set up barricades in front of the American Embassy. In Montmartre the front of the Moulin Rouge was demolished.

In Geneva, the evening before the executions, a mob of five thousand roamed the streets for several hours, overturning American cars, sacking shops displaying American goods, and gutting theaters showing American films. Finally the mob gathered to smash the windows of the Palace of the League of Nations. One rioter was killed, a number injured, after troops with fixed bayonets were sent in.

In Germany *Die Rote Fahne* and other Communist papers appeared on August 23 with black borders. There were demonstrations in Bremen and Wilhelmshaven, and a two-hour torchlight parade in Stuttgart. A marcher was killed in Leipzig; in Hamburg a number of demonstrators were wounded, and a policeman and a worker killed. At one of the largest meetings in the history of the Weimar Republic, Ernst Thälmann compared the murder of Sacco and Vanzetti to that of Karl Liebknecht and Rosa Luxemburg. The playboy mayor of New York, Jimmy Walker, in Berlin on a visit, was booed as he entered the City Hall. *Die Rote Fahne* advised him to spend his vacation on Governor Fuller's farm.

In England forty protestors were injured in a riot at the Marble Arch, and on the night of the executions a crowd gathered before Buckingham Palace and sang "The Red Flag." On the day of the funeral the flag on the building of the Labor Party was at half-mast. Flags were at half-mast throughout the Soviet Union. A street in Moscow was named for Sacco and Vanzetti, and Sovkino, the state motion picture bureau, ordered an Austrian company to start making a film about them. Later the Soviet Government named a pencil factory in their memory and for years produced pencils stamped with their names.

Many were hurt in Oporto, Portugal, when police broke up a demonstration in front of the American Consulate. In Rosario, Argentina, throngs waited in silence and bared their heads when just after midnight the news of the executions reached them. Buenos Aires experienced a general strike. In Mexico City, Diego Rivera spoke at a mass meeting. In Sydney, Australia, a huge procession protested the executions. In South Africa the American flag was burned on the steps of the Johannesburg City Hall.

Nothing comparable occurred in the United States in the six-day interval between the executions and the funeral. A plan of the International Labor Defense and the New York Emergency Committee to have the ashes of Sacco and Vanzetti brought to New York for a Union Square memorial meeting broke up in recriminations between the International Labor Defense and the Boston committee. The Communists blamed Mary Donovan, Michael Gold describing her as "an obscure, spiteful female with a great lust for publicity."

For Boston, on the morning after the executions, the case at last seemed finished. The *Herald* sprinkled its editorial page with relieved metaphors:

The time for all discussion is over. The chapter is closed. The die is cast. The arrow has flown. Now let us go forward to the duties and responsibilities of the common day with a renewed determination to maintain our present system of government, and our existing social order.

The evening *Transcript* viewed the executions more bluntly as "the only possible end."

During the forenoon Dr. Magrath performed the legally required autopsies, and later in the day the bodies of Sacco and Vanzetti were taken to the National Casket Company's room in Merrimac Street. A New Bedford undertaker claimed Madeiros' body.

The committee had planned a ritual lying-in-state, but could find no one in the city willing to rent a hall for the purpose. Mary Donovan wanted the bodies taken to the Hanover Street rooms. When some of the Parlor D people tried to tell her that the rickety building would not stand the strain, she turned on them furiously, shouting "They belong to me now!" As soon as the owner of the building heard that the coffins might be brought there, he barred the entrance with a heavy vertical joist.

While the committee members searched and argued, the bodies remained at the National Casket Company. William Gropper arrived from New York to make the death masks. When it became clear that no halls would be available in the city, Edward Holton James offered the use of his Mount Vernon Street town house. However, the committee decided to use Joseph Langone's funeral parlor at the foot of Hanover Street.

Joseph Langone, the dapper, diminutive North End undertaker, was one of the most prominent members of the Italian colony. In his official capacity he always wore a tail coat and silk hat, and prided himself on the punctiliousness with which he observed the etiquette of death. His two massive Cunningham hearses with their custom-built Brewster bodies and silver flambeaux on the sides were the most elegant in the city. To him were left the funeral arrangements.

Wednesday at midnight he brought the corpses to his workroom, embalmed and dressed them, and placed them in their coffins. Only just in time did Gardner Jackson discover that Langone planned to have Sacco and Vanzetti wearing tuxedos.

Madeiros had gone on display in Rogers & Silvia's undertaking parlor in Providence, and during the day some ten thousand sightseers came to view his corpse. The bodies of Sacco and Vanzetti were not shown until Thursday evening. During the afternoon crowds began to gather in front of Langone's parlor, and the police had to rope off the sidewalks for several blocks. A police guard was posted at the parlor entrance.

At seven o'clock the doors were opened and the spectators flooded through the little room at the rate of thirty-seven a minute. The mahogany coffins were so close together that only a single line could file between them. On each was a laurel wreath from the committee. The dead men's faces were drawn and hollow, the color of bronze. The room was banked to the ceiling with scarlet-flowered wreaths and sprays. One ribbon on a floral piece read ASPETTANDO L'ORA DI VENDETTA—"Awaiting the hour of vengeance." Another read merely REVENGE. Several read MASSACHUSETTS THE MURDERER.

In each corner of the parlor stood a committee member or friend as guard of honor. Eight thousand of the dedicated and the curious passed through Langone's that evening, only the stiff-faced anarchists with their wide black hats and butterfly ties distinguishable in the anonymous throng.

Just as the doors were to open, Mary Donovan posed at the head of the coffins with a sign: "DID YOU SEE WHAT I DID TO THOSE ANARCHISTIC BASTARDS?" —JUDGE WEBSTER THAYER. When Langone, fearing for his license, refused to allow her to continue there, she stalked outside with the placard and showed it to reporters. A police sergeant snatched it from her. There was a scuffle, the placard was torn up, and she was taken to the station, charged with inciting to riot and distributing anarchistic literature.

Thursday, Friday, and Saturday the bodies lay in state from six in the morning until ten at night. A hundred thousand people filed through the narrow parlor—so many that the terrazzo floor and the marble threshold began to crack. Huge floral pieces kept arriving by the hour. The windows of adjoining shops were borrowed to display them. Everyone in the North End, whatever his politics, viewed the bodies at least twice. In after years a common question of the district was: "Were you at Langone's?" Many North Enders dropped by on their way to work. Children made a game of seeing how many times they could dart in and out. Afternoons the line extended up the street beyond the double line of ropes. Evenings it reached over a third of a mile to Waldron's Casino.

It was planned to hold the funeral on Sunday and to have the bodies cremated at the Forest Hills Crematory. The health commissioner granted an extension of the four-day burial law. Saturday, Langone re-embalmed the bodies. Jackson wanted to have a procession with a band, the coffins carried by relays of pallbearers past the State House and through the heart of the city. Superintendent Crowley told Jackson he would allow nothing of the kind. There was to be no band, no filing past the State House, the coffins must be in hearses, and although those who wished might follow on foot there were to be no banners carried or shown.

Sunday morning broke gray and desolate. A line of sightseers and sympathizers still passed through the undertaking parlor for a last look at the now much-darkened faces. At ten o'clock Langone locked his doors and closed the coffin lids.

The procession was to start from North End Park near the Paul Revere House. Five hundred policemen patrolled the North End. Seventy mounted police were assigned to guard the cortège. The police were edgy, resentful of the gadfly agitation that had kept them on twenty-four-hour call for the last two weeks. Just to make certain there would be no gesture before the State House, Crowley had the pavement at Beacon and Tremont streets ripped up. Heavy trucks loaded with sand were placed there, as well as at the corner of Park Street. Police also blocked off the streets behind the State House.

All during the morning crowds collected along Hanover Street, trampling the turf of North End Park into mud. The men—many wearing black neckties, and red carnations in their buttonholes—outnumbered the women eight to one. Four open cars heaped with scarlet blossoms stood in front of Langone's. At 1:30 a column of mounted police cantered over the cobbles of Scollay Square and formed a double line along Hanover Street. Volunteers now began to remove the dozens of floral pieces from the undertaking rooms and the shop windows. Some of the pieces were so large that it took half a dozen men to carry them. At 2:20 the topheavy hearses drew up in front of the funeral parlor, and members of the committee carried out the coffins while Langone supervised them nervously in tail coat and silk hat.

In spite of Superintendent Crowley's order, a group of men in black moved through the crowd, quietly passing out red felt armbands stamped REMEMBER JUSTICE CRUCIFIED! AUGUST 22, 1927. At half past two Alfred Baker Lewis, as organizer of the procession, gave the signal. The two Cunninghams glided from the curb, the cortège advanced up Hanover Street. First came four mounted policemen in black rubber capes. Then a single marcher led the way with the committee's laurel wreaths. Behind him six men, with some difficulty, carried an eight-foot-high floral piece showing photographs of Sacco and Vanzetti and inscribed MARTYRS OF MASSACHUSETTS. Two rows of marchers carrying smaller floral pieces were followed by the hearses, moving side by side and flanked by an honor guard. Behind the hearses more volunteers carried more floral displays—eighteen in all. Then came the open cars heaped with flowers, and two limousines with drawn curtains, one carrying Rosina, Dante, Luigia, and Felicani, the other, members of the committee. Fifteen mounted police rode on either side.

The marchers followed in close-packed ranks, eight abreast, stern-faced, overwhelmingly Italian. Five thousand started from North End Park. It was the most spectacular funeral the city had ever seen.

The sidewalks of Hanover Street were packed with watchers. As the hearses moved up the gradient to Scollay Square, the undertone of muttering was punctuated by the clop of horseshoes on the rain-glazed cobblestones. The marchers, their arms now linked, stretched down the street to the curve of North End Park. On they came, over the cobbles and glistening parallels of car-tracks into Scollay Square, past the pawnshops and the painless dentists, past Waldron's Casino, past the drab lodgings of the American House and the Crawford Chambers, the cheap shoe and clothing shops, the pasticcerias, the shoeshine parlors, the poolrooms, and the bowling alleys. Hundreds of faces clustered in the second- and third-story windows. Along the six-mile route two hundred thousand watched the procession. The March of Sorrow they called it afterward.

At first the attitude of the police seemed neutral, but as the hearses and limousines crossed Scollay Square and turned left into Tremont Street, a detachment of state troopers in trucks cut between them and the massed marchers. Halted momentarily, the marchers surged over the sidewalks, sifted past the subway entrances, picked their way among the stalled vehicles. So great was the crush in Scollay Square that a plate-glass store front caved in. There was a moment of panic as the glass crashed on the pavement. The police now seemed less neutral. Two bystanders were arrested for jeering at them.

Still numbering in thousands, the marchers formed up again on the wide length of Tremont Street, linked twenty-five abreast from curb to curb. As they reached the corner of Park Street they began to put on their arm-bands, and suddenly the dark ranks were bright with scarlet. An occasional marcher would fall out. Others joined in from the throngs lining Boston Common. A fleet of taxicabs followed the marchers, ready to pick up the footsore at a flat rate of a dollar apiece to Forest Hills. Mike Flaherty, near the head of the procession, spotted Felix Frankfurter and his wife in a doorway near Park Street and beckoned to them. They joined with him as far as Boylston Street. At the corner of the Common, those who had carried the largest floral pieces began to tear them apart and strew the blossoms in the street before the oncoming hearses.

From Tremont Street through the slum miles of the South End and the Negro district the police at each intersection directed traffic into the now thinning ranks. Near Roxbury Crossing the hearses unaccountably speeded up to twenty-five miles an hour and were soon over a mile ahead of those on foot. Scrambling to catch up, the marchers broke ranks, many dropping out or taking to cabs. A hardy remnant of a few hundred red armbands reached the elevated station at Egleston Square within sight of Forest Hills and continued along Washington Street under the dripping el structure.

Up to this point the spectators had been impassive, but now, in the Irish Catholic district of Forest Hills, they turned hostile. Jeering faces filled the windows of the three-deckers flanking the el, and there were derisive shouts of "Guineas" and "Go home!"

The remaining marchers were passing the office of the Metropolitan Coal Company, a few hundred feet from the Forest Hills terminal, when the police charged them. No one knew why. At one instant the bedraggled armbanded figures were trudging along in the drizzle, at the next the police were flailing at them with their nightsticks, led by a furious sergeant wielding a heavy-handled umbrella. At the impact the ranks broke, most of the marchers bolting up Washington Street. The charging police seemed to go completely out of control. Anyone with an armband became a fair target. Men were dragged from the running boards of cars and beaten. Others trying to escape on foot were cornered in dead-end alleys. Dozens of fugitives burst into the yard of the Gulf Refining Company in a last attempt to dodge the swinging clubs. A Boston *Post* reporter, himself running, saw several men clubbed and kicked as they fell, and he caught a glimpse of a girl in a doorway, her face in her hands and her split chin dripping blood. The rain began to fall in torrents.

Not more than 150 marchers finally managed to work their way down side streets and back lots to join up on the other side of the terminal. When they arrived at the crematory on Walk Hill Street, a half-mile beyond, the hearses had already arrived, the coffins had been carried into the chapel, and the gates were locked.

Several thousand others who had come safely by car were waiting inside the grounds on the downhill slope in front of the chapel, watched impassively but without anger by the mounted police. The sodden, weary marchers could do no more than stand with bared heads while the cremation took place.

Only the committee and those closest to the defense were admitted to the small chapel. Luigia and Rosina chose to remain outside in the car. There was no formal service. Mary Donovan read five bitter paragraphs by Gardner Jackson, scarcely able to control her voice as she spoke the words over the coffins:

You, Sacco and Vanzetti, are the victims of the crassest plutocracy the world has known since ancient Rome. . . . And now Massachusetts and America have killed you—murdered you because you were Italian anarchists. . . . In your martyrdom we will fight on and conquer.

That was all. At 4:30 the coffins were placed in the retort chambers. The gates were opened, the hearses and the curtained limousines rolled away, the police reined in their restive horses as the crowd dissolved into small groups and individuals making their way unmolested along Walk Hill Street. Those who looked back saw a thin column of smoke rising from the crematory's central chimney, black and unwavering against the low sullen sky.

Like the Dreyfus case to which it has been so often compared, the Sacco-Vanzetti case became a tumult of the intellectuals. As I look back on it, my father and my Aunt Amy in their lesser way were representative of that tumult. For my father Sacco and Vanzetti became a challenge to the institutions he believed in, and he shut his mind against them. After Captain Van Amburgh's testimony convinced him they were guilty he did not concern himself further with the fairness of the trial, although as an honest man he took a thin view of Judge Thayer. My Aunt Amy could not imagine that her friends of the Elizabeth Peabody House and The Women's City Club might be wrong, that John Haynes Holmes, whom she had known as a young man, might be wrong, that liberalism could be wrong. She, too, closed her mind.

For the more extreme partisans on both sides the belief in the guilt or the innocence of the two Italians became a dogma. Just before the 1961 ballistics tests were conducted a member of the Committee for the Vindication of Sacco and Vanzetti told me that even if a test should show indisputably that Bullet III had come from Sacco's pistol, he would still be convinced that Sacco was innocent.

For myself, I found that when I examined the various confessions, they had a way of falling apart. After Sammarco's lie-detector test there was nothing to be said for Silva's Bridgewater tale. Madeiros' various statements about South Braintree had just too many discrepancies in them. Once I had driven and checked the getaway route and found that the license-plate number of the murder car noted down in South Braintree was last identified by Julia Kelliher in Brockton eight miles beyond Randolph, I could no longer believe that the bandits had switched cars in the Randolph Woods. They would not have been foolish enough to go to the useless trouble of putting the telltale plates on a second car and driving away in it. Nor did it seem possible for Madeiros, if he had been in the back seat of the Buick, to have mistaken two metal boxes planted at his feet for a leather bag. And of course if he and the Morellis had not arrived at South Braintree until noon—as he claimed—then who were the men who shadowed Neal, who strolled around the town during the morning, who spoke to Lola Andrews? It has been asserted that Madeiros had nothing to gain by making a fraudulent confession to the South Braintree crime, but in fact by making one he prolonged his life two years.

The hypothesis that the Morelli gang committed the South Braintree holdup is at first plausible, yet it is too closely bound to the Madeiros confession to stand alone. Extraordinary coincidences are brought to light in Ehrmann's book but, just in the matter of the cars, I could not imagine the one that Mike Morelli was casually driving through the center of New Bedford three hours after the crime was the murder car. Nor could I believe that the Morellis would on three separate occasions drive forty miles to an obscure Boston suburb to steal two sets of license plates and a car. Why all the way to Needham when there were so many nearer places? It was as absurd as imagining Mike, the night of the crime, driving the Buick back through those miles of waste land to abandon it in Brockton when all the police in New England were on the alert for it.

As for Joe Morelli's confession, he knew how much money Silva had made with his pseudo-confession, and he may have thought Morris Ernst an easy mark. When he was writing his autobiography in the Lewisburg penitentiary, he used as source material Osmond Fraenkel's 550-page summary of the case. The still-extant volume, inscribed "Joseph Morelli, Nov. 10, 1935," is larded with marginal notes made by Joe and his friends. Yet the later parts of Joe's autobiography were written after he had lost contact with Ernst. To dismiss it completely is to leave a number of intruding questions unanswered. How did it happen that Joe was so familiar with the names Coacci, Boda, and Orciani—all mentioned only casually in the trial record? How did he know that Coacci had worked at Slater & Morrill unless he had had some contact with him? Was there something, after all, in the persistent rumors that Berardelli had recognized the men who shot him? It was hard to imagine Sacco, even harder to imagine Vanzetti, associated with the anthropoid Morellis, but Boda, as a boot-legger, would have needed underworld connections for his supplies. For a time Boda and his brother had run a dry-cleaning shop in Welles-ley, within walking distance of Needham. Boda drove a car. He fits the description of the man who tried to borrow license plates at Hassam's garage. And it is easier to imagine him walking from Wellesley to Needham to steal plates and a car than it is to imagine the Morellis making the successive trips from Providence.

Having begun the writing of this book with the assumption that Sacco and Vanzetti were innocent, I found myself holding to it with an increasingly troubled mind as my work progressed, but I did not begin to consider whether they might not, after all, have been guilty until I learned of what Moore had told Upton Sinclair. That Moore had come to doubt his hotly held convictions made me feel I must at least re-examine mine. Moore, the dedicated radical, the battler for lost and almost-lost causes, was not the man to have denied himself out of pique. His reasons for his change of mind must have been profound. According to Eugene Lyons, he had spent much time following the trail of a criminal group he had reason to believe was involved in the South Braintree crime. "But when he got near the end of the trail," Lyons wrote, "the Italian anarchist members of the Defense Committee called him in and ordered him to 'lay off.' They wouldn't say why, but the inference is that they feared his line of investigation."

One of Moore's investigators told me that Moore had finally come to the conclusion that Boda was the man who engineered the holdup.

As convincing to me as Moore's reluctant reversal was the fact that Upton Sinclair's experience seemed to support it.

I had visited Sacco's family [Sinclair wrote in 1953], and I felt certain that there was some dark secret there. Nobody would be frank with me, and everybody was suspicious even though I had been introduced and vouched for by Mrs. Evans, a great lady of Boston who had led and financed the fight for freedom of these two Italians.

To thousands like my Aunt Amy the innocence of Sacco and Vanzetti appeared so transparent that it should have been obvious to anyone with the slightest knowledge of the case. Yet at the very core of the defense there was disbelief. I was overwhelmed when I discovered that even Carlo Tresca shared it—Tresca, the acknowledged and admired leader of the anarchists in the United States, to whom they turned as a matter of course when they were in trouble. No one, not even the police who arrested him—and he had been arrested thirty-six times—questioned his integrity. He looked after his own. According to Sinclair, when Moore was leaving for Boston in 1920, Tresca—to Moore's annoyance—put two comrades wanted by the police for a robbery in the car with him. In the defense of Sacco and Vanzetti, Tresca played the part of guardian angel or great-uncle. If anyone should have had inside knowledge of the affair, Tresca was the man.

In 1943, a few weeks before Tresca was murdered in New York by the Italian-born Soviet agent Enea Sormenti,* Max Eastman, who had known Tresca for years and had written a profile on him for

* During the Spanish Civil War Sormenti, as Colonel Carlos Contreras, commissar of the Fifth Brigade, conducted the bloodiest of the Communist-directed purges. He was responsible for the execution of the anarchist leader, Andrés Nin, in spite of the protests of the Republican Prime Minister, Juan Négrin. At the end of the war he escaped to Mexico in time to organize the first attempt on the life of the exiled Trotsky. After World War II, under his original name of Vittorio Vidali, he became leader of the anti-Titoist Communists in Trieste. Tresca, in May of 1942, denounced Sormenti-Vidali on the front page of his anarchist paper, *Il Martello*, as a "commandant of spies, thieves and assassins."

It was a long-standing grievance of the Communists that Tresca was able to keep them out of the Garibaldi Society, the leading organization of Italian antifascists. Even in the hothouse period of Russian-American friendship during World War II, he continued to block their infiltration. In 1942 the Office of War Information organized the Italian-American Victory Council to arrange overseas broadcasts and prepare for political changes in Italy after the war. So

The New Yorker, talked with him about the Sacco-Vanzetti case:

I felt close enough to ask him one day, when whispers had reached me concerning Upton Sinclair's distressing experiences in Boston:
"Carlo, would you feel free to tell me the truth about Sacco and Vanzetti?"
He answered: "Sacco was guilty but Vanzetti was not."
At that moment some people entered the room where we were talking and I lost the chance to ask more. I lost it permanently, for I had no opportunity to see Carlo again before he was himself shot by an assassin.

The reasons for Tresca's answer died with him, yet they must have been compelling or he would have skirted the question.

Thirteen years after Tresca's death a new and conclusive series of ballistics tests was to bear him out. Many times postponed, they were finally conducted in the laboratory of the Massachusetts State Police on October 11, 1961, by Jac Weller, the honorary curator of the West Point Museum, and Colonel Frank Jury, a former head of the Firearms Laboratory of the New Jersey State Police.

The one certain method of determining whether two bullets have passed through the same gun barrel is examination with a comparison microscope, which brings the bullets together in one fused image. If the striations match, the conclusion is that both bullets were fired from the same weapon.

Using a comparison microscope and bullets they themselves had just fired from Sacco's pistol, Weller and Jury determined beyond dispute that Bullet III had been fired from that pistol. The other five bullets, they found, had all been fired from a single unknown gun. As for the four shells that Bostock had picked up and given to Fraher, three had been fired in an unknown gun. Weller and Jury agreed, after comparing the breechblock markings of Shell W with those of a newly fired test shell, that Shell W had unquestionably been fired in Sacco's pistol. Thus, the comparison microscope findings of 1961 confirmed the tests made by Major Goddard in 1927.

Turning to the question of a bullet substitution, Weller and Jury found it unlikely that the prosecution or its agents would have

---

great was Tresca's influence that he was able to exclude Communists as well as ex-fascists from the new organization.

Sormenti-Vidali was sent from Mexico on a special mission to get rid of Tresca. "Where he is I smell death," Tresca told a friend a few days before he was shot down on a New York street.

attempted to obtain suitable bullets by firing them from Sacco's pistol into a side of beef; such a deception would not only have been difficult to keep secret, but the method would have offered no certainty of a plausibly lopsided bullet.

Captain Proctor had custody of the bullets and the guns, the bullets from the time of Berardelli's autopsy until they were offered in evidence at the trial. If any substitution was made, Proctor was the only one with the extended opportunity to accomplish it. Van Amburgh was called to the trial as an outside expert; at that time he would have had neither the motive nor the occasion to make such a substitution.

When, just before the ballistics testimony at the trial, Van Amburgh, Proctor, and the defense expert, Burns, test-fired Sacco's pistol, none of them was able to get hold of any obsolete Winchester cartridges similar to Bullet III. Proctor fired three Winchesters of the new type without the cannelure; Van Amburgh fired three Peters; Burns fired eight U.S. cartridges. None of these could have been used as a substitute for the obsolete Winchester Bullet III.

That Proctor made any switch of bullets or shells seems impossible in view of his character and the relevant facts. Proctor was amateurish in his knowledge of ballistics, and it was for other reasons than the bullet evidence that he felt Sacco and Vanzetti were not guilty. At the trial he had not thought Bullet III had come from Sacco's pistol, and in 1923, in his affidavit for Thompson, he still insisted that Sacco's pistol had not fired the mortal bullet. But if the prosecution had somehow replaced the original Bullet III by a falsely marked bullet actually test-fired from Sacco's pistol, there would have been no need for Van Amburgh to be so qualifying in his identification of the bullet, and no need for Proctor to use his ambiguous "It is consistent with." Both he and Van Amburgh would have *known* that the false bullet came from Sacco's pistol and could have said so flatly.

Then, too, there is the matter of motive. When the case first came to trial it was no earth-shaking issue for District Attorney Katzmann or for the State Police. Katzmann, if he had lost, would still have been re-elected district attorney. The case could not have been worth the risk of detection and disgrace for him or for Proctor to forge the evidence for a conviction.

After examining Bullet III, Weller and Jury concluded that it had been fired into a body—though whether a human or animal body, whether living or dead, they could not say. They did not think it possible that the slightly flattened side of the bullet could have been produced in a test firing. In contrast to Ehrmann and Wilbur Turner, Thompson's expert, Weller and Jury did not find that the identifying scratches on the bullet's base varied noticeably from the scratches on the other three bullets.

The inquest record of April 17, 1920, bears out these findings. Eighteen days before Sacco and Vanzetti were arrested, Dr. Frederick Jones testified that the bullet which lodged against Berardelli's hipbone and was subsequently marked III had been slightly flattened as it came to rest against the bone. Dr. Magrath, who performed the autopsy, identified the bullet at the trial a year later by the three scratches he had made on it:

As I found it, it lay sideways against the flat surface of the hip bone, and in my opinion the flattening of the bullet was due its striking that bone side on. The bone is curved at that point, and a very slight amount of impact from the more pointed part of the bullet would bring its side against the bone, if it had not force enough at that point to perforate the bone and go through it, which it did not.

The cumulative evidence is overwhelming that the Colt automatic found on Sacco the night of his arrest was one of the two pistols used to kill Berardelli. Even if one accepts the possibility that someone other than Sacco fired the Colt, Sacco knew who that someone was.

Sacco's defenders have claimed that the evidence of those who testified to having seen him in Boston on the day of the murders is too overwhelming to be shaken by any ballistic evidence. Yet thirty years after the trial, that evidence was to turn paper thin with the admission of a former Boston anarchist, Anthony Ramuglia, that he had been coached to present a false alibi for Sacco. As a young man, Ramuglia was a member of the East Boston anarchist group to which Sacco and Vanzetti belonged. At the request of his comrades, he had agreed to testify that he had seen Sacco in Boni's Restaurant on April 15, 1920. Only when he was about to appear in court did he recall that on that day he had been in jail in St. Louis. On learning this, the anarchists picked another comrade whose perjury would be less liable to discovery.

Vanzetti's innocence is, at least for me, confirmed by my talks with Brini and by Tresca's admission to Eastman, as well as by the contradictions to the court testimony brought out in the Pinkerton reports. Yet it would have been like Vanzetti to go to the chair rather than betray a friend. He had once remarked that it was an evil to be arrested, but a still greater evil to desert a comrade. When Moore was preparing his closing argument at Dedham, he felt that if he sacrificed Sacco he had a fighting chance of persuading the jury to acquit Vanzetti. "So I put it up to Vanzetti," he later wrote; " 'What shall I do?' and he answered, 'Save Nick, he has the woman and child.' "

Both men died bravely, undoubtedly fortified by the thought, expressed by them many times, that they were dying for the working class of the world. Vanzetti, in the death chamber, calmly reasserted his innocence. Yet it is noteworthy that Sacco, who had refused to sign all pleas for clemency, chose rather in his last moment to proclaim his vindicating belief in anarchy.

It is possible that Sacco, whatever his guilt, may have considered himself innocent in the sense that he was serving a higher cause. His dreams were of violence. He was, as he told Thompson, at war with the government. To defend anarchy in the persons of his comrades Elia and Salsedo may have seemed to him to justify Parmenter and Berardelli sprawled in the gravel. The paymaster and his guard would merely be soldiers on the other side of the barricades, their deaths insignificant in comparison with the triumph of the cause. Vanzetti could express his anarchistic beliefs and then say, "Of course, I may be wrong." Sacco could not qualify himself. His was the iron belief, one that has caused so much slaughter in the world, that the cause is more important than the individual. So he turned with fanatic hatred against Moore; so he applied the imagery of the Passion to his dilemma; so he died.

Over forty years have passed since the convictions of Sacco and Vanzetti. Their case was the American case of the century, one that became all things to all men. So divisive was it, that only now is it possible to see it in perspective. The accusations and counteraccusations fade, those who played their roles in it die, but the tragedy—however one may define it—remains.

About
the Author

Francis Russell has contributed historical and critical articles to such periodicals as *American Heritage, Horizon, The Yale Review, The Christian Science Monitor,* and abroad to *The Observer, The Guardian, The Countryman, Irish Writing* and others. He is the author of one of the more intimate books on America's "Roaring '20s," *The Great Interlude,* as well as the best-selling examination of Harding and his times, *The Shadow of Blooming Grove.* In addition he has written a volume of critical essays on Joyce, Kafka and Gertrude Stein, a study of Albrecht Dürer, and the companion American Heritage histories, *The Making of the Nation* and *The Confident Years.* It was while serving on a jury in Dedham, Massachusetts, thirty-two years after Sacco and Vanzetti had been tried and condemned in the same courtroom, that he began his investigation of the written and unwritten history of the case that resulted in *Tragedy in Dedham.*

Mr. Russell was born in Boston. He attended the Roxbury Latin School there and went on to do most of his undergraduate work at German universities. When he returned to America he completed his A.B. at Bowdoin and his A.M. at Harvard. During World War II he served as a captain in the Canadian Intelligence Corps. After the war he was a political intelligence officer with the British 30th Corps in Hildesheim, Germany. On leaving the army he traveled extensively and lived for various periods in France, England, Holland, Ireland and Germany. He held Guggenheim Fellowships in 1964 and 1965 and is a member of the Society of American Historians. With his wife and daughter he lives in a seventeenth-century house, "The Lindens," in Sandwich on Cape Cod.

468

Sources and Acknowledgments

In spite of the great amount of material that may be found in print about the Sacco-Vanzetti case, important new information came to light during the writing of *Tragedy in Dedham*, much of it from the following persons. While many of them hold opposing views, I am grateful to them all for giving me of their knowledge and time:

Ben Bagdikian, Dr. William C. Boyd, Alfonsina Brini, Beltrando Brini, Paul J. Burns, Frank W. Buxton, Albert L. Carpenter, John Conrad, Anthony W. DiCecca, Barbara B. Dolliver, John Dos Passos, Michael J. Dray, Max Eastman, Herbert B. Ehrmann, Aldino Felicani, Michael C. Flaherty, Frank S. Giles, the late James M. Graham, Alden Hoag, John Hurd, Frank J. Jury, Suzanne La Follette, Isaac Don Levine, the Reverend Donald G. Lothrop, Eugene Lyons, Charles A. McCarthy, Robert A. McLean, Robert H. Montgomery, Mary DeP. Murray, Shelley A. Neal, Willis A. Neal, Tom O'Connor, James Rorty, Joseph Sammarco, Charles E. Sands, the late Dr. Warren Stearns, Michael E. Stewart, the Reverend Hillyer H. Stratton, Upton Sinclair, Jac Weller, Otto Zausmer.

For permission to quote passages from their writings about the case I am indebted to Dr. Ralph Colp, Jr., Max Eastman, Eugene Lyons, Robert H. Montgomery, and Upton Sinclair. Permission to quote from the manuscript of John F. Dever was granted by his executor; permission to quote from two letters in *The Letters of Sacco and Vanzetti* was granted by the publisher, The Viking Press, Inc.

I wish also to acknowledge the help of the Braintree Public Library, the Boston Public Library, the libraries of the Boston *Globe* and the Providence *Journal*, the Boston Athenaeum, the Dartmouth College Library, and the Harvard Law School Library.

Among the many sources I consulted, the following were the most pertinent:

Colp, Ralph, Jr. "Sacco's Struggle for Sanity." *The Nation*, Vol. 187, No. 4 (August 16, 1958).

————. "Bitter Christmas: A Biographical Inquiry into the Life of Bartolomeo Vanzetti." *The Nation*, Vol. 187, No. 22 (December 27, 1958).

Dr. Colp consulted the files of the Massachusetts Department of Mental Health in writing these accounts of the periods when Sacco and Vanzetti were confined in mental institutions.

Dever, John F. *Memoirs of the Sacco-Vanzetti Case*. Manuscript, estate of John F. Dever.

Presents the Dedham trial from the jury's point of view.

Dos Passos, John. "Facing the Chair." Boston,. Sacco-Vanzetti Defense Committee, 1927.

Eastman, Max. "Is This the Truth about Sacco and Vanzetti?" *National Review*, Vol. XI, No. 16 (October 21, 1961).

Eastman's account of Carlo Tresca's assertion of Sacco's guilt; incorporates the essence of Upton Sinclair's "The Fishpeddler and the Shoemaker."

Ehrmann, Herbert B. *The Untried Case: The Sacco-Vanzetti Case and the Morelli Gang*. Second edition, New York, The Vanguard Press, Inc., 1960.

A brilliant working-out of the hypothesis that the South Braintree crime was committed by the Morelli Gang of Providence, Rhode Island. It remains, however, only a hypothesis.

Frankfurter, Felix. *The Case of Sacco and Vanzetti*. Boston, Little, Brown & Co., 1927.

Frankfurter, Marion D., and Jackson, Gardner. *The Letters of Sacco and Vanzetti*. New York, The Viking Press, Inc., 1928.

The manuscript originals of most of these letters, plus others, are in the Harvard Law School Library. The published versions have been edited as to spelling and grammar, a number of class-war and anticlerical passages have been suppressed, and in some cases meanings have been altered.

The Good Shoemaker and the Poor Fish Peddler. Four reels of documentary motion picture film. Thought to be lost, discovered in Rockport, Massachusetts, in 1960 by Tom O'Connor, Donald G. Lothrop, and Francis Russell. Now in possession of Brandeis University.

Joughin, G. Louis, and Morgan, Edmund M. *The Legacy of Sacco and Vanzetti*. New York, Harcourt, Brace & Co., Inc., 1948.

At the time of its publication the most balanced and comprehensive study. Morgan wrote the chapters on the two trials and their legal aftermaths; Joughin dealt with the historical, sociological, and literary aspects of the case.

Lyons, Eugene. *Assignment in Utopia*. New York, Harcourt, Brace & Co., Inc., 1937.

Montgomery, Robert H. *Sacco-Vanzetti—The Murder and the Myth*. New York: The Devin-Adair Co., 1960.

The first book attempting to prove that the trial and subsequent proceedings were fair and that the men were justly convicted. While arid in style, it offers a careful analysis of the evidence and presents many telling points requiring detailed answers from those who think otherwise.

Morelli, Joseph. *Autobiography*. Manuscript, 574 pages.

Copies are said to be in the possession of the author's granddaughter, a Providence criminal lawyer, and Louis V. Jackvony, Jr., son of the one-time counsel for the Morellis.

Musmanno, Michael A. *After Twelve Years*. New York, Alfred A. Knopf, Inc., 1939.

An account, by one of the younger defense lawyers, of the last legal maneuvers.

Pinkerton Report on the South Braintree Holdup. Manuscript, Travelers Insurance Company, Hartford, Connecticut.

This report does not appear in *The Sacco-Vanzetti Case: Transcript of the Record . . .*

Record of Public Hearing Before Joint Committee of the Judiciary of the Massachusetts Legislature on the Resolution of Representative Alexander J. Cella, Recommending a Posthumous Pardon for Nicola Sacco and Bartolomeo Vanzetti. Boston, Committee for the Vindication of Sacco and Vanzetti, 1959.

The Sacco-Vanzetti Case: Transcript of the Record of the Trial of Nicola Sacco and Bartolomeo Vanzetti in the Courts of Massachusetts and Subsequent Proceedings, 1920–1927. New York, Henry Holt & Co., Inc., 1928–1929.

The five volumes and supplemental volume include the complete record of the Dedham trial, a nearly complete record of Vanzetti's Plymouth trial, the various appeals and their outcomes, affidavits concerning Madeiros and the Morellis, a partial record of the Lowell Committee hearings, the minutes of the Parmenter-Berardelli inquest, and the Pinkerton report on the Bridgewater holdup.

Sinclair, Upton. "The Fishpeddler and the Shoemaker." New York, *Institute of Social Studies Bulletin*, Vol. 2, No. 2 (Summer, 1953).

Article expressing Sinclair's doubts of Sacco's innocence and reporting Fred Moore's similar doubts.

Vanzetti, Bartolomeo. "The Story of a Proletarian Life." Boston, The Sacco-Vanzetti New Trial League, 1924.

Zelt, Johannes. *Proletarischer Internationalismus im Kampf um Sacco und Vanzetti*. East Berlin, Dietz Verlag, 1958.

Drawing on records in Moscow, this book contains valuable information about the Communist-controlled development of the protest movement in Central Europe and the directed demonstrations inside the Soviet Union. Its balancing of facts, however, cannot always be relied on. Typical of its distortions is Zelt's quotation from *Putj MOPR*, the organ of the International Red Aid, to the effect that "in 1926 the students of the University of Brockton, in spite of a ban by reactionary professors, unanimously chose as their graduation thesis 'The Case of Sacco and Vanzetti.' " There is, of course, no college or university in Brockton, but according to the Boston *Herald* of June 3, 1927, "discussion of the Sacco-Vanzetti case by the class in current events in the local high school has been banned by the history teacher, Miss Sarah McGrory, on the theory the students are not old enough to understand it. The action was taken by the teacher after the class, in its usual manner of selection of a subject for discussion, voted in favor of the Sacco-Vanzetti case."

Index

Adrower, Giuseppe, 124, 173-174, 193
Affe (Afa), Carlos, 183, 196-197
Aiken, John, 127, 128, 216
Anderson, George, 423, 443, 446
Anderson, Maxwell, 8, 13
Andrews, Lola, 12, 32-33, 146-151, 153, 224, 230-232, 390
Andrews motion, 221, 264, 265
Arrogni, Harry, 155
Atwater, Eldridge, 161
Atwood, Alfred, 136, 212
automobile, getaway:
    at Bridgewater, 49, 50, 51-52
    at Dedham trial, 156, 204-205
    in Madeiros' confession, 281, 300, 301, 461
    in Manley woods, 56-57
    at Plymouth trial, 99
    route checked by Francis Russell, 306, 307-308
    at South Braintree, 38, 39, 41, 44-46
    stolen from Francis Murphy, 51

Bagdikian, Ben, 305, 309
Baker, Alta, 44
Balboni, Carlo, 102
Balboni, Rosa, 102
Barone, Bibber, 290, 292, 299, 300
Barr, C. A., 52-53, 56
Barry, John, 267, 268
Bastoni, Enrico, 102
Beal, Fred, 421, 448, 452
Bedard, Alfred, 282
Beffel, John Nicholas, 113, 115, 116
Behrsin, Hans, 34-35, 37, 69, 146
Benchley, Robert, 391, 412
Benkosky, Steve (Steve the Pole), 294, 295, 297, 300
Bent, Silas, 304, 312
Berardelli, Alessandro, 35, 36, 37-38, 39, 40, 42, 43, 46, 314, 462

Berardelli, Alessandro (cont.):
    autopsy on, 47, 158
    revolver of, 26, 142, 160-162, 163, 176
Berardelli, Sarah, 162, 176, 391-392
Bernkopf, Elizabeth, 246-247, 412
Blackwell, Alice Stone, 253
Bloor, Ella Reeve, 436, 448, 451
Boda, Mike, 54, 55, 57-59, 60-61, 70, 88, 91, 92, 96-97, 101, 140, 156, 166, 178, 180, 181, 183, 190, 197, 314, 462
    pistol of, 58, 295 fn.
Boice, Mae, 284, 286-287, 299
bombings, 17, 84-85, 117, 121, 219, 331, 412, 426
Bongiovanni, Adeladi, 103
Borsari, Emma, 103
Bosco, Albert, 172, 182, 193, 395-397
Bostock, Jimmy, 37, 38, 40, 42, 47, 48, 69, 142, 159, 162, 224
Bowles, Benjamin, 49-50, 69, 94, 99
Boyd, Dr. William, 318
Brandeis, Louis, 114, 435
Branting, George, 386
Brenner, William, 39, 146, 307
Brini, Alfonsina, 77, 104, 169-170
Brini, Beltrando, 21-23, 78, 103-104, 369, 392, 466
Brini, Vincenzo, 77, 93, 95, 104
Brooks, Edward, 152
Brooks, Georgina, 95, 99-100
Brouillard, Albert, 51, 52, 57, 58, 118, 148, 356
Broun, Heywood, 419
Bruno, "Doggy," 272-273, 319, 320, 321, 324
Bullard, F. Lauriston, 344-345
bullets, 13, 47, 158-160, 201, 202, 205, 209, 212, 233, 234-235, 242-244, 314-318, 376-377, 402, 415, 461, 464-465

Burgess, Henry, 105
Burke, Frank, 40, 69, 164, 224, 225, 297
Burns, James, 158-159, 160, 163, 295, 376, 465

Cahoon, Dr. Charles, 238
Callahan, Jack, 271, 304
Callahan, William, 68, 93, 94, 139, 164, 166
Campbell, Dr. C. MacFie, 239
Campbell, Julia, 31-33, 149, 151
Cannon, James, 332, 333, 335
Canter, Harry, 253, 405, 416, 421
cap, found near Berardelli, 42, 47, 125, 157, 183, 190, 194, 197, 401, 415
Carbarn Bandits, 349-350
Carbone, Antony, 122, 340
Carpenter, Albert, 224, 231, 253, 278, 279
Carrigan, Mark, 36, 40, 69, 142
Carter, Edward, 164
Casey, Richard, 52, 101
Cellucci, Joseph, 167
Cerro, Henry, 167
Chase, Elmer, 41, 168
Chisholm, George, 44
Christophori, Esther, 103
Cicchetti, Beniamino, 118, 120
Citizens National Committee for Sacco and Vanzetti, 427
Clark, Francis, 45, 301
Cline, Charles, 335-336, 338
Coacci, Ferruccio, 54, 55-56, 57, 96, 97, 112, 140, 287 fn., 462
   pistol of, 58
Codman, John, 114, 253, 382
Coes, Loring, 194, 391
Colarossi, Vincent, 177
Colbert, Maurice, 40
Cole, Austin, 62, 101, 152-153
Collins, John, 315, 316-317
Colp, Dr. Ralph, 241
Communists, and Sacco-Vanzetti case, 6-7, 217-218, 328-329, 330, 332-333, 335-336, 338, 366-367, 454
Connolly, Michael, 62-63, 100, 156, 406
Conrad, John, 324, 325
Constantino, Dominic, 146
Cook, Waldo, 419, 427
Coolidge, Calvin, 406-407, 435

Corl, Melvin, 170, 177
Cox, Alfred E., 49-50, 69, 94, 99, 390, 403
Cummings, Homer S., 250-51

Daley, William, 244, 263
Damato, Nicola, 41, 155
Darroch, Lola, 111, 224, 232, 253
Darrow, Clarence, 336, 338
DeBeradinis, Louis, 41, 69
Debs, Eugene, 326
DeFalco, Angelina, 118-121
Defense Committee, 107, 141, 219, 222, 267, 326, 333-334, 335, 338, 417, 427
   and conduct of defense, 125-126
DeForest, Ralph, 34
Dentamore, Antonio, 182, 196, 395, 396
Department of Justice, 121-123, 340-341, 426-427, 433
Desmond, Walter, 44, 168, 300
Dever, John, 13, 133-136, 137, 138, 143, 144, 145, 148, 150, 153, 155, 159, 163, 164, 170-171, 174-175, 180, 211-212, 233, 413
Devlin, Frances, 35, 36, 40, 69, 143, 144, 165
Di Bona, Candido, 412
DiCarlo, John, 102
DiCecca, Anthony, 319-323
Dodson, William, 270 fn.
Dolbeare, Harry, 31, 151-152
Donato, Narciso, 89-90
Donovan, Mary, 268, 334, 356, 362, 384, 405, 408, 416-417, 424, 425, 436, 451, 454, 456
Dorr, Wilson, 45, 168
Dos Passos, John, 421
Doyle, Tommy, 224, 225, 228, 278
Dray, Michael, 24-26
Dreyfus, Alfred, 381
Driver, Thomas, 285
Duval, Clement, 86

Eastman, Max, 463
eels, delivery from Corso & Cannizzo, 404-405
Ehrmann, Herbert, 3, 286-289, 292-298, 308, 314, 355, 369, 376, 402, 404-405, 411, 461, 466
Elia, Roberto, 12, 88-91

Emerson, Marion, 108
Ensher, Napoleon, 101, 156
Ernst, Morris, 303-305, 308, 309, 310, 314, 462
Ettor, Joe, 109, 326
Evans, Elizabeth Glendower, 114, 139, 157, 165-166, 190, 207, 223, 237-238, 240, 244, 252, 258, 327, 334, 336, 337, 341, 356, 362, 382, 385, 419, 423, 452
Evarts, Richard, 411, 431, 433, 435

Fabbri, Amleto, 267, 333
Falcone, Emilio, 166
Falzini, Luigi, 160, 161
Farmer, Albert, 44, 300, 301
Farnum, George, 433
Faulkner, John, 152, 153
Felicani, Aldino, 14, 15, 16-18, 82, 107, 108, 113, 139, 172, 177, 252, 253, 268, 269, 334-335, 338, 356, 404, 405, 409, 424, 432, 434, 458
and DeFalco episode, 118, 119, 120
and defense funds, 223, 333
Ferguson, Lawrence, 165
Ferrari, Joseph, 282, 298, 299, 322, 356
Field, Elias, 242, 243, 411, 412, 433, 442
Finerty, John, 422, 428, 443, 446
Fiochi, Margherita, 103
Fitzemeyer, George, 162-163
Fitzgerald, J. Henry, 160, 163
Flaherty, Michael, 268, 459
Fleming, Michael, 290-291, 299, 356
Florence, Aldeah, 176
Flynn, Elizabeth Gurley, 108, 109, 113, 116, 268, 269
Flynn, William J., 87, 88, 89
Foley, William, 166
Fortini, Mary, 102, 404
Fraher, Thomas, 47, 48, 370, 401
Frankfurter, Felix, 8, 87, 268, 286, 332, 334, 341, 353-354, 366, 383, 408, 411, 424, 435, 459
Atlantic Monthly article, 352-353
vs. John Wigmore, 371-372
Frantello, Albert, 36, 48, 69, 165
Frazer, Dr. John Chisholm, 46, 141
Fuller, Alvan T., 20, 23, 278, 346, 347, 349, 353, 355, 363, 366-367, 368, 389, 421, 422, 423, 424, 425, 426-427, 441, 446-447
character of, 5-6, 350-351

Fuller, Alvan T. (*cont.*):
investigation by, 369-370, 373, 390-391, 392, 404, 405, 406, 407, 408-409
and Madeiros, 378-379, 388
and Vanzetti, 394
Fuller, Charles, 56-57, 156

Gaines, Mary, 198
Galleani, Luigi, 78, 80, 84, 86, 87, 88
Gallivan, Jeremiah, 43-44, 47, 118, 397, 401, 412, 415
Ganley, John, 131, 212
Gatti, Nicola, 167
Geary, Daniel, 288
Gerard, George, 136, 175, 212
Gill, Augustus, 234, 376, 390
Giovannitti, Arturo, 78, 80, 109, 326
Goddard, Calvin, 376-377, 402, 415, 464
Goodridge, Carlos, 12, 41, 154, 155-156, 224, 228-230, 390
Goodridge motion, 221, 228, 246, 264, 265
Gould, Roy, 36-37, 224-225, 369, 403, 415
Gould-Pelser motion, 221, 224, 263, 265
Govoni, Doviglio, 93, 94, 102
Grabill, Ethelbert Vincent, 367, 371, 431
Graham, James, 94, 95-96, 97, 98, 105, 443
Grant, Robert, 373, 375, 389, 400, 403, 413, 414
Graves, Earl, 49-50, 51, 52, 94
Greenslet, Ferris, 374, 451
Guadagni, Felice, 93, 119, 120, 171-172, 173, 182, 193, 253, 395-397, 405
Guerin, Lieutenant, 198, 199
Guidierris, Sibriano, 167
Guidobone, Angelo, 170

Hamilton, Albert, 233-235, 242-243, 262, 295, 377, 402
and switched pistol barrels, 247-249
Hamilton-Proctor motion, 221, 233, 244, 247, 264, 265
Hapgood, Powers, 436, 441, 442
Harding, Frank ("Slip"), 50, 52, 69, 70, 94-95, 99
Hassam, George, 51, 69, 100
garage of, 96, 271 fn., 462

Hassam, John, 232, 369
Hassam, Lola, 31. *See also* Andrews, Lola
Hawley, Frank, 198, 199
Hayes, James, 195-196
Hayes, Louise, 36, 39, 69, 295, 403
Hays, Arthur Garfield, 428, 433
Hellyer, Henry, 47, 48, 51, 52, 53, 167-168, 198, 339
Henderson, Jessica, 238, 419, 432, 434
Heron, William, 33, 154, 155
Hersey, Wallace, 131, 221
Hewins, Mabel, 45
Hicks, Granville, 332
Hill, Arthur Dehon, 235-236, 244, 245, 327, 411, 412, 419-421, 422, 424, 430-431, 432, 433, 435, 440
Holladay, Paula, 436, 437
Holmes, John Haynes, 366, 427, 452, 460
Holmes, Oliver Wendell, 84, 353, 423, 433, 446
Hunting, Dr. Nathaniel, 46, 141
Hurwitz, Albert, 275-277

Iacovelli, Henry, 197, 198
Iscorla, Pedro, 166
Israel, Harold, 249-250, 251

Jack, Cerise Carman, 139, 166, 238, 258, 326, 327, 346, 382
Jackson, Frank, 397, 398, 400
Jackson, Gardner, 334-335, 338, 383, 384, 392, 404, 405, 406, 408, 424, 451, 456, 457, 460
Jackson, William Schuyler, 428, 433, 446
Jackvony, Louis, 302, 305, 310
Jacobs, Ellsworth, 292-293
James, Edward Holton, 370, 371, 417, 436, 442, 455
Jesse, Frank, 170, 177
Jocomo, John, 274-275
Johnson, Ruth, 60-61, 66, 100, 106
Johnson, Samuel, 57, 331
Johnson, Simon, 57, 59, 60, 61, 64, 66, 100, 106, 178, 181
Jones, Dr. Frederick, 47, 141, 466
Jury, Frank, 464, 465, 466

Kane, Francis Fisher, 428, 433
Kane, William, 69, 95, 97, 98, 124
Karnes, Robert, 288

Katzmann, Frederick Gunn, 8, 20, 22, 24, 68, 93, 96, 114, 118, 121, 122, 282, 340, 353, 354, 395, 401, 465
character of, 4-5, 25-26, 66-67
cross-examination of Sacco, 184-186, 188-191
cross-examination of Vanzetti, 179-181
at Dedham trial, 130, 133, 136, 138, 139, 142, 145, 146, 149, 151, 158, 161, 178, 418 fn.
and DeFalco episode, 119, 120
and Orciani, 162, 190
at Plymouth trial, 97, 98, 99, 101, 103, 104, 105, 106
summation at Dedham trial, 202-205
Katzmann, Percy, 119, 120, 124
Kelley, George, 82, 92, 125, 157, 174, 190, 194
Kelley, Michael, 72, 73, 79, 82, 173, 191
Kelley, William, 290-292
Kelliher, Julia, 45, 301, 461
Kennedy, Minnie, 36, 39, 69, 295, 403
King, Harry, 136, 329 fn.
King, John, 52, 100
Kurlansky, Harry, 150-151

LaBrecque, Alfred, 150, 398
La Guardia, Fiorello, 366, 441, 452
Langlois, Edgar, 39, 144
Laughton, Warren, 61, 62, 64
Lawrence, Bishop William, 363-365, 389, 418
LeBaron, Frank, 55-56, 64
Letherman, Lawrence, 275, 340, 341, 342
Levangie, Mike, 29, 40, 48, 69, 151
Levine, Isaac Don, 426, 427, 428, 442
Lewis, Alfred Baker, 405, 416, 421, 458
Lippmann, Walter, 419
Liscomb, Barbara, 39, 167
Lloyd, John, 45
Longhi, Vincent, 103
Lopez, Frank, 113, 197, 216, 224, 252, 253, 267
Loring, Fred, 42, 47, 157
Lowell, Abbott Lawrence, 2, 5, 372, 373-375, 389, 402, 403, 413
and Bosco-Guadagni alibi, 395-397
Lowell Committee, 315, 373, 376, 388, 389, 395, 402
report of, 407, 413-415, 417, 419

Luban, Jacob, 273, 274-277, 279, 321
Lummus, Henry, 282, 285, 328
Lyons, Eugene, 110, 111-112, 114, 216, 222, 225, 226, 253, 329 fn., 333, 334, 383, 452, 462
Lyons, Fred, 271 fn.

McAnarney, Jeremiah, 25-26, 126, 127, 129-130, 131-132, 135, 139, 140, 147, 153, 155, 171, 174, 176, 179, 185, 192, 200, 220, 221, 307, 341
summation at Dedham, 201-202
McAnarney, John, 126, 127, 132-133, 179, 268, 406
McAnarney, Thomas, 126-127, 130, 159, 164, 213, 215, 245-246
McCullum, Peter, 39, 146, 162, 307
MacDonald, Herman, 369, 373, 390, 392, 407
McGlone, Jim, 37, 42, 144
McHardy, Lewis, 136, 426
McLaughlin, Dr. Joseph, 266, 430, 449, 450
McLean, Bob, 305, 307, 308, 310, 311, 312, 313, 316
MacMechan, Virginia, 258, 259
McNamara, Frank, 136, 221
McNaught, Henry, 152
Madeiros, Celestino, 279-285, 286-287, 289-290, 294, 298, 299-300, 301, 314, 341-342, 377-379, 388, 405, 406, 409, 413, 423, 441, 449-450, 455, 456, 461
Magazu, Peter, 41, 154, 155
Magrath, Dr. George Burgess, 47, 141, 158, 418, 449, 455, 466
Mahoney, Margaret, 31, 35, 142, 162
Malaguti, Terese, 102
Mancini, Tony, 294-295, 296-298, 314
Marden, Frank, 135, 221
Marks, Jeannette, 384, 451
Mede, Jimmy, 271-272, 273-274, 277-278, 320, 321-323, 324
Meyerson, Dr. Abraham, 238, 239, 368
Millay, Edna St. Vincent, 421, 428, 441
Minor, Robert, 116
Moller, Emil, 278-279
Monello, Angelo, 172-173, 182
Monterios, Barney, 284-285, 290, 299, 309
Moore, Fred H., 13, 16, 109, 119, 120, 123, 125-126, 127, 220, 246, 251,

327, 333, 363, 382, 383, 463, 467
and Albert Hamilton, 233-234, 249
and ballistics evidence, 159, 201
and bombings, 219
and Carlos Goodridge, 228-230, 264
as creator of Sacco-Vanzetti case, 108, 110-111, 112-114, 124-125, 252
at Dedham trial, 129-133, 135, 136-137, 139, 140, 144, 145, 153, 154, 164, 166, 191
and defendants' guilt or innocence, 12, 17, 256-257, 462-463
and defendants' radicalism, 179, 221
and Emil Moller, 278-279
and Frank Lopez, 224
and Jimmy Mede, 274, 278, 321
and Joe Sammarco, 322, 325
and Lola Andrews, 146-151, 230-232
and Lottie Tatillo, 398-399, 400
and Louis Pelser, 225-227
and Luban and Silva, 274-277
money problems of, 222-223
and New Trial League, 252-253
relationship with Sacco, 241, 254-256
and Roy Gould, 225
summation at Dedham, 200-201
Moors, John, 332, 363, 374, 392, 427
Morelli, Frank, 293
Morelli, Helen, 312-313
Morelli, Joe, 279, 288, 289, 292, 295-296, 297, 298, 302-303, 308, 311
autobiography of, 304-305, 309-310, 312-314, 461-462
Morelli, Mike, 292, 308, 461
Morelli Gang, 3, 284, 287-288, 289, 290, 293, 294, 341, 461
Moro, Joseph, 333, 384, 406, 408, 421, 424, 431
Mucci, Leon, 112, 196
Murphy, Dr. John, 50, 100
Musmanno, Michael, 15, 391-392, 411-412, 421, 422, 428, 430, 431, 432-433, 435, 443, 446-447, 448
Mussolini, Benito, 380-381

Neal, Shelley, 28-31, 35, 43, 117, 141-142
New Trial League, 252-253, 254, 267
Nichols, Annie, 39, 166
Novelli, Jenny, 34, 69, 167-168, 339

Oates, "Guinea," 272-273, 318, 320, 321, 324
O'Brien, Robert Lincoln, 331, 344, 369-370, 418
O'Connell, William Cardinal, 367, 434
O'Connor, Tom, 338-339, 391, 401, 443, 452
Orciani, Ricardo, 13, 19, 65-66, 69-70, 88, 90, 91, 92, 94, 96, 140, 156, 161, 162, 178, 181, 183, 190, 197, 314, 462

Packard, Lottie, 229, 415. See also Tatillo, Lottie
Palmer, A. Mitchell, 91, 123
  bombing of house, 84-85, 88
  Red raids of, 53, 82, 87-88
Papa, Vittorio, 102
Parker, Dorothy, 421, 432
Parker, Seward, 136, 212, 221
Parmenter, Frederick, 35-36, 37-38, 40, 42-43, 46
Pelser, Louis, 39, 145-146, 224, 225-227, 263, 307, 390
Pieraccini, Ralph, 287, 292
Pierce, Edward Peter, 352, 355
Pierce, Wilfred, 165
Pinkerton reports, 168, 338-340, 392, 466
Pool, Elmer, 45
Pound, Roscoe, 87, 286, 366
Prince, Dr. Morton, 345-346, 363, 417
Proctor, William, 2, 47, 100, 158, 160, 164, 242, 244, 345, 395, 402, 464-465
  testimony re Bullet III, 159, 243, 247, 264-265, 354, 415

Quintiliano, Luigi, 91, 193, 197

Ranney, Dudley, 281, 288, 289, 291, 292, 298, 299, 300, 341, 367, 376, 377, 395, 402, 403, 406
Rantoul, Lois, 139, 157, 194, 341, 412
Ravachol, François, 86
Reading, Arthur, 420, 431, 447
Reed, Austin, 45-46, 152-153, 212
Reid, Robert, 145, 224, 225
Ricci, Angelo, 40, 198
Ricci, Dominic, 174
Richards, John, 287, 293-294, 296, 390
Richardson, James, 265, 412
Ripley, Walter, 135, 140, 163, 212, 214, 221, 244

Ripley motion, 221, 262-263, 265
Robinson, Merton, 235
Rose, Reginald, 329 fn.
Rosen, Joseph, 168-169, 177, 403
Ross, Joseph, 166, 190, 191, 192
Rugg, Arthur Prentice, 285, 352, 355
Ruzzamenti, John, 122

Sacco, Dante, 211, 327, 393, 431
Sacco, Ines, 130, 237, 244, 327, 393
Sacco, Nicola:
  alibi of, 171-174
  anarchism of, 86, 260-261
  arrest of, 63-65
  break with Moore, 254-255
  cap of, 97, 157, 183, 190, 194, 197, 199, 415
  character of, 72-73, 81-82
  and departure for Italy, 91-92
  early life of, 78-80
  and Fuller's decision, 409
  guilt of, 466
  hearing on South Braintree crime, 94 fn.
  hunger strike of, 237, 238
  identifications of, 69, 143-145, 147-148
  indicted, 116
  interpretation of case, 336, 337
  and James Graham, 94, 96
  last words of, 450, 466
  letter to son, 438-439
  and Madeiros confession, 279-280
  mental breakdown of, 239-242
  in Mexico, 81
  in Morelli confession, 314
  pistol of, 8, 64, 73, 139, 158, 183, 189, 203, 233, 234-235, 247-249, 314-316, 415, 464-465, 466
  speech at sentencing, 357-358
  as symbol, 1, 348
  testimony, 181-192
Sacco, Rosina, 72, 80, 91, 92, 97, 112, 125, 211, 214, 238, 240, 244, 306, 327, 341, 356, 386, 392, 409, 419, 424, 425, 430, 432, 434, 438, 441, 446-447, 458, 460
  and Fred Moore, 113, 130, 132, 178, 207
  testimony at Dedham, 197-198
Salsedo, Andrea, 87, 88-91
Sammarco, Joe, 272, 273, 274, 278, 319-325, 461
Sargent, John, 340, 426, 433

Sawyer, Roland, 365-366
Shachtman, Max, 328, 332-333, 338
Shaw, George Bernard, 330, 331 fn.
Shaw, Maynard, 100
shells, 42, 47, 159, 212, 234, 314, 315, 376-377, 464
Shields, Art, 113, 116, 222
Sibley, Frank, 12, 154, 185-186, 211, 233, 334, 412
Silva, Frank, 271-273, 274-278, 279, 318, 320, 321, 322, 324-325, 461
Sinclair, Upton, 17, 256, 304, 463
Sisk, James, 109, 127
Slater, Rexford, 161
Splaine, Mary, 35, 36, 40, 47, 48, 69, 143-144, 165, 297, 345-346
Squires, Francis J., 119, 120, 121 fn., 282
Stearns, Warren, 19-21
Stewart, Michael, 18-19, 50-51, 52, 53, 54, 55, 56, 57, 58-59, 60, 62, 64-65, 69, 94, 96, 97, 100, 101, 118, 125, 148, 158, 198, 199, 394, 398, 418 fn.
Stone, Harlan, 435, 441
Stong, Phil, 386-387, 388 fn.
Stratton, Samuel, 373, 375
Sullivan, Simon, 105-106
Supreme Judicial Court, Massachusetts, 328, 351-352, 354-355, 431

Taft, William Howard, 418, 435
Tatillo, Lottie, 397-400
Thayer, Webster, 4, 5, 13, 54, 123-124, 127-128, 261, 328, 344, 346, 354, 369, 389, 406, 419-420, 460
  and Mrs. Bernkopf, 246-247
  character of, 97-98
  charge to Dedham jury, 8, 205-210
  at Dedham trial, 129-133, 134-135, 136-137, 140, 141, 148, 149, 150, 154, 157, 178-179, 192, 193-194, 199, 210-211
  and Lowell Committee, 414
  and Madeiros motion, 341, 342-343, 351, 353
  at Plymouth trial, 101, 105, 106
  sentencing of Sacco and Vanzetti, 356-359, 361-362
  and supplementary motions, 244-246, 262-265
  and switched pistol barrels, 248-249
Thomas, 280, 281. See also Driver, Thomas

Thomas, Dr. Albert, 238
Thompson, William G., 17, 108, 132-133, 235-236, 243, 244, 245, 247, 257, 265, 268-269, 278, 322, 326, 328, 333, 337, 338, 347, 353, 354, 362, 363, 366, 367, 369, 378, 383, 395, 401, 403, 409, 410, 414, 415, 419, 422, 426
  and Bosco-Guadagni alibi, 396-397, 402
  and Calvin Goddard, 376, 377
  and Department of Justice, 340-342
  and Jimmy Weeks, 289, 291-292
  last talk with Vanzetti, 443-445
  and Lottie Tatillo, 399-400
  and Madeiros, 280, 281, 285-286, 290, 299, 339, 346, 351-352
  opinion of Vanzetti, 73, 327
  and Wilbur Turner, 402
Thorndike, Herbert, 94, 95
Totty, Warren, 51
Tracey, William, 33, 154
Tresca, Carlo, 16, 78, 80, 85, 90, 91, 107-108, 109, 110, 115, 432, 463, 466
Turner, Wilbur, 402, 465

Vahey, James, 274
Vahey, John, 93-94, 95, 96, 97, 98, 100, 101, 102, 105, 106, 282, 443
Valdinoce, Carlo, 88
Valdinoce, Susie, 327
Van Amburgh, Charles, 2, 158, 159-160, 235, 248, 249-251, 295, 460, 464-465
Vanzetti, Bartolomeo:
  alibi for Bridgewater crime, 101-104
  alibi for South Braintree crime, 168-170
  anarchism of, 86, 260
  arrest of, 63-65
  and Back Bay women, 258
  character of, 71-72
  clemency petition of, 367-368
  development in prison, 257, 259-260, 261
  early life of, 73-78
  eulogy of Sacco, 362-363
  and Fuller's decision, 409-410
  identifications of, 69, 94-95, 99-100, 151, 152-153
  indicted for South Braintree crime, 116
  innocence of, 466

480 TRAGEDY IN DEDHAM

Vanzetti, Bartolomeo (cont):
interpretation of case, 336, 337
and James Graham, 95-96
and Jimmy Mede, 273-274
and John Vahey, 93-94, 95, 359, 429
last interviews with Thompson, 422,
443-445
last words of, 450, 467
letter to Dante Sacco, 439-440
and Lowell Committee, 390
mental breakdown of, 266-267
in Mexico, 81
moods in prison, 347
in Morelli confession, 314
revolver of, 8, 15, 19, 26, 64, 68,
139, 142, 160-162, 163, 203, 209,
233, 235, 314-316, 403
speech at sentencing, 358-361
statement for United Press, 428-430
as symbol, 1, 259, 348
testimony at Dedham, 176-181
tried for Bridgewater crime, 97, 98-
106
Vanzetti, Luigia, 393, 416, 424, 432,
434, 438, 441, 446, 458, 460
Vaughn, Earl, 62-63, 156, 406
Ventola, Angelo, 66
Ventola, Joseph, 54, 55, 57, 66, 97
Vernazano, John, 104, 105
Vorse, Mary Heaton, 114-115

Wade, Lewis, 34-35, 38, 48, 69, 142-
143, 162, 297, 307
Wadsworth, Lincoln, 162, 403
Wait, William Cushing, 352, 354
Walsh, Frank, 428, 433
Waugh, Frank, 131
Weeks, Jimmy, 282, 284, 285, 289,
290-292, 296, 297 298, 299
Weller, Jac, 464, 465, 466
Wells, H. G., 381
West, William J., 121, 340, 341
Weyand, Fred, 121, 122, 340, 342
Wiggin, Joseph, 369, 390, 391, 446
Wigmore, John, 371-372
Wilbar, Winfield, 282, 291, 298, 331,
355, 357
Williams, Harold, 215, 227, 247, 248,
249
at Dedham trial, 138, 139-140, 142-
143, 144, 147, 150, 156, 157, 163
and DeFalco episode, 118, 119
Williams, John, 171-172, 182, 193
Wind, Max, 56, 156
Winslow, Gertrude, 238, 356
Witner, Adolph, 273, 274-277

Zagroff, Segris, 123-124
Zelt, Johannes, 217
Zorian, Harold, 121, 340